INTRODUCTION TO CHICANO STUDIES

A Reader

Edited by

LIVIE ISAURO DURAN

and

H. RUSSELL BERNARD

The Macmillan Company, New York

The Macmillan Company
866 Third Avenue, New York, New York 10022

Library of Congress catalog card number: 72–78609

Printing   1 2 3 4 5 6 7 8   Year   3 4 5 6 7 8 9

Contents

iii

INTRODUCTION
La Raza

There are three basic premises on which this book is founded. They were the guides for the selection of the readings and the principles on which the material was organized. Briefly stated they are as follows:

1. Chicano culture is real. We often hear the view that Chicano identity is just now being forged by Chicano intellectual leaders out of cultural fragments. From an anthropological perspective this is false. Chicanos have lacked political power in the past and have been oppressed as a result. But this should never be misconstrued as meaning that they lack a common cultural heritage and identity. For reasons discussed more fully in Part II, Chicanos have remained relatively more culturally intact than most ethnic groups in America. They have a prehistory, a history, and a modern culture.

For this reason phrases such as forgotten Americans and awakening minority are misleading and inappropriate in describing Chicanos. Chicanos indeed have been forgotten (ignored would be a better word) by those segments of Anglo society that distribute the wealth of our complex socioeconomic system. But it would be a mistake to think that they were ever forgotten by those segments that grew wealthy on Chicano land and labor. Since those who accumulate wealth and those who control its distribution tend to be the same in our society, this has required a certain amount of schizophrenic behavior on their part. To say that Chicanos have been forgotten is to emphasize only one side of the schizophrenia. Moreover, Chicanos have never been asleep or unconscious of the conditions of poverty, disease, hunger, and ignorance in which they live, so to say they are "awakening" is inaccurate. They have never been unconscious of the fact that they were forced to live under such conditions by an exploitative society. However, they were unaware that they had the power to change their conditions through such collective political and economic

1

actions as strikes, bloc voting, and boycotts. Thus, aware is a term that more accurately describes their present state; Chicanos have developed a political, not a cultural awareness, that they did not have previously. Chicanos now understand, for example, that they need not accept poverty wages for decent work; they understand that they may call themselves Jesús rather than Jesse even if it offends Anglos; and they understand that they may fight politically and economically to reject discrimination in health care, housing, employment, education, and the administration of justice. But this political awareness is not the beginning of a new Chicano culture—except in the sense that Chicanos are Americans and that all minority movements for self-determination are a vital part of American culture in general. Chicano culture was alive in 1848, when Aztlán was first separated politically from Mexico, and it continues to live, grow, and change in the United States, a product of its own political, economic, and social circumstances. The first principle with which we began, then, was that Chicano culture is real and requires description and analysis rather than justification for being.

2. Our second premise is that Anglo society does not have a "Chicano problem." Rather Chicanos have problems caused by Anglo society. They are poorly housed, poorly fed, and poorly represented in government. There are basically two opposing views as to how this situation has arisen. The dominant view is that Chicanos are at fault because they are either biologically or socially inferior. That is, at worst, they are "naturally adapted to agricultural labor" and at best they are "held back from advancement by their language and culture." The opposing view is voiced in the Report of the United States Commission on Civil Disorders (the so-called Kerner Commission or Riot Commission Report). After studying the riots in the black ghettos during the late 1960's the Commission concluded that, "White racism is essentially responsible for the explosive mixture which has been accumulating in our cities since the end of World War II." White racism, in other words, is the cultural trait of Anglo society that is to blame for the conditions of poverty among Chicanos (and blacks and Indians) as well as for the violence and hatred it breeds.

3. Our third premise is that self-determination—Chicano solutions to Chicano problems—is both the most rapid and the only satisfactory solution to those problems. Traditional Anglo culture dictates that problems, once recognized, should be studied, isolated, and attacked with money, technology, and "good old Yankee knowhow." This traditional wisdom is constantly reinforced because it works so well for solving essentially technological questions like going to the moon, removing soot from smoke, or increasing the protein content of wheat. It is easy to see how we might extend this formula to social issues. In fact, up to a point, it is eminently reasonable. This is, after all, a modern industrial, market-oriented society and Chicanos are part of it. There can be little doubt that proper study and isolation of social problems are a necessary part of any serious attack on them. The same is true for money and technology; it would be point-

less to envision a solution to poverty, hunger, disease, and ignorance without massive application of both of those commodities. But there the formula stops. "Good old Chicano knowhow" is appropriate for solving Chicano problems.

On the basis of these three suppositions we have organized this volume into three main sections: Yesterday, Today, and Tomorrow. The first deals with the ancient and historical roots of Chicano culture from the Maya and the Aztec, through the Spanish conquest of Mexico and the colonial period, the Mexican-American War, and the development of the Chicano population in the United States over the past 125 years. The second section examines Chicano life from two perspectives. Customs, beliefs, world view, and social structure constitute the internal *perspective, and deprivation and discrimination suffered at the hands of a hostile larger system constitute the* external *perspective. Finally, Section III describes some of the most important attempts by Chicanos to control their own destiny, covering such areas as Chicano Studies programs on college campuses and various movements such as those led by César Chávez, Reies Tijerina, and José Angel Gutiérrez to win just wages, land rights, and political power for Chicanos. Because the Chicano movement is committed to bringing about institutional change and because its goals have yet to be fully achieved, we have grouped its activities together as the shape of tomorrow. Nevertheless, these activities must be considered an integral part of Chicano culture.*

In addition to these three main sections, we have provided an introduction containing just three articles: "The Race Problem in Latin America," by José Vasconcelos, a selection by Octavio Paz entitled "The Sons of La Malinche," and "The People of Aztlán" by Armando B. Rendon. These three authors provide an understanding of raza, *Chicano, El Movimiento, and Aztlán, four concepts that are basic to Chicano Studies.* .

The concept of raza *may be understood at two levels: the cosmic and the Mexican–Chicano. In 1916, when Vasconcelos coined the phrase* La Raza Cósmica, *he felt that the New World would see the emergence of a great Cosmic Race, a biological mixture of all the races of mankind resulting from miscegenation in the Americas. Perhaps he felt that the New World could put an end to racism by eliminating racial differences. Racial differences continue to exist, however, and the Cosmic Race has not emerged. In fact, there is little chance that it ever will. Only a very few persons, highly trained human biologists, use the word* race *to mean a biologically definable population. Most people mean a social group of some kind when they speak of races. For example, it makes no biological sense to speak of a "Jewish race," or a "black race," or a "Latin race," though we hear those phrases all the time. The first refers to a religion, the second to skin color, and the third to a common historical background of many different peoples.*

Thus, Vasconcelos' Raza Cósmica has not developed and probably will not develop biologically. In the social meaning of the word race, *however, the story is different. There can be little doubt that a general Latin American culture and psyche has emerged, but what it is and how it should be described continue to be controversial among scientists and philosophers. All we can be sure of is that Latin Amercian culture is composed of Latin (that is, Spanish) and American (that is, Indian) traits. It is a new culture, born in conquest and nurtured on colonialism, wars of independence, and revolutions for social justice. There are nearly 300 million people from California to Chile who are part of this heritage. They are all* raza. *Most are Spanish speakers, but at least 20 million also speak one of more than 400 Indian languages. Perhaps 10 million of them do not speak Spanish at all.*

Most of the members of La Raza Cósmica *are mestizos, or mixtures of Indian and Spanish blood; but there are tens of millions of blacks (called Negroes), mulattos (mixtures of black and Spanish genes), and* zambos *(the offspring of Indian and black matings). All these different people share in the history of Latin America and have contributed to its unique culture. They are all, therefore, part of* La Raza Cósmica, *as are Cubans in Miami, Puerto Ricans in New York, and Chicanos in Aztlán.*

For Chicanos, however, raza *refers more specifically to the Mexican social and biological heritage than to any other in Latin America. This means that, as in Mexico, the emphasis is on the Indian (that is, native American) rather than on the Spanish (that is, Latin) side of the* Raza Cósmica. *When great public buildings are raised in Mexico, such as a coliseum or the national university, the architecture is often markedly reminiscent of Aztec and Maya motifs. The music of rural Mexico is unmistakably influenced by aboriginal themes, and this extends all the way to the works of Carlos Chávez, one of the great composers of the twentieth century. The same holds true for the food: the basic Indian diet of tortillas, chile peppers, beans, squash, and tomatoes is woven into the menus and dishes of the most luxurious restaurants in Mexico City. There can be little doubt that the Spaniards conquered Mexico and that Spanish culture has had the most profound influence on the development of modern Mexican life, but the identity of Mexico remains with the conquered rather than the conquerors. The national heroes are people like Cauhtemoc, the last Aztec emperor, and Benito Juárez, the Indian who became Mexico's first president after its independence from Spain. Cortés may be a hero to the few Spaniards living in Mexico, but there is not a single monument to the conqueror in Mexico City. Octavio Paz, in his article on the Mexican psyche, reminds us that Cortés took a mistress when he landed in Mexico. She was an Indian woman, known as La Malinche (from her Aztec name Malintzin), and she symbolically gave over the Aztec world to the Spanish soldier by the offering of her sexuality. Yet, when Paz describes the character of Mexicans, his fellow countrymen, he calls them (and himself) children of La Malinche and not children of Cortés.*

It is this emphasis on the physically conquered but spiritually vibrant Indian aspect of raza *which is central to the Mexican and Chicano iden-*

tity. For like the Mexicans, Chicanos have chosen their Indian heritage as the symbolic force of their identity. The area where most Chicanos live is not called the Southwest or el Sudoeste, but Aztlán, after the mythical origin of the Aztecs perhaps in what is now New Mexico. The name Chicano itself is derived from Mexicano, the word used in Mexico today to refer to the 600,000 people who still speak Nahuatl (Aztec). (In the original pronunciation the x sounds like sh.) This is not to deny the importance of the Spanish heritage to Chicano life. The Spanish language was used to write El Cid, Don Quixote, and the philosophical expressions of Unamuno. It was used to write the Mexican Constitution, the first in the New World to grow out of a social revolution. And it is used today by Chicanos to write poetry, drama, and political oratory that has galvanized an oppressed minority into social action against its oppressors. In addition, many aspects of Mexican and Chicano family life, religion, and kinship structure have their roots in medieval Catholic Spain. Still, when it came time to select a banner under which Chicano farmworkers would strike against the grape growers of California and under which a new Chicano political party would be formed, it was not the Castilian coat of arms that was chosen. The flag of El Movimiento is a black Aztec thunderbird on a red ground, the same symbol used by Mexico's largest labor union in its strikes.

This does not mean, however, that Chicano culture is a mirror of Mexico's. Mexican national culture cannot be understood as a simple combination of Spanish and Indian traits. Mexican Catholicism is basically derived from Spain and many Mexican saints are derived from earlier Indian deities. But the result of that combination is a new product, different from either of the earlier forms of religion, Spanish or Indian. The same is true of Chicano culture; it cannot be understood as a simple combination of Mexican and Anglo-American customs. Like Mexican culture, it too is new and different from any other raza subculture.

Who, then, are the Chicanos? A Chicano is anyone of Mexican descent now living permanently in the United States. Some Chicanos are still Mexican citizens, having come to this country in the recent past. Most Chicanos, however, are American citizens. Millions can trace their ancestry in this country back well beyond 1848, when the Southwest became United States territory. Most of the European immigrants did not arrive on the East Coast until after the Civil War. Chicanos are part of America, and have been for longer than most whites. They have helped to build America's agricultural industry and have fought and died in her wars. Still America has isolated the Chicano, calling him a foreigner.

In Mexico the Chicano is also called a foreigner. His allegiance to the United States and the Anglo accent in his Spanish brand him a pocho, a fallen Mexican who has given up his culture in favor of the despised gringo's. Manuel Gamio, the Mexican anthropologist, described the Chicano as a man without a country. "The American of Mexican race is really, so far as nationality is concerned, in a difficult and unfortunate position.

Such a person, when he goes to Mexico, wearing American clothes and speaking Spanish with a foreign accent, calls himself Mexican because he is accustomed to being called a Mexican in the United States. Nevertheless, Mexicans in Mexico, knowing nothing of this, become indignant of the idea of such a person being a Mexican, while, on the other hand, Americans find it strange that he calls himself an American, since in the United States he is always a Mexican or a Spanish-American."[1]

In another passage[2] Gamio quotes a Mexican woman recently arrived in the United States who is deeply disillusioned by the culture of the Chicanos. She is divorced; in discussing her future plans she says: "If I do marry someday it would be with a Mexican. The Americans are very dull and very stupid. They let women boss them. I would rather marry an American than a pocho, however." Scorned by white Anglo society as Mexican and doubly scorned by Mexican society as pocho, the Chicano has no choice but to be what he is, a member of a new and totally unique raza subculture born of Mexican and Anglo traits, but neither one nor the other. For this reason we have avoided using the term Mexican-American. In our judgment it conveys the notion that Chicanos are a trivial combination of Mexican and Anglo traits rather than a true subcultural entity. Among some Anglo writers the word Chicano seems to be avoided as something not quite respectable. There is a tendency to feel that the word has only recently crept out of militant rhetoric into common usage. Among Chicanos the word has been in use for at least seventy years, though in earlier years the evidence indicates it may have been used as a term of disrespect, like pocho. In all fairness, the debate is not over yet. There are many writers, including Chicanos (some of whose work appears in this book), whose political sensitivities and messages are in agreement with the principle of self-determination but who continue to use the term Mexican American. It is our view that Mexican American is a gabacho (Anglo) term devised to give Chicanos pseudorespectability in the American ethnic sense. It is also our view that the term Chicano is respectable enough.

---

[1] Mexican Immigration to the United States (Chicago: University of Chicago Press, 1930), p. 129. (Reprinted in 1969 by Arno Press, New York.)

[2] The Mexican Immigrant (Chicago: University of Chicago Press, 1931), p. 162. (Reprinted in 1969 by Arno Press, New York.)

THE RACE PROBLEM IN LATIN AMERICA

José Vasconcelos

Many theories have been advanced as to the origin of the old inhabitants of this New World. The discoveries of Professor Hrdlička, relating to strong similarities between a certain Siberian tribe and the North American Red Indians may be entirely correct, but they do not exclude the possibility of the existence of some more autocthonous stock coming from the very far south, from Patagonia, as the Peruvian legends seem to indicate. Certain similarities that have often been pointed out between the Maya Quiché architecture and the Egyptian manner of building, would tend to confirm the opinion of the believers in the Atlantis of the classic days; and finally, the theory of Professor Wegener regarding the original unity of all continents in one body which has been separated as a result of the earth's rotation would clear away all sorts of difficulties, for it would allow us to state that there is no more mystery attached to the aboriginal American than the mystery that surrounds the whole of the human race. Farther

Reprinted from J. Vasconcelos and M. Gamio, *Aspects of Mexican Civilization*, by permission of The University of Chicago Press. Copyright 1926 by the University of Chicago.

José Vasconcelos was one of Mexico's great social thinkers in the twentieth century as well as a highly controversial statesman and politician. He took his law degree in 1907, participated in the Mexican Revolution, and was appointed rector of the National University by General Obregon. He served as Secretary of Public Education between 1921 and 1924 and in that brief span revolutionized the educational system of his country. In 1929 he made a disastrously unsuccessful try for the presidency and went into exile for eleven years. He returned to Mexico in 1940 as director of the National Library; he remained in this position until his death in 1959.

back than five thousand years we do not know how we lived, nor where.[1]

We can, however, assert that in the New World, just the same as in the Old, a series of civilizations have developed and decayed. Civilizations come and go, but it is very probable that the human stock, the particular race that creates a certain period of cultures, does not disappear with the disappearance of its constructive power. The social development of a certain people may stop entirely while the race itself goes on reproducing its members. The Greeks of the Roman days had disappeared as a ruling type of civilization but continued to exist as a race and traveled and mixed with other races; and the original stock thus became modified but never totally destroyed. The same thing can be said, I am sure, of the Indian. When Cortés arrived on the continent the Indians of Montezuma did not know themselves who had been the builders of the Teotihuacan pyramids that were lying covered with the dust of centuries a few miles away from the old Tenochtitlan—the Mexico City of today. But there is no doubt that a great number of these Montezuma Indians had in their veins the same blood of the builders of the forgotten monuments. The Aztecs, who were comparatively newcomers, may not have had it, but the strata of the older races inhabiting the valley, were no doubt inheritors of the flesh and the soul of the high-type ancestors. The invader never succeeded in destroying all of the subjected population, but had to coexist with them and naturally intermarried and learned from the older inhabitants. In the same manner we can affirm that, although the natives of Yucatan and Guatemala had forgotten all about the history of the builders of the Maya Quiché palaces, they still have in them the soul of the ancient architects. It is absolutely no wonder that a historical tradition should get lost in a time in which there was no written language; and even such written characters as existed were transmitted only through verbal tradition, with consequent danger of a total loss of the key to the symbols through periods of war, emigrations, and calamities.

The fact I am trying to emphasize then is that our race, the Indian races of the tropics at least, do not constitute a primitive stock. Call it, if you will, a decayed stock, but not a primitive stock. The new Mexico Indian may be primitive, although I would rather say that instead of being primitive he is provincial; that is to say, that what remains of his culture is

---

[1] In the 1920's, when Ales Hrdlička proposed that American Indians had first come from Siberia to Alaska, many scholars were skeptical. Research since that time has shown that Hrdlička's observations were correct. There is very strong evidence for trans-Pacific contact with the New World, but no evidence that these contacts were of significant influence in the development of New World civilization (see, for instance, Philip Phillips, "The Role of Transpacific Contacts in the Development of New World Pre-Columbian Civilizations," *Handbook of Middle American Indians*, Vol. 4 [Austin: University of Texas Press, 1966], pp. 296–315). Wegener's theory of continental drift is still under debate. But even if the continents were a single land mass at one time, their separation would have occurred many millions of years before men ever appeared on earth. Vasconcelos' statement that our knowledge of New World prehistory goes back only 5,000 years was correct in 1925. Today, however, we know that *Homo sapiens* came from Siberia, following the great ice age mammals, at least 20,000 years ago and perhaps double that time.—*Eds.*

derived from the little he could obtain, placed at such a distance from the higher civilizations of the southern sections of Guatemala and Mexico. I maintain that the rhythm of civilization at that time, as well as in the time of the Spaniards and way up into the seventeenth century, the rhythm of civilization in the New World was, and had been, from south to north instead of being as it is today and as it has been since the Declaration of American Independence, from north to south. Since the beginning of the nineteenth century, the Latin-American countries began to take from the United States their political institutions, their school systems; and later we have taken the railroads, the machinery, and finally the capital for the development of our resources; but in the preceding centuries, during the day of the Indian and during the day of the Spaniard, it was the native of Arizona who had to march down to the south in search of tools for his wool-weaving and in search of inspiration for the drawings that decorate it. In the time of the Spaniard, the mission and the tillage both came from the better architecture and from the more advanced agriculture of Central Mexico, then the mother of Latin-American culture. In South America we find a similar, though inverted, movement. Civilization there centered about the semitropical and about the temperate plateau of Cuzco and scarcely reached the deserted plains of what is today the great growing Argentine nation. But the Aztec and the Inca sections were at the time, not only the most densely populated but also the centers of the culture of the New World, the creators of civilization of that period.

Our Indians then are not primitive as was the Red Indian, but old, century-tried souls who have known victory and defeat, life and death, and all of the moods of history.[2]

I wish to call your attention to the fact that the Indians of Mexico as well as the Indians of Peru represented a certain type of civilization and consequently were not as the North American Indian simply tribes of natives, wandering tribes of hunters, because this in itself perhaps explains why the Spaniard had to mix with the Indian, while the Englishman did not mix but simply forced the Indian back. Whenever two civilizations meet, one or the other becomes predominant, but they both undergo a change; they both lose certain traits and win others. What had happened to the Spaniard during the Arab invasion, happened to the Indian during the Spanish invasion. There is a difference of course in degree, and, as we shall see later, a very surprising difference in results; but the truth is that the social, the historical process of the Spanish conquest in Mexico was about the same as any of the Asiatic or European

[2] It should be clear that Professor Vasconcelos' use of the word *primitive* is not meant to convey the meaning *inferior*. In anthropology the term *primitive* refers to cultures that have developed outside the sphere of influence of the so-called mainstream civilizations. These include those of the Nile, the Indus Valley, the confluence of the Tigris and the Euphrates, the bend of the Huang-Ho, and the civilizations of nuclear America centered in Mexico and Peru. The Pueblo culture of the southwest was indeed very advanced between 800–1000 A.D. Vasconcelos, however, refers generally to the nonagricultural Indians of North America.—*Eds*.

invasions by which one race obtained control and predominance and the other was subjected, but both going along living in close contact and modifying each other through that contact.

The case of North America, as we all know, was very different. This was not an invasion, at least not a sudden overwhelming invasion, but a long penetration of the territory without conservation of the native stock, and consequently without social contact or any other relation with the Indian.

This difference is the origin of the policy and of the practice of what we may call the one-race standard as against the mixed-race standard. By that I mean this undeniable fact that the civilization of North Amerca is a one-race civilization, a white-race civilization as you insist on calling yourselves, sometimes even to the exclusion of other whites such as for instance the Spaniard. A white civilization that may contain, and does contain, millions of other racial stocks such as the Negro, but does not consider such dissimilar stock as a part of itself and does not as a rule intermarry with it. The Negro here, as well as the Indian, is in a world apart socially and is a body that is connected only politically with the white population. Of course nobody can deny the deep influence, and a gradually increasing influence, of the Negro upon the American mind—an influence that gives you the music to which you dance, and the laughter that helps your happiness, two heavenly gifts, lavishly spread by the socially isolated Negro.[3]

On the other hand we have, in the south, a civilization that from the beginning accepts a mixed standard of social arrangement not only as a matter of fact but through law, since the Indian after being baptized became the equal of the Spaniard and was able to intermarry with the conqueror. The wedding of Cortés—who is accused of having murdered his Spanish wife in order to marry, or at least to live undisturbed with, his Indian love La Malintzin—is symbolical of the new state of affairs and of the whole of the race situation in our country. The example of Cortés in taking an Indian woman for his wife was followed by many others; it went on then and has been going on since; but the first time that the world realized what had happened in America was, I believe, when the first writer of the new race appeared in Peru. About the middle of the sixteenth century the learned public of Spain began to read with curiosity and amazement the works of a celebrated mestizo, surnamed El Inca—El Inca Garcilazo de la Vega, a historian, a man of letters, perhaps the first man of letters of the New World. The writings of El Inca—very entertaining and fascinating reading even today—dealt with childhood memories

---

[3] Today this kind of statement would be unacceptable since it implies that black Americans are innately musical and jovial. Though Vasconcelos was sensitive to the problem of race mixture in Mexico, he was not immune to the predominant prejudices of his time regarding blacks. Remember also that he is speaking here as a Mexican to a North American audience.—Eds.

of the life of his mother, an Indian princess, and his father, a Spanish captain. El Inca also wrote some tales and narratives about the conquest and about the feelings of the defeated natives; he heard and repeated in his writings many old stories taken from the lips of cacique ancestors; he impregnated himself with all the legend and all the sentiment of the dying Indian civilization; and then, while still a young man he traveled through Spain and learned and adopted Spanish ideas and also learned to love Spain and Spanish European culture. His mind, as his own blood, became then the hyphen, the meeting point of this Spanish-Indian Tragedy, all of which through his genius he succeeded in transforming into a new broader concept of life. And it can be fairly said that in the days of Garcilazo there was no greater mind in this New World, either among the Indians or among the Spaniards, than the mind of this half-breed, who was struggling to make one mind of the two conflicting mentalities of the New World. And with Garcilazo the spiritual alliance of, the spiritual blending of, the Indian and the Spaniard was sealed forever.

Since then, more and more every day, the fortunes of the Spanish-American countries have been passing into the hands of men that acknowledge Garcilazo as their spiritual ancestor. We have been at heart Spaniards even when we have had to fight against Spain, and we remain Indian even when our skin accidentally becomes whitened through marriage with the more recent Spanish stock. In this way the half-breed cannot entirely go back to his parents because he is not exactly as any of his ancestors; and being unable to connect fully with the past, the mestizo is always directed toward the future—is a bridge to the future. No country can show, better than Mexico can, all of the signs and the effects of this peculiar mestizo psychology.

Notice the fact, that the mestizo represents an entirely new element in history; for if it is true that in all times the conquered and the conqueror have mixed their bloods, it is also unquestionably true that never before had there come together and combined two races as wide apart as the Indian and the Spanish, and never before had the fusing processes of two such different castes been made on such a large scale. History had never witnessed this process of two unrelated breeds intermingling and practically disappearing in order to create a new one. According to some observers, all of our backwardness, all of our difficulties and unfruitful struggles are derived from the fact of this unsound and even contemptible mixture of races. A noted philosopher, who for a time was the master even in our own mestizo universities, the Englishman Spencer, specifically pointed to us as an example of a hopeless hybrid product of the violation of the sacred scientific rules of a purifying, uplifting evolution. At any rate, the English have always stood for the conservation of an original unmixed human stock and have succeeded in maintaining it; and the Spaniards have always disregarded this purely white prejudice and have actually created the millions of the mestizo stock of America and of the

Philippines. The unlimited progress of the Anglo-Saxons in civilization in the late centuries has led to the belief in the soundness of their policy. Many even among ourselves felt as though we had to admit that racial hybridism could only produce a low type of humanity, an inferior stock that could only be aided by the constant increase of a renewed wave of white people such as has flooded for instance the unpopulated territories of Argentina. Such is still the belief of some Latin-Americans of the purer European stock; and there are many mestizos who feel that all of their vows should favor the elimination of the native strain.

To me this last attitude is nothing but a case of cowardice. We are dazzled by the power of the world's civilization at the present moment; and we forget that there is in hybridism something deeper than can be observed by the superficial thinker. It is very easy to agree with success; it is very easy to philosophize with the partial conclusions of a given moment of history. But if we think with our heads and if we search with our own souls into the mysteries of human destiny, we immediately find that the so-called pure-race theory is nothing but the theory of the dominating people of every period of history. And the pure-race theory leads, very often almost fatally, to the parental marriages, to the incestuous marriages of the Pharaohs. If we observe human nature closely we find that hybridism in man, as well as in plants, tends to produce better types and tends to rejuvenate those types that have become static. If we go through history we find that after a period of adaptation the results of the renewal of blood are always beneficial. Even some of the most modern authors on the subject, such as the Frenchman Pittard, conclude that a pure race is a myth because all nations are the result of numerous mixtures; he goes farther and states that, "it is only the poor devils" that can claim a non-mixed pedigree, because only the lower classes amongst retired nations marry between themselves, while the powerful of any group always enrich their experience by marrying some of the prettiest or more attractive women of the neighboring tribe. The advantages of a mixture of races has then been generally recognized; race prejudice as it exists today is a comparatively modern feeling and originates perhaps from the necessity for the English colonizer of far-distant territories densely populated by dissimilar races. The Englishman with his highly developed social instinct understood that if his colonizers of the distant territory of the Indies began to marry the native women, very soon the European in them would become absorbed and the next generation would become lost for the Empire. The Spaniards were bolder; for the decision to accept the results of intermarrying the native was not without forethought, but perfectly calculated, as is shown by the long discussion that preceded the papal statement to the effect that the Indians were entitled to receive the sacraments of the church, marriage among them.

Now if we compare the results of the English policy in India with the results of the Spanish policy in America, even at a time when the British policy is not yet ripe, not having had the centuries of the Spanish colonization's experience, I believe that we shall be justified in declaring that the cultural results of the Spanish method are superior. The Spanish have succeeded in reproducing their blood in part and their culture in full in twenty nations that are today about as Spanish as Spain itself can be, though independent politically and socially. The English, on the other hand, with their system of not even maintaining social intercourse with the natives of India are today as completely strangers in India as on the day their ancestors first landed; and it does not seem probable that they will ever succeed in eradicating the Indian, to substitute for him the Islander. We find in India a coexistence, a juxtaposition, of cultures that do not mix, in the same manner that the bodies of the two races remain fatally apart. Which system is ultimately the better, even from the selfish point of view of the conqueror, is something that only the future can answer. We do not pretend to give advice, but we are bound to accept the Spanish method which in a way has created our nationalities and is the very reason of our existence as a race and a branch of the human family. We cannot condemn the Spanish method without denying ourselves.

The founders of the United States were fortunate in not finding in this territory a very large Indian population, and so it was easy for them to push the Indian back; but the importation of the Negro has brought to this nation, as we all know, a problem harder, no doubt, than any known before. And the North Americans, who are the result of a mixture of all the European races, have followed the English system in regard to the Negro, that is to say, the system of strict avoidance of matrimonial relations with the colored race. The Spaniards did not obey this rule of abstention even with the Negro, the population of many of our tropical sections is largely mulatto, a mixture of the Spanish and the Negro; the Portuguese have also created a mulatto population in Brazil; so here again, we find the Latin system of assimilation and intermarriage and mixture opposed to the Anglo-Saxon method of matrimonial taboos and pure-race standards.

If the tremendous problem involved in this coexistence of two races that live apart in the same home could be considered as finally solved in this country, then there would a good argument for those who claim that Mexico should try to do away with the mestizo and the Indian population by importing millions of Europeans; but the fact is that you cannot destroy a race, that you cannot change social conditions at will, and that you have to face the problem not only with the brain but also with the heart and the superior instinct of nature. And at least for us in Mexico, it is too late to change our practices. There is nothing left for us to do, but to follow the Spanish tradition of eliminating the prejudice of color, the prejudice of race in all of our social procedures. No matter what our theoretical opinions might be, we have to start from the fact that the mestizo is the predominating element in Mexico.

But the mestizo of Mexico does not hold an undisputed reign over the country. Once in a while you still hear in Mexico an echo of the Indian voice that claims for a return to the past of the race as a means of obtaining strength and inspiration. The claims of the pure Indian sound sometimes almost as distinct in its vision as the creed of the most ardent advocate of the purity of the white in his own country. And the evidence that this is not merely a theoretical feeling is found in the story of our revolutions, which in some cases have developed purely Indian movements with the tendency to reinstate purely Indian standards. The Indian uprisings of Yucatan, known as *guerra de castas*, the "War of Castes," the pure Indian against the mestizo and the *criollo*, against the Spanish-speaking, against the Mexican population, is an old but clear example. The Zapata movement of the last revolution clearly contained the seeds of an Indian revival over the whole extent of our country. There was a time when the European dress was not allowed in the Zapata territory; and those Mexicans of white Spanish skin that happened to join the Zapata armies had to adopt the dress and the manners of Indian, in a certain way had to become indianized before they could be accepted. But the weakness of the pure Indian movement lies of course in the fact that the Indian has no civilized standards upon which to fall back. He has no language of his own, never had a language common to all of the race. And the advantage of the Spanish method of colonization through assimilation is here again demonstrated, I believe, in the fact that the Spanish spirit is still gaining victories over the native Indian spirit through its language, through its religion, and its social forms of living. Even the more radical leaders of the Zapata revolt, pure Indians like the school-teacher Montaño who was the brains of the group, were expressing themselves in good Spanish and were basing their economic theory of the distribution of the land, etc., on the terms of the European manner of life. At the same time the mass of the revolted Indians was carrying, as in the days of Hidalgo, the image of the Virgin of Guadalupe as a banner. They were being Spaniards even against their will and their knowledge; and it is only natural that all of this should happen as they had no other tradition upon which to fall back. On the other hand, the movement, although very conscientiously prepared, was overpowered by the stronger mestizo element of the armies of Carranza, of Obregón, and of Villa, who represented the Mexican rather than the Indian, that is to say, the Spanish American, the Indo-Spaniard who also prevails in Central America, in Peru, and in Bolivia.

You may ask if the *criollo*, the descendant of the pure Spanish blood, has not also tried to gain control in Mexico, and I believe we can answer that the *criollo* has made efforts to predominate and also has failed in such efforts. I believe that such tendencies as those represented by the group that aligned itself with Maximilian were mainly European, Spanish tendencies. And to defeat them, the mestizo and the Indian joined under the leadership of the Indian Benito Juarez. Since that time I am sure that the alliance between the mestizo and the Indian has become final, and of course, there being no dividing line by reason of color or caste, the *criollo* also has entirely adapted himself to a national sentiment, or rather to a

continental sentiment of Ibero-Americanism, that has as a common inde-
structible bond the Spanish language and the Spanish type of culture.

The truth is then that whether we like it or not the mestizo is the dominant element of the Latin-American continent. His characteristics have
been pointed out many a time: a great vivacity of mind; quickness of
understanding, and at the same time an unsteady temperament; not too
much persistence in purpose; a somewhat defective will. It is curious to
note that the blending of two different souls through inheritance has produced broader mental disposition. From a purely intellectual point of
view I doubt whether there is a race with less prejudice, more ready to
take up almost any mental adventure, more subtle, and more varied than
the mestizo, or half-breed. I find in these traits the hope that the mestizo
will produce a civilization more universal in its tendency than any other
race of the past. Whether it is due to our temperament or to the fact that
we do not possess a very strong national tradition, the truth is that our
people are keen and are apt to understand and interpret the most contradictory human types. We feel the need of expressing life through many
channels, through a thousand channels; we are not addicted to local tradition or to the European, but we desire to know and to try all—the East
and the West, the North and the South. A plurality of emotion, an almost
mad desire to try all and to live life from every point of view and every
manner of sense experience—we are perhaps more truly universal in sentiment than any other people. Notwithstanding, we sometimes appear to be
bigoted and patriotically local, but this is a result of the dangerous political position in which we have been placed in recent years. On the other
hand we are unstable, and this I believe can be easily understood by the
biologist, as we are a new product, a new breed, not yet entirely shaped.
I believe such weakness can be overcome by obtaining a clear definition of
our aims and by devoting ourselves to a definite and a great task.

Many of our failings arise from the fact that we do not know exactly
what we want. First of all, then, we ought to define our own culture and
our own purposes, and educate ourselves to them. No nation has ever
risen to true greatness without an ardent faith in some high ideal. Democracy and equal opportunities for every man has been the motto of the
great American nation. Broadness, universality of sentiment and thought,
in order to fulfil the mission of bringing together all the races of the earth
and with the purpose of creating a new type of civilization, is, I believe,
the ideal that would give us in Latin-America strength and vision.

The goal may seem too ambitious, but it is only great, unlimited ideals
that are capable of giving a nation the strength that is required to break
the routine of life and to outdo itself. The more ambitious the goal is, the
more strenuous the effort becomes. Our mystic temperament demands a
task that has, in itself at least, a tendency that is unbounded and almost
impossible. A fiery impetus is our only hope if we are to catch up with the
world. Our struggle is, in a way, the struggle of the future, because every
day mankind will come more and more into contact, and mixtures of all

sorts of blood and thought and sentiment will go on increasing, and with them the phenomena and the problems of "mestisage" (of mixture) will become universal. The time and the opportunity of the one-blood, a pure-blood, group is passing away; everywhere the pure-blood groups are being absorbed; and even if they have been masters, they will not stand long before the increasing wave of the technically educated masses of the complex breed. In a way, the world is coming back to the confusion of Babel, and there will come a long period where mixture, or what we call "mestisage," is bound to be the rule. We cannot then dispose of the problem by declaring, as the evolutionists of the Spencer school declared, that the hybrid type was a degenerate type. Such a statement represents only the short-sighted opinion of prejudice and the view advantageous to the imperialist. Let us remember though, that all imperialisms have been swallowed and overwhelmed exactly by those same masses they despised. The future will have to be prepared for in a different manner if we wish to see not a repetition of history but a new era in human progress.

From our local point of view in Mexico, I have started to preach the gospel of the mestizo by trying to impress on the minds of the new race a consciousness of their mission as builders of entirely new concepts of life. But if the mixed race is going to be able to do anything at all, it is first necessary to give it moral strength and faith in its own ability. The sort of science we have been teaching in our schools was not fit for this purpose; on the contrary it was the science created to justify the aims of the conqueror and the imperialist—the science that came to the help of the strong in their conquest and exploitation of the weak: the aristocracy of the white man and the empire of the white over the world, not only in the name of might but also on the ground of a certain semiscientific theory of the survival and predominance of the fittest, which is popularly known as Nietzschean evolutionism, from Nietzsche, the German. One of the first steps toward our moral regeneration, that I have been advocating in Mexico, is the abandonment of this blind belief in certain hasty deductions from Darwinism and the substitution of Mendelism for Darwinism in our biological philosophy as we might find more racial hope and more individual strength and faith in the Mendelian hypothesis of life. Modern scientific theories are in many cases like the religious creeds of the old days, simply the intellectual justification of fatalities of conquest and of commercial greed. If all nations then build theories to justify their policies or to strengthen their deeds, let us develop in Mexico our own theories; or at least, let us be certain, that we choose among the foreign theories of thought those that stimulate our growth instead of those that restrain it. And so, instead of taking up, for instance, the Indian problem with the point of view of the ethnologist of the evolutionistic school who starts from the *parti pris* of his theory, according to which it will take the Indian about five thousand years to develop up to the mentality of the white, we ought to open our eyes to the fact that the Indian five thousand years ago was building monuments that the mentality of the white is using this very day as an inspiration for its new wonder cities of Chicago and New York. The racial theory to which we ought to subscribe then is the theory that the differences among peoples depend more upon ability to do certain things to the exclusion of other things rather than to differences of degree in their total development. Some races chiefly develop artistic ability; other people develop commercial aptitude; and so on. The conclusion of this theory would then be extremely favorable to the mestizo type of culture, as it tends to complement the weaknesses of a particular stock through interchange and assimilation with all the world. In fact, all of the great periods of history have been the work of a mixture of races, of peoples and cultures, rather than the work of any privileged pure-blood nation.

THE SONS OF LA MALINCHE

Octavio Paz

The Mexican works slowly and carefully; he loves the completed work and each of the details that make it up; and his innate good taste is an ancient heritage. If we do not mass produce products, we vie with one another in the difficult, exquisite and useless art of dressing fleas. This does not mean that the Mexican is incapable of being converted into what is called a "good worker." It is only a question of time. Nothing except a historical change, daily more remote and unlikely, can prevent the Mexican—who is still a problem, an enigmatic figure—from becoming one more abstraction.

When this moment arrives, it will resolve all our contradictions by annihilating them, but meanwhile I want to point out that the most extraordinary fact of our situation is that we are enigmatic not only to strangers but also to ourselves. The Mexican is always a problem, both for other Mexicans and for himself. There is nothing simpler, therefore, than to reduce the whole complex group of attitudes that characterize us—especially the problem that we constitute for our own selves—to what may be called the "servant mentality," in opposition to the "psychology of the master" and also to that of modern man, whether proletarian or bourgeois.

From *The Labyrinth of Solitude* by Octavio Paz (New York: Grove Press, 1961). Reprinted by permission of Grove Press, Inc. Translated by Lysander Kemp. Copyright © 1961 by Grove Press, Inc. (Original edition: *El Laberinto de la Soledad*. Mexico City and Buenos Aires: Fondo de Cultura Económica, 1959.)

Octavio Paz is probably Mexico's greatest contemporary poet and essayist, and an important international contributor to twentieth-century philosophy. In his varied career he has served as special literary envoy to Mexico's French embassy and as Mexico's ambassador to India. He was awarded the International Grand Prize in Poetry in Belgium in 1963. His book *The Labyrinth of Solitude* is considered the classic statement of the Mexican male's world view.

Suspicion, dissimulation, irony, the courtesy that shuts us away from the stranger, all of the psychic oscillations with which, in eluding a strange glance, we elude ourselves, are traits of a subjected people who tremble and disguise themselves in the presence of the master. It is revealing that our intimacy never flowers in a natural way, only when incited by fiestas, alcohol or death. Slaves, servants and submerged races always wear a mask, whether smiling or sullen. Only when they are alone, during the great moments of life, do they dare to show themselves as they really are. All their relationships are poisoned by fear and suspicion: fear of the master and suspicion of their equals. Each keeps watch over the other because every companion could also be a traitor. To escape from himself the servant must leap walls, get drunk, forget his condition. He must live alone, without witnesses. He dares to be himself only in solitude.

The unquestionable analogy that can be observed between certain of our attitudes and those of groups subservient to the power of a lord, a caste or a foreign state could be resolved in this statement: the character of the Mexican is a product of the social circumstances that prevail in our country, and the history of Mexico, which is the history of these circumstances, contains the answer to every question. The situation that prevailed during the colonial period would thus be the source of our closed, unstable attitude. Our history as an independent nation would contribute to perpetuating and strengthening this servant psychology, for we have not succeeded in overcoming the misery of the common people and our exasperating social differences, despite a century and a half of struggle and constitutional experience. The use of violence as a dialectical resource, the abuse of authority by the powerful (a vice that has not disappeared) and, finally, the scepticism and resignation of the people—all of these more visible today than ever before, due to our successive postrevolution disillusionments—would complete the historical explication.

The fault of interpretations like the one I have just sketched out is their simplicity. Our attitude toward life is not conditioned by historical events, at least not in the rigorous manner in which the velocity or trajectory of a missile is determined by a set of known factors. Our living attitude—a factor we can never know completely, since change and indetermination are the only constants of our existence—is history also. This is to say that historical events are something more than events because they are colored by humanity, which is always problematical. And they are not merely the result of other events, but rather of a single will that is capable, within certain limits, of ruling their outcome. History is not a mechanism, and the influences among diverse components of an historical event are reciprocal, as has been said so often. What distinguishes one historical event from another is its historical character: in itself and by itself it is an irreducible unity. Irreducible and inseparable. A historical event is not the sum of its component factors but an indissoluble reality. Historical circumstances explain our character to the extent that our character explains those circumstances. Both are the same. Thus any purely historical explanation is insufficient . . . which is not the same as saying it is false.

One observation will be enough to reduce the analogy between the psychology of the servant and our own to its true proportions: the habitual reactions of the Mexican are not limited to a single class, race or isolated group in an inferior position. The wealthy classes also shut themselves away from the exterior world, and lacerate themselves whenever they open out. It is an attitude that goes beyond historical circumstances, although it makes use of them to manifest itself and is modified by contact with them. The Mexican, like all men, converts these circumstances into plastic material. As he molds them he also molds himself.

If it is not possible to identify our character with that of submerged groups, it is also impossible to deny a close relationship. In both situations the individual and the group struggle simultaneously and contradictorily to hide and to reveal themselves. But a difference separates us. Servants, slaves or races victimized by an outside power (the North American Negro, for example) struggle against a concrete reality. We, however, struggle with imaginary entities, with vestiges of the past or self-engendered phantasms. These vestiges and phantasms are real, at least to us. Their reality is of a subtle and cruel order, because it is a phantasmagoric reality. They are impalpable and invincible because they are not outside us but within us. In the struggle which our will-to-be carries on against them, they are supported by a secret and powerful ally, our fear of being. Everything that makes up the present-day Mexican, as we have seen, can be reduced to this: the Mexican does not want or does not dare to be himself.

In many instances these phantasms are vestiges of past realities. Their origins are in the Conquest, the Colonial period, the Independence period or the wars fought against the United States and France. Others reflect our current problems, but in an indirect manner, concealing or distorting their true nature. Is it not extraordinary that the effects persist after the causes have disappeared? And that the effects hide the causes? In this sphere it is impossible to distinguish between causes and effects. Actually there *are* no causes and effects, merely a complex of interpenetrating reactions and tendencies. The persistence of certain attitudes, and the freedom and independence they assume in relation to the causes that created them, induce us to study them in the living flesh of the present rather than in history books.

History, then, can clarify the origins of many of our phantasms, but it cannot dissipate them. We must confront them ourselves. Or to put it another way: history helps us to understand certain traits of our character, provided we are capable of isolating and defining them beforehand. We are the only persons who can answer the questions asked us by reality and our own being.

In our daily language there is a group of words that are prohibited, secret, without clear meanings. We confide the expression of our most brutal or subtle emotions and reactions to their magical ambiguities. They are evil words, and we utter them in a loud voice only when we are not in control of ourselves. In a confused way they reflect our intimacy: the explosions of our vitality light them up and the depressions of our spirit darken them. They constitute a sacred language like those of children, poetry and sects. Each letter and syllable has a double life, at once luminous and obscure, that reveals and hides us. They are words that say nothing and say everything. Adolescents, when they want to appear like men, speak them in a hoarse voice. Women also repeat them, sometimes to demonstrate their freedom of spirit, sometimes to prove the truth of their feelings. But these words are definitive and categorical, despite their ambiguities and the ease with which their meanings change. They are the bad words, the only living language in a world of anemic vocables. They are poetry within the reach of everyone.

Each country has its own. In ours, with their brief, aggressive, electric syllables, resembling the flash given off by a knife when it strikes a hard opaque body, we condense all our appetites, all our hatreds and enthusiasms, all the longings that rage unexpressed in the depths of our being. The word is our sign and seal. By means of it we recognize each other among strangers, and we use it every time the real conditions of our being rise to our lips. To know it, to use it, to throw it in the air like a toy or to make it quiver like a sharp weapon, is a way of affirming that we are Mexican.

All of our anxious tensions express themselves in a phrase we use when anger, joy or enthusiasm cause us to exalt our condition as Mexicans: "*¡Viva México, hijos de la chingada!*" This phrase is a true battle cry, charged with a peculiar electricity; it is a challenge and an affirmation, a shot fired against an imaginary enemy, and an explosion in the air. Once again, with a certain pathetic and plastic fatality, we are presented with the image of a skyrocket that climbs into the sky, bursts in a shower of sparks and then falls in darkness. Or with the image of that howl that ends all our songs and possesses the same ambiguous resonance: an angry joy, a destructive affirmation ripping open the breast and consuming itself.

When we shout this cry on the fifteenth of September, the anniversary of our independence, we affirm ourselves in front of, against and in spite of the "others." Who are the "others"? They are the *hijos de la chingada*: strangers, bad Mexicans, our enemies, our rivals. In any case, the "others," that is, all those who are not as we are. And these "others" are not defined except as the sons of a mother as vague and indeterminate as themselves.

Who is the *Chingada*? Above all, she is the Mother. Not a Mother of flesh and blood but a mythical figure. The *Chingada* is one of the Mexican representations of Maternity, like *La Llorona* or the "long-suffering Mexican mother" we celebrate on the tenth of May.[1] The *Chingada* is the

---

[1] The "Weeping Woman," who wanders through the streets late at night, weeping and crying out. This belief, still current in some parts of Mexico, derives from pre-Conquest times, when "La Llorona" was the earth-goddess Cihuacóatl. The 10th of May is Mother's Day.—*Tr.*

mother who has suffered—metaphorically or actually—the corrosive and defaming action implicit in the verb that gives her her name. It would be worth while to examine that verb.

Darío Rubio, in his *Anarquía del lenguaje en la América Española*, examines the origins of *chingar* and enumerates the meanings given it by almost all Spanish-American people. It probably comes from the Aztecs: *chingaste* (lees, residue, sediment) is *xinachtli* (garden seed) or *xinaxtli* (fermented maguey juice). The word and its derivatives are used in most of America and parts of Spain in association with drinks, alcoholic or otherwise. In Guatemala and El Salvador *chingaste* means the residue or dregs that remain in a glass. In Oaxaca coffee lees are called *chingaditos*. Throughout Mexico alcohol is called *chínguere*—or, significantly, *piquete*.[2] In Chile, Peru and Ecuador a *chingana* is a tavern. In Spain *chingar* means to drink a great deal, to get drunk. In Cuba a *chinguirito* is a shot of alcohol.

Chingar also implies the idea of failure. In Chile and Argentina a petard *se chinga* when it fails to explode, and businesses that fail, fiestas that are rained out, actions that are not completed, also *se chingan*. In Colombia *chingarse* means to be disappointed. In Argentina a torn dress is a *vestido chingado*. Almost everywhere *chingarse* means to be made a fool of, to be involved in a fiasco. In some parts of South America *chingar* means to molest, to censure, to ridicule. It is always an aggressive verb, as can be seen in these further meanings: to dock an animal, to incite or prod a fighting-cock, to make merry, to crack a whip, to endanger, to neglect, to frustrate.

In Mexico the word has innumerable meanings. It is a magical word: a change of tone, a change of inflection, is enough to change its meaning. It has as many shadings as it has intonations, as many meanings as it has emotions. One may be a *chingón*, a *gran chingón* (in business, in politics, in crime or with women), or a *chingaquedito* (silent, deceptive, fashioning plots in the shadows, advancing cautiously and then striking with a club), or a *chingoncito*. But in this plurality of meanings the ultimate meaning always contains the idea of aggression, whether it is the simple act of molesting, pricking or censuring, or the violent act of wounding or killing. The verb denotes violence, an emergence from oneself to penetrate another by force. It also means to injure, to lacerate, to violate—bodies, souls, objects—and to destroy. When something breaks, we say: "*Se chingó.*" When someone behaves rashly, in defiance of the rules, we say: "*Hizo una chingadera.*"

The idea of breaking, of ripping open, appears in a great many of these expressions. The word has sexual connotations but it is not a synonym for the sexual act: one may *chingar* a woman without actually possessing her. And when it does allude to the sexual act, violation or deception gives it a particular shading. The man who commits it never does so with the consent of the *chingada*. *Chingar*, then, is to do violence to another. The verb

---

[2] Literally, a bite, prick or sting; a picket or stake.—*Tr.*

is masculine, active, cruel: it stings, wounds, gashes, stains. And it provokes a bitter, resentful satisfaction.

The person who suffers this action is passive, inert and open, in contrast to the active, aggressive and closed person who inflicts it. The *chingón* is the *macho*, the male; he rips open the *chingada*, the female, who is pure passivity, defenseless against the exterior world. The relationship between them is violent, and it is determined by the cynical power of the first and the impotence of the second. The idea of violence rules darkly over all the meanings of the word, and the dialectic of the "closed" and the "open" thus fulfills itself with an almost ferocious precision.

The magic power of the word is intensified by the fact that it is prohibited. No one uses it casually in public. Only an excess of anger or a delirious enthusiasm justifies its use. It is a word that can only be heard among men or during the big fiestas. When we shout it out, we break a veil of silence, modesty or hypocrisy. We reveal ourselves as we really are. The forbidden words boil up in us, just as our emotions boil up. When they finally burst out, they do so harshly, brutally, in the form of a shout, a challenge, an offense. They are projectiles or knives. They cause wounds.

The Spaniards also abuse their strongest expressions; indeed, the Mexican is singularly nice in comparison. But while the Spaniards enjoy using blasphemy and scatology, we specialize in cruelty and sadism. The Spaniard is simple: he insults God because he believes in Him. Blasphemy, as Machado wrote, is a prayer in reverse. The pleasure that many Spaniards, including some of their greatest poets, derive from allusions to body wastes, and from mixing excrement with sacred matters, is reminiscent of children playing with mud. In addition to resentment, there is that delight in contrasts which produced the Baroque style and the drama of great Spanish painting. Only a Spaniard can speak with authority about Onan[3] and Don Juan. In Mexican expressions, on the contrary, we cannot find the Spanish duality that is symbolized by the opposition of the real and the ideal, the mystics and the picaresque heroes, the funereal Quevedo and the scatalogical Quevedo. What we find is the dichotomy between the closed and the open. The verb *chingar* signifies the triumph of the closed, the male, the powerful, over the open.

If we take into account all of its various meanings, the word defines a great part of our life and qualifies our relationships with our friends and compatriots. To the Mexican there are only two possibilities in life: either he inflicts the actions implied by *chingar* on others, or else he suffers them himself at the hands of others. This conception of social life as combat fatally divides society into the strong and the weak. The strong—the hard, unscrupulous *chingones*—surround themselves with eager followers. This servility toward the strong, especially among the *políticos* (that is, the professionals of public business), is one of the more deplorable conse-

---

[3] Onan is the biblical character who was killed by God for practicing coitus interruptus.—*Eds.*

quences of the situation. Another, no less degrading, is the devotion to
personalities rather than to principles. Our politicians frequently mix public business with private. It does not matter. Their wealth or their influence in government allows them to maintain a flock of supporters whom
the people call, most appositely, *lambiscones* (from the word *lamer*: "to
lick").

The verb *chingar*—malign and agile and playful, like a caged animal—
creates many expressions that turn our world into a jungle: there are
tigers in business, eagles in the schools and the army, lions among our
friends. A bribe is called a "bite." The bureaucrats gnaw their "bones"
(public employment). And in a world of *chingones*, of difficult relationships, ruled by violence and suspicion—a world in which no one opens
out or surrenders himself—ideas and accomplishments count for little.
The only thing of value is manliness, personal strength, a capacity for imposing oneself on others.

The word also has another, more restricted meaning. When we say,
"*Vete a la chingada*,"[4] we send a person to a distant place. Distant, vague
and indeterminate. To the country of broken and worn-out things. A gray
country, immense and empty, that is not located anywhere. It is not only
because of simple phonetic association that we compare it with China, for
China is also immense and remote. The *chingada*, because of constant
usage, contradictory meanings and the friction of angry or enthusiastic
lips, wastes away, loses its contents and disappears. It is a hollow word.
It says nothing. It is Nothingness itself.

After this digression, it is possible to answer the question, "What is the
Chingada?" The *Chingada* is the Mother forcibly opened, violated or deceived. The *hijo de la Chingada* is the offspring of violation, abduction or
deceit. If we compare this expression with the Spanish *hijo de puta* (son
of a whore), the difference is immediately obvious. To the Spaniard, dis-
honor consists in being the son of a woman who voluntarily surrenders
herself: a prostitute. To the Mexican it consists in being the fruit of a
violation.

Manuel Cabrera points out that the Spanish attitude reflects a moral
and historical conception of original sin, while that of the Mexican,
deeper and more genuine, transcends both ethics and anecdotes. In effect,
every woman—even when she gives herself willingly—is torn open by the
man, is the *Chingada*. In a certain sense all of us, by the simple fact of
being born of woman, are *hijos de la Chingada*, sons of Eve. But the sin-
gularity of the Mexican resides, I believe, in his violent, sarcastic humiliation of the Mother and his no less violent affirmation of the Father. A
woman friend of mine (women are more aware of the strangeness of this
situation) has made me see that this admiration for the Father—who is a
symbol of the closed, the aggressive—expresses itself very clearly in a
saying we use when we want to demonstrate our superiority: "I am your

---

[4] Somewhat stronger than "Go to Hell."—*Tr.*

father." The question of origins, then, is the central secret of our anxiety and anguish. It is worth studying the significance of this fact.

We are alone. Solitude, the source of anxiety, begins on the day we are deprived of maternal protection and fall into a strange and hostile world. We have fallen, and this fall—this knowledge that we have fallen—makes us guilty. Of what? Of a nameless wrong: that of having been born. These feelings are common to all men and there is nothing specifically Mexican in them. Therefore it is not necessary to repeat a description that has been given many times before. What *is* necessary is to isolate certain traits and emotions that cast a particular light on the universal condition of man.

In all civilizations, God the Father becomes an ambivalent figure once he has dethroned the feminine deities. On the one hand, the Father embodies the generative power, the origin of life, whether he be Jehovah, God the Creator, or Zeus, king of creation, ruler of the cosmos. On the other hand, he is the first principle, the One, from whom all is born and to whom all must return. But he is also the lord of the lightning bolt and the whip; he is the tyrant, the ogre who devours life. This aspect—angry Jehovah, God of wrath, or Saturn, or Zeus the violator of women—is the one that appears almost exclusively in Mexican representations of manly power. The *macho* represents the masculine pole of life. The phrase "I am your father" has no paternal flavor and is not said in order to protect or to guide another, but rather to impose one's superiority, that is, to humiliate. Its real meaning is no different from that of the verb *chingar* and its derivatives. The *macho* is the *gran chingón*. One word sums up the aggressiveness, insensitivity, invulnerability and other attributes of the *macho*: power. It is force without the discipline of any notion of order: arbitrary power, the will without reins and without a set course.

Unpredictability adds another element to the character of the *macho*. He is a humorist. His jokes are huge and individual, and they always end in absurdity. The anecdote about the man who "cured" the headache of a drinking companion by emptying his pistol into his head is well known. True or not, the incident reveals the inexorable rigor with which the logic of the absurd is introduced into life. The *macho* commits *chingaderas*, that is, unforeseen acts that produce confusion, horror and destruction. He opens the world; in doing so, he rips and tears it, and this violence provokes a great, sinister laugh. And in its own way, it is just: it reestablishes the equilibrium and puts things in their places, by reducing them to dust, to misery, to nothingness. The humor of the *macho* is an act of revenge.

A psychologist would say that resentment is the basis of his character. It would not be difficult to perceive certain homosexual inclinations also, such as the use and abuse of the pistol, a phallic symbol which discharges death rather than life, and the fondness for exclusively masculine guilds. But whatever may be the origin of these attitudes, the fact is that the essential attribute of the *macho*—power—almost always reveals itself as a capacity for wounding, humiliating, annihilating. Nothing is more natural, therefore, than his indifference toward the offspring he engenders. He is not the founder of a people; he is not a patriarch who exercises *patria potestas*; he is not a king or a judge or the chieftain of a clan. He is power isolated in its own potency, without relationship or compromise with the outside world. He is pure incommunication, a solitude that devours itself and everything it touches. He does not pertain to our world; he is not from our city; he does not live in our neighborhood. He comes from far away: he is always far away. He is the Stranger. It is impossible not to notice the resemblance between the figure of the *macho* and that of the Spanish conquistador. This is the model—more mythical than real—that determines the images the Mexican people form of men in power: caciques, feudal lords, hacienda owners, politicians, generals, captains of industry. They are all *machos, chingones.*

The *macho* has no heroic or divine counterpart. Hidalgo, the "father of the fatherland" as it is customary to call him in the ritual gibberish of the Republic, is a defenseless old man, more an incarnation of the people's helplessness against force than an image of the wrath and power of an awe-inspiring father. Among the numerous patron saints of the Mexicans there is none who resembles the great masculine divinities. Finally, there is no especial veneration for God the Father in the Trinity. He is a dim figure at best. On the other hand, there is profound devotion to Christ as the Son of God, as the youthful God, above all as the victimized Redeemer. The village churches have a great many images of Jesus—on the cross, or covered with thorns and wounds—in which the insolent realism of the Spaniards is mingled with the tragic symbolism of the Indians. On the one hand, the wounds are flowers, pledges of resurrection; on the other, they are a reiteration that life is the sorrowful mask of death.

The fervor of the cult of God the Son would seem to be explained, at first glance, as an inheritance from the pre-Hispanic religions. When the Spaniards arrived, almost all of the great masculine divinities—with the exception of the rain-god Tláloc, a child and an old man at the same time, and a deity of greater antiquity—were sons of gods, like Xipe, god of the young corn, and Huitzilopochtli, the "Warrior of the South." Perhaps it is not idle to recall that the birth of Huitzilopochtli offers more than one analogy with that of Christ: he too was conceived without carnal contact; the divine messenger was likewise a bird (that dropped a feather into the lap of the earth-goddess Coatlicue); and finally, the infant Huitzilopochtli also had to escape the persecution of a mythical Herod. Nevertheless, it would be a mistake to use these analogies to explain that devotion to Christ, just as it would be to attribute that devotion to a mere survival of the cult of the sons of gods. The Mexican venerates a bleeding and humiliated Christ, a Christ who has been beaten by the soldiers and condemned by the judges, because he sees in him a transfigured image of his own identity. And this brings to mind Cuauhtémoc, the young Aztec emperor who was dethroned, tortured and murdered by Cortés.

Cuauhtémoc means "Falling Eagle." The Mexican chieftain rose to

power at the beginning of the siege of México-Tenochtitlán, when the
Aztecs had been abandoned by their gods, their vassals and their allies.
Even his relationship with a woman fits the archetype of the young hero,
at one and the same time the lover and the son of the goddess. Thus
López Velarde wrote that Cuauhtémoc went out to meet Cortés—that is,
to the final sacrifice—"separated from the curved breast of the Empress."
He is a warrior but he is also a child. The exception is that the heroic
cycle does not end with his death: the fallen hero awaits resurrection. It is
not surprising that for the majority of Mexicans Cuauhtémoc should be
the "young grandfather," the origin of Mexico: the hero's tomb is the
cradle of the people. This is the dialectic of myth, and Cuauhtémoc is
more a myth than a historical figure. Another element enters here, an
analogy that makes this history a true poem in search of fulfillment: the
location of Cuauhtémoc's tomb is not known. The mystery of his burial
place is one of our obsessions. To discover it would mean nothing less
than to return to our origins, to reunite ourselves with our ancestry, to
break out of our solitude. It would be a resurrection.

If we ask about the third figure of the triad, the Mother, we hear a
double answer. It is no secret to anyone that Mexican Catholicism is centered about the cult of the Virgin of Guadalupe. In the first place, she is
an Indian Virgin; in the second place, the scene of her appearance to the
Indian Juan Diego[5] was a hill that formerly contained a sanctuary dedicated to Tonantzin, "Our Mother," the Aztec goddess of fertility. We
know that the Conquest coincided with the apogee of the cult of two masculine divinities: Quetzalcóatl, the self-sacrificing god, and Huitzilopochtli, the young warrior-god. The defeat of these gods—which is what
the Conquest meant to the Indian world, because it was the end of a cosmic cycle and the inauguration of a new divine kingdom—caused the
faithful to return to the ancient feminine deities. This phenomenon of a
return to the maternal womb, so well known to the psychologist, is without doubt one of the determining causes of the swift popularity of the
cult of the Virgin. The Indian goddesses were goddesses of fecundity,
linked to the cosmic rhythms, the vegetative processes and agrarian rites.
The Catholic Virgin is also the Mother (some Indian pilgrims still call her
Guadalupe-Tonantzin), but her principal attribute is not to watch over
the fertility of the earth but to provide refuge for the unfortunate. The
situation has changed: the worshipers do not try to make sure of their
harvests but to find a mother's lap. The Virgin is the consolation of the
poor, the shield of the weak, the help of the oppressed. In sum, she is the
Mother of orphans. All men are born disinherited and their true condition
is orphanhood, but this is particularly true among the Indians and the
poor in Mexico. The cult of the Virgin reflects not only the general condition of man but also a concrete historical situation, in both the spiritual

[5] A fuller description of the meeting between the Virgin and Juan Diego is in Wolf's
article, Section IV.—*Eds.*

and material realms. In addition, the Virgin—the universal Mother—is also the intermediary, the messenger, between disinherited man and the unknown, inscrutable power: the Strange.

In contrast to Guadalupe, who is the Virgin Mother, the *Chingada* is the violated Mother. Neither in her nor in the Virgin do we find traces of the darker attributes of the great goddesses: the lasciviousness of Amaterasu and Aphrodite, the cruelty of Artemis and Astarte, the sinister magic of Circe or the bloodlust of Kali. Both of them are passive figures. Guadalupe is pure receptivity, and the benefits she bestows are of the same order: she consoles, quiets, dries tears, calms passions. The *Chingada* is even more passive. Her passivity is abject: she does not resist violence, but is an inert heap of bones, blood and dust. Her taint is constitutional and resides, as we said earlier, in her sex. This passivity, open to the outside world, causes her to lose her identity: she is the *Chingada*. She loses her name; she is no one; she disappears into nothingness; she *is* Nothingness. And yet she is the cruel incarnation of the feminine condition.

If the *Chingada* is a representation of the violated Mother, it is appropriate to associate her with the Conquest, which was also a violation, not only in the historical sense but also in the very flesh of Indian women. The symbol of this violation is doña Malinche, the mistress of Cortés. It is true that she gave herself voluntarily to the conquistador, but he forgot her as soon as her usefulness was over. Doña Marina[6] becomes a figure representing the Indian women who were fascinated, violated or seduced by the Spaniards. And as a small boy will not forgive his mother if she abandons him to search for his father, the Mexican people have not forgiven La Malinche for her betrayal. She embodies the open, the *chingado*, to our closed, stoic, impassive Indians. Cuauhtémoc and Doña Marina are thus two antagonistic and complementary figures. There is nothing surprising about our cult of the young emperor—"the only hero at the summit of art," an image of the sacrificed son—and there is also nothing surprising about the curse that weighs against La Malinche. This explains the success of the contemptuous adjective *malinchista* recently put into circulation by the newspapers to denounce all those who have been corrupted by foreign influences. The *malinchistas* are those who want Mexico to open itself to the outside world: the true sons of La Malinche, who is the *Chingada* in person. Once again we see the opposition of the closed and the open.

When we shout "*¡Viva México, hijos de la chingada!*" we express our desire to live closed off from the outside world and, above all, from the past. In this shout we condemn our origins and deny our hybridism. The strange permanence of Cortés and La Malinche in the Mexican's imagination and sensibilities reveals that they are something more than historical figures: they are symbols of a secret conflict that we have still not resolved. When he repudiates La Malinche—the Mexican Eve, as she was

---

[6] The name given to La Malinche by the Spaniards.—*Tr.*

represented by José Clemente Orozco in his mural in the National Preparatory School—the Mexican breaks his ties with the past, renounces his origins, and lives in isolation and solitude.

The Mexican condemns all his traditions at once, the whole set of gestures, attitudes and tendencies in which it is now difficult to distinguish the Spanish from the Indian. For that reason the Hispanic thesis, which would have us descend from Cortés to the exclusion of La Malinche, is the patrimony of a few extremists who are not even pure whites. The same can be said of indigenist propaganda, which is also supported by fanatical *criollos* and *mestizos,* while the Indians have never paid it the slightest attention. The Mexican does not want to be either an Indian or a Spaniard. Nor does he want to be descended from them. He denies them. And he does not affirm himself as a mixture, but rather as an abstraction: he is a man. He becomes the son of Nothingness. His beginnings are in his own self.

This attitude is revealed not only in our daily life but also in the course of our history, which at certain moments has been the embodiment of a will to eradicate all that has gone before. It is astonishing that a country with such a vivid past—a country so profoundly traditional, so close to its roots, so rich in ancient legends even if poor in modern history—should conceive of itself only as a negation of its origins.

THE PEOPLE OF AZTLÁN

Armando B. Rendon

We are the people of Aztlán, true descendants of the Fifth Sun, el Quinto Sol.

In the early morning light of a day thousands of years old now, my forebears set out from Aztlán, a region of deserts, mountains, rivers, and forests, to seek a new home. Where they came from originally is hidden in the sands and riverbeds and only hinted at by the cast of eye and skin which we, their sons, now bear.

Driven by drought, or enemies, or by the vision of a new motherland, my people began walking toward the south in the hope of founding a new world. Among the earliest of my ancestors were the Nahúas, from whom sprang the most advanced and sophisticated peoples of the North American continent. They made their own wandering journey to Anáhuac, as

Reprinted with permission of The Macmillan Company from *Chicano Manifesto* by Armando B. Rendon. Copyright © 1971 by Armando B. Rendon.

Armando B. Rendon is a free-lance writer and a vice-president of a Chicano-owned and managed communications firm. He has previously been Deputy Information Officer for the U.S. Commission on Civil Rights.

the region of the Valley of Mexico was then known. From about the time that the Christ Passion was unfolding on the other side of the world, and for perhaps a thousand years afterward, a way of life and thought was evolving which the man-god Quetzalcoatl had forged and which the Nahúas, the Toltecs, the Chichimecas, and then the Aztecs nurtured through the centuries.

The Toltecs forged Teotihuacán, the City of the Gods and the center of the Nahuatl religion. Their influence continued for fifteen hundred years, until the arrival of Hernando Cortés, the final inroad of a searching people that was to spell the end of a great, involuted civilization.

The Chichimeca, nomadic tribes who, tradition tells us came from the North, from Aztlán, or what is now the southwestern part of the United States, began moving down by ancient trails into the Valley of Mexico in about the eleventh century A.D. The Aztecs, who derive their name from Aztlán, were the last significant group to arrive in Anáhuac. Those that survived this exodus came among shallow marshes by a lake and in 1325 founded the city of Tenochtitlán. It was there in the marsh waters that they saw a sign, an eagle grasping a serpent in its claw as it perched upon a cactus sprouting from a rock. Tenochtitlán means cactus upon a stone.

Quetzalcoatl gave birth in his people to the Fifth Sun. Four Suns prefigured the coming of el Quinto Sol, which was to destroy and subsume the rest. The Fifth Sun was the epoch of the Aztec civilization. Huitzilopochtli, who led the Aztecs out of Aztlán, personifies this Fifth Sun, but Quetzalcoatl (historically identified with Topiltzin, the last Toltec king, who reigned in the late tenth century) is the creator of the epoch and its spirit. Earth, air, fire, and water preceded the fifth epoch; the Fifth Sun was movement, progress, life vibrant. The people of the Fifth Sun developed a complex system of religion in a region that was to be New Spain, Mexico, and much of present Central America. They developed an elaborate symbolic language to depict their beliefs. To convey the concept of the Fifth Sun a basic pattern was used of five circles, one circle at each of four corners, with the fifth in the center. An intricate refinement is seen in a circular network of human features incorporating the five-circle mode; the great Aztec calendar stone is a huge representation of this principle. (Laurette Séjourné in her book Burning Water provides an invaluable description and interpretation of the religion and language of our ancient forebears.)

Discovering the spirited sensitivity and depth of the people of the Fifth Sun, the Chicano begins to fathom what must be one of the most psychologically important elements in the make-up of the Mexican. Octavio Paz, the Mexican poet and former ambassador to India, comments in The Labyrinth of Solitude that the Aztec religion was notable for its generally being a "superimposition" on older beliefs (the Nahuatl religion was so infused with various primitive ideas and superstitions that the Aztec version suggested a predisposition to Catholicism and its ally, Spanish rule). Paz says unequivocally, "The Mexican is a religious being and his experience of the divine is completely genuine. . . . Nothing has been able to destroy the filial relationship of our people with the divine."

The spiritual experience of the Chicano, in turn, is profound. From the standpoint of the people of Ollin Tonatiuh, the Nahuatl name for the Fifth Sun, the Chicano's religious experience embodies all of nature. The epic of the Four Suns begins with the Sun of Night or Earth, depicted by a tiger, a period that by itself is sterile; then the Sun of Air, or God of Wind, pure spirit whose indwellers became monkeys; the Sun of Rain or Fire, in which only birds survive; and finally the Sun of Water, friendly only to fish.

The Fifth Sun is born out of man's sacrifice. At its center is the spirit; its mode is movement. It is the unity, cohesion, synthesis of all that has come before, bound into the human soul. Thus, the Fifth Sun is the very foundation of life, of spirituality, not in the restricted sense of an organized religion but in the nature of a common bond among all soul creatures. We can speak, therefore, of a union with the cosmos, of a cosmic sense of spirit, of an alma Chicana (a Chicano soul). The concept of *La Raza Unida* is a further reassertion and profession of that principle of a cosmic Chicano existence. We can think of ourselves as a community of the future and of the past seeking its destiny in the present.

My people have come in fulfillment of a cosmic cycle from ancient Aztlán, the seed ground of the great civilizations of Anáhuac, to modern Aztlán, characterized by the progeny of our Indian, Mexican, and Spanish ancestors. We have rediscovered Aztlán in ourselves. This knowledge provides the dynamic principle upon which to build a deep unity and brotherhood among Chicanos. Ties much more profound than even language, birthplace, or culture bind us together—Aztlán represents that unifying force of our nonmaterial heritage. This is not meant to revive long-dead religions, but rather to resurrect still-living principles of brotherhood (carnalismo), of spiritual union, which we have come so close to losing.

A statement composed in March 1969 in Denver, Colorado, during a Chicano youth conference sponsored by the Crusade for Justice, elaborated for the first time the concept of Aztlán. Notably, a young Chicano writer and poet, Alberto Alurista, proposed Aztlán as the fundamental theme, and this inspired a new awareness of self-concept and intent among Chicanos. In brief, the Spiritual Plan of Aztlán asserts:

> In the spirit of a new people . . . *we*, the Chicano, inhabitants and civilizers of the northern land of Aztlán, from whence came our forefathers, reclaiming the land of their birth and consecrating the determination of our people of the sun, *declare* that the call of our blood is our power, our responsibility, and our inevitable destiny. . . .
>
> With our heart in our hand and our hands in the soil, we declare the independence of our mestizo Nation. We are a bronze people with a bronze culture. Before the world, before all of North America, before all our brothers

in the Bronze Continent, we are a Nation. We are a union of free pueblos. We are *Aztlán*.

References to Aztlán as the place of origin of the Mexican Indian peoples are negligible in North American chronicles. Two of the most easily attainable texts by historians in the United States are William H. Prescott's *History of the Conquest of Mexico* (1843) and Alvin M. Josephy, Jr.'s *The Indian Heritage of America* (1968). Prescott, in reviewing the various histories, compiled for the most part by priest-scholars, noted that "The ingenuity of the chronicler was taxed to find out analogies between the Aztec and Scripture histories, both old and new. The emigration from Aztlan to Anahuac was typical of the Jewish exodus." This suggests the legend that the American peoples were derived from one of the lost tribes of Israel. Commenting on another possible source, Prescott wrote:

> The theory of an Asiatic origin for Aztec civilization derives stronger confirmation from the light of *tradition*, which, shining steadily from the far North-west, pierces through the dark shadows that history and mythology have alike thrown around the antiquities of the country. Traditions of a Western, or North-western origin were found among the more barbarous tribes, and by the Mexicans were preserved both orally and in their hieroglyphical maps, where the different stages of their migration are carefully noted. But who at this day shall read them? They are admitted to agree, however, in representing the populous North as the prolific hive of the American races. In this quarter were placed their Aztlan and their Huehuetlapállan, the bright abodes of their ancestors. . . .

In a footnote, he said of the maps: "But as they are all within the boundaries of New Spain, indeed, south of the Rio Gila, they throw little light, of course, on the vexed question of the primitive abodes of the Aztecs."

It so happens that the Rio Gila flows from southwestern New Mexico, starting a few miles west of where the Rio Grande cuts through the center of New Mexico before it forms a border between Texas and Mexico. From there, the Gila connects with the Colorado River at the junction of California, Nevada, Arizona, and Sonora, Mexico, just above the Gulf of California—a convergence of rivers and cultures as significant for the Americas as the confluence of the Tigris and Euphrates in Mesopotamia! Yet Prescott would have us seek a more distant source.

In a comprehensive study of the Indians of the Americas, Josephy recounts the arrival of the Mexica, a Nahuatl-speaking tribe, "weak and relatively primitive," in the Lake Texcoco area in the early thirteenth century, and their settling on the site of today's Mexico City. The historian says that the Mexica took the name Aztec from Aztlán, whence they had come, "somewhere vaguely to the Northwest and may even have been in the present-day United States Southwest."

An analysis and compendium by Mexican historians of the ancient native peoples, *México a Través de los Siglos* (1939), relates, according to its editors, "the pilgrimage of the Mexicans from the time they left Aztlán until they founded the City of Mexico." The first of the three volumes in this work presents a detailed account of the Nahuatl religion and of Nahuatl origins, and notes specifically that the region encompassing Nevada, Utah, New Mexico, Arizona, California, and the Mexican States of Sinaloa and Sonora contain artifacts and remains of living facilities closely related to those of the Aztecs in the Valley of Mexico. That region is also given the name Chicomoztoc, literally, *las siete cuevas* (seven caves), later to become the fabled and much-sought seven cities of Cibola. Huehuetlapállan was the most important of these population centers. But the Mexican scholars clearly identify Aztec and Mexican origins with the southwestern United States. However, aside from the two United States sources cited, further reference to Aztlán is difficult to find in Anglo history; it is obviously of no consequence except to the Chicano. We still know very little about our ancient origins.

The Chicano is unique in America. He is a descendant of the Fifth Sun, bound to the land of Aztlán by his blood, sweat, and flesh, and heir to gifts of language and culture from Spanish conquistadores. But in him, too, is another dimension.

Some observers have said of the Mexican American that he is an in-between, neither Mexican nor American. The truth is that the Mexican American is a fusion of three cultures: a mezcla of Mexican Indian, Spanish, and the North American—yes, even the Anglo-dominated society is his to absorb into himself.

Too many Mexican Americans have invested solely in the Anglo world, cannot see the value in their multiculture, and do not have the courage to reclaim it and fight for it. I refer not to the culture that the gringo has allowed us to retain, of taco chains and fiesta days, but to the culture, which is the indomitable wellspring of our mestizo character, the fusion of Mexican Indian, Spanish, and now even Anglo. In the Southwest, the Chicano, who is the blending of these three elements, personalities, and psychologies, has come to a time of self-assertion. The word Chicano is offered not merely as a term of differentiation (some would say separation or racism) but also as a term of identification with that distinct melding of bloods and cultures. The term Chicano is anything but racist, because it declares the assimilation of bloods and heritage that makes the Chicano a truly multicultured person.

Chicanismo offers a new or renewed adaptation to a reality of life for the Mexican American. Segregated, maligned, despised, subjugated, destroyed for what he is, and barred from becoming what he would be, the Mexican American turns toward a new path. Unleashing the frustrations and emotions of many generations of lifetimes, reviving suppressed memories, and casting off the weighing terrors, he resurrects himself as a Chicano. He can face the onslaught of cultural racism perpetrated by the Anglo, which he has only endured up to now, with new power, new insight, new optimism—if not for himself, at least for his family and the Chicanos that are to come.

By admitting to being Chicano, to being this new person, we lose nothing, we gain a great deal. Any Mexican American afraid to join with the Chicano cause can only be afraid for himself and afraid of the gringo. The black has faced this truth and found that he must make his way as a black or as nothing, certainly not as the white man's "nigger." We can no longer be the Anglo's "Pancho."

The Federal bureaucrat who shies away from being too Chicano or plays down the cause should get out of government and stop being window dressing; he is harming the people he could especially serve *por no tener tripas*. The Mexican American businessman or professional who disclaims his Chicano roots and will have nothing to do with la causa because it might hurt sales or cut down the size of his Anglo clientele has sold out to the gringo dollar long ago and now betrays the very people who probably put him where he is. The people in the barrio who criticize and decry the Chicano revolt because "it's not how we do things" have forgotten two histories, and they lie to themselves if they believe that the gringo will eventually relent and give them or their children an education, a job, a decent home, or a future.

Any Mexican American who can celebrate the Fourth of July and *el dies y seis de septiembre* must realize that revolt, action for change, is not a thing of the past. The Chicano revolt is a marriage of awareness and necessity that must be consummated over and over if justice is to be done. The Chicano revolt embodies old values that have been suppressed over generations. It goes a step beyond the black revolution in that Chicanos assert that they have a personal and a group point of view which the dominant "culture," made up of blacks and whites, must accept now or suffer the consequences. The Chicano insists that the Anglo respect his language and grant it equal value in any educational system where Chicano students are dominant. The Chicano insists that his culture, his way of life, and that *he* as a person be taken into account when housing is built, when industry offers jobs, when political parties caucus.

There has been a two-way infusion of Anglo-Saxon and African elements within the dominant "culture" to the extent that the color of one's skin, unfortunately for both sides, is the sole measure of acceptance or rejection of one's fellow man in American society. If it were not for color there would be little to distinguish black from white. Black people display a cultural perspective and philosophy little different from what the Anglo desires and demands. We Chicanos see the Negro as a black Anglo. But we Chicanos, as we must admit sooner or later, are different from the Anglo and the black in more ways than merely color. Our people range widely from light-skinned *güeros* to dark-skinned Indios. Certainly, we have our share of black blood from the Negroes who escaped into Mexico, a free country, from the southern slave states, and even Arab-Semitic traces from the Moors. The *güeros* remain Chicano by force of cultural attraction; they would rather be Chicano than Anglo, although they could easily pass as a white gringo.

But besides color, the Chicano may be discriminated against because of his Spanish surname, which he may change; or by his Spanish accent, which he may hide by calling himself "Spanish"; or by the effects of past discrimination, which restrict the kinds of jobs or social encounters he will seek; or even by the family structure which, if strong enough, could effectively thwart the desire to break away from the Chicano community. Add to this list of barriers, dark, "swarthy," or "Indian" skin, and economic and social stability may be an impossible objective. Yet there are still too many Mexican Americans who not only refuse to accept who and what they are, but reject the fact that however comfortable and secure they may be in their present situation, they evolved out of days of discrimination. Nor should they be blind to the jeopardy in which they remain, because they will always be different from the gringo.

The impact of discrimination on the Mexican American has been somewhat obscured by our lack of numbers, our generally passive resistance in past years, our dependence on the white man's justice, even our own blind acceptance of the white man's way as *the* way. Time and again I have questioned Chicanos about the discrimination they have experienced. Invariably, every one who began the conversation with the approach that he had never been discriminated against soon reversed his view. Racism, cultural discrimination, has affected every Chicano. Any of us who at some time has denied his heritage by changing his name or birthplace or by purifying his English of any accent, any who has been forced to leave his home alone or with his family for lack of opportunity, and has felt shame in his language, accent, or skin color, or in the food he eats—that Chicano has tasted the Anglo's kiss of death.

The Anglo-American society is a bastard issued from the promiscuous concubinage of several hundreds of ethnic and racial peoples who have cast their cultural identities into the American melting pot. While it may have been easy and necessary for some ethnic, non-Anglo-Saxon people to do, it is not necessary—nor easy—for Mexican Americans to throw away their birthrights. The need is exactly the opposite. We Chicanos, the people of el Quinto Sol, must realize Aztlán in ourselves, individually and as a group. We are part of the land, but we need not seek a geographic center for our Aztlán; it lies within ourselves, and it is boundless, immeasurable, and limited only by our lack of vision, by our lack of courage, by our hesitancy to grasp the truth of our being.

We are Aztlán and Aztlán is us.

Our ancestors also foresaw that after the Fifth Sun another epoch would ensue, but what form it would take they did not know or say. We Chicanos face the same unknown future. We do not know where the Chicano revolt will lead. It must lead somewhere. Will Chicanos have a say in what eventually happens? Was the Aztecs' Sixth Sun the coming of Cortés, of the white man, and the advent of his destruction? Is this also to be the Chicano's Sixth Sun—destruction at the hands of the white man, the Anglo, the gringo?

Suggested Readings

Aguirre Beltran, Gonzalo. 1946. *La Población Negra de México, 1519–1810: Estudio Ethnohistórico.* Mexico City.
 This ethnohistorical account offers the reader the basic information needed in understanding the amalgamation of African, Mexican, and European peoples in Mexico. Both the biological and cultural mixture is discussed.
Allport, Gordon W. 1958. *The Nature of Prejudice.* Garden City, N.Y.: Doubleday.
 An excellent reference on the psychodynamics of prejudice, this volume is basic reading in understanding the nature of racism.
Degler, Carl N. 1971. *Neither Black nor White.* New York: The Macmillan Company.
 Degler refutes Tannenbaum's idea that slavery in the United States differed from the form it took in Latin America. His book is an attempt to understand the nature of black–white relations in the United States by comparing such relations in a different national and social context, in this case Brazil.
Freyre, Gilberto. 1969. *The Masters and the Slaves.* New York: Alfred A. Knopf, Inc.
 This is the single most important volume dealing with the process of race mixture in the Americas. Though Professor Freyre's specific references are to his native Brazil, his devastating treatment of stereotypes is basic reading in the entire field of New World race relations.
Garn, Stanley M. 1969. *Human Races.* Springfield, Ill.: Charles C. Thomas, Publisher.
 A comprehensive and intelligible book written about race and race formation. It deals with the basic evolutionary problems and does not invoke "race" as a social phenomenon, but merely states what is known of man biologically.
Harris, Marvin. 1964. *Patterns of Race Relations in the Americas.* New York: Walker and Co.
 An explanation of the differences between race relations in Latin America and the familiar North American pattern.
Klineberg, Otto. 1951. *Race and Psychology.* From the UNESCO series

The Race Question in Modern Science. United Nations, N.Y.: UNESCO. Discusses the widely and stubbornly held belief that some races and peoples are inferior. Klineberg gives specific examples to illustrate how such distorted beliefs have led to mass executions and discrimination. He also disputes the validity of culturally biased psychological tests for the measurement of native differences in ability.

Mörner, Magnus. 1967. *Race Mixture in the History of Latin America*. Boston: Little, Brown and Company.

This must be the most comprehensive and completely objective account of the evolution of miscegenation and acculturation in Latin America. Mörner deals with the social, religious, psychological, and political implications of the conquest of native peoples.

Steinfield, Melvin. 1970. *Cracks in the Melting Pot: Racism and Discrimination in American History*. Beverley Hills, Calif.: Glencoe Press.

This book shows how racism and discrimination are woven intimately into the fabric of American life. Although much in this book deals with the black targets of white racism, considerable space is devoted also to Native Americans, Chinese, Japanese, and other ethnic minorities. This text creates an awareness of how racism and discrimination have provided rationalizations for territorial acquisition, prejudicial immigration laws, presidential utterances and actions, and brutalities against ethnic minorities.

Tannenbaum, Frank. 1946. *Slave and Citizen*. New York: Alfred A. Knopf, Inc.

One of the most strongly debated issues in the field of New World race mixture is the difference in treatment of blacks in the United States and Latin America. Tannenbaum takes the position that racism in Latin America is based on social rather than color criteria. A thoughtful statement along similar lines is to be found in Charles Wagley (1968), "The Concept of Social Race in the Americas." A biting (and convincing) counterargument may be found in Marvin Harris' essay "The Myth of the Friendly Master" (1964), as well as in Degler, above.

PART I
Yesterday

This section traces the heritage of Chicanos from Mayan and Aztec times, through the Conquest and the Spanish Colonial period, into the modern era of Chicano history itself.

The modern period begins with the Mexican-American War and includes such landmark events as the gold rush of 1849, the Mexican Revolution of 1910, and the Bracero movement, which lasted from 1942 to 1964. These events were primarily responsible for the growth of the Chicano population in the United States. It is a long and complicated history; diagrammatically it might look like the figure shown on the following page.

The worlds of the Aztecs and the Castilians were born in antiquity. The Western, Roman tradition shaped the political and religious structure of Spain; the culture of the Aztecs had its roots in Teotihuacan. By 1000 A.D. the Toltecs, forerunners of the Aztecs, had set the stage for the historic period of native Mexican Indian life. In Iberia, Spaniards began gearing up for the long wars against the Moors and the reconquest of the peninsula.

By 1500 A.D. Spain was unified under the Catholic kings, Ferdinand and Isabella. Central Mexico was held together by the gods and kings of the Aztecs. The first double arrow shows the meeting of those two worlds in Tenochtitlan.

Mexican culture developed during the Colonial period through such institutions as the encomienda, the Church, caciquismo, and the like. Then, in 1810, tired of listening to decrees on how to manage their internal affairs from a king half a world away, the Mexicans revolted and won independence from Spain. This did not change the social injustices in Mexico, of course. Power changed hands from those whose allegiance was to Spain, to those whose allegiance was to themselves. The Indians and lower-class mestizos continued to suffer.

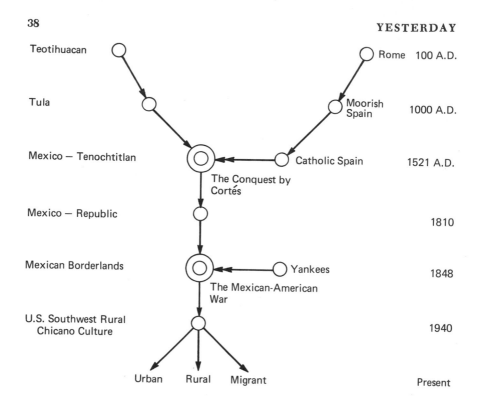

Teotihuacan ○ · · · Rome 100 A.D.

Tula ○ · · · Moorish Spain 1000 A.D.

Mexico — Tenochtitlan ◎ ← ○ Catholic Spain 1521 A.D.
The Conquest by Cortés

Mexico — Republic ○ 1810

Mexican Borderlands ◎ ← ○ Yankees 1848
The Mexican-American War

U.S. Southwest Rural Chicano Culture ○ 1940

Urban   Rural   Migrant   Present

Meanwhile, during the Colonial period, the Church and the last con-
quistadores occupied Indian lands north of the Rio Grande, setting up
towns such as Santa Fe, New Mexico, and St. Augustine, Florida, along
with missions and garrisons as the vanguard of new Spanish colonies.
Then, in 1846 the United States declared war on Mexico and came away
two years later with a good part of Aztlán as part of its territory. The
second double arrow shows the meeting of two worlds again, this time the
Mexican and Yankee cultures rather than Spanish and Indian. Let us con-
sider some of this history in more detail.

Man first came to the Americas about 25,000 years ago, during the last
ice age. At that time the glaciers in the Arctic held a good share of the
water in what is now the Bering Sea between Alaska and Russia. With
much of the sea trapped in the ice sheets the land was exposed, until
about 10,000 years ago, when the land bridge was swamped with the
melting of the ice. These first Americans from Siberia hunted mammoths
and other large animals. But when the ice age was over the climate
changed and the great mammals became extinct, about 7,000 or 8,000
years ago. Just at this time another, more profound source of food became
available.

In Mexico, agriculture, the basis of civilized life, was invented about
7,000 years ago. From very humble beginnings, it slowly became the dom-
inant form of subsistence and by 1500 B.C. there were permanent villages
in the Valley of Mexico and probably on the east coast of Mexico as well.
All over Mexico civilized life flourished, until at about the time of Christ

there were three distinct (but communicating) civilizations. The Mayas inhabited the mountains and lowlands of the Yucatan peninsula, and most of Guatemala and British Honduras. Their capitals were great centers like Tikal and Uaxactun. The Zapotec civilization was centered at Monte Albán in Oaxaca; and the Nahua-speaking peoples (at least we think they may have been Nahua speakers) were centered at the enormous city of Teotihuacan. Teotihuacan is about twenty-six miles from Mexico City, where the Aztecs eventually built their capital. The Aztecs, judging from the size of the city, thought the Teotihuacanos must have been giants. Recent work has shown that, at its height about 300 or 400 A.D., Teotihuacan had a population of 250,000, about the same as Rome at that time.

The Aztecs, however, were not the direct descendants of the Teotihuacanos. By the time the Aztecs arrived, half a millenium had passed since Teotihuacan had been abandoned. For some as yet undetermined reason (there are many good guesses but little scientific agreement) all three of the great classic cultures of Mexico collapsed between 600 and 900 A.D., beginning with the destruction of the great city in the Valley of Mexico.

The accomplishments of the classic cultures is summarized by Bell in her article on the Mayas. The political structure of the Mayan civilization did not last, but the language, architectural styles, art motifs, and other achievements in mathematics and astronomy did survive as part of the American heritage. The Mayas, in fact, were among the first people in the world to invent the zero and their calendar was as precise as our own. There are still about 2.5 million speakers of Maya in Mexico and Guatemala.

The Aztecs, then, acquired a long and great cultural heritage from the classic civilizations. Even though they were not the inventors of this culture, they were expert in adapting it as their own and taking it one step farther, as great civilizations have always done.

When Cortés landed in 1519 near what is today Vera Cruz, he heard about a great civilization in a valley high in the mountains. The people there, he was told, paid homage to a king called Moctezuma and the capital of his domain was called Tenochtitlan. Cortés wanted gold and after he saw the city in November, 1519, he spent the next two years preparing to invade the Aztec capital for it. One of the original conquistadores, Bernal Diaz del Castillo, has left us a moving account, almost a diary, of Cortés' adventures. The Spaniards of that day were very impressed with the grandeur of what is today Mexico City. At that time it was bigger than Madrid and its market place was equal to the greatest trade fairs of the Old World. This was Tenochtitlan, seat of the Aztec Confederacy.

The Aztecs never formed a true empire like the Incas of Peru. The Incas conquered lands and welded them into a single political sphere by allowing local rulers to continue in their positions among their own people. They insured the allegiance of these local rulers by holding members of their family hostage. The Incas had a program to teach Quechua, their language, to all their peoples. They built a massive system of roads and bridges with runners to connect all these provinces with Cuzco, their capital. In short, like the Romans, the Incas did all they could to incorporate the people they conquered into a single state, to make them feel as if they were part of a great political structure while allowing each people to maintain its own customs and identity. When Pizarro conquered the Incas in 1532 their empire stretched out over Peru, Bolivia, Ecuador, and parts of Chile and Colombia, encompassing a population of perhaps 12 million people. Even today there are an estimated 6 million speakers of Quechua, probably as many as there ever were.

The Aztecs, on the other hand, built a loose confederacy of about 6 million people whom they ruled and taxed in the same manner as they conquered them, with terror. S. F. Cook reports that 20,000 captives were sacrificed at the dedication of the great temple at Tenochtitlan in 1487. Thousands more were sacrificed throughout the confederacy each year to celebrate Aztec holy days—and, no doubt, to discourage opposition. The rather uncomplimentary picture Coe paints of the Aztecs in this section reflects the way other tribes in the area probably saw them. This is one of the reasons that the Aztecs were so easily conquered by Cortés and his miniature army. When the Spaniards landed they were joined almost immediately by thousands of Indian allies who counted themselves as enemies of the Aztecs. Still, in spite of its political shortcomings, the Aztec hegemony was a mighty state and a civilization of extraordinary achievement. Its ceramic and lapidary arts, for example, rank among the finest the world has ever produced. And the political structure of Tenochtitlan was more sophisticated and precise than that of any modern U.S. city.

The development of civilization in the New World was generally an extraordinary feat. All four of the other hearths of civilized life in the world (India, China, Mesopotamia, Egypt) had naturally irrigated river valleys to cultivate—the Indus, the Huang-Ho, the Tigris–Euphrates, and the Nile. New World agriculture was forced to develop on steep mountain slopes and in steaming jungles. The New World had no domesticable animals suitable for draught work like pulling a plow. Probably because of this lack the wheel was never used by any New World civilization for work (though the Aztecs did make wheeled toys). Cities and pyramids rivaling the greatest of the Old World were built by many cultures from Missouri to Peru without the benefit of pulleys. Smelting and the use of iron was never invented in the New World, though the Incas were among the great metallurgists of ancient times. They learned to work platinum, for example, a hard metal that defied European technology until the eighteenth century.

All these things make Native American civilization especially noteworthy. But among all the achievements of New World peoples, that of the Aztecs still stands out. As Coe shows, they did not settle in the Valley until the fourteenth century and brought the entire area to its knees between 1367 and 1519. In the space of 142 years the Aztecs rose from a band of starving, wandering hunters to rulers of the greatest state Mexico had ever known.

Admiration of Aztec civilization must be tempered with a consideration of its warlike character and the obvious bloodthirstiness of its religion. There is little that can be said to justify the wholesale slaughter of captives in the name of the Aztec gods. But this should not be misconstrued as an endorsement of medieval Christianity. No one knows how many thousands or millions of "infidels" were killed by the Crusaders in the name of their god. Both civilizations, Aztec and Iberian, achieved greatness in history and both were products of their time. This is an important point in considering one of the most famous stereotypes of all time—the Black Legend and the depopulation of Indians in the decades immediately following the Conquest.

There is little escape from the facts. Between 1519 and 1568, according to Woodrow Borah, the Indian population of central Mexico alone fell from 25 million to 2.5 million, a tenfold reduction in two generations.

Indians were moved from mountains to coastal plantations where they died, unable to adjust to the environment. They were herded off to work in the mines, where they died of exhaustion and malnutrition. And many were just killed outright for refusing to become slaves. The brutal conditions under which Indians were forced to live were described vividly by Juan de Las Casas, a priest who devoted his energies to bringing about legislation to protect the Indians. His writings were very influential, especially in England and Holland, Spain's great colonial era rivals.

Those northern European powers spread the word about Spain's treatment of the aboriginal population in the Americas. Spain became the bogeyman of the colonial era. This was the Black Legend, a historical stereotype that has followed Spain to this day.

Las Casas' writings, however, were also influential in Spain. There, in the sixteenth and seventeenth centuries, a whole series of legislative acts was passed to make slavery and brutality against Indians illegal. If they were ineffectual it was partially because of the great distance between the lawmakers and the colonials whom they tried to influence. In addition, most Spanish colonials were too busy miscegenating and raising families with Indian women to care much about laws regulating their relationships with natives. Latin America is the only part of the New World where a new race (mestizo) was created out of mixing the European and aboriginal peoples. In the United States, by contrast, Indians were neither incorporated racially into the population nor even used to work the lands that were taken from them. They were killed outright, on the theory that "the only good Indian is a dead Indian." Eventually, those who remained were herded onto reservations, totally apart from Anglo-American society—out of sight, out of mind.

It is pointless to try and justify the colonial actions of Spain or of any other European power. Those actions are no less despicable now than they were in the sixteenth, seventeenth, and eighteenth centuries. But it is *important, in taking the historical view, to understand that the Black Legend was as much the result of political and economic rivalry among European colonial powers as it was the result of widespread brutality.*

Most of the Indians who died in the colonial period in fact, were not killed by guns or overwork, but were victims of epidemics. Unaccustomed to the white man's illnesses, they fell easy prey to smallpox, tuberculosis, whooping cough, measles, and venereal disease. That many more Indians died in Spanish America than in British, Dutch, or French America is a function of the fact that the Spaniards got here first and conquered the most populous and wealthy Indian lands, Peru and Mexico. There were more Spanish American Indians to die. And they did.[1]

The actual population of the New World in 1492 and the extent of its destruction after that time remains one of the most controversial issues in Latin American studies. Whatever the exact figures were, the magnitude of the catastrophe is obvious and it shaped much of New Spain's history. As Simpson shows, the encomienda was a device giving land and Indians to colonial noblemen. But what good was land without Indians to work it? As Indians became scarce the repartimiento was instituted. Landowners, mine operators, and cattle ranchers could apply for Indians to the Viceroy, who doled out the scarce commodity to those who needed it. Simpson echoes Rippy's description of Spanish character in the sixteenth century when he says, "Work? Everyone knows that in the great tradition of nobility useful work is degrading."[2]

Ultimately, as more Spaniards came and fewer Indians were left, even the repartimiento did not work. The Spaniards then instituted a free labor market, where landowners would pay their workers and the workers would be free to sell their labor to the highest bidder. Unfortunately, a number of needed safeguards were not built into this plan and the result was a new institution, debt peonage: Indians living in perpetual and increasing cash debt to the landowner and bound to work the land so long as the debt remained unpaid. Thus was born the classic land–man relationship of Latin American society, the latifundio, or hacienda.

As more people came to New Spain and as the need for land and labor increased, the colonials pushed back the frontiers all the way to Kansas and Florida. Some haciendas developed on these lands, but most settlements were centered around a mission or a presidio, or garrison. Gibson and Spicer document this occupation of the frontiers of New Spain and tell us something of the quality of life there.

Early life on the northern Spanish frontier formed one of the immediate elements of Chicano culture. Far from the seat of power in Mexico City,

---

[1] I am indebted to Reymundo Marin of Washington State University for his advice and criticism of an earlier discussion of the Black Legend.

[2] Once again, it is important to point out that this attitude is class specific rather than cultural. The petty nobility of France maintained the same attitude right up to the French Revolution, and there are many aspirants to seminoble status in America today who share the Spanish *caballero's* feelings about work.

and with poor communications between central Mexico and the borderlands, colonization and population growth in the north was slow. Some
very large land grants were established, but, as González shows in Part II,
the true feudal hacienda was never a major component of life in Aztlán.
Thus, the music, art, food, language, farming practices, and the structure
of village life evolved on the Spanish frontier independently from the cultural evolution of central Mexico. By 1845, when the United States Congress voted to annex Texas, the government of Mexico had long since lost
control of life in that territory. But Mexico did try to hold on to her
northern territories and, after refusing to sell them cheaply to the United
States, went to war in 1846.

There are a variety of explanations for the Mexican-American War.
Many historians, Mexicans as well as American scholars, insist that Mexico
wanted the war for her own economic and political reasons. Others take
the view that the war was simply an American land grab. Actually, the
causes of the Mexican-American conflict are not nearly as important as
the treaty which ended it, the Treaty of Guadalupe Hidalgo. By that
treaty some 225,000 Mexicans—75,000 mestizos and double that number
of Indians—became residents of U.S. territories.

Guadalupe Hidalgo is the single most important document in Chicano
history, for not only did it create Chicanos in the first place, but it guaranteed that their land, customs, and religion would be honored. The government of Mexico tried to build safeguards into the treaty which would
ensure that her former citizens would receive protection of their lives and
property.

By international standards Mexico could sue the United States today for
breach of treaty. But that is highly unlikely, for Mexico has continued to
profit from the United States' treaty violations. Guaranteed the protection
of both the U.S. Constitution and the Treaty of Guadalupe Hidalgo, Chicanos are ignored by Mexican and American labor interests alike. Cheap
agricultural labor from Mexico continues to pour into the United States
and compete unfairly with Chicanos for employment. American firms send
parts for radios, appliances, and clothing to Mexico for cheap assembly, at
the expense of American labor.

Chicano property rights have not fared any better. The one article of
the treaty (Article X) which fully and unequivocally guaranteed Chicano
property was stricken by Congress before ratification. The United States
then enacted a law which said that people with Mexican or Spanish deeds
to their land would have to have those titles validated by the American
courts or their land would become public domain. In California alone
during the 1850's former Mexican citizens presented land claims for 12
million acres to the courts; fully one fourth (3 million acres) were denied
—that is, the Mexican and Spanish deeds on which the claims were based
were invalidated (Hammond, 1949).

We have reprinted the most relevant parts of the treaty here, including
the original articles IX and X (IX was significantly modified), the Protocol

of Querétaro, officially explaining the changes made by Congress before ratification, and the Secretary of State's letter to Mexico explaining the changes.

The Mexican–American War was the first event which brought Mexicans into the U.S. political realm. The second was the almost simultaneous discovery of gold in California in 1848. For the next few years the population of the state mushroomed with immigrants from the eastern United States, Mexico, and other parts of Latin America. Leonard Pitt vividly describes the clash between Mexican and Yankee in the wild days of the California gold rush.

The Yankee forty-niners made no distinction between the Chicano citizens of California, Mexican immigrants, or for that matter, migrants from Chile. They were all called foreigners by the invading Anglo-Americans and treated with efficient dispatch both in the California legislature and on the streets. The pattern of relationships established in the gold rush has left its mark on modern Chicano–Anglo affairs. The reader certainly will see a relationship between the violence described by Pitt in California during the 1840's and that described by Carey McWilliams in Part II in the same state during the 1940's.

Between 1848 and World War II Chicano society retained its basically rural character. The degradation of Chicano life and the removal of Chicanos from their land, however, took its toll. By 1940 the major characteristics of rural Chicanos were poverty and lack of land Thus, since that time the thrust of Chicano society has been urban and migratory. With its manpower at war, the agricultural industry of the Southwest needed massive amounts of labor during World War II. The bracero program brought in new thousands of Mexican immigrants and the latest chapter of Chicano population growth was begun. In their article, Grebler, Moore, and Guzman discuss the overall picture of Chicano migration to the United States.

Unfortunately, although we have a fair idea of what the basic components of Chicano society are, we do not have adequate population data. The reasons for this are (1) agricultural migrants are very difficult to count in any census; (2) illegal entry of Mexicans to the United States is a continuing phenomenon which defies accurate measurement;[3] *(3) for most of the United States (outside the Southwest) the United States Census does not count Mexican Americans at all. However, recent evidence shows there may be more than a quarter of a million Chicanos in Michigan and Indiana and another 100,000 in Washington. In those states the question on race in the census questionnaire contained no reference to Mexican Americans (much less Chicanos). The only choices were "White, Negro or Black, Indian (write in Tribe), Chinese, Japanese, Hawaiian, Filipino, Korean, or Other." Those people who checked "Other" were*

---

[3] Last year the Border Patrol deported 280,000 illegal entrants, though how many of these were deported five and six times each we do not know. The Patrol estimates another 500,000 illegals they could not catch.

requested to write in what they considered their "race" to be. Then it was up to the census enumerator to interpret what was written in. The official Bureau of the Census manual took out all the guesswork: "Mexican" or "Hispano" or "Spanish" were counted as white; "Brown" was counted as black; and "Mexican American" or "Chicano" were counted as "other." Altogether, including legal and illegal migrants who were never reached by the census at all, there are probably between 6.5 and 7 million "others" now living in the United States.[4]

---

[4] It is obvious that the actual size of the population of Chicanos in the United States is still a matter of debate. Conservative estimates range from 6 to 7 million. More liberal estimates range from 9 to 10 million. The latter figure includes 7 million Chicanos in Aztlán and 3 million in the northern agricultural states.

The Mexican Heritage

AN APPRAISAL OF THE MAYA CIVILIZATION

Betty Bell

Professor Brainerd, whose task in preparing this concluding chapter has fallen upon me, spoke often of the enigma of the Maya civilization. In this summary and appraisal, I will try to present the unresolved riddles as he saw them.

In recent years, archaeologists and social anthropologists have shown increasing interest in the causes for the development of civilization, and in formulating theories of social and cultural change. A number of analyses have been aimed at determining whether there are any characteristics common to all civilizations, and any series of developmental stages through which they have all passed. The material culture, subsistence basis, technology, religion, social and political structure, and intellectual achievements of the ancient civilizations have been studied, and the causes for their decline have also been ascertained.

Many anthropologists now believe that there are certain criteria by which civilizations can be judged—certain traits common to all of them and certain stages through which they all seem to have passed. In general, progress toward civilization is thought to have been marked by increasing complexity in all aspects of culture and this developmental process is thought to have resulted everywhere in certain distinguishing features by which civilization can be defined. The causes for the decline of civilization, of course, have not been everywhere the same. The decline may have been due to external factors such as military conquest, or to internal weak-

Reprinted from *The Ancient Maya*, Third Edition, by Sylvanus Griswold Morley; revised by George W. Brainerd with the permission of the publishers, Stanford University Press. Copyright © 1946, 1947, 1956 by the Board of Trustees of the Leland Stanford Junior University.

nesses—or to a combination of both—but intensive study will often give at least some indication of the causes.

The Maya, however, cannot easily be made to fit into the pattern which has been developed. As Dr. Brainerd saw it, they present three problems:

1. While their developments in some fields have seldom been surpassed, the Maya lacked a number of traits which have come to be accepted as prerequisites to civilization, and they seem not to have passed through a number of the supposedly necessary developmental stages. Their status as a high civilization cannot be denied, but they lack many of the criteria by which such civilizations are usually defined. If theories of social evolution postulate that certain characteristics are everywhere necessary for the development of a complex society, how are we to account for the Maya?

2. Once the Maya civilization was developed, what kind of authority ruled it? Almost nothing is so far known of Classic-stage political structure. There is no evidence for the ramified political organization and centralized authority which elsewhere marked complex societies. Some method of control must be assumed to be necessary—but what method operated to keep the Maya civilization functioning smoothly through so long a time?

3. The Classic stage was notable for a high degree of homogeneity and stability. In the absence of any strong political authority, this argues for a peaceful and well-adjusted populace, unanimous in its agreement on the cultural values and goals and on the means for attaining them. But despite this presumed placidity, the causes for the decline of Classic-stage civilization must be sought within the society itself; there is no evidence that external pressures hastened its fall. What, then, caused this discontent, this sudden change? Or was it rather the result of some hidden but long-enduring weakness in the society, the culmination of several centuries of small dissatisfactions and the gradual erosion of the sense of cultural community?

In the light of present knowledge, no final answers can be given to any of these questions. We can here summarize the features of Maya civilization, appraise its achievements, and suggest tentative answers—but the enigma remains. Definitive answers must wait upon future studies and investigations, although the answers may never be forthcoming.

Characteristics of Maya Civilization

Let us first recapitulate the features of Maya civilization—its remarkably advanced characteristics and its undeniably primitive ones, as well as its still unknown features.

In comparison with the subsistence bases of other comparably high civilizations, Maya subsistence techniques were almost primitive, and were comparable to the agricultural practices of the Neolithic period in the Old World. The Maya occupied an environment unlike that of most other early high civilizations, and this environment precluded development of the more advanced agricultural techniques upon which most early civilizations have been based. The type of agriculture made necessary by this environmental limitation required the Maya to live scattered throughout the areas surrounding the ceremonial centers.[1] There is as yet no evidence for the concentration of the population into large, permanent settlements of closely packed dwellings. However great their size or elaboration, the sites seem to have been principally the foci of religious ceremonies which drew the populace in from the surrounding countryside, rather than true urban centers.

The character of the Maya area also enforced a degree of isolation unusual among high civilizations. While the dense jungle of the central Maya area may not have been as impassable to the foot-traveling Maya as it is to machine-bound moderns, it must still have cut them off to a large extent from the outside contacts through which new ideas and inventions are diffused, and hindered the development of a large-scale trade which could have supplied resources lacking in the area.

Maya technology was also of a sort which can only be considered rather primitive. Metal was apparently unknown until the Post-classic and then it appears only as jewelry and ornaments, largely imported from other areas. Metal tools were completely unknown; stone tools were used for everything from the cutting of slabs for stelae and building blocks to the execution of the most delicate carving. The wheel was also unknown; there were no wheeled vehicles, nor even the potter's wheel. It might appear that the rollers which were used on the causeways should have suggested the principle of the wheel, but the invention of wheeled vehicles seems to be closely related to the availability of animals for motive power, and the Maya lacked all domestic animals except the dog. This lack of the wheel, however, is general throughout the aboriginal New World, for nowhere except in Peru was there a native domestic animal large enough to serve as a beast of burden or a potential puller of vehicles.[2]

Despite the marked primitiveness of some aspects of their civilization— its isolation, scattered population, simple agriculture, and meager technology—the Maya developed other cultural features to a point of complexity and elaboration unequaled among other early civilizations of the

---

[1] This is one of the principal characteristics of pre-Columbian Mexican civilizations. In general, there were no real cities in the sense of urban complexes, only ceremonial centers whose permanent population consisted mostly of nobles and priests. Teotihuacan and Tikal were spectacular exceptions to this settlement pattern.—*Eds.*

[2] Recent finds indicate that the natives of the New World did invent the wheel, but that they never used it for work. Small animals made of clay were constructed with wheels as toys for children during Aztec times. The fact remains that only the llama in Peru would have served as a beast of burden for pulling wheeled vehicles.—*Eds.*

New World. Although the true arch was never developed, the invention of the corbeled arch permitted the construction of large temples and palaces, occasionally multistoried. The outstanding characteristic of Maya architecture, however, is its emphasis upon skillful and elaborate decoration rather than upon size. The reticulated roof-combs of Tikal and the beautifully carved mosaic façades of Uxmal alike show a preoccupation with the esthetic refinements of architecture rather than with sheer imposing mass. Maya graphic art was also well developed. While the stone sculptures tend to be formal and stylized, and the designs too intricate for modern taste, the skill of their execution is undeniable. The figures on the ceramics are more freely and informally rendered, and many designs, such as that on the famous polychrome plate from Uaxactun, show a degree of sophistication which compares favorably with the most modern ceramic design. Some of the figures in the Bonampak murals, moreover, exhibit a degree of naturalism which Western European art did not achieve until several centuries later.

The Maya religion, which was a focal point for so much of the culture, was complex and formalized. It had a well-developed cosmogony, a large pantheon of gods, and an elaborate cycle of rituals. The Maya had the concept of a creator-god, although he does not seem to have played an important role in the lives of the common people, and of several worlds prior to this one, all of which had been destroyed by floods. In addition to major deities such as the Lord of the Heavens, the gods of rain and corn, and numerous others, each of the thirteen levels of the upper world and the nine levels of the lower world had its patron god. There were also patron deities for each of the katuns, the nineteen divisions of the haab, the twenty day-names of the tzolkin, and the numerals 0 to 13.

The katun endings, the New Year, and each of the months were marked by appropriate ceremonies, which included fasting and abstinence, exorcism, prayers, and sacrifice. Although human sacrifice existed during the Classic stage, the sacrifices were principally of animals and birds; the extensive human sacrifice which characterized Postclassic-stage religion was a Toltec innovation.

This religious complexity is a far remove from the simple pantheon of nature gods which probably existed in the Preclassic. It reflects the increasing complexity of the culture itself, and the growth of a professional priesthood which formalized the religion, elaborated the rituals, and maintained its dominant position in the society by its claim to interpret the wishes of an ever-increasing number of gods.

The most notable characteristic of Maya civilization, however, was its achievements in the abstract intellectual fields of writing, astronomy, mathematics, and calendrics. Alone of New World civilizations, the Maya developed what can truly be considered a system of writing, in which the characters were not merely pictographs or mnemonic devices. Maya hieroglyphic writing was long thought to be entirely ideographic, but recent studies have indicated that many of the elements of the glyphs may be syllabic. It was thus at least in the process of becoming a phonetic system, its characters coming to represent sounds rather than objects or ideas.

Unfortunately, a great deal of Maya writing remains undeciphered, and those portions which have been deciphered have yielded largely calendric or astronomical information. The stelae record the endings of time periods, and the three existing fragmentary codices deal with astronomy, ritual, and divination. Some of the countless codices which Landa prided himself on having destroyed may well have contained the history of the Maya.

Using the simplest of equipment, the Maya calculated the length of the solar year with an accuracy equal to that of modern astronomy, and devised correction fomulae to adjust the discrepancy between the true year and the calendar year which is handled by our leap-year correction. They worked out an accurate lunar calendar and calculated the synodical revolutions of Venus, in each case devising means for correcting the accumulated error.

The Maya vigesimal system of mathematics was a positional system and embodied the concept of zero, a notable abstract intellectual achievement. Elsewhere, this mathematical concept is known to have been developed only in the early Hindu civilization. The ancient civilizations of Mesopotamia employed a positional system of arithmetic, but it seems to have been in existence for centuries before the concept of zero diffused to them from the Hindu world. The ancient civilizations of the Mediterranean area derived many of their cultural features from the civilizations of the Middle East, but they did not take over the well-developed system of computation. This sort of mathematical complex did not penetrate Western Europe until the time of the Arab invasions in the early Middle Ages, several centuries after the Maya had developed their own accurate and flexible system.

The basis of the Maya calendric system was the 260-day tzolkin, with its named and numbered days, and the 365-day haab, with its named months and numbered positions within each month. These two meshed calendars repeated cyclically, and could return to a given starting point only after a lapse of 52 years. The stelae inscriptions, however, involved longer time periods, which, with one exception, were based on the vigesimal system of multiples of twenty. Using these longer periods, the Maya counted the elapsed time since the hypothetical starting date of their chronology. They also recorded in the inscription the fact that the stela was erected on a certain numbered and named day of the tzolkin which occupied a certain position in a particular month of the haab; the accompanying supplementary series recorded lunar information for that date. The information given by these Initial Series or Long Count inscriptions is thus so specific that a day fulfilling all of the prescribed requirements could not recur for 374,440 years.

One of the unknown factors in Maya civilization is the type of authority which governed it during its almost 600 years of existence. Religion was of central importance to the Maya; there is little doubt that it was uniform throughout the area, and that the priests of the various centers must have co-operated closely on religious matters. It is impossible to say how far this control penetrated into political matters. The remarkable homogeneity of Classic-stage civilization would seem to indicate some kind of hegemony over the area, either civil or religious. Priestly control may have sufficed to maintain order, or there may have been some centralized political authority which has so far not been detected.

The other unknown factor, of course, is the reason for the decline of Maya civilization. It was quite clearly not due to outside pressures. There is still no evidence of internal weakness, although it must have existed. It is difficult to believe that so solidly established a civilization could be overturned abruptly, but if dissatisfactions had been accumulating slowly through the centuries, they left no mark by which they can be identified.

Two Theories of Social Evolution

There are certain variations in current definitions of civilization, but all definitions include most of the following requirements: a surplus of food produced by farmers to support nonfarmers; concentrated human settlements (cities); an improved technology; a formal political organization; a society organized into classes, some of which have the leisure for non-utilitarian pursuits; a formal religion and moral order; public works; writing.

From his research on the ancient civilizations of the Old World, archaeologist V. Gordon Childe has concluded that there is a developmental ranking, a causal relationship, among these factors which everywhere makes them prerequisites to the growth of civilization. Childe's most intensive studies have been of the civilizations of the Middle East, and there the evidence does seem to support his theory. In Mesopotamia, for example, large-scale irrigation agriculture was developed on the flood plains of the Tigris and Euphrates Rivers, and large permanent settlements grew up. The availability of surplus food permitted the support of full-time craft and religious specialists, and the existence of craft specialists in turn hastened technological progress. Outside contacts and the development of trade are also cited as necessary to an improved technology, for in this way the society might learn of new technical processes and could also supply resources which might be lacking in its environment.

Religion grew more complex and formalized. The priests were at first the rulers of the cities, later being supplanted in part by the growth of a monarchy and a hierarchy of civil officials. Each city-state was originally an autonomous unit, but as control passed more into civil hands, military conquest and political organization welded a number of city-states into empires.

Within the city-state, order was maintained largely by the ruler's control over the irrigation system which was so vital to the group's existence. The concentration of population facilitated control by a central authority;

the populace could more easily be taxed for the support of the priests, nobles, and king, and conscripted for labor on the palaces and temples.

As social organization became more complex, some classes of society were freed from subsistence activities and had leisure to devote to non-utilitarian pursuits. The priests, supported by the populace, developed mathematics and writing, although it might be argued that these were not entirely devoid of utility since they were developed in connection with keeping accounts of the offerings made to the temples.

In Childe's opinion, then, culture develops with an increased techno-logical efficiency and integrative ability, and an increased control of knowledge. But he believes that the great variety of cultures revealed by ethnographic and archaeological research is a handicap if the objective is to establish general stages in the evolution of cultures. In order to discover general laws descriptive of the evolution of all societies, he feels, we must omit or discount the features peculiar to particular habitats or environments.

Anthropologist Julian Steward believes that this view fails to account for the development of particular patterns among different societies, and he proposes instead a theory of multilinear evolution. This theory admits the existence of distinctive cultural traditions, but does not assume that such traditions are necessarily unique; there is reason to believe that knowledge gained from the analysis of one culture may provide insights useful to the analysis of another. Its emphasis lies not in the uniqueness of cultures but in the similarities that may be found among them. It recog-nizes that cultural traditions in different regions may be wholly or in part distinctive, and merely asks: "Are there any meaningful similarities be-tween two or more cultures that can be formulated?"

Where such similarities are found, it may be possible to determine the causal factors, identical in each case, which led to their development. Such causal relationships need not be universally applicable, for multi-linear evolution presents no pattern into which the cultures of all times and all places must be fitted. Rather, it compares cultural traditions in various parts of the world, attempts to develop a taxonomy of culture types, and to produce significant general statements about the develop-mental process of each type so discovered.

While Childe's theory ignores environmental variations and posits ad-vanced agricultural techniques as being everywhere a prerequisite to the development of civilization, Steward takes account of such variations and suggests that the manner of a society's adaptation to a particular environ-ment may be the significant factor in cultural development. Rather than establish an a priori pattern for the development of all cultures, he sug-gests a possible grouping on an ecological basis. In these terms, he would distinguish as a category or culture type the complex civilizations of Egypt, Mesopotamia, China, Northern Peru, and Highland Mexico, whose subsistence basis was a system of irrigation agriculture on arid lands. These civilizations, scattered as they are in space and time, show quite similar social, political, and technological developments, although the

Inca and Aztec civilizations at the time of European contact had not reached the intellectual heights achieved by the Old World civilizations.

To this extent, Childe and Steward are in agreement. There does seem to have been a parallel development in these arid-land irrigation civilizations which suggests a causal relationship among their culture traits. They exhibit urbanization, similar degrees of technological advancement and social organization, a formalized religion, progress from a theocracy to political organization and a nation-state, and finally, programs of military conquest and empire building. But Steward does not agree that these traits can be considered universal criteria for civilization. He points out that this is but one type of environment, and one type of adaptation. If the manner of a society's adaptation to a particular environment is indeed the significant factor in cultural progress, there can perhaps be many different bases for complex civilizations, and many different paths leading to their development.

Childe's and Steward's Theories Applied to the Maya

Can the Maya be made to fit into Childe's scheme, which seeks to establish universal criteria and developmental stages for high civilizations? A glance at the characteristics of Maya civilization will show that it would be most difficult. They remain, as Dr. Brainerd remarked, an intractable exception.

Maya agriculture was of a rather primitive kind, and it would not have lent itself readily to the centralized control which could be exerted over irrigation systems.[3] There is little doubt, however, that it was capable of producing surpluses, for it obviously supported such nonproducing groups as the priests and nobles. The quality of Maya art and architecture suggests the existence also of craft specialists, who could only be supported if surpluses were available. The free time which the Maya farmer presumably had after filling his family's subsistence needs may have been devoted not only to personal labor on the public works, but also to the production of food for trained artisans who did the highly skilled stone carving for which the Maya are famous.

Although urbanization seems in most areas to have been a significant factor in the development of a complex civilization, true urbanism, in the sense of densely populated settlements, was lacking in the Maya area during the Classic stage. The nature of their agricultural system obliged the Maya to live quite widely dispersed, gathering at the religious centers chiefly for ceremonies. The isolation of the area may have been an important factor in the maintenance of this kind of living pattern through a number of centuries, for such a scattered population, lacking fortified and

[3] Just how efficient or inefficient Mayan farming practices were is one of the great arguments in the field of Mexican prehistory. For a good discussion of this debate, see Bennet Bronson, "Roots and the Subsistence of the Ancient Maya," *Southwestern Journal of Anthropology*, Vol. 22, 1966.—*Eds.*

defensible settlements, might otherwise have been extremely vulnerable to attack and invasion.

Increased technological efficiency is usually a concomitant of civilization, but Maya technology remained unchanged throughout its history. For lack of raw materials, metallurgy never developed; imported gold jewelry and ornaments appeared in the Postclassic stage, but metal tools never replaced stone tools. In the absence of domestic animals, the wheel was not invented, and the nature of the subsistence system offered no opportunity for the invention of improved agricultural equipment.

While Maya society was quite clearly organized into classes, no political organization has so far been detected. The remarkable homogeneity of Classic-stage civilization might indicate some overall political authority, but since religion was so pervasive and important, control might equally well have been theocratic during the entire period. Most high civilizations have evolved into political states, and many have eventually embarked upon programs of military conquest and empire building, but these developments did not appear among the Maya. There is evidence for a certain amount of internecine strife, but no evidence for organized warfare on a nationalistic basis.

The formalized religion which is characteristic of complex civilizations was highly developed among the Maya, and quite obviously the focal point of the culture. Since most Maya public works were religious edifices, the control which urbanization is said to facilitate in conscripting labor may not have been necessary. It is possible that the religion-conscious Maya worked willingly at such tasks.

The most notable Maya achievements, of course, were in abstract intellectual fields, and here they surpassed all other New World civilizations and equaled or surpassed many in the Old World. These achievements, inventions and possessions of the priesthood, seem to have been truly non-utilitarian, not connected with economic activities nor pursued in the hope of economic rewards. Writing, calendrics, astronomy, and mathematics were all parts of the Maya preoccupation with marking the passage of time, a preoccupation which is difficult to explain. The yearly calendar of necessary rituals presumably repeated itself endlessly, but it is not clear what significance the longer time periods had for the Maya, nor why it was so important for them to mark periodically the exact number of years, months, and days which had elapsed since the starting point of their chronology. It must, however, have had a great and central importance to have resulted in an intellectual system of such complexity.

Although the Maya civilization cannot be fitted into any universal criteria or series of developmental stages such as Childe postulates, it can perhaps be approached in Steward's terms, as an example of a highly successful adaptation to a particular environment. The Peten jungle seems an unfavorable setting for the development of a civilization, but the Maya transcended its limitations. The simple agricultural system which it enforced was made not only to fill subsistence needs but also to produce food surpluses. The relative poverty of natural resources prevented a great deal of technological advancement, but the existing technology was employed skillfully enough to fill the needs of a people whose emphasis was largely upon the esthetic refinements of their products rather than upon quantity or mass. The environment and subsistence system precluded any concentration of the population, but the Maya developed a social organization and mechanisms of social control which in other areas have been a consequence of urbanization. With this ecological adaptation successfully accomplished, with satisfactory agricultural, technological, and sociopolitical bases established, the Maya were able to turn their attention to the religious and intellectual developments which characterize most complex civilizations, and which became the hallmark of the Maya civilization in particular.

In a classification of this sort, which attempts to group cultures in terms of their environments and then to find even limited parallels in their development, the Maya must remain, at least for now, the only major culture within their particular ecological category. This may be due in part to the circumstances and difficulties of archaeological investigation. Most of the ancient high civilizations which are well known archaeologically have been located in the drier regions of the world, where climatic conditions have preserved sufficient material to permit quite substantial reconstruction of culture history. Such a degree of preservation is unlikely in humid regions, but more intensive archaeological work in these areas might yield enough information to allow at least limited comparisons of the Maya with other cultures in similar environments. Further archaeological investigation in the jungle regions of southeast Asia might provide material for such a comparison. The remains of at least one apparently high civilization have already been found there, at Angkor Wat in Cambodia. However, the ancient Cambodian civilization has not been studied as intensively as the Maya, and there is at present too little material available for a detailed comparison.

Classic-Stage Government

Much of Maya culture history has now been reconstructed, but the form of Classic-stage government is still problematical. The Classic stage was marked by a high degree of homogeneity and stability throughout the nearly six centuries of its existence. There were regional and temporal variations in such things as architecture and ceramics, to be sure, but the distinctive patterning of Maya culture remained unchanged. The extent of man's obedience to the unenforceable may indeed be one of the marks of civilization, but it is questionable if this alone could maintain order within so complex a society. Some more formal method of control must be assumed to account for the stable and orderly character of Maya civilization over so wide an area and through so long a time.

This widespread homogeneity suggests the presence of one supreme ruler over the area, but there is as yet no evidence for such a centralized political authority. The absence of warfare has been cited in the text as one of the characteristics of the Classic stage, and this might indicate either the importance of religion in government or the presence of a strong civil authority. However, although organized warfare was lacking, there undeniably was sporadic raiding between centers to obtain captives for slaves and for sacrifice. This seems to suggest a certain autonomy for the various centers, and to weaken the case for a central government, which presumably could have prevented such occurrences.

The territorial rulers discussed in the text existed at the time of the Spanish Conquest, but there is no evidence that they were vestiges of some Classic-stage political authority. In all probability, they were part of the political structure introduced by the Toltecs. While much of the social organization and domestic life of the people may have remained relatively unchanged since the Classic stage, the Toltec invasion was in essence a military conquest and so would undoubtedly have destroyed any political institutions which it encountered.[4]

Control may well have been theocratic. Religion was of central importance in Maya life, and authority may have been exercised by a closely co-operating group of priests, each of whom dominated a particular religious center. If the society was thus controlled by means of its adherence to a common religion, the religious bonds were not strong enough to eliminate latent hostility—but at least they were strong enough to ensure that such hostility did not become a disruptive force in the society.

If control was theocratic, it must simply have rested upon the dominant role of religion and ritual in the lives of the common people. The priests held no economically valuable knowledge such as that held by the Egyptian priests, who were able to predict the life-giving floods of the Nile. Nor did the Maya priests control any important economic activity as did the Mesopotamian priests, who held a monopoly on the vital irrigation

[4] At the end of the tenth century the Toltecs were consolidating their empire centered at Tula, about a thousand miles from the heart of the Mayan territory. A civil war between a war faction and a peace faction resulted in the defeat and banishment of the peace leader (Quetzalcoatl) from Tula. Fleeing to Vera Cruz with a few of his men, he set sail to the east and landed in Yucatan. The Mayan civilization had long since collapsed politically (about the end of the eighth century) and Mayan legends tell of the coming of a god called Kukulkan, which means *feathered serpent* in Maya. Quetzalcoatl means *feathered serpent* in Nahuatl. The Mayan city of Chichen Itza was probably ruled by these Toltec outcast leaders. It was this rebirth of Mayan civilization which the Spaniards encountered. An excellent source for the further study of Maya civilization is Sylvanus Morely and George Brainerd, *The Ancient Maya*, Third Edition (Stanford, Calif.: Stanford University Press, 1956), from which the present article is taken. An interesting sidelight to this story of the Toltec invasion concerns the prediction of Cortés' landing. When Quetzalcoatl, who was blond, sailed away he said he would return to take his rightful place as ruler of Mexico. Cortés, also fair haired, landed in the same year of the fifty-two-year cycle as the year Quetzalcoatl sailed away. Moctezuma is said to have presumed that Cortés was the god returning and that is why he handed Tenochtitlan over so readily to the tiny Spanish invasion force.—Eds.

system. Perhaps possession of such specific information or power is not entirely necessary. Some anthropologists have suggested that man turns to religion for aid in matters where his limited empirical techniques are of no avail. The Maya subsistence economy depended upon a favorable combination of natural conditions which was quite outside the farmer's control. The people may well have been convinced that only propitiation of the gods by means of the proper ceremonies, under priestly direction, would ensure their continued well-being and perhaps their very existence. Whatever the means by which control was enforced, it does not seem to have been by the promise of rich economic rewards. The Maya economy was simple and self-sufficient, and apparently it was only necessary for the priests to guarantee its continued existence, although the ceremonial requirements for this guarantee became steadily more elaborate and perhaps even burdensome.

Causes for the Decline of Maya Civilization

Despite this picture of stability and relative placidity, the causes for the inexplicable decline of Maya civilization must be sought within the society itself rather than in outside forces, either natural or human. Earthquake activity, disease, and climatic and vegetation changes have been disposed of as possible causes, and there is no evidence for warfare in the central Maya area. Yet after nearly six hundred years of activity, the great ceremonial centers of the Peten were abandoned. The people may have lived on in the areas around the centers, worshiping fewer gods with simpler ceremonies, but the great religious panoply, the complex cosmogony, the priestly hierarchy, were gone.

Why did this happen? The iconography indicates no change in the all-important religion, no discontentment with the old religion or substitution of a new one. Nor is there any suggestion of the social unrest which has precipitated so many changes in other civilizations. If the causes for the decline were cumulative, they cannot yet be identified in the archaeological record. It must be assumed at present that the change was rather sudden, however strange that seems in the light of religion's central role in Maya life.

It has been suggested by some authorities that perhaps the outwardly placid and well-adjusted populace had merely tired at last of the burdens which its pervasive religion placed upon it. The ceremonies may have become too expensive and the support of the priestly hierarchy too burdensome in proportion to the rewards which religion offered. A new philosophy of life may have arisen which provided new values and goals, or the people may simply have decided that life would go on regardless of priestly intervention with the gods—that their own prayers and offerings, made directly, would ensure the coming of rain and the growing of crops.

This social malaise, whatever its nature, must also have been present in the centers of the northern area, at least to the extent that it weakened the society sufficiently for it to be conquered a short time later by a relatively small number of Toltec invaders. The fact that the Toltec conquest was accompanied by a religious evangelization also suggests some disabling weakness in the Maya religion, or in the people's attitude toward it. Such a ready acceptance of many elements of Toltec religion hardly seems likely had the people still been convinced of the importance of their existing religion.

Thus, five centuries before the Spanish Conquest, this complex civilization which had arisen in an environment unique among the high cultures of the world, and which had flourished for centuries despite its lack of some of the so-called prerequisites of civilization, had fallen into decay.

Appraisal of Maya Civilization

Cultures must be judged not against some absolute scale of achievement, but in relative terms—on the basis of their achievements within the framework of their limitations. In this sort of a classification, the Maya must rank high. Their environment prevented the development of advanced agricultural and technological processes, and inhibited the establishment of concentrated settlements; and this lack of urbanization, in turn, may have prevented the development of complex political institutions and the formation of a political state. But set against this background of limitations and relatively primitive features, Maya esthetic and intellectual achievements have few equals.

The orientation of Maya civilization, its cultural patterning, gives it a unique position among early high civilizations. Others have excelled it in material culture, or have emphasized such traits as political organization or military conquest and empire building, but the remarkable traits of Maya culture are of an intellectual and esthetic order. It is impossible to ascertain the impetus behind this distinctive type of cultural development. So far as is known, it did not depend upon a strong governmental control which could channel cultural developments as it desired. It does not seem to have rested upon stern economic control, nor was it accomplished nor immediately preceded by the invention of new techniques for economic betterment, although this sort of developmental sequence is sometimes assumed to be necessary. The causes behind Maya intellectual progress do not fit easily into the sequences of advancement worked out for other early civilizations, which suggests that we do not yet fully understand the factors that lead a people in the direction of such progress.

While there is some particular emphasis in all cultures, some focal point around which much of the society is organized, this emphasis need not, perhaps, have been deliberately selected; it might equally well be influenced by the limitation of the number of choices available to the society. Thus it might be argued that the Maya cultural emphasis rested upon intellectual florescence at least in part because physical and developmental circumstances denied them the technological and political advancements which other societies emphasized. But this still does not explain Maya intellectual progress. Few if any other cultures with comparably primitive features, however satisfactory their adjustment to their environment, have focused to such a degree upon intellectual attainment. Perhaps the goad, if one be assumed necessary, was the overwhelming importance of Maya religion and the fact that intellectual developments were the inventions of the religious specialists and were closely connected with religious observances.

Whatever the causes of these developments, they are of a sufficiently high order to give the Maya an unchallenged position among complex civilizations. The esthetic refinements of Maya art and architecture, the accuracy of their astronomical system, the intricacy of their calendrics, and the skill and elaboration of their mathematics and writing, are unsurpassed by any other New World civilization and equaled by few in the Old World. The Maya must surely emerge for dispassionate comparison among the great world cultures.

THE POST-CLASSIC PERIOD: THE AZTEC EMPIRE

Michael Coe

The beginnings of the Aztec nation were so humble and obscure that their rise to supremacy over most of Mexico in the space of a few hundred years seems almost miraculous. It is somehow inconceivable that the magnificent civilisation witnessed and destroyed by the Spaniards could have been created by a people who were not many generations removed from the most abject barbarism, but such was the case. It is only through an understanding of this fact, namely the tribal roots of the Aztec state, that these extraordinary people can really be comprehended.

Peoples and Politics in the Valley of Mexico

When any great state collapses, it is inevitable that unless there is another comparable force to take its place, conditions of anarchy will ensue. This is exactly what happened in the Valley of Mexico and surrounding regions in the wake of Tula's destruction in the twelfth century. Refugees

Reprinted with permission from *Mexico: Ancient Peoples and Places* (New York: Praeger Publishers, Inc., 1962).

Michael Coe is professor of anthropology at Yale University. He received his doctorate from Harvard in 1959 and has since participated in archaeological research expeditions in Mexico, British Honduras, Guatemala, Costa Rica, and Tennessee. He is the author of several books, including *Mexico, The Maya,* and *The Jaguar's Children.*

from this center of Toltec civilisation managed to establish themselves in the southern half of the Valley, particularly at the towns of Colhuacán and Xico, both of which became important citadels transmitting the higher culture of their predecessors to the savage groups who were then streaming into the northern half. Among the latter were the band of Chichimecs under their chief Xólotl, arriving in the Valley by 1244 and settling at Tenayuca; the Acolhuas, who founded Coatlínchan around the year 1260; the Otomí at Xaltocan by about 1250; and the powerful Tepanecs, who in 1230 took over the older town of Atzcapotzalco, which it will be remembered was originally founded by Teotihuacán refugees. There is no question that all of these with the exception of the Otomí were speakers of Náhuatl, now the dominant tongue of central Mexico. Thus, by the thirteenth century, all over the Valley there had sprung up a group of modestly sized city states, those in the north founded by Chichimec upstarts eager to learn from the Toltecs in the south.

It was inevitable that a jockeying for power among these rivals would take place, and it was the northern centres which grew at the expense of the southern. Into this uneasy political situation stepped the last barbaric tribe to arrive in the Valley of Mexico, the Aztecs, the 'people whose face nobody knows.' They said that they came from a place called 'Aztlán' in the west of Mexico, believed by some authorities to be in the state of Nayarit,[1] and had wandered about guided by the image of their tribal god, Huitzilopochtli ('Hummingbird-on-the-left'), who was borne on the shoulders of four priests. Apparently they knew the art of cultivation and wore agave fibre clothing, but had no political leaders higher than clan and tribal chieftains. It is fitting that Huitzilopochtli was a war god and a representative of the sun, for the Aztecs were extremely adept at military matters, and among the best and fiercest warriors ever seen in Mexico. They were also among the most bloodthirsty, for their deity demanded quantities of human hearts extracted from captive warriors, and it was not long before they had a very evil reputation for savagery among their more civilised neighbours.

It was not only their unpleasant habits which failed to endear them, but also the fact that they were outright intruders. All the land in the Valley was already occupied by civilised peoples, who looked with suspicion upon these Aztecs, who were little more than squatters, continually occupying territory that did not belong to them and continually being kicked out. It is a wonder that they were ever tolerated since, women being scarce as among all immigrant groups, they took to raiding other peoples for their wives. The cultivated citizens of Colhuacán finally allowed them to live a degraded existence, working the lands of their masters as serfs, and supplementing their diet with snakes and other vermin. In 1323, however, the Aztecs repaid the kindness of their overlords, who had given their chief a Colhuacán princess as bride, by sacrificing the young lady with the hope

---

[1] There is some disagreement among scholars as to just where Aztlán was originally. In Chicano Spanish today, of course, it refers to the five-state southwestern area of the United States.—Eds.

that she would become a war goddess. Colhuacán retaliated by expelling these repulsive savages from their territory.

We next see the Aztecs following a hand-to-mouth existence in the marshes of the great lake. On they wandered, loved by none, until they reached some swampy, unoccupied islands, covered by rushes, near the western shore; it was claimed that there the tribal prophecy, to build a city where an eagle was seen sitting on a cactus, holding a snake in its mouth, was fulfilled.[2] By 1344 or 1345, the tribe was split in two, one group under their chief, *Tenoch*, founding the southern capital, Tenochtitlán, and the other settling Tlatelolco in the north. Eventually, as the swamps were drained and brought under cultivation, the islands became one, with two cities and two governments, a state of affairs not to last very long.

The year 1367 marks the turning point of Aztec fortunes. It was then that the Aztecs began to serve as mercenaries for the mightiest power on the mainland, the expanding Tepanec kingdom of Atzcapotzalco, ruled by the unusually able Tezozómoc. One after another the city states of the Valley of Mexico fell to the joint forces of Tezozómoc and his allies; sharing in the resulting loot, the Aztecs were also taken under Tepanec protection, Tezozómoc giving them their first king, Acamapichtli. At the same time, and in fact probably beginning as far back as their serfdom under Colhuacán, the Aztecs were taking on so much of the culture that was the heritage of all the nations of the Valley from their Toltec predecessors. Much of this was learned from the mighty Tepanecs themselves, particularly the techniques of statecraft and empire-building so successfully indulged in by Tezozómoc. Already the small island kingdom of the Aztecs was prepared to exercise its strength on the mainland.

The Consolidation of Aztec Power

The chance came in 1426, when the aged Tezozómoc was succeeded as Tepanec king by his son Maxtlatzin, known to the Aztecs as 'Tyrant Maxtla' and an implacable enemy of the growing power of Tenochtitlán. By crude threats and other pressures, Maxtlatzin attempted to rid himself of the 'Aztec problem'; and in the middle of the crisis, the third Aztec king died. Itzcóatl, who assumed the Aztec rulership in 1427, was a man of strong mettle. More important, he had in his chief adviser, the great Tlacaélel, one of the most remarkable men ever produced by the Mexicans. The two of them decided to fight, with the result that by the next year the Tepanecs had been totally crushed and Azcapotzalco was in ruins. This great battle, forever glorious to the Aztecs, left them the greatest state in Mexico.

In their triumph, the Aztec administration turned to questions of in-

---

[2] Today the national emblem of Mexico is an eagle, sitting on an organ pipe cactus, holding a snake in its mouth. The symbol of the Chicano labor movement, the Thunderbird, is related to the powerful Eagle symbolism of Mexico and the Aztecs.—*Eds.*

ternal policy, especially under Tlacaélel, who remained a kind of grand vizier to the Aztec throne through three reigns, dying in 1475 or 1480. Tlacaélel conceived of and implemented a series of reforms that completely altered Mexican life. The basic reform related to the Aztec conception of themselves and their destiny; for this, it was necessary to rewrite history, and so Tlacaélel did, by having all of the books of conquered peoples burned since these would have failed to mention Aztec glories. Under his aegis, the Aztecs acquired a mystic-visionary view of themselves as the chosen people, the true heirs of the Toltec tradition, who would fight wars and gain captives so as to keep the fiery sun moving across the sky.

This sun, represented by the fierce god Huitzilopochtli, needed the hearts of enemy warriors; during the reign of Moctezuma I (1440–68), Tlacaélel had the so-called 'Flowery War' instituted. Under this, Tenochtitlan entered into a Triple Alliance with the old Acolhua state of Texcoco (on the other side of the lake) and the dummy state of Tlacopán in a permanent struggle against the Náhuatl-speaking states of Tlaxcala and Huexotzingo. The object on both sides was purely to gain captives for sacrifice.

Besides inventing the idea of Aztec 'grandeur,' the glorification of the Aztec past, other reforms relating to the political-juridical and economic administrations were also carried out under Tlacaélel. The new system was successfully tested during a disastrous two-year famine which occurred under Moctezuma I, and from which this extraordinary people emerged more confident than ever in their divine mission.

Given these conditions, it is little surprise that the Aztecs soon embarked with their allies on an ambitious programme of conquest. The elder Moctezuma began the expansion, taking over the Huasteca, much of the land around Mount Orizaba, and rampaging down even into the Mixteca. Axayácatl (1469–81) subdued neighbouring Tlatelolco on trumped-up charges and substituted a military government for what had once been an independent administration; he was less successful with the Tarascan kingdom of Michoacan, for these powerful people were already equipped with copper weapons and turned the invaders back. Greatest of all the empire-builders was Ahuítzotl (1486–1502), who succeeded the weak and vacillating Tizoc as sixth king. This mighty warrior conquered lands all the way to the Guatemalan border and brought under Aztec rule most of central Mexico. Probably for the first time since the downfall of Tula, there was in Mexico a single empire as great as, or greater than, that of the Toltecs. Ahuítzotl was a man of great energy; among the projects completed in his reign were the Great Temple of Tenochtitlán, for the dedication of which no less than 20,000 captives gained in the 'Flowery War' were sacrificed, and the construction of an aqueduct to bring water from Coyoacán to the island capital.

A more tragic figure in history than his successor, Moctezuma II (1502–20), would be hard to imagine. It was his misfortune to be a very complex person, not the kind of single minded militarist that is so well typified by

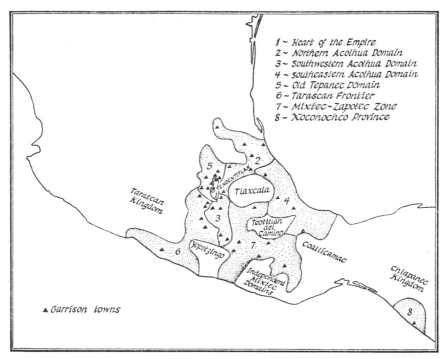

1 ~ Heart of the Empire
2 ~ Northern Acolhua Domain
3 ~ Southwestern Acolhua Domain
4 ~ Southeastern Acolhua Domain
5 ~ Old Tepanec Domain
6 ~ Tarascan Frontier
7 ~ Mixtec-Zapotec Zone
8 ~ Xoconochco Province

Tarascan Kingdom

Tlaxcala

Teotitlan del Camino

Coatlicamac

Xocotzingo

Independent Mixtec Domains

Chiapanec Kingdom

▲ Garrison towns

FIGURE 1. Extent of the Aztec Empire in 1520. The provinces into which the Aztec domains were organised are indicated.

Ahuítzotl. Instead of delighting in war, he was given to meditation in his place of retreat, the 'Black House'—in fact, he was more of a philosopher king, along the lines of Hadrian. Like that Roman emperor, he also maintained a shrine in the capital where all of the gods of captured nations were kept, for he was interested in foreign religions. It is certain that Moctezuma II was deeply imbued with Toltec traditions. This was the cause of his downfall, for when Cortés arrived in 1519, the Aztec emperor was paralysed by the realisation that this strange, bearded foreigner was Quetzalcóatl himself, returned with his Toltecs from the east as the ancient books had said he would, to destroy the Mexican peoples. All of his disastrous inaction in the face of the Spanish threat, his willingness to put himself in the hands of Cortés, was brought about by this dedication to the old Toltec philosophy. It was his destiny, foretold by a series of magical portents, to preside over the total destruction of Mexican civilisation.

The Aztecs in 1519

Let the soldier Bernal Díaz, who was with Hernán Cortés when the Spaniards first approached the island capital of Tenochtitlán on 8th November 1519, tell us his impressions of his first glimpse of the Aztec citadel:

During the morning, we arrived at a broad causeway and continued our march towards Iztapalapa, and when we saw so many cities and villages built in the water and other great towns on dry land and that straight and level Causeway going towards Mexico, we were amazed and said that it was like the enchantments they tell of in the legend of Amadis, on account of the great towers and cues and buildings rising from the water, and all built of masonry. And some of our soldiers asked whether the things that we saw were not a dream.

The island was connected to the mainland by three causeways, 'each as broad as a horseman's lance,' says Cortés, running north to Tepeyac, west to Tlacopan, and south to Coyoacán. These were broken at intervals by openings through which canoes could pass, and spanned by removable bridges, thus serving a defensive purpose; moreover, access to the city by the enemy was barred by manned gatehouses. Across the western causeway ran a great masonry aqueduct carrying water to Tenochtitlán from the spring at Chapultepec, the flow being 'as thick as a man's body.'

The Spanish conquerors called the Aztec capital another Venice, and they should have known, for many of them had actually been to that place. With a total area of about 20 square miles, the city (meaning by this Tenochtitlán and its satellite Tlatelolco) was laid out on a grid, according to a fragmentary sixteenth-century map of one section. Running north and south were long canals thronged with canoe traffic and each bordered by a lane; larger canals cut there at angles. Between these watery 'streets' were arranged in regular fashion rectangular plots of land with their houses. In effect, this was a *chinampa* city.

A brief description of *chinampa* cultivation . . . will not be out of place here. The technique is well known, for it is still used in the Xochimilco zone to the south of Mexico City. The first settlers on the island constructed canals in their marshy habitat by cutting layers of thick water vegetation from the surface and piling them up like mats to make their plots; from the bottom of the canals they spread mud over these green 'rafts,' which were thoroughly anchored by planting willows all around. On this highly fertile plot all sorts of crops were raised by the most careful and loving hand cultivation. This is why Cortés states that half of the houses in the capital were built up 'on the lake,' and how swampy islands became united. Those houses on newly made *chinampas* were necessarily of light cane and thatch; on drier parts of the island, more substantial dwellings of stone and mortar were possible, some of two stories with flower-filled inner patios and gardens. Communication across the 'streets' was by planks laid over the canals.

The greatest problem faced by the inhabitants was the saltiness of the lake, at least in its eastern part. With no outlet, during floods these nitrous waters inundated and ruined the *chinampas*. To prevent this, the Texcocan king Nezahualcóyotl bountifully constructed a ten-mile long dyke to seal off a spring-fed, fresh water lagoon for Tenochtitlán.

FIGURE 2.   The Valley of Mexico in Aztec times.

With its willows, green gardens, numerous flowers, and canals bustling with canoes, Tenochtitlán must have been of impressive beauty, as the Náhuatl poem suggests:

> The city is spread out in circles of jade,
> radiating flashes of light like quetzal plumes,
> Beside it the lords are borne in boats:
> over them extends a flowery mist.

It is extraordinarily difficult to estimate the population of the capital in 1519. Many early sources say that there were about 60,000 houses, but none say how many persons there were. The data which we have, however flimsy, suggest that Tenochtitlán (with Tlatelolco) had from 200,000 to 300,000 inhabitants when Cortés marched in, five times the size of the contemporary London of Henry VIII. Quite a number of other cities of central Mexico, such as Texcoco, also had very large populations; all of Mexico between the Isthmus of Tehuantepec and the Chichimec frontier had about 11 million inhabitants, most of whom were under Aztec domination.

At the centre of Tenochtitlán, the focal point of all the main highways which led in from the mainland, was the administrative and religious heart of the empire. Surrounded by a 'Snake Wall' was the Sacred

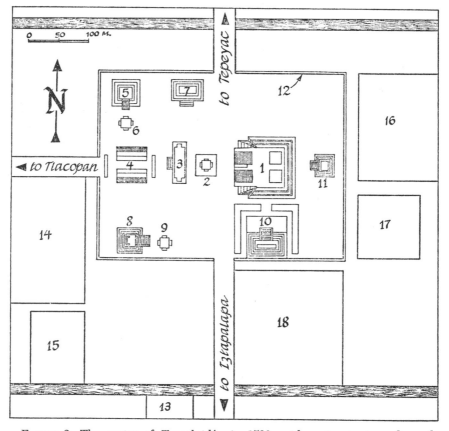

FIGURE 3. The centre of Tenochtitlán in 1520, with main streets and canals. 1. Great Temple of Tlaloc and Huitzilopochtli. 2. Platform for stone of Tizoc. 3. Tzompantli (skull rack). 4. Ball court. 5. 'Eagle House' of the Sun Temple. 6. Platform of the 'Eagle House,' base for Calendar Stone. 7. Snake Temple. 8. Temple of Xipe Totec, God of Spring. 9. Platform for gladiatorial stone. 10. Temple of Tezcatlipoca. 11. Temple of Colbuacán, the former temple of Huitzilopochtli. 12. Snake Wall, enclosing the sacred precinct. 13. 'Black House' of the Temple of Coatlicue. 14. Palace of Moctezuma I (1440–69). 15. 'House of the Songs.' 16. Palace of Axayácatl (1469–81). 17. Royal Aviary. 18. Palace of Moctezuma II (1502–20).

Precinct, a paved area dominated by the 100-foot-high double temple-pyramid, the Temple of Huitzilopochtli and Tlaloc, its twin stairways reddened with the blood of sacrificed captives. Other temples were dedicated to the cults of Tezcatlipoca and Xipe Totec. A gruesome reminder of the purpose of the never-ending 'Flowery War' was the *tzompantli*, or skull rack, on which were skewered for public exhibition tens of thousands of human heads. Having hardly more pleasant associations was a very large ball court, in which Moctezuma II played and lost a game to the king of Texcoco on the truth of the latter's prediction that the former's kingdom would fall. The magnificent palaces of the Aztec royal line surrounded the Sacred Precinct.

Both in Tenochtitlán and in Tlatelolco proper were great market-places, very close to the main temples. The latter market was described by Bernal Diaz in superlative terms; some of the Spanish soldiers who had been in Rome and Constantinople claimed that it was larger than any there. Every product had its own place, the shops being arranged along streets. So many persons came to buy and sell in the daily markets held there that there were market inspectors appointed by the king to check the honesty of transactions and to regulate prices. As for 'money,' cacao beans (which sometimes were counterfeited), cotton cloaks, and transparent quills filled with gold dust served that purpose. Befitting its role as the commercial centre of an empire, in the Great Market of Tlatelolco one could buy luxury products of gold, silver, jade, turquoise, or feathers; clothing of all sorts; foods both cooked and unprepared; pottery, the most esteemed being lovely polychrome dishes and cups from Cholula; chocolate and vanilla; carpenter's tools of copper; cane cigarettes, tobacco pipes, and aromatic cigars; and slaves, human cattle brought in by dealers from the slave centre of Atzcapotzalco and exhibited in wooden cages. The market people had the obligation to furnish war provisions to the state, mainly maize in forms that would not spoil on long marches.

An empire, a tremendous state in place of what had been less than two centuries before but a band of miserable wretches leading a tribal existence—small wonder that the structure of Aztec society was still in a state of transition in 1519. And yet it is utterly false to assert that the Aztecs when first seen by the Spaniards were on the clan level of organization, without any kind of political power greater than that enjoyed by, say, an Iroquois chief. On the other hand, relics of a more simple kind of organization of human affairs certainly persisted in the administration of the empire.

There were four basic social groups in Aztec Mexico. At the top of the ladder were the noblemen or *pilli*, who all belonged to the royal house, 'precious feathers from the wings of past kings,' as one source puts it. It was from their ranks that the imperial administrators were drawn; these had the use of lands belonging to their office and also owned private lands.

The vast bulk of the population were commoners, *macehuales,* organised into *calpulli,* or clans, of which there were about twenty in the capital. All members of a *calpulli* claimed descent from a common ancestor and worked lands which could not be alienated from their group; each family with its plot maintained rights over it as long as it did not lie unused for over two years at a time. As a landholding corporation, each *calpulli* lived in its own ward in the city; Tenochtitlán itself was divided into four great quarters, and every quarter into its constituent *calpulli,* every *calpulli* into *tlaxilacalli,* or streets. Quite obviously, this was an ideal system for administrative control of a large population. The individual *calpulli* had its own temple and some of the more high-ranking of them had schools for the military education of their youth.

At the bottom of the social scale were the bondsmen (*mayeques*), who tilled the estates of the noblemen as serfs; the majority of them would seem to have been the original owners of lands seized from them by Aztec conquest and handed over to be held in severalty by the 'principals.' Another humble group consisted of the *tamime,* porters who hired themselves out to the professional merchants and who may have been semicivilized Chichimecs from the frontier. Slaves as a group were not important; their membership was drawn from captives and from those who had sold themselves to relieve debts. They were well treated and could not be inherited.

In spite of the presence of clans among the Aztecs, there was nothing in the least bit egalitarian about their society. Everybody was ranked according to their contiguity to the ancestral founders of the *calpulli,* quarter, or nation. As a consequence, there were aristocratic families within the *calpulli* who directed its actions and aristocratic *calpulli* within each quarter. The highest ranking *calpulli* of the greatest quarter in Tenochtitlán was that of the nobility, who claimed descent on the distaff side from Quetzalcóatl; within it, the greatest lineage was that of the royal family. A regular system of tribute offering of one third of the products of the soil ensured the maintenance of the clan aristocracies and the nobility, each élite group drawing its support from the units below it.

We see here, then, a society evolved from a more or less primitive organisation in which all lands were originally held by the clans and over which there was no higher authority than clan chiefs, into a fully fledged state with the appearance of a privileged class holding authority by virtue of its wealth drawn from private estates worked by a new lower class, the serfs. Given time, the clans would have certainly declined to total insignificance.

Two other groups were also to a certain degree operating outside the old clan system. Warriors distinguished on the field of battle were often given their own lands and relieved from the necessity of supplying tribute. The *pochteca* were the long-distance traders engaged in the obtaining of exotic products for the royal palace. Travelling into foreign territories hundreds of miles from the capital, they gathered military intelligence as well as needed goods for the crown, in special ports of trade. Like the businessmen-spies of modern days, they often were the vanguard for the Aztec take-over of another nation, acting sometimes as *agents-provocateurs*. While organised into their own *calpulli*, with their own god, they could render tribute to the palace in luxury goods rather than the produce of their lands, and grew rich and powerful as a consequence—perhaps the nucleus of a crystallising merchant class.

Moctezuma II, the emperor, was the greatest landowner of all. Among the Aztecs, the king was elected from the royal lineage by a council composed of the nobles, chief priests, and top war officers; at the same time, the four principal lords who were to act as his executive arm were also chosen. On his installation, the new king was taken by the chief priests to pay homage at the temple of the national god, Huitzilopochtli; while he censed the sacred image, the masses of citizens waited expectantly below, in a din caused by the blowing of shell trumpets. After four days of meditation and fasting in the temple, he was escorted to his palace. To his coronation banquet came even the kings of distant lands, like the rulers of the Tarascan kingdom, the king of the Totonacs, and great personages from as far as Tehuantepec.

The Aztec king was in every sense an absolute ruler, although advised and sometimes guided by his councillors, particularly by the man who filled the office of *Cihuacóatl* ('Snake Woman'), the grand vizier. The descriptions of the Spaniards make it clear that the ruler was semi-divine. Even great lords who entered into his presence approached in plain garments, heads bowed, without looking on his face. Everywhere he went, he was borne on the shoulders of noblemen in a litter covered with precious feathers. If he walked, nobles swept the way and covered the ground with cloths so that his feet would not touch the ground. When Moctezuma ate, he was shielded from onlookers by a gilt screen. No less than several hundred dishes were offered at each meal for his choosing by young maidens; during his repast he was entertained by buffoons, dwarfs, jugglers, and tumblers.

Moctezuma's gardens and pleasure palaces amazed the Spaniards. The royal aviary had ten large rooms with pools of salt and fresh water, housing birds of both lake and sea, above which were galleries bordered by hanging gardens for the imperial promenade. Another building was the royal zoo, staffed by trained veterinarians, in which were exhibited in cages animals from all parts of his realm—jaguars from the lowlands, pumas from the mountains, foxes, and so forth, making an unearthly clamour with their roars and howls. Carefully tended by servants, many kinds of deformed persons and monstrosities inhabited his private sideshow, each with his own room.

Less frivolous activities of the royal household included separate courts of justice for noblemen (and warriors) and for commoners; the overseeing by stewards of the palace storehouse; the maintenance of the state arsenal, officers' quarters, and the military academy; and the management of the empirewide tribute system.

All of these state functions, and the Aztec economy itself, ultimately rested on the agricultural base of the Mexican peoples—the farming of maize, beans, squash, tomatoes, amaranth, sage, and many other cultigens. Thousands of canoes daily crowded the great lake, bearing these products to the capital either as direct tribute or as merchandise to be traded for craft items and other necessities in the market-places. A tremendous surplus for the use of the city was extracted from the rich *chinampas* fringing the shallow lake and from irrigated fields near by.

But the main goal of the Aztec state was war. Every ablebodied man was expected to bear arms, even the priests and the merchants, the latter fighting in their own units while ostensibly on trading expeditions. To the Aztecs, there was no activity more glorious than to furnish captives or to die oneself for Huitzilopochtli:

> The battlefield is the place:
> where one toasts the divine liquor in war,
> where are stained red the divine eagles,
> where the tigers howl,
> where all kinds of precious stones rain from ornaments,
> where wave headdresses rich with fine plumes,
> where princes are smashed to bits.

In the rich imagery of Náhuatl song, the blood-stained battlefield was described as an immense plain covered by flowers, and lucky he who perished on it:

> There is nothing like death in war,
> nothing like the flowery death
> so precious to Him who gives life:
> far off I see it: my heart yearns for it!

Aztec weapons were the terrible sword-club, with side grooves set with razor-sharp obsidian blades; spears, the heads of which were also set with blades; and barbed and fletched darts hurled from the atlatl. The Aztec warrior was gorgeously arrayed in costumes of tiger skins or suits covered with eagle feathers, symbolising the knightly orders; for defence he sometimes was clad in a quilted cotton tunic and always carried a round shield, often magnificently decorated with coloured designs in feathers. Acting as mercenaries, fierce Otomí tribesmen accompanied the army as bowmen.

War strategy included the gathering of intelligence and compilation of maps. On the field of battle, the ranks of the army were arranged by generals. Attacks were spear-headed by an élite corps of veteran warriors, followed by the bulk of the army, to the sound of shell trumpets blown by priests. The idea was not only to destroy the enemy town but also to isolate and capture as many of the enemy as possible for transport to the rear and eventual sacrifice in the capital.

Nations which had fallen to Aztec arms and those of their allies in the Triple Alliance were speedily organised as tribute-rendering provinces of the empire. Military governors in Aztec garrisons ensured that such tribute, which was very heavy indeed, was paid promptly and on fixed dates. It is fortunate that the tribute list in Moctezuma's state archives has survived in the form of copies, for the Spaniards were also interested in what they could extract from the old Aztec provinces. Incredible as it may seem, each year Tenochtitlán received from all parts of the empire 7,000 tons of maize and 4,000 tons each of beans, sage seed, and grain amaranth, and no less than two million cotton cloaks, as well as war costumes, shields, feather headdresses, and luxury products like amber unobtainable in the central highlands. Certainly some of this loot, especially the cloaks, was farmed out by the royal treasury to the *pochteca* as barter goods to carry to distant ports of trade. But a good deal of the tribute acted as the main financial support of the state edifice, since in an essentially moneyless economy state servants had to be paid in goods and land, and artisans had to receive something for the fine products which they supplied to the palace.

Not unsurprisingly, many of the provinces held under such a heavy yoke reacted to the arrival of Cortés by welcoming the invaders from across the sea as a miraculous delivery from a rule which seemed to them a tyranny.

Aztec mythology and religious organisation are so incredibly complex that little justice can be given them in the space of this chapter. The Aztec concept of the supernatural world was a result of the reconciliation by mystic intellectuals of the tribal gods of their own people to the far richer cosmogony of the older civilisations of Mexico, welding both into a single great system. The bewildering multiplicity of Mexican gods were to these thinkers but embodiments of one cosmic principle of duality, male and female, darkness and light, life and death, as personified by the struggle of Quetzalcóatl and Tezcatlipoca, or by Quetzalcóatl and the Death God. It was believed that the world had gone through four cosmic ages or Suns (like the Hindu *kalpas*), each destroyed by a cataclysm; the present was the fifth age, to be extinguished by earthquakes.

Added to the nature gods and culture heroes already familiar to us in Teotihuacán and Tula were the concepts codified by Tlacaélel, comprising the official state cult of the Aztecs. Huitzilopochtli, the terrible warrior god of the Sun, was the miraculous result of the impregnation of his mother, Coatlícue ('Serpent-Skirt'), by a ball of feathers as she was sweeping one day. As she gave birth, her other children, the Four Hundred Gods, killed her by cutting off her head.

All of these deities were thought of as being multiple, that is simultaneously appearing in quadruple form, each constituent placed at one of the four directions of the universe and associated with a particular colour, so that there were white, black, red, and blue Tezcatlipocas, for instance.

The cults were presided over by a celibate clergy. Every priest had been to a seminary at which he was instructed in the complicated ritual which he was expected to carry out daily. Their long, unkempt hair clotted with blood, their ears and members shredded from self-mutilations effected with agave thorns and sting-ray spines, smelling of death and putrefaction, they must have been awesome spokesmen for the Aztec gods.

The daily life of all Aztecs was bound up with the ceremonies dictated by the machine-like workings of their calendar. The Almanac Year (*tonalpohualli*) of 260 days was the result of the intermeshing of twenty days (given names like Crocodile, Wind, House, Lizard, etc.) with the numbers one to thirteen, expressed in their books by dots only. To all individuals, each day in the *tonalpohualli* brought good or evil tidings in accordance with the prognostications of the priests; but the bad effects could be mitigated, so that if a child was born on an unfavourable day, his naming ceremony could be postponed to a better one. For each of the thirteen 'weeks' there were special rites and presiding gods, as well as gods for every day and even for the hours of day and night.

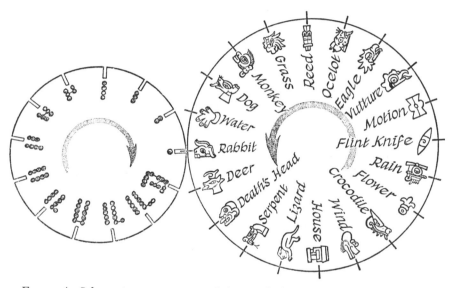

Figure 4. Schematic representation of the *tonalpohualli* or 260-day period of the Aztecs. The twenty named days intermesh with the numbers 1 to 13.

The Solar Year was made up of 18 named months of 20 days each, with an unlucky and highly dangerous period of five extra days before the commencement of the next year. Again, every month had its own special ceremonies in which all of the citizens of the capital participated; given the nature of this kind of cycle, it is hardly surprising that the months were closely correlated with the agricultural year. Such Solar Years were named after the 'Year Bearer,' one of the four possible day names of the Almanac Year which could begin the New Year along with its accompanying numerical coefficient.

All this was recorded in folding-screen books of deer skin or agave paper, kept in the temples by the priests. The state archives also included economic accounts and, possibly, historical works. Curiously, very few truly Aztec codices have survived the Conquest; the finest Post-Classic books which we have were painted in a place that with some confidence can be indicated as Cholula. But about the Aztec script we have some knowledge, for it definitely was of the rebus, 'puzzlewriting' sort; most frequently appearing were place-names, recorded so as to take advantage of common Náhuatl words: thus, the town 'Atlan' was written by combining pictographs of water (*atl*) and teeth (*tlantli*). Numbers up to 19 were expressed by dots, 20 by a flag, 400 by something like a pine tree, 8,000 by a pouch for holding copal incense—that is, the system was vigesimal, increasing in multiples of twenty.

The ritual round must have provided year-long excitement and meaning to the life of the ordinary citizen of Tenochtitlán, with feasts, decoration of the idols, and dances and songs to the accompaniment of two-toned slit drums, upright drums, conchshell trumpets, rattles, and flutes. Homage to the gods prescribed individual penances and burning of blood-spattered paper, burning of perfumed copal incense, and, most dramatically, immolation of thousands of human captives yearly. The victims themselves considered it a glorious death to be seized by the priests and stretched on their backs over a stone on the temple summit, an incision made in the chest with a flint knife, the heart ripped out and placed in the *cuauhxicalli*, or 'Eagle vase,' to be burned for the consumption of the gods. Quickly the head was cut from the corpse, and the body flayed. Priests and those doing penance garbed themselves in the victim's skin, which was worn for twenty days at the end of which the god-impersonator (for they then represented Xipe, the Flayed One) 'stank like a dead dog,' as one source tells us.

Most famous among the Aztec sacrifices was that of the young captive annually chosen to impersonate the god Tezcatlipoca. For one year he lived a life of honour, worshipped literally as the embodiment of the deity; towards the end, he was given four beautiful maidens as his mistresses. Finally, he left them sadly, mounted the steps of the temple, smashing one by one the clay flutes on which he had played in his brief moment of glory, then was flung on his back so that the flint dagger might be plunged into his breast. Most horrible of Aztec practices was the mass sacrifice of small children on mountain tops to bring rain at the end of the dry season, in propitiation of Tlaloc; it was said that the more they cried, the more the Rain God was pleased.

Aztec art and architecture were primarily ecclesiastical, rather than secular in nature. The levelling of the Sacred Precinct of Tenochtitlán by the Spaniards for their own administrative buildings and cathedral destroyed all but the foundations of the major Aztec temples, but some idea can be gained of their magnificence by those that remain elsewhere in the Valley of Mexico, such as the huge double temple at Tenayuca, or the wonderful rock-carved sanctuary at Malinalco, circular and therefore certainly sacred to Quetzalcóatl. To some eyes, Aztec sculpture may be repulsive and there is no doubt that the monumental figures of gods like

Coatlícue may be terrifying, but there is no denying their awesome power. But power is also reflected in the more 'realistic' works such as the seated stone figure of Xochipilli ('Prince of Flowers'), the god of love and summertime, which continue traditions of workmanship perfected by the Toltecs. Or, in the same vein, the lovely sculptured drums from Malinalco, one of which recalls the Náhuatl war song:

> The earth shakes: the Mexica [Aztec] begins his song:
> He makes the Eagles and Ocelots dance with him!
> Come to see the Huexotzinca:
> On the dais of the Eagle he shouts out,
> Loudly cries the Mexica.

Aztec artisans in Tenochtitlán were arranged in an approximation of guilds and were famous for their fine work in feather mosaics; but they were hardly rivals to the great craftsmen of the Cholula area, who under influence from the Mixtecs in the south and Aztecs in the north produced the magnificent Mixteca-Puebla style. Moctezuma himself would eat only from cups and plates of Cholula ware, and it is sure that much of the gold work as well as practically all of the fine masks and other ceremonial paraphernalia of wood encrusted with turquoise mosaic were also manufactured there. The stupendous collection of mosaic pieces once in the hands of Charles V and now in the British Museum and in Florence bears eloquent testimony to late Mexican workmanship in this medum, although most examples were consumed in the *pietre dure* 'laboratories' of Florence in the early nineteenth century.

Highland Mexican artistry radiated to all parts of Mesoamerica in the Post-Classic period, as can be seen, for instance, in the obviously highland-influenced sculptures and fine perforated and incised shell ornaments from the Huasteca, on the northern Gulf Coast.

Lastly, something might be said of the mentality which enabled the Aztec people not only to survive misfortunes, disasters, and privations which would have broken others, but also to create the most advanced political state ever seen in Mexico. Raised in the most austere fashion, trained to withstand cold and hunger, the Aztec individual embodied ideals which would have done credit to an 'old Roman.' Self-restraint and humility were expected even of those whose fortunes soared.

> The mature man:
> a heart as firm as stone,
> a wise countenance,
> the owner of a face, a heart,
> capable and understanding.

Not for him the megalomaniac self-esteem and lust for riches exhibited to the Aztec disgust by the Spaniards!

Furthermore, as a curious foil to this optimistic dedication to war, sacrifice, and puritanical ideals there runs a singular streak of melancholy and pessimism in Aztec philosophy, a theme particularly developed by the closely allied Texcocan royal house. The transitoriness of life on this earth and the uncertainty of the hereafter appear in a song ascribed to King Nezahualcóyotl of Texcoco:

> Even jade is shattered,
> Even gold is crushed,
> Even quetzal plumes are torn . . .
> One does not live forever on this earth:
> We endure only for an instant!

Questions asked in a poem on the same theme:

> Will flowers be carried to the Kingdom of Death:
> Is it true that we are going, we are going?
> Where are we going, ay, where are we going?
> Will we be dead there or will we live yet?
> Does one exist again?

are answered in another place:

> Perhaps we will live a second time?
> Thy heart knows:
> Just once do we live!

The Spanish Heritage

THE IBERIAN BACKGROUND

John Edwin Fagg

Spain Against the World

The feeling that the Spanish are different in their outlooks and ways from other peoples is not limited to the New World. It is age-old in Europe too. Nor is it altogether a matter of foreigners failing to appreciate values cherished south of the Pyrenees. The Spaniards themselves have long agreed with foreign critics or enthusiasts who say they are unlike Europeans and North Americans. Most of them assume, as others do, that Spain is a land where the maxims that govern other peoples do not apply, where the rules are suspended. The mental image of man and his destiny which many Spaniards hold differs in important ways from that accepted by so many of their fellows in the Western world. Their cult of the heroic stance, of action for its own sake regardless of material consequences, their proud refusal to compete with others and to accept rebukes for not playing the game, their long spells of indifference to issues that agitate the outside world—these attitudes fascinate many foreigners and alienate still more. Yet, the Spaniard flaunts his isolation and could not care less what outsiders think.

The Spanish are very much aware, perhaps too much so, of what they call the Black Legend, a collection of myths or facts assembled over a long periods by Spain's foes and victims and perpetuated through prejudice. The list of enemies is long. The Jews and Moslems who were expelled from the peninsula have not forgotten nor forgiven the homeland

Reprinted with permission of The Macmillan Company from *Latin America*, Second Edition, by John Edwin Fagg. Copyright © 1963, 1969 by The Macmillan Company.

John E. Fagg is professor of history and chairman of the department of the Washington Square campus of New York University. He has written extensively on Latin America.

which they loved and, some declare, still long for. Lutherans and Calvinists have added many an item of atrocity to the Black Legend. Italy and the Netherlands were long occupied and mistreated by the Spanish. France and England warred with Spain for generations, and their historians have had much to say of her cruelty and perfidy. Then, the lost colonies have, in the usual fashion, turned on the mother country and blamed it for years of oppression and, often, for most of their own shortcomings. This harsh depiction or misrepresentation of Spain's imperialism persisted until recently and is by no means extinct. It affected public opinion in the United States until well into this century. The Spanish, then, maintain they have been maligned and vilified by spiteful enemies through this Black Legend. It is because of such prejudice that so much of the outside world regards them as unusually cruel, caste-minded, slothful, and given to procrastination or the derided *mañana* habit. Spanish reactions to these criticisms have given them the false reputation for disliking foreigners, though Spain is a proverbially hospitable land to visitors. Finally, in matters of religion there is the least possibility of reconciling critic and apologist. Spain ousted the Jew and Moslem, steadfastly fought the Protestant, and overwhelmed the many paganisms with which she came into contact. The Inquisition has been an evil memory for centuries, and Spaniards have resisted idealistic philosophies not specifically rooted in Roman Catholicism. Mysticism permeates all classes profoundly, to the bewilderment of more worldly outsiders. To charges of bigotry or fanaticism the Spaniard's typical reply is that he takes his religion seriously. And to a degree unknown in the rest of Christendom, he does.

The paradoxes which Spain and its people pose for the foreign student both repel and fascinate. Speculations about national character or collective traits are less fruitful than a study of the locale and history of this people, who have left such an indelible stamp on a great part of the world. Something is to be learned from the period of Roman occupation, the Moslem conquest, the Christian reconquest, and the ultimate unification of Spain. Of more importance for our purposes is the sixteenth century, for this was the time when much of America was conquered and the mold for eighteen Spanish-speaking nations was cast. Some aspects of the sixteenth century are part of the living past today. As the United States traces many of its ideals to the original period of its settlement by seventeenth-century Englishmen who left or fled from a country torn by religious and constitutional troubles, so Latin America shows many effects of Iberian institutions and attitudes of the previous century.

Geographically and in many other ways the Iberian peninsula resembles northern Africa more than Europe, lending foundation to the French taunt that Africa begins at the Pyrenees. Much of Spain is high, arid, and full of great, bleak spaces. Mountain chains almost wall in the country. Spectacular as they are, especially in Granada and in the north, they run wrong for the purposes of rainfall. The dry heartland of the peninsula, Old and New Castile, is therefore suitable more for grazing and mining than for agriculture and forestry. The glare, the winds, the play of shadow and color on the yellow-brown expanses, and the treeless towns give an impression of melancholy which perhaps induces a certain sobriety among the inhabitants. This is Tawny Spain, the Spain which dominates the other sections. These other sections are often beautiful and charming. The northwestern region, Galicia, and the northern coast, Asturias, have a wild, turbulent character with woods, mists, and mountains that run into the sea. The triangle of the northeastern corner, Catalonia, strongly resembles France, which it borders. It is rich and fertile and by far the most European of the several sections. Valencia, to the south of Catalonia on the Mediterranean coast, is something like southern Italy or Greece. Granada and Andalusia, in the south, are semitropical and, when irrigated, lush productive areas of great beauty. Portugal resembles these areas, but it also contains features of the rest of Spain, such as arid stretches and mountains. If nature has not been entirely kind to the Iberians, it still would seem that their peninsula might be as productive as California or Israel if they enjoyed the proper direction.

Ancient Times

This peninsula has been a scene of human activity from time immemorial. The famous drawings of Altamira cave are among the oldest preserved works of prehistoric Cro-Magnon man. We have written records of the Celts, who once occupied the western half of Europe, including Iberia. At some time in the dim past another white group invaded Spain, perhaps from Africa, a people we call the Iberians. The resulting mixture, Celt-Iberian, slowly developed a culture little, if any, more advanced than the ones we have considered in early America. The Celt-Iberians felt the effects of contacts with the more advanced people of the Levant, such as Phoenicians and Hebrews, who occasionally sailed to the peninsula and planted colonies. These Semitic invaders introduced writing and engaged in mining and commerce. Another ancient people, whether invaders or descendants of early man, managed to retain their identity through the ages. These are the mysterious Basques, who still live in the western Pyrenees and speak a language that baffles those who would relate it to any other tongue. Their influence in Latin America has not been light.

After the Greeks began to penetrate the western Mediterranean and venture past the Pillars of Hercules into the Atlantic, important cities and commercial colonies developed along the Iberian coastline. These contacts brought advanced engineering and architecture into the peninsula. Then came the Carthaginians, heirs of the Phoenicians, who in the third century before Christ wrested most of the Greek colonies from their owners and proceeded to conquer the wild inhabitants in the hinterland. This proved a difficult process, for the Celt-Iberians put up a ferocious resistance. One of the earliest Spanish traditions centers about the heroic but doomed defense of the city of Sagunto, a symbol of the warlike fury and spirit of survival that on so many occasions the Hispanic people have demonstrated. Carthage had only a few decades to attempt the colonization of the Iberian peninsula. Her defeats at the hands of Rome during the Punic Wars exposed the region to the legions of the republic, who, to be sure, filled no mere vacuum but fought determinedly for nearly two centuries to overcome the fierce Celt-Iberians. The siege of Numantia in 134 B.C. became another inspiring memory to Spain of a later time, if like Sagunto it was a lost battle.

When at last the peninsula was subdued, it became and remained for about four centuries a firm, loyal component of the Roman Empire known as Hispania. It received a plenitude of new racial stocks and was filled with roads, buildings, theaters, and aqueducts. A leading province of the Roman Empire, Hispania contributed rulers such as Trajan, Hadrian, Theodosius, and Marcus Aurelius; writers such as Seneca, Martial, and Quintilian; as well as soldiers for the legions, officials for the bureaucracy, and fruits and minerals.

The impress of these four hundred years or more of Roman civilization explains much of Spain and Portugal and of Latin America today. Although the strong urban tradition in the Hispanic world has several explanations, a major one was the Roman tendency to civilize and rule through cities, as the Spanish would do in the New World. Roman law still prevails in its fundamental aspects throughout the peninsula and Latin America, the law of a strong empire in which the executive truly rules and tolerates little obstruction from parliaments or courts or local governments. And it is a law which endows the father and husband with great power over the family, which exalts the military and the police and values order more than democratic ideals. Even the languages of the peninsula (except Basque)—Castilian, Catalan, and Portuguese, and the dialects that derive from them—are corrupt Latin. Finally, Hispania became Christianized as Rome did and preserved a special quality of missionary zeal and rigidity that played such a great part in the conquest of America.

The Visigoths

The first crack in the Roman imperial system as far as Hispania was concerned occurred in A.D. 409, when the barbarian Vandals, Alans, and Suevi poured into the peninsula from the north. Five years later came the formidable Visigoths, who had wandered from the Ukraine. Pushing the Suevi up into the rugged northwestern corner of Spain and the Vandals through Andalusia, which took its name from them, into North Africa, the Visigoths occupied with little fighting the places of profit and power from the demoralized inhabitants. They brought little into Hispania but themselves, for their cultural level was low. Scarcely a word of the Visigothic language, very few buildings or articles of utility or artistic value have been preserved. By overpowering the Romans they pushed Hispania into a dark age of semibarbarism and stagnation. The cities all but disappeared, economic life fell to a primitive level, and most men of learning died out or lost touch with the brilliant past. A few decades of Roman or Byzantine restoration on the eastern coasts, from 554 to 621, were not sufficient to revive Hispania.

The Visigothic domination did not signify retrogression in every way. Among many classes the proud Roman tradition persisted, and Latin, though corrupted, remained the basic language of the peninsula. Two of the early "fathers" of the church, Orosius and St. Isidore of Sevilla, were Spaniards who wrote during this period. For all their crudeness the Visigoths brought the Germanic ideal of chivalry and the principle of leadership, by which warriors grouped themselves around admired figures somewhat in the fashion that Latin Americans defer for a time to an outstanding political-military *caudillo*, or leader. Although they debased Roman law along with other aspects of civilization, the Visigoths codified in a *Fuero Juzgo* their own practices so that an eventual amalgamation modified Roman legal traditions with feudal concepts. Kingship was a major contribution of the Visigoths, much as it was to evolve in the subsequent periods of Spanish history.

The Moslems

The Visigoth phase ended abruptly when hordes of North African warriors, fired by the new religion of Mohammed the Prophet and an imperialistic urge to conquer, crossed the Strait of Gibraltar in 711. Although this invasion was a phase of the sensational explosion of the Islamized Arabs and Berbers, who quickly overran territory from France to India, in Spain it was often attributed to Jews seeking relief from Visigothic oppression or to various traitors who intended to spite their enemies. The rotten Visigothic domain, broken by now into many competing local monarchies, collapsed almost at once. A few Visigothic leaders with their more devoted followers took refuge in the mountains of the north while the Moslems swept deep into France. There they were finally checked by Charles Martel in 732 at the battle of Tours and settled back to rule Spain. The only Christian victory in the peninsula was won by Pelayo at the cave of Covadonga, where a few hundred of his men, with divine aid —or so the hallowed tradition has it—defeated thousands of Mohammedans. In any event, it was to prove significant that a few Christians were able to hold out in the mountainous north. The single Christian success did not, however, prevent enormous numbers of North Africans, Arabs, and Levantines—all of whom the Spanish refer to as "Moors"— and many Jews from pouring into the peninsula. This infusion of new blood greatly altered the racial stock of Hispania, and the resulting new culture which flourished accounts more than anything else for the differences between Iberians and other Europeans.

For more than three and a half centuries the Moslems dominated most of the peninsula, and they held rich territories until January 1492. At first their area was an emirate of the Caliphate of Damascus, but in 755, the Abbassid family ousted the Ommayyad dynasty from the throne, whereupon a royal Ommayyad refugee fled to Spain and established himself as monarch. By 929 Ommayyad Spain was powerful enough to rival the older territories in the east and the monarch created the Caliphate of Córdova, which lasted for more than a century before the Moors broke up into splinter monarchies.

While the entire Moorish period was characterized by brilliance and plenty, the century of the Caliphate represented the peak. Córdova was probably the largest and most wealthy city in Europe. The capital with its gorgeous court, mosques, schools, palaces, and business houses was only part of the story. Moslem Spain was heavily populated with hardworking settlers who made this region more productive than it has ever been since. Irrigation, stock breeding, and the cultivation of rice, sugar cane, cotton, silk, and fruits characterized a flourishing economy. So did the thriving towns and cities, supported by an extensive commerce and a great variety of manufacturing. Excellent schools and a large learned class introduced the superior culture of the East and, in time, brought a knowledge of Greek classics to a Christian Europe that had almost forgotten them. Life seemed good in the Caliphate for men of all faiths. The Mohammedans were clearly the ruling class, but they amiably tolerated Jews and Christians as long as there was no likelihood of rebellion and were amazingly gentle when there was.

The contributions of the Moslems to the development of Spain and Portugal were countless. We may note such items as metallurgy, stockraising, and important crops that were to play such a role when the Iberians went to the New World. Much of the Hispanic attitude toward women, both in its chivalric aspects and its harsher phases, has obvious Moorish origin. A list of Arabic words in the Spanish and Portuguese languages would run to many pages. Medical knowledge was advanced and gave the Spanish something of a superiority over other colonizing peoples. Architecture, with the thick walls, patios, fountains, marble and plaster plaques, tiles, brilliant colors, ingenious designs, and other features we think of as typically Hispanic, was greatly influenced or even fashioned by the invaders. The custom of the *siesta* came from the North Africans who moved to Spain. Above all, the racial composition of the whole peninsula was greatly affected by the heavy immigration from Africa and Asia.

The Reconquest

If the brilliant Moslem period brought many peoples and techniques to the Iberian peninsula, the effect of them on the free Christians who finally prevailed after eight centuries was also of enormous importance.

As Américo Castro has described in abundant detail,[1] these eventually victorious remnants of Latin and Visigothic Spain who escaped envelopment in the Moorish tide became what they are largely as a reaction to this Moslem civilization, which inspired them to be different. During the long centuries of contact the Christians outside the Moslem domain learned a great deal from the infidel. But they spurned his industrious ways and his bent for technology. The Christian wanted to be a man of action, a warrior, and not a farmer or artisan or trader. If this attitude implied a weakness on the part of the Christian, he readily translated it into a moral superiority. And the victories came his way. The survival of groups like those who fought with Pelayo ultimately signified the protracted frontier war which resulted in total reconquest of the peninsula.

Some impetus to this Reconquest came with the invasion of northeastern Spain by Charlemagne in 777. While the great monarch abandoned his crusade as too difficult, some of the region we know as Catalonia long remained attached to France and came to resemble that country in many ways. Of much importance was the supposed discovery about 900 of the remains of St. James the Greater on the northwestern coast in Galicia, which was reputed to come about through a miracle of a star remaining still until believers located the grave. Christendom was thrilled by this spectacular event, and the town of Compostela became one of the great attractions for pilgrims during the Middle Ages. The effect on the free Christians was incalculable. They believed St. James protected and blessed their arms, that in difficult battles his white horse would appear in the skies to assure victory. Their war cry, *Santiago* (for Santo Iago or St. James), rang throughout the Reconquest of the peninsula and the Conquest of America.

Before about 1000, when the balance began surely to tip in the Christians' favor, the wars were local and seasonal, a matter of raids not only for the glory of Christ but for land and laborers, and gains were very slow. Urbanism like that of Roman times developed again, for cities with their walls and guards were safer than the countryside. Then, town charters were offered by Christian rulers to encourage growth of such concentrations, and in time the towns became jealous of their privileges and rather independent of outside authority. Furthermore, feudalism of the familiar western European type failed to take shape, for serfs were encouraged by promises of freedom to join the armies, and besides, farm or manor life was unsafe when there were so many raids and so much scorching of the earth. The Christians took on a Moorish custom that was to reach startling proportions in America: the allocation of a fifth of the spoils from a victorious campaign for the monarch. Above all, the character of these early Spanish Christians was affected. They fought with an intensified religious faith that could and did slide easily into a militant fanaticism. They cultivated glory, adventure, striving for the impossible,

---

[1] *The Structure of Spanish History* (Princeton, 1954).

action regardless of risk, and extravagant virility. Physical courage and daring were admired, labor was not. Only infidels and women were supposed to work with their hands.

Despite all the glorification of physical violence and manliness in the Reconquest, we may be sure that many people switched sides, intermarried with the enemy, and ran from combat. The semi-legendary El Cid Campeador, who died in 1099 after a life of heroic achievements romanticized in the medieval epic *El Poema del Cid*, dealt with the Moslems and shifted his allegiance. Yet the tradition of the Reconquest is still a robust influence among the Spanish, affecting them at least as much as the *Drang nach Osten* has the Germans or the more recent westward movement inspires the modern citizen of the United States.

As the momentum of Christian imperialism gathered in the eleventh century, the Moors fell on bad days. The disappearance of the Caliphate of Córdova in 1035 was followed by political fragmentation and then, in 1086, by an invasion from North Africa of warlike, primitive Almorávides. These rude fanatics came with the intention of containing the Christians, but their effect was to dim the brilliance of Moslem culture and to frighten the Christians into more cooperation with one another. Another invasion by the Almohades in 1146 had a similar effect. The Christians were held for a time, but by now the Crusades were stimulating all western Europe and much foreign assistance in the way of pilgrims and knights strengthened the Hispanic faithful. The creation of military orders of devout, crusading knights in the twelfth century introduced a new element into the Reconquest: privileged groups who were competent fighters. These orders of Calatrava, Santiago, and Alcántara proved generally effective, occupied powerful political positions, and disposed of much wealth.

Political power was passing into the hands of Christian monarchs as the institution of kingship developed. The first community to attain the rank of kingdom was Leon in 944. Later in this century Navarre became a kingdom and temporarily united all the Spanish Christian states, only to fall back to the status of a small "saddlebags" state straddling the Pyrenees. In the northeast, Aragon evolved into an aggressive kingdom and absorbed the County of Catalonia. Most important was the growth of Castile, which acquired Leon in the eleventh century, lost it for two periods, and then definitely united with it in the thirteenth century. Castile was to carry out Spain's destiny in the peninsula and America. Playing a tricky game of war and dynastic marriage with its Christian neighbors and often cooperating with Moorish potentates, it absorbed the entire northwest and then thrust itself into the bleak heartland of the peninsula (New Castile).

One accident of the Reconquest was the award of the County of Portugal to a French crusader, Henry of Burgundy, whose heir won complete independence in the twelfth century. Whereas the rulers of Portugal often intermarried with the royal house of Castile and intrigues for union of the two crowns were frequent, the little western state accentuated its own individuality and went its own way.

The expansion of Christendom associated with that most powerful of popes, Innocent III, included momentous triumphs in Spain. The great pontiff fairly compelled the Christian states to cooperate in an offensive against the Moslem which culminated in the battle of Las Navas de Tolosa in 1212. Christian campaigns continued under Fernando of Castile, later canonized as St. Fernando, who in 1236 took Córdova itself and in 1248, Sevilla. Simultaneously, Portugal had completed the task of expelling the Moslem in the western area of the peninsula. All the Mohammedans had left was Granada, a highly developed province with strong natural defenses against the Christians.

Instead of completing the crusade by taking Granada, which managed to remain in Moslem hands until 1492, Castile underwent more than two centuries of medieval anarchy. Some of it was the consequence of the follies of Alfonso the Wise (*El Sabio*), who won the great honor of election to the throne of the Holy Roman Empire but was never able to be crowned or, for that matter, to rule his own kingdom of Castile effectively. He was deposed in 1284, but his reputation as a scientist and man of letters has compensated for his failure as a political leader. Furthermore, he issued an influential codification of laws known as *Las siete partidas* which largely restored the prominent features of Roman law after centuries of Visigothic and Moslem domination. Thus Spain, and eventually Latin America, were to develop within the framework of the ideals of justice and order of the Roman Empire.

The Later Middle Ages

Confusing and depressing as the internal history of Castile was between St. Fernando and Isabel the Catholic, a period extending from 1252 to 1474, it was nonetheless a time of growth and ferment. A weak monarchy was almost the plaything of the great nobles or grandees, but it persisted and eventually came into its own. The lesser nobles, *hidalgos* and *caballeros*, were also powerful and turbulent, engaging in private wars and stealing one another's subjects, so that serfdom practically disappeared. The clergy was numerous and powerful, often a law unto itself, and the great military orders were strong and rich. Franciscans and Dominicans and other regular orders performed much humanitarian and educational work. Towns and cities were largely autonomous. At times they seemed to be developing in a democratic direction. Lands conquered from the Moslem were populated and when Jews and Mohammedans elected to remain in the Christian zones they were comparatively well-treated. Still, the Christians failed to develop much agriculture. They preferred the military life or banditry, the clergy, or mining and ranching. The prestige of livestock raising over farming was stressed in the privileges accorded the *Mesta,* a guild or association of sheepowners who could move their animals across the peninsula irrespective of the damage they wrought on crops. Much of the institutional and psychological preparation for the occupation of America was taking form as empty areas in south central Spain, especially Extremadura and La Mancha, were being populated by Christians. The process was scarcely completed when the New World would offer a larger field for settlement, and a disproportionate number of its colonists would come from these frontier regions in Spain.

On the east coast things were considerably different. Aragon, having absorbed Catalonia, made the ancient city of Caesar Augustus (Zaragoza) its capital. King Jaime the Conqueror won Valencia, Majorca, the chief island of the Baleares, and pushed over the Pyrenees into France during a long reign that spanned the years 1213–1276. Cut off from peninsular expansion by the strength of Castile, the Aragonese later conquered Sardinia, Minorca, Corsica, and Sicily. Interest in overseas territories and an affinity for trade led the Catalans to establish themselves for a time in Greece and Asia Minor while the Byzantine Empire was prostrate. These extensive contacts made the Aragonese monarchy seem more European than the Castilian. Serfdom and other institutions of feudalism gave the kingdom an atmosphere typical of other states of the period, and the northeastern part of Spain still resembles France or Italy in ways that Castile does not. It even seemed for a time that the *cortes,* or assembly of nobles, clergy, and urban delegates, was likely to establish parliamentary rule. But Aragon was not destined to become an England. Cosmopolitan, prosperous, and liberal-minded though it was, Aragon's fate was to be a junior partner of Castile.

The Catholic Kings and the Unification of Spain

In 1469 a highly important royal marriage took place when Fernando, the heir to the throne of Aragon, was united with Isabel, the heiress presumptive to the Castilian crown. This notable couple eventually became *los reyes católicos,* a title given them by the pope, but only after many difficulties and brushes with failure. Isabel's claim was threatened when a daughter was born to the wife of her half-brother, King Enrique the Impotent. In 1474 Isabel won and became queen. This spirited but dignified woman, with her round face, blue eyes, and red hair, was touched with greatness. Her courage and imagination—and her luck— had much to do with Spanish and American history. Fernando was quite different. To his contemporaries he seemed crafty, calculating, tricky, mendacious, and dishonest. These traits brought him the dubious honor of being praised (or obliquely damned) in an entire chapter of

Machiavelli's *The Prince*. But combined with Isabel's qualities, they helped bring unparalleled fortune to the royal couple, their heirs, and to Spain. Fernando did not come into his inheritance until 1479. For that reason, because he enjoyed powers in Castile as Isabel's husband that she did not wield in Aragon as his consort, and because the Castilian monarchy was stronger than the Aragonese, the pair emphasized the more absolutist Castile. Thus Castile's predominance waxed steadily, though for more than a century the Aragonese domains were legally separate, united only by the crown. With the reign of Fernando and Isabel it becomes easier if not altogether accurate to refer to "Spain," since these monarchs and their heirs increasingly ruled the area as one kingdom.

The growth of royal power in Spain was in line with developments in France under Louis XI, England under Henry VII, and Portugal under João II, who were contemporaries of the Catholic Kings. Still, it took much energy, persistence, and skill to accomplish, for it was something new and was by no means inevitable. The nobles found themselves overawed and out-maneuvered by the monarchs and transformed rather rapidly into allies or servants of the royal pair during these years. Many were attracted into a royal guard or into government service. Others were defeated in battle, had their castles razed, their privileges annulled, and their peasants encouraged to move away. The three great military-clerical orders, which had helped establish Isabel, were persuaded or intimidated into naming Fernando as their head, thus bringing more reins into the hands of the monarch. The proud, often defiant towns had to bend before the royal will personified by officials known as *corregidores*, who were later used in America. The *cortes* seldom met, thus discouraging any movement toward parliamentary assertiveness.

Even the formidable forces of the clergy fell under royal control. Beginning in 1482, a series of bulls conceded by popes who needed Fernando's support for Italian or personal affairs made the Church in Spain almost a national organization, subject to Rome only in matters of doctrine. The government supervised ecclesiastical affairs and nominated Church officials. These powers, known as the *patronato real*, were to be employed extensively in creating the great Church establishment in America. To her credit, Isabel was concerned with more than aggrandizing her authority. With the aid of the great Cardinal Ximenes de Cisneros, she disciplined unworthy clergymen and insisted that the Church abide by her own high-minded if intolerant ideals. The effect was to reform the Spanish Church years before the Reformation started, and Protestantism was never to attract many Spaniards. Moreover, the Spanish clergy was zealous and efficient when the discovery of America brought the magnificent challenge to Christianize millions of pagans. In 1478 Isabel, and, in 1481 Fernando, obtained papal permission to establish the Inquisition in their domains under their own control. This agency assisted in the task of eliminating unworthy ecclesiastics and enforcing conformity to doctrine, but under the Grand Inquisitor Tomás de Torquemada it also began the persecution of persons whose Christianity was suspect.

All of this concentration of power in royal hands was facilitated by rallying the soldiers and common people to the cause of the monarchy. This was largely accomplished by a protracted national effort against the remaining Moors in the densely populated kingdom of Granada. This cause, the last stage of the Reconquest that had inspired the Spaniards for nearly eight centuries, was by no means easy to fulfill. An enormous army, many financial sacrifices, the use of gunpowder, and the almost constant presence of Fernando and Isabel were required, and yet it was more than ten years before Boabdil, the last of the Moorish monarchs, surrendered in January 1492. The final victory brought an ecstatic national feeling to Spain and won the applause of Christendom.

So thankful was Isabel for this richly satisfying victory that she decided to illustrate her gratitude by requiring all Jews to become Christians within four months or to leave. Barbarous as the measure was, France and England had done the same thing two centuries before, and while Spain had generally been tolerant and cosmopolitan, popular violence directed at the Jews had been growing rapidly. In any event, Isabel felt righteous about the whole matter. The number of those who became converted, sincerely or otherwise, is not known. Perhaps 150,000 sold out hurriedly and left for Portugal, where they were fleeced further and then sent away to the Ottoman Empire, Italy, the Netherlands, and elsewhere. A large number chose conversion, but this course exposed them to sinister ministrations of the Inquisition and resulted in further sufferings. So successful did the measure seem to Isabel that ten years later she commanded the half-million or more Moslems in Castile to embrace Christianity or leave. In the long run the loss of about a tenth of her population, the most hard-working and skilled element at that, was ruinous.

Great prizes seemed in reach through the dynastic alliances the Catholic Kings made for their children. In some respects they were dogged by bad luck. Their sons died without heirs. Two daughters were "wasted" in a futile effort to bring about a union with Portugal. Another was married to the heir to the English crown, and, when he died, to his brother, the future Henry VIII. This daughter was the unfortunate Catherine of Aragon, who achieved neither marital happiness nor closer ties between England and Spain nor, as it happened, the strengthening of Catholicism. But fortune compensated liberally in the case of another tragic daughter, Juana the Mad, whose marriage with Philip the Handsome of the house of Habsburg greatly changed the destinies of Europe, for better or for worse. For when Isabel died in 1504, Juana and Philip came to Castile to take over the kingdom and the Americas, such as they were then. But Philip soon died and Juana became insane. Her father, Fernando of Aragon, assumed the direction of Castile and her overseas possessions until his death in 1516, a somewhat unedifying period in the early history of America. Meanwhile, his crooked diplomacy and the tough Spanish armies led by the "Great Captain," Gonsalvo de Córdova, brought him Navarre and Naples.

The Emperor Charles V

By the time Fernando the Catholic died, the first son of Juana the Mad and Philip the Handsome was nearly old enough to come into his full rights. From his grandmother, Isabel the Catholic, he inherited Castile and the expanding possessions in the New World. Fernando bequeathed him Aragon, Navarre, much of Italy, and the islands of the western Mediterranean. From his father's mother, Mary of Burgundy, the young heir received lands now included in the Netherlands, Belgium, and parts of eastern France and western Germany, then as now one of the richest areas on earth. His paternal grandfather, Maximilian of Habsburg, left him Austria, assorted territories in central Europe, the likelihood of following him as Holy Roman Emperor, and the prestige of the name of Habsburg. This young man, who became Carlos I of Spain but is better known as Emperor Charles V, eventually acquired titular possession to as much real estate as almost any other person in history. If it proved unfortunate that Spain should become involved in European affairs just as she was taking over much of the New World, the Spanish contemporaries of Charles V were gratified by the majesty of their king and the imperial greatness that had come to their backward and isolated peninsula.

The first visit of young Carlos I to Spain in 1517–1520 was not particularly promising. At that time a clumsy, slow-moving youth, ugly with his pronounced underslung jaw, speaking Flemish, and surrounded by luxury-loving Lowlanders who ate and drank too much, the new king seemed very un-Spanish. As soon as he departed to be crowned Holy Roman Emperor and for his dramatic meeting with Martin Luther at Worms, a serious revolt broke out in Castile. Like so many Spanish rebellions it was called a *comunero* movement, chiefly because its impulse came from towns seeking to cast off royal authority, but it developed the characteristics of a social rebellion against the landed nobility, especially when it spread into Valencia. This feature probably killed the movement, since the privileged groups rallied to monarchical authority, and Spain was to experience little in the way of social or democratic unrest for another three centuries. The monarchy was to be absolute.

Charles V was out of Spain for much of his reign. He had several wars to fight against France, which was almost hemmed in by Habsburg power and had to fight for survival, allying herself with Protestants, Mohammedans, and anyone else who opposed the emperor. Much of the warfare took place in Italy, a circumstance that brought Charles into conflict with the pope on occasion and once, in 1527, resulted in the deplorable sacking of Rome by his unpaid troops. When France associated herself with that formidable infidel, Suleiman the Magnificent of the Ottoman Turks,

Charles became heavily involved in naval warfare in the Mediterranean, land campaigns in the Danube basin, and attempts to seize North African strongpoints. These wars distracted the emperor from his efforts to deal with the Protestant Reformation, which grew more menacing with the Lutheran successes in central and northern Europe and the spread of Calvanism into France and the Low Countries, apart from the peculiar developments in England sponsored by his erstwhile uncle by marriage, Henry VIII, and Edward VI.

When at last Charles V accepted a stalemate with France and the Turks in order to deal with the Protestants, the matter was out of hand. In the 1540's he finally pressed the reluctant pope to undertake the reform of the Roman Catholic Church and collected a great army to deal with the German Lutherans. Victory seemed assured in 1547, and some sort of reconciliation was believed possible, one that would keep the universal church together through concessions to the Protestants. But an unexpected Protestant victory in 1552 undid Charles' labors. Narrowly escaping capture, the emperor had to admit failure. Four years later he astonished the world and grieved his subjects by abdicating voluntarily and retiring to a monastery in Spain, where he died in 1558. Spaniards have always been proud that the great monarch came to regard Spain as his true home, or in his own words, his garden, fortress, treasury, and sword.

In spite of the many distractions that tore at Charles, he devoted considerable time and thought to his overseas empire. It was he who supported, as Isabel the Catholic had, the more humane policies advocated by the clergy to protect the Indians from exploitation and to make them Christians. He wisely backed the conquistadors while they were winning new kingdoms for him and cashiered them as soon as he could in favor of obedient officials who would be scrupulously loyal to the crown. Charles fashioned the fundamental machinery by which Spain would rule the Americas for many generations: the Council of Indies, the viceroys, the missions, the convoys, the mining regulations, and many other instruments. On the other hand, the wealth of the American possessions helped finance his wars in Europe and buttressed the national position of Spain and the international prestige of Habsburgs. The Counter-Reformation, which was to salvage so much from the disintegration of the Roman Catholic Church, owed its beginning to the wisdom of Charles and the financial support he drew from Mexico and Peru. So it was with the cultural greatness of Spain, its *siglo de oro,* partially inspired by the impact of the New World on European imagination and facilitated by the flow of gold and silver from abroad.

Felipe II, the Prudent King

When Charles V abdicated he turned over to his brother Ferdinand the Habsburg possessions in central Europe. The remaining lands were indeed valuable, and the emperor's son had no reason to consider himself disinherited. Felipe II (1556–1598) had assisted his father for years in ruling the spreading Spanish monarchy and was husband of the queen of England, "Bloody" Mary. Now he assumed the thrones of Castile and her expanding empire in the New World and in the countless islands of the Pacific Ocean, Aragon, Navarre, Sardinia, Sicily and Naples, Milan, the Low Countries, and the Franche Comté in eastern France. In 1580 he became king of Portugal and her extensive possessions along the coasts of Brazil, the Atlantic and Indian sides of Africa, and fortified places in Persia, India, Malaya, China, and many islands of the Far East.

By far the most formidable monarch of his time, Felipe II had many enemies. He has long been regarded as the man a modern liberal loves to hate, a gloomy bigot, a despot, a cruel hypocrite. Indeed, he was sober and melancholy and often wrong-headed and self-righteous. But he was keenly aware of his great responsibilities before God and posterity. Felipe worked tirelessly, insisting on knowing everything and deciding everything about his empire, seeking above all to make it operate in accordance with his religious ideals. Greatness is seldom lovable.

Felipe II was not a great innovator but rather a conserver, hence his informal title, "the Prudent." In the New World he created few important institutions, though the establishment of the Inquisition and the dispatch of the Jesuits there had large consequences. For the most part he perfected the operation of the great imperial apparatus that had been in the making since the days of Columbus. The sharp attention Felipe II gave to details and the close supervision he inflicted on administrators affected the way the viceroys, governors, *corrregidores*, bishops, missionaries, treasury officials, and other members of the bureaucracy functioned long after the Prudent King was dead. The very atmosphere of his 42-year reign was too heavy to be dissipated during the remainder of the colonial period. To some students it seems that the spirit of Felipe II still broods over Latin America.

The European problems that Felipe II faced had important repercussions in the Americas. The real force behind the Catholic Counter-Reformation, which became so powerful after the Council of Trent in 1564, the austere king imparted to such faraway places as the Philippines, Mexico, and Peru a passion to hunt down heretics and to keep the faith pure. Along more positive lines, the resurgent Church pursued the conversion of Indians with great energy and improved Catholic education in the New World.

Felipe II continued the wars against the Turks. With the great naval victory of Lepanto in 1572, Christian Spain virtually concluded her eight and a half centuries of warfare against the Moslem. Perhaps with this victory, as many historians have declared, Spain lost that special quality of inspiration which had driven her to greatness. The Dutch rebelled against Felipe II in 1567 and themselves rapidly attained greatness, thriving on the enmity of the detested king. For most of the ensuing eighty years the traders, pirates, and armed expeditions of the doughty Low-landers worked havoc on the Hispanic empires. The long duel between Elizabeth I of England and Felipe II, which culminated in the disastrous experience of the Spanish Armada in 1588, opened a nearly continuous warfare or competition that ended only when Latin America became free, or perhaps with the victory of the United States over Spain in 1898. Felipe's acquisition by force of the crown of Portugal in 1580 had long-range effects, many of them injurious to Spain, that he did not foresee.

In all of these international developments the overseas Spanish posses-sions played a part, sometimes as victim, sometimes as prize, even on occasion as beneficiary. Spain had to tighten her control or risk losing the colonies, and this she did to a degree that fulfilled her purpose, if even-tually it proved burdensome to the Americans. Moreover, the so-called Indies provided much of the treasure that enabled Felipe II to dominate or threaten Europe for so long, and that gave Spain the reputation for power that lasted after the power itself had vanished. The silver galleons helped finance the artistic wonders of the *siglo de oro*, especially the palaces, cathedrals, and cloisters that were erected all over the peninsula. Felipe II chose Madrid for his capital and appropriately adorned it, thanks to American metallic treasures. His personal residence and eventu-ally the tomb of Spanish kings, the bleak Escorial, was testimony of the transatlantic sources of wealth.

The death of this dreaded and strangely admirable king in 1598 is a convenient point to mark the end of Spain's material grandeur. Yet a decline had set in years before. Something had gone wrong in Spain while she was at the peak of her strength. Whatever it was, it rendered the nation sickly for centuries. The mystery of Spain's decline has long tan-talized her own sons and foreign students. Plausible explanations abound, but few agree as to their position in the hierarchy of causes. Looking at the problem from an international point of view, one may insist that Spain was largely diverted from her true destiny in North Africa by Columbus, that she should never have abandoned the land crusade against the Moslems. Or that the inheritance of Charles V embroiled Spain in European affairs so that she wasted her strength on causes that brought her no lasting advantages. The loss of inspiration after the victory at Lepanto has been mentioned. Spain's efforts to hold the Dutch down, to interfere in France, the Germanies, and Italy, and to contain the English drained her while releasing the energies and firing the determination of others. Perhaps she tried to do too much and ended up by collapsing, by becoming, as Ortega y Gasset has said, the dust left by a great people who once galloped down the highway of destiny. Could it even be that Spain was a bogus power, a backward peninsula that through accidents of discovery and dynastic inheritance became inflated, but which always lacked the fundamental resources that nourish greatness? Or should we be content with philosophizing that a century or so of first-rank strength is about all that any modern European nation has been able to sustain?

If one rejects all such explanations a number of reasons related to Spain's internal situation come to mind. The rigid character of her royal autocracy may have been beneficial while the empire was growing but unsuitable for a long period of stability, especially when the caliber of the kings declined so sharply, as it did between 1598 and 1700. The religious intolerance that expelled the Jews and Moslems (and later, the converted Moslems) and badgered the populace into conformity or timidity is a favorite explanation. The emphasis on pastoral and mining industries obstructed the development of agriculture and manufacturing as well as commerce. The influx of treasure from America led to an inflation that injured many groups and, in the long run, enriched Spain's rivals more than herself. Something was at odds in a society which stressed war and religiosity at the expense of plain, humble labor. Does the answer lie in false ideals, collective character defects, or in circumstances the wisest of statesmen could not control? Outsiders and Spaniards alike ponder these imponderables, and no single answer seems to fit.

Having said all this, we must not dismiss Spain too easily after the passing of the Prudent King. For nearly a half-century more Spain, or her ghost, enjoyed great military prestige in Europe. The annihilation of her fleets in 1637–1639 and the catastrophic defeat of her army at Rocroi in 1643 did not altogether overthrow Spain as a respected power. She continued to occupy much of Italy and the Netherlands, and her enormous empire remained loyal and productive. Very little of it was lost to her stronger enemies, the English, Dutch, and French. And then in the eighteenth century Spain underwent a considerable revival under a new dynasty, the Bourbons. Somehow, the vast and peculiar world empire continued operating on the momentum imparted to it by Isabel the Catholic, Charles V, and Felipe II.

Spain's Golden Age

A cultural flowering of large proportions began during Spain's period of overseas expansion and lingered for several generations after the decline had set in, thus offering support both for those who claim that great artistic and literary expression coincides with national greatness and for those who contend it characterizes the aftermath of such periods. It was natural enough that Spanish explorers and conquistadors should write about their achievements, inadequately as they did so for our purposes. They sometimes recorded the facts faithfully but often were partisan and too prone to describe nonexistent marvels and supernatural miracles. Only by inadvertence did they set down most of the facts the modern anthropologist or social and economic historian would like to know. Also, the Spanish wrote books on navigation, geography, metallurgy, and mining that were regarded as authoritative. The collection of important papers dealing with the New World and the recording of its history from the conqueror's point of view were also done with a sense of responsibility. The sudden enrichment of Spain and the profound stimulation of the senses brought about by the great discoveries surely encouraged the establishment of universities. Perhaps thirty or more institutions in the peninsula merited the name of university by the death of Felipe II, and while some of them provided degrees and intellectual pretensions to ignorant graduates, others furthered the growth of academic traditions and standards we can admire.

Such matters, however, constitute no more than the normal or predictable effects of a period of national greatness. There was more to Spain's *siglo de oro* (golden century) than that. Genius, always unaccountable, appeared in many forms during the sixteenth and seventeenth centuries. Above all was Miguel de Cervantes Saavedra (1547–1616), that warrior and man of action whose worthy poems, novels, and essays are overshadowed by his great *Don Quijote*. The dramatist Félix Lope de Vega (1562–1635) wrote so many plays with so many different plots, full of such superlative lyric verse, that he has influenced dramatists of his own and other nations ever since. Pedro Calderón de la Barca (1600–1681), with his lofty absorption in religion and philosophy, was a prolific genius whose lyrical dramas are masterpieces of beauty and profoundly stirring to the spirit. Tirso de Molina (1571–1648) produced an admirable variety of dramas of possibly less depth but often of more interest in the interplay of human passions. Along with these towering figures of literature were great numbers of lesser lights whose verses, stories, and plays enjoyed much popularity in Spain and America. Whether they are chivalrous, pastoral, or picaresque, many of them strike us today as shallow and silly, but then the transient works of literature usually are. Until the appearance of *Don Quijote* in 1605–1611, most Spaniards who read (or listened to readings) were influenced above all by the Portuguese chivalric romance. *The four books of Amadis of Gaul*, with its extravagant treatment of improbable deeds in remote places, was full of meaning to a nation engaged in world-wide explorations. It was fantastic and exaggerated, but the people doted on it. Not a little of the posturing and strutting of the conquistadors may be attributed to the influence of this work.

A plentiful supply of Spanish geniuses rose to the religious issues posed by the Discovery and the Reformation. The political scientists, jurists, and historians we shall consider in later pages as they dealt with the problems of the Americas. St. Ignatius Loyola (1491–1556) and his *Spiritual Exercises* affected many a Jesuit who buttressed the Spanish monarchy in five continents and other devout souls, some of them in high positions of the government, who felt the need of such rigid self-discipline. Spanish mystics have long commanded the respect, often grudging, of the outside world. Outstanding among them was St. Teresa de Jesús (1515–1582), who reformed the Carmelites in the face of many obstacles and wrote powerfully of the blazing ecstasy one may achieve in approaching an awareness of God. St. John of the Cross (1542–1591), her follower and also a Carmelite, described the way to reach spiritual bliss and the joys of mystical experience. While comparatively few people were capable of such discipline, these mystics were loved and respected by the populace at large on both sides of the Atlantic. A strong strain of Spanish mysticism persists in much of the Hispanic world, often serving as another barrier to the sympathetic understanding of this world by outsiders with different religious traditions.

The memorable period of Spanish painting came after the peak of imperial greatness, though the way for it had been prepared by the cultured Charles V and his sponsorship of artists and by Felipe II and his tendency to collect meritorious works of art. El Greco (1541–1614), a Greek or Cretan named Domenico Theotocopuli, painted for years in Toledo his delicate, haunting portraits and scenes that seem to typify the gravity, dignity, and religiosity of the Spaniard. José de Ribera (1588–1652) was able to depict both the spiritual exaltation and the human cruelty that Spaniards displayed in their period of domination. Diego Velázquez (1599–1660) was court painter to Felipe IV and a superlative master of his craft. Serene and realistic, his portraits immortalized the mediocre Habsburgs of the mid-seventeenth century and the characters who frequented their court, something their own achievements fell short of doing. There were many other famous names, certainly those of Zurbarán and Murillo, whose works endowed Spanish painting with its great reputation and furnished inspiration and material for imitation by many artists of the Spanish empire in America, who themselves were often gifted, if not outstanding. In all, the New World partially stimulated and endowed the Golden Age and certainly shared in its glories.

SPAIN: ITS PEOPLE AND ITS RULERS

J. Fred Rippy

Spaniards of the late fifteenth century were a mixture of many peoples, Oriental and North African as well as European, who had come to the peninsula in successive waves during prehistoric and historic times. Civilization was brought to their country by the Phoenicians, the Greeks, the Carthaginians, and the Romans. Spain was a part of the Roman Em-

Reprinted by permission from *Latin America*, Revised Edition, by J. Fred Rippy. Copyright © by the University of Michigan 1958, 1968. University of Michigan Press. All rights reserved.

J. Fred Rippy did his doctoral work on Mexican–U.S. relations at the University of California in 1920. Since then he has taught at the University of Chicago and at Duke University. He is a Guggenheim Fellow and the recipient of numerous awards in the field of Latin American history. He has authored more than a dozen books in this field.

pire for several centuries, and it was during the Roman period that the inhabitants of the country became Christians. Next, shortly after the year 500, the peninsula was overrun by Germanic tribes, especially the Visigoths, who set up a kingdom there, adopted Christianity themselves, and continued to dominate the country until shortly after the Moslem invasion, which began in 711.

During the seventh century the followers of Mohammed, a religious leader of Arabia, had established a vast empire, which included Egypt and northern Africa, from which they entered Spain and conquered most of its inhabitants within a few years. The invaders, mostly Berbers but a good many Arabs, were people of rather high culture, who developed the resources of the country with great skill. They built irrigation systems, fertilized the soil, and imported rice, cotton, sugar cane, citrus fruits, silkworms, and mulberry trees. They worked the silver, copper, lead, and iron mines. They manufactured pottery, glassware, jewelry, and leather goods. Their Toledo swords and their carved leather and ivory were famous. They also introduced the Arabic system of numbers and built the first paper factory in all Europe. Moreover, the Moslem period in Spain is especially noted for its magnificent architecture, its schools, and its science. At a time when nearly all the rest of Europe was just beginning to dispel the darkness of the Dark Ages, the Moorish capital at Córdoba was an impressive cultural center.

But the older inhabitants of Spain, especially those in the mountains of the north who had avoided subjugation, were bitterly opposed to the Moslems both because they were invaders and because they were not Christians. Aided for a time by Frankish neighbors across the Pyrenees, these northern people began a revolt shortly before the year 800, and the uprising soon became a sort of crusade, which continued intermittently for nearly seven centuries! As the invaders were slowly driven back toward Africa, Christian kingdoms and provinces came into existence: the Basque Provinces, Asturias, Catalonia, León, Castile, Navarre, Aragón, Barcelona, and others. The last stronghold held by the Moslems in Spain was Granada, from which they were finally expelled in 1492. By that time, Spanish national unity had practically been achieved. But the Moslems had left a deep impression. Spaniards thereafter were less European than Asiatic, full of mysticism, dignified, proud, sometimes arrogant, and often capable of great self-abnegation.

It was during the reign of Ferdinand of Aragón and Isabella of Castile (1479–1516) that Spanish territorial unity was virtually achieved, that Spanish institutions were crystallized into definite and durable form, and that Spanish nationalism came into being. It was at this time also that Spanish character became so definitely fixed that subsequent centuries did not greatly modify it.

Ferdinand and Isabella, *Los Reyes Católicos*, as they are called in Spain, were sovereigns of extraordinary ability, recognized as such even by their foreign contemporaries. Ferdinand drew forth the admiration of

Machiavelli, who praised him in his *Prince*. Another Italian, Guicciardini, who knew the king personally, describes him at great length.[1]

> The feats that Ferdinand has accomplished, his words, his ways, and his general reputation prove that he is an extremely sagacious man. He is very secret, and unless obliged to, does not communicate important matters; he could not be more patient. He leads a very regular life, assigning times for this and that. He likes to know all about the affairs of the kingdom, great and little, and has them go through his hands; and though he exhibits a willingness to hear everybody's opinion, he makes up his own mind, and directs everything himself. . . . He is good at knightly exercises and keeps them up; he makes a show of great piety, speaks of holy things with great reverence, and ascribes everything to God. . . . In short, he is a very notable king and has many talents; and the only criticisms upon him are that he is not generous and that he does not keep his promise.

The same observer remarked that Isabella was even superior to her husband. "It is said," he wrote, "that she was a great lover of justice, and a lady of the best breeding, and made herself greatly beloved and feared by her subjects. She was generous, of a high spirit, and very ambitious of renown, as much so as any woman of the time, no matter who." Out of deference to her imperial will or excellent judgment, the king often followed her advice. A German visitor once observed that "the Queen is king, and the King is her servant." [2] Her very strenuous life is supposed to have had a fatal effect upon her children; several of them died in infancy; one became insane.

Ferdinand and Isabella founded an absolutism which continued until the opening of the nineteenth century. Turbulent nobles were either attracted to the court or suppressed; the local brotherhoods for defense against highwaymen (the *hermandades*) were organized into royal police; the grand masterships of the great military orders which had been organized during the long struggle against the Moslems, and which not only numbered a million vassals and members but enjoyed a large annual revenue, were taken over by the crown; royal councils were set up; royal judiciaries (*audiencias*) were established; and the old parliaments (called *Cortes* in Spanish) of Castile, Aragón, Valencia, and Catalonia were often ignored or defied. *Visitadores* traveled through the kingdoms and examined the administration of justice and finance, and officials of the crown began to be subjected to the *residencia* (a judicial investigation of their conduct while in office). The captains general, who in earlier times had exercised both military and civil authority in extensive Castilian territory, had been superseded by the *adelantados* (governors), the most important of whom was probably the *adelantado* of the Canaries; but the former office could be resurrected if need should arise. Viceroys (vice-kings) were in charge of Sardinia, Sicily, and Naples. Even the ancient privileges

---

[1] Quoted by H. D. Sedgwick in his *Short History of Spain*, New York, 1925, p. 126.
[2] Ibid., pp. 127–29.

and immunities of the municipalities began to be infringed, for the crown acquired a measure of control over *ayuntamientos* and *cabildos* (town councils) and sent out *corregidores* to inspect the town governments. Finally, the Catholic monarchs reorganized the Inquisition, conquered Granada, recovered Naples (1504), and began those negotiations with the papacy which culminated in the acquisition of royal patronage over the church in Spanish dominions. During the next 200 years, surprisingly few additions were made to the institutional structure which they had set up. Subsequent monarchs modified, perfected, or abused it, but originated little save in the realm of taxation.

Economic conditions in Spain around 1500 were fairly good. Agriculture and stockraising were moderately prosperous and manufacturing industries were spreading to nearly all of the towns, turning out swords, woolens, silks, leather goods, ships, and many other products. A respectable navy and merchant marine were developing, and foreign commerce, encouraged by the crown, was on the increase.

The population, approximately 7,000,000 at this time, was divided into the familiar three classes, upper, middle, and lower, although the middle class, composed of emancipated peasantry and of such members of the lesser nobility as were attracted into business and industry, was rather small. The nobility, higher and lower, and the clergy constituted the upper class. The clergy were wealthy. Spain's seven archbishoprics and forty bishoprics received an income of around $7,000,000, and the annual rents of the secular clergy amounted to about $60,000,000. The regular clergy—there were approximately 9,000 religious houses in the country— were equally rich and perhaps more numerous. At the head of the nobility were the grandees, who either held public office or lived upon the income from the vast estates which they and their ancestors had seized from the retreating Moslems. The lesser nobility—hidalgos and *caballeros*— were neither so wealthy nor so fortunate; but higher and lower alike enjoyed many exemptions and privileges, disdained manual labor, and drew their sustenance mostly from the toil of peasants and others in a semiservile condition. The bottom class was composed of agricultural workers and tenants who were gradually being transformed into a free peasantry, personal servants, industrial laborers in the towns, and a rather large number of beggars. Although serfdom was on its way to extinction, a semifeudal institution called encomienda still persisted in some quarters, where free peasants and smaller landowners "commended" themselves to powerful nobles in the community and rendered them certain services in return for protection.

Of conditions shortly after 1500 Guicciardini gives a vivid, if somewhat unfriendly, description:[3]

> The kingdom is thinly populated; there are some fine cities, Barcelona, Saragossa, Valencia, Granada, and Seville, but they are few for so large a

[3] Ibid., pp. 153–54.

country, and the other towns for the most part are of little account. The southern regions are far the most fertile, but only the land in the neighborhood of the cities is cultivated. Wool, silk, wine, and oil are exported in large quantities. There is sufficient wheat for the home market, and, if the nation were only industrious and given to trade, their iron, steel, copper, hides, and other products would make them rich. But as it is, the country is very poor . . . from the laziness of the people. They are proud, and think that no other nation compares with theirs. . . . They dislike foreigners, and are discourteous toward them. They are more warlike, perhaps, than any other Christian nation; agile, quick, and good at the management of arms, they make a great point of honor, and prefer to die rather than submit to shame. Their light cavalry is excellent, their horses very good; and the Castilian infantry enjoys a great reputation. . . .

Spaniards are thought to be shrewd and intelligent, but they are not good in liberal and mechanical arts; all the artisans at the king's court are French, or foreigners of some sort. All Spaniards look down on trade and put on airs as hidalgos and prefer to be soldiers or (before Ferdinand's time) highwaymen rather than to engage in trade or any other such occupation. It is true that in some parts of Spain they weave and make rich stuffs, as in Valencia, Toledo, and Seville; but the nation as a whole is opposed to industrial life. The country people . . . till the ground much less than they might. Spaniards are fond of show; wear fine clothes abroad; ride a stylish horse; but at home, in the house, they live in a beggarly fashion hard to believe. . . . In outward appearance they are very religious, but not so really. They are very ceremonious, full of fine words and hand-kissings, and everybody is their 'lord' and they are 'at his disposition': but their fair words are not to be taken literally. They are avaricious and great dissemblers.

In short, Spain at the beginning of the sixteenth century had "much of the reality as well as the appearance of greatness," but revealed some symptoms of ill health which, if not remedied, might lead to decline and decrepitude. Political and religious unity had been achieved, an elaborate political organization had been perfected, and the nation was becoming more prosperous. Triumph in a long series of Moslem wars had produced an energetic and optimistic people and a soldiery glowing with crusading zeal, admirably fitted by training and temperament to carve out new dominions across the sea. And intellectually and artistically, Spain was at the threshold of a Golden Age of literature, painting, architecture, and all the fine arts. Yet the very power of the monarchy would become a menace when turned toward unwise policies or when the character of the royal family declined. The intolerance which had deprived the country of the financial and commercial talent of the Jews in 1492 was not to be satisfied until it caused Spain to lose the agricultural and industrial talent of the Moors (1501) and the Moriscos (presumably converted Moors, expelled in 1609) and set up barriers against future immigrants. Disdain for manual labor would result in stagnation when there were no more dominions to subdue. Then an idle nobility would become a pest, fomenting political disorders, living upon administrative graft, and infesting the streets and highways as robbers and beggars. Huge landed estates, held together by mortmain and primogeniture, would retard the growth of the middle class and hamper economic development. The increasing wealth of the church would attract a too numerous clergy, who would succumb to luxury, idleness, and corruption and become a heavy social liability.

Within a single century Spain passed through her Golden Age and entered a long period of moral and material decline. Of the many possible causes to which the decline might be attributed—idle churchmen and nobility; religious absorption and superstition and intolerance; false pride; neglect of science, industry, and public health; vast colonies; exhausting wars; political folly—two need to be emphasized: bad government and the attempt to play an imperialistic role in Europe.

The Spanish monarchy was to blame for both of these. Four of the nine kings who ruled Spain between 1517 and 1808 were corrupt weaklings, and the four who can be described as rather able and energetic—Charles I and Philip II, who reigned during the sixteenth century, and Ferdinand VI and Charles III, who governed during the eighteenth—were stanch exponents of an intolerant absolutism or the devotees of an exhausting imperialism that looked to Europe and the strength of armies rather than to America and the efficacy of industry and sea power. All of Spain's monarchs expended Spanish blood and treasure upon European wars designed mainly to impose Roman Catholicism, or lavished wealth and favors upon an idle and often corrupt nobility. The consequences may be seen in burdensome taxes and economic restraints which contributed to the ruin of commerce and industry, to shrinkage in population, and to the general backwardness and poverty of the nation.

The population of Spain, which had stood at 7,000,000 in 1594, was hardly more than 4,000,000 in 1723. Taking no account of rogues and beggars, who probably numbered no less than 200,000, one Spaniard out of three was now an ecclesiastic, a noble, or a personal servant. Thanks to the attempted reforms of Ferdinand VI (1746–59) and Charles III (1759–88), conditions had somewhat improved before the end of the eighteenth century, but they were still sufficiently bad. Population had increased to a little more than 10,000,000, but the nobility and the clergy still outnumbered the manufacturers, artisans, and merchants, and there were fewer than 2,000,000 farmers and farm laborers. The church and the nobility owned more than half of the arable lands; only one Spaniard in forty was a landed proprietor. Government employees and the army numbered nearly 200,000, and there were still some 140,000 beggars.

These conditions, patterns of value, and concepts of government and the social order will be reflected in that portion of the New World assigned to Spain. (1) An absolute monarchy will claim that the American dominions are the personal possessions of the crown and not of the Spanish nation, and will use them for the benefit of the monarchs and their favorites. (2) Spanish officials and institutions, such as the vice royalty, the captaincy general, the *adelantado,* the *audiencia,* the *visitador,* the *residencia,* the *cabildo,* and the *corregidor,* will be transferred to the colonies. In the presence of an inferior group of people, even the disappearing encomienda will be revived in a somewhat different form. (3) To the religious orders will be entrusted the main task of converting and taming the natives and making them "useful subjects." (4) Farming and grazing lands in America will be concentrated in a few hands as in Spain, and the common people will be hampered by the system of latifundia (large landed estates). (5) Intolerance and hatred of foreigners will close the colonies to heretics and non-Spaniards, destroy priceless relics of aboriginal culture, and retard intellectual and economic progress. (6) A tendency toward municipal autonomy, struggling against monarchal centralization, will reappear, suffer repression, and still persist until the chains of royal despotism are finally broken. (7) Spanish contempt for manual toil, Spanish love of display and fondness for military adventure and official position, will profoundly influence the character and history of the colonies. (8) Spain's monopolistic pretensions with respect to her colonies and her ambition to champion the cause of Roman Catholicism in Europe will not only hamper the progress of Spanish America, but will make it the object of attack by other European nations and even at times the prize in the contest. (9) Although the colonies will feel the heavy hand of the tax farmer and the grafting bureaucrat and suffer the consequences of the decrepitude of the mother country, they will also share the benefits of Spanish higher culture, which was at the dawn of its *Siglo de Oro* (Golden Century) in 1500.

The Conquest

CONQUEST OF UTOPIA

Eric Wolf

In 1492, Christopher Columbus, sailing under the flag of Castile, discovered the islands of the Caribbean and planted upon their shores the standard of his sovereigns and the cross of his Savior. From these islands, the newcomers began to probe the Middle American coast. In Easter week, 1519, a young adventurer, Hernán Cortés—lawyer by professional training and military man through baptism of fire on Santo Domingo—landed in the vicinity of San Juan de Ulua in Veracruz. He brought with him an army of 508 soldiers—32 of whom were crossbowmen and carried harquebuses—16 horses, and 14 pieces of artillery, together with a navy of 11 ships and 100 sailors. In July and August of that year, Cortés beached his ships and embarked on the conquest of Tenochtitlán. Two years later, on August 13, 1521, Tenochtitlán fell into Spanish hands. One cycle of history had come to an end and another cycle began.

How is one to explain this sudden irreversible change in the fate of Middle America? The entire enterprise of the Spanish Conquest seems shrouded in a curious air of unreality. Hernán Cortés conquers an empire embracing millions of people. For lack of holy water, a Fray Pedro de Gante baptizes hundreds of thousands of Indians with his saliva. A Nuñez Cabeza de Vaca sets out to find the golden cities of Cíbola and the

Reprinted from Eric Wolf, *Sons of the Shaking Earth*, by permission of The University of Chicago Press. © 1959 by the University of Chicago.

The author of dozens of articles and books, Professor Wolf is one of America's leading figures in contemporary Mexican cultural studies. He received his doctorate from Columbia in 1951 and has taught at the University of Michigan. He is currently professor of anthropology at Queens College, City University of New York.

Fountain of Youth, to be shipwrecked, reduced to starvation, nearly eaten by cannibals, only to return to the fray as soon as he is rescued. Actors, acts, and motives seem superhuman: their lust for gold and for salvation, their undivided loyalty to a distant monarch, their courage in the face of a thousand obstacles seem to defy simple psychological explanations. They not only made history; they struck poses against the backdrop of history, conscious of their role as makers and shakers of this earth. The utterances of a Cortés, a Panfilo Narváez, a Garay, are replete with references to Caesar, Pompey, and Hannibal. Cortés plays not only at being himself; he is also the Amadís of Gaul celebrated in the medieval books of chivalry. They were not satisfied with the simple act; they translated each act into a symbolic statement, an evocation of a superhuman purpose. Struck with admiration of their deeds and postures, their chroniclers took them at their word. In the pages of the history books these men parade in the guise of their own evaluation of themselves: half centaurs, pawing the ground with their hoofs and bellowing with voices like cannon, half gods, therefore, and only half men.

But their image of themselves obscures the real greatness of their achievement, for greatness can be measured only on a human scale, not on a divine. Part of their greatness was undoubtedly due to the military tactics employed by a courageous and cunning general. The Spaniards used cavalry to break through the massed formations of an enemy that had never before encountered horses; they thus avoided hand-to-hand combat in which gunpowder and iron arms would have been of little avail in the face of the wicked Indian swords, beset with obsidian chips. To counteract the Indian firepower of spears and arrows, the Spaniards used the crossbow, the instrument that gained them such a decisive victory in the great battle of Pavia against the remnants of French knighthood. When Spanish cavalry, artillery, and infantry proved impotent against Indian canoes manned by archers in the canals and lagoons surrounding Tenochtitlán, Cortés again carried the battle to the enemy, attacking the embattled capital across the water, from the boards of thirteen ships built on the spot.

None of these military successes would have been possible, however, without the Indian allies Cortés won in Middle America. From the first, he enlisted on his side rulers and peoples who had suffered grievously at the hands of their Mexican enemies. In a decisive way, as Ralph Beals has put it, "the conquest of Tenochtitlán was less a conquest than it was a revolt of dominated peoples." Spanish firepower and cavalry would have been impotent against the Mexica armies without the Tlaxcaltec, Texcocans and others who joined the Spanish cause. They furnished the bulk of the infantry and manned the canoes that covered the advance of the brigantines across the lagoon of Tenochtitlán. They provided, transported, and prepared the food supplies needed to sustain an army in the field. They maintained lines of communication between coast and highland, and they policed occupied and pacified areas. They supplied the raw materials and muscular energy for the construction of the ships that decided the siege of the Mexica capital. Spanish military equipment and tactics carried the day, but Indian assistance determined the outcome of the war.

In an ultimate sense, the time was ripe for a redress in the balance of power in Middle America. Even Moctezuma, in his abode at Tenochtitlán, must have felt this, for we can read in his hesitations, in his hearkening to omens of doom, evidence of the doubt and uncertainty which was gnawing at the vitals of Mexica domination. The Spaniards provided the indispensable additional energy required to reverse the dominant political trend. Yet they were not mere agents of the indigenous will, mere leaders of an indigenous revolt. Cortés' genius lay precisely in his ability to play this role, to surround himself with charisma in the eyes of the Indians. Cortés played his role to the hilt, but with calculated duplicity. For the Spaniards had not come to Middle America to restore an indigenous society. They acted from autonomous motives which were not those of their Indian allies. Accepting the command of a people deeply accustomed to obedience through long participation in a hierarchical social order, they began to enact their own purposes, to realize their own ends, which were those of Spanish society and therefore alien and hostile to those of the Indians among whom they had begun to move.

To understand these ends, we must try to understand Spanish society of that time, a task in which we moderns experience a particular difficulty. The reduced and impoverished Spain of today obscures our understanding of the once wealthy and powerful empire upon which the sun never set. All too often, we tend to interpret the past by reconstructing it in the image of the present. Again, too often, we view Spain through the lens of a powerful political mythology, a mythology forged both consciously and unconsciously in Protestant countries to advance the liberating cause of Protestantism and republican institutions against Catholicism and monarchical absolutism. According to this mythology, a singularly partisan deity ranged himself on the side of human freedom and economic progress against "feudal" Spain. While in northern Europe right-thinking and industrious men put their shoulders to the wheel of the Industrial Revolution, the Catholic South remained sunk in medieval sloth. But the rise and decline of a society is not explained by recourse to political demonology; the truth is at once simpler and more complex.

Let us not forget that the Mediterranean and not the European North is the homeland of capitalism and of the Industrial Revolution. Italy, southern France, Spain, and southern Germany witnessed the rise of the first factories, the first banks, the first great fairs. At the time of the discovery of America, the Iberian Peninsula harbored thriving cities, humming with expanding wealth and trade. The sources of this prosperity were manifold: the sale of wool to England or to Flanders; the sale of iron wares to the Levant; the seizure and sale of slaves from the African coast; the quick raid on a Saracen stronghold or a pirate's lair. These were enterprises which demanded the utmost in individual stamina and personal valor; they were also exceedingly profitable. And in response the culture which fed upon an extension of these enterprises elaborated its peculiar image of the manly ideal: the overweening personality possessed of skill and courage. This ideal belonged as much to the medieval past as to the commercial future. It was inherently contradictory and revealed in its contradiction the opposing forces at work within the social system that gave it birth. Its heroes act; but the cultural forms of their acts are not only rich in the symbolic pageantry of the medieval knight-crusader but also supreme examples of the exaltation of Renaissance man pioneering on new frontiers of thought and human behavior. Covertly, more than once, the goal of the act is profit, conceived as personal enhancement through the acquisition of gold and riches.

There were in reality two Spains, or two tendencies at work in the Iberian Peninsula. The first tendency was aristocratic, oriented toward warfare and the gain of riches by warfare. It was exemplified most clearly by the armies of Castile, composed of a warlike nobility and a warlike peasantry. These armies had been forged in the fight against the Moors, first in raid and counterraid, later in the systematic reconquest of the Moorish southland. The nobility, partly organized into religious orders of monastic warriors, saw in warfare a ready source of ego enhancement and looted wealth. Its traditional economic interest lay in the extension of grazing range for its herds of cattle and sheep, coupled with a flourishing export trade in wool to northern Europe. The peasantry, on the other hand, consisted of soldier-cultivators, recruited into the army by promises and guarantees of freedom from servile encumbrances and charters of local self-rule. These peasants desired land, free land, to divide among their sons. In warfare, both nobility and peasantry gained their divergent ends.

The other Spain, the other Spanish trend, was less involved in warfare; it pointed toward capital accumulation through rising industry and trade in the hands of a town-based bourgeoisie. Such entrepreneurs existed in all Peninsular towns; but only in eastern Spain, centered in Catalonia, had they gained sufficient power to check the expansionist desires of the aristocratic soldiery. In this part of Spain, a bloody peasant war had smashed the remnants of a feudal system of the classic European kind. Traditional relationships in which a lord exercised economic, judicial, and social control of a group of serfs had given way to new social ties. A free peasantry populated the countryside; a prosperous bourgeoisie, long oriented toward maritime trade, controlled the towns. The country was undergoing incipient industrialization, and the cloth, leather, and iron wares so produced were exchanged in the eastern Mediterranean for the drugs, dyestuffs, and luxury goods of the Orient.

By 1492, these two Spains were headed for collision, a conflict which might well have altered the face of Spain but for the discovery of America. The fall of the last Moorish redoubt put an end to the limitless acquisition of land by conquest and to the easy accumulation of wealth by forceful seizure; 1492 marked the closing of the Spanish frontier. As land became scarce, interests which had run parallel up to that time began to conflict; while the soldier-peasant wanted unencumbered land, the aristocrat wanted open range for sheep and cattle or land for dependent cultivators. With the distribution of the fruits of conquest among the conquerors, moreover, readily available wealth became unavailable. How was new wealth to be produced? To this problem the merchant-entrepreneur of the towns had an answer: capital investment in industry coupled with the reduction of aristocratic power. At this moment, however, the doors to the New World swung wide open to reveal a new frontier: dream cities of gold, endless expanses of land, huge reservoirs of dependent labor. The merchant-entrepreneur receded into obscurity; the knight-adventurer, the visionary of wealth through seizure at sword's point, gained new impetus.

It was this new frontier which settled the fate of Spain. Paradoxically, Spanish industry was to be swamped in a tide of gold from the Indies, which spelled its ultimate ruin; paradoxically, also, the new frontier destroyed the class which might have carried such industrialization to a successful conclusion. For in this New World, all men—peasant, merchant, impoverished noble, noble merchant-prince—could dream of becoming lords of land, Indians, and gold. Men who in Spain might have allied themselves politically and economically with the entrepreneurs and traders of the towns against the aristocrat could in this new venture identify themselves with the ideal of the mounted noble. Men who in Spain might have spurred the growth of the middle classes were here converted into its opponents. The year 1492 might have marked Spain's awakening to a new reality; instead, it marked the coming of a new dream, a new utopia.

Where men of varied pasts and varied interests engage in a common enterprise, belief in a universal utopia renders possible their common action. Utopia asks no questions of reality; it serves to bind men in the service of a dream. Belief in it postpones the day of reckoning on which the spoils will be divided and men will draw their swords to validate their personal utopia against the counterclaims of their comrades-in-arms. Some came to the New World to find gold; others to find order; still others to save souls. Yet in their common dream they asked no questions of one another. For the time being, their dream was validated by their common experience on board ship, by their common sufferings in the face of the enemy, by their common victory.

In the course of their common adventure in utopia they also achieved a set of common usages and understandings which made "the culture of the Conquest" different from their ancestral culture and from the culture still to be in the New World. Their purposes had a transcendental simplicity: gold, subjects, souls. This simplicity patterned their behavior and their thought, some of it conscious, self-imposed. The colonist-to-be in search of his liberty casts off the traditional forms which he has experienced as shackles and encumbrances. The royal official in search of order abhors the tangle of inherited forms of the Old World. The friar leaves behind him a world which is old and corrupt; in utopia he seeks austerity and clarity. The very process of migration produces a simplified stock of cultural forms.

Men drawn from all walks of life, the conquerors were not a complete sample of their ancestral society. They did not bring with them complete knowledge of the gamut of Spanish culture. Some of this age-old heritage they could not reproduce in the New World because they lacked acquaintance with it. Some of it, however, vanished in the crucible of their common experience, in their need to develop a common cultural denominator to facilitate their common task. Spain, but recently unified under one crown, had remained a cultural plural, a mosaic of many parts. Yet the culture of the conquerors was, by contrast, highly homogeneous. This simplification extended to material goods: only one plow, of the many Spanish plows, was transmitted to the New World; only a few techniques of fishing were selected from the plethora of Spanish fishing techniques and transplanted into the new setting. Simplification extended also to symbolic behavior: speech undergoes a leveling, a planing-down of the formalities of Castilian Spanish into a plain and utilitarian idiom. Left behind are the many Spanish folk fiestas in honor of a multitude of beloved local saints; they yield in the New World to the measured and standardized performance of the formal celebrations of way stations in the life of Christ. The culture of the conquest was, as George Foster has pointed out, *sui generis*. In vain one looks in the culture of these men for the rich varied regional heritage of the mother country.

Some of the conquerors wanted gold—gold, the actual tangible substance, not the intangible "promises to pay" of later capitalism. In this they were children of their times, caught in the contradiction between medieval magic and the modern search for profits. All over Europe men longed for gold, encountered gold in dreams, dug for it under trees and in caves, sold their souls to the devil for it, labored over retorts to obtain it from base metals such as iron or lead. It was a kind of illness, and Cortés stated it that way—half cynically and half realistically—in addressing the first Mexica noble he met: "The Spaniards are troubled with a disease of the heart for which gold is the specific remedy." The illness was greed, but beyond greed the desire for personal liberty, escape of the ego from bondage to other men, "spiritual autarchy," as Eliseo Vivas has said, "which is achieved only when you are able to say to another man, *a mi no me manda nadie*—no one bosses me; I am lord because I have land and gold and Indians, and I need not beg any favors from you or any one else." This is the new self-made man talking, the medieval adventurer on the threshold of capitalism, knight-errant in cultural form but primitive capitalist in disguise. The goal is medieval—never again to bend one's will to that of another—but the instrument is modern: the instrument of wealth.

Utopia thus bears at the outset the mark of a contradiction between past and future, a contradiction never wholly overcome. The contradiction is most startlingly illuminated when the Spanish entrepreneur is compared with his contemporary English rival. "The Englishmen," says

Salvador de Madariaga, "though on the surface more self-seeking, were in depth more socially minded; the Spaniards, though in appearance more statesmanlike and creative, more intent on 'enobling' cities and setting up kingdoms, were more self-centered. The Englishman, with his dividends, socialized his adventures, gain, booty; the Spaniard, with his hospitals, foundations, cathedrals, colleges and marquisates, raised a monument to his own self. . . ." The rise of puritanism in the Anglo-American world, so brilliantly analyzed by Max Weber and Richard Tawney, destroyed the contradiction between individual goals and cultural means. For in accepting the Protestant ethic of work and capital accumulation as virtue, the entrepreneur made himself an instrument of production, harnessed himself to the process of capital formation. In Anglo-America, the very means thus became the ends; in Ibero-America, means and ends remained at war with one another, contradictory, unresolved.

If some came in search of gold and its promise of personal liberty, others came in search of order. Their deity was the absolute monarch; their religion the new religion of the reason of state. At the end of the fifteenth century the Spanish crown had just emerged victorious in its political battles against its rivals. With the help of the rising middle classes and the peasantry, it had successfully defeated the attempts of the aristocrats who wished to reduce the king once again to the passive position of a mere *primus inter pares*. Yet this political success but threatened to put the king into the hands of the penny-wise merchants who wished to trade support for a veto over his military and bureaucratic expenditures. The long period of the reconquest had also brought with it a spate of *fueros* or local charters which exempted one or the other local or professional body from the application of the general law; many a king had traded local autonomy for support against the Moorish enemy.

In the conquest of the New World, the crown saw its opportunity to escape the limitations of internal Spanish politics. Gold from the Indies would enrich not only the eager adventurer; a fifth of all gold and silver mined in the New World would be the king's, to finance a royal army, navy, and officialdom, to build the bases of absolutist power upon institutions wholly independent of nobility, middle classes, or peasant cultivators. Wealth from the Indies would underwrite a state standing above all classes, above the endless quarrels of contending interest groups. This state would speak with a new voice, with a new will. It would no longer be bound by precedent; it would set aside solutions which had become traditional, overgrown with the "cake of custom" and with compromise. The New World would not have to grow, piecemeal, in the shadows of ancient complexities: it would be a planned world, projected into reality by the royal will and its executioners. Thus utopia would become law, and law utopian. If Spanish towns had been small, cramped within their rings of fortifications, crowded around small irregular squares, then the towns of the New World would be large, open, unfortified; built upon the gridiron plan; centered upon a spacious square dominated by church and city-hall as twin symbols of sacred and secular power; an architectural utopia conceived by Italian architect-dreamers and built in the New World by royal mandate.

Was it true that many Indians lived in scattered hamlets instead of stationary, circumscribed, concentrated settlements? Then let there be a law to force them to live in nucleated towns, each with its own church, each surrounded by its own fields—within a measured radius of 560 yards from the church steeple—so that they could learn to order their lives to the tolling of church bells and to the commands of royal officers. Land and people of utopia had both been conquered by the sword; but it would be the dry scratching of the goose-quill pen upon parchment that would turn utopia into reality. Let each Indian keep twelve chickens and six turkeys and sell them for no more than 4 reales per turkey and 1½ reales per chicken; let each Indian working in a textile mill receive a daily ration of eighteen tortillas or fourteen tamales, plus chili, chickpeas, and beans. No problem was too insignificant to demand solution, and all solutions were solutions of law. Utopia was to be born also with this fatal deficiency implicit in the contradiction of law and reality. Reality is too protean to be wholly covered by law; it soon grows through, around, and over law, leaving but a hollow shell of words, a gesture of etiquette to gloss over the gap between wish and existence. The Latin American world still bears this legacy of law as a gesture to initiate action, to create a new order, and—when the energy of the gesture is spent—to use the law as wish, to wipe out a reality grown beyond law and order, beyond utopia.

Utopia contained many houses. If some men longed for gold, to build upon it their untrammeled liberty, and if others sought Indian subjects to rule and exercise in the spirit of the new order, so there were men who came to save souls. Upon the ruins of pagan shrines and idols in a new continent filled with souls hungry for salvation, yet uncorrupted by the age-old vices of the Old World, they would erect their own utopia: the prelude on earth of the Kingdom of Heaven. To these prophets of salvation, the conquest of the New World was the call to a great spiritual task: the defeat of Satan in his own redoubt, the redemption of souls languishing in his power, the annunciation of the faith in the one true God. The shock troops of this new faith were the friars, members of the monastic orders, strongly influenced by the reformist religious currents of the times. In some countries, such movements were soon to feed the flames of the Protestant revolution. If this did not happen in Spain, it was not because Spain lacked inflammable intellectual tinder. The economic and political development of the country had given strong impetus to men who began to question long-accepted opinions and to explore new interpretations of Catholicism. Most of these questioners were influenced by Erasmus of Rotterdam (1466–1536), whose teaching de-emphasized the importance of formal ritual and stressed the promptings to piety of an "inner" voice, and by the utopian and reformist thought of Thomas More (1478–1535) and Luis Vives (1492–1540).

The reason that this new religious current did not explode into open rebellion against accepted religious forms is to be found in the character of the Spanish state and the circumstances which surrounded it rather than in the intellectual heterodoxy of the movement. The Spanish state had no need to break with the papacy: it dictated ecclesiastical appointments in its own territory; it possessed the right to read and suppress papal bulls before making them public; it controlled the office of the Inquisition; it even sponsored autonomy in doctrinal matters through its support of the belief in the immaculate conception of the Virgin Mary, long before this belief became official church dogma at the Council of Trent (1545–63). In other European states the hunger for land and capital was one of the chief underlying motives for religious reformation; after the break with Rome, the estates of the church were divided among the members of the Protestant faction. In Spain, the frontiers had not yet closed. Until 1492 land and wealth were still to be had by fighting the Moors in southern Spain in the name of religion, and that year witnessed the opening of the new frontier in the New World, with its promise of gold and glory for all takers.

Under Cardinal Ximénez de Cisneros, the Erasmists received royal approval. The crown saw in their effort to restore the simplicity and austerity of primitive Christianity—in the face of decay and corruption— a spiritual counterpart to its own efforts to centralize Spain and to endow the new empire with a unified sense of mission. Many of the friars who came to the New World had taken part in this religious renewal. The first twelve friars to set foot in New Spain—the so-called Apostolic Twelve— had all worked to spread the gospel of primitive Christendom in southern Spain. Fray Juan de Zumárraga (1461?–1548), the first archbishop of Mexico, was a follower of Erasmus and familiar with the utopian writings of Sir Thomas More. Vasco de Quiroga (1470–1565), the first bishop of Michoacán, actually established a replica of Sir Thomas More's Utopia among the Indian communities of his bishopric. All these soldiers of the faith favored poverty over wealth, communal property over private property. Carefully they labored to purge Catholicism of the accumulation of ritual, selecting from the profusion of religious ritual only the major ceremonials celebrating the way-stations of Christ's life. This desire for purity and simplicity they also expressed in their great single-naved churches symbolic of the homogeneity of primitive Christian worship, uncluttered by devotion to smaller altars and lateral naves.

The utopia of gold and liberty crumbled in the tension between exaltation of the self, through valiant deeds, and wealth, the instrument selected for their validation. The utopia of order remained arrested in the legal gesture, attempting to stem the tide of real behavior. The utopia of faith, too, was to founder, hoped-for morality all too often impotent in the face of stubborn secular demand. And yet, conversion proved a success. The romanticists have long delighted in discovering the idols behind altars, the Gods of the Cave transformed into Christs hanging upon the Cross, the earth goddesses disguised as Catholic Virgins, the braziers burning copal gum on the steps of the churches, and other evidences of pre-Conquest heritage in the religious beliefs and practices of modern Indians. There is much that is Indian in the Catholicism of Middle America; but more surprising than the numerous survivals of pre-Conquest ideas and rituals is the organizational success of the Catholic utopia in a country of different religions and languages. Wherever you go in Middle America, you encounter the images of the Catholic saints and the churches built by the conquerors. Christ and the Virgin may have been transmuted by the adoration of men who had worshipped the Sun and the Moon and the Earth and the Lords of the Four Directions; but when an Indian speaks of a human being today, he does not say "a man"; he says "a Christian," a believer.

How is this success to be explained? It is easy to dismember men with cannons; it is more difficult to tame their minds. Certainly military defeat played a part, because it provided a visible demonstration of the impotence and decadence of the Mexica gods. The Children of the Sun had died by the sword as they had lived by the sword. The old gods had failed. When the Spaniards had demanded that the Totonas of Cèmpoala destroy their idols, the people had recoiled in horror; yet when the conquerors hurled the idols to the ground and broke them to pieces, the idols had remained mute and defenseless. They had not smitten the foreigners; they had failed to show the power that was in them. When the priests released the stones from the Pyramid of Cholula which held back the magic water that was in the mountain so that it would drown the strange men in a flood, the channel remained dry, and their magic deserted them. When the Children of the Sun, the Toltec rulers of Tenochtitlán, called down the wrath of their terrible idol Hummingbird-on-the-Left upon their enemies, Hummingbird-on-the-Left remained silent. The mutilated idols of their gods now rested on the bottom of the lake from which they had set out to conquer the universe for the sun; and the rubble of their temples served as fill for the new city of Mexico which was to arise upon these ruins. The old gods were dead, and powerless.

Not that these old gods had been so greatly loved. We know—or we can guess—that the will of these gods and the burden of human sacrifice rested heavily upon the land. Worship of warrior gods and human sacrifice were religious activities resonant with the military character of Mexica expansion. Inevitably, however, peace and political consolidation brought to the fore alternative religious explanations of a less militaristic character. Quetzalcoatl, the Shining Serpent, served as a symbolic form through which these new interpretations and longings could find expression. His latter-day attributes as a harbinger of peaceful productivity and human wisdom bear surprising similarity to the ideological dictates of

Christianity. Indeed, the Spanish friars came to believe that Quetzalcoatl had been none other than the apostle Thomas, come to the New World to convert the Indians. The longing for peace and for an end to bloodshed provided a fertile soil for the diffusion of the Christian message.

Both religions, moreover, believed in a structured and ordered supernatural world, in which more powerful, unseen, and unfathomable divinities stood above local supernatural mediators of lesser scope and power that were yet more immediately tangible. The Middle American peasant, like his Spanish counterpart, focused his religious interest on these lowlier supernatural helpers. He was more interested in the powers that affected his crops, his children, his family, and the people with whom he was in immediate and personal contact, than in the ultimate powers and their manifestations, which absorbed the interest of the religious specialist. Among the gods of a multi-headed pantheon, his daily concern was with the gods of the earth, fertility, rain and water, with illness, with the immediate short-range future, with the malevolence of his neighbors. Where the Spanish peasant worshipped wooden saints, the Middle American peasant worshipped clay idols; both had recourse to the magical practices of folk medicine; both had a strong sense of omens; and both believed in the reality of witches who could be ordinary everyday people during the day and malevolent spirits in animal disguise at night.

The priests, the specialists of both religions, on the other hand, were the heirs of rich and complex intellectual traditions, trained in the esoteric interpretation of religious symbols whether these symbols concerned multiple incarnations of Tezcatlipoca or the implications of the Revelation of St. John the Divine. The concern of the priest was not the concern of the peasant, and yet the same religious structure could embrace both. As long as the priests remained in command, as ultimate mediators between gods and men and ultimate interpreters of this relationship, men could adapt the manifold religious patterns to suit their personal and local concerns. What was true of religious concerns also held true of gods. A god could be one or triune, unique or multiple, and interpretation could stress his oneness at one time, his multiplicity at another. The Mexica pantheon had embraced many local gods, and the Mexica priesthood had labored to equate these gods with their own inherited deities or with one another. The Catholic Church had a similar tradition of flexibility. Just as the cloak of the Virgin hid many a local Persephone or Isis along the shores of the European Mediterranean, or as an Odin hanging himself from the tree of life became a Christ, so a Hummingbird-on-the-Left became a Spanish St. James riding down upon the heathens; a Tlaloc, a Christian Señor de Sacromonte; a God of the Cave, the Lord of Chalma; and Our Lady Spirit, the Virgin of Guadalupe.

The Catholic Church drove out the priests of the old gods and manned the pivotal points of the religious hierarchy with men ordained in its own cult. It destroyed the old idols and put an end to human sacrifices, burned the sacred picture books and relegated to oblivion much of the calendric and divinatory knowledge of its predecessors; but it also offered the common man a way in which he could cast his traditional attachments into new forms. The Catholic Church, like the solar religion of the Mexica rigid at the heights of command but flexible on the level of the peasant household, built a bridge from the old order to the new. As Frank Tannenbaum has said, "It gave the Indian an opportunity . . . to save his faith in his own gods."

This transition from the old to the new was eased also by an astonishing similarity in ritual and symbol between the old and the new religion. A Nahua or an Otomí would hardly know what to make of a Spanish friar who, hampered by the language barrier, pointed first to the sky to indicate heaven and then to earth to indicate hell, as a first lesson in Catholic catechism. But rituals can be observed and learned by imitation. Both religious traditions had a rite of baptism. In Catholicism, the child was baptized and named, thus including him among the true believers. The Mexica similarly bathed and named the child in a religious rite, and the Maya celebrated with a ceremony the first time the child was carried astride the hip. Both religious traditions had a kind of confession. The Mexica and the inhabitants of the Gulf coast confessed their sexual transgressions to a priest or the earth goddess Filth-Eater; the Zapotec had annual public confessions; and the Maya confessed themselves either to priests or members of their families in case of illness. Both religious traditions possessed a ritual of communion. The Catholics drank wine and swallowed a wafer to symbolize their contact with the divine blood and body of Christ; the Mexica consumed images of the gods made of amaranth and liberally anointed with sacrificial blood. Both people used incense in their churches; both fasted and did penance; both went on pilgrimages to holy places; both kept houses of celibate virgins. Both believed in the existence of a supernatural mother; and both believed in virgin birth. Where Catholics held that Mary conceived immaculately through the power of the Holy Spirit, the Mexica believed that their goddess Coatlícue had given birth to Hummingbird-on-the-Left, impregnated by an obsidian knife which fell from the sky. Both people made use of the cross. A white St. Andrew's Cross, representing the four directions of the universe, often graced the hat and shield of the Shining Serpent, and the Maya made frequent use of the symbol of the foliated cross. The Spaniards represented their sacred stories in passion plays: the Middle Americans represented the annual changes of vegetation and activities in their sacrifices.

The Catholic missionaries well recognized the danger which lay in the maintenance of similar outward forms of ritual upon conversion. Yet they were themselves unable to decide whether these similarities were merely the work of Satan laboring to duplicate in his hellish church the rituals of the church sanctified by God, or whether they might not indeed represent the precipitate of some previous Christian teaching, brought to the New World perhaps by no less a personage than the apostle Thomas. Whatever their doubts, the formal similarities between the two religious traditions permitted an easy transition for the worshipper and gave him continuity precisely in the realm in which continuity was vital: the realm of religious behavior.

Nor did the psychology of Spanish Catholicism differ greatly from the psychology of the Mesoamerican solar cult. The Spanish ideal of the austere knight, defending his honor and the Virgin against Moors or other unbelievers, was not far removed from the Mexica ideal of the jaguar-eagle knight, whose obsidian sword insured victory and sacrificial victims for the hungry deities of war. In both religions cruelty against others in warfare and exalted pride went hand in hand with sacrificial penance— cruelty against the self, performed by a Spanish conqueror in a hairshirt, by a Mexica noble torturing his flesh with the sharp spikes of the century plant.

True to their hierarchical habits, the Spaniards expended their greatest religious effort in converting the nobles, who became their first converts, partly because of the similarity of motivation, partly because of a desire to achieve a secure place in the new Spanish hierarchy through baptism and Christian vows. At Tlaxcala, the first center of the Spanish missionary effort, the local aristocracy strove mightily to reserve for itself a monopoly of all new religious offices, even those of cook, janitor, and gardener in the new monasteries. Their children were the first beneficiaries of Spanish ecclesiastical schooling. They used their power to set the feet of their own tributaries upon the new road to salvation; these tributaries thus came to church, as Fray Mendieta said, "more for the sake of outer appearance, to follow the orders of the *principales* who wanted to deceive them than to find a remedy for their souls." With the nobles firmly dedicated to the worship of the new religion, the commoners could be converted in mass, often with no more than a token understanding of the new divinities they were to worship. Pedro de Gante, exemplary Franciscan and kinsman of Charles V, baptized Indians in Mexico City at a daily rate of 14,000.

To the task of mass conversion, moreover, the church brought an exemplary table of organization. Like the Middle American religion, it drew a line between religious specialists and lay worshippers. In both traditions, the priests were the final spokesmen of the divine realm, in contact with a world to which ordinary men had no access. In both religions, long training was required to make a man worthy of his special role, and in both religions fasts, penances, self-torture, and sexual abstinence were required of priests to maintain their spiritual worth in the sight of the divine powers. Throughout the exercise of their spiritual role on earth, dress, residence, speech, and comportment marked them off from ordinary men. Such parallelism again eased the transition from the worship of the old gods to the worship of the new, maintaining as it did the hierarchy of channels through which supernatural commands were passed down to the lay believer.

To be sure, the Catholic Church was organized internally to take maximum advantage of the opportunities so offered. Its division into holy orders and secular clergy made for great flexibility in a situation where an advance guard was needed to establish new beachheads of the faith, while a rear-guard took over and consolidated the gains. The friars were the advance guard; the abiding missionary work of the sixteenth century which laid the basis for all later religious efforts was probably carried out by no more than one thousand individuals. Established in fortified churches within the core areas of the newly won land, they spread out in "missions of penetration" into areas where Spanish political control was often still in doubt, sometimes ahead of Spanish armies, sometimes in their wake. Always they linked these outposts with their home bases through "liaison missions," to which they could retreat or where they could seek new strength to carry on their task of penetration. The secular clergy, the ordinary priesthood, carried out the work of consolidation.

Inevitably there were quarrels and conflicts of jurisdiction as the work progressed, as well as conflicts of temperament. The holy orders recruited men whose personalities differed markedly from those characteristic of the regular clergy. The friars favored individuals who were more adventurous and utopian in outlook, as well as less amenable to routine and less adapted to the day-to-day life of a going society. The secular clergy showed more conservatism, less of a tendency to sacrifice reality to otherworldly visions and schemes. Thus the larger church benefited by its possession of both kinds of men, both kinds of organization. When the task of conversion was completed, the work of shepherding the flock through its daily tribulations could be turned over to men capable of preserving the gains.

The eventual adjustment of the religious dream to mundane reality was less than utopia, and yet it left an impress on the Indian population such as no other religious or political current has done to this day. Ultimately the message of salvation spelled hope for the Indian, not only hope in the transcendental realm of a supernatural life after death but hope on earth, where utopia was yielding to the pressure of all too secular interests. Men would labor to deny him his humanity, to defend his use as a resource, a tool to be used and discarded at will; but against such claims of politicians, lawyers, and theologians, Pope Paul III would in 1537 assert, in his bull "Sublimis Deus":

> The sublime God so loved the human race that He not only created man in such wise that he might participate in the good that other creatures enjoy, but also endowed him with capacity to attain to the inaccessible and invisible Supreme Good and behold it face to face[;] . . . all are capable of receiving the doctrines of the faith. . . . We . . . consider . . . that the Indians are truly men. . . .

To the Indian, the rite of baptism thus proved an assertion of his essential humanity, to be a man with human claims upon other men. Of this right no colonist or royal official could rob him. When the Indian re-emerges from beneath the wreckage of utopia, we find that he has rebuilt and cemented his new life with bonds drawn from the new religion, at once his opium, his consolation, and his hope of ultimate justice.

THE STORY OF THE CONQUEST AS TOLD BY THE ANONYMOUS AUTHORS OF TLATELOLCO

Miguel Leon-Portilla

The Arrival of Cortes

Year 13–Rabbit. The Spaniards were sighted off the coast.

Year 1–Canestalk. The Spaniards came to the palace at Tlayacac. When the Captain arrived at the palace, Motecuhzoma sent the Cuetlaxteca[1] to greet him and to bring him two suns as gifts. One of these suns was made of the yellow metal, the other of the white.[2] The Cuetlaxteca also brought him a mirror to be hung on his person, a gold collar, a great gold pitcher, fans and ornaments of quetzal feathers and a shield inlaid with mother-of-pearl.

The envoys made sacrifices in front of the Captain. At this, he grew very angry. When they offered him blood in an "eagle dish," he shouted at the man who offered it and struck him with his sword. The envoys departed at once.

All the gifts which the Cuetlaxteca brought to the Captain were sent by Motecuhzoma. That is why the Cuetlaxteca went to meet the Captain at Tlayacac: he was only performing his duties as a royal envoy.

Then the Captain marched to Tenochtitlan. He arrived here during the month called Bird,[3] under the sign of the day 8–Wind. When he entered the city, we gave him chickens, eggs, corn, tortillas and drink. We also gave him firewood, and fodder for his "deer." Some of these gifts were sent by the lord of Tenochtitlan, the rest by the lord of Tlatelolco.

Later the Captain marched back to the coast, leaving Don Pedro de Alvarado—The Sun—in command.

Reprinted from Miguel Leon-Portilla, *The Broken Spears.* Copyright © 1962 by the Beacon Press; originally published in Spanish under the title of *Visión de los Vencidos;* copyright © 1959 Universidad Nacional Autonoma de Mexico. Reprinted by permission of Beacon Press.

Miguel Leon-Portilla received his M.A. from Loyola University in 1951 and his doctorate from the National University of Mexico in 1956. He has taught anthropology at Mexico City College and since 1957 has been professor of history and Nahuatl culture at the National University of Mexico. He has served as director of the *Instituto Indigenista Interamericano* and is a permanent member of the organizing committee for the Interamerican Congress of Americanists. His many works have been translated into a dozen languages.

[1] The Cuetlaxteca were the allied people from Cuetlaxtla in central Mexico.

[2] Gold and silver.

[3] The fourteenth month, October 20–November 8.

The Massacre in the Main Temple

During this time, the people asked Motecuhzoma how they should celebrate their god's fiesta. He said: "Dress him in all his finery, in all his sacred ornaments."

During this same time, The Sun commanded that Motecuhzoma and Itzcohuatzin, the military chief of Tlatelolco, be made prisoners. The Spaniards hanged a chief from Acolhuacan named Nezahualquentzin. They also murdered the king of Nauhtla, Cohualpopocatzin, by wounding him with arrows and then burning him alive.

For this reason, our warriors were on guard at the Eagle Gate. The sentries from Tenochtitlan stood at one side of the gate, and the sentries from Tlatelolco at the other. But messengers came to tell them to dress the figure of Huitzilopochtli. They left their posts and went to dress him in his sacred finery: his ornaments and his paper clothing.

When this had been done, the celebrants began to sing their songs. That is how they celebrated the first day of the fiesta. On the second day they began to sing again, but without warning they were all put to death. The dancers and singers were completely unarmed. They brought only their embroidered cloaks, their turquoises, their lip plugs, their necklaces, their clusters of heron feathers, their trinkets made of deer hooves. Those who played the drums, the old men, had brought their gourds of snuff and their timbrels.

The Spaniards attacked the musicians first, slashing at their hands and faces until they had killed all of them. The singers—and even the spectators—were also killed. This slaughter in the Sacred Patio went on for three hours. Then the Spaniards burst into the rooms of the temple to kill the others: those who were carrying water, or bringing fodder for the horses, or grinding meal, or sweeping, or standing watch over this work.

The king Motecuhzoma, who was accompanied by Itzcohuatzin and by those who had brought food for the Spaniards, protested: "Our lords, that is enough! What are you doing? These people are not carrying shields or *macanas*. Our lords, they are completely unarmed!"

The Sun treacherously murdered our people on the twentieth day after the Captain left for the coast. We allowed the Captain to return to the city in peace. But on the following day we attacked him with all our might, and that was the beginning of the war.

The Night of Sorrows

The Spaniards attempted to slip out of the city at night, but we attacked furiously at the Canal of the Toltecs, and many of them died. This took place during the fiesta of Tecuilhuitl. The survivors gathered first at Mazatzintamalco and waited for the stragglers to come up.

Year 2–Flint. This was the year in which Motecuhzoma died. Itzcohuatzin of Tlatelolco died at the same time.

The Spaniards took refuge in Acueco, but they were driven out by our warriors. They fled to Teuhcalhueyacan and from there to Zoltepec. Then they marched through Citlaltepec and camped in Temazcalpan, where the people gave them hens, eggs and corn. They rested for a short while and marched on to Tlaxcala.

Soon after, an epidemic broke out in Tenochtitlan. Almost the whole population suffered from racking coughs and painful, burning sores.

The Spaniards Return

When the epidemic had subsided a little, the Spaniards marched out of Tlaxcala. The first place they attacked and conquered was Tepeyacac. They departed from there during the fiesta of Tlahuano, and they arrived in Tlapechhuan during the fiesta of Izcalli. Twenty days later they marched to Tezcoco, where they remained for forty days. Then they reached Tlacopan and established themselves in the palace.

There was no fighting of any kind while they were in Tlacopan. At the end of a week they all marched back to Tezcoco.

Eighty days later they went to Huaxtepec and Cuauhnahuac,[4] and from there they attacked Xochimilco. A great many Tlatelolcas died in that battle. Then the Spaniards returned to Tezcoco again.

Year 3-House. The Aztecs began to fight among themselves. The princes Tzihuacpopocatzin and Cicpatzin Tecuecuenotzin were put to death, as were Axayaca and Xoxopehualoc, the sons of Motecuhzoma. These princes were killed because they tried to persuade the people to bring corn, hens and eggs to the Spaniards. They were killed by the priests, captains and elder brothers.

But the great chiefs were angry at these executions. They said to the murderers: "Have we ourselves become assassins? Only sixty days ago, our people were slaughtered at the fiesta of Toxcatl!"

The Siege of Tenochtitlan

Now the Spaniards began to wage war against us. They attacked us by land for ten days, and then their ships appeared. Twenty days later, they gathered all their ships together near Nonohualco, off the place called Mazatzintamalco. The allies from Tlaxcala and Huexotzinco set up camp on either side of the road.

Our warriors from Tlatelolco immediately leaped into their canoes and set out for Mazatzintamalco and the Nonohualco road. But no one set out from Tenochtitlan to assist us: only the Tlatelolcas were ready when the Spaniards arrived in their ships. On the following day, the ships sailed to Xoloco.

The fighting at Xoloco and Huitzillan lasted for two days. While the

4 Present-day Cuernavaca.

battle was under way, the warriors from Tenochtitlan began to mutiny. They said: "Where are our chiefs? They have fired scarcely a single arrow! Do they think they have fought like men?" Then they seized four of their own leaders and put them to death. The victims were two captains, Cuauhnochtli and Cuapan, and the priests of Amantlan and Tlalocan. This was the second time that the people of Tenochtitlan killed their own leaders.

The Flight to Tlatelolco

The Spaniards set up two cannons in the middle of the road and aimed them at the city. When they fired them, one of the shots struck the Eagle Gate. The people of the city were so terrified that they began to flee to Tlatelolco. They brought their idol Huitzilopochtli[5] with them, setting it up in the House of the Young Men. Their king Cuauhtemoc also abandoned Tenochtitlan. Their chiefs said: "Mexicanos! Tlatelolcas! All is not lost! We can still defend our houses. We' can prevent them from capturing our storehouses and the produce of our lands. We can save the sustenance of life, our stores of corn. We can also save our weapons and insignia, our clusters of rich feathers, our gold earrings and precious stones. Do not be discouraged; do not lose heart. We are Mexicanos! We are Tlatelolcas!"

During the whole time we were fighting, the warriors of Tenochtitlan were nowhere to be seen. The battles at Yacacolco, Atezcapan, Coatlan, Nonohualco, Xoxohuitlan, Tepeyacac and elsewhere were all fought by ourselves, by Tlatelolcas. In the same way, the canals were defended solely by Tlatelolcas.

The captains from Tenochtitlan cut their hair short, and so did those of lesser rank. The Otomies and the other ranks that usually wore head-dresses did not wear them during all the time we were fighting. The Tlatelolcas surrounded the most important captains and their women taunted them: "Why are you hanging back? Have you no shame? No woman will ever paint her face for you again!" The wives of the men from Tenochtitlan wept and begged for pity.

When the warriors of Tlatelolco heard what was happening, they began to shout, but still the brave captains of Tenochtitlan hung back. As for the Tlatelolcas, their humblest warriors died fighting as bravely as their captains.

The Tlatelolcas Are Invited to Make a Treaty

A Spaniard named Castaneda approached us in Yauhtenco. He was accompanied by a group of Tlaxcaltecas, who shouted at the guards on the watchtower near the breakwater. These guards were Itzpalanqui, the

---

[5] Not the seed-paste figure described in Chapter 9 [not reprinted here,—Eds.], but the wooden sculpture in the temple on top of the main pyramid.

captain of Chapultepec; two captains from Tlapala; and Cuexacaltzin. Castaneda shouted to them: "Come here!"

"What do you want?" they asked him. "We will come closer." They got into a boat and approached to within speaking distance. "Now, what have you to say to us?"

The Tlaxcaltecas asked: "Where are you from?" And when they learned that the guards were from Tlatelolco, they said: "Good, you are the men we are looking for. Come with us. The 'god' has sent for you."

The guards went with Castaneda to Nonohualco. The Captain was in the House of the Mist there, along with La Malinche, The Sun (Alvarado) and Sandoval. A number of the native lords were also present and they told the Captain: "The Tlatelolcas have arrived. We sent for them to come here."

La Malinche said to the guards: "Come forward! The Captain wants to know: what can the chiefs of Tenochtitlan be thinking of? Is Cuauhtemoc a stupid, willful little boy? Has he no mercy on the women and children of his city? Must even the old men perish? See, the kings of Tlaxcala, Huexotzinco, Cholula, Chalco, Acolhuacan, Cuauhnahuac, Xochimilco, Mizquic, Cuitlahuac and Culhuacan are all here with me."

One of the kings said: "Do the people of Tenochtitlan think they are playing a game? Already their hearts are grieving for the city in which they were born. If they will not surrender, we should abandon them and let them perish by themselves. Why should the Tlatelolcas feel sorry when the people of Tenochtitlan bring a senseless destruction on themselves?"

The guards from Tlatelolco said: "Our lords, it may be as you say."

The "god" said, "Tell Cuauhtemoc that the other kings have all abandoned him. I will go to Teocalhueyacan, where his forces are gathered, and I will send the ships to Coyoacan."

The guards returned to speak with the followers of Cuauhtemoc. They shouted the message to them from their boats. But the Tlatelolcas would not abandon the people of Tenochtitlan.

The Fighting Is Renewed

The Spaniards made ready to attack us, and the war broke out again. They assembled their forces in Cuepopan and Cozcacuahco. A vast number of our warriors were killed by their metal darts. Their ships sailed to Texopan, and the battle there lasted three days. When they had forced us to retreat, they entered the Sacred Patio, where there was a four-day battle. Then they reached Yacacolco.

The Tlatelolcas set up three racks of heads in three different places. The first rack was in the Sacred Patio of Tlilancalco [Black House], where we strung up the heads of our lords the Spaniards. The second was in Acacolco, where we strung up Spanish heads and the heads of two of their horses. The third was in Zacatla, in front of the temple of the earth-goddess Cihuacoatl, where we strung up the heads of Tlaxcaltecas.

The women of Tlatelolco joined in the fighting. They struck at the enemy and shot arrows at them; they tucked up their skirts and dressed in the regalia of war.

The Spaniards forced us to retreat. Then they occupied the market place. The Tlatelolcas—the Jaguar Knights, the Eagle Knights, the great warriors—were defeated, and this was the end of the battle. It had lasted five days, and two thousand Tlatelolcas were killed in action. During the battle, the Spaniards set up a canopy for the Captain in the market place. They also mounted a catapult on the temple platform.

Epic Description of the Besieged City

And all these misfortunes befell us. We saw them and wondered at them; we suffered this unhappy fate.

> Broken spears lie in the roads;
> we have torn our hair in our grief.
> The houses are roofless now, and their walls
> are red with blood.
>
> Worms are swarming in the streets and plazas,
> and the walls are splattered with gore.
> The water has turned red, as if it were dyed,
> and when we drink it,
> it has the taste of brine.
>
> We have pounded our hands in despair
> against the adobe walls,
> for our inheritance, our city, is lost and dead.
> The shields of our warriors were its defense,
> but they could not save it.
>
> We have chewed dry twigs and salt grasses;
> we have filled our mouths with dust and bits of adobe;
> we have eaten lizards, rats and worms. . . .

When we had meat, we ate it almost raw. It was scarcely on the fire before we snatched it and gobbled it down.

They set a price on all of us: on the young men, the priests, the boys and girls. The price of a poor man was only two handfuls of corn, or ten cakes made from mosses or twenty cakes of salty couch-grass. Gold, jade, rich cloths, quetzal feathers—everything that once was precious was now considered worthless.

The captains delivered several prisoners of war to Cuauhtemoc to be sacrificed. He performed the sacrifices in person, cutting them open with a stone knife.

The Message from Cortes

Soon after this, the Spaniards brought Xochitl the Acolnahuacatl,[6] whose house was in Tenochtitlan, to the market place in Tlatelolco. They

---

[6] The Acolmahuacatl was a high priest from the Acolnahuac quarter inside Mexico-Tenochtitlan.

gripped him by both arms as they brought him there. They kept him with them for twenty days and then let him go. They also brought in a cannon, which they set up in the place where incense was sold.

The Tlatelolcas ran forward to surround Xochitl. They were led by the captain from Huitznahuac, who was a Huasteco.[7] Xochitl was placed under guard in the Temple of the Woman[8] in Axocotzinco.

As soon as the Spaniards had set Xochitl loose in the market place, they stopped attacking us. There was no more fighting, and no prisoners were taken.

Three of the great chiefs said to Cuauhtemoc: "Our prince, the Spaniards have sent us one of the magistrates, Xochitl the Acolnahuacatl. It is said that he has a message for you."

Cuauhtemoc asked them: "What is your advice?"

The chiefs all began to shout at once: "Let the message be brought here! We have made auguries with paper and with incense! The captain who seized Xochitl should bring us the message!"

The captain was sent to question Xochitl in the Temple of the Woman. Xochitl said: "The 'god' and La Malinche send word to Cuauhtemoc and the other princes that there is no hope for them. Have they no pity on the little children, the old men, the old women? What more can they do? Everything is settled.

"You are to deliver women with light skins, corn, chickens, eggs and tortillas. This is your last chance. The people of Tenochtitlan must choose whether to surrender or be destroyed."

The captain reported this message to Cuauhtemoc and the lords of Tlatelolco. The lords deliberated among themselves: "What do you think about this? What are we to do?"

The City Falls

Cuauhtemoc said to the fortune tellers: "Please come forward. What do you see in your books?"

One of the priests replied: "My prince, hear the truth that we tell you. In only four days we shall have completed the period of eighty days. It may be the will of Huitzilopochtli that nothing further shall happen to us. Let us wait until these four days have passed."

But then the fighting broke out again. The captain of Huitznahuac— the same Huasteco who had brought in Xochitl—renewed the struggle. The enemy forced us to retreat to Amaxac. When they also attacked us there, the general flight began. The lake was full of people, and the roads leading to the mainland were all crowded.

Thus the people of Tenochtitlan and Tlatelolco gave up the struggle and abandoned the city. We all gathered in Amaxac. We had no shields

---

[7] An Indian from eastern Mexico.
[8] The earth-goddess Cihuacoatl.

and no *macanas*; we had nothing to eat and no shelter. And it rained all
night.

The People Flee the City

Cuauhtemoc was taken to Cortes along with three other princes. The
Captain was accompanied by Pedro de Alvarado and La Malinche.

When the princes were made captives, the people began to leave,
searching for a place to stay. Everyone was in tatters, and the women's
thigh's were almost naked. The Christians searched all the refugees.
They even opened the women's skirts and blouses and felt everywhere:
their ears, their breasts, their hair. Our people scattered in all directions.
They went to neighboring villages and huddled in corners in the houses
of strangers.

The city was conquered in the year 3–House. The date on which we
departed was the day 1–Serpent in the ninth month.[9]

The lords of Tlatelolco went to Cuauhtitlan. Even the greatest captains
and warriors left in tatters. The women had only old rags to cover their
heads, and they had patched together their blouses out of many-colored
scraps. The chiefs were grief-stricken and mourned to one another: "We
have been defeated a second time!" [10]

The Offering of Gold

A poor man was treacherously killed in Otontlan as he was seeking
refuge. The other refugees were shaken by his death and began to discuss
what they could do.[11] They said: "Let us beg mercy of our lord the
Captain."

First the leaders of Tlatelolco demanded gold objects from everyone.
They collected many lip rings, lip plugs, nose plugs and other ornaments.
They searched anyone who might be hiding objects of gold behind his
shield or under his clothing.

When they had gathered everything they could find, they sent the
treasure to Coyoacan in the custody of several chiefs. The chiefs said to
the Captain: "Our lord and master, please hear us. Your vassals, the great
lords of Tlatelolco, beg you to have mercy. Your vassals and their people
are being mistreated by the inhabitants of the villages where they have
taken refuge. They scorn us and treacherously kill us.

"We have brought you these objects of gold, and we beg you to hear
our pleas."

Then they set the baskets of gold objects before him.

[9] July 12–July 31.
[10] The first time by Tenochtitlan.
[11] To avoid the same fate. They wanted to return home.

When the Captain and La Malinche saw the gold, they grew very angry and said: "Is this what you have been wasting your time on? You should have been looking for the treasure that fell into the Canal of the Toltecs! Where is it? We must have it!"

The chiefs said: "Cuauhtemoc gave it to the Cihuacoatl and the Huiznahuacatl. They know where it is. Ask them."

When the Captain heard this, he ordered that the chiefs be placed in chains. La Malinche came to them later and said: "The Captain says that you may leave and speak with your leaders. He is very grateful to you. It may be true that your people are being mistreated. Tell them to return. Tell your people to come back to their houses in Tlatelolco. The Captain wants all the Tlatelolcas to reoccupy their quarter of the city. But tell your leaders that no one is to settle in Tenochtitlan itself, for that is the property of the 'gods.' You may leave now."

Cuauhtemoc Is Tortured

When the envoys from Tlatelolco had departed, the leaders of Tenochtitlan were brought before the Captain, who wished to make them talk. This was when Cuauhtemoc's feet were burned. They brought him in at daybreak and tied him to a stake.

They found the gold in Cuitlahuactonco, in the house of a chief named Itzpotonqui. As soon as they had seized it, they brought our princes—all of them bound—to Coyoacan.

About this same time, the priest in charge of the temple of Huitzilopochtli was put to death. The Spaniards had tried to learn from him where the god's finery and that of the high priests was kept. Later they were informed that it was being guarded by certain chiefs in Cuauhchichilco and Xaltocan. They seized it and then hanged two of the chiefs in the middle of the Mazatlan road.

The Return to Tlatelolco

The common people began to return to their houses in Tlatelolco. This was in the year 4–Rabbit. Then Temilotzin and Don Juan Huehuetzin came back, but Coyohuehuetzin and Tepantemoctzin both died in Cuauhtitlan.

We were left entirely alone when we reoccupied Tlatelolco. Our masters, the Spaniards, did not seize any of our houses. They remained in Coyoacan and let us live in peace.

They hanged Macuilxochitl, the king of Huitzilopochco, in Coyoacan. They also hanged Pizotzin, the king of Culhuacan. And they fed the Keeper of the Black House,[12] along with several others, to their dogs.

[12] See Chapter 1, note 5. [Not reprinted here.—*Eds.*]

And three wise men of Ehecatl,[13] from Tezcoco, were devoured by the dogs. They had come only to surrender; no one brought them or sent them there. They arrived bearing their painted sheets of paper. There were four of them, and only one escaped; the other three were overtaken, there in Coyoacan.

[13] God of the wind, a frequent disguise of Quetzalcoatl.

The Colonial Experience

WORK IN UTOPIA

Lesley Byrd Simpson

*The two Republics, of Spaniards and Indians of which this Kingdom con-
sists, are so repugnant to each other . . . that it seems that the conservation of
the former always means the oppression and destruction of the latter. The
estates, buildings, plantations, mines and herds, the monasteries and religious
orders—I do not know whether it would be possible to maintain them or
improve them without the service and aid of the Indians.*—Viceroy Luis de
Velasco II to his successor, the Count of Monterrey, 1595.

The story of work in New Spain impinges upon all other questions,
because *every part of its economic structure depended in the end upon
the labor of the Indians.* The Indians were not the only ones who worked,
but they formed the great reservoir of labor without which society could
not exist. The Conquest of Mexico was in a real sense the capture of
native labor. The various shifts to which the Spaniards were put to get
necessary work done is relevant to the whole history of Mexico from that
day to this.

Few aspects of the Spanish colonial régime have been the object of
more furious denunciation than its treatment of the Indians. Abuse of the

Reprinted from *Many Mexicos*, Fourth Edition, Revised 1966, by L. B. Simpson.
Originally published by the University of California Press; reprinted by permission of
The Regents of the University of California.

Professor Simpson received his doctorate from the University of California in 1928,
where he continued to teach Spanish and Portuguese until his retirement in 1955. He
has held two Guggenheim Fellowships in Mexico and is considered one of the leading
authorities on colonial Mexican history. His many works include *The Encomienda of
New Spain* and *Many Mexicos.*

Indians was, with few exceptions, tied up with the matter of getting work done. The scowling conquistador lashing the naked and cringing Indian is the traditional picture and one that shows no sign of dying out. On the contrary, the excellent mural decorations which since 1920 have covered the public buildings of Mexico rarely omit it. The lesson to the spectator is that, no matter how bad things may be at present, they are infinitely to be preferred to the slavery of olden times. Like all such facile theses, however, deliberately propounded for indoctrination, this one contains a deal of bad thinking and misinformation. What has been done is to take the desperate plight of the Indian as it was within the memory of many still living and project it back into colonial times. Not that the Indian's life was a continual fiesta under Spanish rule, for it is evident that the elaborate system of protection set up by the Laws of the Indies was evaded as often as not, and that the colonial authorities were in a tacit conspiracy with hacendados, mineowners, and operators of textile mills to keep men securely tied to their jobs. At the same time the necessity of preserving the Indians from extinction made the Audiencia more vigilant in enforcing the laws than is commonly believed. In any case, no part of our survey of Mexico is more important or more necessary to understand than the story of work.

Necessary work always has to be done. In conquered countries, if the population is capable of exploitation, necessary work is always done by the conquered. That may not be sound ethics, but it is history. Our New England ancestors tried to enslave the Pequot Indians of Connecticut and failed only because the Pequots would rather have died than become slaves, and did. The problem of procuring labor had to be faced from the moment Columbus founded his unlucky settlement of Isabella on the island of Española.

The great discoverer, upon his return to Spain in 1493, wrote the Catholic Monarchs a famous letter, which may be considered the first real estate prospectus of the New World. "There are in that island," he wrote,

> mountains and valleys and fields, and beautiful fat lands for planting and sowing, for raising cattle of all kinds, for cities and villages. The ports are such as you would not believe unless you saw them, as are the many broad rivers of sweet waters, most of which are gold-bearing. . . . The people all go naked as their mothers bore them, save only that some of the women cover a single part with a green leaf, or with a cotton cloth made for the purpose. They have no iron or steel or arms, nor are they apt for such things, not because they are not well set up and beautiful, but because they are wonderfully timorous. . . . They are so guileless and so generous with what they possess that you would not believe it without seeing it.

Free rich land and a docile population waiting to be put to work! The appeal to the poverty-stricken and land-hungry soldiers of Spain was irresistible—the same soldiery who had lived on loot in the conquests of Granada and Naples, and had always found the loot too little. There were many thousands of these unemployed warriors in Spain at the close of the fifteenth century. Each was a nobleman in his own mind, for the bearing of arms was a patent of nobility. For many centuries a whole class of society had had no trade but arms and no income but the spoils of the enemy. The Spanish crusader, who became the conquistador of the New World, was a hardy, brave, ruthless, and usually illiterate barbarian. The noble state, however, postulated land and retainers, and he had only his arms. Work? Everyone knows that in the great tradition of nobility useful work is degrading. Cortés himself said that if he had wanted to plow he would have stayed home in Spain.

Small wonder, then, that Columbus had no difficulty in enlisting a considerable army of these adventurers, some fifteen hundred of them, for his second expedition to the Garden of Eden. But one important item had been overlooked, namely, the food supply. In those days armies lived on the country, and Columbus evidently anticipated no difficulty in feeding his men in Española. Native economy, however, was not equal to the added burden. The Indians had got along well enough on a diet of manioc bread, sweet potatoes, and fish, but they produced only what they consumed. The Spaniards ate all the food they could seize, and invaders and Indians alike were soon reduced to a state of permanent starvation. The problem of procuring food was immediate and the situation was heavy with disaster. "Nothing in those days," wrote Las Casas, "gladdened the people here more than to learn that ships were coming with provisions from Castile, for all their sufferings were from hunger." Conditions became so hideous that in the next few years Española was all but abandoned and could be kept up only by sending over shiploads of convicts, *whose sentences of death had been commuted to two years' service in the Indies.* "Indeed," wrote the historian Oviedo, "I saw many of those who at that time returned to Castile with such faces that, if the king had given me his Indies, were I to become as they, I should not have gone thither." The necessity of procuring food, as I shall have occasion to repeat, was the greatest and most continuing modifying factor in the settlement of the Spanish Indies.

Now, the cultivation of manioc (or *yuca,* from which we get tapioca) is extremely laborious, although the yield is generous. The brush must be grubbed up, hillocks built, and the encroaching jungle must be fought back unceasingly. Then the tuberous roots are dug up, grated, and the poisonous juice squeezed out, after which the fibers are made into heavy flat cakes, which have the virtue of lasting indefinitely if kept dry. In that first generation manioc bread was the staple food of the colonists. It was such an important item in the Conquest that it is hardly too much to say that the New World was conquered on manioc. At least, it is hard to see how it could have been conquered without it.

The aversion of the Spanish conquistadores (and others) to manual labor in the tropics is notorious, and the new parasite class insisted on being fed and made rich. What were the heathen for if not to work for their betters? So the Indians of the Antilles were forced to plant manioc and wash gold, and were kept at it so unremittingly, with so little regard for their strength and habits, that the greater part of the population died off in the first twenty years of the Spanish occupation. It was that frightful catastrophe which inspired Las Casas' *Brief Relation of the Destruction of the Indies.* Conditions were so incredibly bad that it may be said that not even Las Casas could exaggerate them.

The Spaniards, however, had not been sent to the Indies merely to drive the Indians to the gold pits. Back in the queen's council were those who remembered that, by the terms of the bull *Inter caetera* of Alexander VI, which gave Spain and Portugal the Indies, she had undertaken to make Christians of the natives. The paradox involved in saving the souls of the aborigines, while using their bodies for profit, agitated the legal minds of Spain for many years, and was solved only after the New Laws of 1542 had come perilously close to destroying the Spanish Empire.

In Española in the time of Columbus the matter was settled summarily by recourse to a proposition which may be somewhat baldly stated as follows: "Is it not just to make the heathen work for us in exchange for the ineffable gifts of Christianity and the profit system?" Lest this proposition shock the reader, it should be added that one of the most persistent criticisms directed for centuries against the Indians was that they had no sense of values. They would not work for wages like Christians, and they exchanged things of great price for things of little price. Their inferiority was manifest. All of which, of course, strikes us as the flimsiest sort of rationalization, but it served. Work had to be done in any case, and Columbus and his successors ground the helpless islanders in a deadly round of unceasing toil. When the despairing Indians resisted (as they did under Queen Anacoana), well, then they were heathen rebels and could legally be enslaved. Columbus's project for establishing a trade in Indian slaves, as I have mentioned elsewhere, was stopped by Isabella herself. The fearful stories of Spanish barbarity which came back from the Indies finally aroused the queen to the necessity of redeeming her pledge to the pope.

So out of starvation, slavery, and death came the first New Deal to the Western Hemisphere. It was entrusted to Don Frey Nicolás de Ovando, Lord Commander of the military order of Calatrava, one of those extraordinary warrior monks who had governed conquered Granada. In 1502 he was made governor of Española, with the mission of repairing the damage done during the misrule of the Columbus brothers, suppressing Indian and Spanish rebels, and restoring order. The old *comendador* was equal to the task. Within the year the Indians who were left alive had been thoroughly subdued, as well as those turbulent spirits among the Spaniards whom Columbus had so signally failed to control.

But Ovando, like every other administrator sent to the Indies, still had to face the problem of feeding the population, getting useful work done, and making Christians and Spanish subjects out of the Indians. It was he who introduced the much discussed and lamented encomienda system (a trusteeship or guardianship) by which the conquered Moorish provinces in Spain had been governed. He divided the Indians into lots of varying size, depending upon the category of the recipient, and put them under the tutelage of presumably God-fearing and high-minded Spanish laymen. Some of the largest encomiendas were given to King Ferdinand and the men of his court. It is well to remember that this was before the establishment of religious missions. The encomendero, in fact, was supposed to assume the obligations of a lay missionary and at the same time to act as collector of the tribute and general overload of the Indians. It was a quasi-feudal arrangement: the encomendero accepted the responsibility of looking after the Indian's soul, while the Indian discharged his end of it by raising foodstuffs and washing gold. *This legal fiction, by one name or another, was behind all measures by which the Indian was coerced into doing work.*

To the conquistador of 1500 it was a reasonable and logical solution of the labor problem. He evidently looked upon the encomienda merely as a contrivance for avoiding the ugly name of slavery. The matter becomes clear in the light of his action after the population had become too scanty to support him. Slaving expeditions to the Bahamas and other "useless" islands (i.e., islands where no gold was to be found) grew to be a profitable traffic. One such expedition, under Francisco Hernández de Córdoba, led to the discovery of New Spain in 1517. The ill-defined status of the encomienda Indians made their lot worse, if possible, than that of the out-and-out slaves. Fray Bernardino de Manzanedo, one of the three Jeronymite governors of the Indies, wrote to Charles V in 1518: "Since no one has the assurance that he will be able to keep the Indians given him in encomienda, he uses them like borrowed goods, and thus many have perished and are perishing."

The blind and fumbling policy of the Spanish Crown during the tragic first thirty years of its government of the Indies makes it easy to drift into a denunciation of the whole Spanish effort. When the policy was not one of squeezing the last *maravedí* out of the natives, as under Ferdinand the Catholic, it was such quixotic nonsense as attempting to restore them to a state of independence under clerical government (the Dominican thesis). The irreconcilable conflict between priest and layman, piety and practicality, was further confused by the fact that Spain had gone into the empire business with no adquate machinery of administration and, naturally, no knowledge of the New World. Moreover, the center of government was so distant that months and even years had to elapse between the recognition of a problem and any remedial measure. The wonder is that anything constructive was ever done.

With all its faults and manifest hypocrisy, the encomienda was a halting but intelligent step toward setting up a stable economy in the colonies. It need not astonish us that it had no immediate beneficial effect on native life, or that the encomendero took his missionary duties lightly. He was too intent upon procuring the necessities of life and the scanty grains of gold that his Indians washed out of the earth, to allow the new legal fiction to alter his murderous course. By 1510, conditions among the

miserable remnants of the population were so ghastly that the first
Dominican missionaries to arrive there were horrified and at once embarked upon their long and heroic campaign to remedy them.

The year 1510 marked the beginning of the curious politico-humani-
tarian pact between the Spanish Crown and the Dominican order, by
which the two were joined in a common effort to suppress the New World
feudalism (the encomienda) of the conquistadores and to preserve the
Indians from extinction. The first target selected by the Dominicans for
attack was the encomienda, to which they ascribed most of the evils of
the Indies. Their violent denunciations of the encomenderos (in which
they were opposed by the Franciscans) brought about a tardy and, in
some respects, ludicrous attempt to save the situation by setting up an
ecclesiastical régime over the Indians. It was embodied in the Code of
Burgos of 1512.

This famous Code, the first written for the New World, is an excellent
example of the idealism, irrationality, and ignorance of the early Spanish
clergymen who legislated for the relief of the Indians. The proper government of the innocent aborigines, according to the reverend lawmakers,
included such measures as teaching them to say their prayers in Latin
and restricting their heathenish custom of taking baths. The Code of
Burgos was stillborn in any case, because the natives of the Antilles were
past saving. It did lay down several principles, nevertheless, which were
never abandoned. The first of them, of course, was that the most imperative duty of the Crown was to convert the Indians to Christianity and
bring them to a "reasonable" (Spanish) way of life. In spite of Dominican
protests, the encomienda was retained as an instrument toward that end.
It may not be coincidental that King Ferdinand held 1,400 Indians in
encomienda. A further reason for its retention was, I suspect, that the
Crown had always rewarded its soldiers with loot taken from the enemy;
indeed, it did not pretend to pay them otherwise. Of great significance to
the subsequent history of the Indies, the Code of Burgos also postulated
the necessity of gathering the Indians in regular European-style communities, in which they should live under Spanish tutelage, and in which
their services would be more readily available for useful work. It was this
typical mismating of economic necessity with humanitarianism which
was to confuse Indian legislation for a century, but which was to result
in that not altogether useless code known as the *Recopilación de las
Leyes de los Reynos de las Indias.*

Cortés and most of his men had lived for years in the Antilles before
undertaking the Conquest of New Spain. They had grown up with the
encomienda, so to speak, and were fully aware that their true wealth was
the labor of the Indians. Cortés had some doubts about the wisdom of
allowing the encomienda to be transferred to New Spain, or, at least, he
so expressed himself to the Emperor. When, however, the Conquest was
accomplished and his men clamored for their reward, there was nothing
to give them but Indians in encomienda, and so they all became little
feudal lords—Cortés really a big one—all this in direct disobedience to

the command of the Emperor, but his edict had come too late. The Crown accepted the *fait accompli,* but from that time on pursued the policy of seizing for itself all the encomiendas whose holders died or otherwise forfeited title. In the Hapsburg system there could be only one logical encomendero, the king himself.

Fortunately for New Spain, the encomienda there turned out to be a very different thing from the disguised slavery it had been in the islands. This was partly owing to the character of Cortés and partly to the character of the mainland Indians. In New Spain the conquistadores found a hardy agrarian people, long inured to the exacting labors of the field, living under primitive feudalism of their native overlords. They accepted a change of masters with some indifference. The status of the pre-Conquest peasant (*macehual*) made the transition easy. There is a curious document in the National Archives of Mexico, a petition sent by the chief men of Huejotzingo (Puebla) to Viceroy Velasco in 1554, begging him to allow them to donate certain of their lands to the peasants.

"We principales," they wrote, "have held our lands from time immemorial, ever since our forefathers left them to us, whereas the macehuales had none; and they cultivated our lands and brought us wood and water, and built all the buildings we had need of, and gave us chickens [turkeys] and chili and everything for our maintenance, and their wives and children served us in everything we commanded. They did all this so that we might allow them to sow their crops on our lands." The macehuales receiving the donation were to bind themselves to cultivate the land of their chiefs.

The reader is not to infer that the Indians of New Spain were better off under the encomenderos than under their native lords, but at least the change was not one from heaven to hell, as we read in the storybooks. And then, as routine and familiarity rubbed some of the sharp edges off mutual intercourse, and especially when the New Laws of 1542 removed the right of the encomenderos to use the labor of the Indians at pleasure, there developed between them and their charges some sort of tolerable relationship, with a healthy basis in common interest, the Indians supporting the encomenderos with tributes, the encomenderos protecting the Indians from the rapacity of other Spaniards.

Bernal Díaz del Castillo was such an encomendero. His encomienda embraced a number of villages in Guatemala. In 1579 a certain Martín Ximénez obtained from the Audiencia of Guatemala a grant of some lands lying within the encomienda of Bernal Díaz, and his Indians appealed to him to stand by. The old conquistador, then eighty-six, took the case to court, and won.

"To this [petition for the grant]," he argued, "I reply and swear that if the said lands could be granted without harm to the Indians, I myself should have asked former governors to grant them to my six legitimate sons. But, as I have said, these lands are the ones on which the Indians have their crops of maize, peppers, and cacao, and from which they pay their tributes, and it is their ancient holding, and that is why I have not asked for them, because it would mean the destruction of the Indians."

Melchor de Pedraza, encomendero of Atotonilco and Zacamal (Hidalgo) in 1580 appealed to the Audiencia to protect his Indians from their own governor and caciques, who were forcing the Indians to work on their lands and in their commerce the greater part of the year, with the result that the Indians had no time for cultivating fields for their maintenance *and for the payment of the tribute*. The frequency of such cases in the fragmentary records leads me to believe that this attitude was fairly universal among encomenderos.

It would be hazardous to assume that the conquistador of New Spain, after the middle of the sixteenth century, turned into a gentle patriarch, intent upon the well-being of his charges. I merely wish to suggest that he did not necessarily continue to be the monster which he had assuredly been in the macabre days of Española. He learned in time that he needed Indians, lots of Indians, live Indians. He had to accept his fuedal obligation toward them, and the Indians themselves recognized this community of interest. Bernal Diaz, who was typical of his class, seems to have settled comfortably into the unexciting life of a country squire, living on his tributes and playing the part of the great white father to the Indians of his encomienda. The encomenderos, it should be added, did not for long continue to be the most numerous or the most representative of the Spanish settlers. In the early days they were a privileged aristocracy, but they were constantly being diminished by death, and their encomiendas were gradually taken over by the Crown. By the end of the sixteenth century the Crown held about three-fifths of all the Indian towns of New Spain. The encomenderos had, in effect, long snce been reduced to the status of pensioners by the law of 1571, which says: "The encomienda is a right granted by Royal Grace to the deserving of the Indies, to receive and collect for themselves the tributes of the Indians given them in trust for their life and the life of one heir . . . with the obligation of looking after the spiritual and material welfare of the Indians and of dwelling in and defending the provinces of their trust, and of doing homage and taking personal oath to fulfill all this."

After the Conquest New Spain rapidly filled up with men from every stratum of Spanish society, and the more there were of them the more acute was the problem of feeding them and getting necessary work done. The conquistador–encomendero class did not disappear—far from it. As a rule they had large families (Bernal Díaz mentions his six legitimate sons on all occasions, leaving the number of his natural children to our imagination), and their offspring continued to enjoy preference in land grants and government jobs. Generally, I suspect, they were spoiled brats, as will appear later on. Out of the needs of this rapidly growing white society of Mexico grew the extraordinary institution of the *repartimiento*, that is, a work allotment, or corvée, in Peru called the *mita*.

It was based on the sound principle that the state might force its citizens to do such work as was necessary for the existence of the commonwealth. It was the eminent-domain principle applied to labor.

Necessary work was defined as the production of foodstuffs, the operation of mines, the erection of public buildings, churches, and convents, the opening and maintenance of roads, harbors, and irrigation ditches, the laying out of new towns and congregations, and the care of travelers. It is apparent that few mechanical services were *not* considered necessary for the good of the commonwealth. The important thing about the repartimiento, however, as far as the Indians were concerned, was that (at least in theory) *no one could be forced to work for private gain and that all services must be paid for in cash.* The authors of the repartimiento were convinced that coercion was an evil, but that at times it was a necessary evil. Anyway, they hopefully believed that it would serve as a stopgap in the transition to a more desirable state of things; that is, it would be an educational interlude during which the Indians would learn to work for wages like civilized human beings. But the repartimiento lasted, at least in agriculture, its field of widest application, for two and a half centuries, and even after Independence coercion was continued for another hundred years under the cheaper and much worse regulated system of debt peonage.

From about 1550 to the repartimiento's codification in 1609, it led to appalling abuses, which excited the condemnation of the Franciscans, especially that of their chief spokesman, Jerónimo de Mendieta. There may be some clerical bias here, but there is none in the most trustworthy of contemporary critics, Don Gonzalo Gómez de Cervantes, who in 1599 addressed a bitter memorial to Don Eugenio de Salazar, Oidor of the Council of the Indies.[1]

Cervantes was corregidor of Tlaxcala and quite likely a member of the powerful Cervantes clan founded by the Comendador Leonel de Cervantes, who achieved fame by bringing his seven daughters to New Spain in 1524 at Cortés' expense and marrying them off to the more prosperous of the conquistadores. Don Gonzalo's indictment of the system clearly reflects the views of the Creole aristocracy and does not pretend to be fair to his opponents. It is, nevertheless, so circumstantial and agrees so closely with Mendieta's account that it commands respect.

In Mexico City, he wrote, there were large numbers of Indian workmen skilled in the mechanical trades: tailors, embroiderers, painters, silk spinners, blacksmiths, cobblers, masons, and carpenters, whose regular wages were four reales (½ peso) to one peso a day; but the juez repartidor made no distinction between them and the unskilled workmen, and pressed them all into work gangs, in which they earned only one real a day. This naturally led to bribery and corruption, for the skilled workmen either hired substitutes or greased the palm of the juez repartidor to let them off, the bribery rate being as high as three or four pesos a week.

The immense amount of labor, he continued, required for the erection

---

[1] This unique document eventually found its way to the British Museum and was published by Alberto María Carreño under the title, *La Vida Económica y Social de la Nueva España al finalizar el Siglo XVI* (Mexico, 1944).

of the four great cathedrals (Mexico City, Puebla, Guadalajara, and Valloldolid), and the large number of churches, chapels, convents, schools, and ecclesiastical edifices of all kinds, kept a veritable army of workmen occupied and aggravated the labor shortage, which was already acute because of the diminishing population. The shortage was especially felt in the haciendas, where the lot of the Indians was grim.

They send a Negro or servant along with the Indians who speeds them up and forces them to work faster than their weak constitutions can support. On top of this, they beat, whip, and mistreat them, and even take away their food and blankets to keep them from deserting. . . . Some farmers, after having kept them for two or three weeks, give them back their bundles of clothing and remove their guards . . . and the miserable Indians, seeing themselves at liberty, leave without collecting their wages, thinking themselves well paid just to get away. . . . These Indians, it should be noted, are assigned to the repartimiento for only one week, but the farmers, faced with the loss of their crops . . . keep them, as I have said, two or three weeks and more. Since the wretched Indian has left his house for [only] a week, his food gives out, and when he returns he finds his wife or his children dead, and his fields ruined for lack of cultivation, or destroyed by cattle.

The Indians are assigned to the mines in the same fashion, and, since the miners have been short of hands since the epidemics of 1575–1576 [*matla-zahuatl* or *cocoliste*, probably spotted fever or typhus, the most deadly of the scourges, which was endemic until well into the eighteenth century], they hold for two or three weeks the Indians who have been assigned to them for one. I am a witness of the abuse that the Indians receive in some of the mining haciendas, especially in those where they are forced to carry the ore to the mouth of the mine, from there to the mill, from the mill to the mortars, from the mortars to the sieves, and thence to the mixing troughs, using their blankets for the purpose, blankets worth at least five or six reales. The rough ore tears the blankets, so the Indian, after serving his week, is paid four reales and left with a ruined blanket that cost him five or six. Thus he works for nothing and even spends his own money.

All officialdom, he wrote, all troops, and all Spaniards who could afford them kept horses in the city, which meant that a large supply of fodder had to be brought in by the Indians pressed into this service.

But only the viceroy and the officers of the Audiencia enjoy this repartimiento, and no citizen or hidalgo does; hence it is of little value to the militia. . . . Every day a great many canoes come in loaded with grass, which is cast into the lake two, four, or six leagues from the city. . . . Many Spaniards make a business [monopoly] of bringing it in canoes, with Negroes in charge of them. . . . The result is that this repartimiento benefits only the [Crown] officers, who thus get their fodder more cheaply than the rest of the citizens. . . . This is a matter that demands correction, because the strength of this kingdom lies in its horses.

It may be a coincidence that Cervantes' *Memorial* was written just after the last petition of the encomenderos to have their encomiendas made perpetual (1597); but they are of a piece, and both repeat the arguments of the Franciscans, that is, that the Indians were better off under the encomienda. However it was, the mounting criticism stirred the Council of the Indies to undertake a complete codification of Indian employment, free or forced.

The Ordinances of 1609 show a great advance in the science of law-making, in their frank recognition of the problem, and in their practical and realistic approach to it. They also afford a glimpse into the working of the paternalistic mind. (It is well to remember that this was in 1609 and the Rights of Man were a long way in the future.) Some of their more important provisions were: (1) Indians might not be brought from excessive distances, more than one day's journey, or from different climates; (2) their wages were to be adequate and proportioned to their work; (3) they must be paid for time spent in traveling to and from their work; (4) they must be paid in cash, in person, and in the presence of a magistrate; (5) their hours of labor were to be fixed by the viceroy; (6) they were to be allowed to go home at night whenever practicable; (7) to prevent their being considered as serfs or bound to the land, they might not be mentioned in any deed as belonging to such and such an estate or mine, for they were by nature "as free as the Spaniards themselves"; (8) they might not be employed, even voluntarily, in sugar mills or pearl fishing, for their weak constitutions unfitted them for such labor; (9) their tributes might not be commuted to personal services (an old prac-tice among encomenderos).

Thomas Gage, that somewhat disreputable but indispensable reporter, has left us a lively and accurate account of the new repartimiento at work:

> The Spaniards that live in that country [Guatemala] . . . allege that all their trading and farming is for the good of the commonwealth, and there-fore whereas there are not Spaniards enough for so ample and large a country to do all their work, and all are not able to buy slaves and blacka-moors, they stand in need of the Indians' help to serve them for their pay and hire, whereupon it hath been considered that a partition of Indian laborers be made every Monday, or Sunday in the afternoon, to the Span-iards, according to the farms they occupy, or according to their several employments, calling, and trading with mules, or any other way. So that for such and such a district there is named an officer, who is called *juez repartidor*, who according to a list made of every farm, house, and person, is to give so many Indians by the week. . . . They name the town and place of their meeting upon Sunday or Monday, to the which themselves and the Spaniards of that district do resort. The Indians of the several towns are to have in a readiness so many laborers as the Court of Guatemala hath appointed to be weekly taken out of such a town, who are conducted by an Indian officer [*mandón*] to the town of general meeting; and when they are come thither with their tools, their spades, shovels, bills, or axes, with their provision of victuals for a week (which are commonly some dry cakes of maize, puddings of *frijoles*, or French beans, and a little chilli or biting long pepper, or a bit of cold meat for the first day or two), and with beds on

their backs (which is only a coarse woolen mantle to wrap about them when they lie on the bare ground), then are they shut up in the town house, some with blows, some with spurnings, some with boxes on the ear, if presently they go not in.

Now being all gathered together, and the house filled with them, the *juez repartidor*, or officer, calls by order of the list such and such a Spaniard, and also calls out of the house so many Indians as by the Court are commanded to be given him . . . and delivereth unto the Spaniard his Indians, and so to all the rest, till they be all served; who when they receive their Indians, take from them a tool, or their mantles, to secure them that they run not away; and for every Indian delivered unto them, they give to the *juez repartidor*, or officer, half a real, which is threepence an Indian, for his fees, which yearly mounteth to him a great deal of money. . . . If the complaint be made by any Spaniard that such and such an Indian did run away from him, and served him not the week past, the Indian must be brought, and surely tied by his hands in the marketplace, and there be whipped upon his bare back. But if the poor Indian complain that the Spaniard cozened and cheated him of his shovel, ax, bill, mantle, or wages, no justice shall be executed against the cheating Spaniard, neither shall the Indian be righted, though it is true that the order runs equally in favor of both Indian and Spaniard. Thus are the poor Indians sold for threepence a week for a whole week's slavery, not permitted to go home at night unto their wives, though their work lie not above a mile from the town where they live; nay, some are carried ten or twelve miles from their home, who must not return till Saturday night late, and must that week do whatsoever their master pleaseth to command them. The wages appointed will scarce find them meat and drink, for they are not allowed a real a day, which is but sixpence, and with that they are to find themselves, but for six days' work and diet they are to have five reals, which is half a crown.

All forms of coerced labor were subject to grave abuses, but even so Gage's indignation is not to be taken at its face value. Gage and his kind, for one thing, lived by virtue of the system. Then, the Indians serving as much as a fourth of their time in the fields for hire were probably no worse off than the peasants of Europe, as Humboldt remarked. They were certainly not slaves. The pittance they received was insufficient to support life at any level; but the Indians did not depend upon their wages for a living. Their wages went toward paying their tribute (a peso a head of family yearly, plus the half-peso of the *real servicio* after 1592) and incidental expenses, mostly connected with their religious life: fees for baptism, marriage, burial, and the like. For the rest, they had their milpas and a good part of their time for cultivating them.

The common criticism of Spanish colonial legislation for the amelioration of the lot of the Indians is that it was evaded as often as not. The labor code of 1609, however, did not aim at the destruction of a system, like the New Laws of 1542, but at a reasonable regulation of long-established practice. It did not, therefore, arouse much opposition. On the contrary, the severity with which the Audiencia came down upon offenders is sufficient proof that it had the support of a substantial majority of its beneficiaries. Labor was getting critically short by 1609 and wastage of manpower could no longer be tolerated, as Gómez de Cervantes had made clear ten years before.

Several factors contributed to make the repartimiento bearable. The first is that it did little violence to native customs. All the evidence we have indicates that before the Conquest the Indian peasant was obliged to contribute part of his time and labor to the cultivation of the common land set aside for the support of priests and officials. He worked the land on a kind of sharecropping basis. He was also accustomed to contributing personal services and tribute in kind. Alonso de Zorita, writing in 1575 in support of the Franciscan thesis against the repartimiento, said of the personal services of the peasants under the Aztecs: "The ordinary daily personal service of wood and water was assessed by the day, by villages, and by districts (*barrios*) in such wise that at most each Indian had to serve only twice a year, and, as has been said, it was assessed among those living close by, and for that reason they were exempted to some extent from the tribute paid by the others."

The pre-Conquest macehual, then, was accustomed to paying tribute and rendering personal services for the support of his rulers. The good-of-the-commonwealth principle must have struck him as right and proper, or, at least, as something to be expected and put up with. In the large number of cases of abuse of the repartimiento heard by the General Indian Court, no objection was ever made to the principle of the thing, but only that such and such a person had violated law or custom. *Costumbre*, let me repeat, was Indian law and was always respected by the Spanish courts so long as it did not run counter to Spanish law.

A second factor in the control of the repartimiento was the endemic shortage of labor. During the century following the Conquest the native population died off at a staggering rate. Smallpox, measles, typhus, and other epidemics wiped out vast numbers of people, while the dislocation of the economy and the normal scourges of famine, flood, and drought made recovery very slow. At the time of the Conquest central Mexico (the settled part of the Plateau) had an estimated population of at least eleven million, of which by 1600 no more than a million and a half remained (Gómez de Cervantes puts the decline at ninety per cent). As a result, competition for labor in the mines raised wages to such a point, even before the Ordinances of 1609, that the miners begged for relief. The same phenomenon occurred in the Spanish towns, where Indian mechanics could earn several times the wage paid in the repartimientos (as we have seen in the memorial of Gómez de Cervantes), and the surrounding agricultural lands were, as a consequence, drained of needed labour. The cry of the hacendados was that the Indians were being spoiled by high wages, a complaint that was repeated for centuries.

A third and very interesting factor in the modification of the repartimiento arose from the nature of New Spain's most vital industry, silver mining. In 1540 a survey of Indian communities was made which showed that a considerable part of the population was being employed in the mines, which at that time were mostly gold placers, in which forced gangs could be used effectively. The huge silver deposits discovered a few years later could not be worked by any such pick-and-shovel technique, but required a specially trained group of men. *By the end of the eighteenth century the silver mines of New Spain were generally operated with free Indian labor,* according to Humboldt. Such an astonishing development demands our attention.

Silver mining was a complicated business of sinking shafts and running drifts, ventilating and draining the mines, and preparing the quicksilver amalgam and roasting it. All these tasks require special skills and cannot be performed by occasional gangs brought in from the fields. Also, the mineral deposits were usually in remote, arid, sparsely settled, nonagricultural regions, to which the repartimientos had to be brought from great distances—a costly procedure and one provocative of much discontent. Moreover, the weekly or fortnightly changing of the labor gangs was destructive of the continuity necessary to efficient operation and prevented the building up of a body of skilled workers, which became progressively more essential as the processes of mining became more complex.

The repartimiento disappeared from mining, then, because it was a clumsy and inefficient device for procuring skilled and specialized labor. A potent cause of discontent with it was the disparity in wages between the free *peóns* (who earned as much as a peso a day) and the men of the repartimiento (who earned an eighth as much). This discontent led to dangerous riots (strikes) in the eighteenth century. But the most powerful factor of all, perhaps, in the elimination of the repartimiento from mining was the unceasing demand for the precious metals (mostly silver) in Europe and Asia, which made it profitable for mine operators, especially in the eighteenth century, to work their properties to capacity and to offer relatively high wages and bonuses to their workmen. Thus it came about that in the course of time the mines gathered about them communities of skilled mechanics, who in turn depended for their subsistence upon the outlying haciendas which had been established to meet this need. The rich farming and stock-raising country in the present states of Guanajuato, Querétaro, San Luis Potosí, Aguascalientes, Jalisco, and Zacatecas was supported by, and supported, the new mining communities.

Baron von Humboldt was struck by the prosperous condition of the mine workers. "In the Kingdom of New Spain," he wrote, in 1803,

> at least within the last thirty or forty years, the labour of the mines is free, and there remains no trace of the mita [repartimiento]. . . . Nowhere does the lower people enjoy in greater security the fruit of their labours than in the mines of Mexico; no law forces the Indian to choose this species of labour, or to prefer one mine to another; and when he is displeased with the proprietor of one mine he may offer his services to another master who may perhaps pay more regularly. . . . The labour of a miner is entirely free throughout the whole Kingdom of New Spain. . . . The Mexican miner is the best paid of all miners; he gains at least from 25 to 30 francs (£1 to

£ 1 4s) per week of six days. . . . The miners, *tenateros* and *faeneros* [ore carriers and piece workers] occupied in transporting the minerals to the place of assemblage (*despachos*) frequently gain more than 6 francs per day of 6 hours (4s 10d).

The miners earned their high wages. In a deep mine, such as La Valenciana at Guanajuato, lack of ventilation was a continual hazard. There was no hoisting machinery available before the late eighteenth century, and the ore had to be carried to the surface, 1,500 feet, on men's backs. This was one of the most expensive operations, for the tenateros could make only five or six trips a day up the long chicken ladders with their 100-pound sacks of ore. By 1790 the hoisting was being done by horse-powered winches (*malacates*).

The determination of real wages in colonial times is a very difficult problem. Average prices do us little good. Maize might be worth two reales a fanega (hundredweight) one season and four times as much the next. It might sell for two reales in an agricultural community, while in a mining community in the mountains it might sell for a peso, that is, four times as much. Prices fluctuated violently from the irregularity of the crops, because there were no adequate storage facilities. The wages of the repartimiento Indian were hardly more than a token wage in any case. In 1550 he earned two and a half reales a week. By 1600 he was earning generally a real a day, and the rate tended to stick at that point. John Stephens found the debt-peonage system working in Yucatan in 1840 on the same weekly quota basis as the old repartimiento, and the men, called *luneros*, that is to say, "Monday men," were still receiving a real a day, which was credited against their "debt." In the repartimientos destined for service in a Spanish town or mine, where expenses were higher and where the men competed with free labor, the pay was substantially better, averaging about two reales a day, although it rarely exceeded half the rate paid for free labor.

One of the arguments by which the repartimiento was rationalized was that it would serve to educate the Indians and elevate them to the status of free workers. Obviously, it did no such thing. A class of free workers did develop in the cities and mines, but it was not through any desire on the part of the employers, who did everything they could to prevent it. The motive, of course, was cheap labor, and the standard excuse was that the Indian would not work without coercion. That assumption was dignified by being made law as early as 1512, when the Code of Burgos postulated: "It has been seen by long experience that the natives are by nature inclined to a life of idleness and vice." The thesis is weakened by the experience of the mining industry, which found it possible to attract workers by paying them adequate wages.

Although in principle the repartimiento was restricted to tasks performed for the benefit of the state, local magistrates took a very broad view of the matter and were prone to define a great many activities within the good-of-the-commonwealth framework. At the same time the law was specific about sugar manufacturing, pearl fishing and the processing of indigo (the fumes from which were supposed to be injurious). It was argued that the Indians were not strong enough for these occupations, so the operators were obliged to employ Negro slaves. The high cost of slaves, however, and the Negroes' tendency to run away and form colonies of dangerous outlaws (*cimarrones*) in the mountains made the employment of Indians more desirable, so Indians were bootlegged into these industries and paid enough to keep them quiet. By the end of the eighteenth century the silver mines were running on free Indian labor, and Humboldt noted that the sugar mills were also.

In the plantations it was necessary to have a dependable labor force, preferably cheap. The problem was serious because, without continuity, it was impossible to operate. Take the case of Don Manuel Garrote Bueno. Don Manuel had a cacao plantation in Guatemala and operated it with Indian workmen under the repartimiento. On March 5, 1798, he addressed a complaint to the Audiencia of Guatemala which illustrates the situation. The Indians, he stated, refused to serve in his repartimiento, alleging that it left them no time to work their own lands. This, he averred, was nonsense, because they were willing to serve for higher pay. In other words, they were striking. "The hope that the superior government," he continued,

> would be able to enforce its provisions [for the repartimiento] had stimulated me to undertake the planting of cacao . . . , but now I am completely discouraged. . . . During the past year I planted 8,000 trees, and at present I have in the nursery more than 9,000. If the repartimiento is going to be enforced I shall be glad to continue planting, but if the stubbornness of these natives and their habit of disobeying the orders of the superior government bring about its suspension, it will expose me to disaster and I shall have to abandon my undertaking. . . .

As resistance to the repartimiento grew, the device of tying men to their jobs by contract and debt came into general use. The practice had been forbidden long ago during the reign of Charles V, but it was too obvious a solution of the labor problem not to be used surreptitiously, and it became so widespread that it was finally accepted as legal.

The working of debt peonage was simplicity itself. What Indian could resist accepting an advance of a few pesos against his wages at the price of putting his cross on a piece of paper which he could not read? Once having done so, he was caught, and the local alguacil could haul him off to work whenever he was needed. Debt peonage became so general that the complete transition to it after Independence was entirely logical. In the nineteenth century, up to the Revolution of 1910, the pulque plantations of the Plateau, the grain and cattle haciendas, the sugar, coffee, banana, cacao, tobacco, henequen, indigo plantations, and the mines all depended upon debt peonage to secure a cheap and constant supply of labor. Meanwhile, after Independence, the Indian little by little lost the land that the Spanish government had wisely set aside for his subsistence and sank to the level of a landless serf, living at the mercy of his employer.

To supply labor for the many textile mills of New Spain, the operators had recourse to other methods which kept the General Indian Court full of complaints. Long before the Conquest the Indians had developed high skill in the manufacture of cotton goods, and after it they continued to supply the country with fabrics, which became one of the most profitable items of tribute collected by the encomenderos and the Crown. Weaving was the most important industry of New Spain, outside of mining, and has continued to be so down to the present day.

Wool began to rival cotton very early. By 1580 the annual commercial clip had attained the imposing figure of 300,000 pounds, and large numbers of people were employed in its manufacture. The ancient problem of ensuring cheap and continuous operation led to the establishment of one of the ugliest of colonial institutions, the *obraje*, which was the worst kind of sweat shop, usually a small affair of a few spindles, dyeing vats, and looms. The commonest means of procuring labor were the press gang, the purchase of convicts from the local jails, contracts, and debt. The men were kept on the job by the simple expedient of locking them in. The textile industry was either too profitable, or the workers were too far beyond the fringe of respectability, to make control effective. Cheap Mexican textiles invaded markets as far away as Peru, but no improvement in the lot of the workers accompanied the growth of the industry.

Father Augustín Morfi, visiting the obrajes of Querétaro in 1777, says of them (in his invaluable *Viaje de Indios*):

> There were once many factories here, where serge, flannel, blankets, and ponchos were made, but they have decayed through the tyranny of the management. Since the majority of the operatives are convicts and are cruelly treated, they do not work with the care which they might otherwise exercise, and the free workers who might make a living in them, will not work because of the horror with which these workshops are regarded.

Humboldt was profoundly shocked by the obrajes. "On visiting these workshops," he wrote,

> the traveler is disagreeably struck, not only by the great imperfection of the technical process in the preparation for dyeing, but in a particular manner by the unhealthiness of the situation, and the bad treatment to which the workmen are exposed. All appear half naked, covered with rags, meagre, and deformed. The doors, which are double, remain constantly shut, and the workmen are not permitted to quit the house. Those who are married are only allowed to see their families on Sundays. All are unmercifully flogged if they commit the smallest trespass on the order established in the manufactory.

In other trades, such as carpentry, masonry, ropemaking, tanning, saddlemaking, and the like, Indian workmen were extensively used, but they were kept in the lower ranks of the medieval guild system brought over by the Spanish workmen. In the hierarchy of apprentice, journey-man, and master, the Spaniards took care to save the better paid jobs for themselves by making it impossible for an Indian to advance beyond the rank of journeyman. It was difficult, in fact, for an Indian to get himself accepted as apprentice, and he was usually employed only in the un-skilled operations. There was nothing to be done about it, because the guilds were powerful and their privileges were sanctioned by laws and customs that reached far back into the Middle Ages.

There was still a wide field for Indian craftsmen in the manufacture of articles for native consumption. Most native crafts survived because they were despised by the white workers, and there was no money in them anyway. So the Indians continued to make and use their own domestic wares without much interruption, and the humble markets of remote vil-lages today are full of handsome pottery, textiles, and leather goods. Native crafts have been discovered in late years by tourists in search of the picturesque, with the unfortunate result that many "Mexican Curious," as one enterprising dealer used to advertise, are now turned out by fac-tories in the capital. The virus has infected crafts along the more fre-quented tourist routes. Some years ago I visited the old textile village of Teotitlán de Valle, Oaxaca, looking for some honest handicrafts, and found the Zapotec workmen weaving hideous imitations of Aztec designs in shrieking aniline colors. "Why," I protested to the *maestro*, "do you make these ugly things instead of your own beautiful blankets?" "That's the way they order them," he answered. "But doesn't anyone make the old blankets?" "No, señor. One maestro refused to change and made the good blankets with cochineal and indigo, but he died. It is all gone now." I found the most dreadful example of this vandalism in the town of Santa Ana, Tlaxcala, one of the oldest textile centers of Mexico, where one shop advertised "Genuine Imitations of Saltillo Blankets!"

This chapter has a happy ending. Twenty-five years later, I am de-lighted to add, Mexican cotton and woolen textiles, silver and lapidary work, leather and pottery, in beauty of design and excellence of work-manship, have taken their place among the best in the world. These flourishing new industries were begun by certain enterprising foreigners (for example, in Taxco, Guerrero, and San Pedro Tlaquepaque, Jalisco) and have been intelligently encouraged by the government's Ministerio de Fomento, whose Museo de Artes Populares in Mexico City is a treat to the eyes.

THE BORDERLANDS

Charles Gibson

The term "Spanish borderlands" refers to northern Mexico and those areas of the southern United States, from Florida to California, that were once colonized by Spain. In the United States Southwest, the Spanish language is widely spoken, and Hispanic toponyms continue to be current as far as Montana and Oregon. In parts of the United States borderlands, land titles and water rights derive from original Spanish grants and surveys. Remnant mission buildings dot the landscape, and the Spanish heritage is still taken seriously in the twentieth century. The tradition embraces Old St. Augustine, Santa Fe, Capistrano, the Alamo, and other appealing elements of our folklore. It is obvious that borderlands culture has influenced our conception of all-Spanish America. But there were important differences between the northern frontier and the more developed parts of the Spanish colony, and it is for this reason, as well as because sections of the United States itself are involved, that we devote our final chapter to this subject.

We do not know who discovered Florida, Juan Ponce de León was the first Spaniard who sought to explore it, in part in response to Indian rumors of the legendary Fountain of Youth (1512–13). Ponce de León coasted Florida on both sides, returned for a second attempt in 1521, lost a number of men on both expeditions, and never established a true colony. Lucas Vásquez de Ayllón and others then explored the Atlantic coast from Florida northward, and in 1528 Pánfilo de Narváez landed on the Gulf coast and continued westward on makeshift rafts. In a famous exploit Núñez Cabeza de Vaca, a survivor of the Narváez expedition, found his way back to central Mexico by water and on foot. Subsequently Hernando de Soto landed in Florida and moved on to discover the Mississippi.[1]

Fifty years after Ponce de León, Florida remained unsettled. Missionary and other expeditions achieved only temporary footholds. Many Spaniards were killed in battles with Indians, and those who survived

Reprinted from *Spain in America*, pp. 182–201, including map on p. 184, by Charles Gibson. Reprinted by permission of Harper & Row, Publishers, Inc.

Charles Gibson is a Guggenheim Fellow. He received his doctorate in 1950 from Yale and served as chairman of the department of history at the University of Iowa from 1963 to 1965, and is now professor of history at the University of Michigan. He is the author of many books and articles on the colonial period in Mexico.

[1] Leonardo Olschki, "Ponce de León's Fountain of Youth: History of a Geographic Myth," *Hispanic American Historical Review*, XXI (1941), 361–385; Morris Bishop, *The Odyssey of Cabeza de Vaca* (New York, 1933); Edward Gaylord Bourne, *Spain in America, 1450–1580* (New York and London, 1904), pp. 159–168.

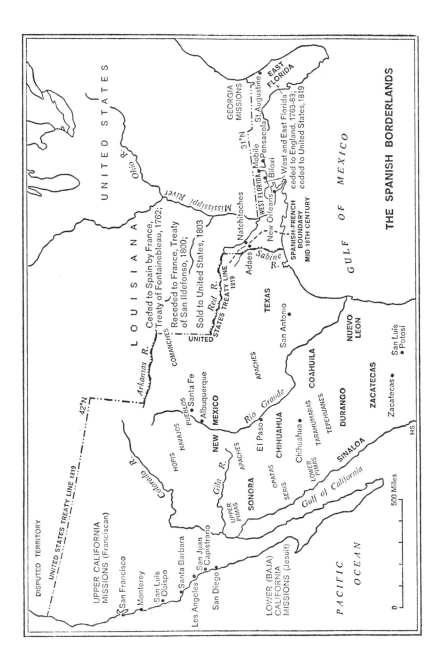

THE SPANISH BORDERLANDS

UNITED STATES

GEORGIA MISSIONS

EAST FLORIDA

St. Augustine

31°N

Mobile
Pensacola

WEST FLORIDA
Biloxi
New Orleans

West and East Florida
ceded to England, 1763-83;
ceded to United States, 1819

GULF OF MEXICO

SPANISH-FRENCH
BOUNDARY
MID 18TH CENTURY

Ohio R.

Mississippi River

Ceded to Spain by France,
Treaty of Fontainebleau, 1762;
Receded to France, Treaty
of San Ildefonso, 1800;
Sold to United States, 1803

Natchitoches

Adaes

Sabine
R.

Red R.

UNITED STATES TREATY LINE
1819

LOUISIANA

Arkansas R.

COMANCHES

TEXAS

San Antonio

APACHES

NUEVO
LEON

San Luis
Potosí

COAHUILA

ZACATECAS

42°N

UNITED STATES TREATY LINE 1819

DISPUTED TERRITORY

Santa Fe
PUEBLOS
Albuquerque
NEW MEXICO

NAVAJOS
HOPIS

Rio Grande

DURANGO

Zacatecas

Colorado R.

El Paso
APACHES

Gila R.

CHIHUAHUA

Chihuahua

TARAHUMARAS

TEPEHUANES

OPATAS

SERIS

LOWER
PIMAS

SINALOA

UPPER CALIFORNIA
MISSIONS (Franciscan)

San Francisco

Monterey

San Luis
Obispo

Santa Barbara
San Juan
Capistrano
Los Angeles
San Diego

UPPER
PIMAS

SONORA

Gulf of California

LOWER (BAJA)
CALIFORNIA
MISSIONS (Jesuit)

PACIFIC

OCEAN

500 Miles

0

HS

went westward or retreated southward. The outstanding failures of the midcentury period were those of Tristán de Luna y Orellano, most of whose fleet was destroyed by storms at Pensacola, and Angel de Villafañe, whose efforts to plant a colony on the Carolina coast were abandoned in 1561. Both these attempts were occasioned by fear that the French would occupy positions on the Florida coast from which attacks might be made upon Spanish shipping in the Bahama Channel.

It was an intensification of the French threat that finally brought about permanent Spanish settlement in Florida. In 1562 a Huguenot party under Jean Ribaut landed in the northern part of the peninsula and settled on an island off the coast of what is now South Carolina. Another party of Huguenots under René Laudonnière constructed Fort Caroline at the mouth of the St. Johns. In immediate response, Pedro Menéndez de Avilés established a Spanish colony in St. Augustine Bay and proceeded to wipe out the Fort Caroline settlers as intruders and Lutherans. (Spaniards frequently had trouble in distinguishing one Protestant group from another.) In 1565, Menéndez de Avilés founded St. Augustine, the earliest continuous settlement within the present limits of the United States, and a base from which Spanish missionaries created additional posts in Florida and Georgia. Further expansion northward was ultimately blocked by the English colonies in Virginia and South Carolina, and after the Georgia missions were abandoned the Spanish occupation came to be concentrated at St. Augustine and a few other nearby locations. In the later colonial period Florida was an impoverished military outpost, incapable of supporting itself by agriculture or the raising of stock, and dependent upon an annual royal subsidy irregularly paid.[2]

New Mexico, the other northern area occupied by Spain in the sixteenth century, was approached overland from the south. The original attraction was wealth, for Spaniards envisioned native civilizations here as lavish as those of the Aztec and Inca empires. Later the purpose became the propagation of the faith and the creation of a frontier mission society. What prompted the earliest colonists in Mexico to believe that rich cultures lay to the north is a historical mystery still unresolved. The fact in any case provides further demonstration of the impact of European myth upon minds predisposed to understand America in exotic terms. Cabeza de Vaca and several other survivors of the Narváez expedition to Florida, arriving back in Mexico City in 1536, gave currency to rumors that seven cities of great size and luxury were situated in the north. Fray Marcos de Niza, leading a party into or toward the Zuñi territory of western New Mexico in 1539, similarly issued exaggerated reports of what he had seen. Finally Coronado on his expedition of plunder and discovery in 1540–42 brought an end to the fanciful rumors and furnished more accurate and more prosaic descriptions of the peoples of the region.[3]

[2] Woodbury Lowery, *The Spanish Settlements within the Present Limits of the United States: Florida, 1562–1574* (New York and London, 1959); John Jay Te Paske, *The Governorship of Spanish Florida, 1700–1763* (Durham, N.C., 1964).

[3] Bourne, *Spain in America*, pp. 169–174; Herbert Eugene Bolton, *Coronado, Knight of Pueblos and Plains* (New York, 1949).

The missionary phase in New Mexico began in 1581, when the Franciscan friar Augustín Rodríguez set out on a campaign of conversion. This and a supporting party under Antonio de Espejo were preliminary to the major colonization movement of Juan de Oñate, who made the first foundations in 1598. Santa Fe, the capital, was founded about 1610.[4] Additional churches were built and new Spanish settlers entered the region in the seventeenth century. In 1680 the great Pueblo revolt forced the white residents to abandon the New Mexican settlements and to retreat to El Paso—one of the notable instances in colonial history of the reversal of an original conquest. Reoccupation took place after military invasion by Spanish soldiers in the 1690's,[5] and from this time on Spaniards preserved a durable, wary control.

Colonial expansion into Arizona and Baja California was for the most part a missionary movement. Baja California had been coasted as early as the 1530's under the direction of Cortés, but the move was premature from the point of view of permanent occupation, and it was not until the late sixteenth century that Jesuits entered the Sinaloa section of northern Mexico. Here also an element of myth intruded. Ignorance and delusion concerning this part of the coast persisted for a long time. "California is an island and not continental as it is represented to be on the maps," soberly declared Vázquez de Espinosa, one of the most informed colonial writers of the seventeenth century.[6]

The foremost pioneer in Arizona and Baja California was a remarkable Jesuit named Eusebio Francisco Kino. Born of Italian parents about 1644, educated in Austria, and sent as a Jesuit missionary to Mexico, Kino arrived in Pimería Alta in 1687. He founded the mission of Nuestra Señora de los Dolores and from there extended the mission frontier into Arizona to the Gila and Colorado rivers. By 1702 he had explored the Colorado from near Yuma to the Gulf of California. Repeatedly he crisscrossed the country between the Magdalena and the Gila.[7] Kino's reputation illustrates again the persistent regionalism of American history. Famous in Arizona, his name is frequently unrecognized in other parts of the country.

In the intermediate region between Florida and New Mexico, Spanish

[4] George P. Hammond and Agapito Rey, *Don Juan de Oñate, Colonizer of New Mexico, 1595–1628* (2 vols., Albuquerque, 1953); Lansing B. Bloom, "When Was Santa Fe Founded?" *New Mexico Historical Review*, IV (1929), 188–194.

[5] Charles W. Hackett, "The Revolt of the Pueblo Indians of New Mexico in 1680," *The Quarterly of the Texas State Historical Association*, XV (1911–12), 93–147; Charles W. Hackett, "The Retreat of the Spaniards from New Mexico in 1680, and the Beginnings of El Paso," *Southwestern Historical Quarterly*, XVI (1912–13), 137–168, 259–276; Charles W. Hackett and Charmion C. Shelby, *Revolt of the Pueblo Indians of New Mexico and Otermín's Attempted Reconquest, 1680–1682* (2 vols., Albuquerque, 1942).

[6] Antonio Vázquez de Espinosa, *Compendium and Description of the West Indies*, Charles Upson Clark, trans. (Washington, 1942), p. 189.

[7] Herbert Eugene Bolton, *Rim of Christendom: A Biography of Eusebio Francisco Kino, Pacific Coast Pioneer* (New York, 1936).

occupation took place in the late seventeenth and eighteenth centuries. In response to French and English settlement in the interior of North America, Spaniards moved both westward from Florida and northeastward from Mexico. The French explorers Joliet and Marquette descended the Mississippi to the Arkansas in 1673, and a decade later Robert Cavelier de la Salle planted a French colony at Matagorda Bay on the Texas coast. In the final years of the century, Pierre le Moyne d'Iberville was commissioned to found the colony of Louisiana on the Gulf of Mexico, and the prompt Spanish reaction was an expedition from Veracruz to establish a stronghold on Pensacola Bay. The French countered with a military fort at Biloxi and moved into Mobile Bay.[8] New Orleans was founded in 1718. The French briefly held Pensacola, and from their garrison at Natchitoches in Louisiana they threatened Texas, Coahuila, and New Mexico. The Spanish borderlands were thus cleanly split by the French in the early eighteenth century between an eastern flank in Florida and a western flank south and west of Texas.

The Spanish response to this new French incursion was to send missionaries and soldiers into east Texas. San Antonio and the Alamo mission were founded in 1718, contemporaneously with New Orleans. A Spanish movement from New Mexico extended as far as the North Platte River, in Nebraska or Wyoming, in search of the French enemy. Additional mission and garrison settlements were introduced into Texas, and the capital of the Spanish province of Texas was fixed at Los Adaes (now Robeline, Louisiana), only a few miles from Natchitoches. Toward the mid-eighteenth century Spain and France faced each other across the boundary of the Arroyo Hondo in Louisiana.[9] Though further French penetration westward was limited by Apache and Comanche tribes, occasional French explorers were able to enter New Mexico from the north.

French-Spanish confrontation in this interior zone was sharply changed by the Seven Years' War. The city of New Orleans and the huge territory of Louisiana, extending from the Gulf of Mexico indefinitely northward and bounded by the Mississippi on the east, were now formally recognized as Spanish possessions. Some local French resistance in New Orleans still had to be crushed, but the war brought an enormous territorial increment to northern New Spain and an effective elimination of the French frontier.[10] Instead of a divided Spanish colony penetrated by

[8] William Edward Dunn, *Spanish and French Rivalry in the Gulf Region of the United States, 1678–1702: The Beginnings of Texas and Pensacola* (Austin, Tex., 1917).

[9] Herbert Eugene Bolton, *Texas in the Middle Eighteenth Century: Studies in Spanish Colonial History and Administration* (Berkeley, 1915). The eastern boundary of Texas became the Sabine in 1819.

[10] Vicente Rodríguez Casado, *Primeros años de dominación española en la Luisiana* (Madrid, 1942); James Alexander Robertson, *Louisiana under the Rule of Spain, France, and the United States, 1785–1807: Social, Economic, and Political Conditions of the Territory represented in the Louisiana Purchase* (2 vols., Cleveland, 1911).

a French wedge on the lower Mississippi, there now emerged a solid Spanish territory to the west and a solid English territory, including Florida, to the east. Though England was to give back Florida in 1783, this new balance of power of the 1760's was to be the decisive one. It was hardly an equal balance. Spain was never able to fulfill the implications of 1763. The interior of North America remained Spanish in name only, and Spain was shortly to return Louisiana provisionally to France and to yield it permanently to the United States. The events of the late eighteenth century thus reveal the practical weakness of Spain's imperial position. A series of complex decisions opened the whole trans-Mississippi west to Spanish occupation, but Spanish physical and human resources were inadequate to the task.

Of all the northern lands available after 1763, only California was settled by Spanish colonists, and here it was not California as we know it but only the coastal strip from San Diego north to San Francisco. This last Spanish move in North America was the result in part of the continuing mission labors organized by Kino and in part of further foreign threats, for Russian traders were moving southward from Bering Strait, and English traders were moving westward from the Great Lakes and the Ohio. These were remote dangers, unlikely in themselves to provoke Spanish counteraction. In the 1760's, however, both the king and his energetic *visitador*, José de Gálvez, who was then conducting a survey and administrative reform in northern Mexico, interpreted the occasion as one requiring new colonization. While investigating Baja California, Gálvez formulated plans for joint occupation of Upper California by missionaries and soldiers, with San Diego and Monterey the principal points of occupation. After the Jesuit expulsion the missionary phase of the movement was entrusted to the Franciscan friar Junípero Serra, who set out for San Diego Bay in 1769. The garrison and mission of San Francisco were established in 1776, San José was founded in 1777, Santa Barbara in 1782. Some twenty California communities were founded during the "mission period" from 1769 to 1823.[11]

All borderland areas have been subjected to intense study. Our summary is a mere skimming of the enormous number of facts known about the region, for it is probable that no other part of colonial Spanish America has stimulated so extensive a program of research. That this is the case is due chiefly to the work of Herbert E. Bolton and his students, who have explored the archives with diligence and reconstructed the course of events in detail.[12] Local historical societies in the United States have done much more than their counterparts in Mexico to make information available. Bolton knew that the borderlands were not a typical or even an

[11] Herbert Ingram Priestley, *José de Gálvez, Visitor-General of New Spain (1765–1771)* (Berkeley, 1916), pp. 253–254; Zephyrin Engelhardt, *The Missions and Missionaries of California* (4 vols., San Francisco, 1908–15).

[12] Bolton was the successor of Hubert Howe Bancroft, who published some of the most thorough studies ever made of borderlands areas. But it was Bolton who first used and emphasized the term and who created the school of borderlands study.

important part of Spanish America.[13] His interest, like ours, depended heavily on the United States connection. But the differences do tell us something of the motives and methods of Spanish expansion elsewhere. At first glance it will seem strange that Spaniards found Florida so difficult to settle and that they took so long to move from central Mexico to California. Florida especially would seem an easy environment for European occupation. Its native inhabitants were sparsely settled, its climate was balmy, and it was far more accessible than the capitals of the Aztec and Inca empires. The apparent advantages, however, implied some of the most practical obstacles. Unlike central Mexico and central Peru, Florida and the other northern regions offered no great incentive. Spaniards needed people to dominate. The borderlands, with few exceptions, lacked wealth and organized civilizations. Their native societies were too loosely structured for Spain to incorporate readily into a functioning colonial organization.[14] Encomienda and *repartimiento,* while they were not entirely absent, never had the importance that they had in the south.[15]

Towns in the north were of smaller size and more distant from one another than the towns of central and southern Mexico. In the Valley of Mexico and its environs, aboriginal peoples were members of pre-existing communities, and they could be utilized in community form for Spanish purposes. In the north, Spaniards found settlements of this kind only in a few places, chiefly among the Pueblos of the Rio Grande and Colorado River region. In Sonora and Georgia and California and elsewhere, original Indian settlements were either far less compact and developed or totally nonexistent, and the Spaniards' task was one of creating settlements in the *reducción,* or mission, form. Tepehuanes and Tarahumaras and most other peoples of northern Mexico lived a half-sedentary, half-nomadic existence. Whether under religious or civil authority, a dominant effort of Spaniards in the north was to establish towns, and the success of Spanish relations with natives could be measured to a considerable degree in terms of town foundation. Spanish failures in controlling native peoples were most pronounced where Indians refused to submit to community life.

The most important towns from the ordinary secular Spanish viewpoint

[13] "With a vision limited by the Rio Grande, and noting that Spain's outposts within the area now embraced in the United States were slender, and that these fringes eventually fell into the hands of the Anglo-Americans, writers concluded that Spain did not really colonize, and that, after all, she failed. The fallacy came, of course, from mistaking the tail for the dog, and then leaving the dog out of the picture. The real Spanish America, the dog, lay between the Rio Grande and Buenos Aires. The part of the animal lying north of the Rio Grande was only the tail. Let us first glance at the dog." The quotation is from a paper by Bolton in 1929. See John Francis Bannon (ed.), *Bolton and the Spanish Borderlands* (Norman, Okla., 1964), pp. 32–64. The point is further developed in Howard F. Cline, "Imperial Perspectives on the Borderlands," in *Probing the American West, Papers from the Santa Fe Conference* (Santa Fe, 1962), pp. 168–174.

[14] Charles W. Arnade, "The Failure of Spanish Florida," *The Americas,* XVI (1959–60), 271–281.

[15] Encomiendas in the borderlands developed chiefly in the Rio Grande valley. For a summary, see Lansing B. Bloom, "The Vargas Encomienda," *New Mexico Historical Review,* XIV (1939), 366–417.

were the mining towns, particularly those in the central corridor north from Zacatecas. Here the dates of foundation reflect the steady movement northward: Zacatecas and Durango in the sixteenth century, Parral in the seventeenth century, Chihuahua in the early eighteenth century. The principal mining towns were also administrative and social centers, as well as markets and depots for supplies other than silver. Their layouts were in the familiar Spanish pattern, with plazas, official buildings, churches, and residential houses clustered around the central plaza. Their Indian inhabitants were laborers or servants in the homes of their Spanish masters. Indian or mestizo mine workers also occupied entire barrios, to which they were attracted by the prospect of wages, for a considerable part of the labor force was "free." A few of the upper Rio Grande towns —El Paso, Albuquerque, Sante Fe—were smaller versions of the towns of Northern Mexico.[16] But the chief economic motive for all northern expansion—mining—was conspicuously lacking in the areas that form part of the United States, and the momentum of town foundation accordingly slowed and eventually ceased altogether.

A distinctive type of Spanish frontier community, on the other hand, was the presidio, or garrison. The line of protective northern fortifications eventually extended across the entire continent from Florida to California. St. Augustine had the largest and most important fortification and the one with the longest tradition, but this came to an end in 1763 with the English occupation, and St. Augustine never regained its former importance for Spain. The Louisiana garrisons of the eighteenth century had the special function of protecting Spanish territory against the French. The characteristic presidios of the inland borderlands were those designed as outposts on the moving frontier for protection against the attacks of marauding Indians. The type first appeared in the sixteenth century, as a safeguard on the roads from Mexico City to Querétaro, Guanajuato, and Zacatecas. In the Chichimeca area of the central plateau, almost all presidios of the sixteenth century were still located south of the northernmost points of Spanish occupation. The chain of forts at this time ran in a northwesterly direction, and a main function of the soldiers was to escort travelers and silver trains from station to station.[17] But with the end of the Chichimeca War and with the more deliberate expansions of the seventeenth and eighteenth centuries, the presidio became a genuine frontier fortress. Presidios of northern Mexico and the United States borderlands were staffed by up to about sixty Spanish soldiers, living in or near small mud fortifications, and surrounded by their families, Indian

[16] France V. Scholes, "Civil Government and Society in New Mexico in the Seventeenth Century," New Mexico Historical Review, X (1935), 71–111; Edward H. Spicer, Cycles of Conquest: The Impact of Spain, Mexico and the United States on the Indians of the Southwest, 1533–1960 (Tucson, 1962), pp. 298–303.

[17] When they were added, new presidios were commonly introduced into the south rather than the far north. In the 1570's the new presidios were constructed on the roads to Panuco and Guadalajara, hundreds of miles south of Zacatecas, and the Chichimeca raiders were attacking farther to the south than ever before. Philip Wayne Powell, Soldiers, Indians, and Silver: The Northward Advance of New Spain, 1550–1600 (Berkeley and Los Angeles, 1952).

servants, and a miscellany of hangers-on. The soldiers were equipped with horses and firearms, with which they went out on punitive expeditions against unpacified Indian peoples. Indian soldiers frequently accompanied the Spaniards in forays against other Indians. In addition to their primary defense function, the soldiers were used as mail carriers, military escorts, police, and guards. Supplying the unproductive presidios was one of the principal administrative problems of the frontier.[18]

In the history of ranches and haciendas as in the history of towns and presidios, an essential pattern was that of expansion northward from southern and central Mexico. Settlement of the Chichimeca area allowed for an extension of cattle raising on a large scale. Fortunes made in mining were invested in land and animals, and the virgin land supported great herds. Single ranchers in some cases had a hundred thousand cows by the late sixteenth century. The immense grasslands of Zacatecas, Durango, and Nueva Vizcaya attracted not only ranchers but herds of wild cattle and horses, which increased so rapidly that they soon outdistanced humans. Herds roamed at will in the unfenced unsettled areas, occasionally invading frontier settlements as wild bands. Herding, horsemanship, the open ranges, the rodeo, the accouterments of silver, the "Charro" psychology, became permanent features of the area.[19]

The rodeo was a Mexican solution to the problem of unconfined animals. The Mexican rodeo has analogies in other parts of the world, but it probably developed independently and in any case it acquired special traits. The original rodeo, not at all the public display of skill in roping and riding that we now know, was literally a roundup, with mounted cowboys arranged in a circle large enough to surround the animals and to enclose them in a progressively smaller area. In the center, different brands were identified and allocations of unbranded animals were made among the owners. The rodeo left a permanent Spanish legacy in the cattle areas of the United States. Some of our most familiar terms—bronco (wild), lassoo (Sp. *lazo*), rodeo itself—are loan words. Others have been modified but can be readily traced to Spanish originals: chaps are *chaperejos*, protective leggings to guard against the chaparral scrub; lariat is *la reata*, the rope; buckaroo is the Anglo-American version of Spanish *vaquero*, or cowboy.

Indians also became raisers of cattle and horses. In the south in the sixteenth century Indians had taken to small-scale sheep farms, but few

[18] Oakah L. Jones, Jr., "Pueblo Indian Auxiliaries in New Mexico, 1763–1821," *New Mexico Historical Review*, XXXVII (1962), 81–109; Max L. Moorhead, "The Presidio Supply Problem of New Mexico in the Eighteenth Century," *New Mexico Historical Review*, XXXVI (1961), 210–229; Te Paske, *Governorship of Spanish Florida*.

[19] Donald D. Brand, "The Early History of the Range Cattle Industry in Northern Mexico," *Agricultural History*, XXXV (1961), 132–139, identifies the periods of cattle expansion and furnishes a map of the expanding cattle frontier. See also Richard J. Morrisey, "The Northward Expansion of Cattle Ranching in New Spain, 1550–1600," *Agricultural History*, XXV (1951), 115–121. There were some cattle ranches in Florida in the period from about 1655 to about 1702. They appear to have been permanently destroyed by English raids in the War of the Spanish Succession. See Charles W. Arnade, "Cattle Raising in Spanish Florida, 1513–1763," *Agricultural History*, XXXV (1961), 116–124.

raised horses or cattle. In the north the Yaquis and Tarahumaras and Pueblos and some other peoples adopted both sheep and cattle. They did so partly under missionary auspices, but partly also because the opportunities were greater, the herding areas larger, and the danger of damage to agriculture by feeding and trampling less. Among the Navajos and Apaches, remote from direct Spanish influence, these animals had far-reaching consequences. Navajo and Apache raiders attacked Spanish and other Indian settlements, taking sheep, cattle, and horses. Some Navajos in the eighteenth century became efficient sheepmen, raising their own herds and developing the techniques for making woolen blankets for which they are celebrated today.[20] The Apaches continued to be nomadic raiders, using their horses for quick attacks and getaways, and generally rejecting the kind of adaptation effected by the Navajo shepherds. On the other hand, the great difference in current reputation between the predatory, merciless Apaches and the gentle, blanket-weaving Navajos is largely a result of later adjustments and selective modern identification. These differences were much less pronounced in the eighteenth century, when both peoples lived by raiding. One of the ironies of borderlands history is that the Apaches were not originally a belligerent or aggressive people. Their raids were the outcome of colonial pressures and opportunities. They became aggressive after Spaniards introduced horses that they could ride and after Spaniards established communities, including Indian communities, that they could attack.[21]

The climactic institution of the borderlands, as everyone knows, was the religious mission. Differing, from the establishments of central and southern Mexico, the mission was appropriate to the frontier region, where, as Bolton observed, Indians "were hostile, had few crops, were unused to labor, had no fixed villages, would not stand still to be exploited, and were hardly worth the candle." [22] Accordingly, in addition to its religious function, the mission served secondarily some of the same objectives as the civilian town and the presidio. Justifications for new mission foundation were expressed in terms both of religious need and of strategic imperial expansion, and missionaries themselves argued the one purpose as well as the other. Both Texas and California had been looked to as mission fields long before the occupations of the eighteenth century; the ultimate timing, however, depending on an assessment of new imperial requirements.[23]

[20] This became an industry catering to a tourist market in the late nineteenth century. At about the same time the Navajos began to use imported, machine-made blankets in their own domestic life.

[21] Spicer, *Cycles of Conquest*, pp. 210–261; Jack D. Forbes, *Apache, Navaho, and Spaniard* (Norman, Okla., 1960).

[22] Bannon (ed.), *Bolton and the Spanish Borderlands*, p. 191.

[23] "It is seen every day that in missions where there are no soldiers there is no success, for the Indians, being children of fear, are more strongly appealed to by the glistening of the sword than by the voice of five missionaries." This is a missionary's statement of 1772, quoted in Bannon (ed.), *Bolton and the Spanish Borderlands*, p. 202. The combined religious-imperialist character of the mission is developed in Bolton's famous article, "The Mission as a Frontier Institution in the Spanish American Colonies," reprinted *ibid.*, pp. 187–211.

Ecclesiastical labor in the missions fell to Franciscans and Jesuits. Franciscans were the principal Spanish missionaries in Florida and Georgia, and they were present at the discovery of the Zacatecas lodes in 1546. Later they carried their labors into other regions of northern and northeastern Mexico—Coahuila, Nuevo León, Nuevo Santander, and the Concho region of Chihuahua—as well as into Texas. Franciscans accompanied the Oñate expedition of 1598 and maintained the New Mexico field continuously after this except for the period of rebellion in the late seventeenth century.[24] Franciscans also were the missionaries among the Pimas, in California, and in other places after the expulsion of the Jesuits.

The Jesuits received a favorable viceregal attention at a crucial time in the late sixteenth century, when the original Chichimeca hostilities were at an end and when the official policies of "pacification" were shifting from a military to a missionary emphasis. Jesuits came to central Mexico first in 1572, rapidly establishing their position and reputation as the most vigorous and disciplined of the missionary bodies. They were in Guanajuato by 1582 and in the San Luis Potosí area in 1592. Though they failed in Florida, they were preferred over the Franciscans by Viceroy Velasco and others on the northern frontier, and from the conclusion of the Chichimeca War until 1767 they dominated the labors in the north central plateau and in the Sinaloa area to the west. Conversion work among the Tepehuan, Tarahumara, Yaqui, Mayo, Pima, Opata, and Seri Indians of the northwest Mexican coast was exclusively a Jesuit undertaking, and it is probable that Jesuits rather than Franciscans would have been the missionaries of California but for the general Jesuit expulsion.[25] Thus although the Jesuits were the principal missionaries of the moving frontier in northern Mexico, a coincidence of causes assigned most of the borderlands of the present United States to the Franciscans.

Of the other two leading missionary bodies in south-central Mexico—Dominicans and Augustinians—neither was a major force in the Chichimeca country or the borderlands. Augustinians were in the Pame region east of Guanajuato and San Luis Potosí, but they did not move northward with the expanding frontier as Franciscans and Jesuits did. The Dominicans were critical of the Chichimeca War from the start, regarding it as the consequence of unwarranted Spanish aggression, and they played practically no role in the frontier movements until the late eighteenth century, when they were selected to substitute for the ejected Jesuits in Baja California.

Spaniards had always conceived of religious conversion in America as a broadly civilizing process, and on the northern frontier as elsewhere

[24] Maynard Geiger, *The Franciscan Conquest of Florida (1573–1618)* (Washington, 1937); John Tate Lanning, *The Spanish Missions of Georgia* (Chapel Hill, N.C., 1935); Powell, *Soldiers, Indians, and Silver,* p. 10; Spicer, *Cycles of Conquest,* pp. 157 ff.

[25] Powell, *Soldiers, Indians, and Silver,* pp. 192, 197, 209; Gerard Decorme, *La obra de los jesuítas mexicanos durante la época colonial, 1572–1767* (2 vols., Mexico, 1941); Peter M. Dunne, *Pioneer Black Robes on the West Coast* (Berkeley and Los Angeles, 1940); Peter M. Dunne, *Pioneer Jesuits in Northern Mexico* (Berkeley and Los Angeles, 1944), and *Early Jesuit Missions in Tarahumara* (Berkeley, 1948).

they aimed at a full social and cultural reorientation of native life. The difference was that on the frontiers Indians had much more to learn. Jesuits and Franciscans were active promoters of the *congregación*, in the belief, undoubtedly accurate, that without it religious conversion would have been impractical or impossible. Community life implied a reorganizing of the economy, and Indians accordingly were taught agriculture and stock raising and a variety of crafts. In some areas, as among the Pimas under Kino's direction, the mission cattle ranches advanced more rapidly than the missions themselves.[26] Franciscans in California developed elaborate economic complexes, the native inhabitants of which built aqueducts, dams, and reservoirs and cultivated gardens, grain fields, orchards, and vineyards. Indians constructed buildings, learned carpentry and masonry, operated gristmills, raised cattle and sheep, tanned hides, wove textiles, and made wine, shoes, soap, and candles, all under Franciscan supervision. Cattle raising was the foremost industry, and hides and tallow the principal sources of income. Not all the missions of the borderlands were so thoroughly involved in economic activities as were those in California. But labor, agriculture, construction, crafts, granaries, cattle, and orchards were features of the Franciscan foundations in Texas[27] and elsewhere, and it was chiefly in New Mexico that the ecclesiastics lacked official control over Indian economic life. Even in New Mexico, however, the friars taught stock raising and crafts, and everywhere in the borderlands they introduced plows, European plants and seeds, and new agricultural techniques in addition to Christianity.

Characteristically the congregated Indian houses were laid out in an orderly pattern within the mission confines. Surrounding the central quadrangle were the smith's shop, workshop, granary, tannery, and stables. The church was the largest building, dominating all others. This standard physical form was developed by Jesuits for northern Mexico and it achieved its culmination in the Franciscan establishments of California. In New Mexico, on the other hand, the tendency was to retain existing Indian communities intact, to build the churches on the edge of the settlements, and to divide Indian life between a town-oriented secular aspect and a church-oriented religious aspect.[28] These differences were less the result of differing preconceptions and philosophies among the religious bodies than of the nature of Indian societies. In New Mexico the Franciscans adapted their methods to sedentary Indian peoples. In California they dealt with natives who had no permanent communities, who knew neither agriculture nor pottery making, and who lived on acorns and whatever else they could gather.

Indians from the south were introduced on the frontiers as aides in these processes of civilization. They came as colonists, teachers, and

[26] Spicer, *Cycles of Conquest*, pp. 126, 131.

[27] Billie Persons, "Secular Life in the San Antonio Missions," *Southwestern Historical Quarterly*, LXII (1958–59), 45–62.

[28] It is perhaps relevant to observe that Pueblo society survived relatively intact to the twentieth century, whereas California Indian society disintegrated in the nineteenth century. There were of course other reasons for this in addition to the differences in mission form.

models, the purpose being to instruct by example in orderly social living, agriculture, and political officeholding. Tlaxcalans were used in this way at various locations in northern Mexico and Texas. Tarascans were moved north to Sonora, and Opatas from Sonora were moved to Arizona. Politically the mission communities came to be organized, as were Indian towns to the south, with offices of *gobernador, alcalde, regidor,* and *alguacil.* Indian officers were appointed by the missionaries or elected by the community. The full native community had judges and police, a *cabildo,* a jail, and other institutions for the maintenance of internal order, all under the supervision of Spaniards. But it should be added that these programs often lapsed, most missionaries had little understanding of the social organization of the peoples among whom they worked, and appointments to native office were sometimes made arbitrarily and thoughtlessly.[29]

In the north, more than in the center and south, the teaching of the Spanish language became an important part of the religious program. The particular problem was that many languages were spoken by a relatively small number of people. In the Valley of Mexico and its surrounding area, only a few languages were spoken, and a friar who learned one or two of these could communicate with thousands of converts. In the north, peoples only a few miles apart might speak mutually unintelligible languages. It was uneconomical, indeed it was impossible, for missionaries to learn all the languages and dialects of the borderlands. Jesuits were more successful in learning languages than were Franciscans and they took the obligation more seriously. But the common effort even among Jesuits was to teach Spanish to Indians. The result for a variety of reasons was only partially successful. The observation of a Franciscan friar in California suggests some of the limitations and frustrations: "They find it difficult to learn to speak Spanish at this Mission, since each year pagans arrive to become Christians and the greater number of these are old people. A suitable method to get them to talk Spanish is the one we follow, namely, we exhort and threaten them with punishment, and in the case of the young, we punish them from time to time. We do not know what reasons keep them from using Spanish." [30]

It is obvious that the religious and civil society of the borderlands contained many potentialities for strife. Conflicts between ecclesiastics and political authorities were common from the beginning. Civil governors sought to take Indians as laborers, to exact extralegal tribute from them, and to profit from them in other ways. Private *hacendados* and ranchers

---

[29] "Usually such appointments were made on the most meager knowledge of the groups. Indians who presented themselves as friendly and helpful to the Spaniards were given the appointments, often immediately with a cane as badge of office, and without any inquiry into the status of the individual in his group." Spicer, *Cycles of Conquest,* p. 390.

[30] Maynard Geiger (ed.), "Questionnaire of the Spanish Government in 1812 concerning the Native Culture of the California Mission Indians," *The Americas,* V (1948–49), 487. For a full summary of the mission language program and its effects in northern Mexico and the United States Southwest, see Spicer, *Cycles of Conquest,* pp. 422–430.

were always alert to the possibilities of sequestering Indians from the religious communities. Conflict with the garrison soldiers was also frequent. Royal administrators and civilian colonists repeatedly criticized the clergy for their severity with Indians, for their exploitation of native labor, and for their laxity in moral behavior, and missionaries in their turn criticized civilians and administrators with these same accusations.[31]

Disputes with outsiders were paralleled by internal tensions within the communities. No matter how benevolent and Christian, conversion was a program designed to impose European standards upon non-European peoples. The common attitude of the clergy was one of authoritarian paternalism, and in various degrees the regime that they imposed was maintained by force, with whipping posts, stocks, and prison cells. Missionaries disagreed among themselves concerning the degree of conformity required, and concerning the degree of compulsion necessary to achieve it. Sudden and arbitrary campaigns against residual pagan practices alternated with periods of toleration and leniency. One of the great strengths of Kino and one of the major reasons for his success was his tolerance of existing Indian practices. But it is obvious that no program could be too tolerant, for this would defeat the purpose and weaken the effort to substitute Christianity for paganism.

Indians responded to Christian life in complex ways. The writings of Franciscans and Jesuits refer repeatedly to the problems raised when Indians accepted some Spanish conditions but not all. The Christian program for individual conversion conflicted with Indian kinship organizations. The Christian concept of sin conflicted with Indian fertility concepts. These and many other differences tended to be understood by the clergy in European terms. Indians were "sly and crafty . . . hypocrites." They had "no diligence, or stability . . . nor capacity to understand the Christian mysteries." Particularly disturbing were the acts of withdrawal, when Christianized or apparently Christianized Indians without warning escaped the mission confines and fled back to their original society.[32]

At other times outright rebellion broke out. The Tepehuanes, the Tarahumaras, the Pueblos, and others rose in serious insurrections, looting and killing, blaspheming holy objects, and maintaining their resistance for long periods. Over a thousand Spaniards were killed in a Yaqui uprising of 1740. The Hopis, Christianized in the seventeenth century, became the most successful of the rebellious peoples, holding out against Spanish counterattack from the time of the New Mexico revolt in 1680 to the end of the colonial period. In California, with the Mexican secularization of 1833, the mission Indians defied the friars, slaughtered thousands of cattle, and fled.[33]

The outstanding differences between borderlands society and the

[31] Spicer, *Cycles of Conquest*, pp. 288–308.
[32] *Ibid.*, pp. 311, 313.
[33] Ray Allen Billington, *The Far Western Frontier, 1830–1860* (New York, 1956), pp. 7–8.

society of central Mexico and Peru were differences of degree and emphasis, and they depended more on Indian society than on Spanish. The fact suggests how sensitively Spaniards responded everywhere in America to the circumstances of native life. Where Indians could be a lower class Spaniards immediately became an aristocratic class, capable of developing the elaborate urban cultures of Mexico City and Lima. In northern Mexico, native peoples were less well equipped to perform this supporting role, and in so far as they could perform it the tendency of Spaniards was to concentrate Indian services in primary economic tasks, especially in the mining of silver. Undoubtedly if rich mines had been discovered in Texas or California, Spaniards would have been stimulated to far greater exertions in their manipulations of native peoples. Without this motive secondary objectives came into play: Christianization and civilization of Indians, resistance to imperial threats by foreign nations, and economic activities involving lesser commodities such as cattle. It should not be forgotten that the borderland was a frontier. What made it a frontier was precisely the reduced intensity of Spanish concern with it, and in this sense it paralleled other frontiers, such as southern Chile and southern Argentina, where Indians were sparse and hostile, and where Spaniards found no mines to work. Borderlands society was naturally selective and diluted in comparison with the central capital society, and all Spanish life in the north was appropriately provincial.

The Christian effort of the borderlands reminds us again that Christianity, though of less interest to many individuals, was an important element in Spanish imperialism. For particular missionary personalities the frontier was a challenge, the more so *because* its Indians were primitive or hostile. Neither the religious nor any other impulse was sufficient to promote expansion farther north, and this means that the Christian effort, like the secular, was defined and limited at fixed points. But the religious drive was strong in northwest Mexico and California, where missionaries were impelled to create wholly new societies, with adjunct economic and political and social institutions. The peculiar features of the frontier called forth and intensified this part of the Spanish purpose, which in the seventeenth and eighteenth centuries was one of self-sacrifice and spiritual values in excess of those of the south.

THE SPANISH PROGRAM

Edward H. Spicer

As they advanced into northwestern New Spain, the Spaniards planned to build towns, or *villas,* which would be centers of Spanish culture. In such towns would be the center of government, including a military garrison, the palace of the governor as the seat of Spanish administration, the homes of officials, the homes and shops of settlers who were engaged in trade and manufacture, warehouses, and churches, seminaries, and all the other structures necessary for the usual activities of a center of Spanish civilization. On the east side of the Sierra Madre Mountains towns were founded in succession as mines were located, the number of settlers increased, and the Indians were reduced. Zacatecas in 1546, Durango in 1563, Santa Barbara in 1567 (although only a mining centre rather than a political capital), Parral in 1631, and Chihuahua in 1709. Meanwhile, as a result of the Spanish thrust into New Mexico bypassing the steady advance in the south, Santa Fe had been set up about 1610, but its citizens were forced by the Pueblo Revolt in 1680 to move temporarily southward to El Paso. On the west a similar advance through Sinaloa took place, culminating in 1598 in the establishment of a presidio and the town of San Felipe y Santiago on the Sinaloa River, from which the reduction of Sonora proceeded. About 1720 San Juan Bautista became the capital town of Sonora and remained so until the seat of government was moved to Arispe in 1786.

Such towns were designed as places in which Spanish officials, civil and military, could live as fully as possible in the Spanish manner. From the late 1500's on, they were sometimes laid out, in accordance with royal directives, as grid-pattern towns with central plazas flanked by a large church, the governor's palace, and other governmental buildings, but often, as in the cases of Parral and San Juan Bautista where mining led to the founding of the town, the topography was such that streets could not be laid out at right angles, and the town followed the topography of the country, as was the case with most cities in Old Spain. None of the

Reprinted from *Cycles of Conquest,* by Edward H. Spicer, Tucson: The University of Arizona Press, copyright 1962.

Edward Spicer received his doctorate from the University of Chicago in 1939. Since then he has taught at the University of Arizona where he is now professor of anthropology. He has been a Guggenheim Fellow twice and a National Science Foundation Senior Fellow for his researches in Mexico. He was editor of the *American Anthropologist.* He is best known for *Cycles of Conquest,* from which the present selection was taken, his edited volume *Perspectives in American Indian Culture Change*; and his work on the Yaqui Indians of northern Mexico.

capitals grew to be larger than four or five thousand population during the Spanish period and most were smaller, including San Juan Bautista, Arispe, and Santa Fe. Unless they were the center of mining activities they did not draw much Indian population. Even if they were mining centers, like San Juan Bautista and Santa Barbara, the bulk of the Indian population was more or less transient. The Indians preferred to maintain their roots in their own villages, including the mission communities.

The capital towns thus became the places of residence of Spanish settlers, chiefly those employed in one way or another in governmental administration and others engaged in trade or mining. Indians went to them to purchase goods, but few Indian families settled there permanently. There was, nevertheless, a type of Indian town resident. In Santa Fe during the 1600's there was a whole barrio of several hundred people consisting of Indians brought by Oñate from Tlaxcala in central Mexico. In addition, the Spanish recruited Indians, by various means, as servants for their households and for common labor. Many of these in Santa Fe and Chihuahua and Sonora towns were Apaches, Navajos, Tobosos, or other non-missionized Indians captured in battles and indentured permanently. How many such servants, consisting chiefly of women and children, there were in any one town is not recorded, but over the whole region their number must have run into the thousands. In all of the towns there were also Indians from the reduced tribes who were serving sentence for crimes under the Spanish judicial system and who were put to work for the Spanish families for longer or shorter periods. There were probably also Indians who for various reasons left their home villages and took up residence voluntarily in the towns where they could get wages or find other means of support. Although many of the Spanish residents were regularly employed in trade or governmental activities, accounts also testify that each town had a considerable population of floating Spaniards who, after working in mines or at other occupations in various places in the frontier country, drifted to the towns to get work. Many of these were reported as mulattos and mestizos. They were most usually described as ignorant, superstitious, and lacking in industry. Efforts were made to control their movement in numbers into the frontier towns, but evidently with little success, despite the agreement of church and civil officials that they were undesirable and a bad influence on the Indians.

Under these circumstances the towns were composed of two groups: a heterogeneous and polyglot population of both Spanish and Indian derivation, and the families of the Spanish officials and the successful commercial men and mine contractors. The latter maintained a relatively high standard of living and occupied large and substantial houses. On the other hand, poverty-stricken Indians and Spaniards completely dependent on the wealthy group for their living and attached to them as servants or laborers lived apart in sharply contrasting circumstances. Many of the wealthier class were almost as transient, however, as the Indians, since officials appointed by the viceroy were frequently changed and, where mining existed, fortunes were made quickly or mines worked out, and those connected with them moved away. We must view the towns as very unstable communities, but in which there developed as the most permanent elements a poor class of racially-mixed people and impoverished Spanish families unable to move away.

The mining towns which did not serve as seats of government were for the most part very similar in character. A number of them, such as for example, Parral in Chihuahua and Alamos in Sonora, were situated in areas of minerals which were not quickly worked out and which consequently persisted throughout the Spanish period, growing into stable communities with considerable Spanish population. The towns of this character were few in number, but where they did develop they became the visible models of Spanish culture for the Indians. In them the Spanish class system with very great differences in living standards between rich and poor was strong. A sharp distinction was made between *gente de razon,* or upper class people of Spanish descent, and others of mixed blood, whether Indian and Spanish, Negro and Spanish, all three, or purely Indian. Only the gente de razon participated in the government and controlled the mines. Only the gente de razon had capital for the development of business enterprise. The intermarriage which took place between Indians and Spaniards involved only the poorer class of Spaniards, and except in the Opata country there was a very limited amount of this. What the Indians met with when they went to the towns was a Spanish way of life which excluded them except as servants and laborers. They encountered distinctions of dress and housing which left no doubt as to their not being encouraged to dress and live like the Spanish upper class. Moreover they encountered an attitude which held that the distinction between rich and poor was a permanent arrangement resting on the sacredness of "pure Spanish blood" and that therefore there was no expectation that Indians and mixed bloods would ever come to behave like wealthy Spaniards. They found an emphasis on rights by inheritance, on authoritarian government, and disrespect for labor with the hands. Very few Indians ever made any contact of course, with this aspect of Spanish culture, while thousands were directly influenced by the Spanish culture of the mission communities.

The mining towns were an especially important influence throughout Sonora. They existed widely through the Opata and Lower Pima country and were the scene of extensive and intensive contacts of those Indians with the Spaniards. We are told that contacts with Opatas were often on a basis of equality and that considerable intermarriage took place as a result.

Another type of Spanish settlement which became of increasing importance in Sonora during the Spanish period was the presidio. This was a military garrison of from thirty to fifty soldiers under a resident commander and subject to the direction of a civil authority. A presidio was composed of an adobe-walled fort, the houses of the soldiers and their families when they had any, and corrals for the horses which were an important part of the military equipment. Soldiers sometimes engaged in small ways in raising crops. Thus, a presidio was an outpost of Spanish culture, but an example of only a few selected aspects. In Sonora, companies of Opatas and Pimas sometimes lived for extended periods in the vicinity of the presidios, ready for campaigns against Apaches with the Spanish soldiers. There was probably a good deal of intermixture of the unattached soldiers with Indian women and some consequent marriages.

Outside of the mission communities, probably the most intimate contacts for the Indians were with Spanish settlers interested in farming or cattle raising. These took several different forms. In New Mexico along the upper Rio Grande Valley, where this kind of contact began immediately with the establishment of Oñate's colony in 1598, there were two types of settlement. Of greatest importance in the beginning were the encomienda grants to soldiers who had participated in the conquest of Mexico, who accompanied Oñate. These were sections of land given outright to individuals to exploit in any manner they could. The encomienda in the early 1600's included the right of repartimiento, that is to say, the right to employ (for compensation) Indians who were resident on the land granted. No encomiendas were granted in New Mexico which included the major pueblo settlements, but grants were made which did include some small settlements of Tewa Indians north of Santa Fe, some Tiwas south of Santa Fe, and many Piros and others north of El Paso on the lower Rio Grande. It was against the law for the person granted the encomienda to live on the land among the Indians, but this law was rather systematically ignored in New Mexico, especially in the Tewa country. New Mexican encomenderos forced Pueblo Indians to work for them, frequently with no, or very small, compensation and were reported to have disrupted the lives of villagers by interfering in their local affairs. Spanish employees of the encomenderos intermarried with Indians and gradually took over Indian lands. An early absorption of scattered Indian families took place up and down the Rio Grande Valley.

In addition, in New Mexico, another type of settlement by Spaniards influenced the Indians. This was the colony of settlers who were granted a piece of land as a village grant. Such settlements were frequently composed of ordinary soldiers who had served in the Mexican campaigns and were given a village grant in return for their service in assisting in the conquest. Some grants of this sort were made alongside existing Indian villages; others were made in uninhabited areas where irrigation was possible and there was land for grazing. At first there were some clashes with Indians over land rights and some Indians were driven away from their old settlements. But gradually peaceful relations prevailed and a great deal of intercourse and contact developed. Intermarriage took place, with Indian women going to live in the Spanish settlements and occasionally the reverse. In this way kinship relations developed between Spanish settlers and Indians and there was give and take on a basis quite different from anything that developed either in mission communities or Spanish towns. There was much cultural borrowing in craft techniques, food preparation, agriculture, language, curing, and many other aspects of culture, under conditions of equality. Here there was probably as much influence from the Indians on Spaniards as the reverse.

Similar situations developed in Sonora and Chihuahua. In these areas colonization took place more gradually than in New Mexico and at a time —the later 1600's—when the encomienda system was no longer in full operation. It took the form of more or less isolated ranches and farms, or haciendas, scattered widely along the edges of the Tarahumara country and through central and northern Sonora in the Opata and Pima country. There was also considerable development of haciendas in the Mayo country. The ranchers and farmers employed Indian labor, to some extent captives, whom they bought, but also voluntary laborers especially at harvest and planting time whom they paid in kind. Living in isolated places, the proprietors were forced to a greater extent than were the mining contractors or residents of Spanish towns to adjust their behavior to a standard which the Indians would accept without rebellion. Hence their ranches and farms were often the scene of peaceful relations and considerable diffusion of Spanish ways to the Indians. Missionaries sought to incorporate into their mission communities such Spanish settlers whenever possible and urged that ranches and haciendas be set up near the missions. Nevertheless Spanish ranchers and hacendados also brought on conflict with the Indians since they frequently, as was the case in New Mexico, appropriated land which Indians had been accustomed to use, and their herds disturbed either the settlements or the water supplies of the Indians.

The authorities in the Spanish towns supported what amounted to a fourfold program for the incorporation of Indians into Spanish society. Their program stood in contrast with that of the missionaries although of course the king required them to recognize the missionary program as essential and many were wholeheartedly convinced that it was essential. The missionary program might be summed up as an attempt to incorporate Indians into Spanish society through a gradual modification of Indian communities, through continuous teaching, demonstration, and instruction, through the acceptance of the missionary as a fatherly guide in the process, and through forcible imposition, when necessary, of church attendance and work routines. In contrast, the civil authorities urged incorporation through the organization of Indians into formal political units of Spain, the forcing of European work habits in mines and agricultural establishments run by Spaniards, the production of tribute, the distribution of tribal land to individual Indians, and the fusion of Spaniards and Indians through intermarriage and living together in the same communities. To say that all Spaniards who urged these measures were thinking in terms of a program of integration into the Spanish Empire, rather than in terms of their own private interests, would be absurd. Most civil authorities who urged the measures were thinking of their own personal interests or were responsive to the interested thinking of the mine contractors, settlers, and other Spanish inhabitants of the frontier. But the official justification of the measures, as expressed in reports of the viceroy's visitors, governors of provinces, and others who formulated official thinking, was that they were basic for the speedy and satisfactory incorporation, of Indians as full Spanish citizens into the Empire.

The effort to organize all Indian villages into formal governments resembling the local governments of Spain was of course official policy from the first in northern New Spain. It involved the appointment by a governor of a province of civil and military officials among the Indians of each village. Canes of office were distributed to such individuals after they had been picked out. They were then held to be responsible for maintaining peace, for enforcing discipline by whipping or use of stocks as the missionary or other official might require, and serving as a communication channel with the Spanish civil authority. There was variation over the region, but the general pattern was the following. Each village was supposed to have a governor as general civil head, a captain as military and police head, and sometimes alcaldes who served as judges. These appointees derived their authority from the Spaniards and were responsible to them. In New Mexico village councilmen (*regidores*) were also required who constituted a governing council of the village. Various kinds of titled assistants were introduced in different areas. Terms were for one year and elections by the village were permitted, although Spanish approval was required.

We have seen that it was frequently the practice for civil authorities to rely on missionaries to select and appoint governors and other village officials and that it was regular practice for the missionary to appoint his own group of church officials. Apparently few provincial governors or even Spanish alcaldes were in close enough touch with the whole group of villages under their jurisdictions to make or check the appointments. Consequently it fell to the missionaries, under delegation from the civil authority, to do this, a situation which must have served to link civil and ecclesiastical government in the minds of the Indians even more closely than they were linked in ideal Spanish practice. It also served to place the missionary in an advantageous position for getting cooperation between civil and church arms of the native government in his mission community. The governor and his associated officials, once appointed (or elected), were, however, under the supervision of the Spanish alcaldes who were the administrative executives set up by a Spanish governor within his province. There is little indication that any but the most fragmentary communication systems were set up during the Spanish period between Spanish and Indian governors. However, channels did exist and were used and the village governorship came to be, if nothing else, an established means of communication outside missionary channels, when Indians wished, between their villages and the Spanish officials. In New Mexico where tribute was required from the Eastern Pueblos, the Spanish authorities made continual use of the native governors and the staffs in collecting taxes. Where tribute was not established in Sonora and Chihuahua, relations between the native governors and Spanish civil authorities were at a minimum. But we may say that generally some degree of political incorporation was achieved through the establishment of this formal organization among the Indians.

The second feature of the civil program consisted of putting Indians to work as soon as possible in Spanish-controlled enterprises, rather than on their own farms. In New Mexico this was quickly done through either the encomienda or tribute system, much as it had been in central Mexico. The same abuses developed as had developed in Mexico, namely, forcing Indians to work to the extent of injuring their own personal interests. The encomienda system had to be curbed by law in New Mexico as it was elsewhere and was eliminated only after the disruption of many Tewa villages and the creation of much hostility against the Spaniards. Tribute likewise became a source of exploitation, causing New Mexico missionaries to bring many charges against New Mexico governors who forced Indians not only to provide the required tribute for the king but also to produce textiles, pinyon nuts, salt, and other goods for the governor's own private commerce. In Sonora and Chihuahua the major form of production within the Spanish economic system was the mining chiefly of silver and gold. No tribute was exacted in the usual form. By 1725 the exaction of tribute was strongly urged by Spanish Alcalde Mayor Manje of Sonora and by other citizens, but the Jesuits were able to prevent these recommendations from being put into effect. Subsequent recommendations by other representatives of the viceroy in the late 1700's seem to have been ignored, chiefly because of fear of arousing the hostility of Yaquis and other Indians who still remained peaceful in Apache-ridden Sonora. Although tribute was not employed as a means to get Indians to work on the European basis in the south, the mines offered the opportunity to put them to work. Labor was at a premium from 1600 on in Chihuahua and from the 1680's (after the founding of Alamos) in Sonora. Spanish migrants could not fill the demand. Hence in the Chihuahua mines of Parral, Santa Barbara, and the later ones, Indians were brought in by whatever means was possible. Hundreds of Tarahumaras were forced into the mines and either not paid at all or paid inadequately. Indians from Sinaloa and later from Sonora also came by the hundreds to the Chihuahua mines. As the Sonora mines developed, as at Ostimuri, Soyopa, Alamos, San Juan Bautista, and dozens of other places during the late 1600's, Indians from all the Sonora tribes, except the Seris and Apaches, also went to work in the mines. Abuses arose as usual—forcing Indians to work, nonpayment of wages, underpayment, delayed payment, and so on. The only recourse which Indians had under the Spanish system was to tell the missionaries who could protest to the civil administration, to hide far away from any recruiting parties, or finally to revolt. All such methods were employed, with the result that abuses seem to have been considerably reduced by the mid-1700's, so that a more or less steady supply of voluntary Indian labor, to a large extent in the form of Yaqui migrants, was increasingly available, in both Chihuahua and Sonora. One is tempted to say that European work habits—a daily unit of labor for a fixed unit of pay—were successfully established only among Yaquis, and possibly the Opatas. The Spaniards spoke of Yaquis as consistent and able workmen in the mines in the early 1700's and had lesser praise for Opata work habits, but no reports by Spaniards (after a few early ones) indicate that the Tarahumaras or any other northern Indians satisfied their standards. The incorporation by work seems thus to have been only partially successful.

The third point in the civil authorities' program was the distribution of land to individual Indians. It had been generally assumed at first that this would be possible any time after the ten-year period of exemption from taxation. As we have seen, it never quite took place anywhere in northwestern New Spain. It began to be urged throughout Sonora, partly as a measure for breaking tribal solidarity of such groups as the Yaquis, as early as the 1760's. It was urged repeatedly thereafter at various times during the Spanish period, and steps were taken among the Yaquis and some others. However, very little Indian land was actually deeded by title to Indians, although a good deal was deeded to Spaniards. The pressures by Spaniards who wanted to acquire the rich lands surrounding Indian villages, such as those on the Mayo, Yaqui, and Sonora rivers was very great. But the process of acquiring the land was never fully legalized by a general land allotment during the Spanish period. Consequently the taking up of Indian lands by Spaniards had to proceed by squatting or illegal methods. Grants to whole Indian villages were made in New Mexico, and a few titles were given to individuals, but in the main this procedure for incorporation was blocked by a sort of passive resistance on the part of the various Indian groups, no doubt stimulated by the methods of corporate land management employed by the missionaries in the mission communities.

The fourth feature of the civil program of integration was also largely blocked—due partly to the difficult character of the environment in the northwest. Colonization was slow from the very start and consequently fusion of peoples either biologically or culturally was retarded. The first colonists to New Mexico turned around within two years and went back home; by the beginning of the 1800's there were only five Spanish towns of over 1000 population and the total non-Indian population was only about eighteen thousand. Towns grew rapidly in eastern Chihuahua where mines were rich, but these were outside the Tarahumara country and resulted in the incorporation of only a very small part of the tribe into an assimilated population. Settlement of Spaniards was slow in starting in Sonora and after fifty years it became so difficult to survive in the face of the Apache raids that the Spanish population began a steady shrinkage rather than increase. Throughout the 1700's reports of visitors and others continued to urge that colonization by a "desirable type of

Spaniard" be pushed. However, settlers could not be attracted to a country in which mines were petering out, Indians were raiding unrestrainedly, and most agricultural development was carried out against considerable odds.

The Conflicts in Spanish Culture

The two major instruments of cultural change on the northwestern frontier—the mission community and the Spanish settlement—were deeply at odds with one another. Conceived as being complementary by the policy makers, they turned out to be increasingly in conflict. The heart of the conflict lay in the fact that the missionaries conceived of a transitional institution, the self-sufficient agricultural community, as a necessary vehicle for bringing Indians into Spanish civilization while the civil administrators wanted prompt and direct integration of Indians into Spanish-type communities.

Granting the need for a transitional phase, the king agreed at first to the ten-year period for missionary work. This turned out to be all too short from the missionary's point of view, although it is not precisely clear what standard of measurement missionaries were using when they urged extensions and held that even Indians who had been under the mission system for forty or fifty years were still not ready for taxation and other forms of participation in the Spanish program. The fact is that the ten-year period of grace did provide sufficient time in most cases for laying the foundations of the corporate communities which the missionaries had in mind. Such communities were created by the dozens in Sonora, and missionaries felt a great stake in maintaining them as they were. In them there was no individual ownership of land, there was no explicit taxation although Indians worked for the mission, there was no clear political integration with Spain, there was no development of Indians as individual wage laborers, there was no obliteration of the Indian as Indian through fusion with the Spaniard; there was, in short, not the sort of situation which made a Spanish alcalde feel that he could go to an Indian village, give an order, and have it understood in a way that would get action immediately to satisfy his superior, the provincial governor. The mission communities were not Spanish political units articulated effectively with the provincial government.

To non-clerical Spaniards generally in Sonora by the end of the 1600's, the practical isolation of the mission communities from Spanish economic life under control of the missionaries was insupportable. They wanted labor which could be employed according to whatever conditions the employers set up. Many wanted land, and Indians were living on the best farm and range land. These Spaniards didn't want to be bothered with what were, to them, alien communities of people with different ways of doing things. In their way stood the mission communities with the missionaries constituting a phalanx of defense, a phalanx whose leaders had the ear of the viceroy. So the two branches of the Spanish government moved into sharper and sharper competition for Indian labor, Indian land, Indian produce, Indian minds, and Indian loyalty.

The missionaries, on the other hand, had developed their interests effectively in the mission communities. Each lived in a little kingdom where he was the authority. He had the ear of the Indians. He had made progress in his teaching and in his building of churches. The life of the mission community, focused on God and spiritual things as defined by the missionary, was a thing apart physically and culturally from the Spanish town. The latter was full of undesirables, as missionaries never tired of pointing out, misfits and failures and drifters without moral foundations, family ties, or spiritual interests. Some Jesuit missionaires in Sonora hesitated to teach the Spanish language to their Indians, because as a later Jesuit historian put it, summing up their views, "If [knowledge of the Spanish language] favored public prosperity and the fusion of races, it was certainly also to the injury of the intellectual, moral, and religious interests of the poor Indians." He referred here to the detribalized and wandering Indians who began to appear in the 1700's as hangers-on around the Spanish mining settlements, poverty-stricken and often demoralized. To distribute the land to individuals, to permit the abuses of labor exploitation, to require regular tribute, to encourage Indians to mingle with the riffraff of the frontier settlements would indeed break up the little kingdoms of God, for in the missionary view the errors of lack of understanding rife in the mission populations were as nothing to the errors of commission to be learned from a disorganized Spanish lower class in a frontier town.

Thus the missionaries held on as long as they could against the breakup of their communities and looked toward secularization as the destruction of much of their work. Eventually, with the expulsion of the Jesuits, the entering wedge for the secular program was provided. The mission communities disintegrated; a new era for Indians began with the assumption of responsibility for the Spanish program by the civil authorities. The conflict in Spanish society between the values of the missionary Orders and those of the political hierarchy was apparently solved.

The Creation of Modern Aztlán

THE SECESSION OF TEXAS

Henry B. Parkes

Prior to 1823 there had been, at the most, three thousand white people in Texas. Otherwise its undulating prairies and richly wooded river valleys—a territory as large as France, with a soil as fertile as any in America—had been left to the savage Comanche Indians, who lived in the mountains of the interior, and to the buffalo and the mustang. Sooner or later it was inevitable that the land-hunger of the Anglo-Saxons—that insatiable expansive force which in less than a century was to people the three thousand miles between the Alleghanies and the Pacific—should be attracted into this inviting vacuum.

After the establishment of the Mexican Republic a native of Connecticut, Stephen Austin, had visited the City of Mexico and obtained a grant of land in Texas and the right to people it with colonists. Similar grants were afterwards made to fifteen other *impresarios*. The settlers were to pay only a nominal price for their land but were to assume all the responsibilities of Mexican citizenship. Such colonies, the Mexican federalists believed, would act as a barrier against annexation by the United States. The offer of cheap land was attractive; and equally attractive was the possibility of escaping from creditors. Within ten years Texas had a white population of from twenty to thirty thousand, in addition to a number of negro slaves who had been imported for work on the cotton fields.

Friction between the two races soon developed. The Americans found

Reprinted from A History of Mexico, pp. 200–221, by Henry B. Parkes. Copyright © 1938, 1950, 1960 by Henry B. Parkes. Reprinted by permission of the publisher, Houghton Mifflin Company.

Professor Parkes received his B.A. from Oxford in 1927 and his doctorate from the University of Michigan in 1929. Since 1949 he has been professor of American intellectual history at New York University.

themselves a part of the Mexican State of Coahuila; they were deprived of trial by jury and the English common law, and their foreign trade was hampered by the scarcity of licensed seaports. Austin respected his duties to his adopted country with a Puritan conscientiousness, but the other *impresarios* were often blunt and aggressive frontiersmen who soon grew impatient with the inefficiency and the dilatory habits of the Mexican officials. When, in 1826, one of them was expelled as a result of controversy about conflicting land claims, his followers rebelled; thirty men paraded through the town of Nagodoches, carrying a red and white flag and proclaiming the independent republic of Fredonia. Upon the arrival of a Mexican army they hurried across the frontier without fighting; but the result was to cause a change in Mexican policy.

When the Mexican authorities studied the situation, they began to regret their blindness in admitting the Anglo-Saxons. Instead of being a barrier to American expansion, the colonies in Texas seemed likely to be its advance guard. For thirty years outlying provinces of the old Spanish Empire had been dropping like ripe fruit into the lap of the United States. The enormous acquisition of Louisiana, followed in 1819 by that of Florida, had merely whetted the appetite of these agrarian imperialists. Joel Poinsett had already endeavoured to purchase Texas, and many Americans were known to regard the territory as rightfully theirs. If the Anglo-Saxons were to absorb Texas, other provinces would follow, and Mexico would be devoured piecemeal. These fears were carefully encouraged by H. G. Ward,[1] who regarded American expansion as a menace to British interests in the Caribbean; and in 1828, by Ward's advice, the former insurgent leader, Mier y Terán, was sent to Texas on a mission of inspection. Mier y Terán recommended that the growth of American influence should immediately be checked.

In 1829 Vicente Guerrero issued a decree for the abolition of slavery. Slavery scarcely existed in Mexico outside Texas, and his primary purpose was to discourage American immigration. Mier y Terán reported, however, that the decree could not be enforced. The next year Lucas Alamán secured the adoption of more drastic measures. On April 6, 1830, it was decreed that no more colonists should be admitted from the United States and that customs duties should be collected along the Louisiana frontier; and Mier y Terán was provided with troops with which to enforce obedience. The duties were a serious burden to the colonists, and the high-handed methods by which Mexican officials endeavoured to prevent smuggling caused a series of riots. By 1832 the Americans were on the verge of rebellion.

When Santa Anna pronounced against Bustamante it occurred to the worried and law-abiding Austin that the activities of the Texans could be passed off as a liberal protest against centralism. A liberal general visited the territory, discovered that its inhabitants were loyal adherents of Santa

[1] H. G. Ward was the British chargé d'affaire in Mexico at this time.—*Eds.*

Anna, collected the troops, and marched them back into Mexico to participate in the revolution. The Texans then organized a convention, at which they asked for the repeal of the Law of 1830 and for separation from Coahuila; and Austin went to the City of Mexico to state their case to the new government. He was unable to persuade Gómez Farías to allow the Texans to govern themselves as a separate state; and when, in a fit of depression, he wrote a letter recommending his friends in Texas to establish a state legislature in defiance of the government, he was put in prison, and not released for eighteen months. Meanwhile the Law of 1830 was not being enforced, and American immigrants were again pouring into the country. Mier y Terán, apparently driven to despair, had committed suicide.

When Santa Anna assumed dictatorial powers, he sent an army under General Cos to Texas, with instructions to enforce obedience to the law and to collect the customs. Lorenzo de Zavala, flying from the wrath of Santa Anna, brought the news to Texas; and the Texans, still professing to be Mexican federalists, resolved to defend themselves. In December, 1835, Cos and his army were besieged in San Antonio, and after five days of street fighting—the Mexicans shooting from the tops of houses, and the Texans breaking through the adobe walls with battering rams—he was driven across the Rio Grande. Meanwhile Santa Anna, hoping to crush the rebellion and afterwards to return in triumph to the capital and take over the presidency from Barragán, was marching northwards across the deserts of Coahuila. His Indian conscripts, badly equipped by grafting contractors in whose profits Santa Anna had shared, exposed alternately to blazing sunlight and to freezing January nights, deserted or died of exposure by scores; but Santa Anna pressed forward implacably.

He found the Texans unprepared for resistance. Among the motley array of freedom-loving farmers and ambitious adventurers from across the American border who had congregated at San Antonio, there had been no agreement on common action. Some had pushed forward for an invasion of Tamaulipas, others were returning to their homes. For a period the commander-in-chief was changed almost daily. Austin had been despatched to Washington to ask for help from President Andrew Jackson. In February, when Santa Anna reached San Antonio with an army of three thousand, he found only one hundred and fifty Texans, commanded by William Barrett Travis, holding the old mission building of the Alamo. Travis refused to surrender and, after he had been besieged for two weeks, the Mexican trumpets sounded the *deguello*—the notes of which dated back to the Moorish wars in Spain and which meant "no quarter"—and the Alamo was taken by storm and all its defenders slaughtered.

A few days previously a convention at Washington-on-the-Brazos, two hundred miles to the east of San Antonio, had drafted a declaration of Texan independence, named David Burnet provisional president of the new republic and Lorenzo de Zavala vice-president,[2] and found its military leader in Sam Houston. Houston, six feet two inches tall and broad in proportion, with a taste for liquor and for magniloquent oratory, was a character out of Homer. A friend and disciple of Andrew Jackson, he had abruptly ended a political career by separating from his wife for reasons never divulged, had consoled himself by becoming an Indian chieftain among the Cherokees—who had given him the sobriquet of "Big Drunk" —and had recently entered Texas with the intention of redeeming his ruined fortunes by leading the movement for independence. In his sober intervals he was capable of a sagacity and a power of command such as the Texans sorely needed.

Houston ordered retreat; and for the next month, under heavy spring rains, the entire population of Texas was flying eastwards in a miserable confusion, among them the army of seven or eight hundred who constituted the last hope of the infant republic. Behind them the Mexicans in four squadrons were beating up the country, confident that all resistance was at an end. Hearing that the provisional government was at Harrisburg, at the mouth of the river San Jacinto, Santa Anna pushed on rapidly with the pick of his army. But the government had taken ship to Galveston, so Santa Anna turned northwards to find a ford, and at Lynchburg Ferry he found Houston waiting for him, encamped on the edge of an oak forest. For twenty-four hours the two armies faced each other across a stretch of prairie, and finally, on the afternoon of April 21, Houston ordered an attack. Santa Anna, after throwing up breastworks, had neglected the most elementary precautions. His men were cooking their dinner, and their commander was enjoying a siesta. With a shout of "Remember the Alamo!" the Texans stormed the breastworks and slaughtered six hundred of the Mexicans, while the remainder were rounded up by Santa Anna's second-in-command, Colonel Almonte, and surrendered. Santa Anna himself fled during the battle, and was captured the next day hiding in some long grass and dressed in a blue shirt, white pants, and red carpet slippers.

The battle of San Jacinto ended the war but did not settle the status of Texas. Santa Anna was willing to promise anything in return for freedom; but he was disavowed by the Mexican Government, which made no attempt to reconquer Texas but refused to recognize its independence. There were disappointments for the Texans also in the United States. They had been hoping to guarantee themselves against attack by securing admission into the American Union; but opposition had developed in the northern states, where it had been decided that the whole episode was a slave-owners' plot to filch slave soil from a freedom-loving republic—an interpretation which had been invented by Almonte and imparted by him to abolitionists who had visited Mexico. Andrew Jackson was personally sympathetic, but he was also thinking of the next election, so he

---

[2] Zavala died the following year, generally regarded in Mexico—then and since—as a traitor.

maintained a most correct neutrality. Santa Anna was finally despatched to Washington to support the claims of Texas, his captors having decided that it would not be in keeping with the dignity of the new republic to have him shot; and after futile discussions Jackson put him on board an American warship and restored him to Mexico.

So the Lone Star Republic was to remain a republic. In 1838 a new president was to be elected, and since the two leading candidates both committed suicide—one by jumping off a boat and the other with a gun— the honor fell to Mirabeau Bonaparte Lamar, whose ambitions, but not his abilities, were worthy of his name. The most conspicuous result of Mirabeau Bonaparte Lamar's attempts to make Texas into a great nation was that the Texan dollar depreciated to a value of three cents. In an effort to redeem the financial fortunes of his government he sent a raiding party to Santa Fe, hoping to seize control of the caravan trade between Chihuahua and St. Louis. The party reached Santa Fe in a state of starvation, capitulated to the Mexican authorities, and was sent in chains to the City of Mexico. The Mexicans retaliated by raiding San Antonio. A Texan army then invaded Tamaulipas, was forced to surrender, escaped into the mountains, and after wandering for weeks without food was duly recaptured; to prevent further escapes, every tenth man was shot and the remainder imprisoned. These hostilities destroyed whatever chance there might otherwise have been of Mexican acceptance of the loss of Texas.

The Centralist Republic

When Santa Anna returned to Mexico he found that his willingness to barter Texan independence for his personal freedom was common knowledge. Unable to regain the presidency, he retired to Manga de Clavo. The conservatives were now firmly in possession of the central government, and in December, 1836, they imposed a new constitution which abolished the liberties of the states and provided for property qualifications for voting. Barragán having died, they could think of no more suitable president than Anastasio Bustamante, who was brought back from his exile in Great Britain and, in April, 1837, replaced in the president's palace.

It was not long before Santa Anna was again in the public eye. Several foreign nations had claims against Mexico for losses suffered by their citizens during the sack of the Parian market in 1828 and subsequent disturbances; and though the Mexican Government might admit its liability, it was in no position to meet it. In 1838 a French fleet appeared off Vera Cruz, demanding payment of claims valued at six hundred thousand pesos. The Mexicans, with their usual love for sarcasm, dubbed this episode the Pastry War: one of the claims was that of a French pastrycook whose restaurant at Tacubaya had been wrecked by some Mexican officers who had dined too well. The French bombarded the fortress of San Juan de

Uloa, which had been considered impregnable two hundred years before and which was supposed in Mexico to be still impregnable; unfortunately artillery had in the interim become more powerful, and the fortress capitulated. The Mexican Government promptly declared war on France, and the *léperos,* somewhat vague as to the nationality of the invaders, raised a shout of "Down with the Jews!" which they subsequently changed to "Down with the Saxons!" Santa Anna, meanwhile, had been summoned to Vera Cruz to give his advice, and had proceeded to assume the command. Early one morning the French raided the city, nearly capturing Santa Anna, who escaped in his underwear; later in the day, when the French were returning to San Juan, he reappeared at the head of his troops, and a cannon ball, fired from one of the French ships, shot away his leg. This occurrence proved to be very fortunate for Santa Anna. In his despatches to the government he explained that he had repulsed the French and that his life was in danger, but that he would die happy in the knowledge that he had consecrated his blood to his country. Having secured a guarantee of their six hundred thousand the French returned to France, and Santa Anna was again a popular hero.

Nevertheless Bustamante succeeded in holding office for four years, chiefly because the difficulties of the government were so insuperable that no other conservative chieftain wanted the presidency. The financial crisis was now chronic, and the annual deficit was rarely less than twelve million pesos. Savage Indian tribes from the mountains of Sonora and Chihuahua had discovered that the rule of the Republic was very different from that of the viceroys, and were raiding creole settlements. Yucatán, under a liberal government, was virtually independent; and liberal chieftains in the northern states were talking of secession. Gómez Farías, in exile at New Orleans, watched events, and in 1840 he returned to head a liberal rising in the City of Mexico. For eleven days there was fighting through the streets; and though the combatants did little harm to each other, cannon balls, hurtling at random about the city, killed a number of civilians. Eventually the news that Santa Anna was on his way, proposing to act as mediator, frightened both parties into an agreement. The liberal chiefs were given safe-conducts, and returned into exile.

Men of intelligence were beginning to despair. The whole country seemed to be disintegrating into anarchy, and the inevitable end seemed to be a gradual annexation by the United States. Memories of Revilla Gigedo and the greatest of the viceroys grew popular, and many began to declare that Mexico ought never to have revolted from Spain. But when there were actual proposals to import a monarch from Europe, there was an outburst of indignation. A Yucatecan congressman, Gutiérrez de Estrada, who had declared that a foreign king would regenerate the country, was compelled to go into hiding. Estrada did not, however, abandon his faith in the virtues of royal blood; twenty years later—an exile in Europe—he was to find ears which were only too receptive.

The army chiefs decided finally that it was time to replace Bustamante

by somebody who would be more efficient in extracting taxes. In 1841
there occurred the most cynical, the most wholly unprincipled, of all
Mexico's revolutions. Paredes, the commandant at Guadalajara, raised
the standard of revolt, and was joined by Santa Anna and by Valencia,
who a few months before had compared Bustamante's suppression of the
liberals to God's creation of the world. The three generals with their followers met in council at Tacubaya, and then bombarded the City of
Mexico for a week. Bustamante, driven to his last resource, turned liberal
and called for a restoration of the constitution of 1824. When this extraordinary *volte-face* failed to win support, he retired into exile. Santa
Anna drove into the city in triumph behind four white horses and
assumed dictatorial powers. Next year a new congress was elected, which
proved to contain a *moderado* majority; so Santa Anna retired to Manga
de Clavo, leaving the invidious task of dissolving it to the man who had
once been the lieutenant of Morelos, Nicolás Bravo. Bravo nominated a
Junta of Notables, which in 1843 produced another new constitution, under which the president was to be virtually a dictator. Santa Anna was
then elected president.

As dictator Santa Anna had ample opportunity to appear in his
Napoleonic rôle and to display the various facets of his richly disharmoni-
ous character. He proved to be remarkably energetic in collecting money.
By exacting forced loans from the Church, by increasing import duties
twenty per cent, and by selling mining concessions to the English, he
raised a revenue twice as large as his predecessor's. These new resources
were then distributed where they would prove most useful; thousands of
new officers were added to the army payroll, and the government contractors found it easy to make fortunes. Santa Anna's amputated leg was
disinterred from its grave at Manga de Clavo and solemnly reburied in
the cathedral. His statue was erected in the plaza, with one hand pointing
towards Texas, which he was still promising to reconquer—though it was
remarked that it also appeared to be pointing towards the mint. A new
theatre, *El Gran Teatro de Santa Anna*, was built and was proclaimed to
be, with one exception, the largest in the world. When the wife of the
dictator was seized with a mortal sickness, a parade of twenty thousand
persons, headed by the archbishop, carried the host to her deathbed.[3]
Santa Anna himself, like Napoleon, wore simple clothes, as though dis-
dainful of personal display, and endeavored to add to their effect by
clothing his staff in scarlet uniforms; when he dined in state six colonels
stood behind his chair, and when he sat in his box at the theatre a glitter-
ing array of generals sat beside him. Those admitted to his intimacy found
the same courteous manners as before, the same melancholy expression,
the same professions of zeal for the greatness of Mexico, and the same
capacity for occasional acts of generosity.

Meanwhile, the taxable potentialities of the country were diminishing,

---

[3] A month later, however, the dictator was remarried—to a girl of fifteen.

and army officers were beginning to grumble that their salaries were overdue. In 1844 Paredes revolted; and when Santa Anna marched against him, a popular insurrection in the City of Mexico restored Gómez Pedraza and the *moderados* to power, a mild but honest general, José Joaquin Herrera, becoming president. The *léperos* celebrated the occasion by digging up Santa Anna's leg and trailing it through the streets on a string, and cast lots for the privilege of overthrowing his statue. Defeated by Paredes, Santa Anna fled into the mountains of Vera Cruz. There, according to legend, he was captured by cannibalistic Indians and was on the point of being eaten when he was rescued by government troops. He was finally allowed to retire to Havana with instructions not to return for ten years.

Herrera remained in office for a year. Finally his apparent willingness to negotiate with President Polk about the status of Texas, which had been annexed to the United States early in 1845, gave the conservatives an excuse to overthrow him. In January, 1846, Paredes marched on the City of Mexico, while Herrera and the entire body of his supporters fled from the city in a single coach. Paredes governed with energy, but having seized power as the spokesman of Mexican national pride, he found himself confronted with the impossible task of fighting a war against the United States.

The War with the United States

For a quarter of a century there had been antagonism between the United States and Mexico. Americans were contemptuous of a republic which could not maintain order, and were in the habit of predicting that it would be the destiny of their country to extend its beneficent rule over the entire continent. Mexicans feared the expansive tendencies of the Anglo-Saxons, and did not distinguish between the speeches of American citizens and the policies of American governments.

American citizens resident in Mexico had lost property through revolutionary disturbances or military confiscations; and finding no redress in Mexican law courts, had appealed to their own government. After peaceful remonstrances had produced no result, the United States had threatened war, and Mexico had then agreed to submit the claims to arbitration. An international court had rejected three quarters of them as illegitimate and had, in 1841, given an award of about two million dollars against Mexico on account of the remainder. Mexico had paid three instalments of this debt and had then defaulted.

More serious was the problem of Texas. Mexicans were apt to regard the Texan rebellion as part of a deliberate plan of expansion concocted by the United States Government, and believed that the loss of Texas would be followed by that of other provinces. Santa Anna, instead of recognizing Texan independence and taking steps to defend the adjacent territories, had aroused public opinion by constant threats of reconquest. This had alarmed the Texans, and since the United States had refused to protect them they turned for assistance to Great Britain. The possibility that Texas might become a British sphere of influence caused alarm in the United States; the opposition of the Northerners to the entry into the Union of another slave state was weakened; and early in 1845 Congress agreed to annexation. Herrera, meanwhile, had consented to recognize Texan independence on condition that she remained independent, but the offer came too late.

Mexican governments, feeling that both honor and national independence must be vindicated, had repeatedly declared that annexation would mean war; and when Texas was annexed, Almonte, now Mexican ambassador in Washington, asked for his passports. Many Mexicans, intoxicated by the rhetoric of newspapers and *pronunciamentos*, were confident that the United States could be defeated. Those better informed hoped for sympathy from New England and for help from Great Britain. Herrera, nevertheless, seems to have been willing to accept the inevitable, provided that Mexico's aggrieved national pride were adequately conciliated. But James K. Polk, who had become American president in March, 1845, was not a conciliatory person; he was a strong-willed and unimaginative small-town lawyer, who was incapable of appreciating the exaggerated sense of honor and the contempt for considerations of profit and loss which prevailed south of the Rio Grande. Moreover, as the Mexicans had correctly anticipated, the United States was not content with Texas; it also wanted California. That empty and attractive territory seemed to be going begging. The tide of Spanish advance, at its high-water mark in the eighteenth century, had flowed into it and then receded, leaving behind a few creole landowners, who lived on broad *haciendas,* among enormous herds of horses and cattle, with a generous and leisurely elegance. The Mexican Government, a couple of thousand miles away to the south, had no effective control over the territory; and Polk was alarmed by rumors that Great Britain was proposing to buy it. His intention was to offer to assume the unpaid claims in return for a satisfactory boundary line between Texas and Mexico, and to attempt also to purchase California. Such a bargain, he believed, would benefit Mexico by enabling it to pay its debts; that the Mexicans would regard the suggestion as an insult was something which he was unable to understand.

He was informed by Herrera that a commissioner to discuss the Texas question would be received. Polk promptly nominated John Slidell as minister. The distinction between a commissioner and a minister seemed meaningless to Polk, but to Mexico it meant the difference between admitting that Mexico had been wronged and resuming ordinary diplomatic intercourse. Herrera was anxious to negotiate, but he knew that if he failed to vindicate Mexico's national honor there would be a revolution; and when Slidell reached Mexico he was almost tearfully besought not to press his demand for official recognition as a minister. Shortly afterwards

Paredes seized power, and Slidell, again pressing for recognition, was given his passports. Polk now prepared for war, feeling that the unpaid claims and the dismissal of Slidell were sufficient provocation. There were already American troops in Texas, and these had been ordered into the no-man's land, claimed but never occupied by Texas, between the Nueces and the Rio Grande. The commander in that section—so decreed by the inscrutable providence who chooses American presidents—was Zachary Taylor, a veteran of forty years of Indian warfare, commonly known as "Old Rough and Ready." Taylor crossed the two hundred miles of sandy plain south of the Nueces and established himself on the Rio Grande. Paredes regarded Taylor's advance as an invasion of Mexican soil, and gave orders that he should be resisted. On April 25, 1846, some American dragoons were attacked and forced to surrender by Mexican cavalry. When the news reached Washington Polk sent his war message to Congress—a message which, to his regret, he had been compelled to draft on the Sabbath; American blood, he explained, had been shed on American soil, and war existed by act of Mexico.

Many New Englanders opposed the war, still faithful to the theory that Texas had been deliberately stolen by the slave-owners. The slave-owners, on the other hand, were willing to defend Texas against invasion but disapproved of Polk's alacrity in declaring war, for they realized that California would never become slave soil. But the Mississippi Valley was swept by the war fever. All that pride in the destiny of the Anglo-Saxon republic, that physical vigor, that restless craving for adventure which characterized the American frontiersman, had found an outlet. The dominions of the former Spanish Empire had always exercised the magnetic pull with which throughout recorded history the warmth and color of the South has attracted the peoples of the North. The young men of the Mississippi Valley wanted, they declared, to "revel in the halls of Montezuma," and in this banal phrase they gave expression to exotic fantasies for which they expected fulfilment in the mysterious land of Mexico. Confronted by such enthusiasm, and by the efficiency of the American artillery, Mexico with her conscript armies and her antiquated weapons was doomed to defeat from the outset.

Zachary Taylor was ignorant of generalship and culpably inattentive to the welfare of his troops; but his physical courage, displayed by sitting on his horse and coolly writing despatches while bullets were flying past him, aroused the enthusiasm of the volunteers. In May, 1846, the Americans defeated General Arista, whose troops could not hold their ground for long against the deadly accuracy of the American guns, crossed the Rio Grande, and captured Matamoros. After spending two months at Matamoros, while several thousands of his men died from dysentery and from an epidemic of measles, Taylor decided to march southwards; he took Monterey by storm from General Ampudia, and finally established himself at Saltillo. Meanwhile the American fleet, in cooperation with a number of American residents, had taken possession of California.

By this time Mexico had undergone another revolution. Paredes had found himself unable to conduct the war, and had turned for consolation to drink. In August Juan Álvarez initiated an insurrection; Gómez Farías and the *puros* returned to power; and the constitution of 1824 was re-established. Farías did not propose to allow Polk to win the war by default, and with characteristic optimism he resolved on a rash experiment. Santa Anna was the ablest of Mexico's generals; he was to be brought back from exile, and while he and his army were busy defeating the Americans the *puros* were to finance the war by confiscating the property of the Church. Santa Anna showed his usual willingness to promise anything; and the alliance which had been broken by his treachery a dozen years before was re-established. Before Santa Anna could resume the presidency, however, he had to devise a method of getting into Mexico; between the cockpit in Havana, where he had been beguiling his exile, and the Mexican coast was the American fleet. This problem was easily solved through a negotiation with Polk. Santa Anna despatched an agent to Washington, promising that if he were allowed to return to Mexico he would make peace on favorable terms, explaining that Mexico needed to be intimidated by an invasion, and drafting a plan of operations for the American War Department. Polk fell into the trap and gave orders that Santa Anna should be allowed to slip through the blockade. In August the Napoleon of the West landed at Vera Cruz, where he had a chilly reception and was lectured for his past misdeeds; and in September he entered the City of Mexico. Farías promptly shuttled him off to San Luis Potosí, where he was to collect an army, while a liberal congress was gathered together, which named Santa Anna acting president and Farías vice-president.

The American Government had meanwhile decided on a change of plan. Polk had been alarmed by Taylor's incompetence, and alarmed still more by the possibility that, in spite of his incompetence, he might continue to win victories; Taylor was a Whig, and Polk had no desire to present the Whigs with a military hero as their next presidential candidate. After searching in vain for a Democratic general, he had determined that Winfield Scott—another Whig—should at least share the glory. Scott was to take half Taylor's army and land at Vera Cruz, while Taylor was ordered to retreat from his exposed position at Saltillo. Taylor grudgingly surrendered the troops, but continued to invite attack by remaining near Saltillo.

By January Santa Anna had collected an army of twenty-five thousand, which he financed partly by wholesale confiscations and partly out of his own pocket. Riding in a carriage drawn by eight mules and accompanied by his fighting cocks, he set off to overwhelm Taylor. Taylor, encamped in open country eighteen miles to the north of Saltillo, was nearly taken by surprise. Such scouting parties as had been sent out were captured by the Mexicans, some of them drunk and others merely asleep. On February

21 a solitary horseman descended the neighboring hills and rode into the American camp with the news that Santa Anna was close at hand. Taylor hastily burnt his stores and retreated a dozen miles to Angostura, close to the *hacienda* of Buena Vista, where the road ran through a broad pass between inaccessible mountains. Santa Anna arrived the next day, and on the morning of the twenty-third he drew up his army in battle array, exhibiting for the benefit of the Americans all the brilliant uniforms of the Mexican cavalry, while priests passed up and down the lines celebrating Mass. When the ceremony was concluded, he flung his men into a gap between the American army and the mountains on the eastern side of the pass, which Taylor, misjudging the nature of the ground, had left undefended. But if Santa Anna was the better general, the Americans had the better guns, and once again the Mexicans were mowed down by devastating artillery fire. By nightfall the gap had been closed and the two armies faced each other in their original positions. The Americans, who were outnumbered by about three to one, awaited with trepidation a renewal of the attack on the following day. Santa Anna, however, decided otherwise; his Indian conscripts, unaccustomed to soldiers who stood their ground so obstinately and to guns whose aim was so deadly, were in no mood for a renewal of the slaughter; he had captured two American standards—enough to make it appear that he had won a victory. During the night, under a crescent moon which soon dropped below the mountains, Santa Anna gathered his army together and stole away towards San Luis Potosí, leaving fires burning to conceal his retreat. Like Napoleon in 1812, he went ahead in his carriage, proclaiming victory; and like Napoleon's army in 1812, the Mexicans, straggling along the road to San Luis Potosí in wintry weather without leadership, were decimated by starvation. When Taylor discovered that Santa Anna had disappeared, he and his second-in-command fell into each other's arms and came to the conclusion that they had won the battle. Despatches to that effect were sent to Washington, which made Taylor the hero of the country and resulted in due course in his election to the presidency. He had foiled Polk after all.

While Santa Anna had been capturing American standards in Coahuila, Farías and his *puro* followers had been encountering difficulties in the capital. The clergy had volunteered to pray for a Mexican victory and had been generous in sponsoring religious processions, but to suggestions that they should contribute some of their money they had turned a deaf ear. Finally congress had authorized the seizure of five million pesos of clerical property. This proposal aroused the usual storm of opposition, and some of the clergy began to look with favor on the invading Americans, who might conquer Mexico but who would at least leave their estates intact. About a million and a half was extracted by force from the coffers of the Church, after which civil war put a stop to confiscations. The militia of the City of Mexico, who had gathered themselves together to defend their country from the Americans, decided instead to defend the Church from the *puros;* and a number of creole regiments, lavishly adorned with sacred medals and scapularies, who were known to the *mestizos*—from their love of dancing and festivity—as the *Polkos,* rebelled against Farías. As Santa Anna approached the city the leaders of every party hurried out to congratulate him on his victory and to secure his support. He decided to repeat his betrayal of 1834. Farías was again ejected, and one of the *moderados,* Anaya, was put up as acting president. Having extracted another two million pesos from the Church, in return for a promise of immunity in the future, Santa Anna turned eastwards to meet Winfield Scott.

Winfield Scott—"Old Fuss and Feathers" to his men—was an arrogant egotist, but he was also a scientific general, who left little to chance. On March 7 he and his army had landed on the sandhills to the south of Vera Cruz; after a devastating bombardment the city had capitulated; and the Americans had then hurried into the interior in order to escape the yellow fever. In the middle of April they found Santa Anna waiting for them at Cerro Gordo, in a strongly fortified position where the road wound upwards into the mountains. Scott's engineers found a way of turning the northern flank of the Mexicans, and a detachment of Americans dragged their guns across deep ravines and through thick woods, which Santa Anna had pronouced inaccessible even to a rabbit. Attacked on front and on their left, the Mexican army was cut to pieces, and the survivors took to their heels, streaming in disorder along the roads back towards Mexico. Scott could now proceed at his leisure to Puebla, a clerical town which refused to allow Santa Anna to defend it. Not until he reached the Valley of Mexico would Santa Anna be ready to meet him again.

The confusion of Mexico City was now indescribable. *Moderados* and *puros,* clericals and monarchists, all bitterly blamed each other, and all were united in suspecting Santa Anna. Stories of his negotiations with Polk had got abroad, and there were questions as to how he had slipped through the American blockade. Survivors of the army which he had abandoned in Coahuila had straggled back to the city, and reported that Angostura had not been the victory which he had described. Yet in spite of the rumors that he had sold his country to the Yankees, he was recognized as the only man capable of meeting the crisis. His military rivals— elderly survivors from the War of Independence like Bustamante and Nicolás Bravo, the intriguing Almonte and the drunken and treacherous Valencia, Arista, who had been in disgrace since his defeat at Matamoros, and Lombardini, who had few qualifications for command except the length of his moustaches—were equally untrustworthy; and they had little of Santa Anna's energy and experience. For once Santa Anna's interests were identical with those of Mexico. So he reassumed the presidency, and the warring factions finally agreed to a semblance of cooperation under his leadership.

Santa Anna might be unable to win battles, but he was still capable of gathering armies. Having lost one in Coahuila and another at Cerro Gordo, he now collected a third, and devoted himself with great energy to preparing the city for defence. He succeeded, moreover, in tricking the Americans into contributing to the cost of his preparations. Polk still believed that Santa Anna was sincerely proposing to make peace as soon as Mexico had been sufficiently intimidated; and he had attached to Scott's expedition a clerk from the State Department, Nicholas Trist, with instructions to negotiate a treaty as soon as Santa Anna should indicate that the process of intimidation need go no further. When, therefore, Santa Anna sent a message to the Americans, explaining that he was anxious for peace but that he needed ten thousand dollars immediately, the money was forwarded to him from Puebla.

In August, having discovered that the Mexicans still needed intim- idation, Scott left Puebla, climbed the pass below the snowbound peak of Popocatépetl, where the Valley of Mexico with its lakes and cornfields and *haciendas* was spread out below him, and descended on the village of Chalco. On the afternoon of August 9 the bells of the Cathedral of Mexico announced the approach of the Americans. The Mexican army was waiting for them on an isthmus between two lakes to the east of the city. Scott swung around to the south, along a waterlogged road between the lakes and the foothills of the mountains, until he came to the highroad from Mexico to Acapulco. Here again Santa Anna was waiting for him. During the next three weeks the Mexicans fought with a courage and an obstinacy which startled the invaders. For the first time the war had begun to eclipse the conflict of parties. The Mexican army consisted no longer of Indian conscripts but of creole and *mestizo* volunteers who were prepared to die in defence of their capital city; and Santa Anna, untiring in his efforts to organize his troops and exposing himself recklessly in the forefront of every battle, seemed almost to have been metamorphosed not into a Napoleon of the West but into something more honorable: a national leader. But the guns and the generalship of the Americans were still irresistible. They repulsed Valencia, who had disobeyed Santa Anna's order to retreat, at Contreras, and took Churubusco from Anaya by storm, capturing an unfortunate regiment of Irish Catholics who had changed sides during the war, only to be shot as deserters. There followed an armistice, during which Santa Anna, still professing to be anxious for peace, hastily strengthened his defences. Meanwhile Valencia, retiring to Toluca, issued a *pronunciamento* calling for the beheading of Santa Anna and war to the bitter end. When Santa Anna rejected the American terms, the Americans, fighting every inch of the road and suffering heavy losses, assaulted Molino del Ray, scaled the heights of Chapultepec, and on the evening of September 13 penetrated within the gates of the city. Santa Anna retired to Guadalupe, and the *ayuntamiento* of the city flew a white flag, while the *léperos* took the opportunity to sack the National Palace. At dawn on the fourteenth a column of grimy and bloodstained Yankees, headed by two generals on foot, one of whom had only one boot, marched into the plaza, and a few minutes later Winfield Scott galloped up at the head of his staff and received the applause of his army. The Mexicans crowded the sidewalks and the roofs of the houses, watching the invaders with interest and without apparent hostility; but when the Americans began to disperse to their lodgings, hidden marksmen opened fire and paving stones were thrown from the housetops. Through the day there was murderous street-fighting, but on the next morning the *ayuntamiento* succeeded in putting a stop to the slaughter and gave orders that the Americans should be provoked no further.

Santa Anna, supported by the *puros,* was eager to continue the war. He planned to gather fresh armies and to cut off Scott from his base at Vera Cruz. Mexico could evade the recognition of defeat indefinitely by resorting to guerrilla warfare. Through the winter, raiding squadrons, half patriot and half bandit, were cutting to pieces detachments of Americans or provoking them to equally murderous vengeance. But after Santa Anna had failed in an attack on the American garrison at Puebla, the *moderados* secured a majority in congress and determined to make peace. The wealthy creoles felt that guerrilla warfare would be even more ruinous to them than it could be to the Americans. The country seemed to be relapsing into anarchy. Half the northern states were on the verge of declaring themselves independent. The Maya tribes in Yucatán, goaded into rebellion by the greed of creole henequen growers and equipped with guns by the British merchants at Belize, had risen against the whites and had seized the whole peninsula except Merida and Campeche. Peña y Peña, the chief justice of the supreme court, assumed the presidency, established a government at Querétaro, and opened negotiations. Santa Anna, deposed from the presidency, fled into the mountains, and after narrowly escaping capture by the Texas Rangers, who were scouring southern Mexico in the hope of avenging the Alamo, was finally given a safe-conduct by the American authorities. After being banqueted by a party of American officers, he retired into exile in Jamaica.

Trist and Scott, in accordance with the instructions which had been given them a year before, proceeded to negotiate peace. Mexico was to cede Texas, California, and the vast expanse of empty territory between them—more than half the entire area of the republic—and was to receive fifteen million dollars, plus the cancellation of the unpaid claims. Threatened with a renewal of hostilities, Peña y Peña and a majority of the Mexican congress gave their assent; and the terms were forwarded to Washington. Demands for American annexation of the whole republic had been growing popular; but since the treaty had been made, Polk decided to accept it. On March 10, 1848, the Treaty of Guadalupe Hidalgo was ratified by the American Senate, and by the last day of July the last American soldier had departed from Mexico. The Mexicans were subsequently to note with pleasure that nemesis had followed imperialism; for the acquisitions of Guadalupe Hidalgo precipitated one of those conflicts between North and South which were to culminate, thirteen years later, in the American Civil War.

"GREASERS" IN THE DIGGINGS: CALIFORNIANS AND SONORANS UNDER ATTACK

Leonard Pitt

Why did the Spaniards and Mexicans fail to discover gold before 1848? What would have happened to them had they done so? These are two of the "iffiest" questions in all California history.

The Mexicans had, in fact, discovered minor deposits of gold in southern California more than a decade prior to the historic Coloma discovery, but they did miss the big find in the Sierra. The causes of their oversight include a fear of Indian attack in the interior and a decision to hug the coast for protection; no population pressure ever drove them inward. The Spanish tradition of looking for signs of *oro* among the Indians, as in Hernán Cortés' conquest of the Aztecs, also played a role, although a negative one, for the California Indians did not manipulate gold. Another cause may have been that the contentment of rancho life after 1834 had sapped the rancheros' energy necessary to explore new territory. Or perhaps the trouble was, simply, bad luck: Captain Gabriel Moraga's forty-six expeditions before 1820 had brought him near, if not directly atop, the Mother Lode, yet no gleam caught his eye. The Spanish Americans generally did not want for daring as explorers or for skill as miners; centuries of experience in both had equipped them ideally for the fateful discovery they somehow failed to make.

As to what might have been their history had they chanced upon the Sierra gold, the possibilities are numerous. They range from the attainment of genuine cultural maturity and political independence to an even more crushing defeat than the one they received after 1849. Perhaps California would have become one of the most populous and heavily defended places in the Spanish Empire or in the Mexican Republic. The Californios might have had genuine Mexican military support in a war with the Yankees, and thus also a better treaty settlement. Conquest by a European power would not have been entirely out of the question either. The answer, of course, depends upon *when* one supposes the gold to have been discovered: the earlier the better for the Californios, from the standpoint of the growth of Yankee expansionism in the 1840's. One suspects,

Reprinted from *The Decline of the Californios: A Social History of the Spanish speaking Californians, 1846–1890*, by Leonard Pitt. Originally published by the University of California Press; reprinted by permission of The Regents of the University of California.

Leonard Pitt is an associate professor of history at San Fernando Valley State College. His book, *The Decline of the Californios*, won the 1967 Commonwealth Club Silver Medal for the best work on California history.

however, that Manifest Destiny somehow was bound to triumph along the Pacific Coast and eventually convert California into a Yankee province.

The Californios themselves scarcely ever engaged in such ruminations, for they were not a people to pine over lost opportunities and were faced with realities that gave them enough food for thought. The discovery of gold in 1948 made an enormous impact on them—the greatest in their brief experience: it brought them riches, for one thing; it threw them together with other Latin Americans, for another; and, most important, it opened them to full-scale Yankee penetration and conquest.

As news of the discovery spread in 1848, Californios speedily converged on the Sierra from all directions and, in a sense, made up for lost time. The experience of the Angeleños was typical. With Don Antonio Coronel taking on the function of patrón, the thirty Californios, Sonorans, and Indian servants had good luck from the outset. They immediately enticed some mountain tribesmen to accept baubles in exchange for gold nuggets and, after spying out the Indians' trove and plying them with more trinkets, they obtained their digging labor into the bargain. In one day Antonio himself ended up with 45 ounces of gold; Dolores Sepúlveda found a 12-ounce nugget; and Señor Valdez discovered a boulder buried only 3 feet down which had once blocked the flow of an ancient alluvial stream and produced a towelful of nuggets in a short time. He sold his claim to Lorenzo Soto, who took out a whopping 52 pounds of gold in eight days and then sold it to Señor Machado, who also became rich. Even a Sonoran servant became fabulously wealthy overnight.[1]

In all, about 1,300 native Californians mined gold in 1848, the year of the bonanzas. If they had missed the opportunity to discover Sierra gold in the past, they did not do so now; nearness to the placers gave them the head start on the thousands of prospectors still getting their wits together for the voyage halfway around the world. The Californios had additional advantages in knowing precisely where and how to find gold and in gladly pooling their resources and dividing their labor. As a result, the organized Californios, though less numerous than the 4,000 individualistic Yankees in the mines that year, probably extracted as much gold as they. Coronel, a struggling Mexican schoolteacher, had pocketed enough gold to become a prominent landowner, viticulturist, and community leader. He and many other Californios resolved to make a second expedition the next year. They dismissed the news that a few Californios had been harried from their claims by fist-swinging Oregon Yankees, who refused to acknowledge that the Treaty of Guadalupe Hidalgo granted some Mexicans full citizenship: in 1848 "everything ended peacefully." [2]

[1] Antonio F. Coronel, "Cosas de California . . . ," 1877, MS, Bancroft Library, pp. 140–186.

[2] Augustin Janssens, *The Life and Adventures in California of Don Agustín Janssens: 1834–1856*, ed. by William H. Ellison and Francis Price (San Marino, Calif., 1953), pp. 136–137.

In the year that followed, the story changed drastically. Coronel's return trip to the mines began badly, with a near-fatal brawl in a Sonora saloon. One day he and *compadre* Juan Padilla were waiting for the wet January weather to clear, when a former Bear Flagger began to bully Padilla for having served as Bernardo García's henchman in the wartime atrocity against Cowie and Fowler. Padilla insisted that the charge was a lie, and the American replied with an assault. After a severe beating, Padilla lay in an upstairs room, hovering near death for several weeks, while below his accuser continued to threaten his life. Only Coronel's good reputation and the intercession of friendly Americans restrained the former Bear Flagger.

After nursing his friend back to life, Coronel returned to the Sierra. He fell in among Chileans, Mexicans, and Germans doing well at dry diggings until confronted with posters declaring that foreigners had no right to be there and must leave the mines at once; resistance would be met by force. Although this threat never materialized, excitement mounted. In a nearby camp, a Mexican gambler's tent had been raided, and some Yankees accused five foreigners of stealing 5 pounds of gold. Coronel's associates doubted the accusation against at least one apparently honorable man and raised 5 pounds of gold to offer as ransom. Coronel conferred with a Yankee delegation and gave them the gold. The delegates then retired to consider the offer but never re-emerged from the drunken and agitated crowd, which by then numbered into the hundreds. The money did no good; all five prisoners were convicted and flogged at once, and two of them, a Frenchman and a Chilean, were charged with a previous murder and robbery. Guilty or not, the pair scarcely understood enough of the proceedings to reply to the accusations. When Coronel next saw them they were standing in a cart, lashed together back to back and pinned with a note warning away defenders such as might come from Coronel's camp. A horse then jolted the cart from under the men, and California had witnessed its first lynching. That incident resulted, Coronel thought, from a declining gold supply and the Yankees' increasing jealousy of successful Spanish Americans.

As quickly as possible Don Antonio led his group away from the newly named "Hangtown," and resettled in the remote northern mines. But even there a hundred gringos appeared with the gruff announcement that the entire riverbed belonged exclusively to Americans who would tolerate no foreigners. Furious, some of Coronel's people who had reached the limit of their endurance planned armed resistance, even at the cost of their lives, but Coronel held back and sadly announced, "For me gold mining is finished." [3]

By July many other Californios had cause to echo Coronel's words. As

---

[3] Op. cit., pp. 125–140; Leonard Pitt, "The Beginnings of Nativism in California," *Pacific Historical Review*, XXX (Feb., 1961), 23–38.

the only true native-born citizens they did have a legitimate place in the mines, yet they knew no way to convince 100,000 hostile strangers of this truth. Fisticuffs or hand combat simply was not the Californians' style. Consequently, one of them carried into the field of combat a safe-conduct pass, signed by the army's secretary of state, which certified him as a bona fide citizen deserving of every right and privilege, of every lawful aid and protection.[4] What good the pass did is not recorded, but the attacks mounted. For most Californios, the best answer was to go home and stay there: "Don't go to the mines on any account," one *paisano* advised another.[5] Out of pride, which prevented them from being converted into aliens by Yankee rogues and upstarts, few Californians ventured back into the maelstrom after 1849.

Musing over the gold rush from a safe distance, the Californians once more concluded that outsiders were, by and large, despicable. Mariano Vallejo said of the forty-niners without sparing any nationality, "The good ones were few and the wicked many." Hugo Reid ticked off the list of troublemakers:

> . . . vagabonds from every quarter of the globe. Scoundrels from nowhere, rascals from Oregon, pickpockets from New York, accomplished gentlemen from Europe, interlopers from Lima and Chile, Mexican thieves, gamblers of no particular spot, and assassins manufactured in Hell for the expressed purpose of converting highways and biways into theatres of blood; then, last but not least, Judge Lynch with his thousand arms, thousand sightless eyes, and five-hundred lying tongues.[6]

The Californians now simply reverted to their customary circular logic, which held that evil came from outsiders, that outsiders were mostly evil, and that evil mothered evil. In no other way could they explain the ugly behavior of so many people, especially Americanos.

After a century of slow population growth, during which the arrival of twenty-five cholos or fifty Americans seemed a momentous occasion, suddenly and without warning California faced one of the swiftest, largest, and most varied folk migrations of all time. More newcomers now arrived each day in California than had formerly come in a decade. Briefly told, the story of the Californians in the gold rush is their encounter with 100,000 newcomers in the single year of 1849—80,000 Yankees, 8,000 Mexicans, 5,000 South Americans, and several thousand miscellaneous

---

[4] Signed Oct. 26, 1849, by Captain Henry W. Halleck; see *California and New Mexico*, 31st Cong., 1st sess., H. Ex. Doc. 17 (Washington, 1850), pp. 869–870.
[5] Hugo Reid to Abel Stearns, April 22, 1849, quoted in Susana Bryant Dakin, *A Scotch Paisano: Hugo Reid's Life in California, 1832–1852* . . . (Berkeley, 1939), pp. 164–169.
[6] Loc. cit.

Europeans—and with numbers that swelled to a quarter million by 1852.[7] Even assuming the goodwill of every last one of these strangers, they outnumbered the Californians ten and fifteen times over and reduced them to feelings of insignificance.

It is the destiny of ethnic groups in the United States to be thrown together with people of "their own kind" whom they neither know nor particularly like—perhaps even despise. This was the lot of the Californios in 1849, with the massive migration of Latin Americans. It was bad enough that by 1850 the Mexican cholos outnumbered the 15,000 Californios; even worse, angry Yankees simply refused to recognize any real distinctions between Latin Americans. Whether from California, Chile, Peru, or Mexico, whether residents of twenty years' standing or immigrants of one week, all the Spanish-speaking were lumped together as "interlopers" and "greasers." In this molding, the Californians, who had always kept aloof from cholos and earlier had won some grudging respect from the Yankees, lost most heavily. Their reputation as a people more heroic, handsome, and civilized than other "Spaniards" now dissolved. Their proximity to the greasers between 1849 and 1852 put them in actual jeopardy of their lives. In essence then, the Latin-American immigrants were a sort of catalyst whose presence caused the sudden and permanent dissolution of the social elements.

The biggest waves of Latin Americans came from Chile and northern Mexico. The Chileans excelled in baking and bricklaying and other skills and thus found themselves in especially great demand in California. They settled down at the foot of San Francisco's Telegraph Hill, in a place called "Little Chile," or went into the mines to dig, until expelled by the Yankees.[8]

Even more prominent and numerous were the northern Mexicans. Distinguishable from other Latin Americans by their billowy white pantaloons, broad sandals, and sombreros, the "Sonoranians" or "Sonorans," as the Yankees called them, first entered the Sierra late in 1848, after either trudging across the Colorado deserts or sailing via Mazatlán. Some had sojourned in California earlier; in 1842, well before the advent of James Marshall, a Sonoran had discovered gold near San Fernando Mission. More visibly mestizo, less consciously Spanish than the Californians, they seemed "primitive" by local standards. Apache raiders kept them from their own mines and pastures, so that the Sonorans pounced on the California discovery as a panacea. The northern Mexican patróns themselves encouraged the migration of the peons by sponsoring expeditions

---

[7] Doris Marion Wright, "The Making of Cosmopolitan California: An Analysis of Immigration, 1848–1870," California Historical Society *Quarterly*, XIX (Dec., 1940), 323–343; XX (March, 1941), 65–79.

[8] The travails of the Chileans in California are presented in Vicente Pérez Rosales, *California Adventure*, trans. by Edwin S. Morby and Arturo Torres-Rioseco (San Francisco, 1947); and Roberto Hernandez Cornejo, *Los Chileños en San Francisco de California* (Valparaiso, Chile, 1930).

of twenty or thirty underlings at a time, giving them full upkeep in return for half of their gold findings in California. The migration included so broad a spectrum of the population of Sonora and Sinaloa and was so large and continuous throughout 1850, that it compelled the governors of northern Mexico to admonish repeatedly about the dangers of life on gringo soil.

The Sonorans came on swiftly, heedless of any warnings, knowing that they had vital services to offer California—as prospectors and hired hands, as supply merchants and mule skinners, also as monte gamblers and prostitutes. The leading merchants of Altar and Horcasitas, Sonoran towns near the international boundary, stripped their shelves in the spring of 1849, loaded up every available pack animal and scurried for the mines. There they sold everything they had brought, dug some gold, and shortly left their followers to return to Sonora for new stock or for quick investment in Mexican securities—much of this accomplished before most of the Yankee Argonauts had even arrived.[9]

Sonorans gravitated mainly toward the San Joaquin River tributaries, called the "southern mines" or "dry diggings," especially near a spot named in their honor, Sonora. Here they introduced Yankees to many of the rudimentary mining techniques that typified the early gold rush era. Sonorans somehow could probe the topsoil with knives and bring up nuggets, or work the *batea* (pan) to great advantage. Where water was scarce and quartz plentiful, as in the southern mines, they had the endurance to sit for hours and winnow dirt in their scrapes, sometimes using their own gargantuan breath if the wind died down. They could also improvise the *arastra* (mill), consisting of a mule harnessed to a long spoke treading in a circle and grinding ore under a heavy, flat boulder. Others eventually caught on to those techniques and machines and later surpassed them, but the Sonorans' sixth sense for finding gold and their willingness to endure physical hardship gave them great advantages. Talent made them conspicuously "lucky"—and, therefore,—subject to attack by jealous Yankees.

Although the Californios quietly withdrew from the Sierra and left the field to the Mexicans and the Yankees, the scene in the mines deserved their closest attention. For, the mines became the staging ground for widespread attacks on their ranchos and pueblos, the rehearsal place for broad-scale assaults on the Spanish-speaking.

The problem of precisely how to react to the remaining "Spaniards" made the Yankees squirm. They shifted from violence to legislation, from legislation to litigation, and back again to violence. Some wished to exploit, others to expel, and still others to control the Latin Americans. On

[9] José Francisco Velasco, *Noticias estadísticas del estado de Sonora, acompañadas de ligeras reflecsíones* . . . (Mexico, D.F., 1850), p. 281 ff. On the Sonoran miners and their technology see Sylvester Mowry, *Arizona and Sonora* (New York, 1864), p. 97 and passim: and Rodman W. Paul, *California Gold: The Beginning of Mining in the Far West* (Cambridge, 1947), pp. 26, 110–113, 212.

occasion, some Yankees even proposed allowing them completely free access to the mines.

It would have given small comfort to Coronel, Vallejo, Reid, and other Californios to learn that good and decent men had inspired the purge trials of the winter and spring of 1849. Yet, in truth, a great deal of anti-foreigner agitation originated from the most reputable new citizens— army officers, lawyers, merchants, clergy, and public officials. It is a fact that the first organized and officially sanctioned outburst against Spanish Americans came from three hundred "white-collar" Yankees. While stranded in Panama in January, 1849, on their way to San Francisco, they heard distressing rumors that "foreign plunderers" from all over the Pacific littoral had already siphoned off $4 million worth of gold in California; how much remained for "true citizens" thus was problematic. On a slight provocation, the Yankees called a public meeting to deal sternly with the interlopers. No less a dignitary than the justice of the Oregon Territory presided over the gathering, and in the background hovered General Persifor F. Smith, traveling to Monterey to take charge of the army. Smith drafted a circular declaring that, in California, he would "consider everyone who is not a citizen of the United States, who enters upon public land and digs for gold as a trespasser." This declaration won him three hundred vows of support.[10]

The miners, who twice confronted Coronel with the charge that "foreigners" had "no right" to dig gold, were simply enforcing Smith's hastily improvised "doctrine of trespass." In April, vigilantes at Sutter's Mill drove away masses of Chileans, Mexicans, and Peruvians; and during a similar purge along the Sacramento River on the Fourth of July lives were lost, property destroyed, and foreigners' goods were sold at auction. More than a thousand victims, mainly Chileans, came pouring down into San Francisco shortly afterward, many of them embarked for home. "General Smith is blamed by everyone as the sole cause of the outrage." [11]

Smith beat a hasty retreat when he discovered that the consequences of the plunderers' activities had been grossly overrated: gold was still plentiful, and most of the dust already exported from California had found its way into the hands of American supply merchants. His successor, Brigadier General Bennet Riley, rode through the mines trying to undo some of the damage caused by the doctrine of trespass by telling Americans that technically all diggers were guests on government land, and that thereafter none should be denied access to its bounty.[12]

Resentment against the "greasers" mounted, however, a product of deep and abiding feelings of nationalism, racism, and despair over the debasement of free labor. The nationalism was partly a hangover from the war. Some men imagined seeing "whole battalions, armed to the teeth . . .

[10] The incident is described in Victor M. Berthold, *The Pioneer Steamer* California: *1848–1849* (Boston and New York, 1932), pp. 37–42 and passim; and by Smith to William Marcy, Jan. 7, 1849, in *California and New Mexico*, pp. 704, 707.

[11] Hugo Reid, July 18, 1849, quoted in Dakin, op. cit., pp. 174–175.

[12] Riley to R. Jones, Aug. 30, 1849, in *California and New Mexico*, pp. 788–789.

moving through the heart of Mexico . . . gotten up by the great capitalists and friends of Santa Anna . . . rising in one solid mass whose cry is 'California's recovery or death!' " [13] Yankee veterans unhappy in the diggings and nostalgic for army comradery saw in the coming of the "greasers" the pretext for a "muss," whether for mayhem or for merriment. Northern Europeans—the Irish in particular—and Australians became implacable foes of the Spanish-Americans, more so perhaps than many native-born citizens of the United States. The notorious San Francisco gang, the "Hounds," for example, which was staffed by former New York Volunteers and Australians, took particular delight in attacking the Chileans who came to San Francisco after fleeing enemies in the mountains.

The forty-niner's xenophobia also stemmed from fear of unfair economic competition. Back home, one could normally see who became rich, how rich, and by what means; a community could use institutional means to regulate the process and keep it fair. But on the periphery of civilization, controls broke down: men sometimes prospered by unfair means; the population upsurge, the ceaseless shuffling of men from camp to camp, and their scrambling for the top of the social ladder defied control by ordinary methods. Thus the forty-niner improvised new devices, even vigilante justice.

Fear of economic competition had some basis in reality. Sonoran peddlers marched into the mines and sold 10,000 pack mules in three years, thereby depressing the prices of mules (from $500 to $150 a head in a matter of weeks) and of freight rates (from $75 to $7 per hundredweight in two months). This reversal of fortunes evoked no complaint from the Yankee miners, who could buy onions, potatoes, and other supplies all the more cheaply and had come to associate Mexican mule bells with savory cooking odors and a few cheap comforts of life; but it brought, in 1850, a pained outcry from Stockton entrepreneurs, who sought mass expulsion of their business rivals. Moreover, when the Mexicans set to work as peons in the employ of their patróns, they did make themselves the target of the prospectors. Miners who began muttering against the Mexicans and plotting violence felt keenly conscious that the Spanish Americans were cheapening the value of labor.[14]

The treatment of immigrant Spanish Americans in the mines hinged also on the slavery question. They came into California precisely when the Yankees felt most irritated on this score and could see most clearly the parallels between Negroes and their masters, on the one hand, and peons and patróns, on the other. Yankee prospectors ejected from the mines with equal vigor any combination of bondsmen and masters. In July a prominent Texan, Thomas Jefferson Green, and his slaves were unceremoniously tossed out of Rose Bar on the Yuba River. These prospectors put

[13] New York *Herald*, April 3, 1849, quoted in Berthold, op. cit., p. 50.
[14] Riley to Jones, Aug. 30, 1849, in *California and New Mexico*, pp. 788–789. See also Bayard Taylor, *Eldorado, or, Adventures in the Path of Empire* (New York, 1949 [1st ed., 1850]), pp. 67, 79.

into effect a local code prohibiting the mining operations of all master-servant teams, whatever their relationship. Three months later this provision cost the life a Chilean and led to the ear cropping and whipping of Chileans and Mexicans who tried to oppose it.[15]

With California's entry into the Union as a free state, the plight of the Spanish Americans in the mines worsened momentarily. Their protagonists proclaimed that, if slaves were prohibited from the mines, then so should be the "refuse population from Chile, Peru and Mexico and other parts of the world [who are] . . . as bad as any of the free negroes of the North, or the worst slaves of the South." The apparent inconsistency in immigration policy annoyed both the friends and the enemies of slavery. In the first California legislature, nativists freely categorized the Pacific immigrants as a race whose morality and intelligence stood "but one degree above the beasts of the field." The State Assembly, in no uncertain terms (by a vote of twenty-two to two), asked Congress to bar from the mines all persons of foreign birth, *even* naturalized citizens.[16]

This extreme nativism soon brought about its own backlash. A fraction of the entrepreneurs in the mines began to worry less about the alleged dangers of unlimited immigration or of competition from "foreign capitalists" and more about the "disgregated, fractioned, broken up" techniques of mining; more about the possibilities of investing capital and hiring Mexican laborers, and less about expelling the interlopers. Usually outshouted at public meetings and outvoted in the legislature, this Yankee faction nonetheless had on its side the logic of economy and the ear of a few outspoken politicians who began a campaign to exploit, rather than exclude, aliens.[17]

Advocates of this new position were most numerous and effective in the southern mines. There, the Sonorans evicted from the northern placers late in 1849 found relative safety, hiring themselves out to Yankees who maintained loaded pistols, "cool eyes . . . [and] steady nerves" against possible opposition by other Yankees.[18] The Yankee patróns especially appreciated the Sonorans' skill and willingness to work for a daily wage of a dollar in food and a fraction of gold. "Greasers" worked speedily, when prompted, although work itself—and riches or savings—bored them, and gambling, drinking, dancing, and indolence cut down their work time. The argument ran as follows: The American, "with all his

---

[15] Allen B. Sherman, ed., "Sherman Was There: The Recollections of Major Edwin A. Sherman," *California Historical Society Quarterly*, XXIII (1944), pp. 351–352, James J. Ayers, *Gold and Sunshine: Reminiscences of Early California* (Boston, 1922), pp. 49–63.

[16] J. Ross Browne, *Report of the Debates in the Convention of California, on the Formation of the State Constitution, in September and October, 1849* (Washington, 1850), p. 143 ff.; *Journals of the California Legislature, 1849–1850* (San Jose, 1850), pp. 803–811, 1013–1018.

[17] San Francisco merchants commissioned Felix P. Wierzbicki's *California As It Is and As It May Be* (San Francisco, 1849), which advocated measures to eliminate adventurism and stabilize the diggings. See also Claude Petty, "John S. Hittell and the Gospel of California," *Pacific Historical Review*, XXIV (1955), 5 ff.

[18] *Marysville Directory* (n.p., 1858), pp. xv–xxvi; Taylor, op. cit., pp. 66, 67, 75.

impatience of control, his impetuous temperament, his ambitions and yearning will . . . [never] be content to deny himself the pleasure of civilized life in the states for the sake of $4.00 to $3.00 per day, to develop the resources of the dry diggings"; the Mexican, on the other hand, is "milder in spirit, more contented to endure, more willing to suffer, more weak spirited, if you please," [19] but for those very reasons he is the man for the job. Although a mere "hewer of wood and drawer of water," [20] he would unlock California's wealth much as the Negro had done in the South. American freight shippers at the same time learned that the Mexican *arrieros* (mule skinners) were the most reliable of hired hands— skillful, proud of their work, and sure to get the pack train through the worst blizzard, over the toughest mountain trail. A genuine paternal fondness sometimes linked the arriero and his new Yankee patrón.

Yankee tradesmen of the southern mines came to see the Spanish Americans as particularly good customers. It occurred to them that, in contrast with the stingy Yankee who saved his money and sent it home, the Latin American invariably wanted to take home goods, not money; he spent all he had. Just as the Spaniard's eccentric work habits could be turned to the operator's profit, so could his spendthrift tendencies be turned to the advantage of the merchant. General Riley discovered that "Americans, by their superior intelligence and shrewdness in business, generally contrived to turn to their own benefit the earnings of Mexicans, Chileans and Peruvians." [21]

The tension between Yankee and Latin-American miners climaxed in the Foreign Miners' Tax Law of 1850, one of the most original if benighted laws ever passed in a California legislature.

Thomas Jefferson Green, its author, boasted that he personally could "maintain a better stomach at the killing of a Mexican" than at the crushing of a body louse.[22] A Texan, he had come to this opinion in a Mexican prison while brooding over the failure of a filibustering expedition. After a harrowing escape from the prison, Green published an account of his exploits, together with a tirade against all things Mexican (and Negro) and a proposal that the United States swallow up all of Mexico. He had come to California in the hope of using slaves to plant cotton, although the episode at the Yuba River smashed that idea completely. Because he had served in three Southern legislatures, however, and had a good reputation among Southerners, he easily won election as state senator from Sacramento.

Green had legendary powers of persuasion, even over men who disliked his social ideals. It was he who always gained adjournment of the California Senate to "more comfortable surroundings"—namely, his own bar—and thus earned his colleagues the sobriquet, "Legislature of the Thousand Drinks." In his tax bill—a kind of personal rejoinder to the men who had expelled him from Rose Bar for attempting to use Negro

[19] *Times* (Stockton), Aug. 17, 1850.
[20] Ibid., Nov. 23, 1850.
[21] To Jones, Aug. 30, 1849, in *California and New Mexico*, p. 788.
[22] *Journal of the Expedition against Mier* (New York, 1845), p. 269.

bondsmen—he proposed to issue mining permits to foreigners at a cost of $20 monthly (he later reduced it to $16). This tax, he thought, would bolster the bankrupt state treasury by $200,000 each month and would also encourage Yankee operators to buy licenses for their operatives, and to employ them "at a fair rate . . . until the labor is performed according to contract." The law would delight Americans no end and discourage mob action, or what Green grandly called "the interruption of the stronger power which is in the people." [23] This possibility so neatly wrapped up all the nagging problems of labor competition, foreign monopolies, taxation, bondage, immigration, and mob violence that the Assembly passed it nineteen to four and the Senate seven to four; the latter house, by a vote of eleven to two, also gave Green a special commendation for originating so "splendid" a plan.[24]

Although later condemned as an intemperate and malicious act, "conceived in drink and brought forth in jollity," the Foreign Miners' Tax Law actually had quite sober intentions. Its main difficulty was that instead of flatly trying to either exploit, expel, or give free rein to the foreign-born, it tried to straddle the issue. It promised something for everybody: the prospector would be able to evict all "unprotected" aliens, the operator would be able to undercut the "agents of foreign bankers" who sponsored immigration, the government would receive money to pay its bills (among them, the expense vouchers of the legislature), the collectors would make a commission of $3 on each permit sold, and the immigrants themselves could claim the protection of the law if they paid their tax. On the face of it, one could hardly have asked for a more equitable solution.

Yet the Foreign Miners' Tax Law hardly worked that way at all. In Tuolumne County, where most of the potential taxpayers were entrenched, the impost caused outright defiance. Printed posters immediately denounced the tax and implored its intended victims to "put a bridle in the mouths of that horde who call themselves citizens of the United States, thereby profaning that country." [25] Two French radicals, schooled in the Revolution of 1848, engineered a rebellion and for its success needed the cooperation of the Mexicans. Although the Mexicans were gun-shy, they nevertheless went to tell the Yankees what was on the mind of all non-Yankees. An impressive array of 4,000 "aliens"—mostly Mexicans—congregated on the outskirts of Sonora on Sunday, May 19, to consider proper action against the law, which was to take effect the next day. To the collector's face the delegation flatly declared that the foreign-born might pay $3 or even $5 monthly, but not $20—a token sum for protection against rowdies, but not an entire fortune monthly. When the collector held his ground and demanded the full amount, most foreigners fled the town.[26] One remaining Mexican threatened the sheriff, or so it seemed to the bystander who killed him with a bowie knife. Local officials

[23] *Journals of the California Legislature, 1849–1850*, pp. 493–497.
[24] Ibid., pp. 232 ff., 1106 ff.; *Cal. Stats.* (1850), p. 221.
[25] *Daily Pacific News* (San Francisco), May 28, 1850.
[26] "Statement of [Collector] L. A. Besançon," *Journals of the California Legislature*, 1851, Senate, App. M, no. 2, p. 660.

prohibited merchants from selling supplies to any foreign miners and spread an alarm to nearby camps to call up reinforcements for the forthcoming "war" at the county seat.

One hundred and fifty war veterans promptly stopped work at Mormon Gulch, selected a captain, put on the remains of their uniforms, and, with regimental colors high, marched to Sonora for action. Sonora received them warmly with fulsome speeches, food, and free liquor. By nightfall the town seethed with inevitable rumors of Mexican incendiarism, assassination, and massacre. Officers posted pickets, stored weapons, and briefed the men for the next day's action. Sonora was under martial law.

Next morning, into the diggings marched four hundred Americans—a moving "engine of terror"—heading for Columbia Camp, the foreigners' headquarters. They collected tax money from a few affluent aliens and chased the rest away, with a warning to vacate the mines. One trooper recalls seeing "men, women and children—all packed up and moving, bag and baggage. Tents were being pulled down, houses and hovels gutted of their contents; mules, horses and jackasses were being hastily packed, while crowds were already in full retreat." [27] The posse finally arrested the two "hot-headed Frenchmen . . . of the red republican order," who started everything, fined them $5 for "treason," and dismissed them. Thus ended the "muss." The men liquored up for the road, hoisted the Stars and Stripes to the top of a pine tree, fired off a salute, and headed for home. Next day, about five hundred French and German forty-eighters stormed into Sonora shouting revolutionary slogans and vowing to liberate the Frenchmen. Upon hearing that the pair had been freed, the would-be liberators dispersed sheepishly. [28]

Sonora had just recovered from the excitement of this "French Revolution" when a new attack broke over the heads of the Spanish-speaking. A series of robberies and violent deaths came to light near town in which the victims were Yankees and the murder weapons *riatas*; this made it easy to blame "foreigners of Spanish-American origin." Next, a Sonoran and his three Yaqui Indian retainers were caught burning two bodies and would have been lynched, but for the timely intervention of the justice of the peace and the sheriff, who remanded the prisoners to the district court. On the morning of the court trial (July 15), the Mormon Gulch veterans again descended on Sonora in military order and spoiling for action. Informed that the prisoners might be hirelings of a "notorious Mexican chief" at Green Flat, they marched there, rounded up practically every male in sight, herded them back to Sonora, and literally corralled them for safekeeping overnight. In the morning, the justice of the peace investigated the "caze of murther against 110 Greasers . . . captured by 80

[27] The quotation is from Walter Murray, a participant, writing in the *Herald* (Sonora), n.d., 1852, and reprinted in the *Pioneer and Historical Review* (San Jose), Aug. 11, 1877; see also *Times* (Stockton), May 19, 25, June 1, 1850; San Francisco *Daily Alta California*, May 24, 1850.

[28] Friedrich Gerstäcker, *Scenes of Life in California*, trans. by George Cosgrave (San Francisco, 1942), pp. 37–66.

brave Americans," [29] but, having determined that the Mexicans were innocent newcomers, he let them go. After a momentary riot scene in the courtroom, the Sonoran, on bended knees, convinced the jury that he and his Indians had killed no one but had accidentally discovered the bodies and were trying to dispose of them according to Yaqui burial custom. The crowd dispersed grudgingly.

Unhappily, another gruesome death, uncovered the very next day, again made Sonora the prey of every rumor incriminating Latin Americans. Since all previous measures had failed to stop the atrocities, it was proposed to cleanse the hillsides thoroughly of every Spanish American with the least tinge of "evil." The present emergency demanded that "all Mexicans should suffer for a few." [30] The "better element" of Yankees in the southern mines, who normally recoiled from drastic measures, now feared that their territory was fast acquiring the reputation of a bandit refuge, which was bad for business, and felt impelled to join the broadside attack. Outshouting one dissenting voice, a large public meeting in Sonora voted to force all foreigners to deposit their arms with Americans and apply for permits of good conduct. All Latin Americans, except "respectable characters," were given fifteen days in which to depart. The Mormon Gulch veterans set to work enforcing these dicta with gusto.

The screening plan to expel the "obnoxious" Spanish Americans worked well. It reduced the danger of *bandido* attack and frightened off economic rivals. Between May and August, from five to fifteen thousand foreign-born diggers scattered from the southern mines. Mexicans went elsewhere looking for surcease of trouble but were dogged everywhere; eventually, they came streaming out of the Sierra, some showing signs of "pinching want." Even those who paid the extortionate $20 found that it bought very little protection, for if the collector neglected his monthly rounds their certificates lapsed, and if the Americans of one county refused to honor permits bought in another, the Spanish-speaking had little recourse but to leave. They knew that they alone of all foreign miners were being subjected to the tax: when they taunted the collectors to tax Irishmen, Frenchmen, and other Europeans they received no satisfactory reply. Masqueraders posing as collectors came into Mexican camps, solemnly tore up valid permits, and demanded money for new ones; when rebuffed, they auctioned off the victim's dirt and installed in his claim a "loyal citizen." One imposter carried off his charade so well at Don Pedro's Bar that he convinced a posse to help him chase away forty peons and their patrón and killed two Mexicans in the action, before his identity was uncovered.[31]

[29] Judge Barry, quoted in Edna Buckbee, *The Saga of Old Tuolumne* (New York, 1935), p. 38.

[30] Enos Christman, *One Man's Gold: The Letters and Journals of a Forty-Niner* (New York, 1930), p. 176 ff.

[31] The tax troubles of the Spanish-speaking and of other "foreigners" are highlighted in the Stockton *Times*, July 27, Aug. 10, 1850; the Sacramento *Transcript* Sept. 21, 1851; and in Richard Dillon, "Kanaka Colonies in California," *Pacific Historical Review*, XXIV (1955), passim.

Even when seeking an escape from California, Mexicans found the Americans lying in wait for them. On the Colorado River, a United States Army lieutenant had express orders "to make all Sonorans passing out of California with gold, pay a duty . . . and for my trouble, to put the whole of it in my pocket." [32] A troop of California militiamen blandly confiscated from homebound Sonorans more than a hundred "stolen" mules and horses, ignoring the brand marks proving ownership and compelling the Mexicans to walk 300 miles, including 100 miles across desert.

In the preceding year misunderstanding, fear, and hatred had created an atmosphere so hostile to "Sonorans" as to sanction fraud and murder. Nonetheless, the argument for both protecting and exploiting the foreign miners once more gathered strength. The earliest and most effective counterattack against prejudice was made by the San Francisco Vigilance Committee of 1849, which summarily expelled the "Hounds" from town and made amends to the Chileans who had been tormented by them. Thereafter many individuals took up the cause, speaking in behalf of civil law or laissez-faire competition or on grounds of simple revulsion against mob violence. Among those spokesmen were judges, editors, lawyers, a sheriff, a brigadier general, merchants, mine operators, and the French consul. Several sympathetic collectors ceased selling permits. Even the state attorney general disliked the tax so thoroughly that he refused to defend the collector prosecuted in the California Supreme Court and ignored the governor's threat to prosecute him for dereliction of duty.[33]

Xenophobia had injured its perpetrators as well as its victims. As Mexicans fled the southern mines in 1850, the profits of Yankee merchants plunged alarmingly. Eight-dollar crowbars in one afternoon dropped to fifty cents; a plot of land worth several thousand dollars went begging "for a few bits." [34] Out of sheer dollars-and-cents self-interest, if nothing else, businessmen collected money, hired a lawyer to sue the local collector, and circulated a mass petition asking the governor to lower the impost to $5; all but one merchant signed the document. In July and August, after the second wave of expulsions caused retail losses as high as $10,000 a day in three southern counties, merchants who had helped expel the "evil characters" during the bandit scare became aware that *all* Mexicans were fleeing, not merely the undesirables. A crowd gathered at Georgetown, down the road from Sonora, and went on record as denouncing antiforeigner vigilantes and as supporting civil law. As a result the Stockton *Times* reported that the screening plan enforced at Mormon Gulch and elsewhere was "speedily held in contempt." [35]

[32] J. Cave Couts, *From San Diego to the Colorado in 1849 . . . Journals and Maps* . . . (Los Angeles, 1932), pp. 47–48.
[33] Stockton *Times*, Aug. 3, 10, Nov. 23, 1850; March 5, 12, 1851; Lang, op. cit., p. 89; *Herald* (Marysville), Sept. 6, 1850; J. Lombard to Patrice Dillon, Oct. 7, 1850, in A. P. Nasatir, ed., "A French Pessimist in California: The Correspondence of J. Lombard, Vice Consul of France, 1850–1852," California Historical Society *Quarterly*, XXI (1952), 143–146; *Alta* (San Francisco), March 5, 7, 22, 1851.
[34] Stockton *Times*, May 25, June 22, 1850.
[35] Ibid., Aug. 3, 10, 1850.

These forces planned to persuade the governor to reduce the tax, the legislature to repeal it, or, best of all, the courts to nullify it. In the state Supreme Court they pleaded that it infringed the exclusive right of the federal government to govern federal lands and abridged the protection granted to aliens by the state constitution and by two treaties with Mexico. Neither of these arguments, however, swayed the high tribunal, which advanced a philosophy of states' rights in all matters relating to the federal government. Two Southern attorneys convinced the court that a state (1) could rightfully tax federal lands, unless specifically prohibited from doing so, and (2) had police powers to defend itself against undesirables. The court, in effect, agreed with the author of the tax act, Green, who had grandly declared that congressional inaction on the California mines had thrown the state back onto "universal laws . . . higher, greater, and stronger than the written constitution." Gratuitously, the court added that even had the law violated a treaty—which had not been demonstrated—it might still be valid, for state laws could take precedence over treaties.[36] Thus, the Spanish Americans had unknowingly become the victims of the imponderable and pervasive sectional controversies of the day.

Notwithstanding its new judicial seal of approval, the tax was a practical failure, as even its original supporters admitted. The Mexican was not the Negro slave; California was not Texas. The governor, aware that the tax was reaping more resentment than revenue, cut the rate to $20 for four months. Even after this corrective, however, the state obtained only $30,000 instead of an expected $2,400,000. The collector in a county that had 15,000 potential taxpayers, sold only 525 permits and was so harassed on his job that he resigned.[37] By 1851 Stockton's leading citizens had developed such loathing for the tax—"a law for the killing of children to get their fat" [38]—that they decided to rally the entire county and lobby in the state capital to obtain its repeal. This they accomplished in 1851.

The tax had failed to make the state wealthy, to prevent mob action, and to convert immigrants into hirelings as promised. It had eliminated the Latin Americans already in California and curtailed new immigration, a result that did not altogether fill the original bill. Now, having pushed the tax aside, the boosters of the foreign miners hoped to summon them back and make amends. The Yankees had a sudden vision that with the law gone, tens of thousands of Latin Americans would come flooding out of Mexico and Chile and the California towns and wash up into the southern mines, thus opening a new era in gold mining.

That dream failed to materialize, however, since the Spanish Americans by now mistrusted the Yankees and suspected that gold was giving out. They withdrew to Los Angeles and other villages or returned home, informing their countrymen of the dangers of venturing forth into Califor-

---

[36] *The People ex rel. The Attorney General v. Naglee* (1851), 1 Cal. 232.

[37] Governor's "Annual Message to the Legislature," in *Senate Journal, 1851,* p. 33; Stockton *Times,* Jan. 18, 1851; "Statement of . . . Besançon," op. cit., p. 616.

[38] Stockton *Times,* March 5, 1851.

nia. Of course, small parties of Spanish Americans continued to enter the diggings, rummaging about on their own hook and staying alert to the possibility of trouble. The one lone Mexican patrón who dared bring in peons in 1852 stood out so conspicuously that he became the center of an international incident. His case made the complete circuit to Mexico City, Washington, and back to California. The district attorney investigated it for the United States Secretary of War, who determined that, although the crowd of Americans who stopped the Mexican was "wholly unprincipled and deserving of punishment," Mexican nationals should seek reparations in the state courts, since the federal government took no responsibility for riots.[39] Thereafter, no patrón was courageous or indiscreet enough to enter the mines, and the Yankees triumph over "foreign capitalists" and "slaves" was complete.

In the long view of California history, the Mexican miners represent merely a link in a long chain of migrants who reach across the "Spanish borderland." They unwittingly followed the trail blazed by the Spanish soldier Juan Bautista Anza and used later by Mexican cholos and colonists. They foreshadowed the coming of the "wetbacks" and the braceros in the twentieth century.

[39] *Alta*, June and July, 1852, passim; I. S. K. Ogier to William L. Marcy, Nov. 15, 1853, in George Cosgrave, "A Diplomatic Incident on the Little Mariposa," California Historical Society, *Quarterly*, XXI (Dec., 1942), 358–362; and Marcy to Manuel Larrainzar, May 25, April 28, 1853, in William R. Manning, ed., *Diplomatic Correspondence of the United States: Inter-American Affairs, 1831–1860* (Washington, D.C., 1937), IX, 129 ff.

LETTER FROM JAMES BUCHANAN TO THE
MINISTER OF FOREIGN RELATIONS OF MEXICO

To His Excellency, the Minister of Foreign Relations of the Mexican
    Republic.

Sir: Two years have nearly passed away since our Republics have been engaged in war. Causes which it would now be vain if not hurtful to recapitulate, have produced this calamity. Under the blessing of a kind Providence, this war, I trust, is about to terminate, and, hereafter, instead of the two nations doing each other all the harm they can, their mutual energies will be devoted to promote each other's welfare by the pursuits of peace and of commerce. I most cordially congratulate you on the cheering prospect. This will become a reality as soon as the Mexican Government shall approve the treaty of peace between the two nations concluded at Guadalupe Hidalgo on the 2nd February, last, with the amendments thereto which have been adopted by the Senate of the United States.

The President, in the exercise of his constitutional discretion, a few

Reprinted from *Treaties and Other International Acts of the United States of America*, Vol. 5 (Washington, D.C.: Government Printing Office, 1937), pp. 253–57.

days after this treaty was received, submitted it to the Senate for their consideration and advice as to its ratification. Your Excellency is doubtless aware that under the Constitution of the United States, "the advice and consent of the Senate" is necessary to the validity of all treaties and that this must be given by a majority of two thirds of the Senators present. Every Treaty must receive the sanction of this august Executive Council in the manner prescribed by the Constitution, before it can be binding on the United States.

The Senate commenced their deliberations on this Treaty on the 23rd February, last, and continued to discuss its provisions until the 10th instant (March) when they finally advised and consented to its ratification by a majority of 38 to 14. Your Excellency will perceive that a change of 4 votes taken from the majority and added to the minority would have defeated the Treaty.

I have now the honor to transmit you a printed copy of the Treaty with a copy, in manuscript, of the amendments and final proceedings of the Senate upon it. This is done to hasten with as little delay as practicable the blessed consummation of peace by placing in the possession of the Mexican Government at as early a period as possible all the information which they may require to guide their deliberations.

In recurring to the amendments adopted by the Senate, it affords me sincere satisfaction to observe that none of the leading features of the Treaty have been changed. Neither the delineation of the boundaries between the two Republics—nor the consideration to be paid to Mexico for the extension of the boundaries of the United States—nor the obligation of the latter to restrain the Indians within their limits from committing hostilities on the territories of Mexico nor, indeed, any other stipulation of national importance to either of the parties, has been stricken out from the Treaty by the Senate. In all its important features, it remains substantially as it was when it came from the hands of the negotiators.

The first amendment adopted by the Senate is to insert in Article 3 after the words "Mexican Republic" where they first occur, the words, *"and the Ratifications exchanged."*

Under this article, as it originally stood, the blockades were to cease and the troops of the United States were to commence the evacuation of the Mexican territory immediately upon the ratification of the Treaty by both Governments. The amendment requires in addition that these ratifications shall have been first exchanged.

The object of this amendment doubtless was to provide against the possibility that the American Senate and the Mexican Congress might ratify the Treaty, the first in its amended and the latter in its original form: in which event peace would not thereby be concluded. Besides, it was known that this amendment could produce no delay, as under the amendment of the Senate to the 23rd article, the ratification of the Treaty may be exchanged at the seat of Government of Mexico the moment after the Mexican Government and Congress shall have accepted the Treaty as amended by the Senate of the United States.

The second amendment of the Senate is to strike out the 9th Article and insert the following in lieu thereof.

[Here follows the English version of Article 9]

This article is substantially the same with the original 9th article; but it avoids unnecessary prolixity and accords with the former safe precedents of this Government in the Treaties by which we acquired Louisiana from France and Florida from Spain.

The Louisiana Treaty of the 30th April, 1803 [Document 28], contains the following article.

ARTICLE 3

The inhabitants of the ceded territory shall be incorporated in the union of the United States, and admitted as soon as possible, according to the principles of the Federal Constitution, to the enjoyment of all the rights, advantages and immunities of citizens of the United States, and in the mean time they shall be maintained and protected in the free enjoyment of their liberty, property, and the religion which they profess.

Again, in the Florida Treaty of 22nd February, 1819 [Document 41], the following articles are contained.

ARTICLE 5

The inhabitants of the ceded Territories shall be secured in the free exercise of their religion, without any restriction; and all those who may desire to remove to the Spanish Dominions, shall be permitted to sell or export their effects, at any time whatever, without being subject, in either case, to duties.

ARTICLE 6

The inhabitants of the territories which His Catholic Majesty cedes to the United States, by his Treaty, shall be incorporated in the Union of the United States, as soon as may be consistent with the principles of the Federal Constitution, and admitted to the enjoyment of all the privileges, rights and immunities of the citizens of the United States.

Under these Treaties with France and Spain, the free and flourishing States of Louisiana, Missouri, Arkansas, Iowa and Florida have been admitted into the Union; and no complaint has ever been made by the original or other inhabitants that their civil or religious rights have not been amply protected. The property belonging to the different churches in the United States is held as sacred by our Constitution and laws as the property of individuals; and every individual enjoys the inalienable right of worshipping his God according to the dictates of his own conscience. The Catholic Church in this country would not, if they could, change their position in this particular.

After the successful experience of nearly half a century, the Senate did not deem it advisable to adopt any new form for the 9th Article of the Treaty; and surely the Mexican Government ought to be content with an article similar to those which have proved satisfactory to the Governments of France and Spain and to all the inhabitants of Louisiana and Florida, both of which were Catholic provinces.

I ought perhaps here to note a modification in the 9th article, as adopted by the Senate, of the analogous articles of the Louisiana and Florida Treaties. Under this modification, the inhabitants of the ceded territories are to be admitted into the Union, "at the proper time (to be judged of by the Congress of the United States") &c.

Congress, under all circumstances and under all Treaties are the sole judges of this proper time, because they and they alone, under the Federal Constitution, have power to admit new States into the Union. That they will always exercise this power as soon as the condition of the inhabitants of any acquired territory may render it proper, cannot be doubted. By this means the Federal Treasury can alone be relieved from the expense of supporting territorial Governments. Besides, Congress will never lend a deaf ear to a people anxious to enjoy the privilege of self government. Their application to become a State or States of the Union will be granted the moment this can be done with safety.

The third amendment of the Senate strikes from the Treaty the 10th Article.

It is truly unaccountable how this article should have found a place in the Treaty. That portion of it in regard to lands in Texas did not receive a single vote in the Senate. If it were adopted, it would be a mere nullity on the face of the Treaty, and the Judges of our Courts would be compelled to disregard it. It is our glory that no human power exists in this country which can deprive one individual of his property without his consent and transfer it to another. If grantees of lands in Texas, under the Mexican Government, possess valid titles, they can maintain their claims before our Courts of Justice. If they have forfeited their grants by not complying with the conditions on which they were made, it is beyond the power of this Government, in any mode of action, to render these titles valid either against Texas or any individual proprietor. To resuscitate such grants and to allow the grantees the same period after the exchange of the ratifications of this Treaty to which they were originally entitled for the purpose of performing the conditions on which these grants had been made, even if this could be accomplished by the power of the government of the United States, would work manifold injustice.

These Mexican grants, it is understood, cover nearly the whole sea coast and a large portion of the interior of Texas. They embrace thriving villages and a great number of cultivated farms, the proprietors of which have acquired them honestly by purchase from the State of Texas. These proprietors are now dwelling in peace and security. To revive dead titles and suffer the inhabitants of Texas to be ejected under them from their possessions, would be an act of flagrant injustice of not wanton cruelty. Fortunately this Government possesses no power to adopt such a proceeding.

The same observations equally apply to such grantees in New Mexico and Upper California.

The present Treaty provides amply and specifically in its 8th and 9th Articles for the security of property of every kind belonging to Mexicans, whether acquired under Mexican grants or otherwise in the acquired territory. The property of foreigners under our Constitution and laws, will be equally secure without any Treaty stipulation. The tenth article could have no effect upon such grantees as had forfeited their claims, but that of involving them in endless litigation under the vain hope that a Treaty might cure the defects in their titles against honest purchasers and owners of the soil.

And here it may be worthy of observation that if no stipulation whatever were contained in the Treaty to secure to the Mexican inhabitants and all others protection in the free enjoyment of their liberty, property and the religion which they profess, these would be amply guarantied by the Constitution and laws of the United States. These invaluable blessings, under our form of Government, do not result from Treaty stipulations, but from the very nature and character of our institutions. . . .

> James Buchanan,
> Department of State,
> Washington, 18th March, 1848.

THE TREATY OF GUADALUPE HIDALGO:
ARTICLES 8–15

Article VIII

Mexicans now established in territories previously belonging to Mexico, and which remain for the future within the limits of the United States, as defined by the present treaty, shall be free to continue where they now reside, or to remove at any time to the Mexican Republic, retaining the property which they possess in the said territories, or disposing thereof, and removing the proceeds wherever they please, without their being subjected, on this account, to any contribution, tax or charge whatever.

Those who shall prefer to remain in the said territories, may either retain the title and rights of Mexican citizens, or acquire those of citizens of the United States. But they shall be under the obligation to make their election within one year from the date of the exchange of ratifications of this treaty: and those who shall remain in the said territories, after the

Reprinted from Hunter Miller, ed., *Treaties and Other International Acts of the United States of America*, Vol. 5 (Washington, D.C.: Government Printing Office, 1937).

expiration of that year, without having declared their intention to retain the character of Mexicans, shall be considered to have elected to become citizens of the United States.

In the said territories, property of every kind, now belonging to Mexicans, not established there, shall be inviolably respected. The present owners, the heirs of these, and all Mexicans who may hereafter acquire said property by contract, shall enjoy with respect to it, guarantees equally ample as if the same belonged to citizens of the United States.

Article IX

The Mexicans who, in the territories aforesaid, shall not preserve the character of citizens of the Mexican Republic, conformably with what is stipulated in the preceding article, shall be incorporated into the Union of the United States and be admitted, at the proper time (to be judged of by the Congress of the United States) to the enjoyment of all the rights of citizens of the United States according to the principles of the Constitution; and in the mean time shall be maintained and protected in the free enjoyment of their liberty and property, and secured in the free exercise of their region without restriction.

[*One of the amendments of the Senate struck out Article 10.*]

Article XI

Considering that a great part of the territories which, by the present Treaty, are to be comprehended for the future within the limits of the United States, is now occupied by savage tribes, who will hereafter be under the exclusive control of the Government of the United States, and whose incursions within the territory of Mexico would be prejudicial in the extreme; it is solemnly agreed that all such incursions shall be forcibly restrained by the Government of the United States, whensoever this may be necessary; and that when they cannot be prevented, they shall be punished by the said Government, and satisfaction for the same shall be exacted; all in the same way, and with equal diligence and energy, as if the same incursions were meditated or committed within its own territory against its own citizens.

It shall not be lawful, under any pretext whatever, for any inhabitant of the United States, to purchase or acquire any Mexican or any foreigner residing in Mexico, who may have been captured by Indians inhabiting the territory of either of the two Republics, nor to purchase or acquire horses, mules, cattle or property of any kind, stolen within Mexican territory by such Indians.

And, in the event of any person or persons, captured within Mexican Territory by Indians, being carried into the territory of the United States, the Government of the latter engages and binds itself in the most solemn manner, so soon as it shall know of such captives being within its territory, and shall be able so to do, through the faithful exercise of its influence and power, to rescue them and return them to their country, or deliver them to the agent or representative of the Mexican Government. The Mexican Authorities will, as far as practicable, give to the Government of the United States notice of such captures; and its agent shall pay the expenses incurred in the maintenance and transmission of the rescued captives; who, in the mean time, shall be treated with the utmost hospitality by the American authorities at the place where they may be. But if the Government of the United States, before receiving such notice from Mexico, should obtain intelligence through any other channel, of the existence of Mexican captives within its territory, it will proceed forthwith to effect their release and delivery to the Mexican agent, as above stipulated.

For the purpose of giving to these stipulations the fullest possible efficacy, thereby affording the security and redress demanded by their true spirit and intent, the Government of the United States will now and hereafter pass, without unnecessary delay, and always vigilantly enforce, such laws as the nature of the subject may require. And finally, the sacredness of this obligation shall never be lost sight of by the said Government, when providing for the removal of the Indians from any portion of the said territories, or for its being settled by citizens of the United States; but on the contrary special care shall then be taken not to place its Indian occupants under the necessity of seeking new homes, by committing those invasions which the United States have solemnly obliged themselves to restrain.

Article XII

In consideration of the extension acquired by the boundaries of the United States, as defined in the fifth Article of the present Treaty, the Government of the United States engages to pay to that of the Mexican Republic the sum of fifteen Millions of Dollars.

Immediately after this treaty shall have been duly ratified by the Government of the Mexican Republic, the sum of three millions of dollars shall be paid to the said Government by that of the United States at the city of Mexico, in the gold or silver coin of Mexico. The remaining twelve millions of dollars shall be paid at the same place and in the same coin, in annual instalments of three millions of dollars each, together with interest on the same at the rate of six per centum per annum. This interest shall begin to run upon the whole sum of twelve millions, from the day of the ratification of the present treaty by the Mexican Government, and the first of the instalments shall be paid at the expiration of one year from the same day. Together with each annual instalment, as it falls due, the whole interest accruing on such instalment from the beginning shall also be paid.

Article XIII

The United States engage moreover, to assume and pay to the claimants all amounts now due them, and those hereafter to become due, by reason of the claims already liquidated and decided against the Mexican Republic, under the conventions between the two Republics severally concluded on the eleventh day of April eighteen hundred and thirty-nine, and on the thirtieth day of January eighteen hundred and forty-three: so that the Mexican Republic shall be absolutely exempt for the future, from all expense whatever on account of the said claims.

Article XIV

The United States do furthermore discharge the Mexican Republic from all claims of citizens of the United States, not heretofore decided against the Mexican Government, which may have arisen previously to the date of the signature of this treaty: which discharge shall be final and perpetual, whether the said claims be rejected or be allowed by the Board of Commissioners provided for in the following Article, and whatever shall be the total amount of those allowed.

Article XV

The United States, exonerating Mexico from all demands on account of the claims of their citizens mentioned in the preceding Article, and considering them entirely and forever cancelled, whatever their amount may be, undertake to make satisfaction for the same, to an amount not exceeding three and one quarter millions of Dollars. To ascertain the validity and amount of those claims, a Board of Commissioners shall be established by the Government of the United States, whose awards shall be final and conclusive: provided that in deciding upon the validity of each claim, the board shall be guided and governed by the principles and rules of decision prescribed by the first and fifth Articles of the unratified convention, concluded at the City of Mexico on the twentieth day of November, one thousand eight hundred and forty-three; and in no case shall an award be made in favour of any claim not embraced by these principles and rules.

If, in the opinion of the said Board of Commissioners, or of the claimants, any books, records or documents in the possession or power of the Government of the Mexican Republic, shall be deemed necessary to the just decision of any claim, the Commissioners or the claimants, through them, shall, within such period as Congress may designate, make an application in writing for the same, addressed to the Mexican Minister for Foreign Affairs, to be transmitted by the Secretary of State of the United

States; and the Mexican Government engages, at the earliest possible moment after the receipt of such demand, to cause any of the books, records or documents, so specified, which shall be in their possession or power (or authenticated Copies or extracts of the same) to be transmitted to the said Secretary of State, who shall immediately deliver them over to the said Board of Commissioners: provided that no such application shall be made, by, or at the instance of, any claimant, until the facts which it is expected to prove by such books, records or documents, shall have been stated under oath or affirmation.

THE TREATY OF GUADALUPE HIDALGO:
ARTICLES 9 AND 10 BEFORE SENATE AMENDMENT

Article IX

The Mexicans who, in the territories aforesaid, shall not preserve the character of citizens of the Mexican Republic, conformably with what is stipulated in the preceding Article, shall be incorporated into the Union of the United States, and admitted as soon as possible, according to the principles of the Federal Constitution, to the enjoyment of all the rights of citizens of the United States. In the mean time, they shall be maintained and protected in the enjoyment of their liberty, their property, and the civil rights now vested in them according to the Mexican laws. With respect to political rights, their condition shall be on an equality with that of the inhabitants of the other territories of the United States; and at least equally good as that of the inhabitants of Louisiana and the Floridas, when these provinces, by transfer from the French Republic and the Crown of Spain, became territories of the United States.

The same most ample guaranty shall be enjoyed by all ecclesiastics and religious corporations or communities, as well in the discharge of the offices of their ministry, as in the enjoyment of their property of every kind, whether individual or corporate. This guaranty shall embrace all temples, houses and edifices dedicated to the Roman Catholic worship; as well as all property destined to its support, or to that of schools, hospitals and other foundations for charitable or beneficent purposes. No property of this nature shall be considered as having become the property of the American Government, or as subject to be, by it, disposed of or diverted to other uses.

Finally, the relations and communication between the Catholics living in the territories aforesaid, and their respective ecclesiastical authorities,

Reprinted from Hunter Miller, ed., *Treaties and Other International Acts of the United States of America*, Vol. 5 (Washington, D.C.: Government Printing Office, 1937).

shall be open, free and exempt from all hindrance whatever, even although such authorities should reside within the limits of the Mexican Republic, as defined by this treaty; and this freedom shall continue, so long as a new demarcation of ecclesiastical districts shall not have been made, conformably with the laws of the Roman Catholic Church.

Article X

All grants of land made by the Mexican Government or by the competent authorities, in territories previously appertaining to Mexico, and remaining for the future within the limits of the United States, shall be respected as valid, to the same extent that the same grants would be valid, if the said territories had remained within the limits of Mexico. But the grantees of lands in Texas, put in possession thereof, who, by reason of the circumstances of the country since the beginning of the troubles between Texas and the Mexican Government, may have been prevented from fulfilling all the conditions of their grants, shall be under the obligation to fulfill the said conditions within the periods limited in the same respectively; such periods to be now counted from the date of the exchange of ratifications of this treaty: in default of which the said grants shall not be obligatory upon the State of Texas, in virtue of the stipulations contained in this Article.

The foregoing stipulation in regard to grantees of land in Texas, is extended to all grantees of land in the territories aforesaid, elsewhere than in Texas, put in possession under such grants; and, in default of the fulfilment of the conditions of any such grant, within the new period, which, as is above stipulated, begins with the day of the exchange of ratifications of this treaty, the same shall be null and void.

The Mexican Government declares that no grant whatever of lands in Texas has been made since the second day of March one thousand eight hundred and thirty-six; and that no grant whatever of lands in any of the territories aforesaid has been made since the thirteenth day of May one thousand eight hundred and forty-six.

THE PROTOCOL OF QUERÉTARO

In the city of Querétaro on the twenty-sixth of the month of May eighteen hundred and forty-eight at a conference between Their Excellencies Nathan Clifford and Ambrose H. Sevier Commissioners of the United States of America, with full powers from their Government to make to

Reprinted from Hunter Miller, ed., *Treaties and Other International Acts of the United States of America*, Vol. 5 (Washington, D.C.: Government Printing Office, 1937).

the Mexican Republic suitable explanations in regard to the amendments which the Senate and Government of the said United States have made in the treaty of peace, friendship, limits and definitive settlement between the two Republics, signed in Guadalupe Hidalgo, on the Second day of February of the present year, and His Excellency Don Luis de la Rosa, Minister of Foreign Affairs of the Republic of Mexico, it was agreed, after adequate conversation respecting the changes alluded to, to record in the present protocol the following explanations which Their aforesaid Excellencies the Commissioners gave in the name of their Government and in fulfillment of the Commission conferred upon them near the Mexican Republic.

First

The American Government by suppressing the IXth article of the Treaty of Guadalupe and substituting the IIId article of the Treaty of Louisiana did not intend to diminish in any way what was agreed upon by the aforesaid article IXth in favor of the inhabitants of the territories ceded by Mexico. Its understanding is that all of that agreement is contained in the IIId article of the Treaty of Louisiana. In consequence, all the privileges and guarantees, civil, political and religious, which would have been possessed by the inhabitants of the ceded territories, if the IXth article of the Treaty had been retained, will be enjoyed by them without any difference under the article which has been substituted.

Second

The American Government by suppressing the Xth article of the Treaty of Guadalupe did not in any way intend to annul the grants of lands made by Mexico in the ceded territories. These grants, notwithstanding the suppression of the article of the Treaty, preserve the legal value which they may possess; and the grantees may cause their legitimate titles to be acknowledged before the American tribunals.

Conformably to the law of the United States, legitimate titles to every description of property personal and real, existing in the ceded territories, are those which were legitimate titles under the Mexican law in California and New Mexico up to the 13th of May 1846, and in Texas up to the 2d March 1836.

Third

The Government of the United States by suppressing the concluding paragraph of article XIIth of the Treaty, did not intend to deprive the Mexican Republic of the free and unrestrained faculty of ceding, conveying or transferring at any time (as it may judge best) the sum of the twelve millions of dollars which the same Government of the United States is to deliver in the places designated by the amended article.

And these explanations having been accepted by the Minister of Foreign Affairs of the Mexican Republic, he declared in name of his Government that with the understanding conveyed by them, the same Government would proceed to ratify the Treaty of Guadalupe as modified by the Senate and Government of the United States. In testimony of which their Excellencies the aforesaid Commissioners and the Minister have signed and sealed in quintuplicate the present protocol.

[Seal] A. H. Sevier

[Seal] Nathan Clifford

[Seal] Luis De La Rosa

THE EBB AND FLOW OF IMMIGRATION

Leo Grebler, Joan W. Moore, and Ralph C. Guzmán

Across a border of great length, easy to cross in numerous places, and quite unreal to many living in its vicinity, a traditional pattern of migration continued unhampered long after the boundary was established. Since 1900, nearly 1.4 million Mexican immigrants were admitted legally. Many others entered illegally or with permits for temporary employment. This mass movement has been part of an experience intrinsic to the development of our society—peoples coming to the United States from many lands. As Oscar Handlin put it, "Once I thought to write a history of the immigrants in America. Then I discovered that the immigrants *were* American history." But the Mexican movement across the border reveals quite distinctive characteristics when compared with immigration from Europe.

Distinctive Features of Migration from Mexico

First, immigration from Mexico is a late chapter in the history of immigration to the United States. Significant numbers of legal immigrants were first recorded in 1909 and 1910, at the beginning of the Mexican

Reprinted with permission of The Macmillan Company from *The Mexican-American People* by Leo Grebler, Joan W. Moore, and Ralph C. Guzmán. Copyright © 1970 by The Free Press, a Division of The Macmillan Company.

Leo Grebler, Joan W. Moore, and Ralph C. Guzmán were the directors of the Mexican American Study Project at UCLA between 1963 and 1968. Dr. Grebler is a Guggenheim Fellow and currently professor of economics at UCLA. Dr. Moore is a sociologist who now teaches at the University of California at Riverside. She is a former research fellow of the National Institute of Child Health and Human Development. Dr. Guzmán has served as associate director of the U.S. Peace Corps in Venezuela and in Peru. He is a political scientist on the faculty of the University of California at Santa Cruz.

Revolution. About this time, total immigration to the United States had reached its peak and started to decline. The influx from Mexico gathered momentum in the 1920s, with nearly half a million legal immigrants, although by then *total* immigration was sharply reduced from pre-World War I levels.

Second, migration across the Mexican border shows an unusual variety of movements. There are permanent legal immigrants as well as people who come for temporary employment but manage to stay. Mexican and United States citizens who live south of the border commute regularly for work in the United States. Agricultural workers come and go with the seasons. In addition there is the usual array of businessmen, visitors, tourists, students, shoppers, and others entering for limited periods. The Canadian border, too, is traversed by varied traffic, but the pull of economic opportunity drawing Mexicans across the boundary—and hence their incentive to enter the United States by any available means—has been much greater than for Canadians.

Third, movements across the Mexican border have been unusually intensive. In the second half of the 1920s, and again in the period from 1955 to 1964, Mexican immigrants accounted for more than 15 per cent of all immigrants coming to the United States. Between 1957 and 1966, more people arrived on visa from Mexico than from any other country. Mexico has long been the largest single source of aliens for temporary farm work. To judge from statistics on expulsions, which show Mexicans consistently at or near the top, Mexico has also been the main single source of illegal entrants. Its great length and generally harsh terrain make the border difficult to control. The problems of control have been compounded by the recruiting efforts of Southwest employers, by pressures on the Border Patrol from growers and other businesses to relax its vigilance and by the availability of friendly hiding places in the *barrios* of the border states.

Fourth, the intentions of Mexicans coming to this country generally seem to have been less certain and more varied than those of the many millions who came from other lands. Physical proximity, the relatively low cost of movement after railroad and highway connections were established, and the varied opportunities for crossing the border made it easier for many Mexicans to view migration to this country as an experiment, an adventure, or a temporary expedient without a momentous commitment. If a Mexican entered on a regular immigration visa, he could return without incurring great emotional or monetary cost. If he came for temporary employment and liked the experience, he often found it easy to stay. The Mexican on the move might even come and go more than once before he decided to accept or reject the new land permanently. As a result, there has been a large volume of return movements from the United States to Mexico, augmented by forced repatriations which at times reached large proportions.

The Record of Immigration

The Period Before 1920

Literature ranging from folklore to historical treatises testifies to substantial movements of people across the Mexican border long before such movements were controlled, classified, and measured. Even in the late years of the nineteenth century, migration was still informal. Controls were so minimal that no records whatever were kept from 1886 to 1893, and even the statistics for subsequent years were rough approximations. This was still the period of our "open door" immigration policy, modified only by some qualitative restrictions and a small "head tax." Admission to the United States was arranged at the border station, and no visa from an American consulate was required.

Mexican nationals came to the United States under a variety of arrangements. About 24,000 were reported as immigrants in the first decade of this century. But many more crossed the border for temporary work. Mexican laborers were employed not only in agriculture but in mining, railroad construction and maintenance, and other jobs. Around the turn of the century, railroads had been built from the interior of Mexico to the United States. Thus, migration became much easier and cheaper. Yet, recorded (presumably permanent) immigration in the 1900–1909 period was of moderate proportions. Most of the foreign labor employed in Southwest agriculture was still supplied by earlier immigrants from Asia. The vast majority of Mexico's population was immobile geographically as well as socially. Nearly nine-tenths lived in rural areas, and large numbers of agricultural workers were held in peonage, which of course restricted their freedom to move.

The Mexican revolutionary period beginning in 1909–1910 spurred the first substantial and permanent migration to the United States (Table 1). The immigrants of this time had backgrounds probably more differentiated than the backgrounds of those who entered before and after this era. They included upper- and middle-class refugees who felt threatened by the Revolution, as well as many others who simply sought escape from a bloody and protracted conflict. The Revolution also had a more important and durable indirect effect on the movement to the United States. By liberating masses of people from social as well as geographic immobility, it served to activate a latent migration potential of vast dimensions.

How many refugees of the revolutionary era went back to Mexico is not known, but family histories show that quite a few decided to stay in the United States. It is perhaps characteristic that a Mexican American in Texas, whose parents had immigrated during this period, remembers continual family discussion of an early return to the homeland, until he himself, at the age of eighteen, recognized that "he was here to stay."

Table 1.   Number of Mexican Immigrants Compared with
All Immigrants, 1900–1968*

Period†	Mexican‡	Total	Mexican as Per Cent of Total
1900–1904	2,259	3,255,149	.07
1905–1909	21,732	4,947,239	.44
1910–1914	82,588	5,174,701	1.60
1915–1919	91,075	1,172,679	7.77
1920–1924	249,248	2,774,600	8.98
1925–1929	238,527	1,520,910	15.68
1930–1934	19,200	426,953	4.50
1935–1939	8,737	272,422	3.21
1940–1944	16,548	203,589	8.13
1945–1949	37,742	653,019	5.78
1950–1954	78,723	1,099,035	7.16
1955–1959	214,746	1,400,233	15.34
1960–1964	217,827	1,419,013	15.35
Annual figures			
1960–1964 (av.)	43,565	283,803	15.35
1965	37,969	296,697	12.79
1966	45,163	323,040	13.98
1967	42,371	361,972	11.71
1968	43,563	454,448	9.59

* The reported figures for the earlier periods should be considered approximations. All of them refer to persons who were legally admitted for permanent residence.
† Fiscal years.
‡ Classified by country of birth, except for the periods 1935–1939 and 1940–1944, in which the data refer to Mexico as the country of last permanent residence. This classification had to be adopted because the reports for several years in these periods do not furnish data by country of birth. The statistics for periods for which both classifications are reported indicate that numerical differences are relatively small. The "country of birth" classification was adopted here as the basic one not only because it is definitionally superior, but also because characteristics of immigrants are reported on this basis.
Source: Annual Reports of the U.S. Immigration and Naturalization Service and its predecessor agencies.

With the advent of World War I, the "push" of the Mexican Revolution was reinforced by the "pull" of American labor requirements. The shortage of domestic workers meant that growers could make a good case for opening the southern border. Mexicans were close at hand. The economic distress of the Revolution meant that a great many of them were willing to work in American agriculture. The labor shortage opened up opportunities in non-agricultural employment as well, and special regulations issued in 1917 to admit temporary farm workers from Mexico were quickly extended to cover jobs in railroad maintenance and mining.

Hence, this period witnessed substantial temporary as well as increased permanent immigration.

The Mass Migration of the 1920s

Immigration from Mexico reached a peak in the 1920s. Close to 500,000 were reported as entering on permanent visas. Mexican immigrants accounted for 9 per cent of all immigrants to this country in the first half of the decade, and nearly 16 per cent of the total in the second half when the quota system, European prosperity, and emigration restrictions in fascist Italy and communist Russia reduced the movement of people from Europe.

In the 1920s, too, migration from Mexico to the United States reached a peak relative to Mexico's own population (Table 2). Mexican literature of this period began to reveal the first fears that Mexico was losing too many of her energetic, skilled, and ambitious people to the big northern neighbor. On the other hand, apprehensions in the United States about the volume and composition of Mexican immigration led to a vigorous Congressional debate over the extension of the quota system to Mexicans and to stricter administrative controls in the late 1920s.

Immigration reached high levels despite the increased difficulty of entry. American consulates were designated as visa-issuing agencies, and entry could no longer be arranged at the border station. Costs alone rose. Many Mexicans wishing to emigrate now had to incur travel expenses to

Table 2. Emigration from Mexico to the United States as a Per Cent of Mexico's Population, 1900–1960

Year	Mexican Population*	Mexican Population, Decade Average*	Emigration During Decade†	Emigrants as Per Cent of Population
1900	13,607			
		14,383	23,991	0.17
1910	15,160			
		14,747	224,705	1.52
1921‡	14,335			
		15,444	436,733	2.83
1930	16,553			
		18,103	27,937	0.15
1940	19,654			
		22,722	54,290	0.24
1950	25,791			
		30,357	293,469	0.97
1960	34,923			

* In thousands.
† Emigration figures as reported in the United States immigration statistics.
‡ The census was taken in 1921 rather than 1920. The corresponding emigration data cover the 11 years from 1910 through 1921. The emigration data for 1921–1930 covers nine years.
Sources: Mexican population: Censos Generales de Población. Immigration: Annual Reports of the U.S. Immigration and Naturalization Service and its predecessor agencies.

file their application, in addition to the fees for Mexican passports and United States visas. That immigration during the 1920s reached such proportions in the face of these obstacles reflected great pressures.

In Mexico, the economic consequences of the civil war continued well into the 1920s. North of the border, the new era of prosperity acted as a strong magnet. The supply of Asian farm laborers had already dried up in the previous decade. In 1930, an official report to the Governor of California stated that the Mexican "is today a principal source of farm labor in California." The report listed certain qualities of this labor supply that would often be repeated for more than a generation. "He does tasks that white workers will not or cannot do. He works under . . . conditions that are often too trying for white workers. He will work in gangs. He will work under direction, taking orders and suggestions."

Also, nonagricultural labor requirements of the rapidly developing Southwest increased sharply. In other parts of the country, the demand for unskilled labor in manufacture and service industries was met in part by Negroes who migrated from the South. Outside Texas, however, the Southwest's Negro population remained quite small. Mexican immigrants provided a growing part of the low-wage work force. The dependence of the South west on Mexican labor was reflected in stepped-up solicitation of Mexican workers by farm and other enterprises through middlemen—a practice already adopted in earlier periods. It was also reflected in the renewal of World War I arrangements for the admission of temporary workers, although the immigration authorities pointedly stated that "so far as the records indicate, many of the laborers never returned to Mexico." Border control was strengthened in 1924. Nevertheless, illegal immigration seems to have reached large dimensions during the decade. The illegal border crosser could save the head tax, the bother and expense of obtaining a visa from an American consulate, and the cost of waiting at border stations; and he could avoid the literacy test. Manuel Gamio has written a graphic description of the ways of the illegal immigrant during this period, of the strategic role of the "coyotes," or professional smugglers and labor contractors, of document forgery, and of American enterprises enticing immigrants and paying commissions to the smugglers.

The Great Depression and World War II

Beginning in 1928, immigration from Mexico dropped sharply as economic conditions in the United States deteriorated. Large segments of American agriculture were in trouble long before the general slump in business. As the Depression took its toll and soil erosion in the Dust Bowl displaced farmers, rural tenants, and workers, Western agriculture found a new source of low-wage labor supply among the "Okies" and the urban unemployed who sought refuge in temporary farm work. During the 1930s only 27,900 Mexicans entered on permanent visas. The share of Mexicans in total immigration was less than 4 per cent as against more than 11 per cent in the previous decade. But the outstanding feature of this troubled era was substantial net out-migration, caused in large part by forced repatriation.

The manpower emergency of World War II made the Mexicans welcome again. However, legal immigrants from Mexico were slow in responding. Mexico enjoyed increased prosperity, and she needed more workers as world demand for some of her export products rose. Besides, immigrants to this country faced the prospect of service in the United States armed forces when they were of draft age, and some of Mexico's manpower was drawn into her own army when she declared war against the Axis nations in 1942.

But the small figures for visa immigrants during the war tell only part of the story, for this was when the *bracero* program was born. A *bracero* is a person who works with his arms [*brazos*]; the word has become the Spanish equivalent of farm hand. The program provided for the government-regulated recruitment of temporary workers. Initiated under an executive agreement between the United States and Mexico and ratified by Congress in August 1942, it included guarantees on working and living conditions and steady employment, which had been lacking in previous arrangements for Mexican field workers. Conceived as a war-emergency measure, it was to be 22 years before the agreement was terminated, in December 1964. It was replaced by the (sharply reduced) importation of agricultural workers under general provisions of the immigration law.

Immigration Since 1950

Immigration on permanent visa began to accelerate in the early fifties, increasing steadily from 6,372 in 1951 to over 65,000 in 1956. Nearly 293,500 were recorded in the decade as a whole, and the share of Mexican in total immigration exceeded 15 per cent in the second half of the 1950s. The increased volume did not reflect a relaxation of the law or its administration; the Immigration and Nationality Act of 1952 recodified existing statutes and introduced changes affecting mainly Europeans, but left the position of Mexican immigrants essentially unchanged.

Temporary migrations, too, increased sharply during the 1950s. For a time after World War II, the *bracero* program was inoperative, but American growers made such a persuasive case for its resumption that Congress, in 1951, enacted Public Law 78, which replicated the earlier arrangement. The familiar arguments for the need to draw on Mexican workers were reinforced by the manpower shortage of the Korean War. In fact, however, the peak of contract labor was reached in the late 1950s (Table 3). The volume declined gradually over several years before the program ended. This served to soften the impact of its termination on the Mexican economy as well as on United States agriculture.

The flood of wetbacks continued even after the 1951 legislation. Although the *bracero* program offered a legal alternative to men sneaking across the border for temporary work, the number of Mexicans who could participate was limited. Moreover, through illegal employment both

Mexican laborers and American ranchers could save money, time, and inconvenience, and avoid regulation. *Braceros* and wetbacks often worked side by side in the fields. In the early postwar years, the situation became so confused that an administrative solution was devised by transporting

Table 3. Number and Annual Average Employment of Mexican Contract Workers Admitted for Temporary Work in U.S. Agriculture, 1942–1967*

Calendar Year	Number Admitted	Annual Average Employment†
1942	4,203	1,300
1943	52,098	15,600
1944	62.170	18,600
1945	49,454	14,800
1946	32,043	9,600
1947	19,632	5,900
1948	35,345	10,600
1949	107,000	32,100
1950	67,500	20,200
1951	192,000	57,600
1952	197,100	59,100
1953	201,380	70,700
1954	309,033	85,300
1955	398,650	112,800
1956	445,197	125,700
1957	436,049	132,200
1958	432,857	131,800
1959	437,643	135,900
1960	315,846	113,200
1961	291,420	95,700
1962	194,978	59,700
1963	186,865	45,900
1964	177,736	42,300
1965	20,284	2,200
1966	8,647	1,000
1967‡	6,125	600

* Numbers of *braceros* and others admitted as reported by the U.S. Department of Agriculture for 1942–1947 and by the Bureau of Employment Security, U.S. Department of Labor, thereafter. The figures vary from those reported by the Immigration and Naturalization Service partly because the latter are for fiscal years. The data of the U.S. Department of Labor are used here because they have been converted by the Bureau of Employment Security to annual average employment for the period 1953–1967. See House Committee on the Judiciary. *Study of Population and Immigration Problems.* Special Series No. 11 (1963), appendix for part II, table 3; and the current reports *Farm Labor Developments* by the U.S. Department of Labor. For the years before 1953, the above data on annual average employment are estimates constructed as follows: The above source shows annual average employment of temporary Mexican workers in agriculture in the 1953–1962 period to equal 30.1 percent of the number of workers admitted. A ratio of 30 per cent was applied to the years prior to 1953. This procedure assumes a constant relationship between admissions and duration of employment.

† Total man-months for the year divided by 12. The figures are rounded.

‡ No Mexican workers were reported in the category for 1968.

the illegal migratory workers back across the border and then readmitting them as "legally contracted." The process was, perhaps inevitably, called the "drying-out" of wetbacks.

It became clear that the attempt to channel the irresistible wave of temporary farm workers into the orderly and regulated *bracero* program had failed. The Annual Report of the Immigration and Naturalization Service for the fiscal year 1953 referred to the human tide of wetbacks as the most serious problem of the agency: "For every agricultural laborer admitted legally, four aliens were apprehended by the Border Control." Of the 875,000 persons apprehended during the fiscal year, 30,000 were found to hold industrial and trade rather than agricultural jobs, and 1,545 were smugglers of alien labor. This situation led to "Operation Wetback" of 1954–1955, which rounded up and returned many thousands.

Legal immigration continued at high levels in the early 1960s and was rising—from less than 33,000 in 1960 to over 55,000 in 1963. At this juncture, the U.S. Department of Labor intervened through an administrative act. In a routine press release of July 1, 1963, the Department announced that job offers to Mexican immigrants would henceforth need to be "certified." The state employment services were required to verify the legitimacy of the prospective employer and of the job, as well as the permanence of employment. No job could be certified if it could be filled by domestic workers or if the alien's employment would adversely affect domestic wages and working conditions. The immediate result was a sharp drop in legal immigration to 33,000 in 1964. The number increased again in subsequent years, but it levelled off at an annual average of about 44,000 in 1966–1968, far below previous peaks. (For annual immigration figures, see Chart 1.)

Although the job-certification procedure was authorized in the 1952 Immigration and Naturalization Act for broad classes of immigrants from any country, it was implemented in 1963 against Mexicans only. Thus, the 1963 restriction and the end of the *bracero* program in 1964 fundamentally altered the conditions under which Mexicans could come to the United States.

Composition of Immigrants

Immigration statistics show only a limited number of characteristics of people who come to the United States: age, sex, and occupation. (The last item may not be fully descriptive, because it relies solely on the immigrant's designation.) Nevertheless, it is instructive to compare the composition of Mexican immigrants with that of all immigrants and with certain characteristics of the Mexican population itself. Broadly speaking, the Mexican immigrant has been younger than his counterpart from other countries, less skilled (as revealed by his occupation), and more likely to be a male. In recent years, however, there have been some notable

Chart 1.   Number of Mexican Immigrants Compared with All Other
Immigrants, 1910–1967

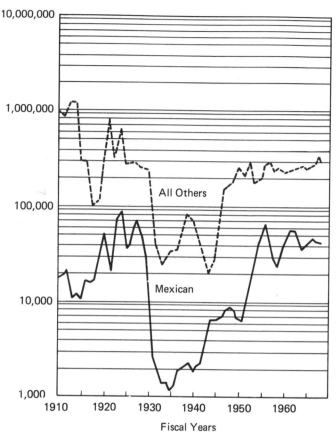

Source: Leo Grebler et al., *Mexican Immigration to the United States: The Record and Its Implications* (Mexican-American Study Project, Advance Report 2, Graduate School of Business Administration, University of California, Los Angeles, January, 1966). Table 25.

changes, probably associated with the job-certification procedure of 1963.[1]

The younger age of Mexican immigrants has persisted, and probably reflects the unusual prevalence of large families in the population of Mexico and a shorter life expectancy in that country. The youthfulness of the group became even more pronounced in 1965–1968, when children and adolescents represented a much greater proportion of Mexican immigrants, than of all immigrants, with the reverse true for the people in "productive" age brackets (Table 4). The breadwinners in the latter

---

[1] For the full array of data on the composition of Mexican and of all immigrants and for comparative figures on the Mexican population, see Leo Grebler *et al.*, *Mexican Immigration to the United States: The Record and Its Implications* (Mexican-American Study Project, Advance Report 2, Graduate School of Business Administration, University of California, Los Angeles, January, 1966), Chaps. 5 and 8. Our description here is based on this source, and the accompanying tables are merely designed to show recent changes.

segment needed the job certificate, whereas the children of previous immigrants who had left their families behind could enter under preference provisions. The sex ratio of Mexican newcomers has also changed. In 1960–1964 the ratio still showed the historical majority of men, especially in the productive age groups. In recent years, however, the sex ratio shows a drastic reversal in favor of women. Again, it seems that wives of previous immigrants have recently accounted for a larger percentage of all admissions, because the entry of male workers has been restricted by the job certification program. It is also possible that the program made it easier for female domestics to immigrate because local supplies in this occupation often fall short of demand.

Table 4.   Age Distribution and Sex Ratio of Mexican Immigrants Compared with All Immigrants, 1960–1964 and 1965–1968*

| | Age Distribution | | | | Sex Ratio† | | | |
| | 1960–1964 | | 1965–1968 | | 1960–1964 | | 1965–1968 | |
Age Group	Mexican, %	All, %	Mexican, %	All, %	Mexican	All	Mexican	All.
Under 10	20.3	16.3	25.4	16.8	101.3	103.0	103.5	103.2
10–19	18.4	15.9	27.4	17.4	96.0	76.0	108.6	83.1
20–29	30.5	33.0	23.2	28.1	134.0	67.2	63.2	59.0
30–39	16.2	17.4	10.5	17.1	162.9	96.0	54.7	87.7
40–59	11.7	13.8	10.1	15.8	116.5	85.5	57.0	77.2
60 and over	2.9	3.5	3.4	4.8	96.8	68.3	83.6	66.0
All ages	100.0	100.0	100.0	100.0	119.5	81.0	82.1	77.4

* Fiscal years.
† Males per 100 females.
Source: Annual Report of the U.S. Immigration and Naturalization Service, 1960–68, tables 9 and 10.

Mexican immigrants have always been more concentrated in low-grade occupations than other immigrants entering *at the same time,* as is shown in Table 5 for recent periods. On the whole, the occupational distribution of Mexican immigrants of the past few decades resemble• that of the European immigrants of *an earlier era* rather than of their counterparts arriving from Europe in the same period. This is a distinction of considerable consequence. In the late decades of the nineteenth century and the early years of this century, the American economy could easily absorb millions of unskilled Irish, Polish, Italian, and Scandinavian immigrants. But since the 1920s (when mass immigration from Mexico began) and particularly since World War II the absorption of people with low-grade job qualifications has become increasingly difficult. The mechanization of industry, the more recent automation of manufacturing and other processes, and the growing importance of consumer and business services have placed a high premium on skills.

The recent occupational distribution of Mexican immigrants shows notable shifts. One is a sharp increase in the percentage of people without occupation, largely women and children (Table 5, Section A). The other is an occupational upgrading of those immigrants whose occupation is reported (Section *B* of the table). There are fewer laborers in the total. White-collar workers have increased—without, however, reaching parity with the occupational composition of all immigrants. The percentage of household workers among Mexican immigrants has risen. These changes seem to be largely attributable to the job certification program.

Table 5.   Occupational Distribution of Mexican Immigrants Compared with All Immigrants,* 1960–1964 and 1965–1968

	1960–1964		1965–1968	
Occupations	*Mexican*	*All*	*Mexican*	*All*
A. Over-all Distribution				
Professional, technical, etc.	1.3%	8.7%	1.5%	10.4%
Farmers and farm managers	0.5	0.8	0.5	0.8
Managers, officials, and proprietors	0.6	2.0	0.7	2.2
Clerical, sales, etc.	2.2	9.4	1.2	7.0
Craftsmen, foremen, etc.	3.1	6.3	2.8	5.7
Operatives, etc.	1.9	4.9	1.5	5.0
Private household	6.6	3.2	6.0	4.4
Service workers except household	1.0	3.3	1.4	3.5
Farm laborers and foremen	9.5	2.3	3.0	1.3
Laborers except farm and mine	17.3	5.1	7.6	3.0
All others†	56.1	54.0	73.8	56.8
B. Distribution of Those Reporting Occupation				
Professional, technical, etc.	3.0%	19.0%	5.7%	24.0%
Farmers and farm managers	1.3	1.7	1.8	1.7
Managers, officials, and proprietors	1.4	4.4	2.6	5.0
Clerical, sales, etc.	4.9	20.5	4.7	16.3
Craftsmen, foremen, etc.	7.0	13.7	10.8	13.2
Operatives, etc.	4.0	10.8	5.7	11.6
Private household	15.1	6.8	23.0	10.2
Service workers except household	2.2	7.2	5.5	8.1
Farm laborers and foremen	21.6	5.0	11.3	2.9
Laborers except farm and mine	39.5	10.9	29.0	6.9

° Mexican immigrants in each occupational class as a percent of all Mexican immigrants, and total immigrants in each class as a percent of all immigrants.
† Housewives, children, and others with no reported or classified occupation.
Source: Annual Reports of the Immigration and Naturalization Service 1960–68, table 8.

According to studies conducted over many years, migration is a selective process. People who move differ from those who do not in such matters as age, sex, education and even in personality characteristics. From a Mexican perspective, one can say that until recent years the United States attracted a disproportionate number of Mexicans of productive age. The emigration rates shown in Table 2 could probably be doubled for persons in the "best years of their lives." Because Mexican immigrants have historically included more men than women, the movement to the United States drained off manpower. Skilled and unskilled industrial workers have been over-represented among immigrants com-

pared to their share in the *Mexican* labor force. However, the net effect of
the movement has probably benefited Mexico, first, by relieving her problems of unemployment and under-employment, especially in agriculture;
second, through the earnings that the visa immigrants and temporary
workers sent home; and third, through the training of those who returned
to Mexico.

Next to nothing is known about the geographic origin of the immigrants. Earlier writings on this subject assert that the majority have come
from Mexico's central plateau, which comprises largely agricultural states.
A secondary locus of migration is said to be the region bordering on
Texas. Information on the geographic origin of *braceros* seems to confirm
these statements, but only on the assumption that *braceros* and permanent
immigrants have largely come from the same areas. Much of the evidence
is not only meager but out of date. According to Mexican observers, the
more recent immigrants include a growing proportion of city dwellers.
Long waiting periods in Mexican border cities also confound the problem of ascertaining the geographic origin of many immigrants.

Commuters: A Growing Problem

Visa entry has been complicated since 1963 by the requirement of a job
certificate, and the *bracero* program was abandoned in 1964, but there remains one special issue affecting border-state conditions and border-state
sentiment on immigration matters: the commuters who live in Mexico but
work in the United States. Commuters may be Mexican nationals, or they
may be United States citizens (including naturalized Mexican Americans)
who live south of the border. If they are aliens they are usually "green-
card holders," that is, at each crossing they present an alien registration
card which evidences that they are legally admitted immigrants and can
therefore work (and live) in the United States. Some of the commuters
are "blue-card holders," who are permitted to cross the border for periods
not to exceed 72 hours and to perform temporary work.

The whimsical aspect of this issue begins with the legal construct under
which green-card holders are considered regular immigrants without
meeting the criterion of continuous *residence* in the United States. A court
decision refers to it as an "amiable fiction." The fictional content is increased by the apparently widespread practice of commuters to establish
residence addresses in the American border cities while continuing to live
in Mexico.

The volume of commuting traffic is not known. The regular statistics of
the Immigration and Naturalization Service cover all legal border-crossers
—shoppers, entertainment seekers, people visiting their relatives, and
and those on business trips, as well as workers. And each entry is counted
separately without recording repeated crossings by the same individual or
his purpose. Thus, United States officials have not produced any contin-

uous, reliable data on the number of Mexicans who commute to *work*. It is astonishing to find that this statistics-minded nation has failed to develop measurements of important border transactions that could be easily supplied by means of modern data-gathering and -processing methods.

In the absence of data, private groups have made widely varying guesses without any firm basis. The estimates (for unspecified recent periods) vary between 30,000 and 100,000 alien commuters to work. The U.S. Department of Labor, in a presentation to a Congressional Committee in 1963, referred to estimates ranging "from about 9,000 to 50,000." The best figures have come from a Mexican government source—the reports of the *Programa Nacional Fronterizo* on Mexican border towns—and they pertain to 1960. On the basis of these reports, we estimate that a minimum of 60,000 persons crossed the border regularly in 1960 from Mexico for employment in the United States. The Immigration and Naturalization Service reported that 40,176 aliens were in this category in November-December 1967, exclusive of commuters who were United States citizens.

Both citizens and aliens, of course, are drawn into international commuting from home to job by higher wages in the United States (even though the earnings may be low by this country's national or regional standards) and by lower living expenses in Mexico (even though prices there may be inflated by the very presence of commuters).

The policy issues posed by this movement are highly complex, and the commuter problem has accordingly received Congressional and other public attention. A drastic curtailment of commuting would have serious repercussions on the economic base of some American border cities. For example, El Paso and Brownsville would probably not be logical locations for garment factories in the absence of the low-wage workers commuting from Mexico. If such businesses closed, the adverse multiplier effects on the entire local economy could reach considerable proportions. Moreover, commuters are important customers of retail stores on the American side of the border. If commuting were blocked, the Mexican government might make it more difficult for Mexican nationals to cross the border for shopping. Thus, on balance the local economy might be stronger with than without the commuting system even if it involved spending more tax money to support unemployed domestic workers and their families.

On the other hand, commuters displace domestic labor, largely Mexican Americans, and depress wages and working conditions. The opposition to the system by organized labor is now reinforced by the antipoverty programs. There seems to be no point in spending public funds to alleviate poverty when the effort is undercut by allowing commuters to take jobs at substandard wages. The employment of Mexican commuters may be considered an indirect form of foreign aid, but the opposition questions the equity of such an arrangement. In this instance, the burden of foreign aid falls mainly on domestic workers competing in local job markets, instead of being distributed more widely.

The commuter system, then, is increasingly under fire from organized labor and welfare groups, particularly since farm enterprises along the border seem to have replaced *braceros* with commuters. For diplomatic if no other reasons, the government will resist the attacks as long as it can, for United States immigration policy vis-à-vis Mexico has always taken international implications into account, perhaps more than for other countries; and the commuter issue is a case in point. In a suit brought in 1962 by the Texas AFL–CIO against the Attorney General of the United States for failure to enforce the immigration law, the Secretary of State intervened by filing an affidavit in which he cautioned that "a sudden termination of the commuter system as the result of a court decision would have a serious deleterious effect upon our relations with Mexico." Meanwhile, Mexico's border development program attempts to anticipate trouble by augmented investment and the establishment of bonded manufacturing districts in Mexican border cities. The objective is to have labor-intensive operations performed south of the border and other operations on United States territory, without customs interference. American firms are increasing their plant investment in Mexican border areas to take advantage of these possibilities. Thus, the free movement of goods and capital could in time replace the movement of workers.

The Outlook

Future Mexican movements to the United States will depend on the migration pressure south of the border and on our own policy. The pressure in Mexico remains high—caused as it is by a compound of fast population growth, low per-capita income, slow if any progress toward more equal income distribution, continued under-employment in the country's large rural sector, and great difficulty in absorbing the migrants into the urban economy. For some time Mexico has been one of the leading countries in terms of over-all economic growth, with a steady increase of about 6 percent per year after adjustment for price changes. But much of this gain has been canceled by the rapid population growth, recently about 3.5 percent per year; and abject poverty is still so widespread that the pressure for emigration is likely to persist for many years to come.

Turning to United States policy, we note that it is clear from the job certification procedure of 1963 and the end of the *bracero* program in 1964 that immigration policy has entered a new, more restrictive era. This is a remarkable change. Until very recently, employers have been able to convince policy makers of the desirability of an ample supply of workers from Mexico, the opposition of labor and civic organizations was to no avail. Now business interests are counterbalanced by considerations of levels of domestic employment, protection of wages and labor standards, and the implications of immigration for antipoverty programs. Under these circumstances, the volume of immigration will unquestionably depend far more on United States policy than on the Mexican migration potential.

The growth of restrictionist sentiment appears in the legislative history and in some of the provisions of the Immigration and Nationality Act of 1965. The original bill was designed mainly to abolish the 41-year-old quota system based on national origin. The position of immigrants from Western Hemisphere countries remained largely unchanged. But in the hearings and congressional debates on the bill, the immigrant from New World countries became a major concern. The outcome was an amendment, taking effect in mid–1968, to allow no more than 120,000 persons a year to enter from Western Hemisphere nations. Thus, the legislators and the Administration who pressed for the abandonment of the traditional quota system could achieve their goal only by yielding to a new regional quota for the Western Hemisphere.

Among the main arguments for the imposition of a maximum was the sharp increase in total immigration from Central and South American countries in recent years, and especially from the Caribbean area (Table 6). Without a maximum, the population pressures associated with the extraordinarily high birth rates in practically all the economically underdeveloped Western Hemisphere nations would produce a flood of immigrants. Other arguments revolved around the difficulty of assimilating people coming from different cultures and absorbing them in an economy in which skills are increasingly essential. These points were often reminiscent of the contentions of the restrictionists on earlier occasions. However, it is notable that the Congressional debates hardly touched on immigration from Mexico or Canada.

Table 6.   Number of Immigrants from Western Hemisphere Countries, 1955–1968*

Fiscal Year	Mexican	Canadian†	All Other	Total
1955	50,772	23,091	22,468	96,331
1956	65,047	29,533	31,683	126,263
1957	49,154	33,203	33,587	115,944
1958	26,712	30,055	35,060	91,827
1959	23,061	23,082	28,389	74,532
1960	32,684	30,990	34,449	98,123
1961	41,632	32,038	45,188	118,858
1962	55,291	30,377	53,150	138,818
1963	55,253	36,003	61,368	152,624
1964	32,967	38,074	73,034	144,075
1965	37,969	38,327	81,395	157,691
1966	45,163	28,358	71,390	144,911
1967	42,371	23,442	90,842	156,655
1968	43,563	27,662	178,811	250,036

* By country or region of birth.
† Including Newfoundland.
Source: Annual Reports of the U.S. Immigration and Naturalization Service.

The effect on Mexican immigration of the ceiling on admissions from Western Hemisphere countries cannot be assessed at this point, but it is safe to predict a continuous tendency toward tighter control of both legal and illegal movements and a policy to reduce the volume of commuting to work. But control will remain a difficult problem. The history of Mexican immigration provides ample evidence that the various kinds of movement across the border are highly interdependent. Thus, when hundreds of thousands of wetbacks were sent home in 1954–1955, many of them returned with "clean papers" or came back as *braceros*. When immigration was curtailed in 1963 and the *bracero* program terminated, one of the immediate results was an increasing number of illegal migrants.

If control were more effective, it would profoundly influence labor-intensive industries in the border states and the Mexican Americans themselves. Agriculture would be forced into increasingly rapid mechanization, thus hastening the migration of Mexican Americans to the cities. Industries would face more effective labor organization. More limited immigration would allow Mexican Americans to consolidate social and economic gains somewhat faster. Their persistent general problem of being identified as an alien and lower-class element would be alleviated. The distance between the minority and the dominant population in education, skills, social status, and English-language competence would probably be reduced more rapidly.

Table A–1. Estimates of White Persons of Spanish Surname and of Mexican Americans, Five Southwest States, 1960

State and Region	White Persons of Spanish Surname	Mexican Americans	Excess of WPSS over MAs	Excess of MAs over WPSS
Arizona	194,356	207,791	—	13,435
California	1,426,538	1,289,008	137,530	—
Colorado	157,173	144,218	12,955	—
New Mexico	269,122	274,531	—	5,409
Texas	1,417,810	1,448,744	—	30,934
Southwest	3,464,999	3,364,292*	150,485	49,778

* The small discrepancy between this figure and the figure of 3,344,292 shown in the earlier estimate for the Southwest is the result of estimating procedures.

An Estimate of the Number of Mexican Americans in 1970

Data available for Mexican Americans permit only the crudest sort of projections. Nothing is known of their age-specific birth or death rates. No numbers are compiled on their interstate migrations. Neither the Federal government nor the various state governments prepare estimates of their number or projections of their future numbers.

The Southwest

One of the two methods used in this estimate for 1970 is a straight-line projection. It assumes that the rate of increase of Spanish-surname persons in the Southwest between 1950 and 1960 continued in the decade of the 1960s. The increase from 2,289,550 in 1950 to 3,465,000 in 1960 was 51.34 per cent. Applied to the 1960–1970 period, this rate produces an increment of about 1,779,000 persons and a total Spanish-surname population of 5,244,000 in the Southwest in 1970.

The other method takes account of the fact that the 1950–1960 rate of increase of the United States population as a whole fell sharply in the 1960–68 period. The decline occurred in both the white and nonwhite segments of the population. The estimates and projections of the U.S. Bureau of the Census in its *Current Population Series, Population Estimates,* P-25 have been revised downward from its previous expectations several times during the 1960s. The revisions were due to the drastic decline in the birth rate. Immigration and death rates have remained almost unchanged. For interstate migration, the movement is still predominantly westward, but at reduced rates. Decreases occurred in the rate of migration to Arizona and California as well as to other states in the West.

None of these observations applies specifically to persons of Spanish surname. Intercensal data for this group are not available. However, to take account of the generally declining rate of increase of the population, the second method of estimation is based upon the proportion of persons of Spanish surname in the total population of the Southwest. It starts with the revised census projections of the total resident population. The arithmetic average of the four census series for 1970 (as given in Series P–25, No. 388) is 37,216,500 persons in the Southwest, as follows:

Arizona	1,811,500
California	20,830,000
Colorado	2,110,000
New Mexico	1,085,000
Texas	11,380,000
Southwest	37,216,500

To estimate the percentage of Spanish-surname persons in the total population in 1970, we use a projection of the 1950 and 1960 relationships:

Spanish surname, 1950	10.87%
Spanish surname, 1960	11.82
Spanish surname, 1970 (est.)	12.69

On this basis, the Spanish-surname population in the Southwest would be 4,722,800 in 1970—a figure substantially below the estimate derived from straight-line projection. The lower figure assumes that the Spanish-surname population also is growing at a declining rate.

The two methods of projection, then, give a range of 4,723,000 to 5,244,000 Mexican Americans in the Southwest in 1970.

The United States

The starting point for the following projection is the number of Mexican Americans in the United States in 1960, as presented previously.

When the 3,842,000 Mexican Americans estimated for 1960 are multiplied by the rate of increase for Spanish-surname persons in the Southwest between 1950 and 1960, 51.34 per cent, the resulting increment is 1,972,483, or a total in 1970 of about 5,814,500. This method merely projects ten years into the future the trend defined by the growth of the Spanish-surname population from 1950 to 1960. The procedure assumes that the rate of increase of the Mexican-American population outside the Southwest was the same as in the Southwest. It is subject to the same reservation that applied to the straight-line estimate for the Southwest. As we noted earlier, the United States population growth rate has generally been slowing down; hence one would expect any straight-line projection to err on the high side.

A second method of projection is somewhat similar to the second estimating method applied to the Southwest, but it necessitates even more assumptions. Foreign-stock Mexican Americans declined from 51.2 per cent of all Mexican Americans in 1950 to 45.2 per cent in 1960. We estimate that this proportion will be about 40 per cent in 1970. By using the census projections of the total United States population for 1970, this method reflects the decline in the rate of growth of the general population. The computation is as follows:

	WHITE STOCK FROM MEXICO	WHITE POPULATION OF UNITED STATES	STOCK FROM MEXICO AS A PER CENT OF TOTAL WHITE POPULATION
1950	1,342,542	135,149,629	.9934
1960	1,724,838	158,831,732	1.0860
1970	2,134,757 (est.)	181,030,432 (est.)	1.1792 (est.)

Applying the projected 40.0 per cent ratio of Mexican stock to the total Mexican-American population, the method yields a projected Mexican-American population in the United States of 5,336,900 (dividing 2,134,757 by .400) by 1970.

The two methods of projection, then, produce a range of 5,340,000 to 5,800,000 Mexican Americans in the United States in 1970. This range is broadly consistent with a census sample survey of November 1969. The census estimate, based on respondents' self-identification, arrived at 5,073,000 people of Mexican descent. Another 1,582,000 identified themselves as "other Spanish Americans" (not of Mexican, Puerto Rican, Cuban, or Central and South American descent). Some of these persons were unquestionably Mexican Americans by our definition. See U.S. Bureau of the Census, *Current Population Reports,* Series P–20, No. 195, Feb. 20, 1970.

Suggested Readings

Pre-Columbian History

Bernal, Ignacio. 1963. *Mexico Before Cortez: Art, History, and Legend.* Garden City, N.Y.: Doubleday & Company, Inc.

The author, the dean of modern Mexican anthropologists, utilizes extensive quotations from the Indian codices, plates, and maps to describe the Indian way of life prior to the conquest. He leaves no doubt in the reader's mind that Mexicans were a people of high civilization and complexity.

Coe, Michael D. 1966. *The Maya.* New York: Frederick A. Praeger, Inc.

This book is an excellent survey of the civilization of the ancient Maya. It gives the reader an insight into the life style, culture, accomplishments, and social stratification of the Mayan peoples.

Covarrubias, Miguel. 1957. *Indian Art of Mexico and Central America.* New York: Alfred A. Knopf, Inc.

This is Covarrubias' finest achievement. In this book he illustrates and delineates Middle America through the use of line drawings, full color plates, and sixty-four pages of photographs. He examines the development of art, architecture, sculpture, and other arts in many of Mexico's most famous archaeological sites.

Leonard, Jonathan Norton. 1967. *Ancient-America,* from the Great Ages of Man series published by Time-Life books. New York: Time, Inc.

This is a series of picture essays, an easy-to-read and factually correct account of American culture history from earliest times through the Aztec and Inca periods. The illustrations used are worth many words.

Morley, Sylvanus G. 1956. *The Ancient Maya.* 3rd edition. Revised by George W. Brainerd. Stanford, Calif.: Stanford University Press.

A basic general work on Mayan civilization. Covers a wide spectrum of the Maya development within an archaeological framework that is in agreement with the most recent findings. It offers a rich sampling of the Maya grandeur.

Newsweek. 1970. National Museum of Anthropology (Mexico City). New York: *Newsweek.* Great Museums of the World.

In 153 color photographs the ancient roots of Mexican civilization are traced. Art and artifacts appear in this volume as they are in the National Museum of Anthropology itself.

Vaillant, G. C. 1965. *Aztecs of Mexico*. Baltimore: Penguin Books, Inc.
Vaillant's work on pre-Aztec archaeology is outdated, but his discussion of Aztec life and culture is still among the most lucid and interesting available. Another excellent source on Aztec culture and religion is Jacques Soustelle's volume *The Daily Life of the Aztecs on the Eve of the Spanish Conquest*. Stanford, Calif.: Stanford University Press, 1970.

Verrill, Hyatt A., and Ruth Verrill. 1967. *America's Ancient Civilizations*. New York: Capricorn Books.
An archaeological account of Mexican and South American civilizations. It discusses great achievements of the Amerindian peoples, e.g., animal and plant domestication, irrigation systems, civil engineering, carvings, tools, textiles, and art objects. Details and interpretations are based on archaeological discoveries throughout Mexico and South America.

Spain in America

De Madariaga, Salvador. 1948. *The Fall of the Spanish-American Empire*. New York: The Macmillan Company.
A historical account tracing 300 years of Spanish tyrannical history in the Americas. He sets the background for the events that took place during the Mexican revolution of 1810.

Gibson, Charles. 1964. *The Aztecs Under Spanish Rule: A History of the Indians of the Valley of Mexico 1519–1810*. Stanford, Calif.: Stanford University Press.
This is one of the most comprehensive studies of the imposition of Spanish institutions during the Colonial period in Mexico.

Hanke, Lewis (editor) 1971. *The Roman Catholic Church in Colonial Latin America*. New York: Alfred A. Knopf, Inc.
An informative source dealing with major religious issues concerning the Catholic Church and the effects on its Latin American pawns. In a series of articles the authors discuss the guiding principles of institutional development of colonial religion from the reign of Ferdinand and Isabella until the independence movements.

Haring, C. H. 1963. *The Spanish Empire in America*. Harbinger Books edition. New York: Harcourt Brace Jovanovich, Inc.
An institutional history of the Spanish colonies in America from 1492 down to the wars of independence. It deals with the transfer of Spanish modes of government and society from the Old World to the New World.

Idell, Albert (translator and editor). 1956. *The Bernal Diaz Chronicles*. Garden City, N.Y.: Doubleday & Company, Inc.
The first English translation since 1705 of an extraordinary historical document, the Conquest as witnessed by one of Cortés' soldiers. Bernal Diaz recorded an eyewitness account of the story of the conquest—its glories and horrors, heroism and tragedies, the greed for gold, and the toppling of a great civilization, climaxed by the death of Moctezuma.

West, Robert C., and John P. Augelli. 1966. *Middle America: Its Lands and Peoples*. Englewood Cliffs, N.J.: Prentice-Hall, Inc.
The geography and culture areas of pre-Columbian and Colonial

America are thoroughly covered. Classifications are based on the interplay of physical environment, historical process, and cultural institutions. The book delves into historical development of man's imprint upon the land through settlement patterns, illustrated with maps, photographs, and distribution charts.

Southwest History and Demography

Alvarez, Jose Hernandez. 1966. "A Demographic Profile of the Mexican Immigration to the United States, 1910–1950," *Journal of International Studies*, VIII, No. 3 (July, 1966), pp. 471–496.

This is a statistically oriented demographic study of Mexican immigration. It deals with geographic distribution, urbanization, language, education, and occupational mobility. It is strengthened by an abundance of census data.

Bolton, Herbert E. 1921. *The Spanish Borderlands.* New Haven: Yale University Press.

This is one of the standard references to southwestern history. Bolton deals mainly with the Spanish experience and cultural contributions to the southwest.

Castañeda, Carlos E., translator. 1970. *The Mexican Side of the Texas Revolution 1836* (2nd ed.). Dallas, Texas: Graphic Ideas, Inc., successors to the P. L. Turner Company.

An important source comprising diaries and dispositions from Mexican leaders prominent in the Texas Revolution, such as General Santa Anna, Ramon Martinez Caro (Secretary to Santa Anna), General Filisola, General Jose Urrea, and General Jose Maria Tornes (Secretary of War). It offers a view of the conflict that is seldom considered in the United States.

Cline, Howard F. 1963. *The United States and Mexico.* Cambridge, Mass.: Harvard University Press.

An authoritative account of historical events and developments between the United States and Mexico.

Gamio, Manuel. 1930. *Mexican Immigration to the United States.* Chicago: University of Chicago Press.

Although this study is outdated by changing immigration policies and new agreements on imported labor, Gamio presents a vivid picture of the various economic and social pressures that forced immigration from Mexico. Gamio deals with the inequalities, abuse, and indignities that the Mexican faces once he enters the arena of exploitation.

Gamio, Manuel. 1931. *The Mexican Immigrant, His Life Story.* Autobiographic documents collected by Manuel Gamio. Chicago: University of Chicago Press.

A collection of statements gathered on fifty-seven immigrants from Mexico during the 1920's. It reveals important reasons why Mexicans left their homes to come to the United States. Further, it shows the discontent in the United States, and the loyalty to Mexico. This book is particularly important in understanding the problems facing the Chicano labor organizations.

Gamio, Manuel. 1960. *Forjando Patria* (*Forging a Nation*), 2nd ed. (1st ed., 1916). Mexico City: Editorial Porrua, S.A.

Mexico's most influential anthropologist expresses deep concern for a movement to revitalize Mexico's Indian culture. Mexico, said Gamio, was not purely European. He believed that in order to bring about unity, Mexico had to forge a new nation based on what was Mexican and what was European.

Rappaport, Armin (editor). 1964. *The War with Mexico: Why Did It Happen?* Chicago: Rand McNally.

A presentation of issues and interpretations of the war in the words of contemporaries. It serves as a companion to *The Mexican War* by Ruiz listed below.

Ruiz, Ramon Eduardo (editor). 1963. *The Mexican War: Was It Manifest Destiny?* New York: Holt, Rinehart and Winston, Inc.

This book of readings treats both sides of the argument over who was responsible for the conflict. There are three essays by Americans and two by Mexicans covering five different versions of what "really happened." The task is for the reader to interpret the war after examining the different views.

PART II
Today

In this section we present a series of articles on modern Chicano culture. Some reflect the internal aspect of Chicano life—family structure, religion, and so on; others deal with the external reality; that is, the relationship of Chicano culture to the larger Anglo society.

THE INTERNAL ASPECT

The first article is by Samuel Ramos, one of modern Mexico's most creative social thinkers. His analysis of the world view of the Mexican male compliments the work of Octavio Paz. And although Ramos' study deals with the Mexican rather than with the Chicano psyche, his perceptive comments on the feelings of the pelado *("the downtrodden") are an excellent introduction to the everyday reality of Chicano life. We have included three articles on religion: an explanation of the significance of the Virgin of Guadalupe, a discussion of the urban parish, and a description through folk tales of Chicano medical practices. This last has both secular and religious components. These are followed by articles on rural social structure, the composition of the Chicano family, and a general overview of Chicano culture in a gringo world by one of the most brilliant Chicano writers, Armando Rendon.*

Three factors have limited our presentation to a few key articles covering the major facets of the culture. The first is that many aspects of Chicano life have been inadequately studied and stereotypically misrepresented in the literature. Two excellent examples are food and language— among the most important areas of everyday life. Research on Chicano foods often begins with the assumption that the diet is inherently inadequate compared with that of Anglos. Alternatively, the diet may be portrayed as an interesting ethnic novelty, something a cook might enjoy toying with once in a while. Serious nutritional studies of individual foods do exist, but there is no comprehensive study of "the black diet" or "the

Chinese diet" or "the American diet." They are far too complex for a single analysis to handle.[1]

It is also often assumed that the general affluence of middle-class whites leads to a healthier diet than that of generally poor Chicanos. Studies of the dietary patterns of white, middle-class college youth, however, have shown serious vitamin and protein deficiencies in many cases, resulting from consumption of abundant quantities of sweets, french-fried potatoes, and other between-meal snacks.[2] Thus, having money to spend on food does not insure an adequate diet. Not having money to spend on food, does insure an inadequate diet. Hot dogs are probably no more nutritional than tacos. What is inadequate about a diet of tacos is that many Chicanos cannot afford to eat enough of them or to provide their families with supplemental high-protein food sources such as meat and fish.

Studies of the language almost invariably start with the assumption that Chicano is a fallen version of a purer form of Spanish. This is a completely unwarranted assumption that makes no linguistic sense. The word troca, meaning "truck," is no more "really" English than the word ketchup is "really" Malaysian or buccaneer is "really" Tupian. Troca is a Spanish word generally confined to the Chicano dialect of that language. All we might say about troca is that it was derived from the English truck. Of course, at the same time we should keep in mind that truck was derived from Greek trochos. There are probably no more English-derived words in Chicano than there are Aztec-derived words in Mexican Spanish or, for that matter, Arabic-derived words in so-called pure Castilian Spanish of the sixteenth century. It would be very appropriate to have a thorough-going study of the Chicano language, but so far very little work has been done in this area. From a sociolinguistic viewpoint, however, one thing does seem to stand out. A Spanish accent in English is generally taken as a sign of backwardness by Anglos, even when the "backward" individual is a native speaker of so-called good Spanish. This is in marked distinction to the reaction many Anglos have toward German ("intellectual"), French ("romantic"), or Chinese ("industrious") accents. These stereotyped ideas on food and speech are all distortions. But they are particularly unfortunate for the Chicano because they are carried over into many other areas of culture. If the Chicano diet and language are inferior, the reasoning goes, then so is Chicano culture generally.

The second factor limiting our selection of articles for this section is that it is too early to tell what effects urbanization is having on Chicano life. Grandfathers and grandmothers of today's Chicano youth came from rural backgrounds. Some were native speakers of Tarascan or Nahuatl.

---

[1] An indication of how complex dietary and nutritional studies are may be seen from the following example: In a recent study of a tiny Otomi Indian village in Mexico (population less than 300) five major dietary patterns of consumption were isolated by the researchers who counted more than 200 foods in the diet of this single group. Furthermore, they found no reason to generalize about the diet of the tribe (whose population is only around 80,000) from their study of a single village.

[2] Reynolds, May S., et al. "The Dietary Habits of College Students," *Journal of Home Economics*, Vol. 34, No. 6 (1942), pp. 379–384.

Today it is estimated that nearly 80 per cent of all Chicanos are urban. Skills derived from rural life may be inappropriate to an urban setting; as a result many shifts are currently underway.

Chicanos from rural New Mexico, for example, were accustomed to a traditional diet containing, among other things, chiles, tortillas, enchiladas, and certain types of beans. Many of these foods (especially the chiles, which are a prime source of vitamins C and D) are not available at reasonable prices in cities. We have no idea how many bologna sandwiches are substituted for traditional meals in the urban setting. Institutions such as donship (giving a title of respect to elderly people) is a characteristic of rural social structure not generally carried into the urban barrio. Compadrazgo, or godparenthood (discussed by Grebler, Moore, and Guzmán in this section), seems to be rapidly declining in importance among city Chicanos. Traditional male–female role relationships are in a state of flux and redefinition as more and more Chicanas work in Albuquerque, Los Angeles, and San Antonio. And so on. These adjustments to urban life are creating greater and greater internal differentiation in Chicano society.

The third factor is that there are so many variations of life style within the population that it is difficult to speak of a single Chicano culture. Which reality shall speak for all Chicanos? The reality of the ghettolike barrio in East Los Angeles? Or the reality of the rural land-owning farmer in northern New Mexico? Or the reality of the migrant farmworker who follows the crops from Texas to Washington, living in an automobile and in labor camps for more than half of each year?

A great deal of research on the internal differentiation among Chicanos is needed before significant generalizations can be made. As Vaca[3] has shown, previous research, mostly by gabacho scholars, has been highly biased. Chicanos have been characterized as lacking internal differentiation[4] and as possessing a culture which hinders them in making social and economic progress. No one would claim that social science research is or can be totally objective and free of bias. But it is only very recently that social science ethics have begun to place the biases of the studied on an equal footing with or better footing than the biases of the studiers. We look forward in the near future to a great deal of excellent scholarship on Chicano culture by both Chicano and Anglo researchers.

THE EXTERNAL ASPECT

Millions of immigrants came to America between 1870 and 1920. They were greeted generally with distrust, hate, violence, and discrimination. They were told to "become American," to "melt" into the American mainstream. Most of them did get into the mainstream but they had to give up

[3] Nick C. Vaca, "The Mexican-American in the Social Sciences," Part 2, 1936–1970, *El Grito* (Fall 1970), pp. 17–51; Part 1, 1912–1935 (Spring 1970), pp. 3–24.

[4] Celia Heller, *Mexican-American Youth: Forgotten Youth at the Crossroads* (New York: Random House, 1966).

their language, religion, and customs to do it, or at least hide those things in the privacy of the home. In other words, they succumbed to the pressures of white racism, stopped being ethnic minorities, and crowded their way into the ranks of the white racists themselves. Then they were "100 per cent American, just like everybody else."

Many members of American ethnic minorities are today discovering the tragedy of those years in their New World heritage. The following comment is a genuine statement, and a common one; it could have been made by anyone. "When my grandfather got here he couldn't say a word of English and people spit on him and made him work as a janitor in spite of the fact that he was a highly educated man. But he learned English and never spoke [fill in any language] in the home so my parents wouldn't learn it. And that's how he got so successful. Why can't the [Negroes, Chicanos] do it just like my grandfather?" There used to be a time when any American would have been proud to have been able to speak of the violence done to his grandparents and how they overcame it by "becoming just like everyone else." Now many people are not so sure. They are coming to realize how tragic their ancestors' situation was.

For Chicanos there was never any significant melting. Some "made it" by essentially the same process as other ethnic groups; they gave up their ethnic identity and pride in favor of "becoming an American," or an American-Mexican, as Gamio[5] called them. But for the most part the overwhelming majority of Chicanos have not assimilated. This is the result of three interrelated factors:

1. White racism in the United States tends to be stronger against physically visible ethnic peoples than against white immigrants. Chicanos, like blacks, are definitely visible as a group; they are also easily recognized by their surname, though this does not appear to be the primary factor, because Jews, Poles, Greeks, and Italians are also recognizable in this way.

2. Unlike the European and Oriental immigrants, the Chicanos were already in the Americas before the Anglos arrived. Thus, they were incorporated into the United States as a vanquished people rather than as participants in the victory over the Southwest.

3. Also unlike European and Oriental immigrants, Chicanos have had a common border with the "old country." Immigrants enter the United States, legally and illegally, on a continuous basis, and the proximity of Mexico has allowed many Chicanos to visit their ancestral homeland often. If not for the constant reinforcement from Mexico of their cultural roots and their exclusion by Anglos from the assimilation process, it is likely that Chicanos would all have become American-Mexican by this time, "just like everyone else."

The study of the external aspects of a minority culture tells us as much about the majority culture as it does about the minority. That racism is an institutional part of Anglo society is only demonstrable through the study

---

[5] *The Mexican Immigrant, His Life Story* (Chicago: University of Chicago Press, 1931).

of minority-group relations with Anglo society. Physical violence is the best known form of racism, because it makes headlines. Fire-trap housing for migrant agricultural workers, beatings by police, and the burning and stealing of Chicano land are well-documented parts of Chicano life, as many articles in this section and the next show. But the most pervasive and encompassing form of racism is "psychic violence," as Ralph Guzmán has called it. It does not make headlines, there are no exposés of it in magazines, and it is everywhere.

Advertising, as Martinez[6] has shown, is a prime offender. How much ethnic pride is lost by a Chicanito who sees the Frito Bandito on television telling all America that Mexicans are thieves and not to be trusted? How many Chicanos are proud to be known as a people who stink? That is what one deodorant company told America in showing its product used by a grubby-looking Mexican outlaw while the announcer said, "If it works for him, it will work for you." Chicanos are portrayed (and betrayed) in the movies and on television as lazy, fat, happy, thieving, immoral creatures who make excellent sidekicks for white heroes. Chicanas are depicted as loose women who are happy to be used by any gunslinger, so long as he is white. The damage to pride and dignity has never been accurately measured. In fact it may not be measurable.

Psychic violence extends into the justice system as the testimony from the Civil Rights Commission and Judge Chargin's transcript both show. Many Chicanos are sent into the armed forces each year (just how many is not known) by judges who offer them that as an alternative to jail for minor infractions.

Nowhere, however, is psychic violence so devastatingly destructive of Chicano dignity as in the public schools. A number of articles in this section reflect this: Ortego shows how Chicanos are made to feel inferior because of their language; Carter demonstrates the systematic neglect that Chicano children experience in public education; Sánchez, in a classic article written in 1934, cautions against the use of certain psychological tests on Chicanitos when the tests have been designed to measure intelligence in middle-class white children. These tests continue to provide white teachers with evidence that Chicano children are backward or mentally inferior, and teacher behavior toward Chicano children reflects these reinforced attitudes.

In a recent experimental study Rosenthal and Jacobson[7] told a group of white teachers that some children in their classes had been shown on psychological tests to be potential "spurters"; that is, children who were expected, according to the tests, to show great progress during the school year. The names of the potential "spurters" were actually chosen in a random fashion designed to make no distinction between Chicanitos and the rest of the children in the class. Almost 80 per cent of the chosen children gained at least ten points on their IQ tests during the year. Only

---

[6] Thomas Martinez, "Advertising and Racism: The Case of the Mexican Americans," *El Grito* (Summer 1969), pp. 3–13.

[7] *Pygmalion in the Classroom* (New York: Holt, Rinehart and Winston, 1968).

50 per cent of the rest of the class gained that much. Thus, if a teacher thinks a child is intelligent, her treatment of that child in the classroom will be reflected on his or her IQ test scores. Other tests show that white teachers have a very negative view of Chicano children's intelligence and ability to learn. The result is that many Chicano children take on the dominant attitude themselves: that is, they believe themselves to be inferior, so they stop learning and become dropouts. (Pushouts would be a better word.)

Psychic violence as an expression of white racism is probably a dominant theme in almost every Chicano child's school experience. Teachers and fellow pupils laugh at them for bringing tortillas and beans in their lunch boxes rather than tuna fish sandwiches on fluffy bread.[8] Guidance counselors encourage them to "learn useful trades" rather than aspire to college. Teachers (even Chicano teachers) may keep them after school and force them to write "I will speak English" 100 times on the blackboard. Throughout the Southwest this practice is known as "Spanish detention."

Psychic violence is often practiced under the guise of aid. For this reason it is the most difficult form of racism to combat. Teachers sometimes tell Chicano children to eat sandwiches so they will "improve their diet." Counselors advise against college because they are "trying to insure the minority member's job security." Judges offer the army as an alternative to jail "in an effort to help keep the young man's record clean."

These forms of racism were practiced in one form or another against nearly all immigrant groups in this country. It is America's shame, not her pride, that most immigrants' self-identity could be broken by it.

---

[8] There is a certain irony in the growing popularity of franchise establishments which sell make-believe tacos to ever more enthusiastic college students.

Internal Culture

PSYCHOANALYSIS OF THE MEXICAN

Samuel Ramos

There is no reason why the reader should be offended by these pages, in which the affirmation is not that the Mexican *is* inferior, but rather that he *feels* inferior. This is quite different. If, in certain individual cases, the sense of inferiority discloses real organic or psychic deficiencies, for the majority of Mexicans it constitutes a collective illusion which results from measuring man against the very high scales of values corresponding to highly developed countries. We ask the reader, therefore, to examine our ideas with absolute equanimity. If, despite these explanations, the reader is hurt, we are sincerely sorry, but we will prove that there exists in our countries of America, as Keyserling puts it, "a propensity to being offended"; thus, an indignant reaction would be the most resounding proof of our thesis.

The *Pelado* [1]

To discover the motivating force of the Mexican soul it was first necessary to review a few of its great collective movements. Plato maintained that the state is an enlarged image of the individual. We shall demonstrate in like manner that the Mexican behaves in his private world the same as he does in public life.

Samuel Ramos, *Profile of Man and Culture in Mexico*, translated by Peter G. Earle (University of Texas Press, 1962). All rights reserved.

Samuel Ramos began his career studying to be an army surgeon and ended it as Mexico's most distinguished professor of social philosophy and esthetic theory when he died in 1959. His philosophic studies included his classic work on the psychoanalysis of the Mexican mind (from which the current selection is taken) and *Toward a New Humanism*, in which he called for a marriage of social theory and social action.

[1] *Pelado.* This past participle and adjective has in Spanish the several literal meanings of "plucked," "bare," "peeled," "treeless," "husked," "penniless." As the designation of a universally familiar social type in Mexico, it defies translation into English. However, the pages immediately following offer a precise characterization of the *pelado.* (Translator's note.)

239

The Mexican psyche is the result of reactions that strive to conceal an inferiority complex. In the first chapter of this book we explained that such concealment is achieved by falsifying the image of the external world, exalting in that way the Mexican's consciousness of his own worth. In his own country he imitates modes of European civilization in order to feel that he is equal to the European, and in order to establish in his cities a privileged group which considers itself superior to all those Mexicans who live beyond the borders of civilization. But this fictional process does not end with exterior things, nor is it enough to restore the psychological equilibrium that the inferiority complex has destroyed. The same process is also applicable to the individual and falsifies his own idea of himself. Psychoanalysis of the individual Mexican is the topic which we shall now undertake.

To understand the mechanism of the Mexican mind, we shall examine it in context that reveals how all its movements are exacerbated; thus the sense of that mind's development will be clearly perceptible. The best model for study is the Mexican *pelado*, for he constitutes the most elemental and clearly defined expression of national character. We shall say nothing of his picturesque aspect, which has been represented to the point of tedium in the popular theater, in the novel, and in painting. Our only interest here is his inner self and the elemental forces that determine his character. His name (*pelado*) defines him accurately. He is the kind of person who continually lays bare his soul, so that its most intimate confines are visible. He brazenly flaunts certain elemental impulses which other men try to dissimulate. The *pelado* belongs to a most vile category of social fauna; he is a form of human rubbish from the great city. He is less than a proletarian in the economic hierarchy, and a primitive man in the intellectual one. Life from every quarter has been hostile to him and his reaction has been black resentment. He is an explosive being with whom relationship is dangerous, for the slightest friction causes him to blow up. His explosions are verbal and reiterate his theme of self-affirmation in crude and suggestive language. He has created a dialectic of his own, a diction which abounds in ordinary words, but he gives these words a new meaning. He is an animal whose ferocious pantomimes are designed to terrify others, making them believe that he is stronger than they and more determined. Such reactions are illusory retaliations against his real position in life, which is a nullity. This disagreeable truth strives to force its way up to the surface of his conscience, but it is impeded by another force which from within the subconscious consistently reduces his sense of personal integrity. Any exterior circumstances that might aggravate his sense of inferiority will provoke a violent reprisal, the aim of which is to subdue his depression. The result is a constant irritability that incites him to fight with others on the most insignificant pretext. But his bellicose spirit does not derive from a sentiment of hostility toward all humanity. The *pelado* seeks out quarrels as a stimulus, to renew the vigor of his downtrodden ego. He needs a support for recovering faith in himself, but since his support is devoid of all real value, he has to replace it with a fictitious one. He is like a shipwreck victim who, after flailing about in a sea of nothingness, suddenly discovers his driftwood of salvation: virility. The *pelado's* terminology abounds in sexual allusions which reveal his phallic obsession; the sexual organ becomes symbolic of masculine force. In verbal combat he attributes to his adversary an imaginary femininity, reserving for himself the masculine role. By this stratagem he pretends to assert his superiority over his opponent.

We should like to illustrate these theories, but unfortunately, the *pelado's* language is so crudely realistic that it is not possible to transcribe many of his most characteristic phrases. Nevertheless, certain typical expressions cannot be ignored. The reader should not take offense at our citation of words which in Mexico are used only in intimate conversations. Beyond their vulgarity and grossness the psychologist can discern a different and more noble sense. And it would be unpardonable to disregard such valuable material for study under the pretext of acceding to a dubiously conceived notion of decency in language. It would be comparable to a chemist's refusing to analyze all substances that smell bad.

The most destitute of Mexican *pelados* consoles himself by shouting at everyone that "he's got balls" (*muchos huevos*)[2] with reference to the testicles. It is important to note that he attributes to the reproductive organ not only one kind of potency, the sexual, but every kind of human power. In the *pelado* a man who triumphs in any activity, anywhere, owes his success to his "balls." Another of his favorite expressions, "I am your father" (*Yo soy tu padre*), intends to assert his predominance unequivocally. In our patriarchal societies the father is for all men the symbol of power. It must also be remarked that the *pelado's* phallic obsession is not comparable to phallic cults and their underlying notions of fecundity and eternal life. The phallus suggests to the *pelado* the idea of power. From this he has derived a very impoverished concept of man. Since he is, in effect, a being without substance, he tries to fill his void with the only suggestive force accessible to him: that of the male animal. He turns this popular concept of man into a dismal view of all Mexicans. When a Mexican compares his own nullity to the character of a civilized foreigner, he consoles himself in the following way: "A European has science, art, technical knowledge, and so forth; we have none of that here, but . . . we are very manly." Manly in the zoological sense of the term, that is, in the sense of the male enjoying complete animal potency. The Mexican is fond of boasting and believes that he demonstrates this potency in courage. If only he knew that such courage is a smoke screen! Appearances must not, therefore, deceive us. The *pelado* is neither a strong nor a brave man. The appearance he shows us is false. It is a camouflage by which he misleads himself and all those who come into contact with him. One can infer that the more show he makes of courage and force, the greater is the weakness that he is trying to hide. However much the *pelado* deceives himself by this illusion, he can never be certain of his power, so long as his weakness is present and threatens to betray him. He lives in distrust of himself and in continuous fear of being discovered. So it is that his per-

---

[2] *muchos huevos*, literally, "many eggs."

ception becomes abnormal; he imagines that the next man he encounters
will be his enemy; he mistrusts all who approach him.

After this brief description of the Mexican *pelado,* an outline of his
mental structure and operation seems advisable for an eventual understanding of the Mexican's psychology in general.

    i. The *pelado* has two personalities: one real, the other, fictitious.

    ii. His real personality is obscured by his fictitious one, or the one that
first appears to himself and others.

    iii. His fictitious personality is diametrically opposed to his real one,
for the object of the first is to raise the psychic level depressed by the
second.

    iv. Since this individual lacks real human value and is powerless to
acquire it, he utilizes a ruse to conceal his sentiments of inferiority.

    v. The fictitious personality's lack of real foundation creates a sense of
self-distrust.

    vi. Self-distrust produces abnormality in the psychic functioning, es-
pecially in the perception of reality.

    vii. This abnormal perception amounts to an unjustified distrust of
others, in addition to a hypersensitivity in his contact with other
men.

    viii. Since our subject lives in falsehood, his position is always unstable
and obliges him to keep constant vigil over his ego, while consequently neglecting reality.

His lack of attention to reality and his correlative preoccupation with
himself lend support to our classification of the *pelado* among the "intro-
verts."

One might think that the *pelado's* inferiority complex is not due to the
fact that he is Mexican, but rather to his proletarian status. Indeed, this
status could be the logical result of the complex, but there are convincing
reasons for assuming that it is not the only decisive factor in the *pelado's*
personality. We also notice that he associates his concept of virility with
that of nationality, creating thereby the illusion that personal valor is the
Mexican's particular characteristic. To see how nationality in itself creates
a feeling of inferiority, one need only note the susceptibility of the
pelado's patriotic sentiments and his pompous expression of words and
exclamations. The frequency of individual and collective patriotic manifestations is symbolic of the Mexican's insecurity about the value of his
nationality. Decisive proof of this affirmation is found in the fact that the
same sentiment exists in cultivated and intelligent Mexicans of the bourgeoisie.

The Mexican of the City

We turn now to the city dweller. His psychology is clearly different
from that of the rural inhabitant, not only because of the kind of life the

latter leads, but because the *campesino* in Mexico is almost always of
the indigenous race. Even though the Indian constitutes a large proportion of the Mexican population, his role is a passive one in the present life
of his country. The active group is that of the mestizos and whites who
live in the city. One supposes, of course, that the Indian has influenced
the soul of the other Mexican group because he has mixed his blood with
theirs. But his social and spiritual influence is today reduced to the simple
fact of his presence. He is like a chorus who silently witnesses the drama
of Mexican life. However, the restricted nature of his intervention does
not mean that it is insignificant. The Indian is like those substances identified as "catalytic," the mere presence of which provokes chemical reactions. Nothing Mexican is immune to this influence, because the indigenous mass is like a dense atmosphere that envelops everything in the
nation. We therefore might think of the Indian as the Mexican's human
"hinterland." But the Indian is not at this moment the object of our
investigation.

The most striking aspect of Mexican character, at first sight, is distrust.
This attitude underlies all contact with men and things. It is present
whether or not there is motivation for it. It is not a question of distrust
on principle, because generally speaking the Mexican lacks principles.
It is rather a matter of irrational distrust that emanates from the depths
of his being. It is almost his primordial sense of life. Whether or not circumstances justify it, there is nothing in the universe which the Mexican
does not see and evaluate through his distrust. It is like an a priori form
of his oversensitivity. The Mexican does not distrust any man or woman
in particular; he distrusts all men and all women. His distrust is not
limited to the human race; it embraces all that exists and happens. If
he is a businessman he doesn't believe in business; if he is a professional
he doesn't believe in his profession; if he is a politician he doesn't believe
in politics. It is the Mexican's view that ideas make no sense and he scorn-
fully calls them "theories." He judges the knowledge of scientific principles
as useless. He seems very confident of his practical insight, but as a man
of action he is awkward and ultimately gives little credit to the efficacy
of facts. He has no religion and professes no social or political creed. He
is the least "idealistic" person imaginable. He unreasonably negates everything, because he is negation personified.

What then does the Mexican live for? He would perhaps reply that it is
not necessary to have ideas and beliefs in order to live—provided that
one does not think. And indeed, this is the situation. In its totality, Mexican life gives the impression of being an unreflecting activity, entirely
without plan. In Mexico each man concerns himself only with immediate
issues. He works for today and tomorrow but never for later on. The future
is a preoccupation which he has banished from his conscience. He is incapable of adventure in projects that offer only remote results. He has
therefore suppressed from his life one of its most important dimensions—
the future. Such are the effects of Mexican distrust.

In a life limited to the present, only instinct can function. Intelligent
reflection can intervene only in those pauses when one is able to suspend

one's activity. It is impossible to think and act simultaneously. Thought presupposes that we are capable of expectation, and one who expects is receptive to the future. Obviously, a life without future can have no norms. Mexican life is accordingly at the mercy of the four winds; instead of sailing, it drifts. Men say that they live as God wills. With neither discipline nor organization, Mexican society not unnaturally finds itself in a chaos in which individual beings move unpredictably like dispersed atoms.

An immediate symptom of this chaotic world is its reliance on distrust which it instills in an almost objective way. When a man feels lost in a realm of instability, where he is uncertain even of the ground he walks on, his distrust increases and makes him hasten to wrest from the present moment its fullest value. Thus the horizon of his life shrinks and his moral sense dwindles to the extent that society, notwithstanding its compatibility with civilization, is like a primitive horde in which men quarrel like hungry beasts.

A trait intimately connected with distrust is susceptibility. The distrustful type is fearful of everything and lives vigilantly, on the defensive. He is suspicious of all gestures, movements, and words. He interprets everything as an offense. In this attitude the Mexican goes to unbelievable extremes. His perception has become clearly abnormal. Because of his extreme touchiness the Mexican quarrels constantly; he no longer awaits attack but steps forward in order to offend. These pathological reactions often lead him to excesses, even to the point of committing needless crimes.

The psychic anomalies just described undoubtedly arise from an insecurity of the self which the Mexican unconsciously projects, converting it into distrust of men and the world. These psychic transformations are instinctive tricks devised to protect the ego from itself. The initial phase of the series is an inferiority complex experienced as a distrust of self, which the individual objectifies in the form of distrust toward strangers. Thus he frees himself from the unpleasantness associated with that complex.

When the human psyche strives to rid itself of a disagreeable feeling, it invariably resorts to illusory processes like the one just described. But in this particular case such processes are unsatisfactory, because the veil covering the unwelcome affliction does not actually suppress it; it only brings about a change in its motivation. The Mexican is continually in a mood that betrays his inner malaise, his incompatibility with himself. He is sensitive and nervous, almost always in a bad humor, and often irate and violent.

The strength which the Mexican attributes to himself, relying on his impulsiveness, is unconvincing. Of course, real energy implies intelligent control of one's impulses, and, at times, suppression of them. The Mexican is passionate, aggressive, and warlike out of weakness; that is to say, he lacks the will to control his actions. On the other hand, the energy evolving from these acts surpasses his vitality, which, more often than not, is weak. How then is the violence of his acts to be explained? Only by considering it as the result of a super-excitation that has caused his psychic disequilibrium.

Knowledge of the psychology of the Mexican would be incomplete without a comparison of his idea of himself with what he really is. We have just spoken of the strength that the Mexican attributes to himself; we consequently assume that he has a favorable idea of his personality. We suspect, furthermore, that some readers of this essay will react against our affirmations, seeking arguments to reject them. The fact is that here we have ventured to uncover certain truths which every Mexican strives to conceal; for he superimposes on these truths an image of himself that does not represent what he is, but what he would like to be. What is the strongest and most intimate desire of the Mexican? He would like to become one who, by dint of his valor and strength, lords it over others. He is artificially exalted by the suggestion of this image, and persuaded to work in harmony with it until such time as he actually believes in the reality of the phantom which he has fashioned out of himself. . . .

. . . In affirming that the Mexican suffers an inferiority complex, I have always meant that this complex affects his *collective* consciousness. If the sense of nationality is undermined by a feeling of inferiority, there is likely to be a pronounced impulsive reaction. In normal situations individualistic tendencies are counter-balanced by the moderating action of collective sentiments. But there can be no normality when this counter-balance is lacking and individualism asserts itself uncontrolled. This very unbalance explains a great number of Mexican character traits, many of which are different and even contradictory. But the common denominator for all of them is their antisocial nature, including distrust, aggressiveness, resentment, timidity, haughtiness, deception, and so on.

I am quite aware that these characteristics were present in Mexicans of the colonial era, who for different reasons developed a similar personality. Social life of that time abounded in injustices which left the Creole at a disadvantage in relation to the peninsular Spaniard, who was always a recent arrival. In his lowly condition the mestizo was worse off still. Because of his inability to get what he wanted he cultivated a kind of reticence in order to cover up his thoughts, and his language had a propensity to falsehood and euphemism. What information we have about Mexicans of the colonial period points up the similarity between their conduct and our own. Quite possibly there were changes for the better in the late eighteenth century, but in the agitated atmosphere of the past century, and for reasons we have already set forth, old attitudes returned. However, in explaining the development of that conduct we showed that it has always been abnormal and misleading, a disguise with which the Mexican has endeavored to conceal his true character. Other investigators have accepted and reaffirmed this point of view; Octavio Paz, for example, calls the Mexican's conduct a mask. Behind this mask he discovers an inclination to solitude which the title of his book expresses, *The Labyrinth of Solitude*.[3] But a more realistic observation would show, contrary to Paz's thesis, that solitude is not the result of voluntary choice, but rather of a disrupting element that makes human character antisocial. Solitude is only a refuge which is sought unconsciously. The Mexican does not desire or enjoy solitude. Rather, solitude afflicts him because of his timidity, his touchiness, and his distrust—all of which are clothed in inhibitions. The love or taste for solitude is the exclusive asset of men endowed with an intense and rich inner life, and only in solitude itself can solitude become a joy. It constitutes an aristocracy of the spirit, the exceptional possession of poets, philosophers, or mystics. It is not cultivated by the common man. . . .

[3] *El laberinto de la soledad*, Fondo de Cultura Económica, México, 1959.

THE VIRGIN OF GUADALUPE:
A MEXICAN NATIONAL SYMBOL

Eric R. Wolf

Occasionally, we encounter a symbol which seems to enshrine the major hopes and aspirations of an entire society.[1] Such a master symbol is represented by the Virgin of Guadalupe, Mexico's patron saint. During the Mexican War of Independence against Spain, her image preceded the insurgents into battle.[2] Emiliano Zapata and his agrarian rebels fought under her emblem in the Great Revolution of 1910.[3] Today, her image adorns house fronts and interiors, churches and home altars, bull rings and gambling dens, taxis and buses, restaurants and houses of ill repute. She is celebrated in popular song and verse. Her shrine at Tepeyac, immediately north of Mexico City, is visited each year by hundreds of thousands of pilgrims, ranging from the inhabitants of far-off Indian villages to the members of socialist trade union locals. "Nothing to be seen in Canada or Europe," says F. S. C. Northrop, "equals it in the volume or the vitality of its moving quality or in the depth of its spirit of religious devotion." [4]

In this paper, I should like to discuss this Mexican master symbol, and

Reprinted from *American Journal of Folklore*, Vol. 71, 1958, pp. 34–39, by permission of the American Folklore Society, Inc., and the author.

[1] Parts of this paper were presented to the Symposium on Ethnic and National Ideologies, Annual Spring Meeting of the American Ethnological Society in conjunction with the Philadelphia Anthropological Society, on 12 May 1956.

[2] Niceto de Zamacois, *Historia de México* (Barcelona-Mexico, 1878–82), VI, 253.

[3] Antonio Pompa y Pompa, *Album del IV centenario guadalupano* (Mexico, 1938), p. 173.

[4] F. S. C. Northrop, *The Meeting of East and West* (New York, 1946), p. 25.

the ideology which surrounds it. In making use of the term "master symbol," I do not wish to imply that belief in the symbol is common to all Mexicans. We are not dealing here with an element of a putative national character, defined as a common denominator of all Mexican nationals. It is no longer legitimate to assume "that any member of the [national] group will exhibit certain regularities of behavior which are common in high degree among the other members of the society." [5] Nations, like other complex societies, must, however, "possess cultural forms or mechanisms which groups involved in the same over-all web of relationships can use in their formal and informal dealings with each other." [6] Such forms develop historically, hand in hand with other processes which lead to the formation of nations, and social groups which are caught up in these processes must become "acculturated" to their usage.[7] Only where such forms exist, can communication and coördinated behavior be established among the constituent groups of such a society. They provide the cultural idiom of behavior and ideal representations through which different groups of the same society can pursue and manipulate their different fates within a coördinated framework. This paper, then, deals with one such cultural form, operating on the symbolic level. The study of this symbol seems particularly rewarding, since it is not restricted to one set of social ties, but refers to a very wide range of social relationships.

The image of the Guadalupe and her shrine at Tepeyac are surrounded by an origin myth.[8] According to this myth, the Virgin Mary appeared to Juan Diego, a Christianized Indian of commoner status, and addressed him in Nahuatl. The encounter took place on the Hill of Tepeyac in the year 1531, ten years after the Spanish Conquest of Tenochtitlan. The Virgin commanded Juan Diego to seek out the archbishop of Mexico and to inform him of her desire to see a church built in her honor on Tepeyac Hill. After Juan Diego was twice unsuccessful in his efforts to carry out her order, the Virgin wrought a miracle. She bade Juan Diego pick roses in a sterile spot where normally only desert plants could grow, gathered the roses into the Indian's cloak, and told him to present cloak and roses to the incredulous archbishop. When Juan Diego unfolded his cloak before the bishop, the image of the Virgin was miraculously stamped upon it. The bishop acknowledged the miracle, and ordered a shrine built where Mary had appeared to her humble servant.

The shrine, rebuilt several times in centuries to follow, is today a basilica, the third highest kind of church in Western Christendom. Above the central altar hangs Juan Diego's cloak with the miraculous image. It shows a young woman without child, her head lowered demurely in her shawl. She wears an open crown and flowing gown, and stands upon a half moon symbolizing the Immaculate Conception.

[5] David G. Mandelbaum, "On the Study of National Character," *American Anthropologist*, LV (1953), p. 185.

[6] Eric R. Wolf, "Aspects of Group Relations in a Complex Society: Mexico," *American Anthropologist*, LVII (1956), 1065–1078.

[7] Eric R. Wolf, "La formación de la nación," *Ciencias Sociales*, IV, 50–51.

[8] Ernest Gruening, *Mexico and Its Heritage* (New York, 1928), p. 235.

The shrine of Guadalupe was, however, not the first religious structure built on Tepeyac; nor was Guadalupe the first female supernatural associated with the hill. In pre-Hispanic times, Tepeyac had housed a temple to the earth and fertility goddess Tonantzin, Our Lady Mother, who—like the Guadalupe—was associated with the moon. Temple, like basilica, was the center of large scale pilgrimages. That the veneration accorded the Guadalupe drew inspiration from the earlier worship of Tonantzin is attested by several Spanish friars. F. Bernardino de Sahagún, writing fifty years after the Conquest, says: "Now that the Church of Our Lady of Guadalupe has been built there, they call her Tonantzin too. . . . The term refers . . . to that ancient Tonantzin and this state of affairs should be remedied, because the proper name of the Mother of God is not Tonantzin, but Dios and Nantzin. It seems to be a satanic device to mask idolatry . . . and they come from far away to visit that Tonantzin, as much as before; a devotion which is also suspect because there are many churches of Our Lady everywhere and they do not go to them; and they come from faraway lands to this Tonantzin as of old." [9] F. Martín de León wrote in a similar vein: "On the hill where Our Lady of Guadalupe is they adored the idol of a goddess they called Tonantzin, which means Our Mother, and this is also the name they give Our Lady and they always say they are going to Tonantzin or they are celebrating Tonantzin and many of them understand this in the old way and not in the modern way. . . . " [10] The syncretism was still alive in the seventeenth century. F. Jacinto de la Serna, in discussing the pilgrimages to the Guadalupe at Tepeyac, noted: ". . . it is the purpose of the wicked to [worship] the goddess and not the Most Holy Virgin, or both together." [11]

Increasingly popular during the sixteenth century, the Guadalupe cult gathered emotional impetus during the seventeenth. During this century appear the first known pictorial representations of the Guadalupe, apart from the miraculous original; the first poems are written in her honor; and the first sermons announce the transcendental implications of her supernatural appearance in Mexico and among Mexicans.[12] Historians have long tended to neglect the seventeenth century which seemed "a kind of Dark Age in Mexico." Yet "this quiet time was of the utmost importance in the development of Mexican Society." [13] During this century, the institution of the hacienda comes to dominate Mexican life.[14] During this century, also, "New Spain is ceasing to be 'new' and to be 'Spain.'" [15] These new ex-

[9] Bernardino de Sahagún, *Historia general de las cosas de nueva españa* (Mexico, 1938), I, lib. 6.

[10] Quoted in Carlos. A. Echánove Trujillo, *Sociología mexicana* (Mexico, 1948), p. 105.

[11] Quoted in Jesús Amaya, *La madre de Dios: genesis e historia de nuestra señora de Guadalupe* (Mexico, 1931), p. 230.

[12] Francisco de la Maza, *El guadalupismo mexicano* (Mexico, 1953), pp. 12–14, 143, 30, 33, 82.

[13] Lesley B. Simpson, "Mexico's Forgotten Century," *Pacific Historical Review*, XXII (1953), 115, 114.

[14] François Chevalier, *La formation des grands domaines au Méxique* (Paris, 1952), p. xii.

[15] de la Maza, p. 41.

periences require a new cultural idiom, and in the Guadalupe cult, the component segments of Mexican colonial society encountered cultural forms in which they could express their parallel interests and longings.

The primary purpose of this paper is not, however, to trace the history of the Guadalupe symbol. It is concerned rather with its functional aspects, its roots and reference to the major social relationships of Mexican society.

The first set of relationships which I would like to single out for consideration are the ties of kinship, and the emotions generated in the play of relationships within families. I want to suggest that some of the meanings of the Virgin symbol in general, and of the Guadalupe symbol in particular, derive from these emotions. I say "some meanings" and I use the term "derive" rather than "originate," because the form and function of the family in any given society are themselves determined by other social factors: technology, economy, residence, political power. The family is but one relay in the circuit within which symbols are generated in complex societies. Also, I used the plural "families" rather than "family," because there are demonstrably more than one kind of family in Mexico.[16] I shall simplify the available information on Mexican family life, and discuss the material in terms of two major types of families.[17] The first kind of family is congruent with the closed and static life of the Indian village. It may be called the Indian family. In this kind of family, the husband is ideally dominant, but in reality labor and authority are shared equally among both marriage partners. Exploitation of one sex by the other is atypical; sexual feats do not add to a person's status in the eyes of others. Physical punishment and authoritarian treatment of children are rare. The second kind of family is congruent with the much more open, mobile, manipulative life in communities which are actively geared to the life of the nation, a life in which power relationships between individuals and groups are of great moment. This kind of family may be called the Mexican family. Here, the father's authority is unquestioned on both the real and the ideal plane. Double sex standards prevail, and male sexuality is charged with a desire to exercise domination. Children are ruled with a heavy hand; physical punishment is frequent.

The Indian family pattern is consistent with the behavior towards the Guadalupe noted by John Bushnell in the Matlazinca speaking community of San Juan Atzingo in the Valley of Toluca.[18] There, the image of the Virgin is addressed in passionate terms as a source of warmth and love, and the *pulque* or century plant beer drunk on ceremonial occasions

[16] María Elvira Bermúdez, *La vida familiar del mexicano* (Mexico, 1955), chapters 2 and 3.

[17] For relevant material, see: Bermúdez; John Gillin, "Ethos and Cultural Aspects of Personality," and Robert Redfield and Sol Tax, "General Characteristics of Present-Day Mesoamerican Indian Society," in Sol Tax ed., *Heritage of Conquest* (Glencoe, 1952), pp. 193–212, 31–39; Gordon W. Hewes, "Mexicans in Search of the 'Mexican'," *American Journal of Economics and Sociology*, XIII (1954), 209–223; Octavio Paz, *El laberinto de la soledad* (Mexico, 1947), pp. 71–89.

[18] John Bushnell, "La Virgen de Guadalupe as Surrogate Mother in San Juan Atzingo," paper read before the 54th Annual Meeting of the American Anthropological Association, 18 November 1955.

is identified with her milk. Bushnell postulates that here the Guadalupe is identified with the mother as a source of early satisfactions, never again experienced after separation from the mother and emergence into social adulthood. As such, the Guadalupe embodies a longing to return to the pristine state in which hunger and unsatisfactory social relations are minimized. The second family pattern is also consistent with a symbolic identification of Virgin and mother, yet this time within a context of adult male dominance and sexual assertion, discharged against submissive females and children. In this second context, the Guadalupe symbol is charged with the energy of rebellion against the father. Her image is the embodiment of hope in a victorious outcome of the struggle between generations.

This struggle leads to a further extension of the symbolism. Successful rebellion against power figures is equated with the promise of life; defeat with the promise of death. As John A. Mackay has suggested, there thus takes place a further symbolic identification of the Virgin with life; of defeat and death with the crucified Christ. In Mexican artistic tradition, as in Hispanic artistic tradition in general,[19] Christ is never depicted as an adult man, but always either as a helpless child, or more often as a figure beaten, tortured, defeated and killed. In this symbolic equation we are touching upon some of the roots of the passionate affirmation of faith in the Virgin, and of the fascination with death which characterizes Baroque Christianity in general, and Mexican Catholicism in particular. The Guadalupe stands for life, for hope, for health; Christ on the cross, for despair and for death.

Supernatural mother and natural mother are thus equated symbolically, as are earthly and otherworldly hopes and desires. These hopes center on the provision of food and emotional warmth in the first case, in the successful waging of the Oedipal struggle in the other.

Family relations are, however, only one element in the formation of the Guadalupe symbol. Their analysis does little to explain the Guadalupe as such. They merely illuminate the female and maternal attributes of the more widespread Virgin symbol. The Guadalupe is important to Mexicans not only because she is a supernatural mother, but also because she embodies their major political and religious aspirations.

To the Indian groups, the symbol is more than an embodiment of life and hope; it restores to them the hopes of salvation. We must not forget that the Spanish Conquest signified not only military defeat, but the defeat also of the old gods and the decline of the old ritual. The apparition of the Guadalupe to an Indian commoner thus represents on one level the return of Tonantzin. As Tannenbaum has well said, "The Church . . . gave the Indian an opportunity not merely to save his life, but also to save his faith in his own gods." [20] On another level, the myth of the apparition served as a symbolic testimony that the Indian, as much as the Spaniard, was capable of being saved, capable of receiving Christianity. This must

[19] John A. Mackay, *The Other Spanish Christ* (New York, 1933), pp. 110–117.
[20] Frank Tannenbaum, *Peace by Revolution* (New York, 1933), p. 39.

be understood against the background of the bitter theological and political argument which followed the Conquest and divided churchmen, officials, and conquerors into those who held that the Indian was incapable of conversion, thus inhuman, and therefore a fit subject of political and economic exploitation; and those who held that the Indian was human, capable of conversion and that this exploitation had to be tempered by the demands of the Catholic faith and of orderly civil processes of government.[21] The myth of the Guadalupe thus validates the Indian's right to legal defense, orderly government, to citizenship; to supernatural salvation, but also to salvation from random oppression.

But if the Guadalupe guaranteed a rightful place to the Indians in the new social system of New Spain, the myth also held appeal to the large group of disinherited who arose in New Spain as illegitimate offspring of Spanish fathers and Indian mothers, or through impoverishment, acculturation or loss of status within the Indian or Spanish group.[22] For such people, there was for a long time no proper place in the social order. Their very right to exist was questioned in their inability to command the full rights of citizenship and legal protection. Where Spaniard and Indian stood squarely within the law, they inhabited the interstices and margins of constituted society. These groups acquired influence and wealth in the seventeenth and eighteenth centuries, but were yet barred from social recognition and power by the prevailing economic, social and political order.[23] To them, the Guadalupe myth came to represent not merely the guarantee of their assured place in heaven, but the guarantee of their place in society here and now. On the political plane, the wish for a return to a paradise of early satisfactions of food and warmth, a life without defeat, sickness or death, gave rise to a political wish for a Mexican paradise, in which the illegitimate sons would possess the country, and the irresponsible Spanish overlords, who never acknowledged the social responsibilities of their paternity, would be driven from the land.

In the writings of seventeenth century ecclesiastics, the Guadalupe becomes the harbinger of this new order. In the book by Miguel Sánchez, published in 1648, the Spanish Conquest of New Spain is justified solely on the grounds that it allowed the Virgin to become manifest in her chosen country, and to found in Mexico a new paradise. Just as Israel had been chosen to produce Christ, so Mexico had been chosen to produce Guadalupe. Sánchez equates her with the apocalyptic woman of the Revelation of John (12: 1), "arrayed with the sun, and the moon under her feet, and upon her head a crown of twelve stars" who is to realize the prophecy of Deuteronomy 8: 7-10 and lead the Mexicans into the Pro-

---

[21] Silvio Zavala, *La filosofía en la conquista de América* (Mexico, 1947).

[22] Nicolas León, *Las castas del México colonial o Nueva España* (Mexico, 1924); C. E. Marshall, "The Birth of the Mestizo in New Spain," *Hispanic American Historical Review*, XIX (1939), 161–184; Wolf, "La formación de la nación," pp. 103–106.

[23] Gregorio Torres Quintero, *México hacia el fin del virreinato español* (Mexico 1921); Eric R. Wolf, "The Mexican Bajío in the Eighteenth Century," *Middle American Research Institute Publication* XVII (1955), 180–199; Wolf, "Aspects of Group Relations in a Complex Society: Mexico."

mised Land. Colonial Mexico thus becomes the desert of Sinai; Independent Mexico the land of milk and honey. F. Francisco de Florencia, writing in 1688, coined the slogan which made Mexico not merely another chosen nation, but the Chosen Nation: *non fecit taliter omni nationi*,[24] words which still adorn the portals of the basilica, and shine forth in electric light bulbs at night. And on the eve of Mexican independence, Servando Teresa de Mier elaborates still further the Guadalupan myth by claiming that Mexico had been converted to Christianity long before the Spanish Conquest. The apostle Saint Thomas had brought the image of Guadalupe-Tonantzin to the New World as a symbol of his mission, just as Saint James had converted Spain with the image of the Virgin of the Pillar. The Spanish Conquest was therefore historically unnecessary, and should be erased from the annals of history.[25] In this perspective, the Mexican War of Independence marks the final realization of the apocalyptic promise. The banner of the Guadalupe leads the insurgents; and their cause is referred to as "her law." [26] In this ultimate extension of the symbol, the promise of life held out by the supernatural mother has become the promise of an independent Mexico, liberated from the irrational authority of the Spanish father-oppressors and restored to the Chosen Nation whose election had been manifest in the apparition of the Virgin on Tepeyac. The land of the supernatural mother is finally possessed by her rightful heirs. The symbolic circuit is closed. Mother; food, hope, health, life; supernatural salvation and salvation from oppression; Chosen People and national independence—all find expression in a single master symbol.

The Guadalupe symbol thus links together family, politics and religion; colonial past and independent present; Indian and Mexican. It reflects the salient social relationships of Mexican life, and embodies the emotions which they generate. It provides a cultural idiom through which the tenor and emotions of these relationships can be expressed. It is, ultimately, a way of talking about Mexico: a "collective representation" of Mexican society.

[24] de la Maza, pp. 39–40, 43–49, 64.
[25] Luis Villoro, *Los grandes momentos del indigenismo en México* (Mexico, 1950), pp. 131–138.
[26] Luis González y González, "El optimismo nacionalista como factor en la independencia de México," *Estudios de historiografía americano* (Mexico, 1948), p. 194.

THE URBAN MEXICAN-AMERICAN PARISH

Leo Grebler, Joan W. Moore, and Ralph C. Guzmán

The trends described in the preceding sections do not mean that the Southwest Church is undergoing a sweeping social-action orientation to-

Reprinted with permission of The Macmillan Company from *The Mexican-American People* by Leo Grebler, Joan W. Moore, and Ralph C. Guzmán. Copyright © 1970 by The Free Press, a Division of The Macmillan Company.

ward the Mexican-American population. The individual territorial parish remains the Church's basic unit of contact with the people. The vast majority of Mexican Americans know the Church through their local parish. Even if many do not attend Sunday Mass regularly, baptisms, marriages, and funerals bring a majority to the Church at one time or another. The chances are that they will meet not the social-action *padre,* much less the bishop, but a traditional parish priest.

Because the parish priest is so important, interviews were held with pastors of Mexican-American parishes in Los Angeles and San Antonio. The main purpose was to test the hypothesis that pastors in Mexican-American parishes, as a group, exhibit status-quo preferences and emphasize strictly pastoral concerns. Fifty-two pastors, 26 in each city, were interviewed between September 1966 and April 1967.

In detail, the interview questionnaire was designed to test the five propositions stated below together with a summary of the responses of those interviewed.

1. *Pastors tend to depreciate suggestions of prejudice and discrimination against Mexican Americans in the larger society.* This proposition was not borne out. A majority of pastors in both cities acknowledged the existence of prejudice and discrimination in the local system, and the majority was greater in San Antonio than in Los Angeles. Instances of past discrimination within the Church were acknowledged by both sets of pastors. "Mexicans were told by 'Anglo' pastors to go to their own church." A few cited instances of a "Mexican church" constructed close to a larger church "so the Mexicans would have some place to go— obviously they weren't wanted in the big church." But denial of present-day discrimination within the Church was practically unanimous.

2. *Pastors are hostile to Protestant churches and view them as the chief enemy in the definition of their jobs.* No pastor interviewed seemed to take Protestant proselytizing seriously. "Not important" and "negligible impact" were opinions commonly expressed. Only 14 pastors in both cities admitted that Protestant efforts attracted "some converts," but very few —and only because of material benefits offered (several spoke of "rice Christians").

3. *Pastors have had little exposure to the social teachings of the Church and preach on this topic infrequently if at all.* In Los Angeles, 73 per cent of the pastors said they had had no exposure to social teachings of the Church in the seminary. In contrast, only 8 per cent of the San Antonio pastors reported no such exposure. Thus, the responses confirm this part of the hypothesis for one locale but not the other. The large discrepancy may be explained partly by the age differentials between the two groups of priests. The Los Angeles pastors were older and may therefore not have been exposed to changed seminary curricula, which include courses in the social encyclicals of recent popes. Also, the majority of San Antonio's clergy consisted of religious-order priests. Religious-order candidates for the priesthood have longer seminary training than diocesan seminarians and are therefore more likely to have had specific courses in social justice.

Acquaintance with this teaching is no guarantee that the priest will preach it. In fact, the majority in both cities did not preach on topics of social justice, confirming the second part of the proposition. When questioned about the reasons, Los Angeles pastors claimed mainly lack of suitable occasions, or that other topics were more important. San Antonio pastors felt that the people were "not ready" to understand the teaching. This inter-city difference may reflect the lower level of Mexican-American educational attainment in San Antonio. Most of the relatively few priests in both cities who stated that they preached "quite often" on the social teachings of the Church did so because it was "prescribed by the Archdiocese."

These findings support the proposition that parish-based priests on the whole do not invest social questions with the urgency felt by their social-action counterparts. In the case of the Mexican American, particularly, they preferred to emphasize "doctrinal and moral" sermons as best meeting the needs of a population poorly instructed in religion.

4. *Pastors take little part in state, civic, or neighborhood organizations and activities.* Generally, this hypothesis is borne out by the responses in Los Angeles but not those in San Antonio. The San Antonio Neighborhood Youth Organization (SANYO), the major war-on-poverty agency in this city, accounts largely for the fact that practically all of the pastors interviewed there mentioned some socioeconomic welfare programs or activities sponsored by the parish. Only 35 per cent of Los Angeles pastors mentioned parallel programs. One Los Angeles parish had a war-on-poverty program initiated by the pastor. Credit unions were mentioned with some frequency, although several pastors in San Antonio reported the failure some years before of a parish credit union.

The pastors in San Antonio showed more participation in state, civic, and neighborhood organizations than those in Los Angeles—54 per cent and 19 per cent, respectively, reporting "some participation." An important factor here may be that more civic leadership is expected of the pastors in San Antonio because there are relatively few qualified lay participants from the Mexican-American community. The wider leadership base of more highly educated Mexican-American laymen in Los Angeles probably diminishes the expectation of clerical representation there. Almost half the nonparticipants in both cities gave no reason for their inactivity; about a third alleged "no time due to pastoral duties"; and the remainder listed "no interest."

No dramatic social protest involving Mexican Americans occurred in Los Angeles to match the "March on Austin" of striking Mexican-American farm workers from the Rio Grande Valley in the late summer of 1966. The marchers came through San Antonio on their way to Austin. They were greeted by Archbishop Lucey and a group of social-action priests. We used this event to probe the San Antonio pastors' attitudes toward a controversial social protest involving Mexican Americans. Only 10 of the 26 San Antonio pastors mentioned the march from the pulpit (all favorably). Four of the sixteen who did not professed to be "confused" about the issues or to lack adequate understanding. Six others expressed dis-

approval of "the method—not the cause." Some were so annoyed by the
social-action priests' participation that this factor qualified their approval
of the march.

5. *Pastors show preference for traditional parish societies as contrasted
with social-action organizations.* This hypothesis was confirmed by the responses in both cities. Organizations ranked first in importance by the
pastors stress traditional parish societies, with some emphasis on the
Confraternity of Christian Doctrine which in each diocese is responsible
for religious instruction programs for Catholic students in public schools.
Doctrinal instruction was given high priority because of the large numbers of Mexican-American elementary and high school students attending
public schools.

Generally, then, the interview results confirm the over-all assumption
that parish-based priests tend to have a narrower view of their functions
and to be wary of new and possibly disruptive activities. At the same
time, the responses highlight once more the inter-area variations which
have been stressed in many other contexts throughout this volume. The
general findings may in part reflect the demands on the time of priests
staffing the low-income parishes in Mexican-American areas. In addition
to the strictly religious functions, acute financial problems require close
attention to management, particularly in San Antonio where the Archdiocese has not been in a position to subsidize low-income parishes.

The parish priest's round of here-and-now activities tends to absorb his

Table 1.   Frequency of Sunday Mass Attendance, Mexican-American
and National Sample Surveys

	Per Cent Attending Once a Week or More	Per Cent Attending Less than Once a Week	Per Cent Never Attending	Total Number (= 100%)
Los Angeles Mexican-American survey respondents, 1965–1966	47	47	6	852
San Antonio Mexican-American survey respondents, 1965–1966	58	41	1	569*
U.S. Catholics, 1966†	67	20	13	n.a.
U.S. Catholics, 1957‡	72	24	4	1,270

* Weighting procedures were used in the San Antonio sample. This means that total numbers
cannot be used as a direct indicator of error. See Appendix H.
† Gallup Survey, reported in the *Catholic Digest*, July, 1966, p. 27.
‡ Survey Research Center at the University of Michigan, reported by Bernard Lazerwitz,
"Religion and Social Structure in the United States," in Louis Schneider (ed.), *Religion, Culture
and Society* (New York: John Wiley & Sons Inc., 1964), p. 430.

time and constrict his perspective, leaving little room for expanding his vision to larger problems in the community. Also, preoccupation with parochial duties means limited contacts with organizations and activities outside the parish. He may be impatient, too, with the protracted discussions of neighborhood and community meetings, for he is used to making decisions on his own and making them rapidly.

Religious Practice and Attitudes of Mexican Americans

Finally, pastors' concern with strictly religious functions is understandable in light of the religious practice and attitudes of Mexican Americans. What was said previously about the clergy's historical perception of the Mexican immigrant applies to contemporary Mexican Americans as well. Large numbers of Catholics in this population do not conform to the norms of the Church. This is evident from our survey data on Mexican-American religious practice and attitudes in Los Angeles and San Antonio.

Mexican Americans in the two cities fall substantially below the national average in weekly Mass attendance (Table 1). According to a recent national survey, even respondents with no Catholic schooling attend Mass more regularly than Mexican Americans (for whom Catholic schooling is not reported). Mexican-American women attend Mass more

Table 2.   Frequency of Mass Attendance, by Sex,
Mexican-American Survey, National Survey, and Schuyler Study

	PER CENT ATTENDING ONCE A WEEK OR MORE		PER CENT ATTENDING LESS THAN ONCE A WEEK		TOTAL NUMBER (= 100%)	
	Men	Women	Men	Women	Men	Women
Los Angeles Mexican-American survey respondents, 1965–1966	39	52	61	48	365	488
San Antonio Mexican-American survey respondents, 1965–1966	56	60	44	40	230*	339*
Schuyler study,† 1960	73	82	27	18	7,354	
U.S. Catholics, 1957‡	67	75	33	25	1,270	

° See note ° in preceding table.
† Joseph B. Schuyler, SJ., *Northern Parish: A Sociological and Pastoral Study* (Chicago, 1960), p. 2020.
‡ See note ‡ to preceding table.

frequently than do men, but both range well below Catholics in other surveys (Table 2). Similar differences appear when age is controlled, with Mexican-American attendance in Los Angeles markedly low in the 20–29 year age group (Table 3). San Antonio Mexican Americans score consistently higher on Mass attendance by age and sex groupings than do Los Angeles Mexican Americans.

National surveys reveal a positive correlation between Mass attendance and education, with a sharp increase for those who have completed high school. San Antonio Mexican Americans generally follow this pattern, while a more complicated pattern holds for Mexican Americans in Los Angeles (Table 4). Los Angeles Mexican Americans living in more segregated neighborhoods appear to practice somewhat more regularly than those in mixed areas, though San Antonio reveals the opposite. Poorer people among Los Angeles Mexican Americans practice more regularly, but income makes little difference in the case of San Antonio Mexican Americans (Table 5). Though no exactly comparable national survey data are available, Lazerwitz sample cited in the tables indicates an opposite pattern: Roman Catholic professionals and other white-collar persons show 81–83 per cent regular Sunday Mass attendance; the attendance of unskilled workers drops, but only to a level of 62 per cent, or more than 10 percentage points above low-income Mexican Americans in Los Angeles.

Further, a study of marriages in Los Angeles County in 1963 revealed a low per centage of Mexican-American marriages originally performed before a Catholic priest (Table 6). This may not be surprising in the case of the foreign born. Mexican law recognizes only a civil marriage, which customarily precedes Church marriage in Mexico. Hence, the foreign born may be ignorant of American practice. However, any impact of American Catholic socialization should appear in an increased percentage of original Church marriages among the native born. This is true for the second generation, but initial Church marriages drop again among natives of native parentage. (Of course, these data do not indicate the proportion of civil marriages later validated within the church.)

Table 3. Per cent Attending Mass Weekly or More Often, by Age and Sex, Mexican-American Survey and Schuyler Study
(Sample size in parentheses)

| | MEXICAN AMERICANS, 1965–1966 | | | | SCHUYLER STUDY* |
| | LOS ANGELES | | SAN ANTONIO | | |
AGE GROUP	Men	Women	Men	Women	Men and Women
20–29	28% (76)	41% (129)	42% (38)	57% (51)	76%
30–39	39 (113)	51 (152)	42 (62)	61 (81)	69
40–49	44 (97)	51 (98)	69 (49)	69 (71)	76
50 years and older	42 (74)	69 (95)	65 (77)	67 (96)	80
Total	(360)	(474)	(226)	(299)	(7,354)

* See note † in Table 2.

Agreement with the teachings of the Church on birth control was far less widespread among the sample of Mexican Americans interviewed in Los Angeles and San Antonio than among a national sample. About 33 per cent of the Mexican Americans expressed agreement as against 68 per cent of the national survey respondents who had complete Catholic schooling, 52 per cent who had some Catholic schooling, and 44 per cent without any Catholic schooling. Moreover, even those Mexican Americans who attend Mass each Sunday or more often were divided in their opinion on birth control; in Los Angeles only 49 per cent expressed conformity to the position of the Church. Disagreement in both cities was particularly striking among those under 30 (65 per cent) and those who had attended college (67 per cent).

The relatively low levels of religious practice and of adherence to some of the fundamental teachings of the Church are at least partially related to the Mexican Americans' low degree of Catholic socialization. This is most evident in their attendance of parochial schools and their participation in religious instruction at public schools. According to estimates for 1966–1967, only 15 per cent of the Spanish-surname school population in grades 1 to 6 were enrolled in the parochial schools of high-density Mexican-American areas of Los Angeles; and only 57 per cent received either parochial schooling or so-called CCD instruction (named after the Confraternity of Christian Doctrine). For grades 7 to 12, the corresponding figures were 23 per cent and 32 per cent. At the junior high and high school level, the Mexican-American participation in CCD classes alone was far below the level for all Catholic students in the same grades. In

Table 4.   Per cent Attending Mass Weekly or More Often, by Sex
and Educational Attainment,
Mexican-American Survey Compared with National Survey
(Sample size in parentheses)

SCHOOL YEARS COMPLETED	MEXICAN AMERICANS, 1965–1966				NATIONAL SURVEY[*]
	LOS ANGELES		SAN ANTONIO		Men and Women
	Men	Women	Men	Women	
0–8 years	49% (164)	57% (232)	58% (139)	60% (191)	63% (436)
Some high school	25 (81)	42 (144)	38 (39)	64 (60)	67 (256)
Four years of high school	30 (67)	48 (77)	62 (34)	72 (28)	80 (397)
One or more years of college	38 (45)	38 (45)	73 (11)	100 (7)	83 (181)
No response	(3)	(5)	(5)	(22)	
Total	(360)	(503)	(228)	(308)	(1,270)

[*] Bernard Lazerwitz, "Religion and Social Structure in the United States," in Louis Schneider (ed.), *Religion, Culture and Society* (New York: John Wiley & Sons, Inc., 1964), table 6, p. 431.

Table 5. Frequency of Mass Attendance in Los Angeles and San Antonio,
by Residential Density and Income, Mexican-American Survey, 1965–1966
(Sample size in parentheses)

| | Residential Density* | | | | | Income of Head of Household† | | | | |
| | Colony | | Inter-mediate | Frontier | | High | Medium | | Low | |
Frequency of Mass Attendance	L.A.	S.A.	(L.A. only)	L.A.	S.A.	L.A.	L.A.	S.A.	L.A.	S.A.
Once a week or more	52% (159)	57% (220)	46% (116)	40% (120)	69% (111)	35% (70)	48% (81)	59% (92)	51% (234)	61% (225)
One to three times a month	25 (77)	30 (113)	22 (56)	30 (89)	24 (40)	30 (60)	28 (47)	28 (44)	23 (108)	28 (104)
Few times a year or less	18 (54)	10 (39)	24 (62)	21 (63)	6 (9)	25 (51)	21 (36)	11 (18)	19 (88)	8 (30)
Never	5 (16)	2 (7)	6 (15)	8 (25)	1 (1)	9 (19)	2 (4)	1 (2)	7 (32)	1 (5)
Total number (= 100%)	(306)	(379)	(249)	(297)	(161)	(200)	(168)	(156)	(462)	(364)

* In Los Angeles, Frontier = tracts with less than 15.0 per cent Spanish-surname individuals; Intermediate = tracts with between 15.0 and 48.8 per cent Spanish-surname individuals; and Colony = tracts with more than 43.8 per cent Spanish-surname individuals. In San Antonio, Frontier = tracts with less than 54.0 per cent Spanish-surname individuals, and Colony = tracts with 54.0 per cent or more Spanish-surname individuals.

† In Los Angeles, high income = > $6,000; medium income = $3,600–$5,999; low income = < $3,600. In San Antonio, medium income = > $2,760; low income = < $2,760.

the city of San Antonio, the Mexican-American enrollment in Catholic schools was only 21 per cent in grades 1 to 8 as against 30 per cent for all Catholic students in these grades, and 14 per cent in grades 9 to 12 as against 23 per cent for all Catholic students. However, their participation in CCD classes matched the general level more closely.

Thus, the parish priest can indeed point to an enormous need for pastoral concern with his Mexican-American flock and rationalize his preoccupation with this task. As was true in earlier periods, the Church cannot assume that the Mexican American will turn to her for comfort and support. Rather, the Church must reach out for him if it is to perform its spiritual role.

Table 6.   Per cent of Marriages Involving Mexican Americans with
            Catholic Ceremony, Los Angeles County, 1963
                   (Neither party previously married)

| | GROOMS | | |
BRIDES	Foreign Born, Mexico	Mexican or Mixed Parentage	Natives of Native Parentage
Foreign born, Mexico	46.7	47.1	43.6
Mexican or mixed parentage	38.6	55.2	52.4
Natives of native parentage	33.3	48.7	45.8

Source: Frank G. Mittelbach, Joan W. Moore, and Ronald McDaniel, *Intermarraige of Mexican-Americans* (Mexican-American Study Project, Advance Report 6, Graduate School of Business Administration, University of California, Los Angeles, November, 1966), Table V–4, p. 43.

Summary

The role of the Roman Catholic Church among the Mexican-American people of the Southwest shows a gradual and uneven trend toward a more involved Church trying to improve their social condition as well as their Church loyalty and their adherence to the norms of religious practice. At the beginning, the legacy of extremely poor resources and the demands made on the Church by the waves of Mexican immigrants necessitated an emphasis on pastoral care. It took considerable time before the Church could turn to social concern.

The study of the dynamics of Church activities suggests that social-action goals may have one of two possible relationships to pastoral goals:

1. Social-action goals may be adopted to further pastoral goals, defending them, legitimating them, making the position of the institutional Church (and therefore its right to exercise its primary religious mission) more acceptable in the larger society. The Archdiocese of Los Angeles, with its relatively early programs to further the Americanization and education of Mexican Americans, is a good illustration of this relationship.

2. Social-action goals may also be adopted as ends in themselves. In this view they are direct concerns of the Church. The betterment of work-

ing conditions, housing, health, education, and so forth is not simply a means to achieve pastoral goals, or a bait to attract new members and re-enlist those who have fallen away. The social-action priests invest their activities with a significance paralleling that of the pastoral concerns. For such priests, encouraging labor-union organization may be no less important than saying Mass.

The most effective and continuous goal reorientation, however, has occurred at the upper levels of the Church hierarchy—statewide bishops' committees and national agencies—as well as in ecumenical groups. For the Church on the parish level is interdependent with the local power centers and subject to immediate constraints, and so is the diocese—it takes a bishop of unusual courage and conviction to resist the strong pressures which can be brought to bear upon him. In contrast, administrative officials operate behind the bulwarks of their multi-faceted institutions.

Most of the parish priests have remained preoccupied with purely pastoral concerns. This explains why writers concentrating on typical parish activities have conveyed the impression of little change in the role performed by the Church. Conversely, an analysis of policies at the upper levels of the hierarchy suggests a cautious revision of the notion that the Church, being basically a conservative force, has retarded the assimilation of Mexican Americans.

FOLK MEDICINE AND THE INTERCULTURAL JEST

Américo Paredes

This paper is a discussion of six jests collected in Spanish at the lower end of the Texas-Mexican border and presented here in English translation. They were part of several hundred texts recorded in 1962 and 1963, during a series of field trips in search of jests and legendary anecdotes that might reveal attitudes of Mexicans and Mexican Americans toward the United States.[1] I will attempt to relate them to Texas-Mexican attitudes toward culture change. They are not peculiar to the group from which they were recorded. Some of them have been collected from other Mexican groups, and their basic motifs are universal. The six were recorded from two informants, one narrator telling five, but I heard the

Reprinted from *Spanish Speaking Peoples of the U.S.*, edited by June Helm (Proceedings of the 1968 Annual Meeting of the American Ethnological Society), by permission of the University of Washington Press.

Dr. Américo Paredes is Professor of English and Anthropology at University of Texas. He was director of the Center for Mexican American Studies there and has served as Editor of Journal of America Folklore.

[1] My field work was made possible by a fellowship from the John Simon Guggenheim Foundation and a supplementary grant from the University of Texas, which I acknowledge with thanks.

same stories from other people during my collecting. It is the circumstances in which the texts were collected that I believe important, and for this reason I will describe them in some detail.

All six texts were collected on tape during two recording sessions at Brownsville, Texas, a bilingual and bicultural community. Jests of this sort are called *tallas* in the regional idiom, and they are told during regular *talla* sessions. Francisco J. Santamaría, the Mexican lexicographer, lists *talla* as a "Texas-Mexican barbarism" for any narrative, anecdote or jest, saying it is derived from the English "tale." This certainly would emphasize the intercultural character of the *talla*, were it not for the fact that Santamaría is wrong. Whatever the origins of *talla*, they certainly are not in "tale," to which it has merely a visual resemblance. Santamaría seems to have known, furthermore, that *talla* is found as far away from Texas as Costa Rica. The term may derive from the verb *tallar*, to rub or to chafe and by extension to tease. The *talla* as it is practiced in South Texas often does have a relationship to the Mexican word play known as the *albur*. Under these circumstances the jests are told as having happened to one of those present, or to one of their close relatives. The victims answer in kind, of course. *Talla* sessions are common occurrences along the border among males of all ages and at occasions varying from wakes to beer-drinking parties. Women rarely are present.

In collecting my first consideration was to recreate as closely as possible the circumstances of a *talla* session in its natural context. In Brownsville the sessions were held at a house just outside of town, which happened to be vacant at the time. A group of men would be invited, enough so that a total of ten to fifteen people were present at one time, including the collector. Sessions began around nine or ten at night and were held outside on the darkened patio or the lawn, with the participants sitting in a circle. Outside the circle was a washtub full of beer and ice. Also outside the circle was the tape recorder, but in a direction opposite to that of the tub with beer and just behind where the collector sat. An empty beer case was placed in the middle of the circle, on which the microphone rested on top of a cushion. The machine was a four-track Revere set at a speed of 3¾ inches per second, recording one hour per track on a 7-inch tape. This made it possible to record four hours on one tape without having to bother with the machine more than three times during the night. Four hours was the usual length of a session, from about ten until two in the morning.

The disadvantages to this method of collecting are the relatively poor quality of the recordings and the extreme tediousness of transcription. A four-hour session might well result in a dozen usable texts. But it is the best method I know for capturing the free, unself-conscious idiom in which the jests are told. The informants knew they were being recorded, of course, but a fairly natural atmosphere could be achieved after the first few minutes. The beer was partly responsible, as was the fact that the microphone was barely visible in the dark, so that the group forgot about it once beer and talk flowed freely. Most important, though, was the presence at each session of one or two assistants planted among the group, whose business it was to make the *talla* session as natural as possible and to elicit the kind of materials I was seeking without having to ask the informants for them. Their first job was to get everybody in the right mood by passing out the beer and making the usual small talk. The main purpose of my collecting, however, was to tape-record jokes and other lore about Anglo Americans. So the "plant" went on to tell some familiar joke on the subject, usually one of the large cycle of jests I have tentatively labeled the "Stupid American" joke. Since those invited were chosen because of their abilities as narrators, they responded with jests of their own, one story suggesting another. The "plant" had one other important function. The party sometimes wandered off in other directions, into small talk or verbal dueling, for example, or into reminiscing and sentimental songs. The "plant" tried to bring things back into line by telling another of his stories, usually texts I had already collected. He could do this as long as he stayed sober himself, something that did not always happen.

The main purpose of my field trip, as has been said, was to collect folklore making covert or direct expression of attitudes toward Anglo Americans and their culture. Materials were recorded in between a series of digressions that the "plants" attempted to control and redirect toward our agreed-on objective. On first examining the transcribable texts I brought back with me, I set aside the six discussed here as belonging with the digressions rather than with the material I was looking for. Americans scarcely appear in them. In No. 6 we do have a character of the "Stupid American" stereotype, but it is the Mexican villagers who appear in a ridiculous light rather than he.

All six of the stories do have in common a general situation: there is a sick person, and a group of people seek a cure for him. It is not the patient himself but his family or the community as a whole that seeks help. A doctor or healer is found, who recommends a cure with varying results. Nos. 1 through 5 all are concerned in one way or another with Mexican folk curing practices. Only in No. 6 is *curanderismo* absent, but the story is a variant of other *curandero* jests known to the collector in which it is the folk healer who recommends the wrong purgative to the patient, or the right purgative to the wrong person. That is to say, all six jests are parodies of a folktale type known to Latin American folklorists as the *caso* and sometimes called the "belief tale" in the United States—a relatively short narrative about miraculous or extraordinary events supposed to have happened to the narrator or to someone he knows. The particular type of *caso* parodied here is based on a formula well known to students of *curanderismo*, a simple pattern pitting the *curandero* against medical science, with science driven from the field in utter confusion.

Somebody falls ill and is taken to a doctor, but the doctor can do nothing for him. The patient gets worse and worse. There may be a consultation attended by several doctors, "a meeting of the doctors," as the *casos* put it, but the men of science cannot find the cause of the disease or recommend a cure. Or perhaps they say the patient is beyond hope of recovery. Again, they may recommend a painful and costly operation requiring a long stay at the hospital. Then someone suggests going to Don Pedrito or Don Juanito or some other *curandero*. The patient's relatives are skeptical at first but they finally agree. The whole group journeys to the *curandero*, who receives them kindly but chides the doubters about their skepticism, which he has learned about by miraculous means even before they arrived. Then he asks a standard question, seemingly unnecessary for his diagnosis but very important to the structured arrangement of the narrative, "And what do the doctors say?"

He is told what the doctors say, and he smiles indulgently at their childish ignorance. Then he prescribes some deceptively simple remedy: an herb perhaps, drinking three swallows of water under special circumstances three times a day, washing at a certain well or spring, or the like. The patient recovers completely. There may be a sequel in which the former patient goes and confronts the doctors. They are surprised, incredible. They visit the old *curandero*, seeking to find out the secret of the cure. The old man tells them nothing, or he will answer in words such as, "God cured him, not I." The doctors leave, chastened and still mystified.

A number of these *casos* have been current in south Texas and northern Tamaulipas for generations, most often in association with the saintly figure of Don Pedrito Jaramillo, the famed healer of Los Olmos, Texas. Ruth Dodson published a number of stories related to Don Pedrito, first in Spanish and later in English translation (Dodson 1934, 1951). More recently, Octavio Romano has studied Don Pedrito as a charismatic figure (Romano 1965). Not all *curandero* belief tales follow the strict pattern of this formula, though it is perhaps the most widely retold. Another important narrative pattern deals with the scoffer who comes to the *curandero* pretending to be ill, merely to ridicule or expose him. The *curandero* punishes him by causing him to have a debilitating and embarrassing case of diarrhea.

The function of the *curandero* belief tale among Mexican folk groups is clear enough. It helps bolster belief in folk medicine; it encourages acceptance by the younger generation of the old traditions, especially when the group must live among an increasingly skeptical majority. This may be equally true whether the Mexican folk group is living in the United States or across the border in Mexico, since Mexican physicians are at times even more intolerant of folk medicine than their Anglo-American counterparts. But this type of *caso* plays an important role among rural and semirural Mexican groups in the United States, who see their folk culture assailed not only by modern science and technology but by the belief patterns of rural Anglo-American neighbors, who may have their own folk beliefs but tend to be contemptuous of those held by foreigners.

It is this type of belief tale that is parodied in jests such as the six we are considering. They quite consciously mock the defenses set up by the *curandero* belief tales, and they express an equally conscious rejection of the folk culture holding such beliefs. On the surface they represent as violent a rejection of Mexican values as that of William Madsen's Mexican American from Hidalgo county, Paul, who wishes he could get the Mexican blood out of his veins and change it for something else (Madsen 1964:43).

Pertinent is the fact that parodies of *curandero* belief tales are widespread among Mexican Americans, certainly one of the reasons why these six intruded into a session of "Stupid American" jokes. The earliest printed example I know of appeared in the *Journal of American Folklore* in 1914 in one of Aurelio M. Espinosa's collections of New Mexican folklore. It is a variant of our No. 6, except that it is a *curandero* rather than a veterinarian who gives the purgative to the wrong person. It works, though, so the *curandero* justifies his action, saying, "*Haciendo la cosa efecto, no importa que sieso sea.*" ("As long as the thing works, who cares whose ass it was?") (Espinosa 1914, Text No. 48). In the late 1920's, when the celebrated Niño Fidencio was curing the sick, the halt and the blind in Nuevo León, Mexico, similar stories were circulated along the border about some of his cures. In one he cured a hunchback by breaking his spine. The hunchback screamed, "I'm dying!"

"But you'll die straight," Fidencio replied.

These are, of course, adaptations of other stories ranging much farther in space and time. All six contain universal motifs found in Stith Thompson's *Motif-Index of Folk-Literature*, either under J2450, "Literal fools" or J2412, "Foolish imitation of healing." Nos. 5 and 6 resemble Spanish folktales about the numskull who is told to bathe his grandmother in hot water and boils her to death instead. Or he is told to clean a child, so he cuts its belly open and takes out the intestines. Nos. 2 and 3, especially No. 2, are based on motifs listed by Thompson under B700, "Fanciful traits of animals." There are several methods by which animals that have introduced themselves into people's stomachs are disposed of. For example, in B784.2.1, reported from Ireland, Italy, and the United States, "The patient is fed salt or heavily salted food and allowed no water for several days. He then stands with mouth open before a supply of fresh water, often a running brook. The thirsty animal emerges to get fresh water." Thompson does not tell us if the animal is then beaten to death. Then there is motif B784.2.1.2, reported from India, about which Thompson tells us, "A husband ties a cock near his wife's feet so that a snake-parasite in her stomach will come out to catch the cock. The snake is then killed by the husband." Thompson does not tell us how the snake comes out of the woman's body, an important omission especially for the psychoanalytically oriented investigator. It might also be worth mentioning that we could find parallels to these jests somewhat nearer at hand; No. 6 is very much like North American sick jokes.

The prevalence of feces and other anal motifs as a source of humor in our jests certainly would interest the psychoanalyst. This characteristic may reflect influence from one type of *curandero* belief tale discussed above, seriously told and believed but causing mirth instead of wonder, when the listener thinks of the discomfiture suffered by the skeptic inflicted with diarrhea. At least, this points to a favorite source of humor among groups telling the same tales. But it is the other *caso* formula—in which the *curandero* vanquishes medical science—that is alluded to in Texts 1 through 5, all beginning very much in the serious belief tale style but becoming *tallas* when the ending takes a ludicrous twist, by means of which the *curandero* and his methods are satirized.

Text No. 1 reproduces the sequel following many of the *casos*, when the doctors come to the *curandero* and humbly seek to know the secret of his powers—truly a triumph of folk healing over medical science. But our *curandero* is not reticent about explaining his methods, nor does he attribute his success to divine power. His answer, in fact, has a logic all its own, based on a folkish kind of empiricism one might say. The hit-or-miss character of many folk remedies, their far-fetched sense of causality, and the actual use of drug in *curanderismo* all come in for ridicule.

Texts Nos. 2 and 3 are variants of the same tale, based on an old and widely traveled motif, B784.2, "Means of ridding person of animal in stomach." It is significant that they were told by the same informant in the order given, 2 before 3, so that No. 3 is an emphatic restatement of No. 2. This jest includes a good part of the belief tale formula: A man falls gravely ill. He is taken to the hospital, where nothing is done for him. Hospital personnel recommend an operation, something the unsophisticated Mexican American dreads. Madsen, for example, reports that for his Hidalgo county informants the hospital is the most dreaded place next to prison and that hospitalization "can become a nightmarish experience when surgery is involved . . ." (Madsen 1964:93–94). Frightened by the prospect of an operation, the relatives take the patient to the *curandero,* who asks the formal question, "And what did they say at the hospital?" The hospital wants to operate, but the *curandero* is reassuring. No operation is necessary; he will cure the patient without much trouble. Up to this point the joke and the belief tale follow more or less identical lines, and it is at this point that the ridiculous is introduced.

There are some other features about Nos. 2 and 3 that should be noted before passing on to the other jests, even though they do not pertain to our belief tale formula. The action is set in Hidalgo county though the story was recorded in the county of Cameron. The narrator first calls the *curandero* "Don Pedrito," evidently in reference to the celebrated Don Pedrito Jaramillo, though he forgets later and calls him "Don Juanito." Still later, in No. 3, the *curandero* becomes "Don Fulanito"— Mr. John Doe or Mr. Such-and-Such, making him just any folk healer. More interesting still is the matter of the hospital. According to the belief tale formula the patient's family refuses to put him in the hospital because of their horror of operations, or the American doctors do get him into the hospital but are unable to find a cure. It is different with our *bracero's* friends, who do want him treated there. Nor do they question at this point the ability of the American doctors to make the patient well. The hospital attendants refuse to admit the patient, and it is because of this that he is taken to the *curandero*. If we keep this in mind, the emphatic character of the second variant, Text No. 3, becomes significant. The same pattern is stated, but in stronger terms. The demand for money on the part of the hospital staff is emphasized by putting it into English, "Who's gonna pay?" pronounced in a drawling, decidedly unpleasant tone. The "All right. Get out!" of No. 2 becomes "All right. Get out, *cabrones!*" [2] Even the gentle old *curandero* suffers a change with his, "There'll be no fuckin operation!" The narrator has warmed up to his theme, whatever his theme may be. At least we can be sure that he intends to be more than merely funny.

Text No. 4 makes an interesting contrast with Nos. 2 and 3. Again the setting is in Hidalgo county, and again the *curandero's* name is Don Pedrito. But in this story the American doctor is sympathetic; he offers to take the sick girl to the hospital. It is the girl's family who decide to take her to Don Pedrito because he "never goes around recommending operations." Up to this point the jest closely follows not only the usual pattern of the *curandero* belief tale but also certain supposedly factual cases reported by nonbelievers in *curanderismo*, in which Mexican Americans are said to have died of such things as appendicitis rather than go to a hospital. Satire begins when Don Pedrito is shown in anything but a humble or saintly mood; he calls the American doctors a bunch of *cabrones*. His diagnosis of what the doctor has called appendicitis is a parody of such folk diseases as *mollera caída* and *susto pasado* (fallen fontanelle and an advanced case of fright sickness).[3] Also satirized is the belief, often encountered by collectors, that only Mexicans can get "Mexican" diseases like *ojo* and *susto*, though it should be mentioned that one encounters just as often belief tales about Anglo Americans who are healed by *curanderos*. Almost twenty per cent of Don Pedrito Jaramillo's cures as related by Ruth Dodson are said to have been done to Anglo Americans (1934:129-146).

At first glance No. 5 seems to be different from the preceding four jests, but it really is based on one small part of the belief tale formula we have been considering: the actual treatment of the patient by the *curandero*. The rubbing down with alcohol is prescribed by *curanderos* and by old-fashioned M.D.'s alike for any number of ailments. In the original Spanish the doctor prescribes that an egg (*huevo*) be put on the patient's forehead, *huevo* being such a common synonym for "testicle" that many prudish people avoid the word altogether, substituting it with *blanquillo*. The use of an egg and of ashes, however, will be recognized by those familiar with Mexican folk medicine as part of the treatment for diseases like *susto* and *ojo*. Even the doctor's reassurance to the patient's family at

---

[2] *cabrón, cabrones* (singular and plural). Literally "he-goat," in formal Spanish usage it is the word for cuckold; in current usage as in the jests, the term is roughly equivalent to the English "bastard."

[3] In Text No. 4 the *curandero's* diagnosis in the original Spanish is *carne juida, sangre molida o pedo detenido.*

the beginning, that "It's not as bad as all that," is part of the *curandero* belief tale formula. Medical science has made a great deal of fuss over the patient's illness, but it will be an easy thing for the *curandero* to make the patient well. It is obvious that the M.D. in this story really is a *curandero* in disguise. The sense of the ridiculous is heightened by having an M.D. playing the part of the *curandero,* or vice-versa, but we must also keep in mind that the doctor to whom the joke is attributed is a Mexican-American. The jest is not identified with any particular doctor, by the way. Even the same narrator will use different names in retelling the story, but the name of a real Mexican-American doctor always is used, most often one that the narrator's hearers know well. I can attest to having heard this same informant tell the same jest downtown, away from a tape recorder, using the name of a different Mexican-American doctor.

Text No. 6 does not seem to go with the others at all; as it stands there is no *curanderismo* involved. But a comparison with No. 5 reveals an identical plot structure: a naive group of Mexicans misinterpret instructions for the treatment of a patient, with fatal results for the patient, the ending in both cases being very much like that of the "cruel" or "sick" joke common in North American urban lore. The characters giving medical instructions in the two stories also bear comparison. The American veterinarian is portrayed as a likable simpleton, along the lines of the "Stupid American" stereotype. But he is working for the Aftosa commission, engaged in slaughtering the Mexican peasant's cattle to control the hoof-and-mouth disease, and thus a much resented figure. The Mexican-American doctor, on the other hand, acts like a *curandero* and thus is comically seen as "one of our boys," but he is also a representative of American medical science and American culture and therefore must share some of the resentments generated by inter-cultural conflicts.

It is this double nature of our texts that makes them especially interesting. In the satirizing of folk medicine and *curandero* belief tales they express a mocking rejection of Mexican folk culture; in their expression of resentment toward American culture they show a strong sense of identification with the Mexican folk.

The texts, as has been said, were recorded during two sessions in Brownsville, Cameron county, Texas, a bilingual and bicultural community with an influential Mexican-American middle class including doctors, lawyers, teachers, well-to-do merchants, and individuals in elective and appointive public office. These are for the most part descendants of the old Mexican settlers of the region, people with their roots in a past when Brownsville was a "Mexican" town rather than immigrants or children of immigrants from Mexico. By usual North American standards they would belong to the middle class; according to Madsen's class divisions for Mexican Americans in Hidalgo county, they would be "upper class" (Madsen 1964:41-43). The participants in the *talla* recording sessions were bilingual males between the ages of twenty-five and fifty-five. They speak good English and have received advanced education in American colleges and universities. They play important roles in community life, not in the life of a "Mexican colony" but in that of the city and the county as a whole. In other words, they would seem to be completely acculturated, having adapted to American culture and functioning in it in a very successful way. At the same time, when they are away from the courtroom, the school, the office, or the clinic and congregated in a group of their own, they think of themselves as *mexicanos*. Not only will they speak Spanish among themselves, but it is quite obvious that they place a high value on many aspects of Mexican culture and are proud of the duality of their background. They do in a sense live double lives, functioning as Americans in the affairs of the community at large and as Mexicans within their own closed circle.

In each of the two sessions groups of about a dozen individuals of the type described told jests of the "Stupid American" type, in which tension and hostility toward the majority culture were expressed in joking situations. The *curandero* parodies were introduced into this context by two of the informants, one at each session. Text No. 5 was told by a lawyer, a friend of the doctor to whom the story was attributed in this particular variant. The doctor was not present at the session. Had he been present the joke might have been interpreted in another way, as part of a verbal duel, with the doctor replying by telling a joke about lawyers in which his friend would have been the main character. This is one way the *talla* is performed, as was said in discussing the probable origins of the word. In this case, however, the doctor's name was used because he is well known and representative. The narrator practices criminal law; his work brings him into contact with many Mexican Americans of the poorer class, much less acculturated than himself, who are usually in trouble when they come to him. His knowledge of Spanish gains him their confidence, and his Mexican background leads him to identify with them in many ways, but his profession demands that he comport himself in the role of an American lawyer functioning in an American court rather than assuming a "Mexican" role as he does when he is with a group of intimates. Many things repressed in the courtroom find an outlet in the *talla* sessions. The lawyer always has amusing anecdotes to tell within his own group, some of them revealing the comic naiveté of his clients, others showing their folk wit and hardheaded common sense.

Texts Nos. 1, 2, 3, 4, and 6 were told by the same person, one of the best narrators I know. Only a sound recording can show his sense of intonation and mimicry, and even then his gestures are lost. He told all five stories in the same session, but not consecutively since he was alternating with other narrators present. It is quite clear, however, that one tale brought another to his mind. These are not his stories any more than No. 5 belongs to the lawyer alone. They are common property, but this informant is recognized as telling them better than most other people do. He works for a school system somewhere in Cameron county, and his job brings him into contact—at times into conflict—with Mexican-American parents of the laboring classes. He also has his anecdotes about his job: the naiveté of some of the parents he deals with, their lack of understanding of American values, their reluctance to keep their children in school. Often he parodies these people when he is among his own group. Just as often he will become exasperated with his job, complaining that his work shows no results, that he is butting his head against a stone wall. He seems sincerely committed in his efforts to raise the educational level of Mexican Americans in the county and is emotionally involved in the situation.

The two informants are typical of their group. They are socially conscious members of the middle class, impatient about the slow acculturation of the average Mexican American and his low economic and social status. At the same time, they reveal a strong feeling of identification with the unacculturated Mexican. They are highly acculturated Mexican Americans who value their ancestral culture in spite of such aspects as *curanderismo,* which they would include among the things the Mexican American must reject in order to compete successfully in an English-speaking world. But their attitude toward the *curandero* is not a hostile one. They will admit that some of these old men are pretty good psychologists in their own way, and they also point out with evident pride that many Mexican herbs have been put to use by modern medical science. Furthermore, the belief in *curanderismo* is something in their own recent past. Such celebrated *curanderos* as Don Pedrito Jaramillo were patronized a half-century ago not only by the poor and illiterate but by many of the land-owning families of the area. Some of those present during the *talla* session I recorded had been treated by *curanderos* in their early childhood. So there is identification on the part of the group not only with the unacculturated Mexican but with *curanderismo* itself. This is most clearly seen in No. 5, in which the *cunandero's* role is given to a highly acculturated Mexican-American physician, an absent member of the group in which the tale was told.

Curanderismo for this group is a subject viewed with a good deal of ambivalence, but the ambivalent attitude is anything but rare in jokes. The best dirty jokes about priests and nuns are told by Catholics; to be truly effective, the contemporary "cruel" or "sick" joke has to be told among people who are highly sensitive to human suffering. The *curandero* jests release a complicated set of conflicting emotions ranging from exasperation to affection in respect to the unacculturated Mexican American, coupled with a half-conscious resentment toward the Anglo-American culture. Also involved is a definite element of masochism, often expressed in the proverbial phrase, "¡Ah, que mexicano!" (Ah, what a Mexican!) used to express jesting disapproval of some bumbling or foolish act. We must keep in mind that members of this group are quite explicit in identifying themselves as *mexicanos,* and that the above phrase is used only in Spanish, never in English.

So these jests are not after all intrusions into a session of stories expressing intercultural conflict; they also are expressions of the same kind of conflict. Only in No. 4 does the doctor, representative of American culture, appear in a favorable light. In Nos. 2 and 3 the matter is quite explicit. The poor *bracero* must go to the folk healer because he is refused treatment at the American hospital. The *curandero* asks for so little—a small fee or a gift, something the poorest laborer can pay. One does not have to be a rich man to visit Don Fulanito. Many such incidents are seriously told by Mexican Americans of the poorer classes. We find the same subject-matter here in jokes, told by people who can afford to be treated at hospitals, but the stories are not quite in the comic vein. There is a good deal of emotional involvement, which members of the group would readily acknowledge among themselves, and that gives an edge to the humor. They may tell you, with a kind of self-directed exasperation, about Mexican laborers who died of appendicitis because they refused to go to a hospital. But they will also tell you other stories of Mexican laborers who died for lack of attention, and it is obvious that these stories arouse their resentment.

Why the events in Nos. 2, 3, and 4 are placed in Hidalgo rather than in Cameron county I am not prepared to say. It may be that Mexican Americans in Cameron county feel that their people in Hidalgo live under worse conditions than they do. It may be a narrative device, placing the action at some distance from narrator and audience. If such is the case, it is worth noting that the device is not a comic one. The comedian uses the opposite approach, relating his story to familiar events and to people close at hand. The introduction of people in the narrator's audience as characters in his jests has been mentioned as typical of one of the aspects of the *talla* session, when it becomes a verbal contest. Narrators tend to place events some distance away for reasons other than comedy. If characters and events are very far away, in a distant time and a distant land, the effect is one of wonder and romance. But to achieve a feeling of verisimilitude, required in the legendary anecdote, events are placed not too far off—in the next town, the next hollow, or the next county. This again is evidence that these jests are not intended to be as funny as they appear on the surface.

This is not, then, a relatively simple case of second-generation Americans ridiculing the culture of their ancestors and thereby rejecting it. As parodies of the *curandero* type of belief tale the jests do express the Mexican American's rejection of his traditional culture. But combined with parody is a good deal of resentment against Anglo-American culture, expressed in a stereotypic view of American physicians and hospital attendants as caring little about Mexican patients of the poorer, less educated class. Since the informants are not poor and badly educated themselves but belong to the middle class, the ambivalence of their attitudes is quite marked. Members of the group telling the jests have not lost the feeling that beneath their Americanized exterior they still are *mexicanos*. There is an underlying conflict between their Spanish-Mexican heritage and an Anglo-American culture they have embraced intellectually without completely accepting it emotionally, in great part because Anglo-American culture rejects part of themselves. The jests help resolve these conflicts brought about by acculturation, involving not only a change from rural to urban values but from a basically Mexican culture to the generalized, English-speaking culture of the majority.

Text I

They tell about an old man who was a *curandero,* that they bought him a patient who was sick in the stomach. And he said, "Give him goat turds."

Said, "But what do you mean, give him goat turds!"

"Yes," he said, "Boiled."

Well, so they did it, and the man got well. And then there was a meeting of physicians. Said, "Listen, man," he said. "We never could find out what was wrong with him. And he got well with goat turds."

So they called the old *curandero.* Said, "Well, why did you give goat turds to this man?"

He said, "It's very simple. Because I knew the ailment he had," he said, "could be cured with some sort of herb. But I didn't know which one," he said. "And since goats eat all kinds of weeds and herbs, I knew the plant that was needed would be there in the shit."

Informant No. 24
Brownsville, Texas
October 20, 1962

Text II

They went to see Don Pedrito about a poor *bracero* who was around there in Hidalgo county, and this poor man got up one night to get a drink of water and he swallowed a spider. Well, he got sicker and sicker, so they took him to the hospital at Edinburg.

And they said, "Who's going to pay?"

"Well, there's no money, I guess."

"All right. Get out!"

"So what can we do?" they said. "Nobody can pay. Let's take him over to Don Pedrito."

Well, so the little old man came and looked him over. "And what happened to him?" he said.

"Well, it's like this." Said, "This boy swallowed a spider."

He said, "And what did they say at the hospital?"

Said, "Oh no! At the hospital they want money to operate on him."

"No," he said, "don't talk to me about operations. I'll take care of him right now. Let's see, turn him over for me with his ass sticking up, with his butt in the air."

They turned him over.

"Now, pull his pants down." They pulled his pants down.

He said, "But bring him out here in the yard." They laid him down in the yard.

He said, "Do you have some Karo corn syrup?"

"Well, yes. Here's some."

Gave his asshole a good smearing with it. "All right, now," he said, "Everybody stand back." And he picked up a stick.

Said, "But what are you doing, Don Juanito?"

He said, "I'm waiting for the flies to gather," he said. "When the flies start buzzing the spider will come out, and I'll kill it with this little stick."

Informant No. 24

TEXT III

And then there was this other guy who drank the kerosene, this other poor man living in a tent around there who picked up a glass. And they had a lot of milk bottles there, made of glass, and they had water and kerosene in them. And this poor man picked one of them up and downed half a liter of kerosene. And he was choking, so there they go to the hospital at Edinburg.

And they took him there. "WHO'S GONNA PAY?" [Part in caps said in English.]

"Well, there's no money, I guess."

"All right. Get out, *cabrones!*"

Well, there was no money, so out! So they took him back, and the poor man was choking. He had downed half a liter of kerosene. Said, "Call Don Fulanito."

So the old man came. "What's the matter?" he said.

"He drank half a liter of kerosene."

"All right. So what did they say at the hospital?"

Said, "Well, at the hospital they want money. For the operation."

"Ah, no There'll be no fuckin operation," he said. "Let's see. Bring him out here for me. Just put him out here and leave him to me." He said, "Don't you have a lantern there?"

"Well, yes."

"Let's see, then. Take the wick out of the lantern." They took out the wick. "Does anybody have a pencil around there?"

"Well, yes. Here's the pencil."

"Now get out of the way," he said. "Pull his pants down." He stuffed the wick in his asshole with the pencil and said, "Let's have a match." He lighted the wick. He said, "All right, now. Everybody stand back. When the fire is gone," he said, "when the wick goes out, then all the kerosene will be out of him."

Informant No. 24

TEXT IV

This is something they say happened in Mission or McAllen or somewhere over there, in Hidalgo county, you see? A girl began to feel very sick in the stomach, and they took her to the doctor. And the doctor said, "This girl has appendicitis." He said, "We'll have to take out her appendix, no other way. If she isn't feeling better by tomorrow at ten," he said, "I'll come for her."

So then a woman said, "Look," she said, "Don Pedrito is in town. He's a *curandero*," she said, "and he's a very wise old man."

Said, "What for?"

"He never goes around recommending operations," she said, "and he never makes a mistake."

Well, so they called him. He said, "Let's see, let's see," he said. "What does the doctor say?"

"Oh, the doctor says it's her appendix."

He said, "Oh, no. Those doctors are a bunch of *cabrones*; all they know is about diseases in English. But this little girl is sick in the Mexican way; she has a Mexican disease," he said. "And it can be only one of three things: fled flesh, bruised blood, or a blocked fart."

Informant No. 24

Z.P. [narrator names a Mexican-American M.D.] went to call on a patient. He examined him and said, "It's not as bad as all that. I'm going to write you a prescription. But I want you to do exactly what I tell you, and I'll come back tomorrow morning. He'll get well, I assure you. But listen very carefully," he says, "because I want you to do it exactly as I am going to tell you."

"Very well, doctor."

He says, "I want you to give him a sponge bath, all right? Soak the sponge in alcohol and give him a good rubbing all over his body. And before the alcohol can evaporate, cover him with a sheet all the way up here to the neck. Then you take a little bit of ashes and sprinkle them around the bed. Pray one Paternoster and three Hail Marys. Then take a ball and balance it very carefully on his forehead," he says. "I'll come back around six or seven in the morning, and I assure you he'll be perfectly all right by then."

Well, so they did as they were told. Next morning the doctor came. But no, the poor man was already dead. "How's the patient?" he says.

"But he already—he's dead."

"But how could he be dead! It wasn't all—it wasn't a fatal disease. You must have failed to do exactly what I told you."

"Oh, no . . . We did, *señor* doctor."

"Well, did you give him the sponge bath with alcohol?"

"Yes, of course. As soon as you left. And we covered him with the sheet so the effect would not be lost."

"And the ashes?"

"Well, see for yourself; there they are. Look there, on the bed; you can still see the ashes there."

"And the ball on his forehead?" he says.

"Well, now there, you see doctor. There's where we had a bit of trouble. We had to call three of the neighbors," he says. "And we tried to do it between us four," he says. "But we couldn't pull it up any farther than his navel."

Informant No. 10
Brownsville, Texas
September 7, 1962

There was a veterinary out there with the Aftosa, a *bolillo* from around here.[4] And then this little old man was very sick; he had indigestion or I don't know what. So they went. "Here's a doctor from the other side of the border. What more do you want!" So they went to see him.

He said, "Oh, no! Me doctor by the cow. But not by the man. NO GOTTA PERMIT." [Vet's dialogue is in heavily accented Spanish, except part in caps, which is in English.]

Said, "No matter, doctor. What do you give the cows when they are sick in the stomach?"

"Well, *hombre*," he says, "me give a little Epsom salts."

---

[4] *bolillo*. One of the many derogatory names for the Anglo American. It seems to have been used originally for the French (*bolillo* is a small loaf of French bread), but later it was transferred to the North American.

Said, "How much Epsom salts do you give the cow?"

He says, "Oh, by one big cow me give her a pound of salts in one gallon of water."

So then they said, "Now we can figure the dose ourselves." They went home and measured half a gallon of water and half a pound of Epsom salts. And they made the old man drink it.

Well, so next morning they came. Said, "Oh, doctor, we came to see you." "How is sick man doing? Is he better?"

"Oh, no, he's dead."

He said, "But how could he be dead!"

"Yes, we came to invite you to the funeral, this afternoon. But don't feel guilty about it, doctor." Said, "It isn't your fault."

He said, "Why you say not my fault?"

Says, "We gave him the salts and the salts worked. He must have died of something else, because even after he was dead he still moved his bowels three times."

Informant No. 24

References

Dodson, Ruth. 1934. Don Pedrito Jaramillo: Curandero. San Antonio: Casa Editorial Lozano.

――――. 1951. Don Pedrito Jaramillo: The Curandero of Los Olmos. *Publications of the Texas Folklore Society*, 24:9–70.

Espinosa, Aurelio M. 1914. New-American Spanish Folklore. *The Journal of American Folklore*, 27:105–147.

Madsen, William. 1964. Mexican-Americans of South Texas. New York: Holt, Rinehart & Winston.

Romano, Octavio Ignacio. 1965. Charismatic Medicine, Folk-Healing and Folk Sainthood. *The American Anthropologist*, 67:1151–1173.

EARLY SETTLEMENT AND TRADITIONAL CULTURE

Nancie L. González

The earliest European settlement of New Mexico was made by a relatively small group led into the area from Mexico by Juan de Oñate in 1598. The descendants of this group and others who had joined them at irregular intervals were completely ejected from the area in 1680 by the Pueblo Indian Revolt. Thirteen years later a successful resettlement was made under the leadership of Diego de Vargas. Both of these conquering

Reprinted with permission from Nancie L. González, *The Spanish Americans of New Mexico* (Albuquerque, N.M.: University of New Mexico Press, 1967).

Nancie González received her doctorate from the University of Michigan in 1958. She has been instructor of nutrition and dietetics at Jamestown College, and is currently professor of anthropology at the University of New Mexico. She has done research and taught in the Dominican Republic and in Guatemala as well as in New Mexico.

groups were composed of a small elite of military leaders, common soldiers, a large number of Spanish-Mexican farmers, some wives, and a
number of Indian retainers (Chavez 1954:xiii; Woodward 1935:28–30).

Three general types of settlement seem to have been made. One was the
administrative and military center, represented by Santa Fe and Albuquerque which were established according to the gridiron plan centering
on a plaza, similar to countless other such towns all over Spanish America.
McWilliams (1943:137) and Loomis (1943:13) suggest that this plaza-
centered town was typical of all Spanish settlements in New Mexico.
Bunting, however, has said that in this area the term "plaza" or "placita"
connoted the idea of a fortified place rather than a central square. By
constructing contiguous houses about a central open area, windowless
outside walls could serve as a defense barrier (1964:3). Weaver also
describes the early settlement of Abajo (a pseudonym for the northern
village which he studied) as follows:

> At first, land was abundant, grazing ranges were open, and the colonists
> settled in three small placitas. Each placita consisted of a series of houses
> built wall-to-wall encircling a small enclosure. Each resembled a small fort-
> ress, and this was probably its early function (1965:13).

Dickey (1949:41) describes the same sort of multiple dwelling unit for
defense. He then goes on to point out that:

> Those communities which experienced little molestation from Apaches and
> Navajos, gradually gave up the fortified patio in favor of houses planned on
> straight lines or an L-shape. When the population of an hacienda approached
> the status of a village, its families separated into small-house units, each
> responsible for a patch of ground. Repeatedly the central government found
> it necessary to warn these settlements against making themselves vulnerable
> by scattering their houses up and down the watercourses.

The last quotation brings us to the second type of settlement pattern—
the *hacienda*. Little is actually known about this particular type in New
Mexico during the early days, although many writers seem to assume that
it was similar to the well-known hacienda complex of Mexico. Thus,
Austin says:

> There was an hacienda with its enclosed *patio* for the *patron* and contigu-
> ous to it, rooms and patios for the servants, two or three such, according to
> the estate, opening into the other, and finally into walled enclosures for the
> domestic animals and the herdsmen. Often there was a *torreon* near the
> entrance for outlook and defense, pierced for the *arcabuceros*. In the later
> times, when the raiding tribes had been subdued, about the middle of the
> eighteenth century, the house of the *hacendado* was two-storied, including
> *salas* for dancing, and extending itself by wings as the sons of the family
> brought their brides home. Every such estate was self contained, manufactur-
> ing its own utilities [1931:142].

Even though it is probable that some haciendas existed on which life was fairly opulent and luxurious, a cautioning note should be made, for it is clear that many of the settlements called haciendas in the literature were in fact merely extended-family multiple dwellings or small villages in which the inhabitants had built their houses contiguously around a central patio for purposes of defense, as described above. Many of these units must have been quite small, as is apparent from reading Bailey's account of a Spanish survey made in 1695 of the region near the town of Chimayo, which had been inhabited before the 1680 revolt. He describes an

> hacienda that once belonged to Miguel Lujan. There the houses were still standing and in them lived the owner with his family. He cultivated and irrigated only sufficient land for one family and raised a suitable number of cattle. This hacienda bordered upon that of Marcos de Herrera, whose family claimed also another hacienda below . . . beyond that was a hacienda belonging to Juan Griego, the most desirable then viewed because of its capacity to house two families and its abundant pasturage . . . (in another) were two excellent pieces of land which were inhabited by three families . . . the hacienda of Pedro de la Cruz was visited, which boasted a one-room abode and only enough land for one colonist and his family [1940:207–208].

The account goes on in this fashion, but quite clearly the term "hacienda" here means "small farm." Most of these were probably inhabited and worked by the members of an extended family. (See also Dickey 1949:1, quoted above.)

Several scholars distinguish between the communal village and the patron dominated village, which might very well be termed an hacienda. Knowlton (1961:451) suggests that the patron-dominated village type predominated in the south and east, while several writers confirm the greater importance of haciendas in the so-called Rio Abajo, or the area from Bernalillo to Socorro.[1] It is also quite likely that the size and elegance of some of these farms increased during the latter part of the eighteenth century and the first part of the nineteenth, when the fear of Indian attacks had lessened. According to Murbarbarger, great haciendas were established in what is now Arizona following the discovery there of precious metals. She writes:

> The Spanish hacienda of San Bernardino, near the present Arizona-New Mexico boundary, about seventeen miles east of Douglas, is said to have embraced, at its peak, around 100,000 cattle, 10,000 horses, and 5,000 mules. Its patron *grande* lived in almost regal splendor in an elegant adobe mansion 100 feet square, surrounded by flower-filled gardens and orchards of oranges, limes, pomegranates, figs, grapes, apricots, peaches, and other fruits suited to this mild climate. Yet, by the time of the Civil War nothing was left of this elegance but ruins, the cause of its demise being laid to the revolt of the Indian slaves engaged in cultivating the attached fields of wheat, corn, beans and fruits [1964:147–148].

[1] See Adams and Chavez (1956); H. Fergusson (1933:81); Zeleny (1944:66).

There are no known ruins in the Rio Grande area which even approach the opulence described above, and even though the "great houses" may have been only a few miles apart between Bernalillo and Socorro (H. Fergusson 1933:81), we have, as yet, little actual knowledge of them. In any case, it does seem clear from a variety of types of evidence, including the landgrant documents as well as other historical and archaeological sources, that the most prevalent type of settlement in this area was the small agricultural and livestock-raising village, which characteristically was founded along rivers such as the Rio Grande and its tributaries, especially in the northern part of the state. Many of these towns were founded close to an already existing pueblo, with which they entered into a symbiotic relationship. In some cases the Spanish simply removed Indians from their villages, taking over the existing houses, cleared fields, and irrigation ditches (Bailey 1940:206).

However, if there was not widespread luxury, neither was the area so desolate and poverty-stricken as has sometimes been assumed. Recent work by the historian Marc Simmons (1965) suggests that the local economy might have been fairly productive. The evidence concerning trade with the Chihuahua and Sonora districts shows that a considerable surplus was achieved, which enabled many to have a fairly decent standard of living. But it should be kept in mind that most of the settlers were peasants living in rural villages and actually working their land themselves. The Indians in the New Mexican area were neither as plentiful nor as productive as those in Mexico, and it was impossible for a Spanish elite to live solely from the surplus of the Indian farmers. Actually, the situation in New Mexico should not be compared directly with that in the Valley of Mexico at the time but with the more northern and outlying districts such as Chihuahua, Sonora, and Durango. Further research may reveal even greater social and cultural similarities between Colonial and present-day New Mexico and areas such as these.

It is not the purpose of this book to describe in detail the beliefs, customs, material culture, and social institutions which are peculiar to and characteristic of the Spanish-Americans of New Mexico. The reader is referred to the bibliography for suggested sources on various topics. Rather, an attempt will be made to describe, in sociological terms, the general parameters of the way of life of these people in the past. Knowlton has appropriately warned against the danger of generalizing about Spanish-Americans. He suggests that further "research may well uncover basic differences in the culture and social structure of the villages of the upper Rio Grande Valley and the Middle Rio Grande Valley in New Mexico, the northern mountain villages, and the plains villages" (1961: 449).

One of the conclusions of the Tewa Basin Study (U.S. Dept. of Agriculture, 1935) was that there appeared to be differences in the social structure of the villages on the east and west sides of the Rio Grande (pp. vii-ix). Certainly it is evident that differences in history and ecological circumstances, plus the relative isolation of the villages, might be conducive to the development of differences among them. Yet it is also clear from a survey of the existing early accounts, and more recent anthropological and sociological studies, that certain themes, patterns, and institutions were fairly common throughout the territory or a certain portion of it. Leonard and Loomis (1941) say, in regard to San Miguel County, "The same problems and characteristics are found in all. Actually, the native villages . . . are strikingly similar" (p. 2). The purpose in delineating these major patterns in the following will be to present a background and context for a discussion of acculturation and a better understanding of the present-day situation in New Mexico.

The small northern Spanish villages were relatively isolated not only from the larger centers such as Santa Fe and Albuquerque but also from each other, and each one formed an almost self-sufficient unit, both in terms of economy and in regard to social structure. Like all peasant communities everywhere, however, they were not, in the final analysis, completely isolated, and they were partially dependent upon a "larger tradition" which gave them certain characteristics (Foster 1953b; Redfield 1953). Even though they produced most of the foodstuffs by which they themselves subsisted, built their own houses of local materials, manufactured furniture and other household items, and even many of their own clothes and ornaments, nevertheless, there were certain trade items which reached even the most remote village. Some of these were such luxuries as the silk shawls, so admired and coveted by the ladies, and the *retablos* or religious pictures portraying favorite saints. It is true that not everyone could afford such items, and local artists and craftsmen produced copies of the imported items, which in time resulted in distinct artistic traditions based upon, but distinguishable from, the European originals. [2]

There were also some items which were necessities for the kind of life led in the village, but which could not be produced locally. Prior to 1779, each incoming settler was given the basic equipment considered essential to successful farming in the region. According to Blackmar each settler was

> . . . entitled to receive a house-lot, a tract of land for cultivation, another for pasture (commons) and a loan of sufficient stock and implements to make a comfortable beginning. In addition to these, he received two mares, two cows and one calf, two sheep and two horses, one cargo mule, and one yoke of oxen or steers; one plow point, one spade, one axe, one sickle, one wooden knife, one musket, and one leather shield [1891:164–165].

Although, as Leonard has noted (1943), this policy was probably seldom carried out with any degree of completeness, it remained an ideal and gives some notion of the kind of basic European technology upon which the early Spanish settlers depended.

[2] Although there are many books and articles dealing with the arts and crafts of New Mexico, the best comprehensive volume on the subject is by R. F. Dickey 1949, *New Mexico Village Arts.*

Most of the plots held by individual farmers were small enough to be cultivated by a man and his immediate family. It appears that grown sons may have remained, together with their wives and children, until the death of the father, at which time the father's land would be divided among them.[3] In some villages daughters also might be given a portion of land as a dowry, the management of which was given to their husbands. In other villages daughters might be given livestock, furniture, and other household goods, but not land, which was reserved for male heirs only (Maes 1941:10). During the first hundred years or so, as settlements gradually increased in size and the land available in the original grant was allotted and subdivided through inheritance, small groups split off from the parent villages and founded new settlements. Frequently such a group would be small in the beginning, but they would request enough land to accommodate additional settlers up to a certain number, after which that village would be closed to newcomers.[4]

By the middle of the eighteenth century the northern limits of Spanish settlement were the village of Chama, on the river of that name, and the villages near the present boundary of Colorado, on the Rio Grande (Culbert 1943:175). But a map of the inhabited places in New Mexico in 1844 shows the Spanish-speaking population still concentrated in an area within a fifty-mile radius of the present town of Santa Fe or at the headwaters of the Rio Grande and Pecos River (Leonard 1943:31). Within this fifty-mile radius, the concentration was evidently quite great, and irrigable land in the river valleys was becoming scarce. Thus, in 1855, the largest farm managed by a single wealthy owner consisted of 1,721 acres in what is now Bernalillo County. Most plots were ten acres or smaller (Dickey 1949:8). Leonard noted that at the time of his study the landholdings of each of the sixty villages in the Upper Pecos watershed were small, ranging from one-fourth of an acre to twenty acres (1943:34).[5]

[3] Although sources differ, this practice may have been of relatively recent origin. Thus, Perrigo says, "Beginning in the Mexican period, when primogeniture had been abolished, the practice of dividing the arable fields among heirs was initiated. A land grant which once sufficed for a family presently was cut up into strips of only a few acres each for the families of sons and grandsons" (1960:370). The practice of leaving all lands to the eldest son would have forced younger sons out of the village, and as long as there was vacant land upon which to settle and form new villages, this would have been an efficient and functional practice. The time of the change in the law suggested here is significant in that it also coincides with the period during which population pressure was becoming a problem. This would have had the effect of increasing the number of persons and families living in any given village, while decreasing the standards of living for all—a situation which did, in fact, develop. E. Ferguson (1940:259) assumes equal inheritance to have been dictated by Spanish law. Atencio (1964:46) says all children always inherited equally in spite of Spanish law favoring primogeniture.

[4] Callon (1962:7) writes, in regard to the town of Las Vegas, "As per the stipulation of the grant they selected a townsite, two community gardens, an easement to a convenient watering place and distributed land to each petitioner. No one was given more land than he could till and keep in good condition. The remainder of the land was for common pasture or to be granted to new settlers who could prove their need of land for the sustenance of their families."

[5] See also Bohannan (1928:4); Burma (1954:14); Rusinow (1938:95); New Mexico Rural Council Study (n.d.:2).

One of the specifications often made in the grants to groups of settlers was that "a person who will not reside in the town with the family belonging to him and who shall remove to another settlement shall lose all right he may have acquired to his property" (Hurt 1941:30). The right of the town officials to exact communal labor from the settlers was also sometimes specifically noted in the petitions. Communal labor and mutual aid seem to have been the primary bases upon which the social structure of these early agricultural villages was founded. Together the settlers built houses, maintained irrigation ditches, grazed their livestock, cared for their sick, buried their dead, and celebrated the holy days of the Catholic religion. Neglected by both church and state, each village developed a relatively autonomous system for maintaining law and order, socializing the children, perpetuating the faith and their culture in general.

The *cofradía* organization of the Catholic church was very early transplanted to New Mexico, as well as to other parts of the New World, and it is likely that the so-called Penitente Brotherhood, a somewhat later development, was an outgrowth of these earlier religious and beneficient societies.[6] Even without the sacraments of the church, which often had to be foregone in the absence of a priest, the rituals of life continued. In addition to the patriarchal extended family, the *compadrazgo*, or system of godparenthood, was also apparently an important institution, serving to strengthen rights and obligations among kinsmen.[7] There seems to have been some tendency toward village endogamy, and marriage between cousins was not frowned upon.

Recreation consisted largely of the celebration of the various life crises and of the holy days of the Catholic calendar, including the day of the village's patron saint. In addition to religious observances, conducted by officers of the *cofradía* or by a priest—if one was available—there was feasting and the inevitable dancing (except in the event of a funeral, which was, however, a kind of social occasion also). For the men and boys, there might be an occasional trip into the nearest larger population center, and for some, an opportunity to accompany the once-a-year *conducta,* or trading caravan, to Mexico.

The necessity to defend themselves from periodic Indian raids was also a factor in the social structure of some of the villages—especially those on the peripheries of the settled areas. The towns of Abiquiu, Belen, and Cebolleta, among others, were continually being attacked and were, in

---

[6] Much of the literature concerning the Penitente Brotherhood is sensational and inaccurate. Myra Ellen Jenkins will soon publish a book based upon the 1935 doctoral dissertation by Dorothy Woodward. In the meantime, this dissertation and a shorter article by Fray Angelico Chavez (1954) are the best scholarly sources.

[7] Only a few of the contemporary sociological and anthropological accounts include much material on the *compadrazgo*. Weaver (1965) is both the most recent and the most inclusive. See also Edmonson (1957) and Kluckhohn and Strodtbeck (1961). A recent Master's thesis (Vincent 1966) at the University of New Mexico outlines and summarizes the existing sources and gives new data on *compadrazgo* in the modern urban environment of Albuquerque.

fact, purposely founded as buffer communities (E. Fergusson 1940:257; Kluckhohn and Strodtbeck 1961:180; Swadesh 1964a, 1964b).

Some villages retained the tightly nucleated settlement pattern, traces of which may sometimes still be seen today. However, in those areas where the Indian menace was not severe, and especially after 1850 in still other areas, the line settlement bordering a stream, and in later days the highway, appeared.[8] Although the flat-roofed, low, box-shaped abode house, a composite of Spanish and Indian ideas and materials, was and still is popular in many areas, another type found in the far north and especially in the more mountainous locations was the large, wooden, often two-storied structure with gabled windows on the second floor, pitched roofs, and covered *porticos* or outside porches, running the length of the building.[9]

Frequently these houses were enlarged as sons brought home wives and increased the size of the extended family. A similar type of arrangement is also observed in the simpler adobe houses, which may have as many as four or five separate doors and compartments extending in an L-shape. A more modern solution, but one which reflects basically the same type of social structure, is the house-trailer. One may find these permanently parked in the backyards of many homes in the rural villages today—one such household visited during the course of this study included three house-trailers in addition to a large two-storied house like that described above. Two married sons and one married daughter lived with their spouses in the trailers, while the elderly head of the household lived in the main structure with an unmarried daughter and three other unmarried kinsmen.

Although livestock was brought into New Mexico by the very earliest Spanish settlers, the primary emphasis in the first century or so was on farming of wheat, maize, beans, chili, and other vegetables, and fruits. Sheep were always more important than any other domesticated animals. Thus, Bancroft says:

> Of live-stock, sheep formed the chief element, these animals being raised in large numbers, both for their wool and meat though there are no reliable statistics extant. Horses and cattle were also raised, but the former were always scarce in the province on account of the numbers sold to and stolen by the wild Indians. I find no definite indications that cattle were raised to any great extent for their hides and tallow [1889:275].

[8] See, for example, *A Pilot Planning Project for the Embudo Watershed of New Mexico* (1961:46–47, 56), hereafter referred to as Embudo Report; Weaver (1965:13, 135).

[9] This style of housing is certainly not the earliest. Thus, the Embudo Report (see note 8) describes Rio Lucio—"Rio Lucio's houses are a good example of the post-colonial changes in local housing construction. Yankee-introduced steel tools were used to shape and ornament the boards which new Yankee-built sawmills began to turn out inexpensively. Adobes began to acquire gabled roofs of wood, wooden floors, front porches, and relatively elaborate wooden trim. Particularly noticeable were paneled doors, louvred or paneled window shutters, and door casings decorated with elaborate mouldings. Pitched roofs replaced the old dirt roofs (*op. cit.*, p. 51).

It is impossible to date exactly the period when sheepherding began to outstrip farming as a way of life for the Spanish *campesino*. However, the population figures given by the official reports and reviewed by Bancroft (1889) indicate substantial increase toward the end of the eighteenth century, and this information coincides with that concerning the founding of many new settlements on the periphery of the former occupied area during this same period. Thus, the population was gradually moving out into the plains around Las Vegas (Town of Las Vegas founded 1835), east of the Sandia and Manzano ranges into the Estancia Valley (Estancia 1819, Manzano 1829), the Upper Pecos watershed (late 1700's) and westward into what is now Sandoval County (Jemez Springs 1798). Some writers have suggested that there was increased use of the available grassland during the Mexican period (1821–1846), and Zeleny (1944:65) notes that by the early part of the nineteenth century sheep and wool had become important exports of the territory. There is even some evidence that there were cases of localized overgrazing at this early date— a forerunner of the disaster which was to befall the state one hundred years later. Thus, E. Fergusson reported that: "In 1827, the stock-raisers of Santa Fe and Albuquerque had two hundred and forty thousand head of sheep on the tax rolls—twice the number that can be supported on that range now" (i.e., 1935) (1935:334).

But it was not until after the annexation by the United States government that stock raising became really big business in New Mexico. Some of the important determining factors were (1) The Indians were gradually conquered—a circumstance which not only opened up new areas for settlement but created a market for meat, since the government agreed to supply rations to many of the formerly nomadic groups. (2) The United States army itself had to be fed. (3) The eastern markets were made more accessible by building of the railroads.[10] (4) Large numbers of settlers and speculators from the east arrived and went into the stock-raising business to turn a quick profit. (5) Continued and increased population pressure sent the Spanish-American population out into the grasslands, and even many of those who remained in agricultural areas turned to herding on a larger scale. Calkins tells us that: "The older generation of settlers in the Cuba Valley (settled between 1868–1878) were farmers, but their sons went into the stock industry. The only cash at a time when money was entering the economy for the first time was to be had in livestock" (U.S. Dept. of Agriculture 1937a:14).

Two well-known social institutions, for which there is little evidence during the early colonial period, seem to have developed along with and

[10] The railroad-building era in New Mexico began about 1875. The Atchison, Topeka and Santa Fe reached Albuquerque April 22, 1880. Not only did the lines of the Southern Pacific establish a junction at Deming, New Mexico, March 10, 1881, but the Santa Fe joined these lines, forming the first all-rail route across New Mexico. For further details, see Arsdale (1932). He says: "Railroad building in New Mexico from 1878 to 1911 brought a fourfold increase in population and a development of resources" (p. 6).

perhaps in consequence of the rise of the livestock industry. The first of these is the *patron* system, which has been highly touted as being typical of Spanish social structure in many areas of the New World, and there are even those who feel that subservient attitudes toward and extreme dependence upon those in authority are part of the personality configuration of those of Spanish descent.[11] However, there is little to indicate that the early farming villages described were anything but egalitarian. Although a few of the landgrants were given to individuals, by far the largest number was in the names of a group of settlers (Leonard 1943). Certainly there were some differences in status, depending upon sex, age, and individual characteristics, but no *patrones* in the true sense of the word. Saunders describes it well when he says:

> Having found a way of life with survival value, the Spanish-American villages continued it generation after generation. One acquired status, prestige, and esteem by conforming to community expectations. In time, if one were of the right sex and belonged to the right family, one might attain a formal or semi-formal position of leadership. If not, it was of no great concern. The privileges were few, but so were the responsibilities. Leadership was nothing to aspire to; neither was it anything to shun [1954:50].

However, there is evidence that with the increasing dependence upon sheep and the influx of population onto the plains and other areas new social forms developed. Toward the end of the Spanish regime and during the Mexican regime many large grants of land were made to individuals for grazing purposes. During this time the power of the *ricos* increased at the expense of the lower classes. Zeleny claims that many of the grants of land to large proprietors during this time deprived the common people of much of their land (1944:82; see also Charles 1940:21). According to Fabiola Cabeza de Baca Gilbert, a native daughter, there was no set pattern for determining wealth and social position, but "on the Llano, in the days of the open range, there were men who ran thousands of head of cattle and sheep. The Baca brothers from Upper Las Vegas—Don Jose, Don Simon, Don Aniceto, and Don Pablo—jointly were running half a million head of sheep in the 1870's" (1954:X). And it is from this period that one begins to get descriptions of types of settlements which sound like the stereotyped Mexican hacienda. Thus, the same writer recalls the following from her childhood:

> Surrounded by the homes of Don Jose's sons and empleados, the Gonzales hacienda was a village in itself. Don Jose ran thousands of cattle on his domain. I remember hearing during conversations that in 1906 he had branded one thousand colts. There were many other ranchos on our way to Las Vegas, but the Gonzales hacienda stands more vividly in my memory than the others [Gilbert, *op. cit.*: 135–137].

[11] Examples of this type of interpretation are found in Hawley and Senter (1946: 137); Russell (1938:36–38).

The town of El Cerrito in San Miguel County was founded in the early part of the nineteenth century. Two of the settler families owned large flocks of sheep, and most of the other families worked for them. Gradually, other families acquired herds of their own, since land was plentiful and sheep multiplied (Leonard and Loomis 1941:10).

The second institution probably deriving from the spread of livestock raising as a major economic base is the *partido* or tenant-herding system. This has been interpreted as a kind of feudal or share system, and it has undoubtedly sometimes worked as such in the case of small operators who, through convenience or necessity, turned over a portion of their herd to a friend or relative on a share basis. However, as has been pointed out by others, when used by the large owners, it was a form of financing which bore a definite relationship to other modern forms of business enterprise. According to studies in the 1930's (U.S. Dept. of Agriculture 1937b), the system operated as follows: The owner supplied a breeding herd to his tenant. The renter agreed to return twenty lambs for every hundred ewes in the herd at the end of an agreed-upon period—usually one year. The tenant further contracted to rent rams from the owner, sell his lambs and wool through the owner, and stand responsible for all operating expenses and losses. The renter was also required to return upon demand a breeding herd of the same size and age as that originally handed over to him.

In exchange, the tenant was entitled to all the wool, all the lambs in excess of the twenty-per-hundred ewes, and the right to graze his own sheep on the owner's land along with the rented sheep. However, he paid for these grazing rights at a specified rate. Clearly, the large owners could not lose!

Although this system sometimes helped a small operator or family to build up a herd,[12] it also effectively maintained a distinction between the large owners and those with small or no herds. Thus, according to a government report, "Tenant herding, as it is now found, begins from a concentration in the ownership or control of the grazing resources which renders the development of independent livestock enterprises virtually impossible and renders the survival of small independent livestock operations difficult in the extreme" (U.S. Dept. of Agriculture 1937b:2). Although there is evidence that the system was known and utilized as early as 1760, it did not become really important until much later. Charles reports, "The general impression of the older sheep men is that the partido system reached its zenith about 1905 and then started to decline" (1940:33). This would correspond with the rise and fall of the sheep industry as a whole in New Mexico. Thus, although sources differ, it appears that the number of sheep in New Mexico increased between 1800 and 1840 to an estimated million and a half, then declined to 377,000

---

[12] This interpretation, as might be expected, is more commonly found among the members of the upper classes involved. See, e.g., Gilbert (1954:57).

in 1850. There was only a slight increase until the 1870's, when the real boom began. By 1880 there were almost four million sheep in the area, a figure which did not appreciably decline until after 1910.[13]

There can be little doubt that the *partido* system was closely related to the *patron* system. Charles says: "The patron looked out for the well-being of the partidario and his family. He encouraged frugality and good management, made advances for subsistence if necessary, attended at weddings and christenings, secured medical attention when needed and always had their interest and comfort at heart" (1940:55).[14]

Several sources indicate that *patronship* was a late development in New Mexico in general. Leonard (1943:118 *passim*) has an especially interesting and illuminating discussion of this. He points out that class distinctions in the early days were based primarily upon family and blood lines and favor with the Spanish crown.

> Later, with the rise of the *patron* class among the Spanish-Americans, however, the channels of circulation between the layers of the social pyramid became more open and the caste element became of less importance. A man with some ingenuity and business acumen might rise within a few years from the laboring class to the exalted status of a *patron*. Economic position came to be a dominant factor in social status [*op. cit.*].

More recent studies seem to confirm this and emphasize the importance of livestock in determining wealth and status.[15] Indeed, even now sheep-herding remains an ideal way of life for the Hispano—although it is no longer a particularly lucrative pursuit. Virtually all contemporary accounts by social scientists comment upon the people's stated preference for this occupation, and Hollywood a few years ago presented a charming, but romanticized, version of such a life which bears little resemblance to the actual circumstances of most Spanish-Americans today.[16]

However, various factors combined to help destroy the basis for the sheepherding industry among Spanish-Americans. There is good evidence that between 1870 and 1900 many Anglos moved into the rich eastern plains area and through force and chicanery deprived the Spanish-Americans of much of their grazing lands. The best-known instances of this maneuvering are described in relation to the so-called Lincoln County wars (1869–1881). Although this wild-west fracas is today best known because of the participation of the famous or infamous Billy the Kid, the real issues seem to have been competition between sheepmen (primarily Spanish) and cattlemen (predominantly Anglo). But even after 1881,

[13] Figures on the number of sheep in New Mexico at various dates up to 1940 may be found in Charles (1940); Donnelly (1940); and, more recently, Irion (1959).

[14] See also U.S. Dept. of Agriculture (1935b:6); Kluckhohn and Strodtbeck (1961: 204).

[15] See especially Edmonson (1957:54); Kluckhohn and Strodtbeck (1961:205); Burma (1954:12).

[16] *And Now Miguel*, Universal Film Exchange, World Premiere, June 1, 1966, Albuquerque, New Mexico.

when some semblance of law and order was established, the Spanish continued to suffer. One authority described the situation in 1885 as follows:

> . . . for several years past, but few Mexicans have been allowed to live within these limits peaceably and without any molestation, for any considerable length of time; that many Mexicans have been killed out-right, without provocation, several have been wounded, and many more driven away from their homes by intimidation and threats of shooting, assassination, and mob violence . . . [quoted in W. A. Keleher 1945:90].[17]

Today this area, along with nearly the whole eastern plains area of the state, is heavily dominated by Anglos, and the term Little Texas is applied to it in recognition of the origin of the majority of the settlers and of their cultural patterns. Dry farming and cattle ranching are today the primary economic pursuits in this area. Although Anglos predominate in the extreme east, it should be pointed out that in the area around Las Vegas, where the plains begin, there are many Spanish-American cattle ranchers as well. It appears that the early conflict was not based entirely upon ethnic differences and that some Hispanos managed to come out quite well. (See p. 284 for descriptions of Gilbert.)

In addition to the loss of land through trickery and deceit, some holdings melted away because the Spanish-speaking population was ignorant of the United States government requirements in regard to registration of land claims and was unable to pay taxes. Much has been written concerning the era of New Mexican history following the U.S. conquest in 1846 and the subsequent difficulties in establishing rightful ownership of lands granted by the Spanish and Mexican governments. In few cases were actual boundaries known with any certainty, and in some instances the same area had been granted to more than one applicant.[18] Furthermore, many of the original titles had been lost or destroyed through the years, and confirming information from the archives of the viceregal and Mexican governments was frequently missing, inadequate, or ambiguous.

In short, the problem of how to secure justice for the previous inhabitants and at the same time open up previously unused or inefficiently used lands to Anglo settlement was enormous. There seems to be little doubt that in spite of good and honorable intentions on the part of most of those who set the policies and made the judgments, there were in fact many individuals who suffered deprivation of lands. Most of the "deals" made were within the letter of the law—but it was a United States law, little understood by most of the people involved. Many, needing cash desperately, sold portions of their land at fantastically low prices within

---

[17] See also Keleher (1957); Shinkle (1964:36).

[18] This occurred, for example, in the well-known case of the Las Vegas Town Grant and in the Estancia Valley at Manzano. In each case a group of settlers was given a grant of land located in the middle of a previous grant to an individual. See Callon (1962:11–16); Bergere (n.d.).

short periods after receiving confirmation of ownership. Others, choosing to live in old Mexico, willingly abandoned or sold cheaply their shares *in absentia*. Most of the buyers were Anglos, but some were also Hispanos who took advantage of their poorer, lower-class countrymen.[19]

The final blows to the economy based upon livestock had their origin in a slow, but inevitable man-made shift in the ecological balance of the area. The tremendous buildup in the number of animals led to serious overgrazing, which effectively destroyed the natural grass and shrub cycle and led to widespread erosion of the topsoils. In addition, the large-scale cutting of timber in the forest areas led to a more rapid runoff and consequent floods, which contributed further to the destruction of the grass cover, made farming more difficult, and destroyed much property. In one case an entire village was permanently destroyed.[20] According to most authorities, the effects of overgrazing occurred prior to 1910 and were recognized by the national government during the first decade of the century, if not before. Johansen (1941b) reported that the Mesilla Valley benefited from a reclamation project which was carried out between 1910 and 1920 and which included the construction of Elephant Butte Dam. Although the area as a whole has developed remarkably since that time, depending largely upon large-scale cultivation of cotton, it is important to note here the effects upon the Spanish population of the area. The overall trend has been in the direction of a more highly commercialized type of farming—larger holdings cultivated with modern machinery and techniques. Johansen says: "While specific quantitative data are not available, there exists evidence that many of the original Spanish-American farmers (most of whom had settled in the area during the Mexican period), in the process of commercialization were removed from their land through foreclosure . . ." (1941:44). Most of these dispossessed persons became part of the farm laborer population, whose ranks were swelled considerably by immigration from Mexico.

Reclamation in the Albuquerque area also led to widespread loss of land by small owners, the majority of whom were Spanish. In 1937, 8,000 people lost their land titles because they were unable to pay taxes and assessments on the Middle Rio Grande Conservancy District Project—a much needed program, true, but one which these people had no part in voting on and no way of paying for. The federal government did try to remedy the situation somewhat by buying some of this land from the

---

[19] The following sources include valuable information and interpretations of various aspects of the land claims problem in New Mexico: Bancroft (1889, Vol. 17); Bloom (1903); Burma (1954); Fierman (1964); Holmes (1967); Horn (1963); Keleher (1929 and 1945); Knowlton (1964); Leonard (1943); Perrigo (1960); U.S. Dept. of Agriculture (1937a); Welch (1950); Westphall (1947). See also a recent account by Rubel (1966) which describes a similar situation in the lower Rio Grande Valley in Texas.

[20] See Harper, Cordova, and Oberg (2943). San Marcial was the village; for details, see Calkins (1937).

state and offering it to those rural communities most in need of assistance.[21]

Another action—designed to aid in reversing the destructive forces then in operation but which has been much resented by the Spanish-American stockmen, among others—has been the creation of national forests from the public lands and the restriction of grazing thereon. As early as 1892 Congress established the Pecos River Forest, now part of the Santa Fe National Forest. Further large amounts of land were set aside during the next sixteen years. In 1906, what is now called the Carson National Forest was formed from all or parts of the Las Trampas, Santa Barbara, Mora, and F. M. Vigil grants.[22] Today roughly 10 million acres, or about one-eighth of the total land area in New Mexico, is within the boundaries of the national forests.[23] Further grants of public lands were made to railroad companies, and some were transferred to the state in aid of public education. Burma (1954:16) and Knowlton (1964:209) say that since 1854 Spanish-Americans have lost 2,000,000 acres of private land and 1,700,000 acres of communal land. Wolff (1950), in describing cultural change in a northern village says, "The most far-reaching event was the establishment of the National Forest early in this century. It eliminated sheep and goats by pre-empting grazing lands and pasture; thus indirectly eliminating spinning, weaving and related skills" (p. 53).

In 1934 the Taylor Grazing Act was passed which set up mechanisms intended to protect the rights of small operators. Permits (termed "preferences" by informants) were issued to the stockmen, the number based on a percentage of the animals already owned. These preferences may not be sold—although they may be "given away" when one sells an animal. A few stockmen have been able to build up their holdings by buying animals—and thus, preferences—from their poorer neighbors who found that the risks involved in owning a very small number of animals simply made their endeavors not worthwhile. Nevertheless, even today the average small livestock owner tends to be suspicious and resentful of the government and its representatives in any matter regarding his animals.

During the summer of 1965 one informant stated that in his opinion the government was trying to drive everyone out of the stock business. In support of his belief he described a number of what he termed "tricks," especially designed to discourage the smaller operators. Among these were the raising of fees, adding of new fees (for such items as fences, e.g.), the reducing of the number of animals each owner was permitted to graze, and the shortening of the grazing season. Other informants expressed distrust of the forest ranger, feeling that his primary function

[21] Laughlin (1940:280 passim). See also U.S. Dept. of Agriculture (1937b, 1937g).
[22] Embudo Report (n.d.:23).
[23] Data from National Forest Areas, U.S. Dept. of Agriculture, Forest Service, June 30, 1964.

was to spy for the government. The local Stock Association, the organization through which many details are handled, was thought by several informants to be dominated by the local forest ranger without whom they are not supposed to meet. However, other informants pointed out that the local townsmen often meet in secret without the ranger in order to hash things out.

It is clear that stock raising, upon which so many have come to depend not only financially but also for status in the eyes of their fellows, has gradually become an illusory and impractical means of achieving either wealth of social position. Still, many cling to a pitiful one or two animals more as a symbol than anything else. Edmonson (1957:47) says:

> New Mexican Hispano culture is firmly based on sheep and cattle ranching and the necessity of change in this fundamental economic pursuit has been a powerful factor in social change generally. The rancheros who are left are scarcely able to support themselves from their small holdings; most of them augment their income by occasional labor for other ranchers, farmers, companies or the government.

Wage labor came to be (1) the means by which the Spanish-American was able to survive while maintaining his unproductive and inadequate fields and herds, and (2) a further agent in the destruction of this way of life. As early as 1909 one astute observer commented upon the effects of wage labor and prosperity:

> With the coming of great American manufacturing concerns, the younger element of the natives is drifting into mechanical employments, yet sheep, goat and cattle raising are still the chief means of livelihood to the many. Since the great advance in the price of sheep and wool a few years ago, the rural New Mexican has grown prosperous beyond all expectation and with this new condition, a change is rapidly coming over him. He is acquiring a fancy for the piano, the phonograph, the Easter bonnet, tinned goods, embalmed hams, steel ranges, modern furniture, granite-ware cooking utensils, and a thousand other things he formerly never dreamed of as being necessary to his happiness [Anderson 1909:158].

It has taken a long time for wage labor to replace sheep-herding; and, indeed, it has not yet completely done so. Yet the story of the gradual decline in this industry is also the story of the change in many other aspects of the sociocultural system of which it was an important integral part, if not its basis. In succeeding chapters some of the specific ways in which this traditional culture has changed during the past five or six decades will be considered. At the same time that the processes of cultural breakdown or disorganization have been going on, there have been trends leading to a new synthesis, a modern reorganization retaining and combining some of the old traits with the new.

Bibliography

Adams, Eleanor B., and Fray Angelico Chavez. 1956 *The Missions of New Mexico, 1776.* Albuquerque: University of New Mexico Press.

Anderson, Arnold M. 1909. "The Native New Mexican," *Great Southwest,* Sept. 1909:156–158.

Arsdale, Jonathan Van. 1937. "Railroads in New Mexico," *Research* 2(1):3–16.

Atencio, Tomas C. 1964. "The Human Dimensions in Land Use and Land Displacement in Northern New Mexico Villages," in *Indian and Spanish American Adjustments to Arid and Semiarid Environments* (ed. by Clark S. Knowlton). Lubbock: Texas Technological College.

Austin, Mary. 1931. "Mexicans and New Mexico," *Survey* 66:141–144, 187–190.

Bailey, Jessie Bromilow. 1940. *Diego de Vargas and the Reconquest of New Mexico.* Albuquerque: University of New Mexico Press.

Bancroft, Hubert Howe. 1889. *The Works of Hubert Howe Bancroft,* Vol. XVII. (*History of Arizona and New Mexico 1530–1888.*) San Francisco: The History Company.

Bergere, A. M. n.d. *Early History of the Estancia Valley.* Pamphlet. New Mexico Archives, Santa Fe.

Blackmar, Frank W. 1891. *Spanish Institutions of the Southwest.* Baltimore: Johns Hopkins Press.

Bloom, Maude E. McFei. 1903. "A History of Mesilla Valley." Unpublished B.A. thesis, New Mexico State University, Las Cruces.

Bohannan, C. D. 1928. *Report on Survey of Chacon, New Mexico Community.* Auspices of the Presbyterian Church in the U.S.A. (mimeo.).

Bunting, Bainbridge. 1964. *Taos Adobes.* Santa Fe: Museum of New Mexico Press.

Burma, John H. 1954. *Spanish-speaking Groups in the United States.* Durham: Duke University.

Callon, Miton W. 1962. *Las Vegas, New Mexico—The Town That Wouldn't Gamble.* Las Vegas: Las Vegas Publishing Company.

Charles, Ralph. 1940. "Development of the Partido System in the New Mexico Sheep Industry." Unpublished Master's thesis, University of New Mexico.

Chavez, Fray Angelico. 1954. *Origins of New Mexico Families.* Santa Fe: Historical Society of New Mexico.

Culbert, James. 1943. "Distribution of Spanish-American Population in New Mexico," *Economic Geography* 19:171–176.

Dickey, Roland F. 1949. *New Mexico Village Arts.* Albuquerque: University of New Mexico Press.

Donnelly, Thomas C. (ed.). 1940. *Rocky Mountain Politics.* Albuquerque: University of New Mexico Press.

Edmonson, Munro S. 1957. *Los Manitos: a Study of Institutional Values.* New Orleans: Middle American Research Institute, Tulane University.

Ferguson, Erna. 1935. "Tearing Down the West," *Yale Review,* n.s., 25:331–343.

———. 1940. *Our Southwest.* New York: Alfred Knopf.

———. 1935. "Tearing Down the West," *Yale Review,* n.s.,

Fierman, Floyd S. 1964. "The Spiegelbergs of New Mexico, Merchants and Bankers, 1844–1893," *Southwestern Studies* 1(4):3–48.

Foster, George M. 1953. "What Is Folk Culture?" *American Anthropologist* 55(2):159–173.

Gilbert, Fabiola Cabeza de Baca. 1954. *We Fed Them Cactus.* Albuquerque: University of New Mexico Press.

Harper, Allen G., A. R. Codova, and Kalervo Oberg. 1943. *Man and Resources in the Middle Rio Grande Valley.* Albuquerque: University of New Mexico Press.

Hawley, Florence, and D. Senter. 1946. "Group Designed Behavior Patterns in Two Acculturating Groups," *Southwestern Journal of Anthropology* 2(2):133–151.

Holmes, Jack Ellsworth. 1967. Politics in New Mexico. Albuquerque: University of New Mexico Press.

Horn, Calvin. 1963. *New Mexico's Troubled Years, The Story of the Early Territorial Governors.* Albuquerque: Horn and Wallace.

Hurt, Wesley Robert, Jr. 1941. "Manzano: a Study of Community Disorganization." Unpublished Master's thesis, Univeristy of New Mexico.

Irion, F. C. 1959. New Mexico and Its Natural Resources, 1900–2000. Albuquerque: University of New Mexico Press.

Johansen, Sigurd Arthur. 1941. "Rural Social Organization in a Spanish-American Culture Area." Unpublished Ph.D. dissertation, University of Wisconsin, Madison.

Kelcher, William A. 1929. "Law of the New Mexico Land Grant," *New Mexico Historical Review* 12(4):350–371.

———. 1945. *The Fabulous Frontier.* Santa Fe: Rydal Press.

———. 1957. *Violence in Lincoln County 1869–1881.* Albuquerque: University of New Mexico Press.

Kluckhohn, Florence R., and Fred L. Strodtbeck. 1961. *Variations in Value Orientations.* Evanston: Row, Peterson and Co.

Knowlton, Clark S. 1961. "The Spanish Americans in New Mexico," *Sociology and Social Research* 45(4):448–454.

Laughlin, Ruth. 1940. "Coronado's Country and Its People," *Survey Graphic* 29:277–282.

Leonard, O. E. 1943. *The Role of the Land Grant in the Social Organization and Social Processes of a Spanish-American Village in New Mexico.* Ann Arbor: Edwards Brothers.

Leonard, Olen, and C. P. Loomis. 1941. *Culture of a Contemporary Rural Community: El Cerrito, New Mexico.* Washington, D.C.: U.S. Bureau of Agriculture Economics Rural Life Studies: 1.

Loomis, Charles P., and Glen Grisham. 1943. "Spanish Americans: The New Mexico Experiment in Village Rehabilitation," *Applied Anthropology* 2(3):13–37.

Loomis, Charles P., and Olen E. Leonard. 1938. Standards of Living in an an Indian-Mexican Village. Washington, D.C.: United States Department of Agriculture, Social Research Report No. 14.

McWilliams, Carey. 1943. *Brothers Under the Skin.* Boston: Little Brown.

Macs, Ernest E. 1941. "The World and the People of Cundiyo," *Land Policy Review* 4:8–14.

Murbarbarger, Nell. 1964. *Ghosts of the Adobe Walls.* Los Angeles: Westernlore Press.

New Mexico Rural Council Study. n.d. San Geronimo. San Miguel County, New Mexico.

Perrigo, Lynn I. 1960. *Texas and Our Spanish Southwest.* Dallas: Banks Upshaw and Company.

Pilot Planning (Embudo Report). 1961. A Pilot Planning Project for the Embudo Watershed of New Mexico. By the Interagency Council for

Area Development Planning and New Mexico State Planning Office. Santa Fe.

Redfield, Robert. 1953. *The Primitive World and Its Transformations.* Ithaca: Cornell University Press.

Rubel, Arthur J. 1966. *Across the Tracks: Mexican Americans in a Texas City.* Austin: University of Texas Press.

Rusinow, Irving. 1938. "Spanish Americans in New Mexico," *Survey Graphic* 27:95–99.

Russell, John C. 1938. "Racial Groups in the New Mexico Legislature," *Annals* of the American Academy of Political and Social Science 195:62–71.

Saunders, Lyle. 1954. Cultural Difference and Medical Care; the Case of the Spanish-Speaking People of the Southwest. New York: Russell Sage Foundation.

Shinkle, James D. 1964. *Fifty Years of Roswell History—1867–1917.* Roswell: Hall-Poorbaugh Press.

Simmons, Marc. 1965. "Spanish Government in New Mexico at the End of the Colonial Period." Unpublished Ph.D. dissertation, University of New Mexico. (Published 1968—*Spanish Government in New Mexico*. Albuquerque: University of New Mexico Press.)

Swadesh, Frances L. 1964. *Property and Kinship in Northern New Mexico.* Boulder: Research Report No. 44, Tri-Ethnic Research Project, University of Colorado (mimeo.).

U.S. Dept. of Agriculture, Forest Service. 1964. *National Forest Areas.* Washington, D.C.: U.S. Government Printing Office.

U.S. Dept. of Agriculture, Soil Conservation Service. 1935. *Rural Rehabilitation in New Mexico.* Reg. Bull. No. 50, Cons. Economic Series No. 23.

———. 1937a. *A Report on the Cuba Valley.* Reg. Bull. No. 36, Cons. Economics Series No. 9.

———. 1937b. *Tenant Herding in the Cuba Valley.* Reg. Bull. No. 37, Cons. Economics Series No. 10.

———. 1937g. Notes on Community-Owned Land Grants in New Mexico. Reg. Bull. No. 48, Consumer Economics Series No. 2.

Vincent, Maria. 1966. "Ritual Kinship in an Urban Setting: Martineztown, New Mexico." Unpublished Master's thesis, University of New Mexico.

Weaver, Thomas. 1965. "Social Structure, Change and Conflict in a New Mexico Village." Unpublished Ph.D. dissertation, University of California.

Welch, Vernon E. 1950. "Las Vegas and the Adjacent Area During the Mexican Period." Las Vegas, N. Mex.: Ms. on file at Highlands University Library.

Westphall, Victor. 1947. "History of Albuquerque 1870–1880." Unpublished Master's thesis, University of New Mexico.

Wolff, Kurt H. 1950. "Culture Change in Luna: A Preliminary Research Report," *Ohio Journal of Science* 50:53–59.

Woodward, Dorothy. 1935. "The Penitentes of New Mexico." Unpublished Ph.D. dissertation, Yale University.

Zeleny, Carolyn. 1944. "Relations Between the Spanish-Americans and Anglo-Americans in New Mexico. A Study of Conflict and Accommodation in a Dual-Ethnic Relationship." Unpublished Ph.D. dissertation, Yale University.

CHANGING SPANISH-AMERICAN VILLAGES OF NORTHERN NEW MEXICO

Clark S. Knowlton

The Spanish-American rural farm villages of northern New Mexico and southern Colorado were first brought to the attention of the public through the writings of tourists, magazine and newspaper correspondents, folklorists, government employees, and military personnel stationed in New Mexico. Their writings exploited the strangeness of Spanish-American culture, the archaic nature of their agriculture, and the imagined romance and color of their adobe villages. It was not until the depression and drought of the 1930's forced large numbers of the village population to seek government assistance that sociologists and other social scientists began to study their culture and social systems. Most of these men either taught at the University of New Mexico or were employed by New Deal agencies.

From their work there came a series of lucid studies and reports describing the impact of depression, land loss, drought, and poverty upon the Spanish-American farm village residents. Although there was a greater focus upon economic problems than upon social systems, these studies provide an important base line against which more recent social change can be measured. They fortunately caught the villages just before the impact of urbanization, industrialization, government defense expenditures, and massive Anglo-American immigration brought about accelerated social change, acculturation, and depopulation. The majority of these publications are extremely hard to find. It is unfortunate that the regional archives of the major New Deal agencies active in the Southwest, such as the W.P.A., P.W.A., Department of Agriculture, and the Department of Interior, were not centralized in a regional library. The archives have now been scattered.

The activities of these New Deal agencies came to an end during World War II. Sociologists connected with them drifted out of New Mexico. Others associated with the University of New Mexico also left. Since then, the Spanish Americans have received but sporadic attention from sociologists and anthropologists who for the most part were teaching or working in New Mexico or Colorado. Most of these scholars did not

Reprinted with permission from *Sociology and Social Research*, July 1969.
Clark Knowlton did his doctoral work at Vanderbilt University in 1955. He has taught at Georgia Southern College, New Mexico Highlands University, and the University of Texas at El Paso, where he is currently professor of sociology. He has done extensive research on Chicano society, southwestern Indians, and Syrian and Lebanese minorities in Brazil.

stay long in the state, and upon leaving shifted their efforts to other areas. As a result, the Spanish Americans, one of the largest and most important Spanish-speaking groups in the Southwest, have never been comprehensively studied.

This is unfortunate, as the rural Spanish-American village culture in northern New Mexico and southern Colorado, one of the few examples of a rural farm village system in the United States, has undergone rapid social and economic changes. The villages at present offer an excellent social laboratory for students interested in population movement, the processes of culture contact and acculturation, and the impact of urbanization and industrialization upon a folktype society, that until recently were quite resistant to acculturation. The Spanish-American villages are an excellent laboratory in which to study the processes that create distressed areas in the United States. The villages would provide considerable data for students of the family, juvenile delinquency, social stratification, folklore, social integration, and small group interaction. These rural communities also offer a field of social experimentation for the development of programs suitable for underdeveloped areas in Latin America.

In this paper, the impact of uncontrolled and undirected social and economic change upon the social integration and the major social systems of the rural Spanish-American villages of northern New Mexico and southern Colorado will be delineated. The Spanish Americans are here defined as a distinct and separate Spanish-speaking group located within perhaps a three hundred mile radius of Santa Fe, New Mexico. It is not often realized that there are a number of diverse Spanish-speaking groups in the Southwest that differ considerably from each other in length of residence in the United States, racial composition, rural urban residence, dialect of Spanish spoken, and degree and type of involvement in Anglo-American society. Subtle variations in basic value orientations and social systems also exist.

Data for this paper have come from a series of village surveys and studies of the rural Spanish-American villages conducted in northeastern New Mexico. The literature has also been perused. The study is divided into two sections. Material is presented in the first section of the traditional structure of the major social systems such as the village community, the extended patriarchal family, the patron-peon system, and village Catholicism. The impact of social and economic change upon these systems is analyzed in the second section.

Traditional Culture

The Village

The Spanish Americans are descendents of early colonizers who moved into New Mexico from Mexico in the late seventeenth and early eighteenth centuries. Living in isolation from other European groups for almost three centuries, they gradually developed a distinctive rural village culture. Settling at first along the Rio Grande River from Taos to Albuquerque, their villages spread into the valleys of the Sangre de Cristo mountains and down along the streams and rivers flowing from these mountains. The ending of Indian raids in the middle nineteenth century led to a rapid expansion of Spanish-American settlement into the plains of eastern New Mexico, western Texas, and southern Colorado, and south along the major river systems toward the Mexican border. This frontier expansion was brought to an abrupt and violent halt by the westward movement of Anglo cattlemen who rolled back the line of Spanish-American ranches and villages in a cloud of violence. This retreat of the Spanish-Americans before the Texan advance is still continuing in northeastern New Mexico.

Spanish American settlement patterns in New Mexico were controlled basically by the same set of rules that governed the formulation of towns and villages throughout Spanish America. Settlements were founded upon land grants made by local representatives of the Spanish Crown and the Mexican government. There were three basic types of land grants. The first and most important in northern New Mexico was the community land grant awarded to a group of villagers requesting land for an agricultural village settlement. The second type, the proprietary grant, was a grant made to a prominent individual who promised to establish a village community, attract settlers, build a church, hire a priest, and provide military protection in return for payments in kind by settlers, control of the local commerce and other privileges. The third type of land grant, the sitio, was given to an individual for a livestock ranch. In general, whatever the original type of land grant, the rural farming village became the dominant type of settlement in the mountain valleys and along the river streams of New Mexico and southern Colorado. Livestock ranches prevailed in the plains east of the Rockies and south of Albuquerque.

Spanish American concepts of land ownership and land use were, unfortunately, quite different from Anglo-American concepts. The Spanish Americans regarded the land as the foundation of family existence, the basis of life itself. It was seldom treated as a commercial commodity to be bought and sold. Every family had the right to receive enough land to sustain itself. Any land not being used by another family could be utilized by families in need of land. Most Spanish-American land claims were based upon possession through traditional use and not through registered land titles listed in a public court of law, a county clerk's office or a state or federal land office. If a family had traditionally used a section of land for a number of years, it had the right of ownership as long as it utilized the land. If the family left, the land after a period of years was open for occupancy by another family. Boundaries were vague and indefinite with large acreages in communal village ownership.

The village community as defined by the Spanish Americans consisted of the village site itself, the plots of irrigated farm land, and the communal ejido. The house lots and farm plots were individually owned. They could be bought or sold, although it was considered wrong to sell them to nonvillage members. The dams and water ditches built by communal labor were under the jurisdiction of a village water master chosen by the village inhabitants. Water rights were not thought of as private property but as belonging to the entire village. Village farmers received a share of water based upon the land that they could cultivate. The village ejido consisting of grazing and timber lands associated with the village land grant belonged to the village as a whole. Every village member had the right to graze livestock and to cut timber in the ejido.

The village with its attached land and water rights was thought of as a single indivisible community. It was regarded as a crime against the moral order of the universe for any political authority to separate the village from its traditional land and water rights. A village community so separated was like a man who had lost an arm or a leg. The villagers that have lost land or water, as most have done, regard themselves as having suffered serious moral wrongs. Even though a hundred years may have passed since a village lost its land, the village inhabitants still know the location of every acre that has been lost. The present owners and users of the alienated land are defined as usurpers who do not have the right to use land that once belonged to the village. There is an aching sense of injustice that will never end until the village is totally abandoned or until the land is restored to the village.

The idea of taxing the land was another foreign concept that was and is extremely destructive of Spanish-American land holdings. Under Spanish and Mexican rule, the produce of the land was taxed but never the land itself. The American conquest of the southwest brought into New Mexico the concepts of carefully delineated individual registered land titles granting perpetual ownership upon payment of taxes, privately owned water rights that could be sold separately from the land, a rigid land tax system based upon payment of specified amounts of money regardless of production from the land, a county system with political control vested in officials elected in periodic elections, and a strong legal dislike of communal property. The Spanish-American villagers were caught up in the spider web of a strange and alien Anglo-American political and legal system that soon stripped them of most of their land.

Each Spanish-American village until quite recently was a small, isolated, self-sufficient, autonomous social cell. Isolated formerly by hostile Indians and until very recently by impassable roads, a village was forced to rely upon its own economic and cultural resources. The majority of the villages developed a subsistence agricultural economy based on wheat, corn, alfalfa, beans, chile, fruit, vegetables, and the grazing of individually owned livestock herds upon nearby communal ranges. It should be emphasized that the Spanish Americans were stock-men as much as they were farmers. There is a tendency in the literature to assume that they depended primarily upon subsistence agriculture. They became subsistence farmers after they had lost their range land to the Anglo Americans. The villages facing the eastern plains engaged in considerable buffalo hunting and trading with the Indians before the twentieth century.

Each village was a strong sociopsychological unit. As Burma has pointed out: "It is impossible to overemphasize the importance of the home village to the Spanish Americans." The past reluctance of the villagers to leave their village even at considerable financial sacrifice to themselves until recently was notorious in New Mexico. The village was the total social universe of its inhabitants. The villager felt emotionally and physically safe and secure in his village. Outside his village, he felt emotionally naked and physically threatened. All strangers, even those from neighboring villages, were felt to be dangerous and potentially hostile. The villager had little sense of identification with any larger social unit than the village community. Regionalism, nationalism, ethnic solidarity, or religious unity have had very little appeal to them until very recently. The village, composed of related extended patriarchal families, met most of the physical, psychological, economic, and social needs of its population.

The social structure of the village was a simple one structured upon four interrelated social systems: (1) the village community itself, (2) the patriarchal extended family, (3) the patron system, and (4) village folk Catholicism. Where these systems still function, the villagers are even now rather resistant toward acculturation toward the dominant society. Where they have vanished or weakened, acculturation is accelerated, and social integration is gravely impaired.

The Extended Patriarchal Family

Dominance and authority within the family were structured upon the related variable of sex and age. Males were dominant over females in every age grouping. Wives were expected to be tolerant, obedient, and faithful to their husbands who had considerable discreet freedom outside the home. The oldest son living with the family came next to the father as a source of authority in the family system. Brothers were expected to protect and care for their younger brothers and sisters. A Spanish-American woman mistreated by her husband would receive some assistance from her brothers, and brothers could expect, if in need, food and shelter from their married sisters. Fathers were expected to be somewhat aloof and formal toward their children. The mothers, on the other hand, knew the hopes, the desires, and the daily behavior of their children. In many Spanish-American families, the mother and children were united in a tacit conspiracy to conceal family secrets from the father who was not expected to be overly inquisitive about doings within the home. All members of the family were expected to work closely together. The strong social drive toward the elimination or repression of sources of conflict that might threaten family unity was an important characteristic of the traditional Spanish-American family system.

Family discipline based upon scolding and shaming rather than physical punishment was in the hands of the mother. Weaning and toilet training were never forced. Each child was taught to be obedient, courteous, and respectful to all adults in the village. Older brothers and sisters played important roles in socializing younger family members. The girls remained under the tutelage of their mothers and seldom left their homes alone before marriage. The boys, defined as young adults at puberty, gradually passed from the authority of the mother to that of their fathers. As young men, they could discreetly sow a few wild oats provided they did not shame the family name or incur diseases. The older men in the family taught them the skills of ranching, farming, hunting, and handicrafts. Relationships between family members were close and based upon reciprocal patterns of mutual assistance. The family subordinating individual welfare to that of the extended family absorbed widows, orphans, and single relatives. Marriage came in early adolescence, and husbands and wives gained social status through high fertility. Few Spanish-Americans were ever alone from birth to death. They tended to live out their lives as members of functioning extended patriarchal families.

The extended patriarchal families residing in a village were caught up in a network of religious obligations by the compradrazgo or godfather system. The godfathers, adult sponsors of children at important religious ceremonies such as baptism, confirmation, and marriage, assumed special obligations toward the parents of the sponsored children as well as to the children themselves. The ramifications of the compadrazgo system frequently unified an entire village population into a functioning system of religious and economic cooperation and responsibility.

The Patron-Peon System

A patron among the Spanish-Americans was and is a prominent individual from a wealthy and powerful family who is able to provide employment, economic security, leadership, decision making, and problem solving for those dependent upon him. His position as patron was based not upon his personal characteristics but upon his ability to perform the institutionalized role of a patron. Two basic types of patrons evolved among the Spanish-Americans. One was the powerful landowner. This type developed primarily in the ranching areas of southern and eastern New Mexico, although scattered patron families of this class were found in almost all sections of the state.

In the areas dominated by large landholders, the patron provided employment and met the economic needs of his workers and their families. He settled conflicts, directed peon labor, cared for the sick, the aged, the orphaned, and widowed, and provided military and political leadership. In return he received absolute obedience from his peons. Until very recently debt peonage existed in New Mexico. Poor families often went into debt to obtain economic security on the large ranches.

The second type of patron was the village patron encountered at one time in almost every Spanish-American village. Usually a merchant, the head of a powerful village family, or a political or military leader, his position as patron rested upon village consensus. The position was not inherited. When a patron weakened or died, another prominent individual able to fulfill the functions of a patron took the role. The position could go to a son but it might also go to an uncle or an in-law, or the head of another family. A village patron was also expected to assist village families, to settle disputes, and to provide leadership. It was expected that he would exploit his position for personal advantages but he should not exploit village families. If he did so, he might lose his position when challenged by another individual.

Religion

The vast majority of Spanish-Americans were Roman Catholics. Their culture was suffused with the beliefs, dogmas, and practices of Roman Catholicism. The village Catholicism, however, was a folk Catholicism evolving in villages rarely visited by a priest. Its focus was upon family worship. Each home had an altar where the village and family saints were worshipped. Village folk Catholicism revolved around the worship of family and village saints. Formal sacraments such as the mass played a minor role in the religious life of the village.

Congregations of Penitentes existed until very recently in the majority of the villages. The Penitente Brotherhood, a unique religious order indigenous to New Mexico, was brought to the area by early Spanish explorers and settlers and by the Franciscan Friars. Its history within the state is rather obscure. The Penitentes were and are organized into local independent village congregations headed by an Elder Brother selected by members on the basis of his piety and social status. In each village the congregation met and meets in a chapter house, the Morada, or in the local church where they were permitted to do so. The Elder Brother saw to it that the brothers, (only men could belong) performed their religious duties, took care of the sick, the widowed, and orphaned, buried the dead, punished those who violated village norms, and settled village disputes. Although the Penitentes maintained a year long cycle of religious activities, their major religious ceremony took place at Easter when a complex passion play commemorating the death and resurrection of Christ was performed. The climax was the hanging of a chosen Penitente brother on the cross to expiate the sins of the village population. The Penitente Order for many served as a mechanism through which Anglo-American dominance was resisted by the Spanish-Americans.

The Impact of Social Change

The Village Community

The traditional Spanish-American village community managed to function, although with decreasing efficiency, until the depression and the drought of the 1930's brought it to an end. The system was literally bled to death through the erosion of its land basis. From the 1880's to the 1910's, the Spanish-Americans lost almost all of their grazing land to the Anglos. One authority estimates that from 1854 to the 1930's, the Spanish-Americans conservatively lost over 2,000,000 acres of private lands, 1,700,000 acres of communal land, 1,800,000 acres taken over by the state, and vast areas lost to the Federal Government without compensation. The loss of their grazing land forced the Spanish-Americans to fall back upon their small irrigated plots. The destruction of wildlife and the ending of Indian trade weakened the village economy. The Spanish Americans were forced into migrant labor toward the end of the nineteenth century in growing numbers. The men left their villages in the spring and returned in the fall. Members of the extended families worked their lands during the absence of the men.

The shifting of the local village economy from a subsistence agricultural and pastoral economy, local handicrafts, and barter to a credit economy managed by Anglo American merchants, was another corrosive force. The merchants opened stores in the majority of the larger villages. They permitted the villagers to open current accounts with them. Dealing with an illiterate population and keeping the only books in the villages, the merchants alone knew the state of the village accounts. When crops and livestock were ready for market, they were sold to the merchant at a price set by him. The villager knew nothing of price fluctuations, of depression or of prosperity, or of the law of supply and demand. The merchant set the retail price of the goods that he sold, the price of the agricultural products that he bought, and the interest rate on village accounts. He frequently built up large landholdings, as some merchants are doing today, by foreclosing on the homes and lands of his clients unable to pay when their accounts were called in at the convenience of the merchant.

Massive erosion and abrading of stream channels generated by uncontrolled grazing of large commercial Anglo-American cattle herds and the cutting of the timber cover on the higher mountains destroyed the farming land and sharply reduced irrigation facilities for a large number of villages. New Mexico is dotted with abandoned Spanish-American villages whose inhabitants witnessed the destruction of their land and water base by Anglo commercial exploitation of the natural resources. The village inhabitants were forced to retreat to urban areas or to join the stream of migrant labor to provide for their families.

The depression of the 1930's temporarily ended the demand for migrant labor and forced the migrants to return to their home villages. The drought destroyed subsistence agriculture. Many villagers would have faced starvation if it had not been for the extended patriarchal family. After several depression years, the extended families exhausted their resources. The villagers were finally rescued by massive programs of government relief. Their village economy had come to an end, destroyed by economic and political forces that they have never managed to understand.

The psychological results of the breakdown of the village economic structure have been as harsh as the social results. The Spanish American village population lost faith in their ability to continue a meaningful way of life in the traditional manner. Sinking into apathy and anomie, thousands fell back permanently upon relief as a way of life. Other thousands began to move reluctantly toward the urban areas of the Southwest and the Pacific Coast. The migration began before World War II, but it was accelerated through defense training programs in the villages during the war. Hundreds were trained and then moved to defense installations in California, Colorado, and elsewhere. The prolonged prosperity of the post-war period outside of northern New Mexico increased the flow of migration. Many northern New Mexico counties lost from fifteen to almost sixty per cent of their total population.

The Spanish-Americans migrating into the urban areas are a semi-literate, unskilled, and what could be called a preindustrial people. They lack the basic personal habits and values to adjust easily to an industrialized urbanized environment. Flowing into the areas of deteriorated housing, they add to the sum of urban problems. Their migratory movement has but transferred economic and social problems from a rural area to an urban area.

The migratory movement is a very reluctant one. Families leaving a village seldom sell their homes or their lands. The adobe houses are boarded up and the land left untilled. Every village in northern New Mexico is marked by crumbling blocked up adobe houses. The land is virtually abandoned. Water rights are lost to the land, and the economic resources of the entire village are thereby diminished. The migrants constantly return to their home villages to visit relatives and to live on unemployment checks received from other states during periods of unemployment. Before they leave the village, they tend to hunt for ways to earn a living that would permit them to stay permanently. Unable to find them, they leave again. Often a child or two will be left behind with their grandparents or other relatives to live in the village.

The rise of largely Anglo-American urban centers in the upper Rio Grande Valley has profoundly modified the social organization of the Spanish American villages around Albuquerque, Los Alamos, and Santa Fe. The villages in this area tend to become bedroom villages, as many of their inhabitants find employment in government and private defense installations in Los Alamos, Albuquerque, and Santa Fe. The employed workers abandon agriculture and introduce Anglo-American type houses and furnishings into the villages. Many Spanish-American workers sink their incomes, however, in orchard and garden plots. Anglo suburbanites have invaded many of the villages. A few of the new Anglo residents try to fit into established Spanish-American patterns of life. The majority, however, tend to superimpose an Anglo-American suburban existence upon the Spanish-American villages. The Spanish-Americans are pushed to the margins of community affairs.

Another unexpected result of the destruction of the Spanish-American village economy has been the creation of a large economically distressed area in northern New Mexico and southern Colorado unnoticed by the rest of the nation. Here, economic conditions often resemble those of Latin America rather than those of the United States. Millions of dollars have been spent since the 1930's by private and public agencies to improve conditions in this area. The majority of the programs have not had the success their administrators envisioned because of their narrow economic individualistic approach. Until the village rather than the individual is adopted as the basic planning unit there is apt to be little success in future programs. Furthermore, few planners and administrators of public agencies in New Mexico and southern Colorado realize that almost every economic problem in northern New Mexico and southern Colorado has its cultural components. These components must be considered before any successful planning can be possible in this distressed region.

Changes in the Spanish-American Family System

The traditional structure of the Spanish-American family system has been seriously weakened by the ending of cultural isolation, the destruction of the traditional village community, emigration, urbanization, and acculturation. Today, the Spanish-Americans resemble the Anglo Americans in that there are a number of different family systems in existence among them. At one end of the continuum are found traditional extended patriarchal families still functioning in the more isolated rural areas and surprisingly enough here and there in the urban areas. At the other end of the continuum can be found deserted mothers and their families as well as aging couples abandoned by their children. The majority of the Spanish-American families are still strongly familistic although acquiring many of the characteristics of the Anglo-American nuclear family system.

The most important factor in the continuous erosion of the patriarchal extended family was the collapse of the traditional village economy. Inability to earn a living and rising expectations among the younger village inhabitants led to the migration of many nuclear family units. A married or a single son usually goes first. If he secures a job, he will send for his family and invite other relatives to visit him. Many stay and in turn try to bring others. Eventually a family nucleus grows up in Denver, Los Angeles, or Pueblo. They cooperate closely together in economic and social matters. Other village families also will come and seek out the nucleus from their villages. The migrating children may leave grand-children to keep company with the grandparents. Many villages tend to have large populations of old people and children.

Inevitably, related nuclear families migrate to diverse urban centers. Every effort is made to keep alive kinship bonds by letters, and frequent visits. A nuclear family in economic trouble can count on assistance from related nuclear families. However, working class families find it difficult to provide the type of economic assistance that could be provided by farming families in a rural village. Inevitably, bonds between distant family weaken. The roles of the grandfather and the older brother are frequently lost through emigration.

Spanish-American families caught up in the rural migrant stream will often migrate in groups of related nuclear families usually under the head of a grandfather or an older brother. The oldest male is almost always the leader of the working group. As migrant labor comes to an end these family groupings settle out of the migrant stream in many different areas from Utah through California to Oregon and Washington. Within the migrating families the traditional roles and statutes of various family members are usually preserved.

Among the anglicizing Spanish-American middle class village families living near the larger urban centers, there is often a conscientious effort to imitate the roles of Anglo-American nuclear families. These roles are often imperfectly learned, and rates of divorce and family breakdown increase. Relationships with unacculturated relatives are deliberately loosened. The nuclear family type is slowly becoming more common among the middle class Spanish Americans.

In general, the Spanish-American family system is still distinguished from the Anglo-American system: (1) greater masculine dominance at all ages, (2) a wife who is just emerging uncertainly from her home, (3) a more rigid control over the behavior of children and teenagers, (4) a more unified and formal ordering of relationships between husband, wife, and children, and (5) a greater tendency toward an extended family.

The erosion of the extended patriarchal family has seriously weakened the ability of the Spanish-American family to perform its traditional role as a producer and consumer unit. Land loss, the destruction of the village economic system, massive unemployment, and emigration have forced many family units into poverty. Other family units have had to turn to the welfare system for support. Families short of land exist in villages where there is much unused land owned by absent families. No mechanism exists to transfer the land except that of the market place. One family refuses to sell because it has the hope of someday returning to the village and the other family may not have the money to buy the land it needs.

The mass media and the public school systems have introduced new patterns of teenage behavior into the village that conflict seriously with traditional village mores. Parents struggling to survive financially are unable to either meet the cultural or the financial needs of their children. As a result rates of juvenile delinquency, family breakdown, wife desertion, illegitimacy, and other indices of social deviation are increasing rather rapidly. The more exposed to anglicization the village is, the higher are the rates of social disorganization.

The village boys have especially suffered. Regarding themselves as adults at the age of puberty, they find it difficult to accept female dominance by the mothers or teachers. Unable to follow the traditional pattern of working closely with their fathers and other male relatives on the land, they have little intimate contact with the adult males of their families. Lacking a knowledge of Anglo values and the skills necessary to find their way in an Anglo-dominated world, they release their frustration through alcoholism, vandalism, and violence against village members.

The compadrazgo system has about lost its original function of integrating extended partriarchal families within the village into a smooth functioning community. There is a growing tendency today to use the compadrazgo system to strengthen the weakening extended family structure rather than to create cooperative relationships with other village families. Young people tend to select cousins, and even closer relations, for the religious sponsors of their children. Among the older generation, emigration often carries a man's compadres to many diverse communities. Inevitably the relationship withers away. The compadrazgo system functions best in a stable community where men and women follow traditional roles.

Impact of Social Change upon the Patron-Peon System

The Spanish-American landowning patron group rapidly disintegrated under constant Anglo-American economic and political pressure. Stripped of their lands by violence, fraud, excessive land tax, unwise use of credit, and the problems of adjustment to a strange economic and political system, they have disappeared as an important social grouping in New Mexico. The entire upper class in many rural areas vanished from among the Spanish Americans. Their going removed a potential buffer from the small Spanish American farmer and peon, exposing them to the full force of the Anglo political and economic systems.

Although the village patrons have survived somewhat better, their influence has been sharply reduced by the intruding Anglo-American merchant, politician, school teacher, and social worker. The merchants played a major role in weakening both the social integration of the village as well as the village patron system. The Anglo merchants came to make money and seldom understood the social systems or cultural values of the Spanish-American rural farm villages. Because of their superior business methods, better wholesale and banking contacts, and the support of other Anglo-American merchants, they were able to drive out competing Spanish-American businessmen.

Through the liberal extension of credit, the encouragement of new wants, and the purchase of village products, the average merchant soon came to dominate the economic life of the village. Without realizing himself what had happened, the merchant gradually destroyed the economic position of the village patron and weakened the social integration of the village. When the Spanish-American patron vanished, the village was left without its traditional system of conflict solution, decision making, articulation with the larger society and leadership patterns. The village world lost its major source of leadership and became even more dependent upon the Anglo society.

Politics was the only system in which the Spanish Americans were able to maintain a minor position of importance. As the Spanish Americans were the majority grouping in the state until the 1940's, Anglo-American politicians were dependent upon their vote. The Spanish Americans seldom understood the Anglo American political system. The village patron usually became the political broker connecting the traditional Spanish-American village community with the dominant Anglo-American political machines in New Mexico. He was known as the "jefe politico" or political boss.

The power of the "jefe politico" rested upon his ability to deliver a substantial block of votes to the Anglo-American political machine. In return, he was allowed to control all public employment in his village or his county from school teaching to employment on the public highways. Usually holding the position of sheriff, he could use his power to intimidate the opposition, to arrest or to release prisoners before an election, to serve or not to serve summons, and to manipulate the county tax rate. County prisoners were frequently fed from a farm and a store controlled by the sheriff's family, and all insurance on public buildings were often carried through family-owned companies. Other members of the extended patriarchal family also held other important political positions such as county clerk, deputies, etc.

The jefe politico is seldom concerned with serious political, social, or economic issues. Deeply involved in bread and butter politics, he is for sale to the politician of any party able to pay his price. He still survives as the major political leader among the Spanish Americans. Many Anglo-American liberals in the Southwest criticize the jefe politico for his short sighted leadership, his corruption, his lack of ideology, his frequent exploitation of his own people, and his willingness to sell out to the highest bidder. Unfortunately, they seldom face up to the major problem of developing an alternative leadership system acceptable to the Spanish-American people.

The patron system rested upon values that for the most part still exist and to a large measure still determine the attitudes of the Spanish Americans toward political leaders, government agencies, welfare, employment, and patterns of conflict solution and leadership. Among them are: (1) a blind loyalty toward traditional ethnic leaders, (2) a tendency to desire to enter into dependent but secure positions of dependency upon an employer or political leader, (3) a reluctance to make decisions and a tendency to postpone decisions as long as possible, (4) a dislike of competition and of personal initiative, (5) a preference for a stable hierarchical social system with well-defined statuses and roles, (6) a preference for a friendly person-to-person primary relationship rather than the formal impersonal relationships of the Anglo world, and (7) a strong dislike for and resistance toward social and cultural change.

In northern New Mexico the jefe politico is still a powerful figure in the rural villages. In other sections of the state, he has tended to disappear. The increase in the English-speaking vote, the rise of a more educated and politically sophisticated younger generation of Spanish-American voters, the increased extension of federal programs beyond the ability of the jefe politico to control, and the slow and halting movement toward a state civil service in time will probably reduce the authority and perhaps even liquidate the position of the jefe politico.

The decline of the patron-peon system has left a vacuum in the social organization of the rural Spanish-American village that has not as yet been filled. The traditional systems of leadership and of decision-making, responsibility for the poor, the solution of family and of group conflicts, and the financing of communal activities, and of maintaining village unity are disintegrating. Spanish-American rural villages are today marked by extreme factionalism. It has been extremely difficult for them to find alternative systems of organizing village families for communal endeavors.

The Impact of Social Change upon Religion

The American conquest of 1847 found a mere handful of Spanish-American priests in the Southwest. Shortly after the annexation of the area, New Mexico was separated ecclesiastically from Mexico. The new religious province was placed in charge of the American Roman Catholic Church. Foreign priests under the direction of Father Lamy from Normandy, France, were brought in to staff the empty churches. Appalled at the folk Catholicism of the Spanish Americans, the new priests tended to identify with the Anglo Americans rather than with the illiterate Spanish-American rural village population.

Local Spanish-American priests were soon excommunicated. The new priests with little understanding of the Spanish Americans set out to eradicate what they defined as paganism from the Spanish-American culture. Religious focus was shifted in the village churches from the local village saints to members of the Trinity and the Virgin Mary. The local adobe churches were often replaced by churches built in the Norman French or Anglo-American styles. The lean, gaunt, suffering Spanish American or Mexican Christ was removed. His place was taken by the Christ Triumphant of American Roman Catholicism. Village fiestas were often terminated, and the Spanish language was replaced by English in many of the villages.

The Penitente Order became involved in politics during the last part of the nineteenth and first part of the twentieth century as a Spanish-American defense organization. Almost every Spanish American politician of any importance belonged to the order. In some communities, the Penitentes split into both Republican and Democratic lodges. Tourist curiosity followed by excommunication of its members by the Roman Catholic Church drove it underground. Its chapels were shifted from the villages into the more isolated rural regions. For many years, the order was viewed by unsympathetic Anglo Americans as a dangerous subversive organization engaged in bloody rituals and constant plotting against Anglo-American interests.

Although the order of excommunication has been lifted, the Penitentes are slowly diminishing in both numbers and importance. In some areas where they once flourished, there are no present Penitente lodges. The majority of prominent Spanish Americans are no longer members. Immigration has carried away many Penitentes into other regions, and the young men are no longer interested in joining. However, the Penitentes continue to exist in the more rural segments of northern New Mexico and southern Colorado. They are still the only voluntary organization found in most of the villages and could serve perhaps as a focus for strengthening the village social organization.

The diminishing strength of the Penitente Order has had its effect upon village and social integration. The yearly calendar of religious ceremonies no longer involves most of the male population, and village social life has become more monotonous and drab. The Elder Brother of the Penitente lodge cannot maintain control of the behavior of those who violate village mores. No other mechanism has yet developed in the villages to fulfill the social or the religious functions of "Los Hermanos Penitentes." Village life, as a result, is marked by vandalism, factionalism, and conflicts between families and individuals.

Many former Penitentes have joined Protestant Churches that are rapidly gaining ground in northern New Mexico. Although the first Protestant Churches were the standard missionary churches, such as the Presbyterian, the Methodist, and the Baptist, they are not increasing as rapidly as the more fundamentalist Pentecostal Churches such as the Assembly of God. The semiliterate Pentecostal missionary supporting himself by his own labor, preaching in Spanish, visiting and exhorting the village population, is in closer harmony with basic village values than either the English-speaking Catholic priest or the middle class Anglo Protestant missionary. The villages are becoming increasingly diversified in religion. Many villages are split into Catholic and Protestant factions. The weakening of the village folk Catholicism, the gulf between the English-speaking priests and the Spanish-speaking masses, the coming of diverse Protestant missionaries, and the loss of power by the Penitentes, have factionalized many villages, and the social integration of the villages has been seriously weakened.

Summary

The breakdown of the isolated, self-sufficient village economy, the passing of political and economic controls into the hands of the Anglo population, the emigration of young adults, increasing religious and acculturational differentiation, the intrusion of a school-system and mass media suffused with Anglo values, and finally the breakdown and mal-functioning of the traditional social systems have created a large, apathetic, poverty-stricken village population bitterly resentful at its inability to live in the traditional manner. So far the village inhabitants have found it impossible to develop the necessary social mechanisms to adjust to the now dominant Anglo-American society. The rural Spanish-American villages are atomistic and factionalized. There are no systems existing now in the villages strong enough to create a sense of community, to break down the barriers of apathy, isolation, and suspiciousness among the village population, and to provide for leadership and conflict solution.

Until sociologists or anthropologists working through government sponsored agencies or the regional universities can either restructure the traditional social systems, or through guided social change bring into existence new ones to integrate the villages, to provide a means of securing the cooperation of the village population, and to better integrate the village region into the economic life of the nation, it is doubtful that any existing government or private programs will be successful in northern New Mexico and southern Colorado. The Negro Civil Rights movement is having its impact. Unrest is growing, and perhaps in time new organizations and new leaders will emerge that can integrate the village population and release them from the current apathy and hopelessness. It is probable that these organizations, if they do come into existence, will be quite militant, and to a large degree will be structured upon the traditional social systems and values of the rural Spanish-American population.

THE FAMILY: VARIATIONS IN TIME AND SPACE

Leo Grebler, Joan W. Moore, and Ralph C. Guzmán

An understanding of the family is strategic to the understanding of stability and change in any social system. Believed by many to be the most critical socializing agency, the family is, therefore, critical in maintaining a social system by producing and sustaining the kind of individual who is most adapted to it. The special importance of the family structure in a minority population in this regard is underlined by the basic thesis of the Moynihan Report as well as by the controversy that followed its publication.[1] The Report emphasized the relationship between "the traditional Negro matricentric family" and the "unmotivated" male personality in maintaining the *status quo* of large masses of Negroes. Some social scien-

Reprinted with permission of The Macmillan Company from *The Mexican-American People* by Leo Grebler, Joan W. Moore, and Ralph C. Guzmán. Copyright © 1970 by The Free Press, a Division of The Macmillan Company.
[1] This chapter draws on an analytic review of the literature prepared by Gerald Rosen.

tists question such a simplified causal chain (which has been even further simplified in this condensation).

Similar issues are the focus of this chapter about the Mexican-American family. Lower achievement levels of Mexican Americans have often attributed to some feature of family structure. In the case of Mexican Americans, it is the special male role *within* the family which is supposed to inhibit the achievement of Mexican-American men. The patriarchal ideal and the cultural ideal of masculinity (expressed in *machismo,* which is discussed later in this chapter) are believed to work together to drain energy into expressive rather than instrumental acts.

Furthermore, it is generally believed that Mexican Americans are exceptionally familistic. Familism has been conceived as curtailing mobility by sustaining emotional attachments to people, places and things. It is argued that extreme attachments to the "old homestead," actual or metaphorical, leads the individual to assume burdens that keep him rooted physically and socially. Among Mexican Americans, familism has been adduced as a prime cause not only of low mobility but of resistance to change of all kinds. In the Mexican-American ethos, familism, along with the special male role, is a source of collective pride. Nevertheless, members of the group and others generally believe that familism also deters collective and individual progress, however defined.

This chapter discusses persistence and change in family-life patterns of Mexican Americans in the face of migration, urbanization, and variations in local milieus. The Mexican-American family will be analyzed here in terms of the always useful but ever equivocal continuum from "traditional" to "modern." As with the folk-urban continuum . . . neither the beginning nor the ending point of the continuum is clear; nor is the continuum one-dimensional. The "traditional" Mexican family as sketched in much of the literature reflects a mixture of upper-status and lower-status ideals and practices. The mixture was made more complex by the minority's adaptation to varied conditions in the United States and by its comparative isolation. The modern end of the continuum usually becomes "the urban middle-class American family," with all of its own complexities. Whether the urban middle-class Mexican-American family is distinguishable from the urban middle-class Anglo family can be explored with the data available in the Los Angeles and San Antonio surveys. The effects of the greater isolation of Mexican Americans in San Antonio can be assayed at each class level. We can analyze whether the lower-class family in either milieu reflects more traditional relationships and values.

THE IMPORTANCE OF FAMILISM

Along with the special features of the male role, the major theme dominating the classic portrayal of the traditional Mexican family is the deep importance of the family to all its members. The needs of the family collectivity supersede the needs of each individual member.

A number of consequences detrimental to individual achievement may follow. To the extent that the family captures all of the significant social relations of the individual, he becomes *less* capable of absorbing new values and of maintaining relations with new kinds of people. Maintenance of "Mexicanness" of both values and ethnic exclusiveness in social relations is therefore achieved largely through familism. Furthermore, in depictions of families following traditional norms, the kin group is the *only* reliable place of refuge from a hostile world. If this were true, the holding power of the family would be intensified. The benefits of the family's "protection" of its individual members, then, may be gained at the price of lowered individual achievement because of isolation from the larger milieu.

In addition to emotional relationships, kinship ties among Mexican Americans are described as avenues of exchanges of a more instrumental nature, as they are in American society as a whole. Mutual financial assistance, exchange of work and other skills, and advice and support in solving personal problems are ideally available within the extended kin group. Though all of these resources are, normatively, also available within the extended kin network of most Americans, reliance on kin is carried to an extreme in the traditional Mexican-American family system. "A kind of family communism" is expected, and anecdotes are told about promising individuals whose potential mobility was undermined by the financial drain imposed by impecunious relatives. Traditionally, it is felt to be shameful to seek aid outside the family circle. This is true especially when the welfare of aging parents is at stake. Thus, again, familism may be a help to the individual in need, but it may be a serious drain on the mobile or potentially mobile individual.

If these functions of the traditional Mexican-American family were in fact prevalent in the past, they might explain some part of the lower collective achievement of the group. However, the extent to which they exist *today* is unknown. But some indication of their persistence may be found in our data on patterns of household composition and of financial and other dependency. The variations in such patterns by income level also give some indication of how "family communism" is related to achievement or mobility, though only extremely tentative causal imputations can be made from the limited data.

Living Arrangements and Visiting Patterns

Whether members of the extended family—grandparents, sisters, cousins—choose to live with each other is a severe test of familism. Extended-family households were not uncommon in the poor Mexican-American communities of urban areas even in the recent past. But all studies, even of the most traditionalistic individuals, reveal a preference for the separate nuclear family household. However permanent such arrangements may turn out to be, doubling up under the same roof for the Mexican-American family appears to be an *ad hoc* solution to temporary problems rather than a valued goal. A newly married couple might move in with the groom's parents, or a widowed mother or father may move in with a son. And, as in other American households, such *ad hoc* arrangements frequently create tensions. In a modification of the extended-family household, observable in many Mexican-American communities throughout the Southwest, several dwelling units are built on the same lot, housing different families of the same extended kin group.

Today, any but the nuclear household pattern or its broken variant (especially the female-headed household) is rare in either Los Angeles or San Antonio (Table 1). Though this finding goes far toward disproving the notion that Mexican Americans are familistic enough to establish joint households in an urban setting, they can still maintain a primary focus on the family, by visiting. In the traditional extended kin group, visiting is especially important for women. For them it is often a major form of recreation, and it tends to be confined to relatives, even to the exclusion of neighbors. Male social relations tend to range more widely and to include non-relatives. While maintaining the kinship system and all of its functions, then, traditional visiting patterns isolate women. Where these patterns survive, they may be important in helping maintain ethnic cohesiveness across potential social distance created by increasing occupational mobility. Any extended kin group is likely to have members scattered over a wide range of jobs and income levels. Thus familism may help prevent a strong social-class cleavage from developing among Mexican Americans. However, several studies have shown that increasing class differentiation within the group does weaken the visiting patterns. And even in homogeneous poor communities, there are generational differences in visiting patterns.

Table 1.   Household Composition of Survey Respondents,
Los Angeles and San Antonio, 1965–1966

	Los Angeles	San Antonio*
Nuclear family households		
Husband, wife, and children	60%	57%
Husband, wife, no children	10	13
Broken families		
Husband and children	2	3
Wife and children	11	12
Single-person households	7	9
Extended-family households†	4‡	3
All others§	6	3
Total number (= 100%)	(947)	(603)

* Weighting procedures were used in the San Antonio sample. This means that total numbers cannot be used as a direct indicator of error.
† Includes both three-generation households and laterally extended households.
‡ Two of these households, or 0.2 per cent of the total, were joint households with two nuclear families.
§ About half of these are single individuals living with a relative. The residual in Los Angeles includes a handful of households with unrelated individuals living with the family, and three households which were extended both vertically and laterally. In both cities, the residual group includes husband-wife families with relatives other than siblings or parents as members of the household.

Though our larger interview sample was not questioned about visiting, the smaller subsample was asked where and with whom they spent holidays. In neither San Antonio nor Los Angeles were there consistent patterns. Some families spent the holidays at home, some with extended kin, some with friends, and one cooperated with its kin group to hire a hall for a Christmas party involving some 100 people.

To judge from the limited data on living arrangements and visiting patterns, then, relationships within the extended kinship group among Mexican Americans have declined in importance with increased urbanization, acculturation, and contact with the dominant system. A similar decline has been found in many societies, although cross-cultural research has shown that neither industrialism nor urbanism *depends* on the decline of familism. Thus, the failure of current Mexican-American urban patterns to conform to Mexican tradition is merely noted here without suggesting unequivocal implications.

The Compadrazgo

No discussion of Mexican-American familism would be complete without consideration of the *compadrazgo*. As in all Catholic groups, godparents have a series of implicit and explicit obligations toward their godchildren, but the structural significance of the *compadrazgo* derives more from the relationship established between the child's godparents and his parents (who become *compadres* or *comadres*) than between the godparents (*padrino* and *madrino*) and the child himself. The bond between *compadres* is supposed to be unusually strong; they can make special claims of all kinds on each other. The functional implications of the *compadrazgo* are complex. To follow one implication, its persistence may be taken to mean that Mexican Americans use a kinship prototype for relationships that other Americans differentiate from their kin. Godparents for a newly-born child are chosen (or nominate themselves) from among two kinds of people—those who are already friends and relatives of the parents, or people of higher prestige. *Compadrazgo* between intimates appears to be far more frequent than the upward-directed relationship. Relatives and friends are invited or offer themselves as sponsors of the children, and existing relationships are reinforced.

Several studies have suggested that early in Mexican-American urbanization the *compadrazgo* retarded change by strengthening bonds between kinsmen. However, there is clear evidence that its function has diminished with urbanization. Few cases of godparents actually taking over the care of an orphaned child have been documented in recent years. Among our samples, less than 2 per cent of the Los Angeles and 3 per cent of the San Antonio respondents had been reared by their godparents. Some research suggests that the mutual obligations of *compadres* are taken far less seriously by younger than by older individuals.

Questions about the *compadrazgo* were asked only of a small subsample of individuals. Relationships with *compadres* were close in some cases but weak in many others and several respondents had not chosen any godparents for their children. Social mobility did not seem to make much difference in the strength of the bonds. One got the distinct impression that the *compadres* were people with whom the respondents would have had close relationships in any case. Only a handful admitted to having received help from their own godparents; most of them were from Mexico (one explicitly stating, as he told how close he was to his *padrinos*, "Aquí no existe tanto el padrinazgo como en México"—The system of godparents is not as common here as it is in Mexico). In the case of one American-born man, his *padrinos* were his grandparents. Occasionally a respondent would indicate that he felt that his *padrinos should have* helped him; one or another complained that they hadn't—"and they were wealthy."

In short, the *compadrazgo*, although undoubtedly still viable, appears to be a minor feature of kinship and community social organization in the major urban centers. It may be changing from an integral feature of the kinship system to an expressive one, beginning to resemble practices found in other Roman Catholic, Greek and Russian Orthodox, and Episcopalian populations in the United States. Its strength among special subgroups of Mexican Americans, such as the politically active, makes the *compadrazgo* interesting. The frequent casual use of the term "*compadre*" among Mexican Americans probably makes the institution more conspicuous than is warranted by its real importance.

Financial Dependency on Kin

If it is the sole resource for financial and other aid (as in the traditional stereotype), the kin group may drain the financial and emotional resources of mobile members. It may also inhibit members from availing themselves of alternative resources in the general society.

As for financial aid, most recent studies show a decline in the sentiment of "family communism" with increasing acculturation and social mobility. The survey data about actual financial exchanges among relatives suggest some interesting amplifications of this statement. Slightly more than half of the Los Angeles respondents admitted having received money from their families—a figure very similar to one found in a general sample of Cleveland. Only about a third of the San Antonio respondents received aid from their families, probably reflecting the city's lower income level, for other data suggest greater traditionalism in San Antonio. On the other hand, about two-thirds of the Los Angeles and about 40 per cent of the San Antonio respondents claimed to have *given* financial assistance to their families. The proportion giving increases with the ability to give, that is, with the family's income.

It is difficult to interpret these data as either supporting or refuting the existence of "family communism." Most of those who had either given or received money were involved in more than one such transaction. Families that help one another seem to do so recurrently, as an expected thing, rather than on a one-time emergency basis. Interestingly, though there are no notable age differences in *giving* aid, younger people are far more likely than older ones to admit to having *received* aid. If one accepts these as valid responses (and not as artifacts of some kind of age-related traditionalistic pride in self-sufficiency), they may be explained by the fact that financial aid was simply less available from relatives in the predominantly poverty-stricken past.

Kin as Source of Advice

Another set of responses shows the extent to which the extended kin group competes with other, more general resources in the urban milieu. Respondents were asked where they would go for advice and help on a variety of problems, ranging from "personal" to "bureaucratic" ("advice on where to go in the city government downtown to get something you want"). Less than half of all respondents would turn to kin sources for help in any kind of problem (Table 2). Kin sources are more popular for personal and financial than for political or bureaucratic problems, and there is little difference between Angelenos and San Antonians at each income level when personal or financial help is involved. In Los Angeles, people's propensity to turn to kin for advice on political and bureaucratic problems varies comparatively little by income. In San Antonio, however, the poor are unexpectedly kin-oriented with regard to maneuvering in city government. Whether people live in predominantly Mexican-American or predominantly Anglo areas makes surprisingly little difference in seeking kinship help for political and bureaucratic assistance, regardless of income

Table 2. Survey Respondents Who Sought Advice or Help from Kin Including Nuclear Family, by Income, Los Angeles and San Antonio, 1965–1966 (Number in parentheses = 100%)

	Personal	Money	Political	City Government*
Higher income†				
Los Angeles	51%	36%	24%	14%
	(345)	(350)	(280)	(316)
Medium income				
Los Angeles	47	43	32	12
	(289)	(279)	(231)	(239)
San Antonio	45	45	23	10
	(273)	(238)	(203)	(199)
Low income				
Los Angeles	41	44	29	12
	(265)	(252)	(192)	(210)
San Antonio	41	40	19	24
	(232)	(196)	(165)	(156)

* "If you needed some advice on where to go in the city government downtown to get something you wanted, who might you go to?"
† In Los Angeles: higher income = > $6,000; medium income = $3,600–$5,999; low income < = $3,600. In San Antonio: medium income ≥ $2,760; low income < $2,760.

level. Women are far more likely than men to turn to kin, most women turning to their husbands.

With regard to financial problems, more than a third of all types of respondents rely on kin. Higher-income people are less likely to do so, however, whether or not they live in a predominantly Mexican colony. (For aid in solving money problems, Colonists are not much different from Frontiersmen at every income level.) Higher-paid people have better credit, and more alternative resources are open to them that permit them to be independent from the kin network. Women are far more likely to turn to family members for financial advice and aid, particularly to their husbands or their children.

On personal problems, family members are particularly frequent sources of advice. However, the survey results show the reverse of what the literature about the Mexican family suggests. *High*-income people with problems are more likely to turn to family for advice than *low*-income people. Furthermore, Mexican Americans living in predominantly *Anglo* areas are more likely to turn to kin than those living in the *barrios*. These differences between Frontiersmen and Colonists are found at the middle-class though not the lower-class levels. (Sex differences, interestingly, are inconsequential.) The data might suggest that the psychological salience of the kin group is enhanced as the individual moves up and out, but closer analysis shows that this would be an oversimplification. The more frequent mention of kin as sources of personal advice among higher-income individuals is largely explained by their mention of husband or wife, *not of extended kin*. In fact, higher-income individuals mention extended kin far less frequently (Table 3). There are more divorced or single individuals, without a spouse to turn to, in poorer *Colonies*. Nevertheless, there seems little doubt that this is the kind of shift found in studies of upwardly mobile individuals in other groups—that is, away from kinship structures which emphasize one-sex relations in the extended kin group (for example, be-

Table 3. Per cent of Survey Respondents Turning to Spouse versus Other Kin on Personal Problems, by Income, Los Angeles and San Antonio, 1965–1966

	Spouse	Other Kin	Non-Kin	Total Number (= 100%)
Higher income				
Los Angeles	27%	24%	49%	345
Medium income				
Los Angeles	23	24	53	289
San Antonio	20	25	56	273
Low income				
Los Angeles	11	30	59	265
San Antonio	7	35	59	232

tween mother and daughter, sister and sister) toward emphasis on the husband-wife relationship of the nuclear family.

In general, the data on sources of advice underscore the point that change is not simply disintegration of family bonds. This has been discovered and rediscovered with regard to the American family system as a whole. Mexican Americans share the national experience of complex patterns of change and of shifts in the structure of family relationships. Though most Mexican Americans themselves believe in their extraordinary familism . . . our findings suggest that they may not be reliable informants. They often do not know the larger system, and thus lack comparative context. Their views also often reflect desired states rather than reality in the urban setting.

The Nuclear Family in the Past Generation

The nuclear family—the biological family of husband, wife and children —is the normal household in present-day Los Angeles and San Antonio. All indications are that it has always been the preferred household type among Mexican Americans. We examine first the so-called "family of orientation" of our respondents—the family in which they were brought up. The discussion here reflects the past, and it will show clearly that the past, characterized by poverty in a rural setting, was not devoid of family problems.

Marital Stability

A measure of the strength of the bond between husband, wife, and children is given by the relative proportions of respondents brought up in intact families. Only about two-thirds of our respondents were reared by both parents—slightly more in San Antonio than in Los Angeles. A large proportion of the remainder were brought up by their mothers alone, and the rest predominantly by one or another relative. (The latter group shows a mixed pattern: Grandparents, or the father alone, or a collateral relative on either the mother's or the father's side were almost equally likely to have been responsible for the respondent during his childhood.) A slightly larger percentage of current higher-income respondents than of low-income respondents were brought up in intact families, but the differences are too small for firm interpretation.

The high proportion of individuals not bought up by both parents suggests either an extraordinarily high death rate among men or, what is more likely, a high rate of desertion or divorce in the parental generation. Studies conducted during the 1930s support the latter interpretation; they picture a situation in which desertion was frequent in both rural and urban settings. The Mexican family was not immune to the disorganizing influences of immigration and poverty.

These findings diverge from the widely accepted impression that the

Mexican-American family has been unusually stable. Even those studies which note that divorce is now increasingly common among Mexican Americans contrast the present incidence of divorce with a presumed prior stablity, both in the United States among older individuals and in Mexico.

Patriarchy in the Rural Past

The Mexican-American family of the previous generation was primarily geared to rural life. This is evident from past research and from our analysis based on the subsample of depth interviews in Los Angeles. But neither our analysis nor past research suggest that these families led an idyllic farm life. Many respondents report a substantial amount of instability. Even in cases where the individual was reared by both parents, the father may actually have been absent for long periods of time, either following the crops (which many men did singly, leaving their families at home) or venturing to new locations to prepare the way for the family's arrival later. Nonetheless, the rural past is significant in that some aspects of its family structure and division of roles appear to have persisted even in urban settings.

Large areas of Los Angeles County, for example, had small farms attached to dwelling units as recently as 15 years ago. Mexican-American men brought up in the county frequently recall that they—like their age peers on Mexican or Texan farms—were exempt from household tasks: They cared for the chickens, chopped wood, and did other outside chores. Household tasks were defined as "women's work." Respondents in the subsample who were brought up in such a setting—whether Mexico or Los Angeles—tended to say that their fathers discouraged school in favor of work that yielded immediate benefits to the family. The dubious gains to the individual from finishing high school were far less important than the survival of the family, especially during the Depression when many of these men were young.

In numerous cases, this kind of family structure adapted itself to the urban setting when the young boy was sent out to work at an early age while the mother and sisters cared for the home. Life histories show many who had part-time jobs, especially in the very poor families or those in which the father had died or deserted. Occasionally, when one parent (especially the mother) had died or left, the boy also helped with household chores, cooking, cleaning, washing dishes. Usually, however, there were enough females around to do the inside chores, and men could grow up firmly convinced of the inherent righteousness of the sexual division of labor. In the intact urban families where there was no need for sons to work, demands were made on them for nothing but trivial errands or help with small household repairs. The sexual division of labor, which is functional in a rural setting, results in a comparatively idle male child and adolescent in a less poverty-stricken urban setting.

The most widely discussed aspect of the sexual division of labor is traditional Mexican patriarchy, in which power and prestige are absolute prerogatives of the male head of the household. When these attributes are delegated, they go through the male line. In the traditional family, the male head makes all important and most unimportant decisions unilaterally, according to the norm. Meanwhile, the submissive wife carries out her husband's decisions unquestioningly or helps to see that they are carried out by the children.

There is considerable evidence that this ideal pattern of decision-making has never been the behavioral norm among Mexican Americans, either in the United States or Mexico, even though it may have been the cultural ideal (at least among men). From the data available on the 27 men in the Los Angeles subsample who were reared in intact families, all but two replied "father" when asked "who ran things" when the respondent was growing up. But this reply was immediately cast in doubt when the same respondents almost universally admitted that their mothers made the day-to-day decisions affecting the children, the running of the household, and so on, and that in most cases decisions about large purchases and similar transactions were made jointly by father and mother.

Further doubt is cast on the image of the patriarch by the fact that only five in the subsample reported that it was the father who normally punished them. In two of these cases the boy worked with the father in the fields, and thus the father had ready access to the miscreant; in certain others, the father was remembered as tyrannical: "My mother practically never spoke; sometimes I wonder how they got married!" In most cases, either the mother or "whoever was closer" punished the children. Actual power in these families was thus largely situationally determined and was exercised by whoever happened to be around when an action or decision had to be taken. Patriarchal values existed, but the families departed from them as a matter of course.

We might suggest, in fact, that the patriarchal values as well as the belief in the stable family became cultural ideals of the Mexican American at least in part *because* of the weakness of both the family structure and the male role. These values might have represented a yearning for an ideally peaceful state of affairs not readily attainable in the poverty-stricken and unpredictable life of the typical Mexican American of a generation ago.

The family, and particularly the nuclear family of orientation, was certainly the primary referende group of our urban samples. In the responses to questions about "who had more influence" over the respondent when he was 13 or 14 old, parents overwhelmingly dominate over teachers, age mates, or other relatives. Overt rejection of parental authority was far from normal a generation ago.

But when respondents were asked whether their father or mother had greater influence over them, more than half of the total sample responding (54 per cent in Los Angeles and 52 per cent in San Antonio) named their mothers. Only 33 per cent in Los Angeles and 41 per cent in San Antonio named their fathers. Thirteen per cent in Los Angeles and eight per cent in San Antonio claimed that mother and father had equal influence. Implications of psychological theory to the contrary, the proportion naming father or mother does not vary with present income level in Los Angeles, but higher-income San Antonians are more likely to state that they have been influenced by their mothers. When we look at cross-sex identification, men naming their mothers are more common than women naming their fathers. This indicates the pervasive importance of the mother.

These data, scanty though they are, suggest the overriding significance of situation for family-role patterns and stability. The situations of the past, of course, still exist in pockets throughout the Southwest and in Mexico itself (the sources of in-migrants to the cities). For this reason, the patterns of the future will probably be of the checkerboard kind. It will become increasingly difficult to generalize about "the Mexican-American family."

The Nuclear Family of the Present Generation

The survey data indicate a substantial departure in the contemporary family from the traditional patriarchy. The departure is greatest among the young, the more well-to-do, and those living outside the Mexican colony. There were generally few differences in attitude by sex; men and women tend to be in greater accord than the old and the young.

Patriarchy in the Urban Present

Respondents were asked their opinions on three statements designed to reflect traditional norms. The first related to the wife's role: Did the respondents agree that "the most important thing" that a married woman could do was to have children? The majority in all categories agreed with the statement, but with a notable age differential—71 per cent in Los Angeles and 76 per cent in San Antonio of those under 30 agreed, whereas 93 per cent in Los Angeles and 94 per cent in San Antonio of those over 50 years of age agreed. There was also a slightly greater tendency for the respondents living in Colonies, especially low-income persons, to agree.

A second statement expressing a traditional sentiment, "A husband ought to have complete control over the family's income," elicited less agreement. Once again, however, the older respondents were notably more traditional in attitude—59 per cent in Los Angeles and 75 per cent in San Antonio of those over 50 agreed, compared with only 38 per cent in Los Angeles and 53 per cent in San Antonio of those under 30. There were substantial, though not systematic, variations among respondents at different income levels in neighborhoods of differing ethnic composition (Table 4).

The third question asked whether respondents agreed that a husband should care for the children when the wife wants time for herself. An overwhelming proportion—91 per cent—of the respondents agreed that the father should baby-sit. There were only minor variations among people of different ages, income, and so forth in Los Angeles, though age differences were noticeable in San Antonio.

These responses—especially the age-related patterns—suggest a substantial shift in the perception of the norms governing the husband's role, if not the wife's. As mentioned earlier, it is doubtful whether the father's control over family matters, such as the budget, was ever as complete as traditional norms would indicate. The responses indicate that the ideas of younger, better-paid, and less ghetto-bound Mexican Americans about the father's role are no longer quite so tenaciously patriarchal as some of the literature suggests. Masculinity is perhaps not quite so associated with dominance as it may have been in the past.

Table 4. Survey Respondents Agreeing that Husband Ought to Have Complete Control over Family Income, by Income and Neighborhood Ethnicity, Los Angeles and San Antonio, 1965–1966

			Total Number (= 100%)	
	Los Angeles	San Antonio	Los Angeles	San Antonio
Higher Income				
Frontier*	24%	—	164	—
Intermediate*	51	—	124	—
Colony*	43	—	77	—
Medium income				
Frontier	29	44%	93	134
Intermediate	48	—	96	—
Colony	52	67	120	190
Low income				
Frontier	42	72	74	47
Intermediate	64	—	75	—
Colony	64	68	126	227

* In Los Angeles, Frontier = tracts with less than 15.0 per cent Spanish-surname individuals; Intermediate = tracts with between 15.0 and 43.8 per cent Spanish-surname individuals; and Colony = tracts with more than 43.8 per cent Spanish-surname individuals. In San Antonio, Frontier = tracts with less than 54.0 per cent Spanish-surname individuals and Colony = tracts with 54.0 per cent or more Spanish-surname individuals.

A similar picture emerges in responses to the question as to who performs certain sex-typed household tasks, ranging from painting rooms to washing dishes (Table 5). Responses to these questions by Mexican Americans are very similar to those of a 1953 sample of the general population of Detroit, suggesting that in this regard the Mexican Americans are close to "typical Americans."

The Mexican-American responses, especially when compared with the Detroit responses, again suggest that egalitarianism occurs more in the masculine sex-typed tasks than in the feminine, just as there is more loosening in the norms regarding the husband's role than in those regarding the role of the wife. Among Mexican Americans, egalitarianism is generally greater within higher-income families and among those choosing to live outside of predominantly Mexican areas. Such differences are insubstantial, however, and so are differences in responses by age and sex. The

Table 5.   Survey Respondents Reporting on Sex Specialization in
Family Roles, Los Angeles and San Antonio, 1965–1966

	WHO PERFORMS TASK							
	Husband (or Husband Might)		Both		Wife (or Wife Might)		TOTAL NUMBER (= 100%)	
	L.A.	S.A.	L.A.	S.A.	L.A.	S.A.	L.A.	S.A.
Painting rooms*	41%	37%	52%	57%	7%	7%	919	593
Expensive purchase†	22	18	68	74	10	9	910	589
Holiday decision‡	14	17	80	77	6	5	905	585
Punishing children§	12	10	71	76	17	13	892	587
Night care of children¶	3	4	38	35	59	61	909	587
Washing dishes‖	6	6	18	11	76	83	900	593

* "Painting rooms in the house."
† "Picking out more expensive things like furniture or a car."
‡ "Deciding where to go for a holiday or celebration."
§ "Punishing the children, if necessary."
¶ "Getting up at night to take care of the children if they cry."
‖ "Washing dishes."

most striking finding relates not to internal variations in the departure
from traditional sex specialization, but rather to the conspicuous presence
of a basically *egalitarian* division of household tasks, with female specialization in a restricted domestic area.

Machismo

In particular, these responses about husband and wife roles in the
Mexican-American nuclear family cast doubt on the common notions of
machismo—at least as expressed within the urban family. The complex of
attitudes and identities associated with this ethnic concept of masculinity
has been well detailed in the literature. In addition to the dominant theme
of sexual virility, *machismo* is also intertwined with the traditional patriarchy; masculinity is said to be demonstrated not only by the man's sexuality—particularly extra-marital—and other activities that suggest a
phallic preoccupation, but by domination over the affairs of his family and
especially over his wife. The female role, which complements this phallic
notion of the "strong Mexican husband," is that of the submissive, naive,
rather childlike "sainted mother," whose purity is preserved by her husband's refusal to bring the world and its sins into the home. Our data
suggest that though the Mexican-American man may still refuse to wash
dishes, in the more important aspects of the husband-wife and father-child
relationship he is willing to admit that he has ceded control; at the same
time he has assumed some of the responsibilities that were traditionally
"feminine."

These attitudinal data are, of course, silent on the actual processes of
change, which have been touched on in some studies of Mexican-American
urban life. The apparently greater persistence of traditionalism with reference to feminine tasks is not surprising; the greater exposure of working

men to norms of the larger society may have an indirect influence on their concepts of masculinity. The availability of television at home may reduce the attraction of the corner bar for a tired working man. We also lack data on actual sexual behavior of our male respondents. But *machismo* as traditionally acted out takes at least two to play—the questing man and the alarmed and excited woman. Whatever the similarity in content of the extra-marital game in American and in traditional Mexican society, the rules of the games are different in the two societies. Acculturation, involving change in self-definition, occurs not only through the inspiration of positive models and interaction conducive to new definitions of appropriate behavior. Such acculturation also occurs in the course of interaction in which expectations are discordant. As isolation declines, the "Mexican" is increasingly in confrontation with the American sex game.

The behaviour classified under the label of *machismo* appears to have much in common with lower-class definitions of masculinity, especially youth-culture definitions, across ethnic groups in American society. The complementary *female* roles appear to differ from one subgroup to another. Though the behavior persists and continues to be fun for those participating in it, it is the target of direct attack by the socializing institutions of the American system. (High school dress and conduct regulations throughout the Southwest are specifically directed to curtailing what many administrators designate as "Don Juan" behavior.) It is also the victim of more subtle attacks in the form of the kind of demands placed on the adult man in his work place. Increasingly, also, urban life offers recreational alternatives to the all-male fantasy-creating and occasionally acting-out group of intimates. The continued isolation of the Colony-based Mexican-American nuclear family from families in the dominant system probably permits the preservation of feminine roles and of some intra-family patterns of interaction. These female roles are not too dissimilar from female role expectations in American society at large, and their persistence is undoubtedly reinforced by this fact.

Birth Control

Another issue related to the family's role structure is its size, which involves attitudes toward birth control. Of course, this issue is intimately associated with *machismo* as well as with norms about the role of women. As noted by students of birth control in other lower-class populations, opposition to the use of contraceptives comes frequently from men. Masculine potency and dominance are symbolized by the fact that men can get women pregnant. Though demonstrating one's virility and potency may be especially significant during adolescence, it may continue, by implication, to be meaningful into adulthood and into the familial role. A brief pilot study conducted in a small California community indicates that among traditionalistic lower-class Mexican-American respondents it was more often the husband than the wife who objected to the use of any contraceptive measures, occasionally going to the extreme of taking away or hiding birth-control pills prescribed for the wife. And at a more affluent level, one of two pharmacists in this small California town stated in an interview that some Mexican-American women would not permit pill purchases to be put on the family charge account. They insisted on paying cash to conceal the purchase from their husbands despite tax advantages that would accrue from evidence of a legitimate medical expense. The study concluded that when contraception was consistently practiced by Mexican-American families its success depended in large measure on a shift in the husband's perception of his own and his wife's role. The shift may have been motivated in part by the young couple's awareness of the problems experienced by relatives, especially mothers who bore large numbers of children. The manifestations of the change, however, appear to lie in the development of increasing egalitarianism and joint discussion of family problems, including family planning.

Of course, religious scruples as well as husband-wife relationships may set important limits on the use of contraceptives. Lack of knowledge may also be a factor and prudishness and dignity are threatened in acquiring

Table 6.   Attitudes of Survey Respondents Toward Birth Control, by Age, Income, and Neighborhood Ethnicity, Los Angeles and San Antonio, 1965–1966*

	Per Cent Saying Always Right or Usually Right		Total Number (= 100%)	
	Los Angeles	San Antonio	Los Angeles	San Antonio
Age				
Under 30	73%	64%	217	96
30–39	68	61	290	165
40–49	63	45	213	131
50 and over	50	39	199	207
Income and neighborhood ethnicity				
Colony				
Higher income	69	—	78	—
Medium income	69	53	122	165
Low income	48	45	118	183
Intermediate				
Higher income	71	—	102	—
Medium income	59	—	98	—
Low income	51	—	75	—
Frontier				
Higher income	76	—	175	—
Medium income	62	65	76	109
Low income	56	40	77	135

* The item read as follows: "Family planning—or birth control—has been discussed by many people. What is your feeling about a married couple practicing birth control? If you had to decide, which one of these statements best expresses your point of view? It is always right; it is usually right; it is usually wrong; it is always wrong."

information about them. Nevertheless, several recent community studies indicate that contraception is far from the unthinkable manipulation implied in some stereotypes of Mexican Americans. Data from our Los Angeles survey reflect general acceptance of birth control, at least at the level of verbal expression, whereas data from the San Antonio sample show the persistence of a more traditional stance. In Los Angeles, the response of Mexican Americans was, in fact, at least as accepting of birth control as a recent sample of the total United States population asked the same question (See Note *, Table 6). Sixty-two per cent of the total United States sample had no moral compunctions about birth control, compared with 64 per cent of the Mexican Americans in Los Angeles and 50 per cent of those in San Antonio. As the United States sample included a far larger proportion of Protestants, the response of urban Mexican Americans to the question on birth control is even more striking. . . .

Interestingly, there were no meaningful sex differences in the over-all sample. In both cities, however, there was a pronounced age gradient, with the large majority of respondents under 40—that is, the fertile population—approving birth control (Table 6). Acceptance was also strongly related to income and ethnic composition of the neighborhood. Higher-income respondents in both Anglo and Mexican neighborhoods expressed stronger approval than did lower-income persons, and the same was generally true for those living in predominantly Anglo areas, regardless of income. Finally, the Los Angeles respondents remained more accepting of birth control than the San Antonians even when most factors were controlled. (The exception—middle-income respondents in the mixed areas of San Antonio included the very small proportion of high-income respondents who were probably as acculturated as the high-income respondents in Los Angeles.)

The Ideal Child: A Suggestion in the Data

Whether or not children are planned, the literature leaves little doubt that they are welcome in most Mexican-American families. As already noted, the bearing and rearing of children continues to be seen as perhaps the most important function of a woman, symbolizing her maturity.

The actual relationships between parents and children are difficult to describe adequately in any population, as are all important human relationships. It is almost impossible not to exaggerate one or another dimension when the observer must select. The present discussion focuses on the expectations that parents have for children (an aspect relevant to the functioning of the patriarchy).

In the traditional Mexican-American family, particularly in the middle-class, there seems to have been a very distinct ideal of what is appropriate behavior for children. The "well-brought-up" child is a model of respect. He knows his place in the family scheme of things and does not trespass in spheres of life where he has no business. This model extends from family life to other roles. A well-brought up Mexican-American girl knows enough not to behave like either a boy or a "bad" girl. She does not press for competitive excellence in school. She does not display initiative outside the circumscribed pathways traditionally reserved for girls. If she does, retribution is swift. Traditional Mexican expectations concerning children and, indeed, adults as well are very similar to the traditional expectations of the larger Catholic community. These expectations as regards decorum have extremely constraining effects on children and adults alike. For Mexicans this code of behavior is expressed positively in the term *disciplina*. It is expressed negatively in the term *malcriado*, which is applied to one who is badly brought up.

In view of the non-traditional responses in other spheres, it was rather surprising to find that *"disciplina"* (or its equivalent) was the most frequent response to the question "In your opinion, what are the main things that children need to be taught in the schools today?" (Table 7). Further, unlike many other values discussed here, this response bore little relationship to the economic or neighborhood status of the parents, or even to their age or sex. The more deprived San Antonians tended at every level to emphasize pragmatic learning more than did Angelenos, but traditional views of child behavior were still held by the plurality.

Table 7.   Opinions of Survey Respondents on the Role of the School, by Income, Los Angeles and San Antonio, 1965–1966

	INCOME				
	Higher	Medium		Low	
	Los Angeles	Los Angeles	San Antonio	Los Angeles	San Antonio
Responses emphasizing traditional roles[*]	37%	42%	36%	45%	41%
Responses emphasizing instrumental skills					
Substantive and technical[†]	32	24	38	27	38
Language	3	5	6	5	6
Responses emphasizing social skills[‡]	16	16	14	10	9
Diffuse responses[§]	12	13	6	13	6
Total number (= 100%)	(330)	(245)	(287)	(221)	(248)

[*] *"Disciplina,"* obedience, respect, good manners, religious training.
[†] Basic school subject-matter skills and technical skills related to job or occupation.
[‡] To get along with others, adapt to society.
[§] E.G. "education"; expression of general satisfaction with the system.

This response pattern must not be interpreted as indicating no change in the ideals held out for children. It may rather reflect the ways in which parents cope—or fail to cope—with their children's schools. Their response pattern may also reflect their desire to be thought of as law-abiding in the face of being stereotyped as recalcitrant to law and order. Furthermore, higher-income parents in Los Angeles show a somewhat greater tendency than their lower-income counterparts to take an instrumental view of the schools for their children. Respondents in San Antonio, however, regardless of income, were about evenly divided as to whether manners or skills were the most important things taught in school. Finally, there is evidence of a marked departure from traditional norms in responses to the next question in the questionnaire: "Do you feel the same for both boys and girls?" A traditional response would have emphasized a sex difference, but respondents in both cities overwhelmingly rejected sex difference in educational goals (87 per cent in Los Angeles and 91 per cent in San Antonio). Whatever the education goals of the parents, they were the same for both boys and girls. School enrollment data as given in the U.S. census show little sex disparity.

The traditionalistic response pattern may reflect the persistence of models of behavior for children that are rather inappropriate in a highly competitive urban setting. It suggests processes within many families that discourage behavior deviating from the expected deference. In view of the limitations of survey data on intra-family processes, research on parent-child relations using other methods is badly needed.[2]

The Family Role in Perspective

This chapter has emphasized those features of the traditional Mexican family life which seem to bear most significantly on the understanding of achievement. In the analysis, we have suggested that the "traditional Mexican family" was in fact far from an integrated whole, and that its fate in the second and third generation involved several kinds of change.

We have suggested that certain aspects of the traditional family might have been the adaptive expedients of a poverty-stricken population with very little access to sources of help in the larger society. These expedients may have acquired a retrospective emotional glow that glorifies the reality. Taking in destitute relatives, and doubling up with other families, for example, were probably felt to be obligations, but the virtual absence of extended-family households in the present, as well as some of the life-history data recorded in our interviews, suggest that the obligations were often felt to be onerous. Poverty emphasizes some kinship obligations, but the general upgrading of material welfare in the population means that the more stressful obligations could be allowed to wither.

We have suggested that in some respects the internal structure of family relationships has been reordered as Mexican Americans have moved more fully into the urban middle-class situation and culture. The family may be no less important now than in the past, but the importance and elaboration of, for example, a woman's relationship to her sister may have declined as the importance of her relationship to her husband became enhanced.

We have suggested the possibility of an actual decline in the importance of some values. These might include the traditional definitions of masculinity as the changing work situation, exposure to new values and models of both masculinity and femininity, and higher levels of living shifted the

---

[2] For example, data were collected for this study on family sanctioning techniques, but they turned out to be so equivocal that no interpretation was possible.

reward structure. We have suggested that some cultural lags persist—for example, the continuation of the boy's "leisured" household role even after outside chores have vanished in the urban setting. The persistence of traditional values in the face of changing circumstances may also reflect the nostalgia of an uprooted population. It may reflect striving after a dimly remembered upper-class mode of life, as, possibly, in the emphasis on *disciplina* of the young. It may reflect the influence of continued immigration from more archaic rural settings.

In general, we have viewed the family as simultaneously embodying and acting out both a transmitted set of traditional norms and a developing set of adaptive norms. An additional aspect of adaptation to the urban situation is relevant both to the achievement and the roles considered in this chapter. This is the process of mobility away from the lower class. Middle-class role models, mentioned elsewhere in this book, are important in the process. Such role models are, naturally, *outside* the normal lower-class family. But the importance of role models *inside* the lower-class family—and the lessons that may be drawn from the presence of older *non*-achieving household members—may be easily underestimated.[3]

The possible importance of the class situation for the young person may be illustrated by contrasting the Negro with the Mexican-American family. At least superficially, the similarity between the "product" of each in the behavior of young males is striking. Both fit the stereotype of the "acting-out" man who takes gratification here and now rather than deferring gratification until occupational attainment gives him the income to satisfy his wishes more "rationally." Both Negro and Mexican-American male personalities have been "explained" in terms of ethnic subculture— that is, of a group of particular structures and/or values especially relating to the family and especially concentrated in the ethnic group. Mexican-American families are "too patriarchal, too clannish, with ties that are too strong" for the male role to change or for individual mobility to take place. Negro families are "too matricentric, too disorganized, and too weak" to provide the youth with adequate male role models necessary for achievement. Though this summary vastly simplifies a complex literature, the fact remains that both families are seen as producing basically the same kind of young man—one who drops out of school because he is preoccupied with immediate pleasures—but producing him from radically different structures and values.

This parallel suggests that our analysis of shifts, disintegration, or persistence of traditional Mexican family features would still leave questions about achievement unanswered even if the data were much richer. There may be a process common to lower-class and especially minority lower-class families—whether they are traditionally patriarchal or matriarchal, clannish or disorganized, weak or strong—that presses toward the emergence of a basically similar low-achieving man.

[3] Lorenzo Campbell contributed to this analysis.

In addition to the familiar discrepancy in total expected lifetime earnings of the well and the poorly educated and of Anglos and minorities, there is a sharp difference in the age-related pattern of earnings, and an equally sharp difference in the age-related pattern of access to a general sense of self-esteem based on social evaluations of peers. In Chart 1, the age-related earnings pattern of the white college-trained professional is contrasted with that of the nonwhite laborer with an elementary school education. (Comparable data for Spanish-surname males were not available.) Generally the income of the poorly educated laborer does not increase appreciably at higher ages. Graphically, it is closer to a *linear* configuration, indicating lack of variation compared with the clearly parabolic income configuration of the white professionals, who can expect peak earnings in late middle age.

It is, of course, the older men in the family that have experienced either the linear income curve or the parabolic ones. Their experience reflects

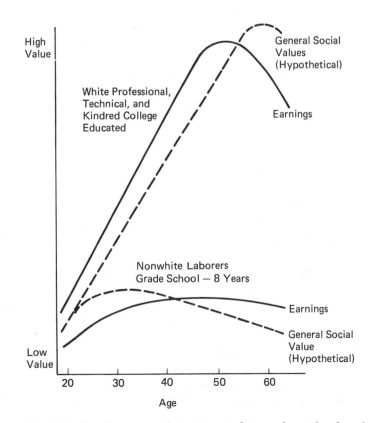

CHART 1. Age-related patterns of earnings and general social value, for white professional college-trained males compared with nonwhite grade-school-educated unskilled laborers.

the opportunity structures of the previous generation without either the economic gains or the civil-rights gains of recent decades. But it is among such older men that today's lower-class young man is reared. The linear income curve may have meant that the family could never "get ahead of itself." The family may be continually vulnerable to unanticipated needs for money because of illness or of unemployment. (Economic disasters are conspicuous in urban minority ghetto life, not only through experiences of relatives and friends, but also in the content of appeals in loan company and insurance company advertisements based on the assumption that economic disaster is just around the corner.) The effect of the contrast between age-and-earnings patterns of the lower and middle classes may be exemplified by the timing of large purchases. For a young laborer of a minority group to make big purchases *before* he acquires the potential burden of a family is "rational," just as it is rational for the young white college man to defer such purchases.

There is also an age-related pattern of more general evaluation. For the middle-class man, the "best years of life" tend to be in middle age. By then he is at the peak of his career and can command maximum general prestige from the community, among other things. On the other hand, for the lower-class man, the "best years of life" tend to be in his youth. At that period, he is just as vigorous and attractive as anyone else—perhaps even more so than the middle-class man of the same age, since he may be more preoccupied with being in good physical condition. General self-esteem is derived more from the world of work for the middle-class man, and more from physical activity for the lower-class man. Although the prestige estimation curve in Chart 1 is schematic, both curves do conform to reality. The income curves are based on empirical observations; the "general social value" curves reflect what is known about the timing and the social and psychological meanings of various age statuses to men of different social class levels.

The implication for behavior of the social-evaluation curve may be illustrated, just as the implication of the income curve was illustrated with the timing of large purchases. If a man perceives his greatest chances for access to general prestige to be to those values emphasizing physical attractiveness, then it is rational for him to maximize his attempts to attain these values during youth. On the other hand, if a young man's greatest chances for access to general prestige are those related to occupational success, then he is far more likely to defer immediate gratification during his youth in expectation of future rewards. (The hippie movement—and this may explain the uproar about it—emphasizes norms like those of the lower class: Middle-class hippies act in some ways like lower-class youths.) Neither "decision"—to "act out" or to defer gratification—need denigrate the values inherent in the other. The upper-status individual may envy the lower-class man's *machismo* or its equivalent as much as the latter envies the former's general prestige. In this respect, unlike that concerning income, the poor young man may be the rich young man's equal.

We are suggesting here that lower-class young people, who perceive that their fathers are already old by the time they reach their late fifties, may view things this way. Experiences in the family may suggest the acceleration of life, and the logical conclusion, perhaps never explicit, may be that one should maximize one's enjoyments in youth. The labeling of purchases as "extravagant" or "prudent," the depreciation of "immediate gratification," and the encouragement of "deferred gratification" are parts of a culture which is based on common middle-class experiences with a highly age-patterned income and prestige curve. If lower-class subcultures, irrespective of ethnicity, are based on common experiences with a linear income and prestige curve, they may applaud the decision to spend on comforts earlier in the life cycle. They may also seek more general gratification in the present rather than wait for a probably *less* propitious time. To be sure, in the present social and political climate, lower-class youth following such reasons may be suffering from a cultural lag. Certainly an important factor in the success of policies encouraging ghetto youth is whether such cultural lag exists, and how lower-class and especially minority youth can recognize the new opportunities opening up and respond to them. "To underestimate the extent of these opportunities would mean that some would be lost; to overestimate them would, in the present political climate, be a self-fulfilling prophecy."

This excurcus on age expectations is designed to supplement whatever insight into achievement may be gained from the analysis of changes in the Mexican-American family. The attempt to attribute achievement too narrowly to subcultural values and norms—family or other—may run the risk of producing yet another puzzle. On many items, for example, we find Mexican-American respondents to be astonishingly close to "acculturation." But Mexican Americans are not only carriers of an ethnic tradition. Large numbers share the situation of the urban lower-class minority-group members in the United States. The exaggeration of one dimension of their position should not lead to the neglect of the other.

THE CHICANO RENAISSANCE

Philip D. Ortego

In *Understanding Media*, Marshall McLuhan explains that "the medium is the message . . . that the personal and social consequences of any medium—that is, of any extension of ourselves—result from the new scale that is introduced into our affairs by each extension of ourselves." [1] Applying McLuhan's proposition to the Chicano movement, for

Copyright 1971 by Family Service Association of America. Reprinted by permission from *Social Casework*, Vol. 52, May 1971. This article also appears in *La Causa Chicana: The Movement for Justice* (New York: Family Services Association of America, 1972).
[1] Marshall McLuhan, *Understanding Media: The Extensions of Man*, 2d ed. (New York: New American Library, 1964), p. 23.

example, we can see that the Chicano movement is the medium for extending ourselves (Chicanos) in American society, and, as such, the Chicano movement becomes the message. Such slogans as *Ya Basta, Venceremos*, and *Chicano Power* are only elements of the total message; they are simply part of the new scale introduced into Chicano affairs by each of our individual thrusts toward greater participation in American society. Indeed, the personal and social consequences of our extensions into American society have been the result of a new scale of values and aspirations that we have created with each extension of ourselves.

In particular, these extensions appeared first in the form of beneficial societies, then social clubs, and, after World War II, as political organizations. Our extension into the arts—generically including painting, sculpture, architecture, music, dance, literature, drama, and film—is a more recent phenomenon, although there were, of course, Mexican-American artists at various times since 1848.

These artists, however, did not reflect any significant thrust by Mexican Americans into artistic endeavors. They represented only individual successes in penetrating the artistic iron curtain because the animosities engendered by the Mexican-American War created Anglo-American resistance to Mexican-American participation in most spheres of American life except at the lower rungs of the societal ladder. Consequently, Mexican Americans became the backbone of such American enterprises as the cattle industry, the railroad, the cotton industry of the Southwest, mining, and, of course, the fruit and produce industry. The Mexican-American way of life paralleled the black-American way of life, although for the former there was no Emancipation Proclamation.

Nevertheless, the Mexican American was nurtured and sustained in spirit and soul by his music, dance, *cuentos* (folktales), and remembrance of things past—all contributing to the maintenance and development of Mexican-American folk music, folk art, and folklore. Unlike other peoples of the United States—except groups with English-speaking backgrounds, such as the Irish, Scotch, and English—Mexican Americans were reinforced continually in their language, culture, and heritage by their very proximity to Mexico and the almost uninterrupted flow of immigration (legal and otherwise) from Mexico.

There are no accurate or reliable population figures from 1848 to 1900, but the census reports for those years indicate a steady and consistent growth of Americans of Mexican descent. Recorded Mexican immigration from 1900 to the present indicates that, because there was no quota on Mexican immigration until 1965, well over one million Mexicans have come to the United States. The actual figure may be closer to one and one-half million if other means of entry into the United States employed by Mexican nationals are considered. It is clear from these statistics and from the fact that now more than ten million Mexican Americans are living in this country that Mexican Americans are essentially a native group, most of whom were born in the United States.

Mexican Americans have always been "Americans" in the true sense of the word because they were very much a part of the landscape when the Anglo Americans arrived in the Southwest. Despite their early settlement and their large numbers, Mexican Americans have been the most shamefully neglected minority in the United States. In the Southwest, where approximately seven of the ten million live, they subsist on levels of survival far below the national norms. The reason for this low subsistence level, many Mexican Americans argue, is that they are victims of the Treaty of Guadalupe Hidalgo—a treaty that identified those who came with the conquered lands of the Southwest as defeated people. Those who came afterwards in the great migrations of the first three decades of the twentieth century have been equally victimized by stereotypes engendered by the Mexican-American War.

In recent years there has been an increasing social and political consciousness, leading to demands for reformation of the socioeconomic structure that has kept Mexican Americans subordinated these many years. With this increasing social and political consciousness has come the awareness of their artistic and literary heritage. Throughout the Southwest the sleeping Mexican-American giant has begun to flex his dormant muscles.

Redefining American Literature

The decade of the 1970s promises to be one in which this awakening, this renaissance, will be manifested by a growing desire of Mexican Americans not only to attain status in sociopolitical and economic areas but to seek a more substantial literary identity in the ever-widening mainstream of American literature. In the 1970s Mexican-American writers, scholars, and teachers will attempt to redefine American literature as a fabric woven not exclusively on the Atlantic frontier by the descendants of New England Puritans and southern Cavaliers, but as one woven also in the American Southwest with marvelous Hispanic threads that extend not only to the literary heritage of the European continent but also to the very heart of the Mediterranean world.

Like the British roots in the new American soil, the Hispanic roots have yielded a vigorous and dynamic body of literature that, unfortunately for us, has been studied historically as part of a foreign contribution rather than as part and parcel of our American heritage. Moreover, we seldom learn about the extent to which the Hispanic literacy tradition has influenced American literature. The works dealing with the southern and southwestern parts of the United States, therefore, have become the neglected aspect of the American experience; the implication is that such works are not properly within the traditional definition of American literature because they were not written in English.

Language, however, is hardly a logical reason for not recognizing non-

English material as American literature, although it was written in the United States—as in the case of Isaac Bashevis Singer—or what has become the United States—as in the case of the chronicles of the South and Southwest by the Spanish and their progeny. In the pluralistic cultural and linguistic context of contemporary America, we can no longer consent to the suggestions of American literary historians that American literature properly begins with the arrival of British colonials in America.

American literature actually begins with the formation of the United States as a political entity. Thus, the literary period from the founding of the first permanent British settlement at Jamestown, Virginia, in 1607, to the formation of the American union represents only the British period of American literature. So, too, the literary period from the first permanent Spanish settlement at Saint Augustine, Florida, in 1565, to the dates of acquisition of these Spanish and Mexican lands by the United States should, in fact, represent the Hispanic period of American literature. More appropriately, the British and Spanish periods should both be listed under the rubric "Colonial American Literature." The Mexican period of the Southwest should simply be labeled "The Mexican Period."

Loss of a Literary Birthright

The neglect of the Spanish and Mexican literature of the Southwest has produced unfortunate literary consequences for Mexican Americans because they have come to see themselves and their Mexican kinsmen portrayed in our national literature by means of racial clichés and distorted caricatures. Like other minority groups, Mexican Americans were and continue to be inaccurately and superficially represented in literature, movies, television, and other mass media. This situation sometimes has been caused by prejudice, but it has also been caused by those well-meaning romanticists who have seriously distorted the image of the Mexican American for the sake of their art.

Mexican Americans have been characterized at both ends of the spectrum of human behavior (seldom in the middle) as untrustworthy, villainous, ruthless, tequila-drinking, and philandering *machos* or else as courteous, devout, and fatalistic peasants who are to be treated more as pets than as people. More often than not Mexican Americans have been cast either as bandits or as lovable rogues; as hot-blooded, sexually animated creatures or as passive, humble servants. The pejorations and generalizations are to be deplored, and Mexican Americans today are beginning to rise up against the perpetuation of such racial clichés.

Whatever the reason for deliberately or inadvertently neglecting the Hispanic aspect of American literature, the fact remains that not only have Mexican Americans been deprived of their literary birthright but all other Americans have been deprived of an important part of a literary heritage that is also rightfully theirs. Mexican Americans actually have a rich literacy heritage. That they have been kept from it bespeaks a shameful and tragic oppression of a people whose origins antedate the establishment of Jamestown by well over a century (and even more, considering their Indian ancestry). Moreover, the shame and tragedy are compounded when Mexican-American youngsters learn about their Puritan forebears but not about their Hispanic forebears about whom they have as much right—if not more—to be proud.

Heretofore, Mexican Americans have been a marginal people in a sort of no man's land, caught between the polarizing forces of their cultural-linguistic Indo-Hispanic heritage and their political-linguistic American context. They have become frustrated and alienated by the struggle between the system that seeks to refashion them in its own image and the knowledge of who and what they really are. As a result, this cultural conflict has debilitated many Mexican Americans.

Mexican-American youngsters are taught about the cruelty of their Spanish forebears and the savagery of their Mexican-Indian forebears; they have been taught about the Spanish greed for gold, of the infamous Spanish inquisition, of Aztec human sacrifices, of Mexican bandits, and of the massacre at the Alamo. They seldom, if ever, learn of the other men at the Alamo, their Mexican forebears—unknown and unsung in American history—who were killed fighting on the Texas side. American children probably have never heard of such men as Juan Abamillo, Juan Badillo, Carlos Espalier, Gegorio Esparza, Antonio Fuentes, José Maria Guerrero, Toribio Losoya, Andres Nava, and other Texas Mexicans at the Alamo.

In order to be fully comprehended, the ethnic phenomenon of Mexican Americans since World War II must be viewed in the more personal context of their literature. What we have seen instead has been the myriad educational, sociopolitical, and socioeconomic accounts by Anglo investigators and researchers who have pursued the phenomenological chimeras of the queer, the curious, and the quaint. To understand the significance of human movements, we must assess the evidence from the arts. There is little doubt that the contributions to the American experience by Mexican Americans and their forebears have yet to be understood and measured.

In the Southwest the relationship between Mexican Americans and Anglo Americans is similar to that of a legally adopted child and adoptive parents. The analogy describes the circumstances of Spanish-speaking peoples in all the Hispanic territories acquired by the United States. To pursue the analogy to its proper conclusion, we must ask whether, in trying to educate the child about his proper past, we talk about the heritage of the adoptive parents or the *actual* heritage of the adopted child? To indoctrinate the child with the heritage of his new parents as if it were his own is to perpetrate the grossest kind of fraud at the expense of the child.

Information about the literary accomplishments of Mexican Americans during the period from the end of the Mexican-American War to the turn of the century, for example, has been negligible. As Américo Paredes has pointed out, "With few exceptions, documents available for study of the region are in English, being for the most part reports made by officials who were, to put it mildly, prejudiced against the people they were trying to pacify." [2]

American writers have tended to minimize the literary achievements of Mexican Americans in the Southwest for reasons ranging from jingoism to ignorance. It should be noted, however, that no sooner had the Spanish established their hold on Mexico than they started a printing press in Mexico City in 1529, more than a century earlier than any established in the British colonies of North America. Indeed, there was a substantial Spanish-reading public in New Spain and Mexico, including the North Mexican states, until the lands were ceded to the United States in 1848. Spanish literature was read and written in both the Spanish peninsula and in the New World. Such Spanish playwrights as Pedro Calderón de la Barca and Lope de Vega extended their literary influence to Spanish America just as the Mexican-born playwright Juan Ruiz de Alarcón extended his literary influence to Spain.

Oral Transmission of Heritage

In the Southwest the people who had come with the land continued to tell and retell the tales that their forebears had brought from the Old World and from Mexico. These folk-tales had been passed on from generation to generation until they became a decidedly strong oral tradition. Mexican Americans were therefore not "absorbed" into the American "culture" without a literary past and heritage of their own, as so many Americans believe.

To be sure, much of what they knew about that literary heritage had been acquired orally. Folk drama, for example, was immensely popular among the Mexican Americans, who continued to stage the old plays in much the same fashion as the early English folk dramatists had staged their plays in town squares, churches, or courtyards. In the Mexican Southwest, liturgical pastorals depicting the creation and fall of man and of Christ's resurrection evolved into "cycle plays" similar to those of Spain and England. Like the developing culture on the Atlantic frontier, the Southwest brought forth a new literature by New World men.

By the time of the Mexican-American War, the Mexican Southwest had been thoroughly nurtured on drama, poetry, and folktales of a literary tradition of several hundred years. Mexicans who became Americans continued the Indo-Hispanic literary tradition not only by

[2] Américo Paredes, Folklore and History, in *Singers and Storytellers*, ed. Mody C. Boatright, Wilson M. Hudson, and Allen Maxwell (Dallas: Southern Methodist University Press, 1961), pp. 162–63.

preserving the old literary materials but also by creating new ones in the superimposed American political ambiance. To cite only one sphere of literary activity, by 1860 there were a number of Mexican Americans engaged in newspaper work. In New Mexico alone, ten out of eighty journalists of the period were Mexican Americans because most Anglo-American papers published bilingual editions for the vast numbers of Spanish readers in the Southwest. Moreover, Mexican Americans were employed to translate the English-language news into Spanish.

Disparaging Images of Mexican Americans

Nevertheless, Mexican Americans were poorly regarded by the vast majority of Anglo Americans who came in contact with them, and many of the literary portraits of Mexican Americans by Anglo-American writers exerted undue influence on generations of Americans down to our own time. The disparaging images of Mexican Americans were drawn by such American writers as Richard Henry Dana, who, in *Two Years Before the Mast*, described Mexican Americans as "an idle, thriftless people" who could "make nothing for themselves." [3] In 1852 Colonel John Monroe reported to Washington:

> The New Mexicans are thoroughly debased and totally incapable of self-government, and there is no latent quality about them that can ever make them respectable. They have more Indian blood than Spanish, and in some respects are below the Pueblo Indians, for they are not as honest or as industrious. [4]

Four years later W. W. H. Davis, United States Attorney for the Territory of New Mexico, writing of his experiences with Mexican Americans said that "they possess the cunning and deceit of the Indian, the politeness and the spirit of revenge of the Spaniard, and the imaginative temperament and fiery impulses of the Moor." He described them as smart and quick but lacking the "stability and character and soundness of intellect that give such vast superiority to the Anglo-Saxon race over every other people." He ascribed to them the "cruelty, bigotry, and superstition" of the Spaniard, "a marked characteristic from earliest times." Moreover, he saw these traits as "constitutional and innate in the race." In a moment of kindness, however, Davis suggested that the fault probably lay with their "spiritual teachers," the Spaniards, who never taught them "that beautiful doctrine which teaches us to love our neighbors as ourselves." [5]

[3] Richard Henry Dana, *Two Years Before the Mast* (New York: Bantam Books, 1959), p. 59.
[4] U.S., Congress, *Congressional Globe*, 32d Cong., 2d sess., January 10, 1853, Appendix, p. 104.
[5] W. W. H. Davis, *El Gringo: Or, New Mexico and Her People* (New York: Harper & Brothers, 1857), pp. 85–86.

In 1868 the *Overland Monthly* published an article by William V. Wells, "The French in Mexico," in which he wrote that "in the open field, a charge of disciplined troops usually sufficed to put to flight the collection of frowzy-headed mestizos, leperos, mulattoes, Indians, Samboes, and other mongrels now, as in the time of our own war with them, composing a Mexican Army." [6] In our time Walter Prescott Webb characterizes the Mexicans as possessing "a cruel streak" that he believes was inherited partly from the Spanish of the Inquisition and partly from their Indian forebears. Webb asserts:

> On the whole, the Mexican warrior . . . was inferior to the Comanche and wholly unequal to Texans. The whine of the leaden slugs stirred in him an irresistable impulse to travel with, rather than against, the music. He won more victories over the Texans partly by parley than by force of arms. For making promises and for breaking them he had no peer. [7]

Even John Steinbeck in *Tortilla Flat* portrayed Mexican Americans as lovable carousers claiming Spanish blood in the face of their color, "like that of a well-browned meerschaum pipe." [8]

That the defenders of the besieged Alamo were flying the Mexican flag of 1824, not the Texas flag, had been forgotten by the time of the Civil War. Forgotten too is the great heroic effort of Mexican Americans in the Union Army during the Civil War. In Texas, the fact that José Antonio Navarro's "Memoirs" are part of Mexican-American literature has been obscured by time and ethnic myopia. [9] Most Americans probably are unaware that Navarro, a Mexican American, was a member of the first Texas State Senate or that his son Angel III was graduated from Harvard in 1849. In the commemoration of the Texas heroes we hear little about Lorenzo de Zavala, another Mexican American, who served as the first vice-president (ad interim) of the Texas Republic. Instead we hear about the "outrages" of Juan Cortina and his revolt of 1859, despite the fact that Cortina was actually a Union-inspired guerrilla fighting both the Texas Confederates and the French Mexicans.

Neglected Writers

There were many Mexican American writers in the last half of the nineteenth century, but they have remained as neglected as the people they represent. In New Mexico, for example, Donaciano Vigil, editor of the newspaper *Verdad*, compiled a *History of New Mexico to 1851;* [10]

---

[6] William V. Wells, The French in Mexico, *The Overland Monthly*, 1:232 (September 1868).

[7] Walter Prescott Webb, *The Texas Rangers: A Century of Frontier Defense* (Austin: University of Texas Press, 1965), p. 14.

[8] John Steinbeck, *Tortilla Flat* (New York: Bantam Books, 1965), p. 2.

[9] Jose Antonio Navarro, Memoirs, Archives Division of the Texas State Library.

[10] Donaciano Vigil, *History of New Mexico to 1851*, New Mexico State Archives, Santa Fe, New Mex.

and in 1859 Miguel Antonio Otero wrote *The Indian Depredations in the Territory of New Mexico.*[11] In California, Juan Bautista Alvarado completed a "History of California." [12] In northern California, Mariano Guadalupe Vallejo wrote prolifically on a number of topics, composing sonnets for his children and for special occasions. He culminated his literary activities with a five-volume "History of California" that Herbert E. Bancroft hailed as standing without rival among its predecessors in thoroughness and interest.[13] Many Mexican Americans kept diaries (a major type of Hispanic literature) and wrote letters to each other about their day-to-day activities. These letters—most of them unpublished— reveal as much about the Mexican-American experience as the letters of John Winthrop and Roger Williams reveal about the Puritan experience in America.

Historical Background

Quest for Statehood

What most characterized the post-Civil War period in the Southwest was the quest for statehood by the territories of Colorado, Utah, Oklahoma, Nevada, Arizona, and New Mexico. The admission of Texas into the Union had of course precipitated the Mexican-American War, but the *fact* of statehood allowed Texas a measure of "progress" that was not realized in the other territories until later in the nineteenth and twentieth centuries. California became a state in 1850; Colorado, in 1876; Utah, in 1896; and Oklahoma, in 1907. Arizona and New Mexico, however, did not become states until 1912. The delay has been attributed to the fact that the preponderance of Mexican Americans made statehood unpalatable to the rest of the nation.

Although Mexican Americans had proved their loyalty to the United States in both the Civil War and the Spanish-American War (more than half of the Rough Riders in Cuba were Mexican Americans), ethnic hostilities toward Mexican Americans did not lessen. For example, Senator Albert J. Beveridge of Indiana, an outright anti-Hispano, led the resistance against statehood for Arizona and New Mexico on the grounds that Mexican Americans were unaspiring, easily influenced, and totally ignorant of American ways and mores and that, although fifty years had passed since the Mexican-American War, Mexican Americans were still aliens in the United States, most of them having made no effort to learn English.[14] According to Beveridge, such linguistic resis-

---

[11] Miguel Antonio Otero, *The Indian Depredations in the Territory of New Mexico*, Library of Congress, Washington, D.C.

[12] Juan Bautisa Alverado, *Historia de California*, 1876, Bancroft Library, Berkeley, Calif.

[13] Mariano Guadalupe Vallejo, *Recuerdos historicos y personales tocante a la Alta California: historia political del pais, 1769–1849,* 1875. Translated as *History of California*, by Earl R. Hewitt, Bancroft Library, Berkeley, Calif.

[14] In 1902 Beveridge filed a majority report for his committee investigating statehood for New Mexico and Arizona. The report objected to statehood.

tance was treasonous, to say the least, despite the fact that for part of the first decade of the twentieth century Miguel Antonia Otero, a Mexican American, was governor of the Territory of New Mexico (1897–1906), having been appointed by President McKinley and then reconfirmed by President Roosevelt after the assassination of McKinley in 1901.

Mexican Americans strove to become part of the United States in their own way, but they were regarded with disdain by a sizable segment of the Anglo-American population of the Southwest. Ironically, although Mexican Americans were being rejected by American society, the turn of the century saw the creation of "Spanish heritage and landmark" societies that vigorously espoused the restoration of "Spanish" missions in the Southwest. Mexican Americans were the butt of injustice after injustice while their lands, goods, properties, and persons were craftily secured by squatters, unscrupulous lawyers, and con artists who shamelessly bilked them because of their language handicap. Despite the fact that Mexican Americans constituted the majority of the population in the Southwest at first, they were quickly eased down the social rung with the increase of Anglo Americans in the area. By 1870 Mexican Americans ceased to be the majority in California. They had become a minority very early in Texas, although in New Mexico they held on until after the turn of the century. Nonetheless, Mexican Americans were slowly but surely reduced to conditions of peonage approximating the level of servitude into which the blacks had been forced.

Rags-to-Riches Mystique

Against this background emerged the rags-to-riches mystique that was to influence American life well into the twentieth century. Horatio Alger's characters, Tattered Tom, Ragged Dick, and Phil the Fiddler, became the American standard for success through hard work. A Mexican American's "wealth," however, was judged as the product of connivance rather than of fortitude and application. For instance, when the Mexican-American Lugo family of southern California lost its wealth in 1865, Benjamin Hayes quickly suggested that the finger of Providence was responsible for the decay of the Mexican Americans.[15]

Not even Mariano Vallejo's "true history of California," which was meant to show Anglo Americans that Mexican Americans were not as they were caricatured in conversation and literature, could counteract the firmly lodged prejudices of Anglo Americans toward Mexican Americans.[16] Perhaps Leonard Pitt best summarizes the situation of Mexican Americans at the end of the nineteenth century when he writes,

[15] Benjamin D. Hayes, *Pioneer Notes . . . 1849–1875*, ed. Marjorie Tisdale Walcott (Los Angeles: Marjorie Tisdale Walcott, 1929), p. 280.

[16] In 1875 Vallejo wrote to his son, Platon, that he was completing his "true history of California" to serve as a guide for posterity. See Nadie Brown Emparan, *The Vallejos of California* (San Francisco: Gleeson Library Associates, University of San Francisco, 1968), p. 129.

"By emphasizing injustice, violence, and broken promises in their memoirs, the Californians [Mexican Americans] came closer to a meaningful truth than the Yankees who spoke of Providence." [17]

Indeed, the providence of the Yankee was fraught with peril for the Mexican Americans, despite the fact that the Yankees had guaranteed them full citizenship and had agreed to regard them as equals rather than as conquered people. The Yankee rationalization for broken promises that Vallejo bemoaned was simply that "progress has its price" or that the Mexican Americans were "culturally unsuited to the new order" or else that the Mexican Americans had "brought it on themselves." The American pretense at ethical behavior appears all the more reprehensible because of blatant bigotry.

By 1900 Anglo Americans in the Southwest had so taken over the Mexican Southwest that what had once been Mexican and Spanish had been neatly appropriated and transformed into an American "tradition." Mexican water and mining laws were retained in toto by Anglo-American settlers and governments. Spanish words were transformed into English equivalents. *La riata* became *lariat; juzgado* became *hoosegow; calabozo* became *calaboose; chiapas* became *chaps*, and so forth. The American *cowboy* became simply an altered reflection of the Mexican *vaquero*, saddle, ten-gallon hat, and all. The language of America had absorbed a considerable number of expressions, but Mexican Americans themselves were kept at arms-length as "outsiders," to be forgotten for another fifty years.

Resistance to Anglo Aggression

It would, however, be an egregious error to conclude that Mexican Americans were passive in defending themselves against Anglo-American "aggressions." In 1883, for example, Mexican-American agricultral workers went on strike for better wages and working conditions in the Panhandle; in 1903, Mexican-American sugar beet workers went on strike for similar reasons in Ventura, California.

To counter their exclusion from Anglo-American schools, many Mexican Americans formed private and parochial schools, such as El Colegio Altamiro, founded in Texas in 1897. To overcome rural depredations, Mexican Americans in New Mexico formed the Knights of Labor in 1890, a mutual assistance and protective organization. Some Mexican-American organizations, such as Los Gorras Blancos (the White Caps) of New Mexico, were called marauders by Anglo Americans, but their purpose was primarily to protect themselves from such violent repressions as that which in 1904 took the life of Colonel Francisco J. Chaves, a surgeon and Civil War veteran who had become a Mexican-American spokesman, leader, and territorial superintendent of public instruction.

[17] Leonard Pitt, *The Decline of the Californios: A Social History of the Spanish-Speaking Californians, 1846–1890* (Berkeley and Los Angeles: University of California Press, 1970), p. 283.

Migration from Mexico

As has already been noted, La Raza in the United States was to be culturally and linguistically renourished as no other group—save English-speaking—had been. In the decades between 1880 and 1940, almost three-quarters of one million Mexicans officially migrated to the United States. Mexican migration to the United States was one of the truly major mass movements of people in the Western Hemisphere. The phenomenon reflects "the failure of roots," as Ernesto Galaza explains.[18]

At the same time, however, Mexican migration to the United States reflects the growth of technology in North America. From 1880 to 1910, for instance, President Porfirio Díaz sped the construction of 15,000 miles of railroad lines linking the mineral wealth of Mexico to American smelters just north of the border. Mexicans not only worked the rails but were caught by the mystique of something better at the end of the tracks. Unquestionably the railroad provided the best escape for Mexicans in their exodus from war-torn Mexico. "Al norte!" was frequently the best alternative for Mexican refugees. Although the "depopulation" of Mexico was of great concern to the Liberal Party of Mexico, which had effectively brought Porfirismo's administration to an end and had promised to repatriate Mexicans in *el destierro*, the political and socioeconomic situation worsened in Mexico, thereby swelling instead of diminishing the ranks of fleeing Mexicans.

Travel either way across the Mexican-American border was relatively easy until the 1920s. It was not until 1924 that the Border Patrol was established to curb the illegal entry of Mexicans into the United States. Devoid of really natural barriers, the Mexican-American border is no more than a line staked out by markers from the Pacific to El Paso, or a barbed wire fence in places, or, during certain seasons, an almost dry river bed from El Paso to the Gulf of Mexico supporting the ubiquitous undergrowth of chapparal and mesquite. Mexicans settled easily in the Southwest, for, unlike European immigrants, Mexicans were really migrating to an area similar to that from which they came and that was peopled by their kinsmen. Indeed, there was *mucha raza en el norte*.

Significance of the Renaissance

Perhaps the significance of the Chicano Renaissance lies in the identification of Chicanos with their Indian past. It matters not what etymologies are ascribed to the word "Chicano"; the distinction is not in whether the word is a denigration but in that it has been consciously and deliberately chosen over all other words to identify Mexican Americans who regard themselves as Montezuma's children. They have thus cast off the sometimes meretricious identification with the Spanish templar tradition

---

[18] Ernesto Galarza, *Merchants of Labor: The Mexican Bracero Story* (Santa Barbara, Calif.: McNally & Lofton, 1964), p. 17.

foisted on them by Anglo-American society because of its preference for things European. To reinforce their identification with their Indian past, Chicano writers have appropriated for their literary symbols Aztec and Mayan figures, including the great Aztec calendar stone.

Significantly, a literature draws from the history and myths of its people's past. Those of Mexican-Indian ancestry are well aware of the extent to which the myths and history of their Indian past are operating in the Mexican-American ethos. Understandably, it is to the Mexican-Indian past that the Chicano Renaissance has turned for its most meaningful literary symbols and metaphors. The selection of Quinto Sol as the name of a publishing group is itself a manifestation of the Chicano writers' deliberate identification with their Indian past, for the Aztecs were the people of the Fifth Sun (*Quinto Sol*). According to their mythology, there had been four previous epochs, each governed by a sun. The first epoch ended with the inhabitants of earth devoured by ocelots; the second world and sun were destroyed by wind; the third, by a rain of fire; and the fourth, by water. According to the Aztecs, the sun and world in which they lived—the fifth sun—was destined to perish as a result of earthquakes and famine and terror.

Chicano Publications

Mexican Americans have been struggling within the predominantly Anglo-American culture of the United States for over 122 years. Although Mexican Americans have been writing all that time, the realization of Mexican-American literature as the *élan vital* in the life-styles of the people themselves has happened only within recent years. In the fall of 1967, a cohort of Mexican-American writers at Berkeley, California, formed Quinto Sol Publications in a tiny office over a candy store. Their purpose was "to provide a forum for Mexican American self definition and expression on . . . issues of relevance to Mexican Americans in American society today." [19]

Alternatives is the key word in what has since blossomed into the Chicano Renaissance. Mexican Americans had been completely disenchanted with the plethora of writings about them, writings that depicted them in a variety of literary contexts resorting to the most blatant stereotypes and racial clichés, all of them by "intellectual mercenaries" as the Quinto Sol group called them in the first issue of their literary quarterly magazine, *El Grito: A Journal of Contemporary Mexican American Thought*.[20] The promise of *El Grito* was that it would be the forum for Mexican Americans to articulate their own sense of identity. Even more important, the printed word was seen as a very important medium in the Chicano struggle for equality.

To compound the problem, Mexican Americans have not only been deprived of their literary birthright but they have effectively been kept

[19] Editorial, *El Grito* 1:4 (Fall 1967).
[20] Ibid.

from articulating their experiences in American literary outlets. In the last twenty years, for example, few Mexican Americans have published in the "leading" American literary quarterlies. In 1947 Mario Suarez published two sketches entitled "El Hoyo" and "El Señor" in the *Arizona Quarterly*, a literary journal that published the fiction of such other Mexican-American writers as Arnulfo D. Trejo and Amado Jesús Muro and the prose works of such Mexican-American scholars as Rafael Jesús Gonzalez.

Some Mexican-American writers had managed to find literary outlets, but at the expense of their art as Mexican Americans. Understandably, the greatest outpouring of Mexican-American writing since 1900 has been in prose, all of it essential in laying the foundation for what was to erupt as the Chicano Renaissance in the last years of the 1960s. The prose (much of it cast as polemics and rhetoric) helped to refashion first their psychological image and then their literary image. Mexican-American writers who sought to break the long-standing and readily accepted stereotypes about Mexican Americans in print found little or no favor with magazine editors because the images of the "Mexican" in American literature were hard to put aside.

As recently as 1968 an editor of a high school multiethnic text who was looking for material on Mexican Americans rejected a "nonfolk story" by this writer and suggested that the ninth-year reader in which J. Frank Dobie's popular "Squaw Man" appeared would provide an idea of the kind of material he was seeking for the reader. Of course, what he really wanted was the "queer," the "curious," and the "quaint" kind of "folksy" stories most editors have come to expect about Mexican Americans.

At another time, this writer suggested to the editor of a prestigious midwest literary quarterly the idea of publishing an issue on Mexican-American literature because he had just devoted an issue to American-Indian literature. The response betrayed the editor's lack of knowledge about Mexican Americans and their literary achievements, for he indicated he had heard that Quinto Sol Publications had published an anthology of Mexican-American writing but that he had not seen it. Because this writer had indicated he was working on an anthology also, the editor wondered if there would be anything of special significance left over for a special issue with two anthologies available.

Until the 1960s, fiction, such as Floyd Salas's *Tattoo the Wicked Cross* and John Rechy's *City of Night*, was rare.[21] Both authors are Mexican-American writers who have penetrated the literary iron curtain not as ethnic writers but just as writers. This success simply attests to the fact that, as black writers who have written nonblack works, Mexican-American writers are capable of writing non-Mexican-American works. Like the market for black works, the market for Mexican-American works was limited to those who wrote what most editors expected; and

---

[21] Floyd Salas, *Tattoo the Wicked Cross* (New York: Grove Press, 1967); and John Rechy, *City of Night* (New York: Grove Press, 1963).

what most editors had come to expect was the image of the Mexican American as an indolent, passive, humble servant who lived for *fiestas* and *mañana*. Chicano writers, however, are no longer struggling to penetrate the literary iron curtain; they have come to realize that the only viable outlets for their works are those that they create for themselves. In this way was born the Chicano Renaissance and hundreds of literary outlets, from mimeographed magazines to such slick publications as *El Grito* and the Los Angeles-based *Con Safos*.[22]

El Grito has become to the Chicano Renaissance what *Partisan Review*, for example, became to the New Criticism. It has published a variety of fiction, poetry, and prose appealing to the wider Mexican-American community. Principally, however, it has sought to show the patent falsity of Anglo-American works that purport to "explain" the Mexican American in terms of debilitating profiles and criteria. From the beginning, Octavio Romano and Nick Vaca, founders and editors of *El Grito*, have attempted to rearticulate the identity of Mexican Americans from the perspective of Mexican Americans. They have taken American social scientists, in particular, to task for perpetrating false images of Mexican-American culture. In addition, *El Grito* has provided an outlet for emerging Mexican-American writers.

Perhaps *Con Safos* best articulates Chicano life in the barrio. (Most Mexican Americans are still in the barrios or have come from them.) *Con Safos* has a slick news magazine format, and, like *El Grito*, runs first-rate exposé pieces. Although *Con Safos* is more pictorial, *El Grito* regularly has provided space for portfolios of Mexican-American artists. Both magazines are essentially experimental in approach; they publish what reflects the Chicano community however it may be written—in Spanish or English or both—and rely heavily on striking covers employing Mexican-Indian motifs. There is no question of which magazine better articulates the Chicano experience, for both magazines articulate the essential problems of Chicanos everywhere.

Other Chicano magazines are springing up as Chicanos become increasingly aware of the power of the pen and the persuasiveness of print. For several years Francisca Flores, a fiery and undaunted Chicana from Los Angeles, published *Carta Editorial* by herself and at her own expense, commenting on the ills besieging Mexican Americans. What the Anglo-dominated mass media failed to cover in the Chicano community, Francisca Flores reported fearlessly in her small four-page newsletter. To be properly informed on what was happening in Mexican-American affairs, one had to read *Carta Editorial*. In 1970, *Carta Editorial* was absorbed into *Regeneración*, still edited by Francisca Flores but with a news magazine appearance and an expanded core of commentators and contributors.[23] What makes the venture of *Regeneración* significant is

---

[22] *Con Safos*, P.O. Box 31085, Los Angeles, Calif. (Published irregularly as sufficient material becomes available for an issue.)

[23] *Regeneración*, P.O. Box 54624, T.A., Los Angeles, Calif. (Published monthly.)

that the "new" magazine is really a revival of the journal that Ricardo Flores Magon, the Mexican exile, published in the United States while keeping clear of Porfirio Díaz's secret police. Magon started out by publishing *Liberación* in Mexico until he was forced to flee Díaz's wrath.

In the United States, Magon found refuge first in the Mexican-American community of San Antonio, Texas, and then in St. Louis, Missouri, where he founded *Regeneración*. Later, forced to leave St. Louis, he made his way to Los Angeles, where he continued his attack on Porfirismo. He was finally taken into custody by American federal agents on the charge of having violated American neutrality laws. He was imprisoned at San Quentin, where his health failed and where he died. There is no doubt that *Regeneración* was instrumental in the downfall of Díaz.

There has been a special literary relationship between Mexicans and Mexican Americans, for when Mexican intellectuals and writers have fled from Mexico, they invariably have come to the United States and to Mexican-American communities. Many successful and abortive plans involving Mexico have been hatched in Mexican-American homes and communities. Benito Juarez's successful recapture of Mexico from the French was made possible by Mexican-American assistance in the form of money and material—and sometimes men. Porfirio Díaz himself launched his political career from Texas. During the Mexican Revolution of the twentieth century the Mexican-American Southwest provided asylum for many revolutionaries. It is little wonder that the heroes of the Chicano movement are Pancho Villa and Emiliano Zapata and that the Mexican revolutionary writers, Mariano Azuela, José Vasconcellos, and Martin Guzman, are read voraciously by Mexican Americans seeking their own liberation. No contemporary Mexican writers have influenced the Chicano movement so much as has Octavio Paz and his *Labyrinth of Solitude*, a work that goes far in exploring the Mexican mind and thought, not in its Hispanic origins so much but in relation to the Indian origins of Mexico.[24]

The Chicano Theater

El Teatro Campesino, the Chicano migrant theater that grew out of the *Huelga* at Delano in 1965, has transformed the ancient Aztec myths for the *campesino* stage to Chicano relevancy. In one magnificent *acto* entitled "Bernabe," the Chicano link to the ancient Indian heritage is strengthened and articulated masterfully. This message is being carried everywhere in the United States (and abroad) by El Teatro Campesino in its various annual tours. Luis Valdez, director of the company, describes Chicano theater as "beautiful, *rasquachi*, human, cosmic, broad, deep, tragic, comic, as the life of *La Raza* itself." [25] The consequence of

[24] Octavio Paz, *Labyrinth of Solitude* (New York: Grove Press, 1961).
[25] Luis Valdez, Notes on Chicano Theater, *El Teatro* (Official newspaper of El Teatro Campesino, published by El Centro Campesino Cultural, P.O. Box 2302, Fresno, Calif.), p. 4.

El Teatro Campesino has been the creation of similar theatrical companies elsewhere, including universities with as few as a dozen Chicano students.

The distinctive character of Chicano theater lies in its seeming "artlessness." There is no attempt to create setting or atmosphere or character. Valdez, for example, employs *calavera* (skull) masks to create the illusion of temporality. All the skull masks are identical. Only the actions, dress, and voices of the actors differentiate them as characters. The end result is a kind of stylized theater resembling the Japanese Kabuki theater or the Greek mask plays.

In 1969, El Teatro Campesino filmed Rodolfo "Corky" González's stirring epic poem, "I Am Joaquín." Although the poem created considerable impact on the Chicano community, the film version has elevated it to a new dimension. Few, if any, Chicanos who view it are left unstirred because González has skillfully woven myth and memory and desire into a masterwork of poetry. Joaquín becomes the enduring spirit of the Chicano soul and spirit buffeted by alien winds in the country of his forebears where he walks as if he were a stranger. Joaquín's final words are not an empty incantation but a promise that he will endure.[26]

Chicano Poetry

The heart of Chicano poetry lies in the imperative cry of Joaquín. The works of such other Mexican-American poets as Luis Omar Salinas, Abelardo Delgado, Miguel Ponce, and José Montoya reflect the existential problems of survival that Chicanos face day in and day out. There is anguish and frustration in the vision of Chicano poets, but there is also determination bred from the knowledge of who they are. In "Aztec Angel," for example, Salinas glorifies the beauty of the Aztec mother and child, thus encouraging pride in the heritage of the Chicano.[27] In the poem "The Chicano Manifesto," Delgado writes of the impatient *raza*, but tempers that impatience with an appeal for brotherhood.[28]

The message from Chicano poets for change is loud and clear. There is no mistaking the insistent plea for reformation. Although the spirit of Chicano poetry may be considered revolutionary, its intellectual emphasis, however, is on reason as it attempts to move the hearts and minds of men by appealing to their better natures.

The Chicano Novel

The Chicano Novel is a post-World War II phenomenon. José Antonio Villarreal's novel, *Pocho*, was published in 1959.[29] At that time it received scant attention and quickly went out of print. Although it appeared

---

[26] Rodolfo González, I Am Joaquín, *El Gallo* Newspaper, 1967.

[27] Luis Omar Salinas, *Crazy Gypsy* (Fresno, Calif.: Origenes Publication, La Raza Studies, Fresno State College, 1970), p. 51.

[28] Abelardo Delgado, *Chicago*: 25 *Pieces of a Chicano Mind* (Denver: Migrant Workers Press, 1970), pp. 35–36.

[29] José Antonio Villarreal, *Pocho* (Garden City, N.Y.: Doubleday and Co., 1959).

a decade too early, it stands in the vanguard of the Chicano novel for depicting the Chicano experience in the United States. Villarreal's style was influenced by the American "pop" novel of the 1950s, and his portrayal of the linguistic characteristics of Chicanos was clearly influenced by the work of Ernest Hemingway and Steinbeck. The novel's strength, however, is in the author's skillful presentation of the Mexican background of the Chicano migration to the United States.

Two recent novels by Chicanos represent the nexus between the Chicano and Anglo worlds at this time and indicate the direction the Chicano novel will probably take. Richard Vasquez's novel, *Chicano*, will be of special interest to Chicano readers because, in a manner similar to that of *Pocho*, it deals with the substance of their lives and experiences.[30]

Chicano details the odyssey of Hector Sandoval from Mexico to the United States during the Mexican Revolution and the travails of his children, Neftali, Jilda, and Hortencia, and their heirs in California. *Chicano* is an important novel for its portrayal of the Chicano migration, although some critics contend that the values of the novel have been misplaced in a rendition of the traditional fictions about Chicanos.

On the other hand, Raymond Barrio's *The Plum Plum Pickers* is a more exciting work, not because it is experimentally in the same mold as *Cane* —a novel that figured prominently in the Negro Renaissance of the 1920s —but because Barrio has been concerned less with presenting a panorama of Chicano life than with dealing entirely with the contemporary situation of the migrant couple, Manuel and Lupe, caught in the grip of agricultural exploitation.[31]

Essentially, *The Plum Plum Pickers* focuses on the proletarian view of life. Lupe is drawn as a significant figure in the novel, not as a female trifle caught at the edges of that fictive *machismo* so dominant in *Pocho* and *Chicano*. In *The Plum Plum Pickers* Barrio has gone beyond the form of the "pop" novel to create a significant work of American literature.

The Linguistic Aspect

Another important aspect of the Chicano literary renaissance to consider is the linguistic aspect. Chicano writers are expressing themselves on the printed page in their Chicano language, evolved from Spanish and English, and their particular experiences in American barrios, *colonias*, and ghettos. Like black English, the Chicano language is at the heart of the Chicano experience; but unlike black English, the Chicano language deals not only with dialects of American English but with dialects of American and Mexican Spanish. Moreover, it has produced a mixture of the two languages resulting in a unique kind of *binary*

---

[30] Richard Vasquez, *Chicano* (Garden City, N.Y.: Doubleday and Co., 1970).
[31] Raymond Barrio, *The Plum Plum Pickers* (Sunnyvale, Calif.: Ventura Press, 1969).

phenomena, in which the linguistic symbols of two languages are mixed in utterances using either language's syntactic structure.

For the bilingual (Spanish-English, for instance) writer, this structure involves using either his English or Spanish idiolect at will to produce a "stereolect." For example, Alberto Alurista's poetry in *El Espejo-The Mirror: Selected Mexican American Literature* (published by Quinto Sol) reads as follows:

> Mis ojos hinchados
>   flooded with lagrimas
> de bronce
> melting on the cheek bones
> of my concern
>   razgos indigenes
> the scars of history on my face
>   and the veins of my body
> that aches
>   vomito sangre
> y lloro libertad
>   I do not ask for freedom
> I am freedom.[32]

In order to understand contemporary Mexican-American literature, it is important to understand the function of binary phenomena in Chicano communication and expression. It is equally important, however, to understand that these phenomena are not of Mexican-American origin, for binary phenomena occur wherever there is linguistic contact and coexistence. In New York, for example, binary phenomena ("stereo-lecticism") occur among American speakers of Yiddish. In literature, such contemporary American writers as Philip Roth and Saul Bellow use many Yiddish expressions in their works.

Linguistically, it is important to keep in mind the primacy of language in the life of an individual or of a society or culture because the language we speak shapes our particular view of the world. Thus, to comprehend the Chicano experience, one must critically examine the language of Chicanos, not with preconceived notions of what is correct or standard in language usage in Spanish or English but with knowledge of the role language plays in human intercourse. We can no longer tag the Chicano language as "poor Spanish" or "poor English" or as "Mex-Tex," "Spanglish," "Pachuco," or other such denigrations. We must guard against stupidities that suggest that Mexican Americans are nonlingual because they speak neither English nor Spanish. We must bear in mind that we do not depreciate the language of Chaucer's time by calling it "Frenglish," though more French than English was spoken by the upper classes.

Ironically, California proved to be the birthplace of the renaissance that Aurora Lucero had hoped New Mexico would produce. In 1953 she wrote optimistically:

---

[32] Octavio I. Romano-V, ed., *El Espejo-The Mirror: Selected Mexican American Literature* (Berkeley, Calif.: Quinto Sol Publications, 1969), p. 172. Reprinted by permission of the poet.

There now remains but one renaissance to be effected—the literary. With the happy accident that New Mexico possesses more traditional literary materials than any other Hispanic region it should be possible to bring about such a rebirth in the reenactment of the lovely old plays, in the keeping alive the lovely old folk dances and in the singing of the old traditional songs.[33]

The Chicano Renaissance came into being not in relation to the traditional past but rather in the wake of growing awareness by Mexican Americans of their Indian, not Hispanic, identity. The Chicano Renaissance is but the manifestation of a people's coming of age. It has been long overdue, and in another country, like Milton's unsightly root, it bore a bright and golden flower.

[33] Aurora Lucero, *Literary Folklore of the Hispanic Southwest* (San Antonio, Tex.: The Naylor Company, 1953), p. 210.

CHICANO CULTURE IN A GABACHO WORLD

Armando B. Rendon

The concept of raza derives from a belief in the inherent relationship of one man to another, with each man willing to take the initiative, but at the same time insisting on an individual independence. The interdependence of men is another way to look at it, while each man must accept blame or praise for what he does. While raza look to the future, they willingly accept the present situation to a great extent as preordained, so that each individual understands a role that he is to carry out in his position. When a great adversity befalls us, we may tend to accept it, wait it out, hope for the best or for another chance later on. Such a complexity of thought may establish a general attitude of wait and see, *lo que Dios quiera* (as God wishes). How does a revolution touch such a Chicano, move him to action?

Although less and less a factor, but still demonstrative of the Chicano mind, is the attitude toward sickness. While Chicanos will readily admit to a modern acceptance of diseases caused by a more or less obvious contact with something or someone from which disease may be contracted, it is harder to bring out their reversion to age-old views such as the presence of *el mal ojo* (the evil eye) or *susto* (fright), which can produce maladies such as sudden fevers and headaches that raza may find otherwise unexplainable. An old remedy is cotton thread tied around the right wrist and another around the left ankle; another protection is amulets worn by adults and children to ward off el mal ojo. I recall as a child my grandmother placing an egg cracked into a bowl under my bed when I was suffering from a fever, or having someone massage my fore-head and temples with a fresh egg to relieve head pains. Because it resembles an eye, the egg was meant to draw out *el mal ojo*, whatever was causing the illness. Certain herbs or roots might be prescribed for sickness allied with a psychological trauma, although it was never called anything like that by past generations. I've drunk bitter-tasting teas as a youth which were meant to cure almost anything, and looking back they did seem to work, perhaps more so because of the threat of having to drink more of the acrid brew if one didn't recover. Of course, in regard to health problems, less attention is given nowadays to the old folk cures, although there are still curanderas, old women with a unique and mysterious aura about them, who prescribe cures for everything from a boil to impotence.

In a survey conducted a few years ago by Sister Mary Immaculate of Our Lady of the Lake College in San Antonio, Texas, the growing disparity between first and third-generation Chicanos is quite apparent. The trend is toward increased Anglicization of mores in regard to family life, education, courtship, and marriage. Notably, there is a trend toward smaller families; greater individual functioning rather than functioning as family members; an increase in the desire for education and better work opportunities; somewhat more participation in clubs; a preference, still, for family celebrations; a devotion to *la virgen de Guadalupe*, but anti-pious religiosity still among the males; and a stronger role for women in schooling and work, along with a greater sharing of authority and responsibility in the family. A detailed analysis of this and other studies, such as that of Dr. Ramirez, would indicate that there is a strong tendency toward assimilating certain Anglo influences, but also retaining a number of Chicano values, a kind of ambivalence which is the other side of the coin in regard to the Chicano liberation efforts. The overall effect can be described as a trend toward middle-class orientation—adopting Anglo values in order to be more in tune with nonraza friends made at higher educational levels or on the job, thus a tendency to avoid boat rocking, to avoid asserting a style of life that one has tried to forget because one may be embarrassed in front of non-Chicano acquaintances or one's employer.

In the field of folklore, tales such as that of *La Llorona* convey a variety of sentiments and beliefs of the Chicano people. *La Llorona* is the story of human frailty and divine vengeance. In a small Mexican village long ago, a woman discovered her husband in an affair with another woman and in revenge she killed her three little children and hid their bodies. But she hid them so well and in such a jealous rage that afterward she could not find their tiny bodies. God condemned her to search for the bodies so they could have proper church burial or she would never have peace.

With that story firmly implanted in my little mind, should I be naughty as a little boy, my mother would shush me, tell me if I heard the wind in the trees or noises outside the house, it might be *la llorona* searching, searching, for her *niñitos*, and unless I behaved, *la llorona* would carry me away. If you listen to the wind in the trees, particularly in the Southwest, it does seem to be a woman calling out for someone, for rest, at least it does to me.

Another story, *The Little Serpent and the Girl*, imbues a creature with powers of speech and magic and a girl with great beauty and innocence. It seems that a little girl found a tiny snake and took him home, feeding and caring for him. One day, the snake, grown quite large, said to the girl, "I am too much for you to feed and care for, let me go now to the forest." Though very fond of the snake, the girl knew it would be best for him to return to his forest home. As she left him in the woods, the snake told her, "If you ever need help, just call me." As the girl grew into maidenhood, she became very beautiful. Two neighbor women grew envious and plotted to tell the king that the young maiden had said she could turn anything into gold or silver. The king had rocks piled high and brought the young woman, demanding that she make them gold. She denied that she had such a power, and insisted that she was only a poor, innocent girl. The king, enraged, had her eyes taken out, left her in the forest, and gave the eyes to the two wicked neighbors. The maiden remembered what the snake had said and called to him. He came, but by this time he had grown immense, with a head here and a tail there beyond the horizon. Hearing her plight, he licked her hands. One hand would turn things to gold; the other, to silver, he told her. She heard a woodsman nearby and when she called him he took her home, but his wife refused to help her because they were so poor. The girl told the man to bring two rocks, and when he did, she changed them to gold. With the gold, she asked that he go out and buy her a pair of eyes, even a dog's or cat's—it didn't matter. This he did. In fact, the same old women sold him the girl's very own eyes, which they had kept in a little box. The woodsman brought the dried-up eyes to the girl and she asked him to take her back to the spot in the forest where she had found him. When he left, she summoned the snake again. Shown the eyes, the snake licked them and replaced them. They were even more brilliant and attractive than before! Upon returning to the woodsman's home, she heard that the king was sending his soldiers to slay a giant snake that had been devouring the forest animals. She rushed to the woods and told the snake that he must flee for his life. Right away he left, slithering through the forest. The young maiden lived in her little home in peace from then on, but often she would recall her old friend, the little snake, with sadness.

These and hundreds of other stories and fables convey part of the rich cultural background on the folk level. They suggest that the Chicano has inherited a diverse folk background, an ageless, word-of-mouth form of knowledge, a rich resource for the genius of art in Chicanos.

The function of culture in a person's life is "all-encompassing," according to Marcos de Leon, a California educator. "Culture," he has written,

comprises a group's ideas, habits, values, attitudes, institutions; it possesses physical and material aspects with sanctions in technology and
economics. To give the group cohesion and direction, it provides social
institutions, education, and political structures; culture sets up systems of
belief, relating men to the universe. Aesthetics is very much an integral part
of it . . . the graphic and plastic arts, folklore, music, drama and dance. And
finally, there is language, the symbolism of abstract thought, the vehicle of
knowledge, of belief, of legal systems, and of tribal institutions.

"A culture," Dr. Ernesto Galarza has similarly described, "is characterized by (a) the uses it makes of its material environment; (b) the accepted or tolerated relations between the individuals that compose it;
(c) the symbols, conventional signs, and utilities of everyday behavior;
and (d) the values by which the society measures itself as to moral performance." Dr. Galarza concludes that according to this pattern there is
but one culture in the United States, the culture of the American people.
There are no subcultures, as some observers would posit, but an "entire
society that is manifestly capable of spawning slums and breeding
poverty." Dr. Galarza adds that "it is not the subcultures that are in
trouble. It is the culture, the American culture itself."

Dr. Galarza thereby spreads the blame around, but from my point of
view, because one of the functions of culture is evaluating conduct, placing the blame for the destructive efforts directed against the Chicano's
life style is certainly in order. Thus we must consider, as Dr. Galarza
rightly says, the entire structure to ascertain where the roots of conflict
and division lie. Examining the Anglo American "culture," or that predominance of thought and activity in the United States that passes for
culture, I contend that the intimately connected prejudices against people
of other colors and other cultures are at the center of Anglo genocidal
tendencies. The instances of rejection of the Chicano and discrimination
against him because of his different culture, that is, language, life style,
and so on, are numerous and variously recounted here.

Anglo "culture" has resulted in the creation of huge industries around
the goal of a kissing-sweet breath. A value system based on such goals as
this is then projected through commercialization in the mass media to a
degree that the male is castrated and the female desexed. One must
smoke a certain kind of cigarette to be manly or use a special cologne
that comes with karate lessons to be attractive. A female must wear a
brassiere that crosses her heart or use a deodorant that lasts five days in
order to be womanly. One can almost feel pity for the Anglo who, in
order to be part of the Pepsi generation, must drink an uncola, use left
guard, drive a horse transformed into a car, pull on a cigarette that filters
out almost all the cancer-dealing tars, rinse his mouth so he'll be kissed
again, and slick his hair with a cream so that she'll be glad he came back.

Let an Anglo describe his own kind. Nicholas Johnson, a member of
the Federal Communications Commission, writes in his book, *How to
Talk Back to Your Television Set* (1970):

We learn that the great measure of happiness and personal satisfaction is consumption—conspicuous when possible. "Success is signified by the purchase of a product—a mouthwash or deodorant. How do you resolve conflicts? By force and by violence. Who are television's leaders, its heroes, its stars? They are the physically attractive, the glib, and the wealthy, and almost no one else. What do you do when life fails to throw roses in your hedonistic path? You get "fast, fast, fast" relief from a pill—headache remedy, a stomach settler, a tranquilizer, a pep pill, or "the pill." You smoke a cigarette, have a drink, or get high on pot or more potent drugs. You get a divorce or run away from home. And if, "by the time you get to Phoenix" you're still troubled, you just "chew your little troubles away."

It does appear that enough Mexican Americans have perverted themselves to accept wholly the Anglo "culture," a poor substitute for the Chicano way of life, so as to achieve economic and social success. It is almost impossible to avoid Anglo influences, nor are all Anglo ways and advances in science, psychology, and the arts to be rejected out of hand; but in the light of the profile I've just sketched, the Chicano must be very selective. Consistently, I place quotation marks around the word culture when it is preceded by the word Anglo because America has yet to develop a culture worth emulating and passing on to posterity. For the Chicano to accept the Anglo "culture" or to lose his own identity in it would be tantamount to our glorying in the Aztecs because they invented a ball game that almost all Indian tribes played in Mexico and Central America. Culture is made of more than that.

The North American culture is not worth copying: it is destructive of personal dignity; it is callous, vindictive, arrogant, militaristic, self-deceiving, and greedy; it is a gold-plated ball-point pen; it is James Eastland and Richard Nixon; it is Strom Thurmond and Lyndon Johnson; it is a Mustang and old-folks' homes; it is Medicare and OEO; it is an $80 billion defense budget and $75 a month welfare; it is a cultural cesspool and a social and spiritual vacuum for the Chicano. The victims of this culture are not merely the minority peoples but the dominant Anglo group as well; everything that passes for culture in the United States is symptomatic of a people so swept up in the profit motive and staying ahead of the Joneses that true natural and humanistic values may be destroyed without their knowing it. Nationalistically, Anglo America has come to believe that it is the supercountry, that it can do no wrong, that its might does make right. The United States suffers from a lack of perspective, a lack of humility; it is spoiled and immature without showing any signs that it is growing out of that stage.

But the Anglo problem can be seen even more clearly from the standpoint of the discrimination and injustice perpetrated upon the Chicano because of his color. For many decades, the issue of color has been suppressed by both the Chicano and the Anglo as a real substantive cause for conflict and difference. Jack D. Forbes, a California historian who claims he is descended from Powhatan (chief of the Indian tribe that first had contact with the Pilgrim Fathers), has incisively struck to the heart of this issue, pointing out that "scholars and social workers dealing with the Mexican Americans ignore their Americanoid racial characteristics and regard them as simply another European-type minority group with certain cultural and linguistic problems; in doing so, they help the Mexican Americans in *their* escape from the realities of their native American heritage." Color is as much a part of our culture as is language —this distinction is forced upon us; it is inescapable in American society. In a negative sense, the proof of this fact is that Chicanos have been discriminated against for both reasons, among others. In other words, the Anglo recognizes various components in other peoples as different from him; he assumes these qualities to be a cause for him to discriminate, that is, to give preference to those who do not have these different qualities. In so doing, the corollary follows—that to be non-Anglo is to be inferior; to speak other than English is to be inferior; to be brown or black or yellow is to be inferior. Convey the idea that all the good things of life belong to those who are not inferior in those certain ways, and, by and by, those other-than-Anglo people will make every effort to disavow their different traits. But color is extremely difficult to conceal, so all manner of subterfuges are invented—what Carey McWilliams and Jack Forbes refer to as the "White-Spanish myth." Within the Chicano community itself, the prejudice of color operates detrimentally. The lighter-complexioned will be favored over the darker-skinned children. A young girl will have made a better marriage for having married the guero instead of the Indio suitor. A light-complexioned Mexican American girl rejects offers of marriage from two Anglos for fear that "if there should be any dark children, I don't want my husband blaming me and calling them 'my children.'"

"Border City," the pseudonym for a town along the Texas-Mexico border, revealed a number of insights about the value of Mexican American culture to Ozzie G. Simmons, who conducted a study in the border locale in 1958. Simmons perceived that Anglo stereotypes of what Chicanos are tend to be reciprocated by Chicano stereotypes of the Anglo. Chicano stereotypes of the Anglo, however, "take into account the Anglo Americans' conflict as to their [Chicanos'] potential equality and present inferiority," but are much less elaborate than those of the Anglo toward him because Chicanos "feel no need of justifying the present intergroup relation . . . the very nature of their dependent position forces them to view the relation more realistically than Anglo Americans do." Chicanos, Simmons indicates, tend to fulfill the conduct expected of them by the Anglo. Anglos, in turn, expect Mexican Americans to be assimilated, but only if Mexicans become "just like Anglo Americans"; there no middle road for the Anglo. The sociologist concludes:

If the full acceptance of Mexicans by Anglo Americans is contingent upon the disappearance of cultural differences, it will not be accorded in the foreseeable future . . . in viewing cultural differences primarily as disabilities, we

(Anglos) neglect their positive aspect. Mexican American culture represents the most constructive and effective means Mexican Americans have yet been able to develop, for coping with their changed natural and social environment. They will further exchange old ways for new only if these appear to be more meaningful and rewarding than the old, and then only if they are given full opportunity to acquire the new ways and to use them.

We come full circle to the little Chicana's poem about "Brown, brown, brown." Accept our color, the poem says, have pride in it as part of our culture along with language, history, tradition, folklore, land and blood. How well this is understood by Chicano youths is evident in the statement issued by activist youth groups at a liberation conference in Denver:

> Nationalism is an awareness that we are not Caucasian, not Mexican-American or any label the system puts upon us, but that we are a people with an ancient heritage and an ancient scar on our souls. We are oppressed first because we are Chicanos, because our skin is dark. But we are exploited as workers by a system which feeds like a vulture off the work of our people only to enrich a few who own and control this entire country. We suffer a double oppression. We catch a double hell.

The essence of cultural nationalism is the full acceptance of this fact, that we are oppressed because of the color of our skin and because of the nature of our being, and that as a consequence, inevitably, our sole means of preservation and equality before all men is in that color and in that raza. Gonzales has said that anyone who would wish to become a part of Anglo society is "sick, because Anglo society is sick." His epic poem, "I Am Joaquin," published in 1967, relates the internal effects of Anglo society on Gonzales as well as the counter influences and the realization of a new direction for the rebirth of a new spirit:

> I——am, Joaquin.
> I am lost in a world of confusion,
> caught up in the whirl of an Anglo-Society.
> Confused, by the rules
> Scorned, by the attitudes,
> Suppressed by manipulation,
> and destroyed by modern society.
> My fathers,
>   have lost the economic battle
> and won,
>   the struggle of cultural survival
> and now!
>   I must choose . . .
>   between, the paradox of
>   . . . .Victory of the spirit despite
> physical Hunger
>   Or
>   To exist in the grasp of the
> American Social neurosis, sterilization
> Of the soul and a full stomach.
> - - - - - - - - - - - - -
> And in all the fertile farm lands
>   the barren plains

```
The mountain villages, smoke
                smeared cities
                we start to move
Mejicano, Español, Latin, Hispano, Chicano
                I look the same
                I feel the same
                I cry and. . . .
                Sing the same.
I am the masses
      of my people and I refuse to be
      absorbed.
I am Joaquin
The odds are great
but my spirit is strong.
                My faith unbreakable
                My blood is pure
                I am an Aztec Prince
                and Christian Christ
      I SHALL ENDURE!
      I WILL ENDURE!
```

When the Poor People's march advanced to Washington, D.C., Juanita
Dominguez, of the Crusade, wrote new words to a corrido called "La
Rielera," composed during the 1910 revolution. It is in the spirit of a new
people with a new awareness of themselves. It says as much of what
nationalism and what the Chicano revolt is about as anything else that
can be written or said:

```
Chorus I:
      Yo soy Chicano, tengo color
      Americano pero con honor
      Cuando me dicen que hay revolución
      Defiendo mi raza con mucho valor.
  1.  Tengo todita mi gente
      Para la revolución
      Voy a luchar con los pobres
      Pa' que se acabe el bolon.                         Chorus I.
  2.  Tengo mi par de caballos
      Para la revolución
      Uno se llama el canario
      El otro se llama el gorrion.                        Chorus I.
  3.  Tengo mi orgullo y machismo
      Mi cultura y corazon
      Tengo mi fe y diferencias y
      Lucho con gran razon.
Chorus II:
      Soy diferente, soy color cafe
      Tengo cultura, tengo corazon
      Y no me los quita, a mi ni un cabron.
```

```
CHORUS I:
      I am Chicano, brownskinned, an American but with
      honor. When they tell me the revolution has started, I will
      defend my people with all my courage.
  1.  My people are all united, for the revolution. I will
      fight with the poor to end oppression.
                                                           Chorus I.
  .2.  I have my pair of horses for the revolution, one is
      called the Canary, the other, the Sparrow.
```

Chorus I.

3. I have my pride and manliness, my culture and love,
    I have my faith, I'm different, and I fight with great
    reason.

CHORUS II:
    I have my pride, I have my faith, I'm different,
    my skin is brown. I have a culture, I have a heart,
    And no one can take them from me, no, not any bastard.

The fact that a young woman composed those words illustrates an aspect of Chicano culture undergoing radical change from the internalized force of group assertiveness—the relationship between men and women in the Chicano movement. I would be writing but half a book if the Chicana were accorded no special credit in these pages. The Chicana is half the movement. It may seem that when reference is made to Chicano activism, the emphasis is on the masculine alone. That tendency is mainly attributable to my being macho (male) and naturally viewing the Chicano revolt as a male-dominated phenomenon, but I must caution myself every so often, for that could not be further from the truth. Organizations and headlines certainly are dominated by the men, but the Chicanas, Mexican American women, have been beside their men, sometimes even shoving them forward a little bit. What Chicano in recent years has not experienced at some conference or meeting the scathing but truthful words of a Chicana, demanding to know why the men don't take action on this or that issue, "or must the women lead the way and the men hide behind our skirts."

Chicanas today are far different from their grandmothers and even their mothers in certain aspects as a result of the explosion of the small universe which once enveloped the Chicano community. The woman of the Chicano revolt believes that Chicano liberation must also include Chicana liberation. Thus within the overall Chicano movement toward self-determination and creation of a new identity, a struggle is going on between our women and our men. It is not a mortal struggle nor a divisive one, because the women are saying that they want to be recognized by the Chicano macho as a companion in the revolution. Young girls are relating to the folk heroines of the Mexican Revolution—*La Adelita*, subject of a revolutionary *corrido*, who exemplified the *soldaderas* (women who accompanied the rebel armies as camp soldiers, sometimes taking arms themselves). They recall the name of Juana Gallo, a *mexicana* who led the men of her village to avenge a *federales* attack against her village, and of *La Marieta*, Maria del Carmen Rubio de la Llave, a guerillera under Francisco Villa.

Chicanas have even more recent history of their contributions to the reassertion of Chicanismo among our people. A weeks-long strike in the early 1950s against a zinc mining corporation in southern New Mexico seemed on the verge of collapse. The struggling miners, predominantly Mexican Americans, faced certain defeat when a court injunction forbade them from picketing the entrances to the mines. Their wives and daughters took over the picket signs and although many were arrested others replaced them until the company conceded. The union men, in co-operation with their women, secured a significant victory, but the women also won something. As the movie depicting the strike, *Salt of the Earth*, so vividly expresses, the women gained a new respect from their husbands, fathers, and sons. The crisis forced the women to overstep restrictions that had persisted in the traditional macho mentality of the Chicano but which had to fall in the face of pressures that threatened to engulf the entire family. These were the *Adelitas* of the mines.

In the Delano grape strike, women, among the most skillful workers in the vineyards, played a major role from the beginning. Dolores Huerte, a slight, slender Chicana and the mother of seven children, had been active in Community Service Organization projects in the early sixties and had aided Cesar Chavez in the formative two or three years before the huelga began in 1965. She has figured as a strong negotiator for the union in several bargaining sessions with grape-growers and had been effective as a boycott organizer and speaker, particularly before women's groups. Her petite size is disarming, for she is an uncommon Chicana, one of the most formidable personalities in the Chicano movement. She was at Robert Kennedy's side when he claimed victory in California and steps away when the fatal bullets struck him.

Five Mexican American women, members of the National Floral Workers Association, knotted themselves in a twenty-five-foot chain fastened to posts at the entrance to a flower farm they had struck eight months before for union recognition, better wages, and better working conditions. Considered agricultural workers, they were not included under National Labor Relations Act protections. It was an early morning in February 1969 near Brighton, Colorado, when they made their desperate move in violation of a court injunction which had strictly forbidden further picketing of the farm. A morning fog hung in the dawn air. A farm employee cut the chain, but the women didn't budge. Suddenly, a sheriff's deputy approached and sprayed the women with tear gas. The noxious vapors lingered in the foggy, still morning, felling the women, who were unable to move quickly enough because of the chain and the gassing which had rendered them nearly sightless. Other women rescued them by dragging them from under the cloud of gas. With no recourse to the law which had enjoined the picketing and ordered the gassing, the strikers were forced to quit.

There will be Juana Gallos before long, and it's not a question of whether the Chicanos will allow them to appear; they will appear regardless of macho sentiment. It's evident, in the presence and activism of Chicanas at conferences and in demonstrations, that they no longer want to play a passive role in the Chicano community—"to limit her world to domesticity, making frijoles, tortillas, *limpiando la casa, cuidando los niños*," as young Elvira Saragoza has written in *Bronce*, an Oakland barrio newspaper. "She wants to expand, to have the domestic role together with the intellectual role. She wants to be able to use her *cerebro* (mind) because she knows that she too can think, and be creative. She is not an inferior, insubordinate being and she is tired of being treated as one."

Perhaps the most overwhelming reason that machos of the Chicano movement must understand what a girl like Elvira is saying comes, naturally, from a woman, Enriqueta Vasquez, a writer for *El Grito del Norte*, a Chicano newspaper published in Española, New Mexico. "The Mexican American movement is not of just adults fighting the social system, but it is a total commitment of a family unit living what it believes to be a better way of life in demanding social change for the benefit of mankind." Because the Chicano is at the center of the Chicano revolt, Enriqueta points out in *El Grito*:

> . . . there should not have to be a woman's liberation movement within it. . . . When the man can look upon "his" woman as human and with the love of brotherhood and equality, then and only then, can he feel the true meaning of liberation and equality himself. When we talk of equality in the Mexican American movement we better be talking about total equality beginning where it all starts, at home.

The Chicano macho has to concede that he has usually relegated la mujer to the kitchen or to having kids and has never allowed her to express herself. Perhaps it is true, as some Chicanas say, that the Chicano passes on to his woman the frustrations and mierda that befall him during the day. Being unable to fight back at the Anglo boss and to assert his manhood for fear of economic reprisal, he, as the breadwinner, the one most immediately subject to the gringo's supremacist attitude and actions which assail the Chicano mind and spirit, may lash out at the one person who is not at all to blame, or he tries to exert his machismo within the four walls of his home. And when he becomes involved with a cause that encourages, insists upon, and challenges his manhood and pride in *la raza*, he tends to forget that the bountiful cup of *la raza* is the Chicana and that the love and spirit of our people is perpetuated by her love and her spirit.

When I first picked up a tabloid newspaper called *El Rebozo*, my first reaction was that here was a waste of effort and resources which could have been put to better use as part of a total Chicano community newspaper. Two San Antonio Chicanas, Andrea Gomez and Sylvia Gonzales, were primarily responsible for its first issue and they made it clear that the newspaper was intended, along with arousing Chicanas to *la causa*, to make Chicanas aware of las mujeres in the movement. Even the name, *El Rebozo*, strikes a uniquely Chicana tone, as the editors explain: "The traditional garment of the Mexican woman symbolizes the three roles of the Chicana . . . 'la señorita,' feminine, yet humble . . . 'la revolucionaria,' ready to fight for *la causa* . . . 'la madre,' radiant with life."

What Chicanas have to answer for themselves, individually, is whether they can live more than one of these roles at a time. For many Chicanas it is apparent that the traditional role of "radiant mother" is no longer enough to fulfill her womanhood. Nor does the idea of merely being a helpmate appeal any more to some of the Chicanas who wish to be liberated from the home. What does inspire them is the challenge of working for *la causa* side by side with the men, of being appreciated for their ideas and their spirit, of being entrusted with important duties besides handling registrations or taking minutes. *La mujer Chicana* is asking that the men experience a cultural shock—the fact that Chicanas themselves will no longer be docile. Chicanas want to improve themselves, to continue their education into college, to break from the strict family bounds that have suppressed their own aspirations for generations.

I don't for a moment doubt that the Chicana is also conscious of the attrition that has occurred among Chicanos who have gone to college and met for the most part only *gabachas* (Anglo women), and, too often, married them. In a sense, the Chicano culture has suppressed the full development of our women. Then, because they lack the opportunity of other women who take higher education for granted, they are excluded from the best setting for catching a promising young Chicana. Miss Saragoza cries:

> What does this pale creature have which attracts our machos? Do our men feel that they have mastered something? Tamed something? Or that they have mastered white racism? What is it? We don't know. We don't understand! We just say to our men, "Look at what you have, your brown women. Help them! Don't abandon them because when you do, you are throwing away a great deal of yourself!"

Such questions or accusations as these are troubling enough, for they arise out of basic psychological problems within machos who have not come to terms with themselves, or derive from circumstances such as educational barriers which are even greater for Mexican American women than they are for the men. But even more disturbing is the subordination of our women into the most menial tasks, even in the movement. We don't throw her away, but we abuse her spirit and belittle her worth.

A brilliant exposition of the Chicana's role in the movement, and perhaps of women in society generally, is from Mary Lou Espinosa of Milwaukee, Wisconsin. In "La Madre de Aztlán," a statement composed in the fall of 1969, she says:

> Equality respects the function of
> man as father
> woman as mother
> and both as an independent
> human capable of change.
>
> A Chicana woman springs out of her
> Indian and Spanish cultural and
> historic heritage.
> From Indian comes strong mother figure
> From Spanish comes dominant father figure.
>
> True woman's liberation must happen first
> in the mind of the woman. . . .

Socio-economic and political
conditions can help the process of woman's full
assertion in the movement and
in society, but the woman has first
to want to make herself free.

A woman, a mother, knows life
from within because of her function.
Our society is sadly masculine oriented;
it does not know life from within
because men alone make it.

Creative solution to social change
comes with people who have
creative life within themselves,
a free woman can creatively
contribute with racial solutions
because she knows life from within.

Well, the Mexican Revolution might never have carried forward as far as it did had it not been for the soldaderas. I've heard one story about them. At first the macho rebels would scoff at the women who wanted to accompany them, saying there was no place for them in the *revolución*; but many women persisted, following their men at a distance. When men returned from a battle, wounded and hungry, the tender care and nourishing food provided by the women soon won them over. Many *soldaderas* must have fallen victims to combat which enveloped the camps or from the hunger and deprivation which were frequent camp mates in the winters of the revolución. By the same token, it probably will avail *los machos* nothing to reject *las mujeres* who are insisting on becoming *revolucionarias*; they will do so in spite of opposition. I cannot speak for la Chicana nor will I presume to delineate her role in the new Chicano community; she will play the traditional roles, but there will be new ones which she will carve out for herself. But, just as in the Mexican Revolution, I suspect that the Chicano revolt, in all its phases and its efforts, will have to draw upon the indomitable energy and commitment to the Chicano family of *la mujer de la raza*.

External Culture: Relationships with the Gabacho World

COLONIALISM: THE CASE OF THE MEXICAN AMERICAN

Joan W. Moore[1]

American social scientists should have realized long ago that American minorities are far from being passive objects of study. They are, on the contrary, quite capable of defining themselves. A clear demonstration of this rather embarrassing lag in conceptualization is the current reassessment of sociological thought. It is now plain that the concepts of "acculturation," of "assimilation," and similar paradigms are inappropriate for groups who entered American society not as volunteer immigrants but through some form of involuntary relationship.[2]

The change in thinking has not come because of changes within sociology itself. Quite the contrary. It has come because the minorities have begun to reject certain academic concepts. The new conceptual structure is not given by any academic establishment but comes within a conceptual structure derived from the situation of the African countries. In the colonial situation, rather than either the conquest or the slave situation, the new generation of black intellectuals is finding parallels to their own reactions to American Society.

Reprinted from *Social Problems*, Vol. 17, No. 4 (Spring 1970), by permission of The Society for the Study of Social Problems and the author.

[1] I would like to thank Carlos Cortes for his very helpful comments on an earlier draft of this paper.

[2] Oddly enough it now appears that the nature of the introduction into American society matters even more than race, though the two interact. I think this statement can be defended empirically, notwithstanding the emergence of, for example, Japanese-American *sansei* militancy, with its strong race consciousness (see Kitano, 1968).

This exploration of colonialism by minority intellectuals has met a varied reaction, to say the least, but there have been some interesting attempts to translate these new and socially meaningful categories into proper academic sociologese. Blauner's (1969) article is one of the more ambitious attempts to relate the concept of "colonialism" as developed by Kenneth Clark, Stokely Carmichael and Elridge Cleaver to sociological analysis. In the process, one kind of blurring is obvious even if not explicit: that is, that "colonialism" was far from uniform in the 19th century, even in Africa.[3] In addition, Blauner (1969) makes explicit the adaptations he feels are necessary before the concept of colonialism can be meaningfully applied to the American scene. Common to both American internal colonialism of the blacks and European imperial expansion, Blauner argues, were the involuntary nature of the relationship between the two groups, the transformation or destruction of indigenous values, and, finally, racism. But Blauner warns that the situations are really different: "the . . . culture . . . of the (American black) colonized . . . is less developed; it is also less autonomous. In addition, the colonized are a numerical minority, and furthermore, they are ghettoized more totally and more dispersed than people under classic colonialism."

But such adaptations are not needed in order to apply the concept fruitfully to America's second largest minority—the Mexican Americans.[4] Here the colonial concept need not be analogized and, in fact, it describes and categorizes so accurately that one suspects that earlier "discovery" by sociologists of the Mexican Americans, particularly in New Mexico, might have discouraged uncritical application of the classic paradigms to all minorities. The initial Mexican contact with American society came by conquest, not by choice. Mexican American culture *was* well developed; it *was* autonomous; the colonized *were* a numerical majority. Further, they were—and are—less ghettoized and more dispersed than the American blacks. In fact, their patterns of residence (especially those existing at the turn of the century) are exactly those of "classic colonialism." And they were indigenous to the region and not "imported."[5]

In at least the one state of New Mexico, there was a situation of comparatively "pure" colonialism. Outside of New Mexico, the original conquest colonialism was overlaid, particularly in the 20th century, with a grossly manipulated voluntary immigration. But throughout the American Southwest where the approximately five million Mexican Americans are now concentrated, understanding the Mexican minority requires understanding both conquest colonialism and "voluntary" immigration. It also

[3] For a good analysis of the variation, and of today's consequences, see the collection of papers in Kuper and Smith, 1969.

[4] Mexican American intellectuals themselves have persistently analyzed the group in the conquest frame of reference. For a significant example, see Sánchez (1940).

[5] "Indigenous" by comparison with the American blacks. Spanish America itself was a colonial system, in which Indians were exploited. See Olguín (1967), for an angry statement to this effect.

requires understanding the interaction between colonialism and voluntarism.

In this paper I shall discuss a "culture trait" that is attributed to Mexican Americans both by popular stereotype and by social scientists—that is, a comparatively low degree of formal voluntary organization and hence of organized participation in political life. This is the academic form of the popular question: "What's wrong with the Mexicans? Why can't they organize for political activity?" In fact, as commonly asked both by social scientist and popular stereotype, the question begs the question. There is a great deal of variation in three widely different culture areas in the Southwest. And these culture areas differ most importantly in the particular variety of colonialism to which they were subjected. In the "classically" colonial situation, New Mexico, there has been in fact a relatively high order of political participation, especially by comparison with Texas, which we shall term "conflict colonialism," and California, which we shall term "economic colonialism." [6]

New Mexico

An area that is now northern New Mexico and parts of southern Colorado was the most successful of the original Spanish colonies. At the beginning of the war between the United States and Mexico, there were more than 50,000 settlers, scattered in villages and cities with a strong upper class as well as a peasantry. There were frontier versions of Spanish colonial institutions that had been developing since 1600. The conquest of New Mexico by the United States was nearly bloodless and thus allowed, as a consequence, an extraordinary continuity between the Mexican period and the United States period.[7] The area became a territory of the United States and statehood was granted in 1912.

Throughout these changes political participation can be followed among the elite and among the masses of people. It can be analyzed in both its traditional manifestations and in contemporary patterns. In all respects it differs greatly in both level and quality from political participation outside this area. The heritage of colonialism helps explain these differences.

On the elite level, Spanish or Mexican leadership remained largely intact through the conquest and was shared with Anglo leadership after the termination of military rule in 1851. The indigenous elite retained considerable strength both in the dominant Republican party and in the state legislature. They were strong enough to ensure a bilingual provision

---

[6] Of course, we are not arguing that colonialist domination—or for that matter the peculiar pattern of voluntary immigration—offers a full explanation of this complex population, or even of the three culture areas which are the focus of this paper. Mexican Americans and the history of the region are far too complexly interwoven to pretend that any analytic thread can unravel the full tapestry. For other theses, see the analyses developed in Grebler et al. (1970).

[7] This account draws on González (1967); Lamar (1966); Holmes (1964); and Donnelly (1947). Paul Fisher prepared a valuable analytic abstract of all but the first of these sources while a research assistant. I have used his document extensively here.

in the 1912 Constitution (the only provision in the region that guarantees Spanish speakers the right to vote and hold office). Sessions of the legislature were—by law—conducted in both languages. Again, this is an extraordinary feature in any part of the continental United States. Just as in many Asian nations controlled by the British in the 19th century, the elite suffered little—either economically or politically.

On the lower-class level, in the villages, there was comparatively little articulation of New Mexican villages with the developing urban centers. What there was, however, was usually channeled through a recognized local authority, a *patrón*. Like the class structure, the *patrón* and the network of relations that sustained him were a normal part of the established local social system and not an ad hoc or temporary recognition of an individual's power. Thus political participation on both the elite and the lower-class levels were outgrowths of the existing social system.

Political participation of the elite and the *patrón* system was clearly a colonial phenomenon. An intact society, rather than a structureless mass of individuals, was taken into a territory of the United States with almost no violence. This truly colonial situation involves a totally different process of relationship between subordinate and superordinate from either the voluntary or the forced immigration of the subordinate—that is, totally different from either the "typical" American immigrant on the eastern seaboard or the slave imported from Africa.

A final point remains to be made not about political participation but about proto-political organization in the past. The villages of New Mexico had strong internal organizations not only of the informal, kinship variety but of the formal variety. These were the *penitente* sects and also the cooperative associations, such as those controlling the use of water and the grazing of livestock.[8] That such organizations were mobilized by New Mexican villagers is evidenced by the existence of terrorist groups operating against both Anglo and Spanish landowners. González (1967) mentions two: one functioning in the 1890's and one in the 1920's. Such groups could also act as local police forces.

Let us turn to the present. Political participation of the conventional variety is very high compared to that of Mexican Americans in other states of the Southwest. Presently there is a Spanish American in the United States Senate (Montoya, an "old" name), following the tradition of Dennis Chavez (another "old" name). The state legislature in 1967 was almost one-third Mexican American. (There were no Mexican American legislators in California and no more than six per cent in the legislature of any other Southwest state.) This, of course, reflects the fact that it is only in very recent years that Mexican Americans have become a numerical minority in New Mexico, but it also reflects the fact that organized political participation has remained high.

Finally, New Mexico is the locus of the only mass movement among

[8] González (1967:64) concludes that *moradas*, or *penitente* organizations, "were found in most, if not all, of the northern Spanish settlements during the last half of the 19th century and the first part of the 20th."

Mexican Americans—the *Alianza Federal de Mercedes*, headed by Reies Tijerina. In theme, the *Alianza*, which attracted tens of thousands of members, relates specifically to the colonial past, protesting the loss of land and its usurpation by Anglo interests (including, most insultingly, those of the United States Forest Service). It is this loss of land which has ultimately been responsible for the destruction of village (Spanish) culture and the large-scale migration to the cities.[9] In the light of the importance of the traditional village as a base for political mobilization, it is not really surprising that the *Alianza* should have appeared where it did. In content the movement continues local terrorism (haystack-burning) but has now extended beyond the local protest as its members have moved to the cities. Rather than being directed against specific Anglo or Spanish landgrabbers, it has lately been challenging the legality of the Treaty of Guadalupe Hidalgo. The broadening of the *Alianza's* base beyond specific local areas probably required the pooled discontent of those immigrants from many villages, many original land grants. It is an ironic feature of the *Alianza* that the generalization of its objectives and of its appeal should be possible only long after most of the alleged land-grabbing had been accomplished.

Texas

Mexican Americans in Texas had a sharply contrasting historical experience. The Mexican government in Texas was replaced by a revolution of the American settlers. Violence between Anglo-American settlers and Mexican residents continued in south Texas for generations after the annexation of Texas by the United States and the consequent full-scale war. Violence continued in organized fashion well into the 20th century with armed clashes involving the northern Mexican *guerilleros* and the U.S. Army.

This violence meant a total destruction of Mexican elite political participation by conquest, while such forces as the Texas Rangers were used to suppress Mexican American participation on the lower status or village levels. The ecology of settlement in south Texas remains somewhat reminiscent of that in northern New Mexico: there are many areas that are predominantly Mexican, and even some towns that are still controlled by Mexicans. But there is far more complete Anglo economic and political dominance on the local level. Perhaps most important, Anglo-Americans outnumbered Mexicans by five to one even before the American conquest. By contrast, Mexicans in New Mexico remained the numerical majority for more than 100 years after conquest.

Texas state politics reflect the past just as in New Mexico. Mexican Americans hold some slight representation in the U.S. Congress. There are two Mexican American Congressmen, one from San Antonio and one from Brownsville (at the mouth of the Rio Grande river), one of whom is

---

[9] González (1967:75) analyses the *Alianza* as a "nativist" movement, and suggests that its source is partly in the fact that "*for the first time* many elements of Spanish-American culture are in danger of disappearing" (emphasis added).

a political conservative. A minor representation far below the numerical proportion of Mexican Americans is maintained in the Texas legislature.

It is on the local level that the continued suppression is most apparent. As long ago as 1965 Mexican Americans in the small town of Crystal City won political control in a municipal election that electrified all Mexican Americans in Texas and stirred national attention. But this victory was possible only with statewide help from Mexican American organizations and some powerful union groups. Shortly afterward (after some intimidation from the Texas Rangers) the town returned to Anglo control. Some other small towns (Del Rio, Kingsville, Alice) have recently had demonstrations in protest against local suppressions. Small and insignificant as they were, the demonstrations once again would not have been possible without outside support, primarily from San Antonio. (The most significant of these San Antonio groups have been aided by the Ford Foundation. The repercussions in Congress were considerable and may threaten the future of the Ford Foundation as well as the Mexican Americans in Texas.)

More general Mexican American political organizations in Texas have a history that is strikingly reminiscent of Negro political organization. (There is one continuous difference: whites participated in most Negro organizations at the outset. It is only very recently that Anglos have been involved with Mexicans in such a fashion. In the past, Mexicans were almost entirely on their own.) Political organization has been middle class, highly oriented toward traditional expressions of "Americanism," and accommodationist. In fact, the first Mexican American political association refused to call itself a political association for fear that it might be too provocative to the Anglo power structure; it was known as a "civic" organization when it was formed in Texas in the late 1920's. Even the name of this group (LULAC or the League of United Latin American Citizens) evokes an atmosphere of middle-class gentility. The second major group, the American G.I. Forum, was formed in an atmosphere of greater protest, after a Texas town had refused burial to a Mexican American soldier. In recent years, increasing politicization has been manifested by the formation of such a group as PASSO (Political Association of Spanish Speaking Organizations). But in Texas, throughout the modern period the very act of *ethnic* politics has been controversial, even among Mexican Americans.[10]

California

The California transition between Mexican and American settlement falls midway between the Texas pattern of violence and the relatively smooth change in New Mexico. In northern California the discovery of gold in 1849 almost immediately swamped a sparse Mexican population in a flood of Anglo-American settlers. Prior to this time an orderly transition was in progress. Thus the effect was very much that of violence in

[10] This discussion draws on Guzmán (1967) and Cuéllar (1970).

Texas: the indigenous Mexican elite was almost totally excluded from political participation. A generation later when the opening of the railroads repeated this demographic discontinuity in southern California the Mexicans suffered the same effect. They again were almost totally excluded from political participation. The New Mexico pattern of social organization on a village level had almost no counterpart in California. Here the Mexican settlements and the economy were built around very large land holdings rather than around villages. This meant, in essence, that even the settlements that survived the American takeover relatively intact tended to lack internal social organization. Villages (as in the Bandini rancho which became the modern city of Riverside) were more likely to be clusters of ranch employees than an independent, internally coherent community.

In more recent times the peculiar organization of California politics has tended to work against Mexican American participation from the middle and upper status levels. California was quick to adopt the ideas of "direct democracy" of the Progressive era. These tend somewhat to work against ethnic minorities.[11] But this effect is accidental and can hardly be called "internal colonialism," coupled as it was with the anti-establishment ideals of the Progressive era. The concept of "colonialism," in fact, appears most useful with reference to the extreme manipulation of Mexican immigration in the 20th century. Attracted to the United States by the hundreds of thousands in the 1920's, Mexicans and many of their U.S.-born children were deported ("repatriated") by welfare agencies during the Depression, most notably from California. (Texas had almost no welfare provisions; hence no repatriation.) The economic expansion in World War II required so much labor that Mexican immigration was supplemented by a contract labor arrangement. But, as in the Depression, "too many" were attracted and came to work in the United States without legal status. Again, in 1954, massive sweeps of deportations got rid of Mexicans by the hundreds of thousands in "Operation Wetback." New Mexico was largely spared both waves of deportation; Texas was involved primarily in Operation Wetback rather than in the welfare repatriations. California was deeply involved in both.

This economic manipulation of the nearly bottomless pool of Mexican labor has been quite conscious and enormously useful to the development of California extractive and agricultural enterprises. Only in recent years with increasing—and now overwhelming—proportions of native-born Mexican Americans in the population has the United States been "stuck" with the Mexicans. As one consequence, the naturalization rate of Mexican immigrants has been very low. After all, why relinquish even the partial protection of Mexican citizenship? Furthermore the treatment

[11] Fogelson (1967) gives a good picture of political practices which had the latent consequence of excluding Mexicans from Los Angeles politics—a fact of great importance given the very large concentrations of Mexican Americans in that city. Political impotence in Los Angeles has affected a very significant fraction of California's Mexican Americans. Harvey (1966) gives a broader picture of California politics.

of Mexicans as economic commodities has greatly reduced both their motivation and their effectiveness as political participants. The motivations that sent Mexican Americans to the United States appear to have been similar to those that sent immigrants from Europe. But the conscious dehumanization of Mexicans in the service of the railroad and citrus industries in California and elsewhere meant an assymmetry in relationship between "host" and immigrant that is less apparent in the European patterns of immigration. Whatever resentment that might have found political voice in the past had no middle class organizational patterns. California was structurally unreceptive and attitudinally hostile.

Thus in California the degree of Mexican political participation remains low. The electoral consequences are even more glaringly below proportional representation than in Texas. There is only one national representative (Congressman Roybal from Los Angeles) and only one in the state legislature. Los Angeles County (with nearly a million Mexican Americans) has no Supervisor of Mexican descent and the city has no Councilman of Mexican descent. Otherwise, the development of political associations has followed the Texas pattern, although later, with meaningful political organization a post-World War II phenomenon. The G.I. Forum has formed chapters in California. In addition, the Community Service Organization, oriented to local community political mobilization, and the Mexican American Political Association, oriented to state-wide political targets, have repeated the themes of Texas' voluntary association on the level of the growing middle class.

How useful, then, is the concept of colonialism when it is applied to these three culture areas? We argue here that both the nature and extent of political participation in the state of New Mexico can be understood with reference to the "classical" colonial past. We noted that a continuity of elite participation in New Mexico from the period of Mexican rule to the period of American rule paved the way for a high level of conventional political participation. The fact that village social structure remained largely intact is in some measure responsible for the appearance of the only mass movement of Mexicans in the Southwest today—the *Alianza*. But even this movement is an outcome of colonialism; the expropriation of the land by large-scale developers and by federal conservation interests led ultimately to the destruction of the village economic base—and to the movement of the dispossessed into the cities. Once living in the cities in a much closer environment than that of the scattered small villages, they could "get together" and respond to the anti-colonialist protests of a charismatic leader.

Again following this idea, we might categorize the Texas experience as "conflict colonialism." This would reflect the violent discontinuity between the Mexican and the American periods of elite participation and the current struggle for the legitimation of ethnic politics on all levels. In this latter aspect, the "conflict colonialism" of Texas is reminiscent of black politics in the Deep South, although it comes from different origins.

To apply the colonial concept to Mexicans in California, we might usefully use the idea of "economic colonialism." The destruction of elite political strength by massive immigration and the comparative absence of local political organization meant a political vacuum for Mexican Americans. Extreme economic manipulation inhibited any attachment to the reality or the ideals of American society and indirectly allowed as much intimidation as was accomplished by the overt repression of such groups as the Texas Rangers.

To return to Blauner's use of the concept of "internal colonialism": in the case of the Mexicans in the United States, a major segment of this group who live in New Mexico require no significant conceptual adaptation of the classic analyses of European overseas colonialism. Less adaptation is required in fact than in applying the concepts to such countries as Kenya, Burma, Algeria, and Indonesia. Not only was the relationship between the Mexican and the Anglo-American "involuntary," involving "racism" and the "transformation . . . of indigenous values," but the culture of the Spanish American was well developed, autonomous, a majority numerically, and contained a full social system with an upper and middle as well as lower class. The comparatively non-violent conquest was really almost a postscript to nearly a decade of violence between the United States and Mexico which began in Texas.

The Texas pattern, although markedly different, can still be fitted under a colonialist rubric, with a continuous thread of violence, suppression, and adaptations to both in recent political affairs.

The Mexican experience in California is much more complicated. Mexicans lost nearly all trace of participation in California politics. Hence, there was no political tradition of any kind, even the purely negative experience in Texas. Then, too, the relationship between imported labor and employer was "voluntary," at least on the immigrants' side. The relationships were much more asymmetrical than in the "classic colonial" case.

If any further proof of the applicability of the idea of "colonialism" were needed, we have the developing ideology of the new *chicano* militants themselves. Like the black ideologies, *chicanismo* emphasizes colonialism, but in a manner to transcend the enormous disparities in Mexican American experience. Thus one of the latest versions of the ideology reaches out to a time *before* even the Spanish colonialism to describe the Southwestern United States as "Aztlán"—an Aztec term. "Aztlán" is a generality so sweeping that it can include all Mexican Americans. Mexican Americans are the products of layer upon layer of colonialism and the overlay of American influence is only the most recent. That the young ideologues or the "cultural nationalists" (as they call themselves) should utilize the symbols of the first of these colonists, the Aztecs (along with Emiliano Zapata, the most "Indian" of Mexican revolutionaries from the past), is unquestionably of great symbolic significance to the participants themselves. But perhaps of more sociological significance (and far more controversial among the participants) is the attempt to legitimate *chicano* culture. This culture comes from the habits, ideas, and speech of the most despised lower-class Mexican American as he has been forced to live in a quasi-legal ghetto culture in large South-western cities. These symbols are all indigenous to the United States and are neither Mexican, nor Spanish, nor even Aztec. But they *do* offer symbols to all Mexican Americans, after a widely varying experience with Americans in which, perhaps, the ideologues can agree only that it was "colonialist."

References

Blauner, Robert. 1969. "Internal colonialism and ghetto revolt." Social Problems 16 (Spring, 1969): 393–408.

Cuéllar, Alfredo. forthcoming. "Perspective on politics." In Joan W. Moore with Alfredo Cuéllar, Mexican Americans. Englewood Cliffs, N.J.: Prentice-Hall, Inc.

Donnelly, Thomas C. 1947. The Government of New Mexico. Albuquerque: The University of New Mexico Press.

Fogelson, Robert M. 1967. The Fragmented Metropolis: Los Angeles, 1850–1960. Cambridge, Mass.: Harvard University Press.

González, Nancie L. 1967. The Spanish Americans of New Mexico: A Distinctive Heritage. Advance Report 9. Los Angeles: University of California, Mexican American Study Project.

Grebler, Leo et al. 1970. The Mexican American People. New York: Free Press.

Guzmán, Ralph. 1967. "Political socialization." Unpublished manuscript.

Harvey, Richard B. 1966. "California politics: Historical profile." In R. B. Dvorin and D. Misner (eds.), California Politics and Policies. Reading, Mass.: Addison-Wesley, Inc.

Holmes, Jack E. 1964. Party, Legislature and Governor in the Politics of New Mexico, 1911–1963. Ph.D. Dissertation, Chicago: University of Chicago.

Kitano, Harry H. L. 1968. The Japanese Americans. Englewood Cliffs, N.J.: Prentice-Hall, Inc.

Kuper, Leo and M. G. Smith (eds.). 1969. Pluralism in Africa. Berkeley and Los Angeles: University of California Press.

Lamar, Howard Roberts. 1966. The Far Southwest, 1845–1912: A Territorial History. New Haven: Yale University Press.

Olguín, John Phillip. 1967. "Where does the 'justified' resentment begin?" New Mexico Business offprint, July 1967.

Sánchez, George I. 1940. Forgotten People. Albuquerque: The University of New Mexico Press.

FORD AND LA RAZA: "THEY STOLE OUR LAND AND GAVE US POWDERED MILK"

Rees Lloyd and Peter Montague

When the invading armies entered New Mexico in 1846, U.S. General Stephen Kearny grandly announced to the natives, "I come among you for your benefit, not your injury."

Now, more than 100 years later—in the wake of the assault of Reies Tijerina and forces of La Raza against Anglo colonials in the celebrated 1967 Tierra Amarilla "courthouse raid"—there has been a new invasion of the Southwest. This time it is the Ford Foundation, not the U.S. Army, and it is backed by dollars, not soldiers. But the intent is the same as it has always been: to "benefit" the natives—this time with a pacification program aimed at heading off the new militancy, creating a poverty-foundation complex, and building up a "safe" leadership for La Raza akin to the NAACP or the Urban League. Ford's single largest investment has been a $1.5 million loan to establish a huge cattle feedlot in La Jara, Colorado. But after this multi-million dollar business was created, it was surreptitiously handed over to the brother-in-law of the same Ford executive who had publicly announced the feedlot as an example of the Foundation's bounty.

This is a major scandal that has been covered up. As a result, the Anglo benefactors get good publicity, while the poor, as usual, get nothing.

I

In New Mexico, only the people are poor; the land is rich. It contains a wealth of resources and in the north possesses a beauty and rhythm found in few other places. The land in the north has been the focus of a resistance movement which has persisted for more than a century since the U.S. invasion. The land and the communal way of life it once supported remain the essence of this struggle, which has never ended.

"Why do they say the land was conquered? The land was never conquered; it was only *occupied*," said Jose Madril of Velarde, New Mexico. "They must mean something different when they say 'conquered.' I don't know, it's that language [English]. It really has no value. But this land, it's never been 'conquered.' No. Only occupied—the land still be-

Reprinted from *Ramparts Magazine*, September 1970. Copyright Ramparts Magazine, 1970. By permission of the Editors.

Rees Lloyd and Peter Montague are free-lance writers in New Mexico and are associated with El Grito del Norte, a newspaper published in Española, N.M.

longs to the people. And my people, *mi Raza*—they have never conquered my people."

Jose Madril is one of those who rose at Tierra Amarilla on June 5, 1967, and went to the courthouse to make a citizen's arrest of District Attorney Alfonso Sanchez, then the most visible engineer of police repression against the landgrant movement led by Reies Lopez Tijerina.

Madril, now an editor of El Grito del Norte ("The Cry of the North"), the Raza movement paper in the north, is one of the eight Alianza defendants who still face charges in connection with the Tierra Amarilla incident. All eight—Juan Valdez, Baltazar Martinez, Geronimo Borunda, Tobias Leyba, Moises Morales, Salomon Velazquez, Esequiel Dominguez and Madril—are poor, and Raza, and heirs to the land under ancient Spanish landgrants supposedly protected by the Treaty of Guadalupe-Hidalgo which ended the so-called Mexican-American War. "That language, I told you, it has no value," said Madril.

What the armies of the U.S. gained with the gun, the government attempted to control by importing a legal and economic system, value system and educational system. It attempted to wipe out a people's culture, history, heritage and language, while it swallowed up their land.

The colony which the government ruled was huge: New Mexico, fifth largest state, sprawls across 78 million acres. Of these, 27 million (34.6 per cent) are held in the name of the United States government, and another 10 million (12.5 per cent) in the name of the State of New Mexico. Anglo mining, oil, ranching and speculative interests have ripped off most of the rest. Indians now hold only 7,313,600 acres (9.4 per cent). And the people of the north, La Raza, have little left. They have been forced into the cities or migrant labor, poor jobs, no jobs at all. In Rio Arriba County, where Tierra Amarilla is the county seat, the original landgrant covers just under 595,000 acres; an estimated 80 per cent of the people are Raza and more than 50 per cent of them today have incomes of less than $2000 a year.

"To understand it," says Jose Madril, "you have to be able to look at it with Raza eyes, with a Raza heart. Anglo eyes, an Anglo heart, they don't see things the way we do, they don't see what the land means to the people. It's like the *viejo* [old man] said in El Grito: 'The land is our mother. If we lose the land we are orphans. Where will we go?' "

To the Anglo-Americans, the land was perceived as *property*, as real estate to be exploited. Last year, New Mexico's oil industry, which is based in the southern part of the state, extracted $632 million from the land. In all, New Mexico's extractive interests reaped nearly a billion dollars in 1969 alone. The timber industry cut 154 million board-feet from the forests in 1969, almost all of it in areas held by the U.S. Forest Service, the chief official agent of the occupation.

Robert O. Anderson bases his huge Atlantic-Richfield Oil Co. (ARCO) in Rosewell, in southern New Mexico (the area known as "Little Texas" for its overt racism, where signs reading "No Dogs or Mexicans Allowed" used to be found). Though Anderson's tentacles reach deep into Latin America and the Alaskan slope, his crews are at this very moment busy in the government forests in the north of New Mexico looking for more treasure, while the rangers of the Forest Service—"crackers" all—stand guard to keep the people away from their land. Tourists, of course, are welcomed with a smile. Mr. Anderson no doubt also accepted with a smile his appointment this year by President Nixon to the National Council on the Humanities and the National Advisory Commission on Pollution.

It is a political truism that an effective imperialist power will substitute the psychological control of its institutions for the physical control of its armies, but that when the psychological control falters, the gun is always ready. When the bonds of colonial psychology were snapped on June 5, 1967, at Tierra Amarilla, the National Guard of New Mexico invaded the north with troops, bayonets and bullets, tanks and even helicopters. The families of *Alianzistas* were herded into a barbed-wire corral at the home of Tobias Leyba in Canjilon and held there under guard. The indignities were great. Suspected Alianzistas were dragged from their homes. All benevolent pretense concerning the "natives" was dropped. When the National Guard finally put out food (C-rations) for the people it had penned up, the food remained untouched, sitting in the rain when the people refused to take it. "I was very proud of *mi Raza* that day," says Jose Madril, whose wife, two children and infant daughter were held in the pen and refused to eat the food of the foreign army.

Although the U.S. Civil Rights Commission recently admitted in its timid way that overt political police repression of the Alianza had "culminated" in the Tierra Amarilla courthouse incident, the leader, Reies Lopez Tijerina, has been a political prisoner for more than a year.

Tijerina was charged by the State of New Mexico with over 150 separate crimes stemming from the single courthouse incident. In December 1968, Tijerina—brilliantly conducting his own defense—was found innocent of the first three charges brought by the State, including kidnapping, then a capital crime. The State brought three more charges against Tijerina to trial last October, and finally won a conviction on two of the charges, though the jury strangely amended their verdict to say they really believed Tijerina was "like a man guilty of going through a red light taking his wife to the hospital to have a baby"—morally right but technically guilty. The State admitted privately that it would try Tijerina on three charges at a time until he was finally locked up. After the second trial, he was sentenced to one-to-five years on one charge, and two-to-ten years on another. The case is on appeal.

But before the State ever won a conviction, the federal government had already put Tijerina away. In 1966, the Alianza had moved on part of the Forest Service's Echo Amphitheatre Park, which occupies the San Joaquin Landgrant. They declared it the Free City State of San Joaquin in an attempt to force the courts and the Congress to face the issue of the landgrants, the treaty which was supposed to protect them, and the claims of the people to the lands. Two forest rangers, both of whom were known to the angry crowd, were given a mock trial, found guilty of trespassing, and released. The mock trial was more than anything else a move by the leadership to alleviate the tension and to preserve the rangers' health and safety. Neither man was brutalized in any way, nor injured, nor even struck. Nevertheless Tijerina and four others were convicted of assault on federal officers, and Tijerina drew a two-year sentence. The presiding judge at the trial, U.S. District Judge Howard Bratton, characterized Tijerina as "the leader of a mob" in imposing sentence. Tijerina was still free pending his appeal, but in June 1969 a similar incident at Coyote in northern New Mexico served as a pretext for the federal government to revoke Tijerina's bond on the 1966 conviction.

As the anniversary of the "courthouse raid" approached, Tijerina had called for a four-day gathering at Coyote. Alianza supporters arrived from around the country, while Tijerina flew off to Washington to preface the Coyote meeting with a "citizen's arrest" attempt on Warren E. Burger, then being sworn in as Nixon's Chief Justice of the Supreme Court. Arrest warrant in hand, charging Burger with judicial violation of civil rights (a felony), Tijerina waited outside the barred chamber doors as Senator James O. Eastland of Mississippi led Burger away down a deserted back hall. Tijerina filed the warrant with the clerk of the court and departed.

National publicity followed, and though Tijerina's citizen's arrest tactic has been denounced by the media in New Mexico as sham, in reality the tactic has had no small effect. "You see," Tijerina used to say, "the government is very powerful, very powerful, like a lion. And we are like a little cricket, that's all. The lion, he's big and powerful, but the cricket, he sneaks up and gives him a little tickle, then another, and another. What can the cricket do against the lion? The lion is so big and strong, he has so many weapons. But the cricket," Tijerina woud say, his voice dropping almost to a whisper as he leaned forward intently, "maybe one day the cricket will just . . . walk . . . into the big . . . lion's . . . ear . . . and . . . TICKLE HIM TO DEATH!"

The citizen's arrest provisions of the United States common law have long been recognized as valid, but no one before Tijerina had used them as a political weapon against the police and judicial oppression. At the gathering in Coyote, Tijerina led a caravan to Los Alamos, birthplace of the atom bomb, to place the Atomic Energy Commission's Dr. Norris Bradbury under citizen's arrest for "crimes against humanity." Bradbury did not respond to a knock on his door; Tijerina left the warrant there, and his group, followed and monitored by a caravan of State Police, departed. The following day, Tijerina led his caravan in pursuit of New Mexico's Governor David F. Cargo for arrest on similar charges. A government plane whisked the governor away from a barbecue and deposited him at a secret destination. On June 8, Patsy Tijerina, Reies's wife, set fire to two U.S. Forest Service signs in the north—one at Coyote, one at Gallina—announcing to the press that the burning was "a symbolic act of protest against the occupation of the people's lands." State Police watched as the signs went up in flames. Then a band of armed rangers descended on the unarmed crowd—led by James Evans, the Forest Service's chief of law enforcement, packing a special World War II automatic carbine with a 30-bullet clip.

Evans, ignoring Patsy, who was arrested later almost as an after-thought, went straight for Reies. "I wanted to shoot the sonofabitch," Evans told fellow officers in Albuquerque later. Tijerina was arrested June 8 and jailed on June 11 on the previous charge, his bond having been revoked. On June 18, a bond revocation hearing was held at which time affidavits, signed by two witnesses, were introduced, stating that an undercover agent for the State Police, Jack Johnson, attempted to "assas-sinate" Tijerina, but that Johnson's gun misfired twice. Johnson denied this but testified in court that should the opportunity arise, he would suffer no remorse in killing Tijerina. Another State Police undercover agent, Robert Gilliland, testified, "If I had been at Tierra Amarilla . . . I would have shot him. . . . Yes, I hate him." Gilliland is the man the New Mexico State Police have assigned to investigate the bombings and shoot-ings at the Alianza headquarters, where Tijerina lives.

Tijerina, Patsy and six others were arraigned for destroying govern-ment property and assaulting a government officer (Evans). The next day, released on his own recognizance since he already had more than $42,000 in bonds outstanding on other charges, Tijerina announced that Evans had 24 hours to leave New Mexico or he would face citizen's arrest for violating the civil rights of the people at Coyote. Tijerina read the provisions of the law which grant the use of arms to citizens who are making a citizen's arrest. He said Evans could be shot if he resisted arrest and cited the law, chapter and verse.

When the 24 hours elapsed, the arrest party went out. At the heavily guarded home of Evans (who was hiding out in a motel), the spotlights of the police flashed over riot-gun barrels and caught the advancing Alianzistas in the light. Wilfredo Sedillo, vice president of the Alianza, inquired as to Evans's whereabouts, saying the party had come to arrest him. The police said he wasn't there. Sedillo tacked the warrant to Evans's door and left.

Tijerina wasn't even there; he had gone for a ride. Yet the incident served as a pretext for the revocation of his bond and Tijerina was sent to jail on June 11, 1969. On the very same day the Ford Foundation an-nounced its $1.5 million feedlot loan to benefit the poor of northern New Mexico, the same people who are the strength and numbers of the land-grant movement and the Alianza.

II

This was not Ford's first initiative in New Mexico. The way had been paved for some time. The government had developed its own acronymic

"AID" pacification through the Office of Economic Opportunity (OEO)
with its Community Action Program (CAP) and the Home Education
Livelihood Program (HELP), a statewide agency funded by OEO and
sponsored by the New Mexico Council of Churches to assist migrant and
seasonally employed farmworkers.

Tijerina's activities did not make pacification easy. "They took your
land and gave you powdered milk," he roared. As Tijerina's strength continued to grow, the screws of the police repression machine were tight-
ened. OEO, CAP and HELP staff collected information on what was
happening with the Alianza, information which found its way to the
police. Police and government agents were everywhere; files were bulg-
ing in the attorney general's office, the state OEO, the district attorney's
office. The director of the State Archives in the Colony of New Mexico
admits that she regularly turned over to the attorney general the names
of suspected Alianzistas who came in to study the landgrant records.

Into this situation stepped Ford. According to one well-placed Ford
man:

> Ford's first direct contact in New Mexico was in the spring of 1967. The
> key [Ford] man here was Bill Watts, who was active head of the Office of
> Government and Law. Ford was very anxious even at that point to build
> some reasonable alternative to Tijerina and the Alianza. Within a month after
> the raid [sic] at Tierra Amarilla, a team was dispatched to New Mexico.
> Their purpose was to create as quickly as possible a leadership structure
> alternative to Tijerina.
>
> Actually, the team had two objectives: The first was to divert attention
> from Tijerina and the land question by creating an alternative leader, some-
> one to whom they could point as a spokesman for the Mexican-Americans in
> New Mexico. The HELP program was existent, under the direction of Alex
> Mercure, so Ford decided to make Mercure that leader. A few months after
> the team was sent to New Mexico, Ford approved a $453,450 R&D [research
> and development] front to HELP as part of the program to knock out
> Tijerina and create this alternative leadership structure.

After Ford's initial $453,450 grant, OEO stepped up its grants to
HELP. Alex Mercure became known as "The Empire Builder" among his
poverty program colleagues and was named to national commissions,
advisory boards and panels as a "Mexican-American leader." When Congress called hearings after the Tierra Amarilla incident to find out why it
had happened, it called Mercure to testify, not Tijerina or the Alianzistas.
At the same time, Ford and the government were increasing their funds
for HELP's migrant work. Orders went out to the HELP staff to avoid the
subject of Cesar Chavez and the farmworkers' strike, the *huelga* in
California. The budget of Mercure's HELP program fattened to nearly
$3 million by 1969.

Ford's funding of HELP and its involvement in New Mexico was hardly
a matter of treading upon political toes. The political establishment in
the colony was all behind it. Governor David F. Cargo, a Republican,

reached out with open arms, and his predecessor, former (Democratic) Governor Jack Campbell, who at one time had worked for the FBI, took time out to write a "Dear Bill" letter to Watts which, according to the Ford man already quoted, "was fairly explicit in encouraging Watts to bring Ford into New Mexico to put down Tijerina." Campbell now holds a "half-time" job at $15,000 a year as director of the Institute for Social Research and Development at the University of New Mexico, which is in charge of the University's "poverty work." Watts is no longer with Ford; at last report he was working as staff secretary of the National Security Council in the Nixon Administration under Henry Kissinger, an old personal friend of Ford Foundation President McGeorge Bundy.

Ford's benevolent involvement in New Mexico did not, however, draw universal applause. Gilberto Ballejos, editor of El Papel, the Raza movement paper in Albuquerque, denounced Ford's move in the beginning as "Ford's political Edsel. They're trying to create *Vendido* Power (Sellout Power), *Lame* Power (Ass-kisser Power), and they want the poor Raza to pay the price . . . It's Bundy's bullshit, he's trying to bring Vietnam to New Mexico and trying to create 'leaders' the system can use as tools. But it hasn't worked with the Vietnamese and it's not going to work with Raza here in the United States."

Ford did not confine itself to the northern New Mexico area. In the fall of 1967, Ford moved, under a $21,830 grant, to bring together a select group of Mexican-Americans at a meeting in Los Angeles. Out of that gathering eventually came the Southwest Council of La Raza, designed as an umbrella organization covering the Southwest, funded by Ford to the tune of $630,000 in February 1968. The Council's first executive director was Herman Gallegos, who resigned his job as a Ford Foundation consultant to accept the new position. Alex Mercure was immediately appointed to the Council's Board of Directors.

In Texas, Ford invested $2.2 million to establish the Mexican-American Legal Defense and Education Fund, generally known as MALD. Patterned after the NAACP Legal Defense Fund, MALD was intended by Ford to be Southwest-wide, and perhaps national, in scope. In New Mexico at least, MALD has been conspicuously absent from the more controversial issues. One of its first acts was to deny legal assistance to the eight impoverished Tierra Amarilla defendants.

Among Ford's other investments in Texas was the funding of the Mexican-American Unity Council in San Antonio, which in turn financed the small ($8527) budget of the Mexican-American Youth Organization. MAYO's existence has been anathema to the political establishment and especially to Congressman Henry B. Gonzales [D-Tex.], who attacked it and the Ford Foundation on the floor of Congress last year.

Ironically, Gonzales's attack on Ford for funding "militants" provided the best articulation to date of the reasons Ford had provided $630,000 for the Southwest Council of La Raza (Congressional Record, April 16, 1969, p. H2734): "One thing that surprised the Ford analysts was that the Mexican-American population had no effective national organization; there was no equivalent of the NAACP or the Urban League. . . . The foundation concluded that one prime requisite for progress was national organization and national leadership; such an organization would define goals toward which the whole group could aspire, and could coordinate the efforts of all groups toward those national goals." The Southwest Council of La Raza, said Gonzales, "would be the new national leadership organization."

Gonzales's attack on MAYO and Ford, which was widely publicized, lent Ford an image of embattled liberalism at the same time as it provided Ford with an opportunity to withdraw its miniscule funds from MAYO, which had developed a militant momentum of its own and was therefore not a valuable investment for Ford.

McGeorge Bundy himself clarified what business Ford was in when he personally announced, on March 16, 1970, that the Ford Foundation had funded the Southwest Council of La Raza—at $1.3 million—for another two years. Bundy said that while the "council's leaders" had encountered great problems, still they had succeeded in creating "a visible organization with a sense of permanence and stability" and had ". . . taken the first steps toward converting the long pent-up anger and frustration of its people, ever in danger of explosion and violence, into beneficial programming and planning. We are glad to assist in this pioneering effort to provide constructive direction to the growing energy and momentum of the Mexican-American movement."

It was Bundy—formerly Special Assistant for National Security under Presidents Kennedy and Johnson, a major architect of the Vietnam pacification program and the Bay of Pigs Invasion, and now President of the Ford Foundation—who had brought about the coupling of government and foundation efforts at pacification. Under Bundy, wrote The New York Times on September 23, 1968, the Ford Foundation "has come to see itself . . . increasingly as an agent for the resolution of civil conflict." In the same month, Ford announced "a major policy shift"; it would, the Times reported, "place part of its investment portfolio in ventures aiding the poor and minority groups and land conservation rather than enterprises offering greater financial return."

The model of Ford's "constructive direction" is the multi-million dollar cattle feedlot which Ford set up in La Jara, Colorado, with satellite feedlots to be built in northern New Mexico. The feedlot sprawls across 200 acres, with 120 feeding pens capable of accommodating 15,000 cattle. It contains an ultra-sophisticated push-button feed-mixing mill, whose superstructure and three large silos rise before the gleaming new offices which Ford has built for the management, headed by Claude Lowry, an Anglo cattle trader from New Mexico. Decked out in cowboy attire, Lowry is short, balding, and pleasant in the style of Southwest colonial gringoism. Outside his carpeted office at La Jara, the sun glints off the shiny new mixing mill and the small red-and-white single-engine plane tied down nearby. "Yupf," Lowry snuffs at a visitor, "we got a landing strip." Lowry is the brother-in-law of Boudinot P. Atterbury, the same Ford Foundation executive who arranged the benevolent enterprise.

Dr. Manuel Ferran, head of research and development with the HELP program, was the man principally responsible for the design of the feedlot, which was planned as a $4 million operation, with Ford's $1.5 million serving as the financial backbone. Ferran had conducted more than a year's work on feasibility studies for the feedlot project. Ferran—who incidentally had been an employee of the CIA in the Dominican Republic before becoming Mercure's right-hand man in the New Mexico HELP program—saw the fruits of his work appropriated by Ford.

The people in La Jara, Colorado, as in northern New Mexico, are poor and mainly Raza. The border between northern New Mexico and southern Colorado is arbitrary, a white man's demarcation. Part of the Tierra Amarilla Landgrant straddles the line, and the Conejos Landgrant begins where the other ends.

The economy in the San Luis Valley, as in the mountains of the north, is controlled by Anglos, with the difference that many of those in the valley are Mormons, who have raised racism to the position of religious doctrine. But it was the existence of the poverty in the valley and the mountains of the north—official "hunger counties" all—that provided the justification for building the feedlot.

"I guess it all really began," said a rancher expressing the consensus view of valley inhabitants,

> with this meeting they had here in a tavern in La Jara. The way I hear it. Claude Lowry was there with his brother-in-law, fella named Atterbury from the Ford Foundation. Claude Lowry had the good luck to marry his [Atterbury's] sister. Anyway, they say they were in this tavern—Lowry, Atterbury, Harry Immel (he runs a slaughterhouse out at the feedlot), Myron Peterson; lemme see, I guess that's all—anyway, they were in this tavern having a drink and they say Claude Lowry was talking to his brother-in-law about setting up a feedlot. Well, they say after a while Myron Peterson just pointed a finger at Atterbury and said: 'Why don't you get the money for us?' Well, from what I hear, Atterbury just said 'Okay,' he'd try, and that was that. . . .

Of course it was not that simple; private and public interests had to come together before so neat and expensive a deal could be culminated. After the take-over at Echo Amphitheatre and the raising of the flag of the Free City State of San Joaquin, and Tijerina's conviction, the landgrant movement of the Alianza had continued to gain momentum. . . .

III

It was under Bundy's new flag of "aiding the poor" and reaping a "high social yield" from financial investments that Boudinot P. Atterbury of the Ford Foundation flew into Albuquerque and announced a $1.5 million grant for the feedlot in La Jara on the day that Tijerina was sent to prison. Blond and blue-eyed, tailored in corporate dress, Atterbury sat in the office of Albuquerque attorney John Eastham, Ford's legal counsel in New Mexico, together with Frank Martinez, HELP's legal counsel, and Dr. Ferran. To a reporter from the Albuquerque Journal, Atterbury gave glowing and unequivocal assurances that the small, poor, struggling ranchers and farmers of the north would be the most direct beneficiaries because Ford's $1.5 million investment would go, Atterbury said, to "the South-Southwestern Producers Cooperative," which was to be a co-operative comprising essentially the same small, poor ranchers and farmers. As Atterbury himself stressed, "The important thing, in the Ford Foundation's viewpoint, is the integration of the urban and rural, the haves and the have-nots, and the cultures, in a common economic effort. . . . If it succeeds, it could be magnificent."

Atterbury also drew attention to the "bi-culturalism" of the project, praising his brother-in-law Lowry and Ford protegé Mercure as "the two key men [who] represent the bi-culturalism." And, Atterbury added sharply, eyebrows arched, "We're going to show these people like Reies Tijerina, we're going to show these advocates of violence, that Ford has a better way."

Following Atterbury's announcement in Albuquerque, the foundation's headquarters in New York released statements to the national media concerning the New Mexico project and a similar project for blacks in Mississippi, calling them ". . . a new approach to the problem of poverty in rural America."

However, according to a special report made for the OEO, a little less than a month after Atterbury's announcement in Albuquerque and Ford's in New York a separate Corporation was quietly established in Colorado—again, by Atterbury's brother-in-law, Lowry—and *it* became the sole recipient of Ford's bounty. HELP was squeezed out. The South-Southwestern Producers Cooperative never materialized.

Though the fiction of Ford's feedlot has been carefully maintained by HELP, HELP was aware even when Atterbury came to town with Ford's announcement on June 1 that something was amiss in La Jara. But while Tijerina was being locked away, Ferran and Atterbury worked out their differences in an agreeable deal, according to the OEO report, wherein HELP would be "solely" responsible for the project and receive Ford's funds. "Unfortunately, Ford Foundation officials subsequently overlooked all the points of this informal agreement, when more pressure was applied at a meeting July 3," the report says. ". . . Mr. Lowry contacted his brother-in-law . . . apparently he convinced Mr. Atterbury that Mr. Ferran was a HELP 'plant' involved in the project for the purpose of eroding Mr. Lowry's authority. Mr. Lowry and Mr. Atterbury then made the decision to set up a new Colorado corporation, with the intention of freezing out HELP."

The OEO report also described the arrival, on July 9, 1969, of two more Ford officials, Richard Brooke and David Shulte, who had flown into

Albuquerque as evaluators of HELP's $453,450 research and development grant. According to the report, their primary business did not include the feedlot, but Brooke went to La Jara with HELP's Dr. Ferran and spoke with Lowry, who admitted to Brooke that the real purpose in setting up the new corporation was to freeze out HELP. At that point, Ferran warned that if the Colorado corporation was set up, HELP would withdraw all the federal and private funds it had pulled together for the project, but Lowry dismissed the threat and set up the corporation the same day. On July 10—the day after Lowry's feedlot was legally incorporated in La Jara—Brooke, Mercure and Ferran held a strategy meeting. At Ferran's suggestion, it was decided that they would tell the Foundation that a press release would be forthcoming with the following headline: "FORD FOUNDATION OFFICIAL FUNDS FEEDLOT FOR BROTHER-IN-LAW." It was never done. As for Mercure, much of his time was spent away from HELP, in a special staff position with Ford's Southwest Council of La Raza as an "expert" in economic development and "entrepreneurship."

However, apparently in response to the threatened exposure, the Ford Foundation notified HELP on July 14 that Atterbury had "voluntarily" withdrawn from the La Jara project. Naturally this had no effect on the program which Atterbury had created.

"The problem seems to lie," the OEO report said, "in the rather unusual relationship to the project of Mr. Claude Lowry. Mr. Lowry is a brother-in-law of Mr. B. P. Atterbury, a Ford Foundation official who is responsible for the feedlot program." From there the report goes on to describe the nitty-gritty of Ford's "better way" as it evolved under Lowry's guidance in the La Jara venture.

Once in the saddle bought by Ford, Atterbury's brother-in-law apparently played the role of "grand *gringo*" in his $25,000-a-year job. Commenting on their "visit" to the feedlot itself, the writers of the report said Lowry had larded the place with "what could well be called his cronies," that he overrode and ignored the advice of the feedlot's paid consulting firm, and let out construction contracts on his own. Moreover,

> We could not help but note the lackadaisical atmosphere surrounding this multi-million dollar project. . . . We could not detect any form of adequate record keeping, filing or other sound business practices. It was also disappointing to observe the whimsical attitude of this management team toward the project. Outsiders who are not involved in the project, such as local bankers, feed salesmen, friends and visitors, all seemed to be in on discussions of the project's business.

As for the vaunted benevolence-through-business for the poor, the report says:

> Furthermore, he [Lowry] refuses to purchase cattle from small producers. To date [July 31, 1969], he apparently has dealt only with the largest cattle growers. For example, he recently purchased 600 head of yearlings from one

of the best known ranches in the area. . . . Some of the grounds that the new feedlot is being built on were purchased from Mr. Harry Immel, who operated a small stockyard and slaughter plant on the premises. Unfortunately, Mr. Lowry insisted that the project purchase the slaughter plant (against the advice of the research firm working with the feedlot, which said the slaughterhouse would be a "hindrance" to the feedlot) for $100,000. . . . It was also agreed that Mr. Immel would continue to act as manager of the slaughter plant, at a salary of $20,000 a year.

Immel had been in on the earliest discussion with Atterbury and Lowry. According to the report, Immel's $20,000 salary is $3,000 greater than the amount he made when he owned and operated the slaughterhouse himself. Furthermore, meat inspectors retained by HELP appraised the slaughterhouse at only $50,000 (the OEO consultants appraised the surrounding stockyards as possibly worth an additional $20,000) and said the facilities wouldn't meet federal meat inspection standards.

This revealing report commissioned by the OEO has disappeared into the federal bureaucracy, and HELP has maintained a discreet and stony silence. Mercure, with his national and presidential advisory boards, panels and commissions, described as a "leader" and called upon to testify for the poor, has done nothing to draw attention to Ford's fiasco. Privately, he has whispered that HELP no longer has anything to do with the feedlot and has withdrawn its federal and private funds from the project. Publicly, Mercure has said nothing—nor has the New Mexico Council of Churches, which is HELP's sponsor.

The government, too, has kept its silence, even though OEO poured an initial $708,000 into the feedlot program with no small fanfare. In addition to suppressing the report, the government announced, on May 4, 1970, through the office of U.S. Senator Joseph M. Montoya [D-N.M.], that OEO was providing a "supplemental grant of $252,374 to HELP for a satellite feedlot program." Satellite to what? To Ford and its La Jara feedlot fraud. Moreover, to replace HELP funds withdrawn from the project, the government's Production Credit Association has leapt in to provide more than $1.5 million in loans to the feedlot in La Jara. (Not surprisingly, a new publication called "Feedlot News," which the La Jara feedlot started putting out in May, says that the new president of the board is Harold Linger of Alamosa, who is identified in the story as having been an "administrator of the Production Credit Association of Colorado" before joining the feedlot.)

The colonial press in New Mexico, no stranger to suppression and manipulation, has done nothing to expose the federal/Ford axis and its antics. Not a word has appeared in New Mexico on Ford or its feedlot or HELP which even hints at the reality, save for articles in the Raza movement press. The Albuquerque Journal has continued to aim dark innuendo and open distortion at such things as a Raza farming cooperative and people's medical clinic in Tierra Amarilla, while simultaneously holding up as a model Ford's feedlot in La Jara. The Santa Fe New Mexican, which gleefully headlined "CITIZENS ARREST TIJERINA" on the day of Ford's announcement, ran an editorial preface to a story on the feedlot on May 3, 1970, which advised the public in bold-face type that "the impoverished situation of the people of the North was . . . being changed thanks to help of a $2 million Ford Foundation grant, which is being used to set up La Jara Feedlot."

Only the Raza movement press in New Mexico has exposed the Ford program. Last April, El Papel and El Grito del Norte, both members of the Chicano Press Association, became aware of an attempt to draw Raza movement people into a conference in southern New Mexico connected with Ford's Southwest Council of La Raza. The designers of the conference used the names of movement people without bothering to talk to them. To meet this new pacification move, the two Raza papers put out a special issue headed "CONFERENCIA PARA HACER TITERES [Conference to Create Puppets]—FORD FOUNDATION'S PACIFICATION PROGRAM" and containing articles by the movement people whose names had been used, blasting the conference and its pacification efforts.

Ford meanwhile has allowed the release of such information as the addition of four members to the La Jara board, three of them with Spanish names. Even that is a fraud. The legal status of the La Jara Feedlots, Inc., has never changed, according to the Secretary of State in Colorado. There have been no amendments, no changes to the original incorporation, and no name has been added to the controlling trustees.

Ford Foundation President Bundy was LBJ's chief hawk advisor. And despite its billions, Ford's pacification program in the Southwest has been failing as surely as the program in Vietnam, and for the same reason. All across the Southwest, signs of a growing movement toward self-determination and liberation can be seen.

Less than a mile from Ford's feedlot in La Jara, Raza workers at the potato growers' warehouse walked out this year in the first strike in memory in La Jara. The warehouse workers picketed in a late March blizzard, carrying signs which read "Chicano Power!" and "Viva La Raza!"

In El Centro, a small town north of La Jara in the valley, lettuce pickers went out on strike in June in the first farmworkers' strike there in memory. Support for the strikers was spontaneously mobilized from Raza communities in the valley, and the strikers sought their own leaders from among themselves. Ford's manufactured spokesmen were ignored. When the strikers sought organizational assistance, it was from Cesar Chavez of the United Farm Workers' Organizing Committee. When the strikers sought a voice from the outside, it was that of Rudolph "Corky" Gonzales of the Crusade for Justice in Denver, who has called for creation of the independent nation of Aztlan in the Southwest.

And in Tierra Amarilla itself, where it all began in 1967, the people have moved to reestablish the Raza way which once existed, farming their remaining bits of land communally in the Cooperativa Agricola de Tierra Amarilla, which has sent shudders through the colonial powers and made the Cooperativa the subject of police and press attack. But the Cooperativa, comprised of the small, struggling, impoverished Raza ranchers and farmers of the north—the people Ford said it was coming to benefit—are in their second year of planting, despite moves by the power structure, the police and the press to bury them and the Raza way they are resurrecting.

At the same time that it was drawing in its first harvest last year—a harvest which wouldn't be sold, but shared among the people—the Cooperativa moved to open a low-cost people's clinic at Tierra Amarilla. Although the federal government last year poured $1.47 *billion* into New Mexico—including an ongoing $56 million nuclear weapons project in Los Alamos—there has been no medical facility available for the people of the north within a 60-mile radius.

On September 4, 1969, the people's clinic at Tierra Amarilla was destroyed by arsonists. All the rooms were gutted, all medicines destroyed, and most of the equipment either destroyed or extensively damaged. The State Police have been unable to solve the crime. (When a loan was offered by the United Auto Workers, U.S. Senator Joseph M. Montoya reportedly intervened to cut it off. Henry Santistevan of the UAW was then a member of the Southwest Council of La Raza. He is now the Council's executive director.)

But on June 21, 1970, three years after Ford came into New Mexico with a benevolence epitomized by its monument in La Jara, the people in the Cooperativa, almost all heirs to the land and all now desperately poor, held a grand opening of La Clinica del Pueblo de Rio Arriba (The People's Clinic of Rio Arriba), the first and only medical clinic in the colony of New Mexico created and controlled by the people it is intended to serve.

In New Mexico, Ford's million-dollar political fraud is turning into an expensive failure. The phalanx of petty power brokers it attempted to establish, the "leadership" it attempted to create, stand largely impotent, bypassed by the source of power the Foundation in the end couldn't tap: the people.

"Our people have a saying in Spanish, 'Aunque la carcel sea de oro, no deja de ser prison,'" said Jose Madril.

> In English it means something like, "Even though the jail is made of gold, it is still a prison." I guess that's what this Ford Foundation thought it was going to build here. But the people know better.
>
> Our people here in the north have been on the land for years, generations, centuries. They know what Ford was trying to do, it really didn't matter. They want to starve the people and give their money to the *vendidos* [sellouts]. We have seen it all before. It's like spreading fertilizer, manure, you know. You spread it around and what you put it on, it sprouts, it grows out in the open where you can see it, it shows itself. It's just a matter of time. That's what happened here. The only thing that surprises me is that they grew out so fast, they exposed themselves so fast. With all that money, you'd think they would have been smarter, *qué no?*

THE MUTUAL IMAGES AND EXPECTATIONS OF ANGLO-AMERICANS AND MEXICAN-AMERICANS [1]

Ozzie G. Simmons

A number of psychological and sociological studies have treated ethnic and racial stereotypes as they appear publicly in the mass media and also as held privately by individuals.[2] The present paper is based on data collected for a study of a number of aspects of the relations between Anglo-Americans and Mexican-Americans in a South Texas community, and is concerned with the principal assumptions and expectations that Anglo- and Mexican-Americans hold of one another; how they see each other; the extent to which these pictures are realistic; and the implications of their intergroup relations and cultural differences for the fulfillment of their mutual expectations.[3]

The Community

The community studied (here called "Border City") is in South Texas, about 250 miles south of San Antonio. Driving south from San Antonio,

Reprinted by permission from *Daedalus*, Journal of the American Academy of Arts and Sciences, Vol. 90, No. 2 (Spring 1961).

Ozzie Simmons received his doctorate from Harvard in 1952. He has taught at Harvard in the School of Public Health and at the University of Colorado, where he is professor of sociology. He has done extensive research in the area of mental health and is the author of *Social Status and Public Health* and *The Mental Patient Comes Home*, which won the award in 1963 from the American Psychiatric Association for outstanding creative research in human behavior. In addition to his work in the United States, Dr. Simmons spent four years of teaching and research in Peru and Chile from 1949–1953.

[1] Based on an address at the annual meeting of the Mexican Christian Institute at San Antonio in 1958.

[2] See John Harding, Bernard Kutner, Harold Proshansky, and Isidor Chein, "Prejudice and Ethnic Relations," in Gardner Lindzey (ed.), *Handbook of Social Psychology* (Cambridge, Addison-Wesley Publishing Company, 1954), vol. 2, pp. 1021–1061; and Otto Klineberg, *Tensions Affecting International Understanding*, New York, Social Science Research Council, 1950, Bulletin 62.

[3] The term "Anglo-American", as is common in the Southwest, refers to all residents of Border City who do not identify themselves as Spanish-speaking and of Mexican descent. The Anglo-Americans of Border City have emigrated there from all parts of the United States and represent a wide variety of regional and ethnic backgrounds. The terms "Mexican-American" and "Mexican," as used here, refer to all residents of Border City who are Spanish-speaking and of Mexican descent. The term "Spanish-speaking" is perhaps less objectionable to many people, but for present purposes is even less specific than Mexican or Mexican-American, since it also refers to ethnic groups that would have no sense of identification with the group under consideration here.

TODAY

one passes over vast expanses of brushland and grazing country, then suddenly comes upon acres of citrus groves, farmlands rich with vegetables and cotton, and long rows of palm trees. This is the "Magic Valley," an oasis in the semidesert region of South Texas. The Missouri Pacific Railroad (paralleled by Highway 83, locally called "The longest street in the world") bisects twelve major towns and cities of the Lower Rio Grande Valley between Brownsville, near the Gulf of Mexico, and Rio Grande City, 103 miles to the west.

Border City is neither the largest nor the smallest of these cities, and is physically and culturally much like the rest. Its first building was constructed in 1905. By 1920 it had 5,331 inhabitants, and at the time of our study these had increased to an estimated 17,500. The completion of the St. Louis, Brownsville, and Mexico Railroad in 1904 considerably facilitated Anglo-American immigration to the Valley. Before this the Valley had been inhabited largely by Mexican ranchers, who maintained large haciendas in the traditional Mexican style based on peonage. Most of these haciendas are now divided into large or small tracts that are owned by Anglo-Americans, who obtained them through purchase or less legitimate means. The position of the old Mexican-American landowning families has steadily deteriorated, and today these families, with a few exceptions, are completely overshadowed by the Anglo-Americans, who have taken over their social and economic position in the community.

The Anglo-American immigration into the Valley was paralleled by that of the Mexicans from across the border, who were attracted by the seemingly greater opportunities for farm labor created by the introduction of irrigation and the subsequent agricultural expansion. Actually, there had been a small but steady flow of Mexican immigration into South Texas that long antedated the Anglo-American immigration.[4] At present, Mexican-Americans probably constitute about two-fifths of the total population of the Valley.

In Border City, Mexican-Americans comprise about 56 per cent of the population. The southwestern part of the city, adjoining and sometimes infiltrating the business and industrial areas, is variously referred to as "Mexiquita," "Mexican-town," and "Little Mexico" by the city's Anglo-Americans, and as the *colonia* by the Mexican-Americans. With few exceptions, the *colonia* is inhabited only by Mexican-Americans, most of whom live in close proximity to one another in indifferently constructed houses on tiny lots. The north side of the city, which lies across the railroad tracks, is inhabited almost completely by Anglo-Americans. Its appearance is in sharp contrast to that of the *colonia* in that it is strictly residential and displays much better housing.

In the occupational hierarchy of Border City, the top level (the grow-

---

[4] For the historical background of the Valley, see Frank C. Pierce, *A Brief History of the Lower Rio Grande Valley*, Menasha, George Banta Publishing Company, 1917; Paul S. Taylor, *An American-Mexican Frontier*, Chapel Hill, University of North Carolina Press, 1934; and Florence J. Scott, *Historical Heritage of the Lower Rio Grande*, San Antonio, The Naylor Company, 1937.

ers, packers, canners, businessmen, and professionals) is overwhelmingly Anglo-American. In the middle group (the white-collar occupations) Mexicans are prominent only where their bilingualism makes them useful, for example, as clerks and salesmen. The bottom level (farm laborers, shed and cannery workers, and domestic servants) is overwhelmingly Mexican-American.

These conditions result from a number of factors, some quite distinct from the reception accorded Mexican-Americans by Anglo-Americans. Many Mexican-Americans are still recent immigrants and are thus relatively unfamiliar with Anglo-American culture and urban living, or else persist in their tendency to live apart and maintain their own institutions whenever possible. Among their disadvantages, however, the negative attitudes and discriminatory practices of the Anglo-American group must be counted. It is only fair to say, with the late Ruth Tuck, that much of what Mexican-Americans have suffered at Anglo-American hands has not been perpetrated deliberately but through indifference, that it has been done not with the fist but with the elbow.[5] The average social and economic status of the Mexican-American group has been improving, and many are moving upward. This is partly owing to increasing acceptance by the Anglo-American group, but chiefly to the efforts of the Mexican-Americans themselves.

Anglo-American Assumptions and Expectations

Robert Lynd writes of the dualism in the principal assumptions that guide Americans in conducting their everyday life and identifies the attempt to "live by contrasting rules of the game" as a characteristic aspect of our culture.[6] This pattern of moral compromise, symptomatic of what is likely to be only vaguely a conscious moral conflict, is evident in Anglo-American assumptions and expectations with regard to Mexican-Americans, which appear both in the moral principles that define what intergroup relations ought to be, and in the popular notions held by Anglo-Americans as to what Mexican-Americans are "really" like. In the first case there is a response to the "American creed," which embodies ideals of the essential dignity of the individual and of certain inalienable rights to freedom, justice, and equal opportunity. Accordingly, Anglo-Americans believe that Mexican-Americans must be accorded full acceptance and equal status in the larger society. When their orientation to these ideals is uppermost, Anglo-Americans believe that the assimilation of Mexican-Americans is only a matter of time, contingent solely on the full incorporation of Anglo-American values and ways of life.

These expectations regarding the assimilation of the Mexican are most clearly expressed in the notion of the "high type" of Mexican. It is based

---

[5] Ruth D. Tuck, *Not with the Fist*, New York, Harcourt Brace and Company, 1946.
[6] Robert S. Lynd, *Knowledge for What?* Princeton, Princeton University Press, 1948.

on three criteria: occupational achievement and wealth (the Anglo-American's own principal criteria of status) and command of Anglo-American ways. Mexican-Americans who can so qualify are acceptable for membership in the service clubs and a few other Anglo-American organizations and for limited social intercourse. They may even intermarry without being penalized or ostracized. Both in their achievements in business and agriculture and in wealth, they compare favorably with middle-class Anglo-Americans, and they manifest a high command of the latter's ways. This view of the "high type" of Mexican reflects the Anglo-American assumption that Mexicans are assimilable; it does not necessarily insure a full acceptance of even the "high type" of Mexican or that his acceptance will be consistent.

The assumption that Mexican-Americans will be ultimately assimilated was not uniformly shared by all the Anglo-Americans who were our informants in Border City. Regardless of whether they expressed adherence to this ideal, however, most Anglo-Americans expressed the contrasting assumption that Mexican-Americans are essentially inferior. Thus the same people may hold assumptions and expectations that are contradictory, although expressed at different times and in different situations. As in the case of their adherence to the ideal of assimilability, not all Anglo-Americans hold the same assumptions and expectations with respect to the inferiority of Mexican-Americans; and even those who agree vary in the intensity of their beliefs. Some do not believe in the Mexican's inferiority at all; some are relatively moderate or sceptical, while others express extreme views with considerable emotional intensity.

Despite this variation, the Anglo-Americans' principal assumptions and expectations emphasize the Mexicans' presumed inferiority. In its most characteristic pattern, such inferiority is held to be self-evident. As one Anglo-American woman put it, "Mexicans are inferior because they are so typically and naturally Mexican." Since they are so obviously inferior, their present subordinate status is appropriate and is really their own fault. There is a ready identification between Mexicans and menial labor, buttressed by an image of the Mexican worker as improvident, undependable, irresponsible, childlike, and indolent. If Mexicans are fit for only the humblest labor, there is nothing abnormal about the fact that most Mexican workers are at the bottom of the occupational pyramid, and the fact that most Mexicans are unskilled workers is sufficient proof that they belong in that category.

Associated with the assumption of Mexican inferiority is that of the homogeneity of this group—that is, all Mexicans are alike. Anglo-Americans may classify Mexicans as being of "high type" and "low type" and at the same time maintain that "a Mexican is a Mexican." Both notions serve a purpose, depending on the situation. The assumption that all Mexicans are alike buttresses the assumption of inferiority by making it convenient to ignore the fact of the existence of a substantial number of Mexican-Americans who represent all levels of business and professional achievement. Such people are considered exceptions to the rule.

Anglo-American Images of Mexican-Americans

To employ Gordon Allport's definition, a stereotype is an exaggerated belief associated with a category, and its function is to justify conduct in relation to that category.[7] Some of the Anglo-American images of the Mexican have no ascertainable basis in fact, while others have at least a kernel of truth. Although some components of these images derive from behavior patterns that are characteristic of some Mexican-Americans in some situations, few if any of the popular generalizations about them are valid as stated, and none is demonstrably true of all. Some of the images of Mexican-Americans are specific to a particular area of intergroup relations, such as the image of the Mexican-American's attributes as a worker. Another is specific to politics and describes Mexicans as ready to give their votes to whoever will pay for them or provide free barbecues and beer.[8] Let us consider a few of the stereotypical beliefs that are widely used on general principles to justify Anglo-American practices of exclusion and subordination.

One such general belief accuses Mexican-Americans of being unclean. The examples given of this supposed characteristic most frequently refer to a lack of personal cleanliness and environmental hygiene and to a high incidence of skin ailments ascribed to a lack of hygienic practices. Indeed, there are few immigrant groups, regardless of their ethnic background, to whom this defect has not been attributed by the host society, as well as others prominent in stereotypes of the Mexican. It has often been observed that for middle-class Americans cleanliness is not simply a matter of keeping clean but is also an index to the morals and virtues of the individual. It is largely true that Mexicans tend to be much more casual in hygienic practices than Anglo-Americans. Moreover, their labor in the field, the packing sheds, and the towns is rarely clean work, and it is possible that many Anglo-Americans base their conclusions on what they observe in such situations. There is no evidence of a higher incidence of skin ailments among Mexicans than among Anglo-Americans. The belief that Mexicans are unclean is useful for rationalizing the Anglo-American practice of excluding Mexicans from any situation that involves close contact with Anglo-Americans, as in residence, and the common use of swimming pools and other recreational facilities.

Drunkenness and criminality are a pair of traits that have appeared regularly in the stereotypes applied to immigrant groups. They have a prominent place in Anglo-American images of Mexicans. If Mexicans are inveterate drunkards and have criminal tendencies, a justification is provided for excluding them from full participation in the life of the

[7] Gordon W. Allport, *The Nature of Prejudice*, Cambridge, Addison-Wesley Publishing Company, 1954.

[8] For an analysis of Mexican-American value orientations and behavior in the occupational and political spheres, see Ozzie G. Simmons, Anglo-Americans and Mexican-Americans in South Texas: A Study in Dominant-Subordinate Group Relations (unpublished doctoral dissertation, Harvard University, 1952).

community. It is true that drinking is a popular activity among Mexican-Americans and that total abstinence is rare, except among some Protestant Mexican-Americans. Drinking varies, however, from the occasional consumption of a bottle of beer to the heavy drinking of more potent beverages, so that the frequency of drinking and drunkenness is far from being evenly distributed among Mexican-Americans. Actually, this pattern is equally applicable to the Anglo-American group. The ample patronage of bars in the Anglo-American part of Border City, and the drinking behavior exhibited by Anglo-Americans when they cross the river to Mexico indicate that Mexicans have no monopoly on drinking or drunkenness. It is true that the number of arrests for drunkenness in Border City is greater among Mexicans, but this is probably because Mexicans are more vulnerable to arrest. The court records in Border City show little difference in the contributions made to delinquency and crime by Anglo- and Mexican-Americans.

Another cluster of images in the Anglo-American stereotype portrays Mexican-Americans as deceitful and of a "low" morality, as mysterious, unpredictable, and hostile to Anglo-Americans. It is quite possible that Mexicans resort to a number of devices in their relations with Anglo-Americans, particularly in relations with employers, to compensate for their disadvantages, which may be construed by Anglo-Americans as evidence of deceitfulness. The whole nature of the dominant-subordinate relationship does not make for frankness on the part of Mexicans or encourage them to face up directly to Anglo-Americans in most intergroup contacts. As to the charge of immorality, one need only recognize the strong sense of loyalty and obligation that Mexicans feel in their familial and interpersonal relations to know that the charge is baseless. The claim that Mexicans are mysterious and deceitful may in part reflect Anglo-American relations to actual differences in culture and personality, but like the other beliefs considered here, is highly exaggerated. The imputation of hostility to Mexicans, which is manifested in a reluctance to enter the *colonia*, particularly at night, may have its kernel of truth, but appears to be largely a projection of the Anglo-American's own feelings.

All three of these images can serve to justify exclusion and discrimination: if Mexicans are deceitful and immoral, they do not have to be accorded equal status and justice; if they are mysterious and unpredictable, there is no point in treating them as one would a fellow Anglo-American; and if they are hostile and dangerous, it is best that they live apart in colonies of their own.

Not all Anglo-American images of the Mexican are unfavorable. Among those usually meant to be complimentary are the beliefs that all Mexicans are musical and always ready for a fiesta, that they are very "romantic" rather than "realistic" (which may have unfavorable overtones as well), and that they love flowers and can grow them under the most adverse conditions. Although each of these beliefs may have a modicum of truth, it may be noted that they tend to reinforce Anglo-American images of Mexicans as childlike and irresponsible, and thus they support the notion that Mexicans are capable only of subordinate status.

Mexican-American Assumptions, Expectations, and Images

Mexican-Americans are as likely to hold contradictory assumptions and distorted images as are Anglo-Americans. Their principal assumptions, however, must reflect those of Anglo-Americans—that is, Mexicans must take into account the Anglo-Americans' conflict as to their potential equality and present inferiority, since they are the object of such imputations. Similarly, their images of Anglo-Americans are not derived wholly independently, but to some extent must reflect their own subordinate status. Consequently, their stereotypes of Anglo-Americans are much less elaborate, in part because Mexicans feel no need of justifying the present intergroup relation, in part because the very nature of their dependent position forces them to view the relation more realistically than Anglo-Americans do. For the same reasons, they need not hold to their beliefs about Anglo-Americans with the rigidity and intensity so often characteristic of the latter.

Any discussion of these assumptions and expectations requires some mention of the class distinctions within the Mexican-American group.[9] Its middle class, though small as compared with the lower class, is powerful within the group and performs the critical role of intermediary in negotiations with the Anglo-American group. Middle-class status is based on education and occupation, family background, readiness to serve the interests of the group, on wealth, and the degree of acculturation, or command of Anglo-American ways. Anglo-Americans recognize Mexican class distinctions (although not very accurately) in their notions of the "high type" and "low type" of Mexicans.

In general, lower-class Mexicans do not regard the disabilities of their status as being nearly as severe as do middle-class Mexican-Americans. This is primarily a reflection of the insulation between the Anglo-American world and that of the Mexican lower class. Most Mexicans, regardless of class, are keenly aware of Anglo-American attitudes and practices with regard to their group, but lower-class Mexicans do not conceive of participation in the larger society as necessary nor do they regard Anglo-American practices of exclusion as affecting them directly. Their principal reaction has been to maintain their isolation, and thus they have not been particularly concerned with improving their status by acquiring Anglo-American ways, a course more characteristic of the middle-class Mexican.

Mexican-American assumptions and expectations regarding Anglo-Americans must be qualified, then, as being more characteristic of middle- than of lower-class Mexican-Americans. Mexicans, like Anglo-Americans, are subject to conflicts in their ideals, not only because of irrational thinking on their part but also because of Anglo-American inconsistencies between ideal and practice. As for ideals expressing democratic values, Mexican expectations are for obvious reasons the counterpart of the Anglo-Americans'—that Mexican-Americans should be accorded full acceptance

[9] See *ibid.*, for a discussion of the Anglo-American and Mexican class structures.

and equal opportunity. They feel a considerable ambivalence, however, as to the Anglo-American expectation that the only way to achieve this goal is by a full incorporation of Anglo-American values and ways of life, for this implies the ultimate loss of their cultural identity as Mexicans. On the one hand, they favor the acquisition of Anglo-American culture and the eventual remaking of the Mexican in the Anglo-American image; but on the other hand, they are not so sure that Anglo-American acceptance is worth such a price. When they are concerned with this dilemma, Mexicans advocate a fusion with Anglo-American culture in which the "best" of the Mexican ways, as they view it, would be retained along with the incorporation of the "best" of the Anglo-American ways, rather than a one-sided exchange in which all that is distinctively Mexican would be lost.

A few examples will illustrate the point of view expressed in the phrase, "the best of both ways." A premium is placed on speaking good, unaccented English, but the retention of good Spanish is valued just as highly as "a mark of culture that should not be abandoned." Similarly, there is an emphasis on the incorporation of behavior patterns that are considered characteristically Anglo-American and that will promote "getting ahead," but not to the point at which the drive for power and wealth would become completely dominant, as is believed to be the case with Anglo-Americans.

Mexican ambivalence about becoming Anglo-American or achieving a fusion of the "best" of both cultures is compounded by their ambivalence about another issue, that of equality versus inferiority. That Anglo-Americans are dominant in the society and seem to monopolize its accomplishments and rewards leads Mexicans at times to draw the same conclusion that Anglo-Americans do, namely, that Mexicans are inferior. The questioning of their own sense of worth exists in all classes of the Mexican-American group, although with varying intensity, and plays a substantial part in every adjustment to intergroup relations. There is a pronounced tendency to concede the superiority of Anglo-American ways and consequently to define Mexican ways as undesirable, inferior, and disreputable. The tendency to believe in his own inferiority is counterbalanced, however, by the Mexican's fierce racial pride, which sets the tone of Mexican demands and strivings for equal status, even though these may slip into feelings of inferiority.

The images Mexicans have of Anglo-Americans may not be so elaborate or so emotionally charged as the images that Anglo-Americans have of Mexicans, but they are nevertheless stereotypes, overgeneralized, and exaggerated, although used primarily for defensive rather than justificatory purposes. Mexican images of Anglo-Americans are sometimes favorable, particularly when they identify such traits as initiative, ambition, and industriousness as being peculiarly Anglo-American. Unfavorable images are prominent, however, and, although they may be hostile, they never impute inferiority to Anglo-Americans. Most of the Mexican stereotypes evaluate Anglo-Americans on the basis of their attitudes toward Mexican-Americans. For example, one such classification provides a two-fold typology. The first type, the "majority," includes those who are cold, unkind, mercenary, and exploitative. The second type, the "minority," consists of those who are friendly, warm, just, and unprejudiced. For the most part, Mexican images of Anglo-Americans reflect the latter's patterns of exclusion and assumptions of superiority, as experienced by Mexican-Americans. Thus Anglo-Americans are pictured as stolid, phlegmatic, cold-hearted, and distant. They are also said to be braggarts, conceited, inconstant, and insincere.

Intergroup Relations, Mutual Expectations, and Cultural Differences

A number of students of intergroup relations assert that research in this area has yet to demonstrate any relation between stereotypical beliefs and intergroup behavior; indeed, some insist that under certain conditions ethnic attitudes and discrimination can vary independently.[10] Arnold M. Rose, for example, concludes that "from a heuristic standpoint it may be desirable to assume that patterns of intergroup relations, on the one hand, and attitudes of prejudice and stereotyping, on the other hand, are fairly unrelated phenomena although they have reciprocal influences on each other. . . ."[11] In the present study, no systematic attempt was made to investigate the relation between the stereotypical beliefs of particular individuals and their actual intergroup behavior; but the study did yield much evidence that both images which justify group separatism and separateness itself are characteristic aspects of intergroup relations in Border City. One of the principal findings is that in those situations in which contact between Anglo-Americans and Mexicans is voluntary (such as residence, education, recreation, religious worship, and social intercourse) the characteristic pattern is separateness rather than common participation. Wherever intergroup contact is necessary, as in occupational activities and the performance of commercial and professional services, it is held to the minimum sufficient to accomplish the purpose of the contact.[12] The extent of this separateness is not constant for all members of the two groups, since it tends to be less severe between Anglo-Americans and those Mexicans they define as of a "high type." Nevertheless, the evidence reveals a high degree of compatibility between beliefs and practices in Border City's intergroup relations, although the data have nothing to offer for the identification of direct relationships.

[10] Robert K. Merton, "Discrimination and the American Creed," in R. M. MacIver (ed.), *Discrimination and National Welfare* (New York, Harper and Brothers, 1949), pp. 99–128; John Harding, Bernard Kutner, Harold Proshansky, and Isidor Chein, *op. cit.*; Arnold M. Rose, "Intergroup Relations vs. Prejudice: Pertinent Theory for the Study of Social Change," *Social Problems*, 1956, 4: 173–176; Robin M. Williams, Jr., "Racial and Cultural Relations," in Joseph B. Gittler (ed.), *Review of Sociology: Analysis of a Decade* (New York, John Wiley and Sons, 1957), pp. 423–464.

[11] Rose, *op. cit.*

[12] Simmons, *op. cit.*

In any case, the separateness that characterizes intergroup relations cannot be attributed solely to the exclusion practices of the Anglo-American group. Mexicans have tended to remain separate by choice as well as by necessity. Like many other ethnic groups, they have often found this the easier course, since they need not strain to learn another language or to change their ways and manners. The isolation practices of the Mexican group are as relevant to an understanding of intergroup relations as are the exclusion practices of the Anglo-Americans.

This should not, however, obscure the fact that to a wide extent the majority of Mexican-Americans share the patterns of living of Anglo-American society; many of their ways are already identical. Regardless of the degree of their insulation from the larger society, the demands of life in the United States have required basic modifications of the Mexicans' cultural tradition. In material culture, Mexicans are hardly to be distinguished from Anglo-Americans, and there have been basic changes in medical beliefs and practices and in the customs regarding godparenthood. Mexicans have acquired English in varying degrees, and their Spanish has become noticeably Anglicized. Although the original organization of the family has persisted, major changes have occurred in patterns of traditional authority, as well as in child training and courtship practices. Still, it is the exceedingly rare Mexican-American, no matter how acculturated he may be to the dominant society, who does not in some degree retain the more subtle characteristics of his Mexican heritage, particularly in his conception of time and in other fundamental value orientations, as well as in his modes of participation in interpersonal relations.[13] Many of the most acculturated Mexican-Americans have attempted to exemplify what they regard as "the best of both ways." They have become largely Anglo-American in their way of living, but they still retain fluent Spanish and a knowledge of their traditional culture, and they maintain an identification with their own heritage while participating in Anglo-American culture. Nevertheless, this sort of achievement still seems a long way off for many Mexican-Americans who regard it as desirable.

A predominant Anglo-American expectation is that the Mexicans will be eventually assimilated into the larger society; but this is contingent upon Mexicans' becoming just like Anglo-Americans. The Mexican counterpart to this expectation is only partially complementary. Mexicans want to be full members of the larger society, but they do not want to give up their cultural heritage. There is even less complementarity of expectation with regard to the present conduct of intergroup relations. Anglo-Americans believe they are justified in withholding equal access to the rewards of full acceptance as long as Mexicans remain "different," particularly since

[13] For cultural differences and similarities between Anglo-Americans and Mexicans, see Simmons, *op. cit.*; Tuck, *op. cit.*; Lyle Saunders, *Cultural Difference and Medical Care*, New York, Russell Sage Foundation, 1954; Munro S. Edmonson, *Los Manitos: A Study of Institutional Values* (New Orleans, Middle American Research Institute, Tulane University, 1957, Publication 25), pp. 1–72, and Margaret Clark, *Health in the Mexican-American Culture*, Berkeley, University of California Press, 1959.

they interpret the differences (both those which have some basis in reality and those which have none) as evidence of inferiority. Mexicans, on the other hand, while not always certain that they are not inferior, clearly want equal opportunity and full acceptance now, not in some dim future, and they do not believe that their differences (either presumed or real) from Anglo-Americans offer any justification for the denial of opportunity and acceptance. Moreover, they do not find that acculturation is rewarded in any clear and regular way by progressive acceptance.

It is probable that both Anglo-Americans and Mexicans will have to modify their beliefs and practices if they are to realize more nearly their expectations of each other. Mutual stereotyping, as well as the exclusion practices of Anglo-Americans and the isolation practices of Mexicans, maintains the separateness of the two groups, and separateness is a massive barrier to the realization of their expectations. The process of acculturation is presently going on among Mexican-Americans and will continue, regardless of whether changes in Anglo-Mexican relations occur. Unless Mexican-Americans can validate their increasing command of Anglo-American ways by a free participation in the larger society, however, such acculturation is not likely to accelerate its present leisurely pace, nor will it lead to eventual assimilation. The *colonia* is a relatively safe place in which new cultural acquisitions may be tried out, and thus it has its positive functions; but by the same token it is only in intergroup contacts with Anglo-Americans that acculturation is validated, that the Mexican's level of acculturation is tested, and that the distance he must yet travel to assimilation is measured.[14]

Conclusions

There are major inconsistencies in the assumptions that Anglo-Americans and Mexican-Americans hold about one another. Anglo-Americans assume that Mexican-Americans are their potential, if not actual, peers, but at the same time assume they are their inferiors. The beliefs that presumably demonstrate the Mexican-Americans' inferiority tend to place them outside the accepted moral order and framework of Anglo-American society by attributing to them undesirable characteristics that make it "reasonable" to treat them differently from their fellow Anglo-Americans. Thus the negative images provide not only a rationalized definition of the intergroup relation that makes it palatable for Anglo-Americans, but also a substantial support for maintaining the relation as it is. The assumptions of Mexican-Americans about Anglo-Americans are similarly inconsistent, and their images of Anglo-Americans are predominantly negative, although these are primarily defensive rather than justificatory. The mutual expectations of the two groups contrast sharply with the ideal of a

[14] See Leonard Broom and John I. Kitsuse, "The Validation of Acculturation: A Condition to Ethnic Assimilation," *American Anthropologist*, 1955, 57: 44–48.

complementarity of expectations, in that Anglo-Americans expect Mexicans to become just like themselves, if they are to be accorded equal status in the larger society, whereas Mexican-Americans want full acceptance, regardless of the extent to which they give up their own ways and acquire those of the dominant group.

Anglo-Americans and Mexicans may decide to stay apart because they are different, but cultural differences provide no moral justification for one group to deny to the other equal opportunity and the rewards of the larger society. If the full acceptance of Mexicans by Anglo-Americans is contingent upon the disappearance of cultural differences, it will not be accorded in the foreseeable future. In our American society, we have often seriously underestimated the strength and tenacity of early cultural conditioning. We have expected newcomers to change their customs and values to conform to American ways as quickly as possible, without an adequate appreciation of the strains imposed by this process. An understanding of the nature of culture and of its interrelations with personality can make us more realistic about the rate at which cultural change can proceed and about the gains and costs for the individual who is subject to the experiences of acculturation. In viewing cultural differences primarily as disabilities, we neglect their positive aspects. Mexican-American culture represents the most constructive and effective means Mexican-Americans have yet been able to develop for coping with their changed natural and social environment. They will further exchange old ways for new only if these appear to be more meaningful and rewarding than the old, and then only if they are given full opportunity to acquire the new ways and to use them.

THE MYTHS OF THE MEXICAN AMERICAN

Glen Gaviglio

The Mexican Americans, or "Chicanos," have been referred to as the forgotten minority. They are supposedly a quiet, docile, passive, somnolent, and satisfied group of fatalistic near peasants. Therefore they have been erased from the conscience of most Americans. They have been invisible; they have been wiped from history, like the Indians. Yet Chicanos have not lost themselves, even though they have lived in a hostile environment for decades. Why have they been overlooked, ignored, and oppressed?

This brief essay is an attempt to synthesize some of the major sociohistoric factors that have influenced the development of *La Raza*. For

Reprinted with permission of The Macmillan Company from *Society As It Is* by Glen Gaviglio and David E. Raye. Copyright © 1971 by The Macmillan Company. Glen Gaviglio teaches at Solano College and is co-editor of *Society As It Is*.

purposes of analysis, this essay is arranged into four deeply ingrained myths of the Mexican American: (1) The Myth of the Border, (2) The Myth of the Docile Peasant, (3) The Myth of Ethnic and Racial Assimilation, and (4) The Myth of Mexican American Similarity.

Myths are important for societies; they influence every individual's definition of reality. People act in relation to the mythology of their society. Therefore myths are significant behavior inducing and shaping devices. (The social reality of the mind comes in all flavors of distortion.) The influence of some of these distortions is examined in each of the following myths.

The Myth of the Border

Historically, cries of "Spic," "Greaser," "Wetback," or "Taco Bender, go home" were very typical of the American Southwest. The cries are more subdued and sophisticated now, but invariably eruptions occur. For example, in 1969 in the Santa Clara Valley, just south of San Francisco, a venerable judge publicly excoriated a Chicano youth in court, saying that Hitler had a good thing going with the Jews and that a similar program should be undertaken with Mexicans. (At this writing that judge is still on the bench.) [See pp. 482–484.—Eds.]

There is a political boundary separating Mexico and the United States, but the winds of change have modified that boundary immensely. In a very real sense that border does not exist. The border is totally artificial from a geographical perspective. It does not separate climatic or agricultural regions; in fact, it cuts across the natural topography of the area. The difference between Calexico and Mexicali, El Paso and Juarez, and Brownsville and Matamoros is economic and political, not geographical. The border does not really exist for the Chicano. It never has.

At one time the Southwest was part of Mexico. It was inhabited by a mixture of Spaniards and Indians; it was naturally an arid region that was sparsely settled. The region was the frontier or borderlands of Mexico, and it was never an integral part of that country. When the Spanish did come to settle this region, there actually were very few pure Spaniards in the expeditions. Most of the settlers who came north from Mexico were Mestizo and Indian. The Indians who were living in this area had already been strongly influenced by the Aztec civilization. On the eve of the Mexican–American War (1848), there were only about 82,000 Spanish-speaking people living in the Southwest, but they had been there for generations. (There were also an untabulated number of Indians and Mestizos in the area.) In California in 1848, there were 21,000 Spanish-speaking in a population of about 100,000. When California became a state (1850), the constitution was written in Spanish. This constitution, created in part by people of Spanish ancestry, established California as a bilingual state (and it remained bilingual until 1878). In southern California there were bilingual schools until the 1870's. In other words,

California has gone from bilingual schools to denial to the Chicanos of the right to vote, because they cannot read the Constitution. (This has been recently changed by the California Supreme Court.)

When the United States wrested the Southwest from Mexico, many Spanish-speaking people automatically became residents of the United States. They did not immigrate from anywhere. Therefore, when an Anglo tells a Chicano to go home, he is less than amusing; he is grossly misinformed. The Chicano is more firmly rooted in the American past than an Anglo who may have just recently migrated from Europe.

The Treaty of Guadalupe Hidalgo (1848), which terminated the Mexican-American War, was supposed to protect and guarantee the rights of self-determination for the Spanish-speaking people in the newly acquired United States territory. In actuality the treaty did little to protect the rights of the Mexicans in this region. The Anglos immediately displayed a tremendous hostility and resentment toward these Hispanos. The creed of American racism became brutally apparent in the systematic oppression that followed. For example, in California the antagonism between Spanish-speaking and Yankee miners culminated with the Foreign Miners Tax Law of 1850, which effectively drove the Spanish-speaking from the gold fields. (Note the word *foreign*.) In 1851 the Federal Land Tenure Act was passed. This act made possible the systematic and gradual extraction of land from the hands of the Hispanos.

No Chicano is really an immigrant in America. When they "moved north," they felt that they were moving in an environment that was geographically, culturally, and historically familiar. I would even say that in a political sense the border has been a nebulous entity. There was no border patrol until 1924 and there was not even a quota on Mexican immigration until 1965. The reason the border did not exist in a political or economic manner for either the Anglo or Chicano was the need for cheap labor in the fields. As long as there was a ready supply of bodies toward the south, the indigenous labor force could not organize and demand higher wages. When the field workers did try to organize, their leaders were quickly "deported." The farm workers could not effectively unionize until the Bracero program was terminated in 1965. (The program allowed Mexican nationals to reside temporarily in the United States in order to harvest the crops.) The Delano movement still has not completely succeeded, because the border is still quite open. Migrant workers can enter both legally and illegally. "Green Card Holders" are now entering the United States to pick crops in times of emergency (meaning "during strikes"). In reality, the border has always been exactly what the United States has wanted it to be.

The Myth of the Docile Peasant

The Chicano has been stereotyped as a passive peasant. This is absurd on statistical grounds alone. Over 80 per cent of all Chicanos reside in urban areas and over 1 million Chicanos live in Los Angeles. The image of the Chicano is not really a static one. According to the stereotype, the Chicano can be either a fat and lazy peon, slumbering under a cactus and wearing his sombrero and poncho, or he can be a stinking, ferocious, foul-mouthed, greasy bandito. The stereotype of the Mexican American stems from two basic sources: (1) the popularized folk mythology of traditional American racism and (2) the distorted sociological image. We can expect the first; it bears no surprises, but the latter is more repulsive to us, because it comes from unbiased sociological sources.

There is nothing unique in saying that the society of America is racist, but when we confront the historical record of past American racial atrocities, the present looks as though peace and brotherhood abound (if you choose to ignore Vietnam). American literature, with but few exceptions, is filled with condescending racist drivel. One example from *The Oregon Trail* by Francis Parkman (Doubleday, 1948) will provide the proper flavor:

> Two or three squalid Mexicans, with their broad hats, and their vile faces overgrown with hair, were lounging about the bank of the river in front of (the gate of the Pueblo). They disappeared as they saw us approach [p. 260].
> A few squaws and Spanish women, and a few Mexicans, as mean and miserable as the place itself, were lazily sauntering about [p. 260].
> There was another room beyond, less sumptuously decorated, and here three or four Spanish girls, one of them very pretty, were baking cakes at a mud fireplace in the corner [p. 261].
> The human race in this part of the world is separated into three divisions, arranged in the order of their merits: white men, Indians, and Mexicans; to the latter of whom the honorable title of "whites" is by no means conceded [p. 263].

Usually the racism is not even this "subtle." Our history is replete with speeches of major political figures proclaiming a hypocritical and altruistic imperialism. We have always had an inclination to save the ignorant and backward colored masses of the world from themselves, witness this speech delivered by John C. Calhoun in the Senate on January 4, 1848 (after we had defeated Mexico in a war):

> We have never dreamt of incorporating into our Union any but the Caucasian race—the free white race. To incorporate Mexico, would be the very first instance of the kind, of incorporating an Indian race; for more than half of the Mexicans are Indians, and the other is composed chiefly of mixed tribes. I protest against such a union as that! Ours, sir, is the government of a white race. The greatest misfortunes of Spanish America are to be traced to the fatal error of placing these colored races on an equality with the white race. That error destroyed the social arrangement which formed the basis of society. The Portuguese and ourselves have escaped—the Portuguese at least to some extent—and we are the only people on this continent which had made revolutions without being followed by anarchy. And yet it is professed, and talked about, to erect these Mexicans into a territorial government, and

place them on an equality with the people of the United States. I protest
utterly against such a project.

But . . . suppose all these difficulties removed; suppose their people attached to our Union, and desirous of incorporating with us, ought we to
bring them in? Are they fit to be connected with us? Are they fit for self-
government and for governing you? Are you, any of you, willing that your
states should be governed by these twenty-odd Mexican states, with a population of about only one million of your blood, and two or three million of
mixed blood better informed—all the rest pure Indians, a mixed blood
equally ignorant and unfit for liberty, impure races, not as good as the
Cherokees or Choctaws?

Calhoun did not even believe in spreading the faith to the ignorant
colored masses, because they were too inferior even to govern themselves
and accept the gospel of Americanism.

The mythology of American racism has been updated and perfected
since the heyday of blatant expansionism and imperialism. The myths
may be a little more subtle but they are still extremely harmful. It can be
effectively argued that the myths are even more destructive because of
the pervasive influence in the mass media. The world is being turned into
a McLuhanesque global village; therefore more people are influenced by
the racist stereotypes portrayed in the mass media. At the moment one of
the worst offenders is the advertising industry. One particularly offensive
commercial was for Arrid deodorant. It shows a Mexican bandito spray-
ing his underarm while a voice says, "If it works for him, it will work for
you." Do Chicanos stink worse than blacks? Can you envision that same
commercial with a sloppy, fat ghetto black wearing a dirty and torn T-
shirt? Or is the black movement too powerful (or too violent) to allow
that kind of defamation? . . .

These stereotypes are extremely important because people act upon
these myths. Very insipid and disastrous self-fulfilling prophecies can be
initiated by racial and cultural myths. If the dominant group treats the
minority group as an inferior race or culture, the minority can become
just that. In a political and economic sense racial oppression is very
obvious, but it has more subtle manifestations. What happens in the
school system when students are "tracked" or when the teacher has lower
expectations for some students? What happens to the minds of minority
group members? Can a people be taught to hate themselves? Can a
minority group believe the myths the majority perpetrates? One of the
most sickening aspects of race relations in America is that the preceding
questions must be answered in a very negative manner.

Another form of stereotyping is of a more insidious variety because it is
generated by the academic community and therefore carries with it
scientific validity. In particular the work of Heller (*Mexican-American
Youth*), Tuck (*Not with the Fist*), and Madsen (*Mexican-Americans of
South Texas*) should be mentioned. The studies have some very major
defects. The most obvious deficiency from a traditional sociological per-

spective is a methodological one, the authors over-generalize from a biased or partial sampling of Chicanos. These studies list "characteristics" or "attributes" of the typical Mexican American. Some of these character-istics seem like a sociological updating of racial mythology. Is being passive, accepting, and fatalistic much different from being lazy? Do all Chicanos display these traits? We cannot be sure of the limited regional sample of Chicanos in these studies. Another glaring omission in these studies is their completely historical nature. They speak of the Chicano as existing in the eternal present, as if his traditional culture were static and unchanging. The Chicano may not try to change his environment in the same manner as the robust and enterprising Anglo, for he has found that passive adjustment to his social milieu is necessary to his survival. This passiveness creates another blatantly false stereotype. Were those who rode with Villa and Zapata during the Mexican Revolution passively accepting their fate? Were the Chicanos who organized numerous strikes in the Southwest for the past seventy-five years accepting their fate? Are Reies Tijerina, Cesar Chavez, and Corky Gonsalez leaders of a passive and somnolent bunch of poncho-clad peasants?

The last significant error in these books is their tendency to equate and confuse ethnic and class characteristics. Many of the characteristics at-tributed to Mexican Americans in these studies are shared by all lower-class people. Cohen and Hodges, in a study done in California, found that lower-lower-class Chicanos, blacks, and Anglos all shared some basically similar characteristics: extended families, marked anti-intellectualism, *machismo* (a supermasculine, double-standard-type male), use of phys-ical force, and a type of fatalism. Oscar Lewis has argued that throughout the world the lower classes generally share these traits. Lewis terms these characteristics a "culture of poverty"; he sees it as a functional adaptation to their oppressive social conditions. Therefore there is nothing unique in these traits that are supposedly typical of the Mexican American. Some statistical validity resides in the fact that a fairly large percentage of Chicanos live below the poverty level (16 per cent of the Anglos, 27 per cent of the blacks, and 37 per cent of the Chicanos). These figures may understate the degree of Chicano poverty. That 37 per cent basically represents United States citizens. According to the U.S. Department of Immigration, there are 1.5 million alien residents and 4.5 million illegal aliens below the poverty level.

The concept of the culture of poverty can also be interpreted in a very negative manner. It can be used to conclude that the cultural character-istics of the poor people themselves are responsible for their socio-economic status. For example, take the noted fatalism of the lower classes. They feel that they have little control over the institutions and events that shape their lives. It is very possible that the pessimism, apathy, and fatalism of the lower classes is a valid adjustment to a historical social reality. The life chances of a minority group member have been severely and systematically restricted; these people have not had and still do not have very much control over the decisions that affect their lives. Is it really so hard to imagine accepting a religion, whether it is a folk Catholicism or a revivalist Protestantism, that promises an internal reward when the present and future look so bleak? When reality is unbearably ugly, fatalism may be the only answer among rotten alternatives.

It would be wise not to apply the concept of culture of poverty to minority groups unless its sociohistorical component is considered. Why is there a culture of poverty? How did it start? Why do so many different societies have subcultures of poverty with similar traits? The answer lies in an analysis of how people adjust to the conditions of poverty, racism, and oppression.

The Myth of Ethnic and Racial Assimilation

The huddled and hungry hordes of the world streamed to the shores of America, where golden opportunities awaited them. The saga of America is sometimes told as though it were a giant, bottomless cauldron where the oppressed masses of humanity mingled and produced an egalitarian and tolerant democratic society. This is the great myth of the melting pot. It is a romantic and nostalgic vision of the American past that does very little justice to reality. Assimilation in the American melting pot was meant for whites only. For example, Indians were almost exterminated like vermin, instead of being melted, and of course enough has been said recently of black Americans. The Chicano still forms an unassimilated and distinct cultural entity in America.

Glazer and Moynihan (*Beyond the Melting Pot*, 1963) argue that ethnic homogenization never completely took place in America. New York is a veritable hodge-podge of racial and ethnic groups that still function as political interest groups. Glazer and Moynihan succinctly conclude, "The point about the Melting Pot . . . is that it did not happen." Every act of racism and discrimination is a painful contradiction of the concept of the melting pot.

Why have the Chicanos not been assimilated into the American mainstream? The most obvious reason for this lack of assimilation is the dominant Anglo group itself; it has not been willing to let the Chicano assimilate. The Mexican American is in a caste position similar to that of the black man after emancipation. There are other factors that have contributed to the cultural distance between the Chicano and the Anglo. First, there is the fact that Mexico is adjacent to the United States. The homeland for many Chicanos is never far away. There is a continual cultural regeneration and reinforcement. Many Mexicans come to America "temporarily" and never psychologically divorce themselves from the values of Mexico. Then there is the continual immigration, both legal and illegal, from Mexico. There are also visits from relatives going in both directions. The communal and extended nature of the Chicano family further reinforces certain cultural values, like language. Three and four generations may live in the same household. This pattern can be contrasted with many white immigrant groups who left the homeland far behind in Europe, geographically if not psychologically.

Another reason why the Chicano has not been and may never be totally assimilated is that he does not want to be. Why accept the dominant culture? If Anglo youth rebellion is any indication of the viability of mainstream, middle-class American values, Chicanos may be correct in refusing to assimilate. In fact, many of the criticisms that young people level at America have been part of the Chicano cultural and historical tradition. Chicanos have never been "materialistic," or what the Anglo considers "property oriented." The land was usually for all to use or hold communally; their agricultural practices and use of the land were in harmony with nature. Chicanos have always displayed a sense of community, a tendency toward mutual aid, and a strong communal or extended family. They have always nurtured an emphasis on warm interpersonal relationships and a respect for people as individuals.

The Myth of Mexican American Similarity

As with most minority groups, the Mexican American has been stereotyped. The stereotype is usually one of a lower-lower-class Chicano, a rigid caricature which allows a minimum of diversity. The stereotype, as mentioned in a previous section, has negative and racist connotations, and as a valid characterization of social reality, it is sadly lacking.

There are some statistical generalizations that can be made in relation to Chicanos. Many have parents or grandparents who migrated from Mexico, and as a consequence, many speak Spanish, Pocho (a combination of Spanish and English), or English with an accent. As a group, Chicanos tend to be Catholic (easily over 50 per cent). As a population they tend to be young (twenty years of age). The average yearly income for the Mexican American family is the lowest in the nation, except for the income of the reservation Indian. There are more Chicanos (60 to 70 per cent) living in poverty and more Chicanos with less education than blacks (less than eight years, on the average, for those over twenty-five). Chicanos as a group share certain cultural values, but within the broad contours just mentioned there is immense variety.

There are many physical differences in the Chicano population. Although Chicanos tend to be darker than the Anglo population, they range from swarthy to light skinned. All types of ethnic and racial groups have mingled in Mexico with the indigenous people, from black slaves to French immigrants. There are also Filipinos and Puerto Ricans who are culturally Chicano. There are rural and urban differences, generational conflicts, geographical differences, and class differences between Chicanos. Who is a Mexican American? How can you really stereotype the Chicano?

Here lies the strength and weakness of the Chicano. On one hand he is confronted in America with a severe "identity crisis." He is the true marginal man caught between cultures. Historically, he represents the

uneasy compromise between the Hispano and the Indian who was delivered into a hostile Anglo world. Yet as a people, *La Raza* has developed
a deeply ingrained humanism. The term *La Raza* does not simply mean
the race or people, but the community or the family. *La Raza* stands in
striking contrast to the cold and impersonal Anglo world.

A CITY FOUNDED, A PEOPLE LOST

Anthony Gary Dworkin

The story of the Mexican-American[1] in Los Angeles is as old as the
city itself. Many of the Mexican-Americans in Los Angeles today are the
descendants of the city's earliest residents.

An understanding of the condition of the Mexican-American and of the
city he built and lost must go back to a time when there were no free-
ways, or bustling crowds, or smog. Instead, all that existed were grasslands, desert, a few Spaniards, a few Christianized Indians, a few other
Indians, a few missions spaced a day's horse ride apart, and a dusty trail
called *El Camino Real*—The King's Highway.

The Spanish had been in the West for two centuries and the Indians for
two hundred more when forty-six adventurers of mixed Indian, Negro,
and Spanish descent founded Los Angeles. The exact date of the founding
is uncertain; however, the city fathers officially recognize it as September
4, 1781. It is said that the first building the Spaniards established was a
jail to guarantee that the settlers would not escape from their new home.
From out of wastelands a city was carved.

Los Angeles flourished through the nineteenth century. With the overthrow of Spanish rule, the independence of Mexico in 1810, and the
subsequent secularization of the California missions in 1834, the countryside around the pueblo of Los Angeles became a vast spread of great
ranchos.

All this came to an end when gold was discovered in California.
General Winfield Scott's capture of Vera Cruz, Mexico, and the exploits
of General John C. Frémont spelled defeat for the Mexicans in 1848.
Within two years California was a state. The United States paid off its
claims to Mexico and guaranteed that the grant deeds would be honored

From *Our Children's Burden*, edited by Raymond Mack. Copyright © 1968 by
Raymond W. Mack. Reprinted by permission of Random House, Inc.
    Gary Dworkin received his doctorate from Northwestern University in 1970 and has
since taught sociology at the University of Missouri in Columbia. He has done extensive research in Los Angeles, concentrating especially on the failure of public institutions to serve the Chicano population. He has published on Chicano and Mexican
stereotypes of one another and is currently preparing a volume entitled *Double Identity: Mixed Race Peoples Around the World*.

    [1] "Anglo," derived from the term Anglo-Saxon, refers to a person living in the United
States of European, but not Spanish ancestry.
    A Mexican-American is a person living in the United States who was born in Mex-
ico, or whose ancestors came from Mexico, no matter how many years ago.

and the Mexican families could hold their great ranchos. But with the drought of 1862–1864, which killed the cattle, and with the heavy United States land taxes against the ranchos, the *gente de razón*, or the great families from the days of Spanish rule, lost their land. Enormous ranchos, like the 265,000-acre Los Alimitos, were sold for $152 in delinquent taxes.

During the land boom of the 1880s many Midwesterners moved into Los Angeles and bought land. The poverty-stricken Mexicans retreated into the ghetto of East Los Angeles, especially into an area known as the Flats.

With the overthrow of the Diaz regime in 1910 and the Mexican revolution that ensued, a new stream of Mexican immigrants flowed into the expanding city of Los Angeles. These were the landlords and the middle class, abandoning a Mexico that no longer welcomed them.

In the 1920s, with the political and economic unrest in Mexico, a third wave of Mexican nationals migrated to Los Angeles. Many Mexicans were employed in the fields by Anglo fruit growers.

When the Depression came in the 1930s, the Anglo discovered that the Mexicans had not gone back to Mexico between harvests, but had settled in the East Los Angeles ghetto to crowd the relief rolls. While the Anglo was intolerant of the idea that Mexican "nationals" were getting relief, he was even more incensed by the fact that in the depths of the Depression the Mexican laborers were attempting to unionize.

The state decided to deport the laborers. From California about two hundred thousand Mexican-American laborers, their wives, children, and pets were boarded on trains and sent back to Mexico. In some cases the children of the field hands were American citizens, born in the Los Angeles ghetto. However, because they could not speak English and could not show proof of citizenship, they were "repatriated."

Most of the Mexican-Americans in East Los Angeles were not deported. Throughout World War II, with the zoot-suit riots of 1943, and after the war, the migratory laborers continued to move into the cities; by 1960 the Mexican-American was 80 per cent urban.

In many respects the condition of the Mexican-American has improved. He no longer is required to sit in segregated movies, ride in separate sections of buses, and has been given the vote and a partial education. But the wounds inflicted for more than a century do not heal quickly. There is much bitterness in the ghetto.

The Mexican Ghetto Today: The Hard Data of Discrimination

There are more individuals of Mexican descent in Los Angeles than in any city in the world except Mexico City. Mexican-Americans comprise Los Angeles' second largest minority group, and represent 11.5 per cent of the city's 2.5 million residents.[2] Only the Negro, who makes up 14 per cent of the city's population, is larger in numbers. However, for the

[2] Statistical data on the city of Los Angeles are taken from Fair Employment Practice Commission report, "Los Angeles City Schools," October, 1964.

county of Los Angeles,[3] Mexican-Americans are the largest minority group. Of the county's 6 million residents, 9.6 per cent are Mexican-Americans, while 7.6 per cent are Negro. The Mexican population increases on the average by 2,250 new residents per month.

The reason Mexican-Americans outnumber the Negro population in the county but not in the city may be explained by three facts. First, much of the largest Mexican-American ghetto in Los Angeles is not in incorporated territory, but lies just east of the city's boundary. Second, the Negro population has been in the city a shorter length of time and migrated from the South to a concentrated ghetto in the south and central parts of the city; while the Mexican-American, because of his long tenure in Los Angeles, has become dispersed throughout the county as well as concentrated into several ghettos. In fact, most of the incorporated suburbs in the county have sizable Mexican-American populations. Third, because the Mexican-American is a Caucasian, the lighter-skinned members of the population have found it much easier to escape from the ghetto and assimilate in to the Anglo middle-class communities, attend Anglo schools, and share in the dominant culture.

Table 1 presents the social characteristics of the Anglo and Spanish surname[4] populations in Los Angeles County. As might be expected the Anglo's condition is considerably better than the Mexican-American's. More Anglos are married; but fewer people of Spanish surname are widowed or divorced. The divorce rate among the Mexican-American is considerably higher, however, than the statistics or Catholicism would indicate. As one Mexican-American newspaperwoman noted:

Today, as never before, women are going down to Mexico to get divorces from their husbands if they are not satisfied. Before, the woman would just endure, but now women are freer. They go to Mexico for a divorce and it never gets recorded by the State of California. Therefore, population figures could never tell you anything about the shifts.

[3] Statistical information on the county of Los Angeles and for the Mexican-American ghetto are derived from the Research Department of the Welfare Planning Council, Los Angeles Region report, "Background for Planning," 1963.

[4] The United States Census does not adequately differentiate the Mexican-American population from other Spanish-speaking groups. The term "Spanish surname" is employed instead by the census. Hence, Mexican-Americans, Puerto Ricans, Cubans, and Central and South Americans comprise Los Angeles' population of 576,716 people with Spanish surnames. However, this does not present too much of a problem. Over 90 per cent of the Spanish-surname population of Los Angeles are Mexican-Americans, and so the data on Spanish surnames are fairly accurate for Mexican-Americans as well. If anything, the data present a more conservative estimate of the Mexican-American plight as the Cuban population, most of whom are escapees from Castro's regime and were former professionals in Cuba, are better educated, earn better incomes, and have better jobs. However, because the Spanish-surname population who are not of Mexican descent represent only a small fraction of the total category, the discrepancy between statistics on Mexican-Americans and on all Spanish surname groups is slight. If anything, the total number of Mexican-Americans with Spanish surnames is an underestimate of the total Mexican-American population because some Mexican women change their surname by marriage to Anglo men, and some Mexican men Anglicize their surnames.

Table 1.   Characteristics of the Anglo-White and Spanish-Surname
Populations: Los Angeles County, 1960*

	ANGLO-WHITE	SPANISH-SURNAME
Marital Status		
Population 14 and over	3,617,761	361,877
Per cent Single	19.1	25.3
Per cent Married	67.1	65.6
Per cent Married but Separated	11.5	2.7
Per cent Widowed	8.6	5.3
Per cent Divorced	5.1	3.8
Family Income		
All families	1,302,933	128,018
Per cent <$4,000	16.9	25.7
Per cent $4,000–5,999	17.5	27.8
Per cent $6,000–7,999	21.9	22.5
Per cent $8,000–9,999	16.5	12.2
Per cent ≥ $10,000	27.3	11.7
Median Income	$7,433	$5,759
Education		
Population 25 and over	2,966,703	265,928
Per cent no school	1.0	7.0
Per cent 1–7 yrs.	9.1	30.0
Per cent 8–11 yrs.	33.3	37.0
Per cent 12 yrs. (high school)	30.3	17.5
Per cent 1–3 yrs. college	15.4	5.9
Per cent 4 or more yrs. college	10.8	3.0
Median school yrs. completed	12.2 yrs.	9.0 yrs.
Employment Status		
Male, 14 and over	1,728,419	179,181
Per cent in labor force	80.4	80.0
Per cent unemployed	5.1	7.6
Female, 14 and over	1,892,023	182,696
Per cent in labor force	37.5	34.4
All occupied units	1,692,567	146,230
Per cent owner occupied	56.6	47.0
Per cent deteriorated or dilapidated	6.8	19.8
Owner occupied units	958,583	68,686
Per cent value $10,000	8.0	21.7
Per cent value $10,000–19,999	61.7	66.8
Per cent $20,000 or more	30.3	11.5
Median value	$16,900	$13,100
Median gross rent	$85	$68

*Adapted from Table 10, *Background for Planning*, Research Department of the Welfare Planning Council, Los Angeles Region, Research Report No. 17, February 1964.

The Anglo, however, has a higher income (a median of $7,433 for the Anglo and $5,759 for the Mexican-American); he is better educated (the Anglo has completed 12.2 years of school while the Mexican-American has completed only 9); the Anglo is less affected by unemployment (5.1 per cent of the Anglos are unemployed as compared to 7.6 per cent of the Mexicans). And finally, the Anglo lives in a better home; the Anglo's home is worth $16,900 while the Mexican's is worth $13,100; further, 19.8 per cent of the Mexican homes are dilapidated or deteriorated, while only 6.8 per cent of the Anglo homes are in such condition.

The present paper is based upon research in one of the ghettos in the county—East Los Angeles and Boyle Heights. Within this area reside 180,000 people, of whom 67 per cent are of Spanish surname. This ghetto represents the largest single concentration of Mexican-Americans, is a center of Poverty Program work, produces the most militant Mexican-Americans, and is an area in which social scientists have been studying for the past twenty years, thus providing an invaluable storehouse of data.

It was in this area that the 1943 "zoot-suit riots" raged. Here in East Los Angeles and Boyle Heights, situated on the east and traditionally the wrong side of the Los Angeles River and Southern Pacific Railroad tracks, is the infamous Flats. The Flats has been the home of gangs and the repository for successive waves of immigrants. From the 1880s to the post-World War II period the Flats has been occupied by newly immigrated Irish, Armenians, Molokans, Slavs, Jews, and finally Mexicans. Each group turned the Flats into an interstitial area plagued with problems of crime, delinquency, tuberculosis, and human decay—physical, psychological, and social.

In order to make this report more meaningful, at times we shall not restrict our discussion simply to the ghetto itself. Instead, we shall discuss the ghetto in relation to the county as a whole, the Anglo communities to which the successful Mexicans migrate, and Watts, one part of the Negro ghetto.

There is a distinct path taken by the mobile Mexican family as it flees the ghetto. The stages seem to be as follows: out of the ghetto to El Sereno, then to Montebello and Monterey Park, and then, often with the name change and complete Anglicization, into eastern San Gabriel Valley and other Anglo areas. In terms of social class, as judged by income, education, occupation, living conditions, delinquency rates, property values, etc., the class shift is roughly from lower-lower to upper-lower to lower-middle to upper-middle. As one sociologist who has worked with East Los Angeles Mexicans for fifteen years notes:

> There is a mass exodus from East LA to El Sereno. While East LA is lower class, El Sereno is upper-lower and lower-middle class. Thus, as the Mexicans get more money they move out of the LA ghetto and into the El Sereno ghetto. Another reason for the movement to El Sereno is the fact that it has a powerful Catholic church and parochial school. The pattern of

migration is into East LA, to El Sereno, and then finally into Montebello and Monterey Park and east.

Table 2 presents the 1960 statistics on population density and ethnic concentration. It should be noted that there exists a linear relationship between these characteristics and the progressive movement out of the ghetto into successively higher socioeconomic levels. That is, as one moves out of the Mexican ghetto of East Los Angeles and Boyle Heights, population density and percentage of ethnicity decrease. In addition the ratio of Mexican-Americans to Anglos decreases. Furthermore, while Watts has approximately the same high population density as the Mexican-American ghetto, it is more segregated. East Los Angeles is 70.9 per cent and Boyle Heights is 78.5 per cent ethnic, while Watts is 94.5 per cent ethnic. Further, Watts is more homogeneously ethnic. Eighty-five per cent of Watts is of the same race (Negro), while only 67 per cent of the Mexican ghetto is of the same ethnic group (Spanish surname).

The traditional indices of social rank and socioeconomic status also demonstrate a linear relationship between the progressive steps taken out of the Mexican ghetto and increasingly favorable economic, educational, and occupational conditions. The median incomes for the ghetto and the three steps beyond are as follows: the ghetto of East Los Angeles and Boyle Heights, $5,437 and $5,053, respectively; El Sereno, $6,461; Montebello, $7,351; Monterey Park, $7,650. In comparison, the median income in Watts is $4,365, a figure even lower than in the Mexican ghetto.

The median school years completed for East Los Angeles and Boyle Heights are eight each; for El Sereno it is ten years; for Montebello it is eleven years; and for Monterey Park it is twelve years. The educational level in Watts is nine years, and thus is higher than in the Mexican ghetto. As will be discussed later, the difference between the ghetto and Watts may be attributed to an extreme difference in the value system of the Mexican ghetto and that of the school system.

Unemployment rates also demonstrate the linear relation and the fact

Table 2.   1960 Census, Population Density, and Ethnic Distribution*

Area	1960 Population	Persons per Sq. Ml.	Per Cent Negro	Per Cent Other	Per Cent Spanish Surname	Per Cent all Minorities
East Los Angeles	105,464	12,379	<1.0	3.8	67.1	70.9
Boyle Heights	75,065	14,463	3.7	8.0	66.8	78.5
El Sereno	29,477	6,110	1.2	3.8	37.4	42.4
Montebello	32,097	4,312	<1.0	1.6	22.6	24.2
Monterey Park	37,821	5,352	<1.0	2.9	13.1	16.0
Watts (comparison population)	72,203	13,818	85.7	<1.0	8.8	94.5
L.A. County	6,038,771	1,479	7.6	2.0	9.6	19.2

* Compiled from Tables 2 and 7 of *Background for Planning*, Research Department of the Welfare Planning Council, Los Angeles Region, Research Report No. 17, February 1964.

that conditions in the Mexican ghetto are somewhat better (except for education) than in Watts, the Negro area. In East Los Angeles and Boyle Heights the unemployment rates are 6 and 6.6, respectively; while the values for El Sereno, Montebello, and Monterey Park are 3.7, 3.5, and 3.9, respectively. The apparent deviant case of Monterey Park is confounded by the higher percentage of college students in the area. This group enters the ranks of the unemployed during the summer but are "employed" during the school year. Unemployment in Watts is much higher than in the Mexican ghetto. In fact, it is 50 per cent greater, with a 9.4 per cent rate.

Lastly, we note that housing conditions and values improve as we move out of the ghetto into the three other areas. In East Los Angeles and Boyle Heights, respectively, 29 and 23.5 per cent of the homes are deteriorated or dilapidated, and median property values are $11,861 and $11,563, respectively. In El Sereno 17.8 per cent of the homes are deteriorated or dilapidated, and the median property value is $12,581. In Montebello only 4.5 per cent of the homes are deteriorated or dilapidated, while the median property value is $16,834. And in Monterey Park 3.2 per cent of the homes are deteriorated or dilapidated, and the median property value is $17,833. Fewer homes in Watts (22.6 per cent) are deteriorated or dilapidated than in the Mexican ghetto; however, property value ($10,208) is less than in the Mexican ghetto. All of these statistics indicate that the path taken by the Mexican-American as he leaves East Los Angeles and Boyle Heights is one of upward mobility, as measured by these traditional indices.

While no statistics are available on the actual number of Mexican-Americans who escape from the ghetto, we can be sure that the percentage is small. One index is the relatively low percentage of people with Spanish surnames found in the more Anglo areas. Even the phenomenon of passing and name changing is not sufficiently frequent to allow us to conclude that most Mexican-Americans escape the ghetto. Rather, we must conclude that the majority of Los Angeles' Mexican-American population is destined to remain in the ghetto where one may live and die without the need for English, without knowing that the world outside is any better, without leaving the "culture of poverty."

"But They're Just Different"[5]

The educational level of the Mexican-American in the ghetto is lower than in the more disadvantaged Negro ghetto of Watts, because the Mexican value system is so much more at odds with the school system than is that of the Negro. In this section we shall discuss the cultural factors which make the Mexican seem so strange to the Anglo teachers.

[5] A frequently heard statement among Anglo teachers in the Mexican-American ghetto in Los Angeles. One teacher elaborated on the statement by pointing out that "the reason Mexican kids get into so much trouble is that they are born Mexican."

There is a sharp split between the Anglo's and Mexican's culture. The Anglo is secular, practical, objective, competitive, materialistic, and future-oriented. Traditionally the Mexican was not.[6] The new Mexican-Americans are changing, but a viable culture, reinforced by generations of ghetto life and discrimination, and centuries of life in Mexico does not die easily. A conglomeration of Spanish, Indian, and Roman Catholic in origin, the Mexican-American culture has served as a defense against the exploitation by the Anglo. One Mexican-American teacher, who feared that busing Mexican children from the ghetto to Anglo schools out of the ghetto would cause the children to lose their grasp of the Mexican culture, proclaimed:

[The Mexican American] has a culture upon which he can fall back. . . . The actual fact is that the Mexican-American individual, the Spanish-speaking individual, would much rather stay within his own realms of his own neighborhood because he speaks Spanish, he is at home there, why should he want otherwise? [7]

Since there is time to touch upon only a few aspects of Mexican culture, our concern shall be with those aspects which are of maximal importance to the Mexican-American in Los Angeles with respect to his educational opportunities. As such, our discussion shall touch upon the mystical belief in *La Raza* (the race), the Mexican world view; the dominance of *machismo*, or the male-oriented society; the importance of one's parents and extended family; and the cohesion-producing effect of speaking only Spanish in a society whose language is English.

In his discussion of the *Mexican-Americans of South Texas*,[8] William Madsen stated that:

The Mexican-American thinks of himself as both a citizen of the United States and a member of *La Raza* (the Race). This term refers to all Latin-Americans who are united by cultural and spiritual bonds derived from God. The spiritual aspect is perhaps more important than the cultural. . . . The

---

[6] Of the sociological models available to explain the differences between the Mexican and Anglo societies, the most frequently used among researchers in Mexican-Anglo relations is that of the Folk-Urban asymtotic dichotomy. Born in the nineteenth-century tradition of Tönnies, Maine, and Durkheim, the distinction was tested empirically by Redfield, with data from villages in Mexico. Redfield characterized the ideal-typical folk society as follows: "Such a society is small, isolated, nonliterate, and homogeneous, with a strong sense of group solidarity. The ways of living are conventionalized into that coherent system which we call 'a culture.' Behavior is traditional, spontaneous, uncritical, and personal; there is no legislation or habit of experiment and reflection for intellectual ends. Kinship, its relations and institutions, are the type categories of experience, and the familial group is the unit of action. The sacred prevails over the secular; the economy is one of status rather than of market." (Robert Redfield, "The Folk Society," *American Journal of Sociology,* 52, 1947, p. 294.)

[7] From the transcript of "Human Relations—Yesterday, Today, and Tomorrow," Part 1-B (Education), aired on KNBC/television, Channel 4, Los Agneles, Sunday, October 4, 1964, 11:15–11:55 P.M.

[8] New York: Holt, Rinehart and Winston, 1964.

spirit of the Spanish-speaking people, however, is taken to be divine and infinite. As one Latin expressed it, "We are bound together by the common destiny of our souls."

In Mexico, the concept of *La Raza* carries the idea of a splendid and glorious destiny. Mexicans see their greatest national strength in the spiritual vigor of *La Raza*. In Texas, the history of discrimination and economic subordination has modified the concept of the ultimate destiny of *La Raza*. Many Spanish-speaking Texans would say that God had originally planned a glorious future for the Mexican-American, but it probably will never be attained. The failure of *La Raza*, he would continue, is due to the sins of individual Latins. Some believe that *La Raza* is held back by the sins of all Mexican-Americans. . . . Other Latins think that only the worst sinners are holding back *La Raza*. . . . I once asked a Latin if he thought the Anglos were in any way responsible for holding back the Mexican-Americans from their God-given destiny. "Of course not," he replied. "If we lived by God's commands we would be so strong that no one could block us. Of course, the Anglos take advantage of our weakness but it is we who make ourselves weak, not the Anglos."

Not all Mexican-Americans believe that *La Raza* has failed. The militant members of the Mexican-American middle class, most of whom have escaped from the Los Angeles ghetto Anglo neighborhoods, often speak with pride of their Mexican heritage. One Mexican-American businessman who is a member of that category maintained: "If you show the prejudiced Anglos what an advanced culture the Mayans and Aztecs had and prove to them that the Mexican has a great cultural heritage, they will wish that they were Mexicans and respect us. In fact many will want to leave the North and move to Mexico to live."

He is so confident that the Anglo would prefer to live in Mexico once he learned about the culture and history of the land that he has begun to manufacture phonograph records which tell of the Mexican heritage and contain guitar renditions of popular Mexican songs. He sells these at cost to the Anglos who can afford the two dollars, and gives them free to Anglos who are in economic straits.

A second component of Mexican-American culture is *machismo*, the cult of masculinity. The Mexican family, like the Catholic Church, is patriarchal and authoritarian. There is a double standard in which the restrictions upon the male are significantly less. Education is for the man, sexual liberties are for the man, material comforts are for the man, and politics are for the man. The woman is subordinate. She must be faithful to her husband and her children. She is controlled by her parents until she marries; then she is dominated by her husband. In theory and in practice the woman's role in life is one of wife and mother—and nothing more.

The cult of masculinity is at odds with the egalitarian material relationship of the Anglo. Within the ghetto, which is isolated from the Anglo community, strains are less apparent. Still, *machismo* affects female participation and support of such Anglo-operated activities as the school and P.T.A. As the East Central Area Director of the Los Angeles Region Welfare Planning Council observed:

> In the United States the two sexes are on a fairly equal basis. In the culture of Mexico the man is head of the household. The term *machismo* is oftentimes attributed to that trait in the Mexican male where he is the dominant figure in the family. When this characteristic exists, it is the man— the husband—who generally decides if the wife is to attend a P.T.A. meeting, or if she is to participate in a community or civic activity. Thus, because of his own indifference or aloofness, neither he, nor she, becomes actively involved in the community.[9]

When, however, the Mexican-American moves from the ghetto into areas more heavily populated by Anglos, the cultural factor of *machismo* becomes dysfunctional. Mexican-American women compare their relationship with their husbands to that of their Anglo neighbors, and marital unrest often results. As we noted previously, divorces are on the increase and *machismo* is declining. A Mexican-American social worker whose specialty is marriage counseling pointed out that:

> An American middle-class tradition is rough on Mexican husbands. The de-emphasis of *machismo* goes against the strong cultural traditions. Husbands feel the pressure and often leave their wives. For the women the situation is better. It is the first time that they are independent. But both conditions affect the parent-child relationship. Many Mexican kids came to this country when they were very young. They never learned to speak either proper Spanish or proper English. They can't communicate with their parents or their teachers, and vice versa. They feel alienated at home and thus turn to gang life. Only here can they find a peer group that understands them and their problems.

It is in the area of family relations that the dichotomy between the Anglo and Mexican value systems is most apparent, and where its effects upon Mexican educational opportunities are most devastating. The Anglo family is child-centered, while the Mexican family is family-centered. This presents problems with the schools. The social worker continued:

> The schools can't understand why a mother would keep her kid home to tend her brothers and sisters and her cousins while her mother takes her aunt to the hospital. The middle-class parent defines his child's education as the most important thing. But the Mexican parent says that it is the family welfare and family solidarity, including the extended family, that is most important. School is less important than family life, but the middle-class schoolteacher would not understand this.

Couple this with the belief that the woman's place is in the home and that *machismo* is of great importance, and one can understand why there are so few Mexican-Americans in public education. Out of the eight

[9] Martin Ortiz, "Mexican Americans in the Los Angeles Region," unpublished report, 1965.

thousand teachers in the in-service training program in Los Angeles, only seventy-five are Mexican-Americans. Public school teaching is not a masculine occupation in the ghetto, and women are not encouraged to become professionals.

In addition, the school is a symbol of Anglo authority. It is the force which Mexicans see as trying to dissolve family ties. The school demands that the parents obey its wishes. If Juanita's mother wants to have her stay home from school and tend her twelve siblings, the school can seek an injunction against her. The school demands that the child forsake his familial obligations for the needs of the larger society—a demand that rubs against the values of the culture. This is one of the factors which contribute to the high dropout rate among Mexican-American youth. As one Anglo social scientist with an extensive knowledge of the Mexican-American commented:

> Actually you are not going to affect dropout rates as long as the school stands as a symbol of Anglo-Saxon superiority. The Mexican community doesn't trust the schools. The schools threaten to take away the patriarchal rule in the families. A father cannot decide the fate of his children, because the women teachers do so. There is a good deal of paternal pressure on the kids to drop out of school.

Unlike the Anglo-American family, which puts a premium only upon loyalty to the nuclear family, the Mexican family ties extend to all relatives and even close friends. In a report to a group of public school teachers one sociologist noted:

> [In the Mexican-American community] there is the extended family, not just parents, grandparents, children, uncles, aunts, cousins, but also other formal ties with close friends. You may be asked to officiate at the baptism of a child of your friend. I guess the closest role Anglos have to it is a god-parent. Of course this is a great honor. It means that you will be a foster parent, *Padrino* or *Madrina* to the child and *compadre* or *comadre* to its parents. It means that the two families are very closely tied. The *compadre* is technically responsible for the religious instruction and for the vocational or professional training of the child. If there is any kind of trouble, he is considered to be a substitute parent. We do not have this relationship in the Anglo family system. I recall talking about a certain judge with a man who is prominent in the Los Angeles Mexican-American community. He said proudly, "I am *compadre* to him." That means he is a godfather to his children and has a formal relationship to the father. These are extensive family ties where everybody is close to everybody else.[10]

There is little question that the symbols which maintain a culture are best communicated through language, both written and spoken.

---

[10] Paul M. Sheldon, "Mexican Americans and the Public Schools: Some Contrasts in Culture and Social Class," in the report of the Conference on Understanding and Teaching Mexican-American Children and Youth, California State Department of Education, 1964, p. 8.

Buttressing the culture of the ghetto is the Spanish language. The predominant number of members of the older generation of Mexican-Americans speak no English. Nearly 20 per cent of the entire population of the ghetto are functionally illiterate.[11] Among the school-age generation many are barely literate and barely fluent in either English or Spanish. In some sections of the ghetto it is not necessary to be able to speak English. A Mexican-American newspaperwoman observed:

> Did you know that many Mexicans live and die in the East LA ghetto without ever learning English or even leaving the ghetto? Many have never even seen downtown Los Angeles, which is about five miles away. They don't realize that the rest of the world is not a run-down dilapidated slum. I think that if they realized that things were better in other areas, they might get even more militant and would demand their rights. What is keeping the Mexican from overcoming his problems partly is the fact that he doesn't know that things are any different anywhere else.

Because many Mexicans speak little or no English, they have little opportunity to interact with the dominant society. Instead, they seek the security of the ghetto.

Anglos ask why the Mexican-American insists on speaking Spanish. One Anglo teacher observed:

> Mexican-Americans want to be different. They don't want to be American. They insist on speaking Spanish in school. Don't they think that American is good enough for them? If you ask me, it's too good for them!

This is not the issue; rather there is security in speaking Spanish. Ruth Tuck once observed that because Spanish is often the language spoken in the Mexican-American home, lapsing into this language often makes the Mexican-American feel more at ease. Besides, many idioms and turns of the tongue lose their meaning and significance when translated into English.[12]

In addition, there is considerable pressure within the community among the older generation to retain the Spanish language. As Madsen points out:

> From the Anglo viewpoint, Spanish is the primary symbol of "foreignness" of the Mexican-American. For the Latin, Spanish is the primary symbol of loyalty to La Raza. The Mexican-American who speaks English in a gathering of conservative Latins is mocked and regarded as a traitor to La Raza. Among members of the lower class such linguistic disloyalty is forgiven only when a man is drunk.[13]

[11] This, of course, does not mean that all members of this segment cannot read or communicate. Rather, it means that they cannot read English; however, an unknown percentage of this segment can read neither English, nor Spanish.

[12] *Not with the Fist* (New York: Harcourt, Brace, 1946).

[13] William Madsen, *The Mexican-Americans of South Texas*, p. 106.

Furthermore, Spanish allows the culture to flourish. Spanish permits the Mexican-American to maintain cultural pluralism and ties with his family in Mexico. There is reluctance to learn English, the language of the Anglo conquerors, the language of the Yankees who took Mexican land and forced the Mexican into the ghetto, stripping him of everything but his culture—his defense mechanism. As Sheldon notes:

> . . . Among a large part of the Spanish-speaking community English has always been labelled the language of authority spoken by the cop on the beat. English is spoken by the sheriff's deputies. English is spoken by the social worker who controls the mother's allotment. English is spoken by the Anglo teacher.
> . . . There is a carry-over of the Mexican image of the teacher. The *maestro* is much more a disciplinarian and authority figure than American figures. He is also a government figure in Mexican culture. Especially among new arrivals from Mexico, the teacher is held in awe, an attitude which, in a nation of almost universal literacy, is difficult to understand.[14]

We may thus conclude that the explanation for the difference between the educational level of the Negro and the Mexican-American can in part be accounted for by the fact that (1) because of the cult of masculinity, *machismo*, the father of the household determines whether or not his children will go to school, and girls are not encouraged to attend classes; (2) the school, being child-oriented, demands that the child forsake his family at times in order to attend classes, while the Mexican family is family-centered, and insists that the child not go to school if there are too many chores at home to do; and (3) that English, which has been the only language spoken in schools, is the language of the Anglo, the language of the person who conquered the Mexican, attempting to rob him of his culture.

The problems of ghetto life and the dichotomized world in which the Mexican-American lives do not affect the older generation as severely as they do the youth. The Mexican who came to the United States with his family may encounter discrimination in terms of socioeconomic variables, but he has his Spanish-speaking community and Mexican folk culture in the ghetto to fall back upon. He can find shelter in the ghetto. The youth, however, find themselves in a situation unique to children of immigrants in a pluralistic ghetto. In school they are taught to abide by the Anglo child-centered individualistic value system; at home they are reminded of their Mexican heritage and the emphasis on family loyalty. To satisfy the demands of one group is to reject the other. This is the plight of the marginal man. He is marginal to both societies, having full citizenship in neither. There are few cultural symbols available to him with which he can identify. There are few rewards offered for taking either stance. If he sides with the school, he loses his parents' support, but the Anglo community will not accept him, and so he is out of work and without a

[14] Sheldon, *op. cit.*, p. 7.

reference group and culture upon which to rely. If he sides with his parents, he must reject the schools and live his life in the slum—granted, with a culture—but a culture of the slums, and a culture of poverty.

The culture of poverty and the failure of the schools to realize the importance of the family unit in the Mexican culture has taken a great toll among the Mexican-Americans. The Mexican-American has "hyphenated citizenship." He is neither a Mexican nor an American, As a Mexican-American social worker pointed out:

> The biggest source of strain is not with the school or the police. It is with the culture of poverty. Mexican-American kids are marginal men—marginal to their parents' generation and marginal to the Anglos. The Mexican kids can't speak English and they can't speak Spanish. They lack identity. Everything is defined for them in such a way that they cannot belong to either group. They are not wanted or accepted by the Anglos, and they are not wanted by their parents. The Mexican kid is in search of himself. He feels lost. Only in the gang participation does he find a group that understands him and sympathizes with his problems. It is only through gang activity and peer group activity that he can find himself.

But not all Mexican-American kids find themselves in gang activity. Sometimes the marginality is too much to overcome. One eighteen-year-old East Los Angeles girl wrote:

> You can't really win. If you want to be a Mexican you are going to be secluded from the dominant society and you don't have a chance. If you want to be an American you are not going to get any help at home. After a while you get the feeling it isn't worth it. Then you take whatever you can get and have fun—there's nothing else to do.

Despite what she said, she did choose a course of action. One month after writing this she committed suicide.

Aside from taking his life, the Mexican has recourse to changing his name to escape the marginaliy, but even this doesn't work. A social worker told me of the following case:

> I had one case of a Mexican-American about twenty-three who had tried to beat the stigma of being a Mexican and tried to assimilate into the Anglo world by changing his name. He ceased calling himself José Vasquez and became Robert Martindale. But he is still short, dark, and can't speak English very well. Changing his name didn't help. He still can't find work, and now neither the Anglos nor the Mexicans will talk to him.

The social worker suggested a plan of correcting the cultural poverty aspect of the culture of poverty:

> One cultural disadvantage of the culture of poverty is the fact that there are few sources of intellectual stimulation in the Mexican community. There are no legitimate theaters, no music halls where classical music is played; there are only a couple of Mexican movie houses. The only contact with the classics from Mexico are through these two movie houses. One of the Poverty

Program projects in northern California is bringing Mexican literature to the people so that they can be proud of their heritage. There is a need to teach the kids about Mexican art and history. The Japanese community provides classes for their children to teach them Japanese and to educate them about their heritage. This gives them a sense of identity. There ought to be a similar program for the Mexican kids, so that they can learn something about their heritage.

PACHUCOS AND THE ZOOT-SUIT RIOTS

Carey McWilliams

The Origin of *Pachuquismo*

In Los Angeles, in 1942, if a boy wished to become known as a "gangster" he had a choice of two methods. The first, and by far the more difficult, was to commit a crime and be convicted. The second method was easier, although it was largely restricted to a particular group. If you were born of Mexican parents financially unable to move out of certain specific slum areas, you could be a gangster from birth without having to go to all the trouble of committing a crime. For Los Angeles had revised the old saying that "boys will be boys" to read "boys, if Mexican, will be gangsters." The only reservation to be noted, of course, consists in the definition of a "gang."

Adolescent boys in the United States are among the most gregarious groups in our society. American boys traditionally "hang out with the gang." Their association is based, of course, on common interests. The boys in the "gang" may go to the same school, live in the same neighborhood or have the same hobbies. There is, however, a difference in the degree to which the members of various "gangs" feel a sense of solidarity. A boy who belongs to a club for those who make model airplanes may have little loyalty toward the club. It serves a particular interest and beyond this interest he must have other associations. But a "gang" of Mexican boys in Los Angeles is held together by a set of associations so strong that they outweigh, or often outweigh, such influences as the home, the school, and the church.[1]

The various teen-age clubs in the better parts of Los Angeles often get

Reprinted from *North from Mexico* (Philadelphia: J. B. Lippincott Co., 1949), by permission of the author.

Carey McWilliams is from Steamboat Springs, Colorado. He received his LL.B. from the University of Southern California in 1927 and was admitted to the bar. He practiced law until 1938 and then began his long career as a writer and editor of *The Nation*. He has written a dozen books and countless articles for national magazines, many of which, like "Anti-Semitism in America" and "North from Mexico," deal with prejudice and racism in the United States.

[1] This is *palomilla*, or age set, referred to in Rubel's article.—*Eds.*

together and spend an evening dancing in Hollywood. But the respectable places of entertainment will often refuse to admit Mexicans. The boys and girls who belong to the "Y" often make up theater parties. But the "best" theaters in Los Angeles have been known to refuse admission to Mexicans. Many youngsters like to go rollerskating or iceskating; but the skating rink is likely to have a sign reading "Wednesdays reserved for Negroes and Mexicans." Wherever the Mexicans go, outside their own districts, there are signs, prohibitions, taboos, restrictions. Learning of this "iron curtain" is part of the education of every Mexican-American boy in Los Angeles. Naturally it hits them hardest at the time when they are trying to cope with the already tremendous problems of normal adolescence. The first chapters are learned almost on the day they enter school, and, as time passes and the world enlarges, they learn other chapters in this bitter and peremptory lesson.

Most of the boys are born and grow up in neighborhoods which are almost entirely Mexican in composition and so it is not until they reach school age that they become aware of the social status of Mexicans. Prior to entering school, they are aware, to a limited extent, of differences in background. They know that there are other groups who speak English and that they will some day have to learn it, too. But it is at shool that they first learn the differences in social rank and discover that they are at the bottom of the scale. Teachers in the "Mexican" schools are often unhappy about their personal situation. They would much rather be teaching in the sacroscant halls of some Beverly Hills or Hollywood school. Assignment to a school in a Mexican district is commonly regarded, in Los Angeles, as the equivalent of exile. Plagued by teachers who present "personality problems," school administrators have been known to "solve" the problem by assigning the teacher to "Siberia." Neither in personnel nor equipment are these schools what they should be, although a definite attempt to improve them is now under way.

Discovering that his status approximates the second-rate school has the effect of instilling in the Mexican boy a resentment directed against the school, and all it stands for. At the same time, it robs him of a desire to turn back to his home. For the home which he knew prior to entering school no longer exists. All of the attitudes he has learned at school now poison his attitude toward the home. Turning away from home and school, the Mexican boy has only one place where he can find security and status. This is the gang made up of boys exactly like himself, who live in the same neighborhood, and who are going through precisely the same distressing process at precisely the same time.

Such is the origin of the juvenile gangs about which the police and the press of Los Angeles were so frenetically concerned. Gangs of this character are familiar phenomena in any large city. In Los Angeles, twenty years ago, similar gangs were made up of the sons of Russian Molokan immigrants. They have existed in Los Angeles since the city really began to grow, around 1900, and they will continue to exist as long as society creates them. Thus "the genesis of pachuquismo," as Dr. George Sanchez has pointed out, "is an open book to those who care to look into the situations facing Spanish-speaking people" in the Southwest. In fact, they were pointed out over a decade ago in an article which Dr. Sanchez wrote for the *Journal of Applied Psychology*.[2]

The *pachuco* gang differs from some other city gangs only in the degree to which it constitutes a more tightly knit group. There is more to the *pachuco* gang than just having a good time together. The *pachucos* suffer discrimination together and nothing makes for cohesiveness more effectively than a commonly shared hostility. Knowing that both as individuals and as a group they are not welcome in many parts of the city, they create their own world and try to make it as self-sufficient as possible.

While the fancier "palladiums" have been known to refuse them, even when they have had the price of admission, there are other dance halls, not nearly so fancy, that make a business of catering to their needs. It should be noted, however, that Mexican boys have never willingly accepted these inferior accommodations and the inferior status they connote. Before they have visited the "joints" on Skid Row, they have first tried to pass through the palatial foyers on Sunset Boulevard. When they finally give up, they have few illusions left about their native land.

It should also be remembered that *pachuquismo* followed a decade of important social change for Mexicans in Los Angeles. During the depression years, thousands of Mexicans had been repatriated and those remaining began to adjust to a new code of existence. The residence of those who had been migratory workers tended to become stabilized, for residence was a condition to obtaining relief. Thousands of Mexicans were replaced, during these same years, by so-called Okies and Arkies in the migratory labor movement. A greater stability of residence implied more regular schooling, better opportunities to explore the intricacies of urban life, and, above all, it created a situation in which the Mexican communities began to impinge on the larger Anglo-American community.

During the depression years, one could watch the gradual encroachment of Mexicans upon downtown Los Angeles. Stores and shops catering to Mexican trade crossed First Street, moving out from the old Plaza district and gradually infiltrated as far south as Third or Fourth streets. The motion picture theaters in this neighborhood, by far the oldest in the city, began to "go Mexican" as did the ten-cent stores, the shops, and the small retail stores. Nowadays the old Mason Opera House, in this district, has become a Mexican theater. Being strangers to an urban environment, the first generation had tended to respect the boundaries of the Mexican communities. But the second generation was lured far beyond these boundaries into the downtown shopping districts, to the beaches, and above all, to the "glamor" of Hollywood. It was this generation of Mexicans, the *pachuco* generation, that first came to the general notice and attention of the Anglo-American population.

[2] *See* comments by Dr. George Sanchez, *Common Ground*, Autumn, 1943, pp. 13–20.

Thus concurrently with the growth of the gangs there developed a new stereotype of the Mexican as the *"pachuco* gangster" the "zoot-suiter." Many theories have been advanced and reams of paper wasted in an attempt to define the origin of the word *"pachuco."* Some say that the expression originally came from Mexico and denoted resemblance to the gaily costumed people living in a town of this name,[3] others have said that it was first applied to border bandits in the vicinity of El Paso. Regardless of the origin of the word, the *pachuco* stereotype was born in Los Angeles. It was essentially an easy task to fix this stereotype on Mexican youngsters. Their skin was enough darker to set them apart from the average *Angeleno.* Basically bilingual, they spoke both Spanish and English with an accent that could be mimicked by either or both groups. Also there was an age-old heritage of ill-will to be exploited and a social atmosphere in which Mexicans, as Mexicans, had long been stereotyped. The *pachuco* also had a uniform—the zoot-suit—which served to make him conspicuous.

Mexican-American boys never use the term "zoot-suit," preferring the word "drapes" in speaking of their clothes. "Drapes" began to appear in the late thirties and early forties. In general appearance, "drapes" resemble the zoot-suits worn by Negro youngsters in Harlem, although the initiated point out differences in detail and design. Called "drapes" or "zoot-suit," the costume is certainly one of the most functional ever designed. It is worn by boys who engage in a specific type of activity, namely, a style of dancing which means disaster to the average suit. The trouser cuffs are tight around the ankles in order not to catch on the heels of the boy's quickly moving feet. The shoulders of the coat are wide, giving plenty of room for strenuous arm movements; and the shoes are heavy, serving to anchor the boy to the dance floor as he spins his partner around. There is nothing esoteric about these "sharp" sartorial get-ups in underprivileged groups, quite apart from their functional aspect. They are often used as a badge of defiance by the rejected against the outside world and, at the same time, as a symbol of belonging to the inner group. It is at once a sign of rebellion and a mark of belonging. It carries prestige.[4]

For the boys, peg-topped pants with pleats, high waists up under the armpits, the long loose-backed coat, thick-soled bluchers, and the duck-tailed haircut; for the girls, black huaraches, short black skirt, long black stockings, sweater, and high pompadour. Many of the boys saved their money for months to buy one of these get-ups. The length of the coat and the width of the shoulders became as much a mark of prestige as the merit badges of the Boy Scout. But, it should be noted, that the zoot-suit was not universal among Mexican boys. Some never adopted it, while others never adopted it completely. There were all varieties of acceptance. The newspapers, of course, promptly seized upon the zoot-suit as "a badge of crime." But as one zoot-suited boy said to me, with infallible logic, "If

---

[3] The town referred to is *Pachuca* (*a* not o), the capital of the state of Hidalgo. It is located about 50 miles to the northeast of Mexico City.—*Eds.*

[4] *See* comments by Albert Deutsch, *PM,* June 14, 1943; *Racial Digest,* July, 1943, pp. 3–7; New York *Times,* June 11, 1943.

I were a gangster, would I wear a zoot-suit so that everyone would know I was a gangster? No, I'd maybe dress like a priest or like everyone else; but no zoot-suit."

With the backdrops all in place, the curtain now rolls up on an interesting tableau in Our City the Queen of the Angels which was founded in the year 1781 by Mexican *pobladores* under the direction of Spanish officers who wore costumes far more outlandish than those worn by the most flamboyant *pachucos*.

Blood on the Pavements

On Thursday evening, June 3, 1943, the Alpine Club—made up of youngsters of Mexican descent—held a meeting in a police substation in Los Angeles. Usually these meetings were held in a nearby public school but, since the school was closed, the boys had accepted the invitation of a police captain to meet in the substation. The principal business of the meeting, conducted in the presence of the police captain, consisted in a discussion of how gang-strife could best be avoided in the neighborhood. After the meeting had adjourned, the boys were taken in squad cars to the street corner nearest the neighborhood in which most of them lived. The squad cars were scarcely out of sight, when the boys were assaulted, not by a rival "gang" or "club," but by hoodlum elements in the neighborhood. Of one thing the boys were sure: their assailants were not of Mexican descent.

Earlier the same evening a group of eleven sailors, on leave from their station in Los Angeles, were walking along the 1700 block on North Main Street in the center of one of the city's worst slum areas. The surrounding neighborhood is predominantly Mexican. On one side of the street the dirty brick front of a large brewery hides from view a collection of ramshackle Mexican homes. The other side of the street consists of a series of small bars, boarded-up store fronts, and small shops. The area is well off the beaten paths and few servicemen found their way this far north on Main Street. As they were walking along the street, so they later stated, the sailors were set upon by a gang of Mexican boys. One of the sailors was badly hurt; the others suffered minor cuts and bruises. According to their story, the sailors were outnumbered about three to one.

When the attack was reported to the nearest substation, the police adopted a curious attitude. Instead of attempting to find and arrest the assailants, fourteen policemen remained at the station after their regular duty was over for the night. Then, under the command of a detective lieutenant, the "Vengeance Squad," as they called themselves, set out "to clean up" the gang that had attacked the sailors. But—miracle of miracles! —when they arrived at the scene of the attack they could find no one to arrest—not a single Mexican—on their favorite charge of "suspicion of assault." In itself this curious inability to find anyone to arrest—so strikingly at variance with what usually happened on raids of this sort—raises an inference that a larger strategy was involved. For the raid accomplished nothing except to get the names of the raiding officers in the newspapers and to whip up the anger of the community against the Mexican population, which may, perhaps, have been the reason for the raid. . . .

Thus began the so-called "Zoot-Suit Race Riots" which were to last, in one form or another, for a week in Los Angeles.

The Taxicab Brigade

Taking the police raid as a official cue,—a signal for action,—about two hundred sailors decided to take the law into their own hands on the following night. Coming down the center of Los Angeles from the Naval Armory in Chavez Ravine (near the "Chinatown" area), they hired a fleet of twenty taxicabs. Once assembled, the "task force" proceeded to cruise straight through the center of town en route to the east side of Los Angeles where the bulk of the Mexicans reside. Soon the sailors in the lead-car sighted a Mexican boy in a zoot-suit walking along the street. The "task force" immediately stopped and, in a few moments, the boy was lying on the pavement, badly beaten and bleeding. The sailors then piled back into the cabs and the caravan resumed its way until the next zoot-suiter was sighted, whereupon the same procedure was repeated. In these attacks, of course, the odds were pretty uneven: two hundred sailors to one Mexican boy. Four times this same treatment was meted out and four "gangsters"—two seventeen-year-old youngsters, one nineteen, and one twenty-three—were left lying on the pavements for the ambulances to pick up.

It is indeed curious that in a city like Los Angeles, which boasts that it has more police cars equipped with two-way radio than any other city in the world (Los Angeles *Times*, September 2, 1947), the police were apparently unable to intercept a caravan of twenty taxicabs, loaded with two hundred uniformed, yelling, bawdy sailors, as it cruised through the downtown and east-side sections of the city. At one point the police did happen to cross the trail of the caravan and the officers were apparently somewhat embarrassed over the meeting. For only nine of the sailors were taken into custody and the rest were permitted to continue on their merry way. No charges, however, were ever preferred against the nine.

Their evening's entertainment over, the sailors returned to the foot of Chavez Ravine. There they were met by the police and the Shore Patrol. The Shore Patrol took seventeen of the sailors into custody and sent the rest up to the ravine to the Naval Armory. The petty officer who had led the expedition, and who was not among those arrested, gave the police a frank statement of things to come. "We're out to do what the police have failed to do," he said; "we're going to clean up this situation. . . . Tonight [by then it was the morning of June fifth] the sailors may have the marines along." [5]

The next day the Los Angeles press pushed the war news from the front

[5] Los Angeles *Herald-Express*, June 5, 1943.

page as it proceeded to play up the pavement war in Los Angeles in screaming headlines. "Wild Night in L.A.—Sailor Zooter Clash" was the headline in the *Daily News*. "Sailor Task Force Hits L.A. Zooters" bellowed the *Herald-Express*. A suburban newspaper gleefully reported that "zoot-suited roughnecks fled to cover before a task force of twenty taxicabs." None of these stories, however, reported the slightest resistance, up to this point, on the part of the Mexicans.

True to their promise, the sailors were joined that night, June fifth, by scores of soldiers and marines. Squads of servicemen, arms linked, paraded through downtown Los Angeles four abreast, stopping anyone wearing zoot-suits and ordering these individuals to put away their "drapes" by the following night or suffer the consequences. Aside from a few half-hearted admonitions, the police made no effort whatever to interfere with these heralds of disorder. However, twenty-seven Mexican boys, gathered on a street corner, were arrested and jailed that evening. While these boys were being booked "on suspicion" of various offenses, a mob of several hundred servicemen roamed the downtown section of a great city threatening members of the Mexican minority without hindrance or interference from the police, the Shore Patrol, or the Military Police.

On this same evening, a squad of sailors invaded a bar on the east side and carefully examined the clothes of the patrons. Two zoot-suit customers, drinking beer at a table, were peremptorily ordered to remove their clothes. One of them was beaten and his clothes were torn from his back when he refused to comply with the order. The other—they were both Mexicans—doffed his "drapes" which were promptly ripped to shreds. Similar occurrences in several parts of the city that evening were sufficiently alarming to have warranted some precautionary measures or to have justified an "out-of-bounds" order. All that the police officials did, however, was to call up some additional reserves and announce that any Mexicans involved in the rioting would be promptly arrested. That there had been no counterattacks by the Mexicans up to this point apparently did not enter into the police officers' appraisal of the situation. One thing must be said for the Los Angeles police: it is above all consistent. When it is wrong, it is consistently wrong; when it makes a mistake, it will be repeated.

By the night of June sixth the police had worked out a simple formula for action. Knowing that wherever the sailors went there would be trouble, the police simply followed the sailors at a conveniently spaced interval. Six carloads of sailors cruised down Brooklyn Avenue that evening. At Ramona Boulevard, they stopped and beat up eight teenage Mexicans. Failing to find any Mexican zoot-suiters in a bar on Indiana Street, they were so annoyed that they proceeded to wreck the establishment. In due course, the police made a leisurely appearance at the scene of the wreckage but could find no one to arrest. Carefully following the sailors, the police arrested eleven boys who had been beaten up on Carmelita Street; six more victims were arrested a few blocks further on, seven at Ford

Boulevard, six at Gifford Street—and so on straight through the Mexican east-side settlements. Behind them came the police, stopping at the same street corners, "to mop up" by arresting the injured victims of the mob. By morning, some forty-four Mexican boys, all severely beaten, were under arrest.

Operation "Dixie"

The stage was now set for the really serious rioting of June seventh and eighth. Having featured the preliminary rioting as an offensive launched by sailors, soldiers, and marines, the press now whipped public opinion into a frenzy by dire warnings that Mexican zoot-suiters planned mass retaliations. To insure a riot, the precise street corners were named at which retaliatory action was expected and the time of the anticipated action was carefully specified. In effect these stories announced a riot and invited public participation. "Zooters Planning to Attack More Servicemen," headlined the *Daily News*; "Would jab broken bottlenecks in the faces of their victims. . . . Beating sailors' brains out with hammers also on the program." Concerned for the safety of the Army, the Navy, and the Marine Corps, the *Herald-Express* warned that "Zooters . . . would mass 500 strong."

By way of explaining the action of the police throughout the subsequent rioting, it should be pointed out that, in June, 1943, the police were on a bad spot. A man by the name of Beebe, arrested on a drunk charge, had been kicked to death in the Central Jail by the police officers. Through the excellent work of an alert police commissioner, the case had finally been broken and, at the time of the riots, a police officer by the name of Compton Dixon was on trial in the courts. While charges of police brutality had been bandied about for years, this was the first time that a seemingly airtight case had been prepared. Shortly after the riots, a Hollywood police captain told a motion picture director that the police had touched off the riots "in order to give Dixie (Dixon) a break." By staging a fake demonstration of the alleged necessity for harsh police methods, it was hoped that the jury would acquit Dixon. As a matter of fact, the jury did disagree and on July 2, 1943, the charges against Dixon were dismissed.

On Monday evening, June seventh, thousands of *Angelenos*, in response to twelve hours' advance notice in the press, turned out for a mass lynching. Marching through the streets of downtown Los Angeles, a mob of several thousand soldiers, sailors, and civilians, proceeded to beat up every zoot-suiter they could find. Pushing its way into the important motion picture theaters, the mob ordered the management to turn on the house lights and then ranged up and down the aisles dragging Mexicans out of their seats. Street cars were halted while Mexicans, and some Filipinos and Negroes, were jerked out of their seats, pushed into the streets, and beaten with sadistic frenzy. If the victims wore zoot-suits, they were stripped of their clothing and left naked or half-naked on the streets, bleeding and bruised. Proceeding down Main Street from First to Twelfth, the mob stopped on the edge of the Negro district. Learning that the Negroes planned a warm reception for them, the mobsters turned back and marched through the Mexican east side spreading panic and terror.

Here is one of numerous eye-witness accounts written by Al Waxman, editor of *The Eastside Journal*:

At Twelfth and Central I came upon a scene that will long live in my memory. Police were swinging clubs and servicemen were fighting with civilians. Wholesale arrests were being made by the officers.

Four boys came out of a pool hall. They were wearing the zoot-suits that have become the symbol of a fighting flag. Police ordered them into arrest cars. One refused. He asked: "Why am I being arrested?" The police officer answered with three swift blows of the night-stick across the boy's head and he went down. As he sprawled, he was kicked in the face. Police had difficulty in loading his body into the vehicle because he was one-legged and wore a wooden limb. Maybe the officer didn't know he was attacking a cripple.

At the next corner a Mexican mother cried out, "Don't take my boy, he did nothing. He's only fifteen years old. Don't take him." She was struck across the jaw with a night-stick and almost dropped the two and a half year old baby that was clinging in her arms. . . .

Rushing back to the east side to make sure that things were quiet here, I came upon a band of servicemen making a systematic tour of East First Street. They had just come out of a cocktail bar where four men were nursing bruises. Three autos loaded with Los Angeles policemen were on the scene but the soldiers were not molested. Farther down the street the men stopped a streetcar, forcing the motorman to open the door and proceeded to inspect the clothing of the male passengers. "We're looking for zoot-suits to burn," they shouted. Again the police did not interfere. . . . Half a block away . . . I pleaded with the men of the local police sub-station to put a stop to these activities. "It is a matter for the military police," they said.

Throughout the night the Mexican communities were in the wildest possible turmoil. Scores of Mexican mothers were trying to locate their youngsters and several hundred Mexicans milled around each of the police substations and the Central Jail trying to get word of missing members of their families. Boys came into the police stations saying: "Charge me with vagrancy or anything, but don't send me out there!" pointing to the streets where other boys, as young as twelve and thirteen years of age, were being beaten and stripped of their clothes. From affidavits which I helped prepare at the time, I should say that not more than half of the victims were actually wearing zoot-suits. A Negro defense worker, wearing a defense-plant identification badge on his workclothes, was taken from a street car and one of his eyes was gouged out with a knife. Huge half-page photographs, showing Mexican boys stripped of their clothes, cowering on the pavements, often bleeding profusely, surrounded by jeering mobs of men and women, appeared in all the Los Angeles newspapers. As Al Waxman most truthfully reported, blood had been "spilled on the streets of the city."

At midnight on June seventh, the military authorities decided that the local police were completely unable or unwilling to handle the situation, despite the fact that a thousand reserve officers had been called up. The entire downtown area of Los Angeles was then declared "out of bounds" for military personnel. This order immediately slowed down the pace of the rioting. The moment the Military Police and Shore Patrol went into action, the rioting quieted down. On June eighth the city officials brought their heads up out of the sand, took a look around, and began issuing statements. The district attorney, Fred N. Howser, announced that the "situation is getting entirely out of hand," while Mayor Fletcher Bowron thought that "sooner or later it will blow over." The chief of police, taking a count of the Mexicans in jail, cheerfully proclaimed that "the situation has now cleared up." All agreed, however, that it was quite "a situation."

Unfortunately "the situation" had not cleared up; nor did it blow over. It began to spread to the suburbs where the rioting continued for two more days. When it finally stopped, the Eagle Rock *Advertiser* mournfully editorialized: "It is too bad the servicemen were called off before they were able to complete the job. . . . Most of the citizens of the city have been delighted with what has been going on." County Supervisor Roger Jessup told the newsmen: "All that is needed to end lawlessness is more of the same action as is being exercised by the servicemen!" While the district attorney of Ventura, an outlying county, jumped on the bandwagon with a statement to the effect that "zoot suits are an open indication of subversive character." This was also the opinion of the Los Angeles City Council which adopted a resolution making the wearing of zoot-suits a misdemeanor! On June eleventh, hundreds of handbills were distributed to students and posted on bulletin boards in a high school attended by many Negroes and Mexicans which read: "Big Sale. Second-Hand Zoot Suits. Slightly Damaged. Apply at Nearest U.S. Naval Station. While they last we have your Size."

When the Devil Is Sick . . .

Egging on the mob to attack Mexicans in the most indiscriminate manner, the press developed a fine technique in reporting the riots. "44 Zooters Jailed in Attacks on Sailors" was the chief headline in the *Daily News* of June seventh; "Zoot Suit Chiefs Girding for War on Navy" was the headline in the same paper on the following day. The moralistic tone of this reporting is illustrated by a smug headline in the Los Angeles *Times* of June seventh: "Zoot Suiters Learn Lesson in Fight with Servicemen." The riots, according to the same paper, were having "a cleansing effect." An editorial in the *Herald-Express* said that the riots "promise to rid the community of . . . those zoot-suited miscreants." While Mr. Manchester Boddy, in a signed editorial in the *Daily News* of June ninth excitedly announced that "the time for temporizing is past. . . . The time has come to serve notice that the City of Los Angeles will no longer be terrorized by a relatively small handful of morons parading as zoot suit hoodlums. To delay action *now* means to court disaster later on." As though there had been any "temporizing," in this sense, for the prior two years!

But once the Navy had declared the downtown section of Los Angeles "out of bounds," once the Mexican ambassador in Washington had addressed a formal inquiry to Secretary of State Hull, and once official Washington began to advise the local minions of the press of the utterly disastrous international effects of the riots, in short when the local press realized the consequences of its own lawless action, a great thunderous cry for "unity," and "peace," and "order" went forth. One after the other, the editors began to disclaim all responsibility for the riots which, two days before, had been hailed for their "salutary" and "cleansing" effect.

Thus on June eleventh the Los Angeles *Times*, in a pious mood, wrote that,

> at the outset, zoot-suiters were limited to no specific race; they were Anglo-Saxon, Latin and Negro. The fact that later on their numbers seemed to be predominantly Latin was in itself no indictment of that race at all. No responsible person at any time condemned Latin-Americans as such.

Feeling a twinge of conscience, Mr. Boddy wrote that "only a ridiculously small percentage of the local Mexican population is involved in the so-called gang demonstrations. Every true Californian has an affection for his fellow citizens of Mexican ancestry that is as deep rooted as the Mexican culture that influences our way of living, our architecture, our music, our language, and even our food." This belated discovery of the Spanish-Mexican cultural heritage of California was, needless to say, rather ironic in view of the fact that the ink was not yet dry on Mr. Boddy's earlier editorial in which he had castigated the Mexican minority as "morons." To appreciate the ironic aspects of "the situation," the same newspapers that had been baiting Mexicans for nearly two years now began to extol them.[6]

As might have been expected, this post-mortem mood of penitence and contrition survived just long enough for some of the international repercussions of the riots to quiet down. Within a year, the press and the police were back in the same old groove. On July 16, 1944, the Los Angeles *Times* gave front-page prominence to a curious story under the heading: "Youthful Gang Secrets Exposed." Indicating no source, identifying no spokesman, the story went on to say that "authorities of the Superior Court" had unearthed a dreadful "situation" among juvenile delinquents. Juveniles were using narcotics, marihuana, and smoking "reefers." Compelled to accept drug addiction, "unwilling neophytes" were dragooned into committing robberies and other crimes. Young girls were tatooed with various "secret cabalistic symbols" of gang membership. The high pompadours affected by the *cholitas*, it was said, were used to conceal knives and other "weapons." Two theories were advanced in the story by way of "explaining" the existence of these dangerous gangs: first, that "subversive groups" in Los Angeles had organized them; and, second, that

---

[6] "Imported Mexican Workers Save Millions in Citrus Crops," reads a headline, Los Angeles *Times*, June 30, 1943.

"the gangs are the result of mollycoddling of racial groups." In view of the record, one is moved to inquire, what mollycoddling? by the police? by the juvenile authorities? by the courts? Backing up the news story, an editorial appeared in the *Times* on July eighteenth entitled: "It's Not a Nice Job but It Has to Be Done." Lashing out at "any maudlin and misguided sympathy for the 'poor juveniles,'" the editorial went on to say that "stern punishment is what is needed; stern and sure punishment. The police and the Sheriff's men *should be given every encouragement* to go after these young gangsters" (emphasis mine).

Coincident with the appearance of the foregoing news story and editorial, the Juvenile Court of Los Angeles entered a most remarkable order in its minutes on July 31, 1944. The order outlined a plan by which Mexican wards of the Juvenile Court, over sixteen years of age, might be turned over to the Atchison, Topeka, and Santa Fe Railroad for a type of contract-employment. A form of contract, between the parents of the youngsters and the railroad, was attached to the order. The contract provided that the ward was to work "as a track laborer" at 58½¢ per hour; that $1.03 per day was to be deducted for board, $2.50 per month for dues in a hospital association, and 10¢ a day for laundry. It was also provided that one-half of the pay was to be turned over to the probation officers to be held in trust for the ward. That this order was specifically aimed at *Mexican* juveniles is clearly shown by the circumstance that the court, prior to approving the arrangement, had first secured its approval by a committee of "representative" leaders of the Mexican-American community.

The Strange Case of the Silk Panties

All of this, one will say,—the Sleepy Lagoon case, the riots, etc.,—belongs to the past. But does it? On the morning of July 21, 1946, a thirteen-year-old Mexican boy, Eugene Chavez Montenegro, Jr., was shot and killed by a deputy sheriff in Montebello Park on the east side of Los Angeles. The deputy sheriff later testified that he had been called to the area by reports of a prowler. On arriving at the scene, he had stationed himself near a window of the house in question and had played his flashlight on the window. A little later, he testified, "a man" lifted the screen on the window, crawled out, and ran past him. When the "man" failed to halt on order, he had shot him in the back. At the coroner's inquest, the same deputy also testified that he had seen another officer remove a pair of "silk panties" from the dead boy's pocket and that the boy was armed with "a Boy Scout's knife."

While incidents of this kind have been common occurrences in Los Angeles for twenty years, in this case the officers had shot the wrong boy. For it turned out that young Montenegro was an honor student at St. Alphonsus parochial school; that his parents were a highly respectable middle-class couple; and that the neighbors, Anglo-Americans as well as Mexicans, all testified that the boy had an excellent reputation. Accepting the officers' version of the facts, it was still difficult to explain why they had made no effort to halt the boy, who was five feet three inches tall, when he ran directly past them within arms' reach. Before the hearings were over, the "silk panties" story was exposed as a complete fake. Despite a gallant fight waged by Mr. and Mrs. Montenegro to vindicate the reputation of their son, nothing came of the investigation. "Raging Mother Attacks Deputy Who Slew Son" was the *Daily News* headline on the story of the investigation.

. . . On January 23, 1947 the attorney general of California ordered the removal of two police officers for the brutal beating of four Mexican nationals who, with eight hundred of their countrymen, had been brought to Oxnard to harvest the crops. . . . On March 30, 1946, a private detective killed Tiofilo Pelagio, a Mexican national, in a café argument. . . . On the same day affidavits were presented to the authorities that confessions from four Mexican boys, all minors, had been obtained by force and violence. . . . Esther Armenta, sixteen years of age, complained to her mother that she was being mistreated by Anglo-American classmates in a Los Angeles junior high school. "They would spit on her," said Mrs. Catalina Armenta, the mother, "and call her a 'dirty Mex.' Esther would come home in tears and beg me to get her transferred." A few weeks later the girl was in juvenile court charged with the use of "bad language." She was then sent to the Ventura School for Girls, a so-called "correctional" institution. When Mrs. Armenta finally got permission to visit her daughter, in the presence of a matron, the girl had "black and blue marks on her arm" and complained that she had been whipped by one of the matrons. . . . On April 10, 1946, Mrs. Michael Gonzales complained to the Federation of Spanish-American Voters that her daughter had been placed in the Ventura School without her knowledge or consent and that when she had protested this action she had been threatened with deportation by an official of the juvenile court. . . . On the basis of a stack of affidavits, the San Fernando Valley Council on Race Relations charged on May 16, 1947 that the police had broken into Mexican homes without search warrants; that they had beaten, threatened, and intimidated Mexican juveniles; and that they were in the habit of making "wholesale roundups and arrests of Mexican-American boys without previous inquiry as to the arrested boys' connection—if any—with the crime in question." . . . In 1946 a prominent official of the Los Angeles schools told me that she had been horrified to discover that, in the Belvedere district, Mexican-American girls, stripped of their clothing, were forced to parade back and forth, in the presence of other girls in the "gym," as a disciplinary measure. . . [7]

The Politics of Prejudice

I reported the zoot-suit riots in Los Angeles for *PM* and *The New Republic* and had a hand in some of the hectic events of that memorable

---

[7] For a detailed account of still another "incident," see *Justice for Salcido* by Guy Endore, published by the Civil Rights Congress of Los Angeles, July, 1948.

week. Following the June seventh rioting, I chaired a meeting of a hundred or more citizens at which an emergency committee was formed to bring about, if possible, a return to sanity in Los Angeles. The same evening we communicated with Attorney General Robert W. Kenny in San Francisco by telephone and urged him to induce Governor Earl Warren to appoint an official committee of inquiry. The next day the governor appointed a committee of five which included four names from a panel which I had submitted. The fifth member was the governor's own selection: Mr. Leo Carrillo. Mr. Carrillo, like the sheriff of Los Angeles, is a descendant of "an early California family." The committee immediately assembled in Los Angeles where Mr. Kenny presented to them a proposed report, with findings and recommendations, which I had prepared at his request. With some modifications, this report was adopted by the committee and submitted to the governor. Out of the work of our emergency committee there finally emerged, after a year of negotiation, the present-day Council of Civic Unity.

Praising the report of the governor's committee—which I had prepared —the Los Angeles *Times* devoted several harsh editorials to certain "reckless" individuals, myself included, who had suggested that "racial prejudice" might have had something to do with the riots! "When trouble arose," said the *Times* in an editorial of June 15, 1943, "through the depredations of the young gangs attired in zoot-suits, it was their weird dress and not their race which resulted in difficulties. That is a simple truth which no amount of propaganda will change." In the same editorial, the charges of unfairness which I had raised in connection with the Sleepy Lagoon case were branded as "distortions," "wild charges," and "inflammatory accusations" (charges later confirmed in minute detail by the District Court of Appeals).

When Mrs. Eleanor Roosevelt innocently remarked in her column that the zoot-suit riots were "in the nature of race riots," she was severely taken to task by the *Times* in an editorial of June eighteenth under the caption: "Mrs. Roosevelt Blindly Stirs Race Discord." Even the president of the Los Angeles Chamber of Commerce felt compelled to reply to Mrs. Roosevelt. "These so-called 'zoot-suit' riots," he said, "have never been and are not now in the nature of race riots. . . . At no time has the issue of race entered into consideration. . . . Instead of discriminating against Mexicans, California has always treated them with the utmost consideration." [8]

The zoot-suit riots in Los Angeles were the spark that touched off a chain-reaction of riots across the country in midsummer 1943. Similar "zoot-suit" disturbances were reported in San Diego on June ninth; in Philadelphia on June tenth; in Chicago on June fifteenth; and in Evansville, Indiana, on June twenty-seventh. Between June sixteenth and August first, large-scale race riots occurred in Beaumont, Texas, in Detroit, and in Harlem. The Detroit riots of June 20-21 were the most disastrous

[8] Los Angeles *Times*, June 18, 1943.

riots in a quarter of a century. The swift, crazy violence of the Harlem riot resulted, in a few hours' time, in property damage totalling nearly a million dollars. The rapid succession of these violent and destructive riots seriously interfered with the war effort and had the most adverse international repercussions. The spark that ignited these explosions occurred in *El Pueblo de Nuestra Señora La Reina de Los Angeles de Porciúncula,* founded by Felipe de Neve in 1781, settled by Mexican *pobladores.*

None of these disturbances had more serious international consequences than the zoot-suit riots. On April 20, 1943, President Roosevelt had held his historic meeting with President Camacho on the soil of Mexico. At the time the riots occurred, Mexico was our ally in the war against Germany, Italy, and Japan. Large-scale shipments of Mexican nationals had just begun to arrive in the United States to relieve the critical manpower shortage. "Our two countries," President Roosevelt had said, "owe their independence to the fact that your ancestors and mine held the same truths to be worth fighting for and dying for. Hidalgo and Juárez were men of the same stamp as Washington and Jefferson." President Camacho, replying to this toast, had said that "the negative memories" of the past were forgotten in the accord of today. And then in the largest city in the old Spanish borderland had come this explosion of hatred and prejudice against Spanish-speaking people.

In response to a request from the Mexican ambassador, Secretary of State Hull had asked Mayor Fletcher Bowron for an official explanation. With a perfectly straight face, the mayor replied that the riots were devoid of any element of prejudice against persons of Mexican descent! The same edition of the newspapers that carried this statement also carried another statement by the mayor under a headline which read: "Mayor Pledges 2-Fisted Action, No Wrist Slap"—a reference to police action contemplated against the Mexican minority. On June ninth Mr. Churchill Murray, local representative of the coordinator of Inter-American Affairs, wired Mr. Rockefeller that the riots were "non-racial." "The frequency of Mexican names among the victims," he said, "was without actual significance." If all this were true, asked Dan G. Acosta in a letter to the Los Angeles press, "Why are we consistently called hoodlums? Why is mob action encouraged by the newspapers? Why did the city police stand around saying very nonchalantly that they could not intervene and even hurrahed the soldiers for their 'brave' action? Not until these questions are answered, will the Mexican population feel at ease."

What the riots did, of course, was to expose the rotten foundations upon which the City of Los Angeles had built a papier-mâché façade of "Inter-American Good Will" made up of fine-sounding Cinco de Mayo proclamations. During the riots, the press, the police, the officialdom, and the dominant control groups of Los Angeles were caught with the bombs of prejudice in their hands. One year before the riots occurred, they had been warned of the danger of an explosion. The riots were not an unexpected rupture in Anglo-Hispano relations but the logical end-product of a hundred years of neglect and discrimination.

The riots left a residue of resentment and hatred in the minds and hearts of thousands of young Mexican-Americans in Los Angeles. During the rioting, one Los Angeles newspaper had published a story to the effect that the *cholitas* and *pachucas* were merely cheap prostitutes, infected with venereal disease and addicted to the use of marihuana. Eighteen Mexican-American girls promptly replied in a letter which the metropolitan press refused to publish: "The girls in this meeting room consist of young girls who graduated from high school as honor students, of girls who are now working in defense plants because we want to help win the war, and of girls who have brothers, cousins, relatives and sweethearts in all branches of the American armed forces. We have not been able to have our side of the story told." The letter, with a picture of the girls, was published in Al Waxman's *Eastside Journal* on June 16, 1943. Still another group of Mexican-American girls—real *pachucas* these—bitterly protested the story in another letter which the metropolitan press did not publish. These girls insisted that they should be examined, as a group, by an officially appointed board of physicians so that they could prove that they were virgins. Long after the riots, I have seen Mexican-American boys pull creased and wrinkled newspaper clippings from their wallets and exhibit this slanderous story with the greatest indignation. Four years have now passed since the riots, but the blood has not yet been washed from the pavements of Los Angeles.

SOME CULTURAL IMPLICATIONS OF A MEXICAN AMERICAN BORDER DIALECT OF AMERICAN ENGLISH

Philip Darraugh Ortego

There is no accurate measure of the number of Spanish-speaking Americans and immigrants in the United States, but the most consistent figures suggest a population of approximately 10 to 12 million. This, then, would make Spanish-speaking Americans and immigrants the second largest linguistic group in this country next to the speakers of the national language, with all of its various dialects. While there are significant numbers of Spanish-speakers in such urban centers as New York, Miami, and Chicago, most of the Spanish-speakers in the United States are concentrated in the five-state area of Texas, New Mexico, Colorado, Arizona,

Reprinted by permission from *Studies in Linguistics*, Vol. 21 (1969–70).

Philip Ortego received his doctorate from the University of New Mexico. He now teaches at the University of Texas at El Paso, where he is professor of English and executive director of the Chicano Affairs program. He is a critic, poet, and linguist and has authored many articles on the subject of Chicano affairs as well. He has recently been active in promoting the development of bilingual curricula in the public schools.

and California, with the single largest concentration in Los Angeles. And along the 1600-mile U.S.-Mexico border, particularly, Spanish-speaking Americans and immigrants constitute the majority population.[1] In a recent report issued by the U.S. Office of Education, five and a half million Spanish-speaking children were reported attending schools in the Southwest.

There is a wide range of opinion regarding the nature of the language problem of Spanish-speaking children in the Southwest. Holland, for example, views the problem as being essentially rooted in the "language barrier" imposed upon the learner.[2] Anderson and Johnson, on the other hand, emphasizes the "home environment" as a determinant of English language achievement among Spanish-speakers.[3] Forbes points to race and culture as the significant factors.[4] Also to be considered, of course, are the determinants of individual differences.

In a study of the intellectual development of slum children, Vera P. John confirmed the linguistic truism that "words may be one of the primary and perhaps most essential methods by which the child pools his varied experiences in order to process incoming stimuli effectively."[5] Not only is language "the primary means by which the child is inducted into the life of society," [6] but it is the factor which shapes his entire view of the world. In fact, linguistic research now supports the proposition that all languages produce distinctive conceptual systems or *Weltanschauung*; in other words, that "modality" in the human experience is predicated by the language we speak.

Few people would doubt that the linguistic disabilities of the under-privileged and minority groups represent their most serious handicap. Sufficient studies have shown that there is a specific pattern of difficulties in educational and vocational performance among members of the poorer classes, both of which are linguistic difficulties, essentially. For example, Mexican Americans in the Southwest are plagued with the difficulty of English pronunciation. In other parts of the country differences in grammar have been considered as social differentials; but in the Southwest, when the pronunciation of Mexican Americans is compared with the pronunciation of Anglo-Americans, the general assumption is that the

---

[1] Ortego, Philip D. The minority on the border. *The Nation*, 205:20, December 11, 1967.

[2] Holland, William R. Language barrier as an educational problem of Spanish-speaking children. *Exceptional Children*, 27:42.

[3] Anderson, James C. and William H. Johnson. Sociocultural determinants of achievement among Mexican American students. A paper prepared for the National Conference of Educational Opportunities for Mexican Americans. Sponsored by ERIC/CRESS, Austin, Texas, March 1968.

[4] Forbes, John D. *Mexican Americans: a handbook for educators*. Berkeley, California, 1968.

[5] John, Vera P. The intellectual development of slum children: some preliminary findings. *The psychology of language, thought, and instruction*. [(eds.) John P. De-Cecco et al.] New York, 1967, p. 120.

[6] Deboer, John J. Some sociological factors in language development. *Elementary English*, 29:482, 1952.

difference reflects ethnic and cultural retardation on the part of Mexican Americans.

Some social scientists insist that an accent can be a serious linguistic handicap in the realization of full educational and economic achievement. They may be right, but for the wrong reason. To begin with, an accent can be a serious linguistic handicap only if the auditor chooses to make it a handicap. Admittedly an accent could create transmission interference, but it is insurmountable only if the auditor so chooses. The real problem is that an accent sometimes evokes a certain attitude, a prejudice or bias on the part of the auditor that is somehow unmistakably conveyed to the speaker. The result can be a sense of frustration, hostility, and even a sense of inferiority. Yet most of what we call accent is really *dialect*, or, at the very least, pronunciation audibly different from the pronunciation of other members of a speech community. Fortunately, linguistic science has pointed out that we all speak differently, that we all speak a dialect of some kind or other, that we all speak our own idiolects.

In the American Southwest, Mexican Americans have been particularly singled out and penalized for their accents; that is, for their "spanglish," as their border brand of English is sometimes called. Mexican American kids are indoctrinated early in the goal-concept of achieving Standard American dialect (whatever that is). In fact, most high schools of the Southwest still have special English courses (usually identified as English X, for want of a better euphemism) designed to help Mexican American students overcome (and "hopefully" eliminate) their accents. This means concentrating on special lists of words that always include the word "sheet."

It is important to point out that the single most cultural force influencing the pronunciation of English by Mexican Americans in the Southwest is the proximity of the Spanish-speaking country of Mexico. The result is that many Mexican Americans continue to speak Spanish as their first language and English only as a second language. And the fact that many Mexican Americans can trace their American roots considerably before the treaty of Guadalupe-Hidalgo hardly alters the fact that they will regard Spanish as their first language. It is true that many of the more educated and sophisticated Mexican Americans have become truly bilingual, speaking both Spanish and English without a trace of "accent" in either. But the English pronunciation of the vast majority of Mexican Americans who speak English either as a first or second language is unmistakably influenced by Spanish phonology.

Sometimes, only out of necessity, Mexican Americans have acquired English as a second language. And the learning (for kids especially) has oftentimes been a vicious and degrading experience. But the height of linguistic "imperialism" in the Southwest occurs in the form of penalties imposed upon Mexican American students for speaking Spanish in the schools or their environs. There still exists in many Southwestern public schools one form of punishment known as "Spanish detention." This is an after-school detention for having broken the "no-Spanish" rules. The teachers identify and inform on the students. All of this simply makes the Mexican American feel that Spanish is an inferior language. And it has become fashionable among some Anglo-American educators to speak of Spanish-speaking Mexican Americans as being "illiterate in two languages," failing to realize that for many Mexican Americans a part of learning Spanish as their first language involved learning to read it.

Considering the sociological, psychological, cultural, and linguistic factors in the acquisition of language and reading skills by Spanish-speaking children in the Southwest, the most significant factor appears to be the socio-economic level and status of the family. For despite equal educational facilities, improved socio-economic circumstances tend to enhance the educational development of children. In her study of New York school children, Lazar found that bright students came from better home environments than average or dull students.[7] Thus, the success of language programs for the disadvantaged does not seem to be necessarily dependent or predicated upon a technique or methodology, but, rather, upon the socio-economic milieu of the students. This conclusion was supported by the report of the National Council of Teachers of English Task Force on teaching English to the disadvantaged. They found that regardless of racial or ethnic background, the circumstances of disadvantaged children were identical, all coming from families existing on annual incomes falling below the established national minimum subsistence level.[8]

Yet, for the most part, current views about language, culture, and behavior are still influenced by historical and traditional concepts. In most cases, these concepts insufficiently explain the intricate relationship between language, culture, and behavior. Unfortunately, because of this umbilical dependence upon historical and traditional views, much cultural-linguistic and psycholinguistic research has all too often been simply a "quest for the quaint,"[9] thus producing highly questionable conclusions. Equally unfortunate is that these conclusions tend to reinforce existing stereotypes about groups of people.[10] For example, too many researchers in cultural anthropology keep turning up the same generalizations about Mexican Americans of the Southwest. The most pejorative (and perhaps the most damaging) of these is that Mexican Americans are philosophically "fatalists" and that they are enveloped by a cultural mystique called "machismo," which controls their sexual animation. As generalizations about a people, these are tenuous, to say the least. Yet these generalizations are used unsparingly (it seems) in documenting

[7] Lazar, May. *Reading interests, activities, and opportunities of bright, average, and dull children.* New York, 1937.

[8] Corbin, Richard. Literacy, literature and the disadvantaged. *Language programs for the disadvantaged.* Report of the NCTE Task Force on Teaching English to the Disadvantaged. Champaign, Illinois, 1965, p. 6.

[9] Guzman, Ralph. Ethics in federally subsidized research—the case of the Mexican American. Testimony presented at the Cabinet Committee Hearings on Mexican American Affairs, El Paso, Texas, October 26–28, 1967.

[10] Ortego, Philip D. The green card dilemma. *The Texas Observer*, 60:5, 1968.

a variety of psycho-cultural propositions about Mexican Americans.[11] While one cannot accuse all of these researchers of dishonesty, one cannot fail to bring their methods to task. It's amusing that Otto Jesperson himself believed that the Hawaiian language was simple, which simplicity he attributed to climatic circumstances. And many of these "quaint" conclusions are still with us.

The great failing in the educational assessment of Spanish-speaking children, though, lies in the failure of most educators to understand the multifaceted role of language, that language is not only an intimate part of people but that it is the vehicle of the child's cultural system and perhaps the most important variable.[12] However, the education of Spanish-speaking children centers more on approach than on methodology; that is, more on the question of conventional beginnings versus radical innovations. This conflict invariably yields a cross-purpose of objectives. The implicit assumption of those who favor the retention of the conventional approach is that all children begin school with the same advantage, thus belying, for the most part, the reality of the linguistic situation in the Southwest. The fact of the matter is that the Spanish-speaking child starts school with a deficit, with a decided disadvantage. This is not, however, "linguistic impoverishment" as some educators call it, but simply a handicap in an educational system geared specifically to the dominant national language. Traditionally the resultant (and in most cases inevitable) conclusion on the part of non-Spanish-speaking teachers and educators has been simply to identify Spanish-speaking children as "retarded."

Thus, in considering the psycho-cultural factors in the acquisition of reading and language skills by Spanish-speaking students in the Southwest, the most critical factor to be considered is the school environment. Despite the conclusions of the Coleman Report,[13] which cites the differences in the background of students as a significant variable in their education, it is the differences in the background of teachers which in fact becomes the essential variable in the education of children from diverse backgrounds, especially Spanish-speaking children. For example, in their research for *Pygmalion in the Classroom*, Rosenthal and Jacobson[14] deceived a group of teachers into believing they were working with "gifted" Mexican American students, when in fact the children had been selected randomly from various achievement groups. The upshot of the deception was that the "gifted" children actually progressed more rapidly than the other students simply because of the "positive attitude" of the teachers. Unfortunately, in the Southwest too many teachers approach their Spanish-speaking students with attitudes that engender only failure and disappointment instead of achievement.

[11] Ortego, Philip D. The Mexican-Dixon line. *El grito: a journal of contemporary Mexican American thought*, 1:4, 1968.
[12] Ortego, Philip D. The people of Sanchez. *The Nation*, 209:15, 1968.
[13] Coleman, *et al*. *Equality of educational opportunity*. Washington, U.S. Government Printing Office, 1966.
[14] Rosenthal, Robert and Leonore Jacobson. *Pygmalion in the classroom*. New York, 1968.

Of course the training of the teachers of English to speakers of other languages in elementary and secondary schools has been about as precise as the training once given to army sharpshooters, whose last instructions were to crank in "Kentucky windage" before squeezing off their second shot at the target. The first shot was just to see whether or not they were on target. So, too, TESOL teachers in the public schools "fire away" at their Mexican American students, using about as much judgment about their sharpshooting teaching techniques as "Kentucky windage."

But the linguistic situation in the Southwest today is still pretty much where it was yesterday, and the day before, and the day before that.[15] For example, most classes in the methodology of teaching English as a second language are simply exercises in the repetition of the problem— few solutions emerge. And those that do emerge are seldom implemented.

Unfortunately, these TESOL methodology courses for teachers of Mexican Americans concentrate on linguistic analysis at the most superficial level. The inevitable conclusions of these "methodology" courses consistently point out the same facts: that Mexican Americans are linguistically disadvantaged. NDEA Language Institutes help to make some English teachers aware of the specific linguistic difficulties of Mexican Americans, but little if anything happens in their classrooms when they get back to their schools. But the teacher is all too often only a pawn in the community game of scholastic upsmanship. Supervisors and administrators establish standards in English which the teachers are required to meet. And sometimes it is easier for teachers to conform to the requirements of the syllabus than to the principles of their profession.

Thus it is not uncommon for a teacher to spend a summer studying the latest techniques of teaching English as a second language and the application of linguistics to the teaching of English, only to go back to his or her school and take up the old ways and old prejudices. Linguistic truths give way to invidious fallacies. And before long, Mexican American students are considered once more as lazy, unambitious, stupid, and retarded because they fail to meet the linguistic standards of the schools. We are faced, then, with the question of whether the teacher of Mexican Americans is concerned with language as communication or language as group identification.[16]

Therefore, Mexican Americans have found themselves at the bottom of the language heap, more often than not condemned by the abuses of (perhaps?) well-meaning but misguided teachers and administrators. And it is not surprising that over the years Mexican Americans have come to believe the linguistic doctrine perpetuated by the schools. Yet, while linguists have been mining the eastern sector of the U.S. for the Linguistic Atlas, very little—if anything—has been done in the Southwest in map-

[15] Rosen, Carl L., and Philip D. Ortego. Language and reading problems of Spanish-speaking children in the Southwest. *Journal of Reading Behavior*, 1.1–70.

[16] Rosen, Carl L., and Philip D. Ortego. *Problems and strategies in teaching the language arts to Spanish-speaking Mexican American children*. U.S. Office of Education (ERIC/CRESS), February 1969.

ping out and explaining the linguistic variations of its inhabitants, especially Mexican Americans. The studies that have been conducted in the Southwest by linguists and anthropologists have focused on the languages of American Indians. Studies by others have focused on the quaint, the curious, and the queer, specifically the languages of the Curanderos, the Pachucos, and the Tirilongos, three hardly representative groups. But the various dialects of the 4½ million Mexican Americans of the Southwest have been ignored. That in an area covering over five states 4½ million Mexican Americans would speak almost as many dialects of English as are spoken along the Atlantic seaboard seems not to have aroused much interest on the part of linguistic researchers.[17] It seems to me that genuine linguistic research [18] in the Southwest can help considerably in reducing language prejudice by pointing out that differences in pronunciation are as much a part of natural phenomena as run-off and erosion. And that the English spoken by Mexican Americans of the Southwest United States is as much English as the English spoken by a New Englander or a native of the Bronx.

[17] These figures are now out of date; latest estimates for the Southwest alone range from 7 to 10 million. See p. 45 for clarification.

[18] Rosen, Carl L., and Philip D. Ortego. *Issues in language and reading instruction of Spanish-speaking children.* International Reading Association: Newark, Delaware, 1969.

BILINGUALISM AND MENTAL MEASURES:
A WORD OF CAUTION

George I. Sánchez

The great development shown in objectivity in education during the last two decades has led to the conception among those over-zealous to demonstrate the scientific accuracy attained in this field that we are at a point where mental capacities of children can be determined accurately by the mere *application* of the newly devised measuring instruments— standardized mental tests. While sound thinkers in the field of tests and measures have constantly cautioned against the superficial and unanalytical use of these instruments, the quest for a short-cut to critical and exhaustive study of the abilities of school children has led to numerous

Reprinted from *Journal of Applied Psychology*, December 1934, by permission of the American Psychological Association.

Professor George Sánchez is one of the most accomplished Chicano scholars in the country. He began his distinguished career as an educator by teaching and serving as principal in rural New Mexico schools between 1923 and 1930. He received his doctorate in education at the University of California in 1934. Since then he has taught at many American colleges and universities, including the University of Texas, where he holds a joint appointment as professor of history, philosophy of education, and educational psychology.

abuses and errors in the use of mental tests. This is especially true of those who, blindly accepting the doctrine of individual differences, fail to recognize the importance of the fundamental personal, social, and cultural differences of the pupils and of the extremely important question of differences in milieu.

While the misapplication of tests is a matter of general concern and evident in education generally, it is in the treatment of the problems presented by bilingual, or environmentally handicapped, children that the gravest mistakes have been made. The caution with which such prominent students as Terman, Garrett, Otis, Pintner, Freeman and others have approached the use of tests in instances where language or environmental problems enter into the testing situation has been largely ignored or misinterpreted by those, who, equipped with the mechanical technique of application and scoring, have failed to place due weight on the analysis and evaluation of personal differences and of environmental problems.

The fact that tests have in a measure fulfilled their function of checking on the community of experience of children and on the extent to which children vary in profiting from common experiences has seemingly led many to assume that there is a universality in community of experiences. However, a test is valid only to the extent that the items of the test are as common to each child tested as they were to the children upon whom the norms were based. Only when community of experience actually exists can checks based on that assumption be valid, even if we grant that such checks do symbolize intellectual capacity—an "if" that has serious questions in itself.

The controversial nature of "intelligence" as such and of intelligence as a predetermined, hereditary faculty can easily be appreciated when one reads such works as Spearman's *Abilities of Man*[8] or Chapter X of Beard's (editor) *Whither Mankind*.[1] The latter reference is an illuminating and extremely readable treatment of the question of the relationship between "race" and intellectual achievement. Geo. A. Dorsey, in a humorously satirical manner, is unrelenting and even vicious in his attack upon those who have garbled the facts of genetics, eugenics, and heredity to champion the superiority of "Nordic" or "Aryan" "race." In unequivocal terms the glaring inconsistencies of the doctrine that "like begets like" and that civilization and intellectual accomplishment are linked irrevocably with Nordic heredity are set forth and ridiculed. In addition, outstanding anthropologists and geneticists are cited as authorities for the evidence against the deterministic assumption of a Nordic "corner" on brains. The chapter is a refreshing antidote to the widespread acceptance of the superiority of nature over nurture.

Yet, in spite of the uncertain basis upon which the fundamentals of mental tests rest, time and again students of the bilingual question insist on applying tests and accepting the results uncritically. To be sure tests are tools that should be used for what they are worth. The problem confronting the examiner is that of determining their worth in a particular situation. The worth of test-results lies in their proper interpretation and in the assistance which such interpretation lends to furthering the educational needs of the pupil. An IQ ratio, as such, *has no value*. It is only when that measure is used critically in promoting the best educational interests of the child that it has any worth-while significance to the educator. This means that an IQ of 70 is valuable only in relation to the hereditary, cultural, social, and educational background of the child and the way in which that past history can be utilized and improved in making the child the *best possible person he is capable of being.*

While on the surface an IQ of 70 means "moron," actually it means that only to the extent that the past history of the child has been assayed by the test in equal manner, with equal justice, and in equal terms as were the past histories of the children used as the criteria of the test. Even so, it is being granted for purposes of argument that such an assay is a valid one —that what is being sampled really represents evidence of "intelligence."

A few years ago Dr. T. R. Garth[2] of Colorado tested about 1,000 ("Mexican"?) Spanish-speaking children from different communities in Texas, Colorado, and New Mexico. He found that the median IQ of these children was 78, slightly above the point of demarcation for morons. In fact, 50 per cent of the fourth-grade children tested were of 71.8 IQ or below! Uncritical evaluation might lead to the conclusion that at least 50 per cent of the Spanish-speaking children represented by this large sample was unfitted to participate in any but the simplest tasks of life. Such a wholesale indictment of a people would be indefensible—yet such are the results of test *application.* Who would champion the thesis that half or more of the Spanish-speaking, *or any other such,* group is dull, borderline, and feeble-minded when it is generally accepted that only 7 per cent of "normal" groups may be so classified? However, such a champion would find test-results to support his cause!

The writer tested a second-grade group of bilingual children and found the median IQ to be 72.[5] Working on the assumption that the tests reflected a function of the school, remedial instruction in language and language arts was given over a two-year period with the result that the median IQ was "raised" to approximately 100, or normal. Thus the tests served a very useful purpose as tools—though their value as yardsticks of "intelligence" was questionable throughout the entire procedure. The class proved to be a slightly superior group of students throughout later development. If initial test results had been accepted at face value, a large percentage of the children would have been classified as belonging in special classes for the dull and some even as belonging in institutions for the feeble-minded!

The Binet Tests, when evaluated for vocabulary difficulty,[6] have been found by the writer to contain many words that do not even appear in the best of recommended word lists for bilingual children—to say nothing of the possibilities that such lists do not represent actual word mastery on the part of the pupils. If many of the words of the tests are unknown, and many but casually familiar or just recently acquired, what can be said as to the experiences and operations, the background and rapport, presupposed by the very nature of the tests? While language handicap in all probability transcends mere speech or vocabulary difficulties, it seems evident that at the very least the removal of such difficulties is a prerequisite to the beginnings of proper measurement. Even so, it is dangerous to assume that by supplying word knowledge the language handicap has been removed.

One investigator[7] used a makeshift "translation" of a test and found that there was no language handicap because the IQ's were not raised by such procedure! What assurance did he have that the IQ's obtained from the "translated" test were comparable to the norms? Why should the IQ's be raised by his procedure? And, is the evidence conclusive that the IQ's were not raised? The whole question is that of whether or not the revised test was the same test as the original in terms of difficulty, suitability, validity, reliability, etc. Similar tactical errors are common in testing programs and in the thinking of many who deal with the bilingual problem.

Of particular interest is the use to which measures or estimates of abilities have been put in other phases of education. Too often professional and scientific use of measures of evaluation is circumvented by attitudes and emotions which have no place in the educational program. From the standpoint of educational theory there are considerations which transcend the practical questions of sentiment, desirability, opposition or acquiescence, etc. Miss Reynolds,[4] of the United States Office of Education, quotes a graduate student who argues for segregation because "the two nationalities do not associate much . . . Mexican children . . . do not want to play with American children," etc. She also quotes a Los Angeles school official: "Our educational theory does not make any racial distinction between the Mexican and native white population. However, pressure from white residents of certain sections forced a modification of this principle to the extent that certain neighborhood schools have been placed to absorb the majority of the Mexican pupils in the district"! Dr. Paul Taylor[9] quotes a Texas school official: "We don't enforce the attendance on the whites because then we would have to on the Mexicans." Many other such expressions are common and are clearly presented in the studies made by Dr. Taylor. How such attitudes can go hand-in-hand with scientific instruments is incomprehensible, if such instruments are to produce worth-while results. That this condition is one which contributes to the impairment of educational opportunity cannot be denied.

Though not necessarily attributable to questions of attitudes and prejudices, it is apparent to any one who takes the time to examine the records that the state educational system in New Mexico is not functioning efficiently with respect to the bilingual problem. For example, in 1932–33 there was a total of 24,810 Spanish-speaking children enrolled in the first and second grades of the public school system.[3] However, only 540 were enrolled in the twelfth grade—two per cent as compared with a percentage of fourteen for other children. In other words, and in spite of any and all excuses that might be offered, *the Spanish-speaking group is not receiving a comparable education.* Some might counter with the argument that the Spanish-speaking group does not have the capacities to continue in school, so they drop out or are eliminated. It could be granted, only for the sake of argument however, that the group has an average IQ of 85. This means that 50 per cent of the group is above that level and that certainly a number much greater than 540 is capable of doing twelfth-grade work. Then, who has failed—the child or the school? What of compulsory education? What of the duty and responsibility of the State? What of the democratic theory of education?

The flagrant violations of the fundamental aspects of the theory of education and of the social and economic goals of America that are observed in the practice of education among bilinguals point to the urgent need for greater real professionalization of the educational practitioners and of further public enlightenment. The frequent prostitution of democratic ideals to the cause of expediency, politics, vested interests, ignorance, class and "race" prejudice, and to indifference and inefficiency is a sad commentary on the intelligence and justice of a society that makes claims to those very progressive democratic ideals. The dual system of education presented in "Mexican" and "white" schools, the family system of contract labor, social and economic discrimination, educational negligence on the part of local and state authorities, "homogeneous grouping" to mask professional inefficiency—all point to the need for greater insight into a problem which is inherent in a "melting pot" society. The progress of our country is dependent upon the most efficient utilization of the heterogeneous masses which constitute its population—the degree to which the 2,000,000 or more Spanish-speaking people, and their increment, are permitted to develop is the extent to which the nation should expect returns from that section of its public.

It appears that to those whose interest lies in the field of technical evaluation of the question of the school and the bilingual child there has come the time when fundamentals must be determined. The relative responsibility of the school and of the child in the achievement of desirable goals must be examined. Is the fact that a child makes an inferior score on an intelligence test prima facie evidence that he is dull? Or is it a function of the test to reflect the inferior or different training and development with which the child was furnished by his home, his language, the culture of his people, and by his school? When the child fails in promotion is it *his* failure or has the school failed to use the proper whetstone in bringing out the true temper and quality of his steel?

The school has the responsibility of supplying those experiences to the child which will make the experiences sampled by standard measures as common to him as they were to those on whom the norms of the measures were based. When the school has met the language, cultural, disciplinary,

and informational lacks of the child and the child has reached the
saturation point of his capacity in the assimilation of fundamental experiences and activities—then failure on his part to respond to tests of
such experiences and activities may be considered his failure. As long as
the tests do not at least sample in equal degree a state of saturation that
is equal for the "norm children" and the particular bilingual child it
cannot be assumed that the test is a valid one for that child. Under our
theory of education *the Child cannot fail*. Nevertheless, for comparative
purposes, a child or a group may be classed as inferior or superior by
measures which do equal justice to the criterion and the child or group.
The fundamental questions in mental tests of bilingual children, then, are
primarily questions of validity, to wit:

I. Do the tests measure *in that particular child* what they purport to
   measure? The tests may be valid for the "average" child and still lack
   validity for an individual or for a particular group. Questions of culture, schooling, socioeconomic status, etc., loom big in this phase of
   the problem.
II. Are the assumptions on which the test was based for the original
    "norm" children applicable with equal justice to the particular case?
    If the use of a radio were assumed to sample intelligence, would a
    Navajo Indian living in a hogan be equally subject to such an assump-
    tion as average children, or would the tallying of sheep be a more
    desirable measure? Is "intelligence" abstract reasoning, memory, "g,"
    "s," etc.? Whatever it is, are the assumptions of what it is justified
    universally?

While it would be shortsighted to propose the abandonment of mental
tests in the bilingual problem, and nothing herein contained should be so
interpreted, a note of caution in their use is in order. It should be borne in
mind that a mental test is not a measure in the same sense that yardsticks or meters are measures. Mental tests are professional instruments
which must be supplemented by intelligent and professional application
and evaluation for the best interests of the child or group concerned.

Citations

1. Beard, C. H. *Whither Mankind*. Longmans, Green, 1928.
2. Garth, T. R. The Intelligence of Mexican School Children. *School
and Society*. XXVII, 1928; pp. 791–794.
3. N. Mex. Dept. Educ., Division of Information and Statistics. *Annual
Financial and Statistical Report—1932–33*.
4. Reynolds, Annie. The Education of Spanish-speaking Children. *U.S.
Office of Education Bulletin*. No. 11, 1933.
5. Sánchez, Geo. I. Scores of Spanish-speaking Children on Repeated
Tests. *Ped. Sem. and Jr. Genetic Psych*. March, 1932; pp. 223–231.

6. Sánchez, Geo. I. The Implications of a Basal Vocabulary to the Measurement of the Abilities of Bilingual Children. To appear: *Jr. Social Psych.*

7. Sheldon, W. H. The Intelligence of Mexican School Children. *School and Society.* XIX, 1924; pp. 139–142.

8. Spearman, Chas. *The Abilities of Man.* Macmillan, 1927.

9. Taylor, Paul S. Mexican Labor in the United States. *U. of Calif. Publications in Economics.* Vol. 6, No. 5.

MEXICAN AMERICANS: HOW THE SCHOOLS HAVE FAILED THEM

Thomas P. Carter

The socioeconomically disadvantaged and subordinate status of the Mexican American in the Southwest has been recognized by the Anglo population for years. Educators have been aware that "Mexican kids do poorly in school"—that both academic achievement and school attainment have been very low in the past. They continue to be low in the present as well.

Concomitant with this recognition was, and is, the belief that such a situation is in the natural order of things, and that "Mexicans" are doomed by their genetic or cultural inheritance to occupy second class citizenship. Racists explain the minority's subordinate position on the grounds that they possess less innate intelligence. The somewhat less biased rationalize it by recourse to the omnipresent stereotype of the lazy, apathetic, incompetent and noncompetitive "Mexican." Schoolmen have reworked this latter perspective into the Southwestern version of the cultural deprivation theory, arguing that Mexican American children fail in school due to the inadequate, inappropriate, or "foreign" socialization afforded by home and *barrio*. Laymen and educators seem to agree: "Mexicans do poorly in school and society because they are so obviously inferior—they are inferior because they are so obviously Mexican."

While the social usefulness of such "arguments" is understandable, it is difficult to take them seriously. Although cultural difference of some Mexican American groups is obvious, sole reliance on group characteristics

Reprinted with permission from *College Board Review*, published by the College Entrance Examination Board, New York, No. 75 (Spring 1970). Copyright © 1970 by College Examination Board.

Thomas Carter was a member of the Mexican American Study Project at UCLA, where he received his doctorate. He was Scholar in Residence for the U.S. Commission on Civil Rights and is the author of *Mexican Americans in School: A History of Educational Neglect*. He is currently Dean of the School of Education at Sacramento State College.

(usually stereotyped) to explain low acculturation and assimilation is untenable. The Mexican American minority's situation can only be understood by in-depth analysis of numerous interrelated factors; I call on educators and others to initiate serious analysis of this kind.

I am going to suggest in this article that school and society have served to keep the Mexican American in his place, and that Southwestern society has functioned best with a pool of cheap, unskilled labor and a subordinate ethnic "caste." A poorly schooled "Mexican" fitted admirably into such a social system. The school, reflecting and functionally related to its parent society, unconsciously developed policies and practices, and promoted conditions that discouraged academic achievement and encouraged early dropping out. Many of these practices and conditions have persisted into the present. A large share of the responsibility for the Mexican American minority's "failure" must be borne by the school, and the school must modify its present approach from efforts *to change the home and child* to efforts *to change itself*, if Mexican American performance is to be improved.

Southwest Society and the School

Most Mexican immigrants, as well as those of Spanish ancestry resident in the Southwest for generations, became well-integrated cogs in the social system dominated by Anglos. Most of them possessed the skills, experience, and perhaps temperament demanded to mesh into the rural agricultural economy. The economic system was (and still is in many areas) characterized by a "*hacienda*-like" social structure (by *latifundismo*) and a dual "caste" system reminiscent of the social arrangements of the plantation system of the South. With the continuing disappearance of the traditional *hacienda*, a new form emerged—agricultural industry. This system is socially not unlike the *hacienda*, except that the paternalism of the *patrón* is not continued by modern management. Mexican Americans who did not enter the agricultural system in earlier periods usually meshed equally well, since they had the skills and knowledge essential for the closed social systems spawned by mining and railroading. In a sense, the Mexican immigrant "never left home"—the social, economic and even perhaps political arrangements on both sides of the Rio Grande in the past were very much alike.

Society and its schools produced an adult Mexican American population prepared for participation in the agricultural economy and relatively closed society of the older Southwest. The school was, and in many geographic areas still is, "successful" in equipping most Mexican Americans with the knowledge and skills appropriate to low status: minimum English language ability, rudimentary reading and figuring skills, and the values necessary to be a "law abiding," although non-participating, powerless, and essentially disenfranchised, citizen.

The fact that the school failed to Americanize or to raise group social

Table 1.   Median Years of Schooling Completed 1950 and 1960
(Adults over 25 Years of Age)*

	1950 Tot. Pop.	wpss†	1960 Tot. Pop.	Anglo	wpss	Nonwhite
Arizona	10.0	6.0	11.2	12.1	7.0	7.0
California	11.6	7.8	12.1	12.2	8.6	10.6
Fresno	9.8	5.6	10.4	10.7	6.1	8.8
Sacramento	11.3	7.9	12.2	12.3	9.1	10.9
Colorado	10.9	6.5	12.1	12.2	8.2	11.2
New Mexico	9.3	6.1	11.2	12.2	7.4	7.1
Texas	9.3	3.5	10.4	11.5	4.8	8.1
Lubbock	11.0	1.7	11.6	12.1	3.1	8.3
Beaumont-Port Arthur	9.7	7.0	10.8	11.7	8.7	7.1

* Data taken from Mexican American Study Project Advance Report # 7, The Schooling Gap: Signs of Progress, Leo Grebler. (From the 1950 and 1960 United States Census)
† wpss represents White Persons of Spanish Surname, a census category analogous to Mexican Americans in the Southwestern states.

status of so many Mexican Americans was evidence of its success, since local society functioned best with an easily controlled, politically impotent and subordinate minority. School practices evolved that functioned to perpetuate local society by unconsciously encouraging the minority to fail academically, drop out early, and enter society at the low status traditional for Mexican Americans—thus producing exactly the human types necessary to perpetuate local society. Mexican American failure to achieve well in school contributed to the Anglo's "foregone conclusion" that "Mexicans" were innately less intelligent, lazy, passive, fatalistic, and lacked initiative. Formal educational institutions and local society were mutually supportive—this functional integration helped perpetuate the social and economic status quo.

Since the middle 1930s, the Southwest has changed radically. It has: (1) become predominantly urban; (2) rapidly industrialized; (3) in the rural areas, replaced earlier arrangements with "agricultural industry"; and (4) placed much less emphasis on mining and railroading. The majority of Mexican Americans, like their Anglo counterparts, now live in metropolitan areas and must compete in the urban industrial job market. Far too many minority members find it difficult or impossible to compete with others due to the substandard and inappropriate schooling they have received, and job discrimination. The stability of the older social system is disappearing though, and the radical and rapid demographic, economic and social changes are contributing to grievous personal social and economic maladaptations and malfunctions.

While these social changes are occurring rapidly, the school is rarely able to keep up by modifying its practices or policies, its teaching staff or their attitudes and perceptions. Too often school conditions "appropriate" to past social circumstances persevere into the present with devastating influence on children as well as society in general. The history of the Mexican American's contact with the Anglo Southwest is not pleasant, nor is their contact with that society's institutions of formal education.

The School Situation Now

Improved schooling represents one avenue that can enhance a minority's social status. There are two major ways of looking at a group's performance in school: by examining school success or failure as measured by academic achievement, and by examining the quantity of participation in schools. In both cases Mexican Americans are doing very poorly, and massive efforts are needed to alter the situation.

Table 2.   Drop-Out Rates by Grade Level
(in Per Cent of Enrollment by Grade)*

GRADE	ANGLO	MEXICAN AMERICAN	NEGRO
7	4.8%	17.6%	7.2%
8	7.0	17.1	8.9
9	15.0	22.5	19.2
10	28.5	23.2	26.7
11	27.4	13.7	23.6
12	17.4	5.9	14.4

* Data taken from *The Challenge and the Chance*, Report of the Governor's Committee on Public School Education, Austin, Texas, August 31, 1968, p. 38.

Minority children are not reaching standard norms in any area of academic achievement. In language arts, the group achieves at a rate substantially lower than either national norms or those of their local Anglo counterparts. In no aspect of reading are their scores "normal." While their general ability in language arts is low, two areas are reported to be partial exceptions: Mexican American children approach (but rarely reach) local or national norms in spelling and fundamentals of grammar. Their achievement in arithmetic is also low, though it is generally better than in the language arts. When total arithmetic achievement is broken down into "problem solving" (involving language skills) and "fundamentals," differences are apparent. The Mexican American group does better in areas not dependent on the English language. As with members of other economically disadvantaged groups, the Mexican American falls progressively behind in measured achievement as he continues in school. He is generally closest to the majority group in the first year of school. Then there is partial closing of the gap during the last years of high school, probably attributable to the heavy drop-out of low achievers.

Another measurement of achievement is Intelligence Quotient, for my purposes a measurement of learned culture and not intellectual capacity or potential. The minority is severely underrepresented at the "gifted" level and overrepresented at the slow or "retarded" level. For example, a recent California study found an approximate two-fold overrepresentation of Mexican American children in special education classes (classes for the mentally retarded). I would suggest that it would be more than three times overrepresented in other states and perhaps four times in Texas. The minority overpopulates low ability tracks and underpopulates high ones. Rigid ability grouping (tracking) often results in rooms or sections that approximate 100 per cent Mexican American concentration. It is hard to tell whether such segregation is due to ability or the fact that they are Mexican American. Some educators argue that, considering the low average IQ of Mexican Americans, they achieve about as well as can be expected, and that there is a normal number of overachievers and underachievers.

Achievement and the Home

School achievement, as measured by whatever standard, is highly related to social class and to home background. Parents with more education, income, or higher status occupations tend to produce children who do well in school. Higher social status minority families tend toward the acculturated end of the continuum—that is, the family orientation is away from the "Mexican," or traditional folk culture. The more middle class the Mexican American child, the more he meets the expectations of teachers and school and thus the better his chances. On the other hand, the more foreign or culturally distinct the orientation of the home the less the child's chance of school success.

The degree a group participates in the institutions of society is a good measure of assimilation or social integration. Mexican American participation in Southwestern institutions of formal education is exceedingly low when compared with the participation of either the Negro or Anglo populations. This is true of the past as well as of the present. Table 1 points up the extreme "underschooling" of the Mexican American minority in the five Southwestern states and selected metropolitan areas within them.

A number of points are obvious: (1) there is extreme disparity among the three groups; (2) while Anglo attainment shows some differences, it is quite constant among the states and cities; Mexican American attainment varies greatly; and (3) substantial improvement did occur from 1950 to 1960. Although signs of progress are evident, the schooling level of the group remains very low. Current studies indicate that the younger elements of the Mexican American population (under 25) are surpassing their older peers in years of schooling completed. Although Mexican Americans are completing more school, so are other groups, and their relative position remains constant. The Mexican American is probably gaining slightly. Nevertheless, he is still the poorest schooled of the three groups, with only the American Indian in a lower position in the Southwest.

The Census of 1960 revealed the interesting fact that Mexican American men and women have the same approximate level of schooling—a rather startling finding considering the almost universally held belief that Mexican Americans discourage formal education for women. As with all groups, income and schooling are related. However, the Mexican American median income in 1960 tended to be slightly higher than that of the Negro. Analysis suggests that this odd circumstance can be attributed to more universal and blatant discrimination against blacks.

Another way to view participation is to compare percentages of enrollment at given age or grade levels. At all ages a lower percentage of Mexican Americans attend school than either Anglos or Negroes. However, the percentages of participation are roughly comparable until the "drop-out" ages of 16–17: in California 83.3 per cent and in Texas 76.3 per cent of the total population at these ages were attending school in 1960. Only 73.7 and 58.6 per cent, respectively, of the Mexican Americans were in school. More current studies indicate that the low Mexican American participation and high drop-out rate continues. Table 2 reports the official estimates of drop-out rates for the three major groups in Texas. The very large percentage of Mexican Americans leaving school during grades seven and eight is particularly puzzling to those unfamiliar with Texas schools. Most of these children are probably two or three years over-age, having been held in lower grades a number of years.

Texas tends more than other Southwestern states to promote students on the basis of rigid grade level requirements. This overeagerness contributes strongly to Mexican American school withdrawal. The same Texas source (not shown in Table 2) estimates that 66 per cent of the Anglo, 52 per cent of the Negro, and 40 per cent of the Mexican American boys graduated in the 1966–67 school year. Thus, 60 per cent of the Mexican American boys left school prior to high school graduation for some reason.

The same research (also not shown) projects "Percentage of Graduates" to 1978–79, where it predicts that 55 per cent of the Mexican Americans will graduate. Mexican Americans will then be just about as "successful" as are Negroes at present. Estimates by the United States Office of Education are even more pessimistic: ". . . in Texas, 89 per cent of the children with Spanish surnames drop out; in California . . . more than 50 per cent of Mexican American high school students drop out between grades 10 and 11. . . ." The drop-out rates of Mexican Americans are probably highest in Texas and lowest in California. However, the rate is much too high in all five states. The magnitude of the problem should be obvious. But few educators seem to realize, that children with only near literacy schooling are suitable only for very low skill occupations—jobs that will probably disappear in the near future due to technological advances.

Higher Education

Mexican American enrollment in institutions of higher education, a significant indicator of group upward mobility, is very low. According to the Census of 1960, at ages 20–21 about 20 per cent of the total population in the Southwest was attending some form of college, while only approximately 12 per cent of the Mexican Americans were. Colleges or universities serving geographic areas of high ethnic concentration enroll approximately half the percentage of Mexican Americans they should. In other words, if the local population served by an institution is 50 per cent Mexican American, only about 25 per cent of the college enrollment would come from this minority group.

Even this is deceiving since most of the Mexican American college students are either freshmen or sophomores. The Mexican American percentages are even lower in major state universities than they are in regional state colleges and lesser institutions. For example, the undergraduate Mexican American student body at The University of Texas at Austin during the 1966–67 academic year was only about 2 per cent, and the percentage at The University of California at Berkeley would have been even less.

Leadership in the Southwest presently recognizes that the maintenance of a rapidly increasing Mexican American population with low group status and such low levels of schooling and achievement represents a serious threat to societal stability. Although such a population may have served the old rural Southwest well, presenting little threat to the social equilibrium, its continued presence now contributes to many undesirable conditions. Even the more politically and socially conservative Anglo elements see these conditions as alarming, and are pressuring schools to eliminate the overt manifestations of the Mexican Americans' low social status. The school must "raise the group" by insuring that the young persevere and achieve academically in school. It is hoped that improved school achievement and attainment will lead to higher group status, and the subsequent elimination of such conditions as underemployment and dependence on welfare.

But if pressures from within society are forcing action to resolve some of these grave problems (problems partially created by the fact that schools have inadvertently functioned to maintain Mexican Americans in a subordinate position), it must be regrettably acknowledged that it is not the altruism of educators that is at play. Rather, the controlling political elements have seen that societal peace and balance are threatened and are encouraging or demanding whatever school action is evident. A low status Mexican American is no longer functional—the Southwest has changed.

The Community

The community and its formal educational institutions are inexorably related; it is impossible to separate institutions from the society they serve. Each functions for, and contributes to, the maintenance and continuity of society. The dependency of the American school on local society for direction, as well as economic support, almost guarantees that little initiative will be forthcoming from educators. While this "democratic local control" is deemed essential, it nonetheless discourages attempts by school-men to substantially modify their institutions or to use them as agents of social change. Educational leaders are all too often members of the conservative establishment or are dominated by it—impotent to counter its wishes. If these controlling elements manifest little interest or concern about the status of minority groups and see the situation as *natural* (and the minority groups remain mute and powerless) little initiative will be forthcoming from the educational establishment. If no group or problem is "rocking the boat," the school comfortably assumes it is performing adequately.

These conditions characterized the Southwest in the recent past. The few in the past who raised their voices to advocate school reform (like George I. Sánchez of The University of Texas at Austin) found they had an unresponsive, though polite, audience. But Southwestern society has and does determine educational practices, and as society changes slow changes can be anticipated in the schools. Many of the school's practices so perfectly mirror the local society's mores that any substantial modification must probably await changes in the community. Legal intervention to force local school practices into alignment with national values are usually countervened, subverted, or evaded by local schools, as is exemplified by attempts at enforced racial desegregation. Other school practices are not so closely aligned with community mores but are nonetheless exceedingly difficult to modify due to "institutional habit," and the inability of the highly bureaucratized school to modify itself. For many reasons, educators and schools resist change, whether the force for change emanates from within or without institutional walls.

The School's Position

The search for the reasons for the low school achievement of the Mexican American minority has resulted in the isolation of three complex and interrelated sets of factors. There is *no one* explanation of why Juanito can't read, is "poorly motivated," and flees the school early to assume the low status traditional for his group. Rather, the factors become obvious by careful examination and analysis of: (1) the natures of the diverse Mexican American subcultures and the socialization afforded their young, (2) the kind and quality of formal education provided and the school social climates promoted by local practices, and (3) the nature of the local and regional social systems and the equal or unequal opportunity they provide the Mexican American. No simplistic or single explanation is possible. Yet, unfortunately, most authorities fail to recognize the latter two points and stress that the minority's low status, lack of assimilation and acculturation, and school failure are due to the group's distinctive culture. The widespread (if not almost universal) acceptance of this "theory" is easily understood, as it exonerates society and school from complicity in the situation.

The failure of the minority to "succeed" in the United States society or its institutions of formal education is seen as due to the "peculiar" socio-cultural characteristics of the group. This perspective is a common one in our nation. Low status of minority groups and continued "foreignness" are situations caused by innumerable social and economic factors within the dominant society, as well as the cultural characteristics of the minority. However, Americans generally see low assimilation and acculturation as due solely to failure of the minority in question. Our tendency is to consider the "Negro problem," "Indian problem," or "Mexican problem" as the sole responsibility of each ethnic group. We blame the minority for its own low status—for being the cause of its own "problem." The cultural deprivation "theory" in education supports and reinforces this perspective.

There is a strong tendency to over-react and, by rejecting this simplistic argument of "cultural disadvantagement," fail to understand the inter-relationship between the three major factors involved. The nature of the subcultures or subsocieties are influenced in untold ways by society and its institutions, as indeed the inverse is the case. We are dealing with a complex whole not amenable to facile separation or clear definition. It is a total social and institutional situation that produces low school achievement and attainment among Mexican Americans.

"Standard" Students Succeed

One not-so-startling conclusion can be drawn from an analysis of the kind of children who succeed in schools: those who do so tend to be children who are culturally and personally similar to what the school expects. They are almost invariably the "standard" children from "normal" homes —average middle-class American youngsters. The "different child," whether he be Anglo, Negro, lower class or what have you, rarely measures up at school entrance or exit to the normal or "standard child." It is more than simple to conclude from this reality that such cultural, social class, or personality differences can account for a child's poor school performance. Indeed, given such different children faced with an undifferentiated or standard middle-class oriented school, their differences can be seen as *causing* school failure. However, the assumption that these children are less intelligent, culturally deprived or psychologically abnormal is an uncalled for by-product of this sort of reasoning.

Most educators (with the support of the vocal elements within the middle class) assume that the school is adequate and validly represents the core values, content, and mores of American culture. This assumption is reaching the proportions of a self-evident conclusion. Therefore, it is not difficult to understand that the school, when given a choice between seeing the Mexican American's poor school performance as attributable to either his home socialization or the conditions within school and society, readily opts to blame the home and the socialization it provides.

In order to support this position, educators have developed elaborate and detailed descriptions of the life-style and personalities of Mexican Americans and their children, containing the assumed differences in world view and life-style that "account" for the minority group child's lack of school success. Mexican American children are regularly (almost always) perceived as being, among other things: fatalistic (often attributed to Catholicism), present-time oriented, from patriarchal homes, superstitious, and generally as bearers of a "traditional" or "folk" culture. Unfortunately, these common beliefs of educators about minority children: (1) are based on little, if any, current objective evidence; (2) are derived from older, though probably valid ethnographic descriptions of rural "folk culture;" (3) demonstrate little insight into the nature of culture, society or language; (4) describe *one* monolithic Mexican American culture, where, in reality, great diversity exists; (5) picture a static minority culture, changing little over time; and (6) correspond beautifully with the common Anglo stereotype of "Mexicans" in general.

Armed with this formidable arsenal of false or exaggerated beliefs, schoolmen find the reasons for minority school problems and, in so doing, pass the buck to the Mexican American's home and culture. The stereotyped culture provides educators with a plausible and sufficient explanation of Mexican American school failure. In reality there is no *one* Mexican American culture—immense cultural diversity exists. Only three universal tendencies can be attributed to the Mexican American: he *tends* to speak Spanish, *tends* to profess Roman Catholicism, and *tends* to be poor.

With the blame settled securely on the Mexican American home and culture, school personnel proceed to remedy the situation in the only way their logic allows. Since cultural difference or "deprivation" is the problem, the school must eliminate it, thereby insuring school and social success. This position is fortified by the widespread acceptance by educators of the proposition that the American school was a principal agency in the acculturation of other foreign or immigrant groups. Most educators argue that a prime function of the school is the rapid, perhaps ruthless, Americanization of children of foreign backgrounds. In this regard, the school is supportive of the general American concept of minorities as being wonderful at the point that their members cease to be culturally distinct—the idea that the immigrant is acceptable within our society as soon as he is indistinguishable from the rest of us.

Altering the Home Culture

Compensatory education and remedial programs to "meet the needs" of deprived Mexican American children (to reorient, reconstruct, retool, or remodel them) are undertaken. Such programs and projects are the result of the combination of the three prevalent educational assumptions: that the home culture is the cause of school failure, that the school is presently satisfactory, and that a principal function of the school is to Americanize the foreigner by eliminating his alien cultural orientation. I contend that school programs *based exclusively* on these three highly questionable assumptions are doomed to failure, and that there is little or no objective evidence indicating otherwise.

In spite of the dearth of evidence of success, vast sums of federal and local money have been and are being spent in efforts to reorient the lowest social classes and other groups into a model of middle-class desirability. In a sense, federal funds contribute to the highly questionable assumption that children of such groups are intellectually inferior, culturally deprived, or both. In addition, federal efforts implicitly support the questionable propositions that minority children can be successfully remodeled into "standard Americans," and that society will then willingly accept and offer them equal opportunity. Financial aid from Washington tends to reinforce the local educational *status quo*. Governmental financial assistance has only very rarely resulted in substantial school reform or modification.

Two major factors impede the Mexican American's ability to use the school instrumentally to raise his socioeconomic status. School factors discourage his achievement and attainment, and discrimination and the limited number of statuses open to his group in much of the Southwest discourage his usually high educational aspirations. Local society often does not reward the Mexican American for his efforts to move upward. The school is presently charged with raising achievement and attainment of the group in order to insure their incorporation into the rapidly changing society. Yet in many areas, the present society provides only limited social or occupational slots, thus eliminating the reward crucial to school perseverance, achievement, and motivation.

In a sense, the school must produce Mexican Americans who are able to occupy statuses presently or locally unavailable to them, and to learn roles that are not appropriate in the local community. This indeed is a big order. Few would contend that the school *can* change the social system, since the institution is too closely related to, and controlled by its parent society. The school cannot provide the open statuses necessary to encourage postponement of reward—only changes in the socioeconomic order can.

Nevertheless, the school can make institutional participation rewarding to the degree essential to encourage Mexican Americans to persevere in preference to exit at early ages. However, the school is usually seriously hampered by its inability to modify conditions and practices as these reflect local mores and attitudes. Not only are the attitudes of the educators themselves conservative and often biased, but the practices and curriculums of the school are as well, reflecting the older and controlling generation's beliefs. The school continues practices that tend to lower achievement and attainment, encourage early mental and physical withdrawal, and, in general, cause school participation to be of little intrinsic reward. The very school conditions that have "successfully" maintained a caste-like society are still regularly encountered.

Unfortunately, the school has reached, or is reaching a stage that makes substantial institutional modification most difficult. A contributory factor encouraging the maintenance of the institutional *status quo* is the fact that the very practices that inhibit Mexican American achievement and attainment tend to be supported as essential by the powerful conservative elements controlling schools. These groups usually demand the continuance of: instruction in English only, strong reliance on IQ scores, rigid tracking, *de facto* segregation, the inculcation of idealized middle-class values and norms, the suppression of the behavioral manifestations of foreignness, the exclusion of Mexican or Mexican American culture from the curriculum, and strong authoritarianism within the schools. The very practices that contribute to minority school failure have become almost "core educational values." The aggregate of these practices creates the negative school social environment seen as a crucial factor in low achievement.

Although exceptions exist, the majority of Southwestern educators are unable either to objectively analyze their schools or to make the modifications necessary to encourage minority group achievement and attainment. The majority of institutions seem static. They are approaching formalism, a stage, in Willard Waller's words, ". . . where the structure has become too intricate, or too rigid, or the idea of function has faded from the minds of the functionaries." The functionaries of the school appear to be overly concerned with the maintenance of their own positions, a condition seen to be guaranteed by the continuance of the institutional *status quo*.

The professed objectives of American education (equal opportunity, the child reaching his maximum potential, and others) are increasingly voiced by educators, but all too often they appear only as shallow utterances. The means by which such ends are to be attained too often function to impede their realization. School practices, curriculums, over-reliance on testing, and rigid ability grouping often inhibit the reaching of such exemplary goals. These conditions are difficult to modify. While extolling its professed objectives, the on-going function of the school seems all-too-often to be self-preservation and self-justification. A difficult situation exists. Nevertheless, modification of certain practices and conditions represents a possible avenue to the enhancement of the Mexican American minority's performance in school, and thus in American society.

The school must change. To do this, a new breed of educators must appear who are free to make the essential school modifications. There is little sign of their impending arrival. In spite of the rhetoric, (about the "innovative programs" and other suggested panaceas) few significant changes are taking place in Southwestern schools. We need imaginative institutional self-study (perhaps from the consumer's point of view) and massive changes in the policies, practices, curriculums and staffing of schools. The school must be encouraged to change, and that change must result from careful analysis, if we are to offer the Mexican American minority in the Southwest its educational due.

THE ADMINISTRATION OF JUSTICE IN THE SOUTHWEST
U.S. Commission on Civil Rights

Treatment of Mexican Americans

Complaints of Excessive and Discriminatory Use of Force

A peace officer in making an arrest has the right only to use that amount of force reasonably necessary to effect the arrest and to detain the prisoner. . . . All peace officers should remember that generally the sole purpose of an arrest is to bring the alleged culprit before a court of law and not for the purpose of giving any peace officer the opportunity of wreaking the public's or his personal venegance upon the prisoner.[1]

This rule, from the Texas Law Enforcement Officers' "Handbook", reflects the law of most American jurisdictions, including Arizona, California, Colorado, and New Mexico, the other Southwestern States included in this study.[2] Despite these official State policies, the Commission and its staff during the course of the present study received numerous complaints of excessive force by law enforcement officers against Mexican Americans. Many of the complainants believed they would not have been subjected to such treatment had they been Anglos.

Reprinted with permission from *Mexican Americans and the Administration of Justice in the Southwest* (Washington, D.C.: U.S. Commission on Civil Rights, March 1970).

In 1968 the U.S. Civil Rights Commission held a series of hearings and closed meetings throughout Aztlán. The hearings were in response to the growing number of reports received by the Commission concerning brutal treatment of Chicanos by members of the criminal justice system. In guarded, cautious statements the Commission failed to condemn the justice system in strong terms. But its investigations speak for themselves and we have selected some of its most important findings for reprinting here.

[1] Handbook for Texas Law Enforcement Officers, prepared by the Texas Commission on Law Enforcement Procedures (1967) at 25.

[2] See e.g., Ariz. Rev'd. Stats., R. Crim. Proc. 14(b) (1956): Cal. Pen. C. §§ 835, 843 (West Cum. Supp. 1968); Tex. Stats. Ann. § 15.24 (1966). New Mexico and Colorado do not specify by statute that the force used shall be reasonable. However, the courts have applied the same rule in those jurisdictions. *Colorado v. Hutchinson*, 9 F. 275 (8th Cir. 1925) (Colorado); *Mead v. O'Connor*, 66 N. M. 170, 344 P2d 478 (1959) (New Mexico); *Padilla v. Chavez*, 62 N. M. 170, 306 P2d 1094 (1957) (New Mexico); Restatement (Second) Torts § 132.

The most extreme allegations were made by residents of small towns where, according to many Mexican Americans, such incidents are not unusual. Matt Garcia, a Mexican American lawyer who has practiced for many years in San Antonio, Texas and other cities in south and west Texas, testified at the Commission's San Antonio hearing in December 1968. He related the following incident involving a Mexican American in south Texas which he alleged occurred in that area in 1965: [3]

> . . . a man went to the courthouse to inquire as to his father's case. He was told that he was going to be tried at 7. So he went to find out whether or not the man was going to be tried at 7 a.m. or 7 p.m. And this inquiry was made of the justice of the peace.
>
> When this inquiry was made, the sheriff walked in and said: "What do you want, Mexican?" Of course they don't call you "Mexican" . . . they call you "Meskin," and the man said: "Well, this is none of your concern," and they proceed to pistol-whip him. Both the sheriff and the judge. The man had a very severe gash across his scalp. He was beaten about the face, and he was dragged from the court. . . . And he kept yelling that he was going to die, that he was bleeding to death. [4]

Garcia testified that the victim was hospitalized because of the injuries resulting from the beating and that no criminal charges were filed against him. [5]

Another Mexican American lawyer testifying at the hearing stated that conditions in south Texas have not changed during the past few years and that law enforcement officials are determined to suppress any attempts by Mexican Americans to challenge abuses of their authority:

> And they think that they have a right to. They think that laws are made for them to use as they like. And I honestly think that these people believe that they have a right to expect the Mexican American to take everything that they dish out.
>
> And when you stand up and speak for your rights . . . they think that you're infringing on their rights. [6]

Alfred Figueroa, a businessman and a lifelong resident of Blythe, California (population about 20 per cent Mexican American) told the Com-

[3] Mr. Garcia was asked not to disclose names and places involved in this incident because the officials involved were not present to rebut the statement made about them.

[4] *Hearing Before the U.S. Commission on Civil Rights,* San Antonio, Tex., Dec. 9–14, 1968 at 669–70 [hereinafter cited as San Antonio Hearing].

[5] The Department of Justice investigated this case on the basis of the victim's complaint. The sheriff stated that the victim became "loud and abusive" in the office of the justice of the peace, called him a coward and refused to leave. The sheriff admitted poking the victim in the stomach with his pistol. This led to a fight in which the sheriff and the justice of the peace admittedly beat the victim with a pistol on the head. A local doctor confirmed that the victim suffered lacerations on the head and that the sheriff suffered cuts and bruises. The Department of Justice decided that this case lacked prosecutive merit because the victim's statements were uncorroborated.

[6] San Antonio Hearing at 672.

mission's California State Advisory Committee of being beaten by the local police in 1963.[7] According to Figueroa, he was having a soft drink in a bar when three police officers told him to come outside to talk to them. At that time, Figueroa said, there were many migrant farm workers in town. Believing he was being mistaken for one of them, he told the policemen that "they were barking up the wrong tree." When Figueroa refused to leave the bar, he stated, one of the policemen said that he was "just another smart Mexican," threw him on the floor, kicked him and handcuffed him. Figueroa claimed that he made no move to resist the arrest, yet the officers threw him in a car and when he could not get in because of the narrowness of the door, slugged him and kicked him inside. By this time, according to Figueroa, a great crowd had gathered because he was well known in town.

He gave the following account of the incident to the Committee: "In the process of trying to get me in they kicked me and kicked me and kicked me and I would get up and I said why are you doing this to me . . . and they would say: 'Get in there, you damn Mexican'." [8]

Figueroa was taken to jail and charged with drunkenness. He was acquitted of this charge. With great difficulty, he found a lawyer who was willing to bring a civil action against the police officers and obtained recovery against one of the officers.[9]

Figueroa stated that he and his brothers have been subjected to constant harassment at the hands of the local police. According to a complaint filed in April 1968 by his brother, Gilbert, against law enforcement officials of the city of Blythe and the county of Riverside, such an incident occurred in October 1967 in Riverside County. The complaint[10] alleges that two off-duty Blythe plainclothesmen assaulted Gilbert Figueroa and falsely arrested him "because he is a Mexican American and . . . one of the Figueroa brothers whose opposition to police malpractice and . . . activities in urging and aiding Mexican Americans and other minority persons to assert their rights are well known in the Blythe area." [11] The complaint further alleges that two Riverside County Sheriff's officers, who were on duty, refused to protect the plaintiff from the

---

[7] Closed meeting held by the California State Advisory Committee to the U.S. Commission on Civil Rights in Los Angeles, Calif. on Aug. 17, 1968, stenographic transcript at 264–301 (hereinafter cited as Los Angeles T.).

[8] Los Angeles T. at 268.

[9] *Figueroa v. Mackey* (Blythe) Riverside Superior Ct., April 1967 jury verdict for plaintiff $750 (reported in Civil Liberties Docket, Vol. XIII, 1967–1968, p. 76, published by Ann F. Ginger, Berkeley, California).

[10] *Figueroa v. Krupp*, Civil No. 68–648–AAH (C. D. Cal., filed Apr. 22, 1968). This is a suit under 42 U.S.C. 1981, 1983, 1985–89 for violation of civil rights, assault, and false imprisonment against the city of Blythe and the county of Riverside, as employers of the individual defendant police officers and against responsible officials of the city and county. The complaint was dismissed against all the defendants except the individual defendant law enforcement officers. An appeal has been taken from those orders. The action against the remaining defendants has not yet been set for trial.

[11] *Figueroa v. Krupp, Id.*, complaint, para. 19.

Blythe plainsclothesmen when he asked them to do so and that the Blythe Chief of Police refused to let the plaintiff lodge a complaint against these men.[12]

At the Commission's San Antonio hearing, Mrs. Frances Alvarez and Mrs. Margarita Contreras testified that on the evening of June 9, 1968, at the Pecos Memorial Hospital in Pecos, Texas, Officer Floyd South of the Texas State Highway Patrol struck both of them, causing a serious head injury to Mrs. Alvarez.[13] The alleged assault arose out of an argument with Officer South, after he had accused Mrs. Contreras' 16-year-old son, who had been in an automobile accident, of smoking marijuana. According to Mrs. Alvarez, [the young man's aunt] she and her husband and the boy's parents became very upset at this allegation and challenged Officer South to prove that the boy was an addict. Officer South denied that he had made the accusation and when the boy's mother insisted, he allegedly slapped her, hit Mr. Contreras, and struck Mrs. Alvarez with his fists. Mrs. Joan Kerr, a nurse who was on duty at the hospital at the time of this incident, testified at the hearing that she heard a woman scream outside the hospital and ran out to investigate:

> I saw [Officer South] hit Mrs. Contreras. And Mrs. Alvarez was bleeding profusely from her forehead . . . the four of them were huddled together and Mr. South . . . kept motioning his hands and telling them: "Come on, come on, who wants to be next?" [14]

Officer South, who testified at the hearing, denied that he struck Mrs. Alvarez or Mrs. Contreras. He claimed that Mrs. Contreras, Mr. Contreras, and Mr. Alvarez "jumped on him" outside the hospital and that he hit Mr. Contreras once in self defence. When asked how Mrs. Alvarez received her wound, he replied that he had "no idea." [15]

Allegations of unjustified use of force by police against Mexican Amer-

---

[12] Id.

[13] San Antonio Hearing at 686–95. Two other persons, Mrs. Miriam Starley, a night supervisor, and Slim Heath, the father of a boy being treated at the hospital that evening, were present and observed part of this incident. Id.

[14] San Antonio Hearing at 690.

[15] Id. at 709. The local grand jury, when presented with these facts, failed to return an indictment against Officer South (see discussion below, p. 45). A complaint was made to the Department of Justice of possible violation of 18 U.S.C. 242, the principal Federal criminal statute protecting citizens against violations of their civil rights by law enforcement officers. The statute provides that:

> Whoever, under color of any law, statute, ordinance, regulation or custom, willfully subjects any inhabitant of any State . . . to the deprivation of any rights, privileges or immunities secured or protected by the Constitution or laws of the United States, or to different punishments, pains or penalties, on account of such inhabitant being an alien, or by reason of his color, or race, than are prescribed for the punishment of citizens, shall be fined not more than $1,000 or imprisoned not more than one year or both and if death results shall be subject to imprisonment for any term of years or for life.

As of Mar. 31, 1969, the complaint was under investigation by the Department of Justice.

icans also were voiced in interviews in major southwestern cities. Howard Rosenberg, general counsel of the Legal Aid Society of Denver, Colorado, said that some Denver policemen abuse Mexican Americans and treat them with contempt.[16] As an example, he gave the following account of the experience of an elderly Mexican American client: When the client's automobile steering wheel became loose one evening he stopped and requested the assistance of a policeman. The policeman pulled alongside but instead of coming over to the client's car, told him to come into the police car. When the client explained what had happened, the officer said that there was nothing wrong with the car, that the man was just drunk. The client denied this. During the discussion, the officer lit a cigarette and the client asked if he could have one. "There are no cigarettes for you, Mexican," the officer allegedly replied. When the client, who was offended, tried to walk away, he was arrested and jailed. At the station, Rosenberg stated, the client was insulted. In the jail he reportedly was put into the "drunk tank" and received a broken jaw from a beating administered by a deputy sheriff.

The client was tried and convicted of drunkenness. His testimony and that of the arresting officer conflicted and the judge chose to believe the latter. Rosenberg believes the client was not drunk and had a good case against the Denver police, but the client became so discouraged by his conviction, which he appealed unsuccessfully, that he was unwilling to bring a civil action based on his arrest and mistreatment.[17]

Paul Phillips, an attorney in Albuquerque, stated that in March of 1967 he saw from his office window a policeman and a man in civilian clothes chasing a young boy whom they had caught in a parking lot. Phillips said that the man in civilian clothes "dragged the kid down and the cop jumped on his back and started riding piggy-back on him and started to push his head against the pavement." [18] Phillips reported that he was so outraged by what seemed to be the use of excessive force than he ran down to the street to investigate the incident. He said he followed the arresting officer to the precinct and complained about the officer's treatment of the youth. According to Phillips, the victim, a 16-year-old Mexican American accused of shoplifting who had tried to run away from the officers, claimed that his head had been smashed against the pavement seven times. Phillips stated that the youth's family did not wish to pursue the matter and that the police said Phillips could not have seen

---

[16] Interview with Howard Rosenberg, Oct. 16, 1967.

[17] Telephone interview with Howard Rosenberg, Feb. 27, 1969. According to Rosenberg, the client filed a complaint about his treatment with the Denver Police Department but without any results. On Mar. 31, 1969, a Commission staff member interviewed George Seaton, chief of police of Denver, to give him an opportunity to investigate this incident. (Mr. Seaton promised to write to the Commission concerning the incident. As of publication of this report, he had not responded.)

[18] Closed meeting of the New Mexico State Advisory Committee to the U.S. Commission on Civil Rights in Albuquerque, N. Mex., May 4, 1968, stenographic transcript at 41 (hereinafter cited as Albuquerque T.).

what had happened from a fifth floor office window.[19] Police investigation of Phillips' complaint exonerated the officer involved.[20]

Some of the incidents reported to the Commission had resulted in death. These generally involved resistance to arrest or an attempt to escape from police custody. Mexican Americans have asserted that the police officers would not have used deadly force against an Anglo under similar circumstances.

One such incident occurred in Stanton, California. According to one of the leaders of the local Mexican American community, two young men en route home late one night were stopped, questioned, and searched by a police officer. The officer reportedly assigned no reason for his actions but said he was going to take them to jail because they lacked identification. At that point, it was reported, one of the young men, aged 18, started to run away from the officer, whereupon a cruising police car stopped and an officer who saw the youth running fired his revolver, killing the young man. The officer was prosecuted on a charge of involuntary manslaughter, but the case was dismissed after the prosecution presented its case.[21]

A similar incident occurred in Alpine, Texas, in June 1968. According to reports of local residents, a police officer was chasing Henry Ramos, a 16-year-old Mexican American driving a car, in order to get information about his brother. The officer, it was reported, had a reputation for being rough and abusive and had been accused in the past of harassing Ramos, his brother, and other Mexican Americans. The chase ended when the boy stopped his car and fled on foot and the pursuing officer shot him once—fatally. A police investigation resulted in the filing of a charge of murder without malice against the officer and an indictment by the local grand jury.[22]

The Commission heard many other allegations that law enforcement officers in the Southwest use excessive force against Mexican Americans. There were other allegations of brutality in the cities previously men-

[19] Mr. Phillips expressed the opinion that the Albuquerque Police Department is unable to take care of the "mildest upset" in a reasonable way. Albuquerque T. at 40. As an example of the common use of excessive force, he cited an incident that occurred in 1967 which involved a dispute between two families in which two women and the children of one of the women were severely beaten by the police. One of the women was part Mexican. Although Mr. Phillips was not sure that her nationality played a role, an investigation of the incident by a Subcommittee of the Commission's New Mexico State Advisory Committee convinced the Chairman of the Committee that there were racial overtones in the incident. Alburquerque T. at 46 and interview with Gene Hill, Feb. 5, 1968.

[20] Albuquerque Journal, Apr. 19, 1967.

[21] Los Angeles T. at 302–310. The officer involved resigned from the force because of public pressure (id.). A complaint was made to the Department of Justice and as of Mar. 31, 1969, was under investigation for possible violations of 18 U.S.C. 242. Investigative files of the Department of Justice.

[22] Interviews in Alpine, Texas, Sept. 8–13, 1968. As of Aug. 19, 1969, the case had not come to trial. Telephone conversation with Felix McGaugh, County Judge, Brewster County, Texas.

tioned—Los Angeles,[23] Denver,[24] and Albuquerque[25]—as well as in other major cities—including Tucson, Arizona,[26] San Antonio, Texas,[27] El Paso, Texas,[28] Austin, Texas,[29] and small towns visited in the Southwest.[30]

Although the Commission cannot establish the validity of each of these complaints—this is the function of a court—their prevalence suggests the existence of a serious problem. This conclusion is confirmed by the fact that between January 1, 1965 and March 31, 1969 the Department of Justice received 256 complaints of police abuse, mostly of a serious nature, from Spanish surname persons in the five Southwestern States.[31] The conclusion also is supported by the receipt of 174 complaints of serious police brutality against Mexican Americans by the American Civil Liberties Union of Southern California during the past 2 years.[32]

Unequal Treatment of Juveniles

The Commission received many complaints alleging discriminatory treatment of Mexican American juveniles by law enforcement officers. One of the most common was that Anglo juvenile offenders were released without charge to the custody of their parents, while Mexican American youths were charged with offenses and jailed or sent to a reformatory.

For example, a counselor for the State employment office in Roswell, New Mexico, told the Commission's New Mexico State Advisory Committee:

> I know that when we were brought up, there were young people in Roswell who were friends of ours and the boys would get into minor skirmishes, breaking up signs or something like this. They would be taken to the police department, picked up, but they would be released in the custody of their parents. As far as we know, no charges were ever made against these people. This is why, I think, I was very shocked when I became involved in working with these [Mexican American] young people, especially with my young friends, and found that charges were made against them, such as stealing cantaloupes out of a farmer's field, curfew violations, being truant from

[23] Los Angeles T. at 86–89, 133–135.

[24] Interview with James R. Carrigan, Nov. 13, 1967.

[25] Albuquerque T. at 140–45.

[26] Interview with Alex Sanchez, Mar. 7, 1968.

[27] Interview with a resident who did not wish to be identified, Oct. 10, 1968. Other confidential interviews shall be hereinafter referred to as staff interview.

[28] Interview with Clark Knowlton, June 1968.

[29] Interview with Mario Obledo, Apr. 8, 1968.

[30] Interviews with Natividad Fuentes, Uvalde, Tex., Apr. 12, 1968 (discussed in chap. 4, infra); Jose Val Vede, Fort Sumner, N. Mex., Feb. 28, 1968; Gilbert Garcia, Roswell, N. Mex., Feb. 11, 1968.

[31] Commission staff review of Department of Justice investigative files. Of these complaints, 149 concerned law enforcement officials in Texas. The geographical distribution of the rest of the complaints was as follows: 8 from Arizona, 44 from California, 14 from Colorado, and 41 from New Mexico.

[32] Institute of Modern Legal Thought, Law Enforcement: The Matter of Redress, a report of the American Civil Liberties Union of Southern California (1969) at 55 (hereinafter cited as ACLU Report).

school and things like this. These would all be on record and they all have quite extensive juvenile records.

Among the Anglo people I work with, these just aren't done. I don't think Anglo children are this much better. I think this just happens, and this is the way it is.[33]

Arthur Esquibel, the former chief of police of Las Vegas, New Mexico, told the Committee that when he was chief between 1962 and 1966, local officials proposed to give two trouble-making young gangs in his community—one Mexican American and one Anglo—widely differing types of punishment. The community was concerned by acts of vandalism, believed to be the work of the Mexican American gang. Asked to investigate, the police found that both gangs were involved, apparently competing to see which gang could be the most destructive. At first Esquibel had difficulty persuading the community that there actually was an Anglo gang in addition to the Mexican American gang. Subsequently, local public officials called a meeting of the parents and members of both gangs and proposed that since most of the Mexican American boys had arrest records, charges should be filed against them. The punishment proposed for the Anglo boys was that they be disciplined in school by being forbidden to play basketball for 3 weeks.

Esquibel, as chief of police, insisted that, since all of the boys had committed the same offenses, all or none should be charged. As a result, no charges were brought against any of the gang members.[34]

Mrs. Jesusita Vigil of Silver City, New Mexico, stated than in February 1968, her 16-year-old son was arrested for truancy and placed in jail. The school principal and the probation officer reportedly offered the boy his choice of going to the State reformatory, joining the Job Corps, or leaving the State.[35] Willie T. Gonzales, a resident of Silver City, commented on this incident: "They do this for Spanish-speaking people, they give them this kind of choices. To Anglos, it is just a matter of going to their parents and solving this between them. That is the way it's done for one group and done differently for another." [36]

It was alleged that Mexican American parents often are not notified when their children are arrested. Mrs. Vigil said that after her son had been arrested for truancy and jailed, 2 days elapsed before she could find out where he was.[37] Mrs. Amelia Zamora, a resident of Portales, New Mexico, claimed she was never notified when her son was arrested and jailed for truancy.[38] Carleton Crane, a former policeman, said that in

---

[33] Closed meeting of the New Mexico State Advisory Committee to the U.S. Commission on Civil Rights in Roswell, N. Mex. Apr. 20, 1968, stenographic transcript at 108 (hereinafter cited as Roswell T.).

[34] Albuquerque T. at 131–34.

[35] Roswell T. at 32.

[36] *Id.* at 33.

[37] *Id.* at 31.

[38] Interview with Amelia Zamora, Feb. 28, 1968.

Portales, parents of Mexican American children are seldom informed that their children have been arrested. A young Mexican American from Portales reportedly was going to the movies with his mother when he heard his brother yell down from the city jail that he had been arrested. This was the first notification the family had of the arrest which apparently had occurred a day earlier.[39]

Discriminatory treatment of young Mexican Americans was alleged in other areas of the Southwest. Mose Trujillo, under sheriff of Denver County cited the case of a young Mexican American who had just bought a BB gun and was arrested upon leaving the store for illegal possession of the weapon. He contrasted this incident with another in which a young Anglo, who had been shooting at windows with his BB gun, was sent home by the police.[40] Minori Yasui, director of the Denver Commission on Community Relations, said that different treatment of Anglo and Mexican American youths is common in Denver. Yasui was concerned that, as a result of unwarranted police action against them, many Mexican American juveniles build up arrest records which jeopardize their employment prospects.[41]

Mike Gonsalez, an attorney in Del Rio, Texas, stated that there was unequal treatment of Mexican American and Anglo youths in south Texas. According to Gonsalez, some young Mexican Americans, recently caught breaking into a beer distributors' store in a small town in Texas, were arrested and charged with burglary. At about the same time some Anglo youths, according to Gonsalez, also broke into a store, stole some beer, and held a drunken orgy which resulted in their arrest. According to Gonsalez, because they were the sons and daughters of prominent Anglo members of the community, the incidents were not reported in the local newspapers and the young people were not charged.[42]

Other Forms of Discriminatory Treatment

A common complaint was that Mexican Americans are treated with less respect and less regard for their rights than Anglos. These allegations related largely to the manner and tone of voice used by law enforcement officers in approaching Mexican Americans, the treatment by law enforce-

---

[39] Roswell T. at 133. Lack of modification may be attributable in some areas to the view of law enforcement officials that Mexican American parents do not care about their children. Jerry Thomas, chief of police of Center, Colorado, and Richard Walker, a local patrolman, argued that "Spanish" parents "spend money on a six pack or a bottle of wine rather than buy cookies for their kids." Interview with Jerry Thomas, Dec. 14, 1967.

[40] Interview with Mose Trujillo, Nov. 13, 1967.

[41] Interview with Minori Yasui, Oct. 16, 1967. Interviews with Peter Mirelez, Nov. 14, 1967, and Dennis Santistevan, Dec. 11, 1967.

[42] Interview with Mike Gonsalez, Dec. 3, 1968. Also, San Antonio Hearing at 667–68. Mr. Gonsalez heard about this case from a Mexican American deputy sheriff in the town who did not wish to be identified. Many of the complaints regarding the use of excessive force, such as those described above, involved juveniles as victims. There were also numerous complaints from juveniles about being stopped by the police on "suspicion" (see below, pp. 10–11).

ment officers of Mexican American traffic offenders, and the frequent stopping of Mexican Americans on suspicion. . . .

Rev. Charles R. White, program director of a settlement house in a Mexican American neighborhood in Los Angeles, compared police enforcement of the curfew around the settlement house and his recollection of police action at curfew hour in his own [Anglo] community.[43] According to Reverend White, if Mexican American youths are standing on the sidewalk near the settlement house at 9:30 to 10 o'clock, the police stop, tell them in forceful terms to leave, and threaten them with arrest if they do not clear the street by 11 o'clock. Reverend White's own recollection of police enforcement of the curfew in his youth was quite different. "Now, my experience growing up in an Anglo community is that when it got close to curfew hour, they would come by and they would kind of motion out of their windshield, you know, and you knew what that small motion meant." [44] He added that young people in East Los Angeles were afraid to hold a dance at his settlement house for fear the police would break it up and arrest them. . . .[45]

In San Antonio, Mexican American youths complained that some officers address them as "Pachuco" or say "Hey, punk, come here", and that they are arrested if they protest.[46] One young man said, "There is always something they can stick you with if they want." [47] Some Mexican American high school students in San Antonio alleged that while they are on their way home from school, officers tell them to tuck in their shirt tails and to stop wearing pointed shoes.[48]

---

[43] Los Angeles, Calif., Municipal Code § 45.038 requires young people under 17 to be off the streets by 10 p.m.

[44] Los Angeles T. at 30–31.

[45] Los Angeles T. at 32.

[46] Interview with six young men who did not wish to be identified, because of their fear of the police, Dec. 10, 1968. A Mexican American from San Jose, Calif. also suggested that policemen provoke defiant behavior leading to arrests:

The questions are such that they want you to defy them . . . As a result, they are able to charge you with resisting [arrest] and even attack you.

Interviews conducted by the University of California's Western Center on Law and Poverty for its study "Sentencing of Mexican Americans" (1969), prepared for the Commission under contract, unpublished manuscript at 163 (hereinafter cited as Western Center Study).

[47] Id. Councilman Thomas Bradley of Los Angeles, a former police lieutenant, commented on the large number of "false arrests" in Negro and Mexican American areas, where the only charge is resisting arrest or assaulting an officer:

. . . this happens, I would say almost entirely because somebody resists the abuse of an officer or demands to know why the officer is stopping the person or speaking out, in interference, and saying, 'I know my constitutional rights!' Well, that's the worst mistake they can make. This brings out some kind of reaction when they are being arrested, and if they resist in any way; they then charge battery against the officers. . . . Los Angeles T. at 108.

See also, Task Force Report: The Police, The President's Commission on Law Enforcement and Administration of Justice (1967) at 179–80; Chevigny, Police Power (1968).

[48] Interview with Roy Valdez and group of young men from West San Antonio, Dec. 10, 1968.

Mr. Rosenberg, of the Denver Legal Aid Society, reported that a young Mexican American was stopped by a Denver policeman as he was escorting a blonde Anglo girl home from a party. The girl was driving, Mr. Rosenberg stated, and the officer told her she was speeding. The policeman then asked her escort: "Mexican, what are you doing with a white woman?" and arrested him. The young man was charged with four traffic violations which were dismissed in court since he was not driving the car. According to Mr. Rosenberg, the officer called the girl's mother to tell her that her daughter was out with a "Mexican".[49]

Inequalities in Treatment of Traffic Violations. Several persons, including some law enforcement officials, charged that Mexican Americans are treated more severely than Anglos for traffic violations. Such allegations were received from residents of Arizona, New Mexico, California, and Colorado.

The chief of police of Tucson, Arizona, reported that Anglo police recruits who had just completed training duty with regular officers observed that "a Mexican American was much more likely to be ticketed for a traffic violation than an Anglo." [50] The chief stated that he believed these observations to be accurate and was endeavoring to correct the situation. As of March 1968, traffic tickets in Tucson allegedly carried racial designations. These included "M" for Mexican until a protest was made by a Mexican American city councilman, resulting in the inclusion of Mexican Americans in the group labeled "Caucasian." [51]

Other such observations came from Philip Flores, a high school student in Las Cruces, New Mexico, who said that many Mexican American youths believe the police are more severe with them than with others in connection with motor vehicle offenses[52] and from Don Sosa, Jr., a lawyer in Las Cruces, who agreed.[53]

Several persons reported harassment of Mexican Americans by the police under the pretext of automobile safety checks. The Lohman report gives a first-hand account of an incident in San Diego in which a young Mexican American was stopped and questioned at length for having a loose tail-light connection on his automobile. The person who saw this concluded that "the cop was just looking for the boy to do something or say something so he could lay him out".[54] A resident of Albuquerque said that in 1967 his 18-year-old son was stopped by the police, searched, and checked for needle marks without any apparent reason. When the young man asked the officers why he was being stopped, they reportedly said that he had a defective plastic cover on his automobile license plate. . . .[55]

[49] Interview with Howard Rosenberg, Oct. 16, 1967.
[50] Interview with Bernard L. Garmine, Mar. 6, 1968.
[51] Interview with Hector Morales, Mar. 6, 1968. Mr. Morales was continuing his efforts to eliminate all racial designations from traffic tickets, but at the time of this interview he had not yet succeeded.
[52] Interview with Philip Flores, Feb. 7, 1968.
[53] Interview with Dan Sosa, Jr., Feb. 26, 1968.
[54] Lohman report at 83.
[55] Staff interview.

Participation by Mexican Americans in Law Enforcement Agencies

Importance of Participation

In the course of this study, the opinion was voiced that fear and distrust of Mexican Americans toward law enforcement agencies could be reduced by increasing the number of Mexican American law enforcement officers. For example, a Mexican American probation officer who had been a policeman in Phoenix for 6 years, stated that more Mexican American police officers were needed in that city.[56] He thought police teams could operate more effectively in Mexican American neighborhoods if at least one of the members was a Mexican American. The Mexican American officer, he believed, could put Mexican American citizens at ease, serve as an on-the-spot interpreter when necessary, and thus defuse tense police-citizen encounters and avoid miscarriages of justice.

The director of public safety for the city of Las Cruces, New Mexico, a Mexican American, stressed the importance of placing Mexican American law enforcement personnel at many levels of responsibility to secure the trust and confidence of the Mexican American community. He pointed out that in Albuquerque, no Mexican American law enforcement officer held a high ranking or policy-making position. In the same city the Spanish-speaking community continuously complained of police misconduct. By way of contrast he pointed to another large city in New Mexico where Mexican Americans held positions as police lieutenants and captains. Here police-community relations were excellent because the Spanish-speaking community, represented at all levels within the police department, was convinced that it would receive fair treatment from the police.[57]

Extent of Participation. In order to obtain information on the employment of Mexican Americans in law enforcement agencies, the Commission included questions on employment statistics in the questionnaire sent in October 1968 to 793 law enforcement agencies. These included 616 police departments, 168 county sheriffs, and nine State agencies in Texas, Arizona, California, Colorado, and New Mexico. The communities represented by these agencies ranged in size from less than 10,000 population up to and including metropolitan areas of more than 500,000 persons. The larger cities included Phoenix and Tucson, in Arizona; Los Angeles, San Francisco, San Diego, Oakland, and Sacramento, in California; Denver, Colorado Springs, and Pueblo, in Colorado; Albuquerque and Santa Fe, in New Mexico; Dallas, Houston, Ft. Worth, San Antonio, El Paso, and Austin, in Texas. Responses were received from 280 law enforcement agencies—about 35 per cent of the recipients. There were 243 responses from police departments, 32 from sheriffs' offices, and six from State law enforcement agencies.

[56] Interview with Sam Romero, Apr. 24, 1968.
[57] Albuquerque T. at 193–94.

Police Departments

Total employment in 243 police departments—uniformed, plainclothes, and civilian—was 34,717. Of this number, 1,989 or 5.7 per cent, were Mexican American. This contrasts with the Mexican American proportion of the five-State region's population—11.8 per cent.[58] There were found to be 23,944 uniformed officers, of whom 1,247 or 5.2 per cent were Mexican American. Of the uniformed policemen, 10,648, or 45 per cent, had never been on duty with a Mexican American officer at any time in their police careers.

Among plainclothes officers, 244 or 9.3 per cent were Mexican American out of a total of 2,398. Of the 8,375 civilian employees, Mexican Americans totaled 518, or 6.11 per cent.

Significant variations appeared in the extent to which Mexican Americans were employed by police departments. In some cities the Mexican American proportion of the police force approached the Mexican American proportion of the population. For example, in a Texas city with a Mexican American population of about 40 per cent, 165 of the 623 uniformed police officers, or 26.5 per cent, were Mexican Americans, and 40 of the 131 plainclothesmen [30 per cent] were Mexican American. In a large city in New Mexico, with a 28 per cent Mexican American population, about 20 per cent of the uniformed policemen and 31 per cent of the plainclothesmen were Mexican Americans.

Other cities—and these were in the large majority—had significantly poorer records. In a large Texas city which estimated its Mexican American population at 7 per cent of the whole, less than 3 per cent of the uniformed policemen and only 2 per cent of the plainclothesmen were Mexican American. A large Colorado city with an approximate 30 per cent Mexican American population had a uniformed police force that was 13.4 per cent Mexican American.

Ethnic breakdowns were not received from the police departments of either Los Angeles or San Francisco—the two largest cities in California. The Los Angeles Chief of Police sent a letter to the Commission's Acting Staff Director in October 1968, in which he stated that much of the requested information was unavailable in his office, and that the assembling of what information he did have would require excessive man-hours. He further indicated that if the Commission would send a staff member to Los Angeles, a representative from his community relations office would assist him in gathering some of the information. According to the Los Angeles Human Relations Bureau, total employment in the Los Angeles Police Department for 1968 was 5,937 persons. The bureau was unable to provide any ethnic breakdown of this total, stating that employment statistics by race and ethnic origin were no longer kept by the police department.[59] An official Los Angeles publication for fiscal year 1967–68

[58] See introduction, p. x. (Not reprinted here.—*Eds.*)
[59] Telephone interview with Charles Sierra, Advisor to the Director, Los Angeles Human Relations Bureau, June 4, 1969.

Police Employees—Uniformed, Plainclothes, and Civilian

Position	UNIFORMED			PLAINCLOTHES			CIVILIAN EMPLOYEES		
	Total	Mexican American	Per Cent Mexican American	Total	Mexican American	Per Cent Mexican American	Total	Mexican American	Per Cent Mexican American
Patrolman	17,946	1,001	5.6	1,554	151	9.7	8,375	518	6.11
Detective	2,625	132	5	396	33	8.3			
Sergeant	898	29	3.2	133	11	8.3			
Lieutenant	413	25	6	95	6	6.3			
Captain									
Inspector	68	3	4.4	33	None	0			
Chief Inspector	27	2	7.4	4	None	0			
Deputy Chief	60	2	3.3	32	2	6.3			
Chief	195	12	6	52	1	2			
Unclassified	1,712	41	2.4	99	20	20			
Totals	23,944	1,247	5.2	2,398	224	9.3			

Total civilian employees	8,375
Total police employees	26,342
Total all employees	34,717
Total Mexican American civilian employees	518
Total Mexican American police employees	1,417
Total MA employees	1,989
Per cent MA's overall total	5.7

NOTE. Cumulative statistics obtained from answers to Commission October 1968 questionnaires.

indicates that there were 1,844 new appointments to the police department during that year, of whom 153, or 8.3 per cent, were Mexican Americans.[60] The 1960 census indicates that 10.5 per cent of the Los Angeles' population is Mexican American.

The Human Rights Commission of San Francisco informed the Commission that as of May 31, 1968, there was a total of 2,240 police department employees in San Francisco, of whom 33—slightly over 1.4 per cent —were Spanish surnamed. There were 1,722 uniformed policemen, of whom 22—slightly under 1.3 per cent—were Spanish surname.[61] Seven per cent of San Francisco's population is Mexican American, according to the 1960 census.[62] In May 1967, the Commission held a public hearing in the Bay Area cities of San Francisco and Oakland. A staff report prepared in connection with that hearing concluded that: "In the Bay Area, Spanish Americans are underrepresented in local governmental employment as well as in Federal employment. . . . Of 1,722 uniformed policemen, only 22 are Spanish-speaking, of whom 19 are policemen-entrants. [There are 1,253 persons in the police-entrants' category.]"[63] According to 1967 figures collected by the Commission for its study of patterns of minority group employment in State and local government, in Oakland, which had a Spanish surnamed population in 1960 of 6.8 per cent, only 0.6 per cent of the uniformed police were Mexican American.[64]

In another large California city, where Mexican Americans constituted an estimated 10 per cent of the population, only 23 of the 700 uniformed officers, or 3.3 per cent, and only two of the 123 plainclothes officers, or 1.6 per cent, were Mexican American. In another large city in California, the Mexican American percentage was 15 per cent of the total population. Of this city's 370 uniformed policemen, 14, or 3.8 per cent and of its 79 plainclothes investigators, four, or 5 per cent, were Mexican American.

A number of inquiries in the questionnaire related to recruitment and selection practices. The first question asked was whether the agencies had established qualifications for appointment. Of the 277 agencies which responded, 274 answered affirmatively. The requirements of only 164 agencies, however, were in printed form and available to the public.

A majority of the responding agencies required that as a condition of employment officers live in the jurisdiction. Of 271 agencies responding to a question regarding minimum educational requirements for initial appointment, 193 required high school graduation. The great majority of

---

[60] Los Angeles City Personnel Department—Fair Employment Practices Survey, 1967–68.

[61] Telephone interview with Jack Casford, Human Relations Analyst, San Francisco Human Rights Commission, June 4, 1969.

[62] San Francisco has a number of Filipinos and persons from Central and South America, the majority of whom have Spanish surnames. *Id.*

[63] *Hearing before the U.S. Commission on Civil Rights, San Francisco, Calif., May 1–3, 1967, and Oakland, Calif., May 4–6, 1967* at 823.

[64] U.S. Commission on Civil Rights, *For ALL the People . . . By ALL the People,* A Report on Equal Opportunity in State and Local Government Employment, (1969) [hereinafter cited as For ALL the People] at 25.

agencies stated that applicants were required to take physical, written, and oral examinations.

More than 40 per cent of the responses listed failure to pass written examinations as the primary reason for disqualification of Mexican American applicants. Nearly 30 per cent listed failure to meet physical requirements,[65] 25 per cent reported failure to meet educational requirements, almost 25 per cent listed inadequate character references, and about 17 per cent mentioned lack of facility with the English language as the primary reason for disqualification.

There were 56 agencies which stated that no Mexican American applicants had applied in the previous 3 years; 157 responded that from 1 to 10 per cent of their applicants had been Mexican Americans. These 213 responses constituted almost 80 per cent of the 271 responses to this question.[66] The questionnaire asked the agencies for their views as to the reason why relatively few applications had been received from Mexican Americans. Inability to meet the educational requirements was the most frequent response. Of the 271 respondents, 193 indicated that a high school degree was required for police applicants. The second most important factor was the existence of written examinations. The third factor, cited in almost as many responses as the second, was an unfavorable impression of police work by Mexican Americans.

This last factor frequently was cited during the Commission's field investigations. Rev. John Luce and Rev. Charles White stated that Mexican Americans in Los Angeles were reluctant to become policemen for fear of being regarded with disfavor by other Mexican Americans. The main reason for this fear, they said, is that Mexican Americans do not trust the Los Angeles police and are convinced that the police do not trust them. Most of the Mexican American police officers in Los Angeles, they

---

[65] On Aug. 17, 1968, the Commission's California State Advisory Committee held a meeting on administration of justice problems in Los Angeles. One of the Committee members, Daniel L. Fernandez, questioned city councilman Thomas Bradley about the physical requirements for police recruits and what could be done to make them less restrictive. Councilman Bradley responded:

. . . the Civil Service Commission establishes the standards but they take directions from the police department. For a long time Chief Parker was unwilling to drop the minimum height from five-ten down to five-nine, and finally down to five-eight. This was a long and agonizing fight that went on. Now, I have not seen that the officers . . . were handicapped by the fact that their height was reduced. There was a time when they have—I've forgotten the exact number of teeth, but the question was asked one time, "What are they going to do, bite people?"

Councilman Bradley further pointed out that at one time the police department required that a recruit have a four-inch chest expansion, and that one almost had to be a good athlete to meet this standard. He concluded his comments on physical requirements by observing, "I think the reduction in the height from five-eight to five-seven would not impair the ability of the officer to do his job. They don't need muscle and massiveness so much as they need tact." Los Angeles T. at 106–08.

[66] Twenty-four responses showed applications from Mexican Americans amounted to between 11 and 25 per cent of the total; 12 responses indicated that Mexican American applicants constituted between 26 to 50 per cent of the total, 10 responses indicated that the Mexican American applicants constituted between 51 to 75 per cent of the total; and 12 responses indicated that more than 75 per cent of their applicants were Mexican Americans.

said, are looked upon as "sell-outs" and are often described as having become anglicized in their attitudes and practices.[67]

Similarly, a Spanish surnamed police officer in Denver, referring to the attitude of the Mexican American community toward any Mexican American police applicant, stated: "He is considered to be a defector." [68] The officer's superior, an Anglo division chief, supported this view, saying: "A stigma attaches to a minority individual when he becomes a member of a police department." [69] According to an official of the community action program in Roswell, New Mexico, Mexican American community leaders there are unwilling to furnish names of potential Mexican American applicants to the police chief because the leaders are apprehensive of subsequent criticism and abuse by the Mexican American community.[70]

Community leaders in each of the five States suggested that special efforts must be made to attract qualified Mexican Americans into law enforcement work. A majority of the departments, however, have no recruitment program, much less programs designed to attract Mexican American and other minority applicants. Of the 272 agencies responding to the question as to whether the agency had a recruitment program, 162 stated that they had none, and 177 said they had made no special efforts to recruit Mexican American applicants during the past 2 years.

Queried as to which methods the agency utilized to inform the Mexican American community of its desire to receive applications, 56 out of 141 agencies responding, or 40 per cent, indicated that they had made announcements which were distributed by Mexican American community organizations. Only nine agencies, however, indicated that they had arranged for the publication of such information in local Spanish language newspapers; only 16 had made arrangements for such announcements to be broadcast over local Spanish language radio and television stations; and only two had printed such announcements in Spanish and had had them distributed in the Mexican American communities.

The larger cities have the poorest records. Of the 141 responses, 17 came from cities with populations of 250,000 to 500,000. Of these 17, only one stated that it had made an announcement in a Spanish language newspaper or on a Spanish language radio or television station.[71]

---

[67] Los Angeles T. at 39. Arthur Garcia of the Police Malpractice Complaint Center of the Los Angeles American Civil Liberties Union, stated that Mexican American police officers are often more brutal than Anglo officers in their treatment of Mexican Americans. Both Luce and White expressed the belief that this is one way in which the Mexican American officer tries to show Anglo officers that he thinks as they do and is not prejudiced in favor of his own people. *Id.* at 61, 71–72.

[68] Staff interview.

[69] Staff interview.

[70] Roswell T. at 157–58.

[71] Sixteen of the 141 responses came from cities in the 100,000 to 250,000 population category. Only one response indicated that an announcement had been made in a Spanish newspaper and only three indicated that Spanish radio and television stations had been utilized. Cities in the category of 50,000 to 100,000 population accounted for 18 of the responses; of the 18 agencies only two had made announcements in the local Spanish language newspapers, and only one had used the local Spanish language radio and TV stations.

Sheriffs

Twenty-seven of the 32 responses from county sheriffs furnished statistics concerning their law enforcement personnel by ethnic category. Eleven came from Texas, seven from California, four from New Mexico, three from Colorado, and two from Arizona. In these 27 counties the sheriffs and their deputies and other law enforcement personnel totalled 5,251. Of this number 292, or 5.5 per cent, were Mexican American.[72]

In several counties in Texas the Mexican American proportion of the deputies in the sheriff's office equaled or exceeded the Mexican American proportion of the county's population. Thirty-seven out of 39 sheriffs' deputies in Webb County [Laredo] Texas—where Mexican Americans constitute 77 per cent of the population—and 36 out of 73 in El Paso County [49 per cent Mexican American] were Mexican Americans. In both of these counties, the sheriffs also were Mexican Americans. In Bernalillo County, New Mexico—where Albuquerque is located—15 of the 27 sheriff's deputies were Mexican Americans.

These are exceptions to the rule, however. Commission staff members received information that a relatively low number of Mexican Americans were employed as law enforcement personnel by sheriffs in the majority of areas visited.

For example, in both of the two largest cities in Arizona, the sheriffs had only token numbers of Mexican Americans on their staffs.[73] One Mexican American attorney in Texas pointed out that there were few Mexican American deputy sheriffs in many of the counties located in the Rio Grande Valley, where Mexican Americans constitute a significant portion or even a majority of the population.[74]

A Texas county where the population exceeds 22,000, of which Mexican Americans constitute about 25 per cent, had no Mexican American deputies on the sheriff's staff, according to a community leader.[75] The sheriff's response to the questionnaire confirmed this statement. A similar situation existed in Reeves County, Texas [population approximately 14,000], where the population is about 50 per cent Mexican American. According to a prominent community leader in Pecos, the county seat of Reeves County, there had not been a Mexican American deputy sheriff for many years.[76] Similarly in Culberson County, Texas, where 45 per cent of the population is Mexican American, the sheriff had no Mexican Americans on his staff.[77]

State Law Enforcement Agencies

Six State law enforcement agencies responded to the Commission questionnaire—two from California and one from each of the States of

---

[72] Unlike police departments, which use the merit system for appointment and promotion, many deputy sheriffs are hired on the basis of political patronage with merit and qualifications considered to be of secondary importance.

[73] Staff interviews with representatives of sheriffs' offices.

[74] Staff interview.

[75] Staff interview.

[76] Staff interview.

[77] Staff interview.

Arizona, Colorado, New Mexico, and Texas. The response of the Texas Department of Public safety indicated that 28 of its 1,740 uniformed and plainclothes officers were Mexican Americans—1.6 per cent of the total officer force—in sharp contrast to the Mexican American proportion of the State's population [14.8 per cent].

Testifying at the Commission's San Antonio hearing, Col. Wilson Speir, director of the Texas Department of Public Safety, reported that there were no Mexican Americans among the 62 Texas Rangers in his department. He said that there were 38 Mexican American patrolmen and two Mexican Americans on the intelligence staff.[78] In response to the Commission's questionnaire, the total number of patrolmen was given as 1,432, of whom only 26 were Mexican Americans—1.8 per cent. At the hearing, in response to Commissioner Hector Garcia's questioning, Colonel Speir admitted that he arrived at the figure 38 by classifying uniformed officers serving in the drivers license service and the motor vehicle inspection service as "patrolmen."

At the hearing Spier testified: "We have had in past years a captain of the Texas Rangers that was a Mexican American, Captain Gonzales, one of the most famous of all Ranger captains, who is now retired after 30 years of service."[79] In response to a question by Commissioner Garcia, himself a Texan, about the spelling of this former Ranger's last name, Speir responded "G-o-n-z-a-u-l-l-e-s." When Commissioner Garcia expressed the view that this man was never considered to be a Mexican American by the statewide Mexican American community, Speir responded that he was considered to be a Mexican American by the Texas Department of Public Safety.[80]

The name of the former Ranger captain actually was spelled "G-o-n-z-a-u-l-l-a-s."[81] In a newspaper account of an interview with Gonzaullas, [which took place the day after the hearing], who had retired in 1951 after 30 years' service with the Texas Rangers, he is reported to have stated that his father was of Spanish-Portuguese descent, that his mother was of German descent, and that he considered himself to be an American. He also was reported to have said that he could never recall a Mexican American holding a high rank in the Texas Rangers during his 30 years' service although he did know of one regular Mexican American Ranger.[82]

The California Highway Patrol listed an overall total of 5,010 uniformed officers, including 4,364 State traffic officers. It failed to indicate whether any of these uniformed personnel were Mexican American. Its covering letter accompanying its response stated in part: "Under State law, race, descent, or ethnic group affiliation has no bearing on securing employment with this Department." Similarly, the California Department of Justice, which returned the Commission's questionnaire

[78] San Antonio Hearing at 717, 726.
[79] *Id.* at 719.
[80] *Id.* at 728.
[81] San Antonio Express & News, Dec. 15, 1968 at 3–A.
[82] *Id.*

unanswered, stated in a letter that it had two law enforcement bureaus within the department—the bureau of criminal identification and investigation with 33 special agents, and the bureau of narcotics enforcement with approximately 100 peace officers. It did not indicate how many were Mexican American, stating only that there were a "substantial number" of Mexican Americans in each of these bureaus.

The Colorado State Patrol response indicated that it had 418 uniformed officers of whom 350 were patrolmen. All of the 12 Mexican Americans were patrolmen and they constituted slightly more than 2.8 per cent of the total 418.

The New Mexico State Police response showed 248 law enforcement personnel. Sixty-one of the 229 uniformed officers and 13 of the 19 plainclothesmen were Mexican American. Thus, Mexican Americans constituted 74 of the 248 personnel—or nearly 30 per cent of the law enforcement officers in the agency. The statistics from this one agency compare favorably with the 1960 Population Census for New Mexico which indicates that 28.3 per cent of its total population is Mexican American. . . .

Participation by Mexican Americans in Agencies of Justice

The relative shortage of Mexican American lawyers is reflected in the scarcity of Mexican American judges and prosecutors. In turn this may contribute to the lack of confidence which Mexican Americans have in the judicial system and the administration of the civil and criminal laws. To determine the extent to which Mexican Americans serve as judges in the Federal and State courts of Arizona, California, Colorado, New Mexico, and Texas a Spanish surname check was made, using the Spanish surnamed list of the U.S. Immigration and Naturalization Service of the Department of Justice and the appropriate Federal and State legal directories.[83] While it is possible that there are judges of Mexican ancestry who do not have Spanish surnames, the margin of error would not be great enough to substantially change the stated percentages.

United States District Courts

The 1969 Directory of the United States Court Officials[84] lists a total of 59 Federal District judges sitting in the 12 districts of the five States.[85]

---

[83] *1969 Directory of U.S. Court Officials; 1968 Calif. Roster; 1968 Texas Legal Directory; 1968 New Mexico Attorney Roster of the Bench and Bar; Arizona Courts 1969–70* compiled by Sec'y of State, Jan. 1969; and *Court List* furnished by Colorado Bar Ass'n, May 1969.

[84] Published by the Administrative Office of the U.S. Courts, Washington, D.C.

[85] Arizona, Colorado, and New Mexico each comprise one Federal District. California is divided into five districts, and Texas into four.

Of the 59 judges only two are Spanish surnamed—one in California and one in Texas. Both are comparatively new on the Federal bench.

State Courts[86]

Of a total of 961 judges serving on State courts in the five States only 32 or 3.0 per cent are Spanish surnamed.[87] There are 32 supreme court justices in the five States. Only one of these, the chief justice of New Mexico, is Spanish surnamed.

The five States have a total of 183 judges at the next intermediate or appellate level. Five of these (three in New Mexico and one each in Colorado and Texas) are Spanish surnamed.

At the State court trial level, there are a total of 746 judges; 26 are Spanish surnamed. California has seven, Colorado three, New Mexico 14, Texas two, Arizona none.

The following chart shows the number and location of State court judges by ethnic origin:

State Courts

	MEXICAN AMERICAN	OTHER	TOTAL
Arizona[88]	0	61	61
California[89]	7	430	437
Colorado[90]	4	166	170
New Mexico[91]	18	39	57
Texas[92]	3	233	236
Total	32	929	961

District Attorneys and Public Prosecutors

Because of the importance of the role district attorneys and public prosecutors and their staffs play in the administration of justice, a Commission staff member obtained information, through telephone conferences, regarding the number of Spanish surnamed attorneys employed in these offices in 22 southwestern cities.

Of 590 State district attorneys and public prosecutors and their assistants, in these cities, only 20, or slightly more than 3 per cent, are Spanish

[86] All of the judges of the State courts of Arizona, California, New Mexico, and Texas are elected for terms of varying length. In Colorado all State court judges are appointed by the Governor of the State. Ariz. const. art. VI §§ 3, 5; Ariz. Rev. Stats. § 12–120.02; Calif. const. art. VI § 26; N. Mex. const. art. IV §§ 4, 12; Tex. const. art. 5 §§ 2, 4, 5, 6, 7, 15; Colo. const. art. VI, §§ 7, 8, 12, 21, 22.

[87] Id.

[88] Includes Supreme, Appellate, and Superior Courts.

[89] Id.

[90] Includes Supreme, District, County Courts, and Probate Courts.

[91] Id.

[92] Includes Supreme, Civil and Criminal Appellate, and District Courts.

surnamed. Of these 20, there are none in Arizona or Colorado, one in New Mexico, eight in Texas, and 11 in California.

The following chart shows the cities for which information is available and their district attorneys and public prosecutors by ethnic origin:

Attorneys Employed in Offices of District Attorneys and Public Prosecutors

	MEXICAN AMERICAN	OTHER	TOTAL
Arizona:			
Phoenix	0	8	8
Tucson	0	6	6
Yuma	0	1	1
California (counties):			
Alameda	1	58	59
Fresno	1	19	20
Los Angeles	5	291	296
San Diego	2	56	58
San Francisco	1	35	36
Santa Clara	1	46	47
Colorado:			
Colorado Springs	0	15	15
Denver	0	22	22
Pueblo	0	9	9
New Mexico:			
Albuquerque	0	9	9
Las Cruces	0	5	5
Roswell	0	5	5
Santa Fe	1	6	7
Texas:			
Austin	1	10	11
Brownsville	1	1	2
Corpus Christi	1	1	2
El Paso	0	6	6
Houston	0	7	7
San Antonio	5	12	17
Total	20	570	590

Department of Justice

The Federal Government has a long established policy of equal employment opportunity. This policy has undergone a number of recent implementations and at the present time agencies are required to take affirmative action to recruit and promote minority employees. The Commission requested employment statistics from the Department of Justice for the five-State area to determine what progress it had made in recruiting and promoting Mexican Americans.

The Department of Justice statistics include employees of the legal divisions, including U.S. attorneys and U.S. marshals; the Federal Bureau of Investigation; the Bureau of Prisons; the Immigration and Naturalization Service; and the Bureau of Narcotics and Dangerous Drugs. The total number of all Department of Justice employees in the five States as of November 30, 1967 (excluding the Bureau of Narcotics and Dangerous Drugs, which was only transferred from the Department of the Treasury to the Department of Justice on April 8, 1968) was 6,079. Of this total 448, or 7.36 per cent, were Mexican American.[93]

In the General Schedule grades, which comprised 5,608 employees, Mexican Americans held 400, or 7.1 per cent, of the jobs. The overwhelming majority of their positions, however, were found in the lower Grades GS–1 through GS–8. For example, in Grades GS–1 through GS–4, Mexican Americans held 136 of the 823 jobs, or 16.5 per cent. In Grades GS–5 through GS–8, they held 219 of the 2,280 jobs, or 9.6 per cent. Thus, of the 400 jobs, 355 were concentrated in the lower paying categories.[94]

In Grades GS–9 through GS–11, where junior supervisory and junior executive positions are located, there were 36 Mexican Americans out of 1,437 total employees—only 2.5 per cent. In the executive and higher supervisory Grades of GS–12 through GS–18, only nine of 1,068 employees—about one-third of 1 per cent—were Mexican American.[95]

None of the 53 legal division employees in the five States, occupying Grades GS–12–18—where all the lawyers and other top professionals are found—was Mexican American. Nor were there any Mexican Americans among the 47 Bureau of Prisons employees in these grades.[96]

Mexican Americans constituted only three of the 772 FBI employees in Grades GS–12–18 and only three of the 365 FBI employees in Grades GS–9–11. Of the 1,811 FBI GS classified employees in the five States, only 48—or 2.7 per cent—were Mexican Americans.[97]

In the Bureau of Immigration and Naturalization, only 25 of the 856 employees found in Grades 9 through 11—less than 3 per cent—and only six of the 196 employees in Grades 12 through 18—slightly more than 3 per cent—were Mexican Americans.[98]

The Bureau of Narcotics and Dangerous Drugs was transferred from the Department of the Treasury to the Department of Justice on April 8, 1968, in accordance with President Johnson's Reorganization Plan. The Assistant Director for Administration of this Bureau furnished the Commission with the following employment statistics for the five-State Southwestern region: [99]

[93] Letter from Kenneth J. Stallo, Director of Personnel, U.S. Department of Justice, to Robert Amidon, U.S. Commission on Civil Rights, Mar. 27, 1969 (with attachments).
[94] Id.
[95] Id.
[96] Id.
[97] Id.
[98] Id.
[99] Letter from N. B. Coon, Assistant Director for Administration of the Bureau, to the General Counsel, U.S. Commission on Civil Rights, Mar. 20, 1969.

STATE	TOTAL CLERKS	SPANISH SURNAMED CLERKS	TOTAL AGENTS	SPANISH SURNAMED AGENTS
Arizona	1	none	2	none
California	25	none	96	6
Colorado	9	none	18	1
New Mexico	1	1	4	none
Texas	15	2	39	3
Totals	51	3	159	10

NOTE. As these statistics indicate, only about 6 per cent of the narcotics agents are Spanish surnamed.

IN THE SUPERIOR COURT OF THE STATE OF CALIFORNIA IN AND FOR THE COUNTY OF SANTA CLARA

JUVENILE DIVISION

HONORABLE GERALD S. CHARGIN, Judge   Courtroom No. 1

In the Matter of
PAUL PETE CASILLAS, JR.,
a minor.

No. 40331

STATEMENTS OF THE COURT

San Jose, California   September 2, 1969

APPEARANCES:
For the Minor: FRED LUCERO, ESQ.
                                          Deputy Public Defender

For the Probation Department: WILLIAM TAPOGNA, ESQ.
                                          Court Probation Officer

Official Court Reporter: SUSAN K. STRAHM, C.S.R.
September 2, 1969   10:25 A.M.

Statements of the Court

THE COURT: There is some indication that you more or less didn't think that it was against the law or was improper. Haven't you had any moral training? Have you and your family gone to church?

THE MINOR: Yes, sir.

THE COURT: Don't you know that things like this are terribly wrong? This is one of the worst crimes that a person can commit. I just get so disgusted that I just figure what is the use? You are just an animal. You are lower than an animal. Even animals don't do that. You are pretty low.

I don't know why your parents haven't been able to teach you anything or train you. Mexican people, after 13 years of age, it's perfectly all right to go out and act like an animal. It's not even right to do that to a stranger, let alone a member of your own family. I don't have much hope for you. You will probably end up in State's Prison before you are 25, and that's where you belong, any how. There is nothing much you can do.

I think you haven't got any moral principles. You won't acquire anything. Your parents won't teach you what is right or wrong and won't watch out.

Apparently, your sister is pregnant; is that right?

THE MINOR'S FATHER, MR. CASILLAS: Yes.

THE COURT: It's a fine situation. How old is she?

THE MINOR'S MOTHER, MRS. CASILLAS: Fifteen.

THE COURT: Well, probably she will have half a dozen children and three or four marriages before she is 18.

The County will have to take care of you. You are no particular good to anybody. We ought to send you out of the country—send you back to Mexico. You belong in prison for the rest of your life for doing things of this kind. You ought to commit suicide. That's what I think of people of this kind. You are lower than animals and haven't the right to live in organized society—just miserable, lousy, rotten people.

There is nothing we can do with you. You expect the County to take care of you. Maybe Hitler was right. The animals in our society probably ought to be destroyed because they have no right to live among human beings. If you refuse to act like a human being, then, you don't belong among the society of human beings.

MR. LUCERO: Your Honor, I don't think I can sit here and listen to that sort of thing.

THE COURT: You are going to have to listen to it because I consider this a very vulgar, rotten human being.

MR. LUCERO: The Court is indicting the whole Mexican group.

THE COURT: When they are 10 or 12 years of age, going out and having intercourse with anybody without any moral training—they don't even understand the Ten Commandments. That's all. Apparently, they don't want to.

So if you want to act like that, the County has a system of taking care of them. They don't care about that. They have no personal self-respect.

MR. LUCERO: The Court ought to look at this youngster and deal with this youngster's case.

THE COURT: All right. That's what I am going to do. The family should be able to control this boy and the young girl.

MR. LUCERO: What appalls me is that the Court is saying that Hitler was right in genocide.

THE COURT: What are we are going to do with the mad dogs of our society? Either we have to kill them or send them to an institution or place them out of the hands of good people because that's the theory —one of the theories of punishment is if they get to the position that they want to act like mad dogs, then, we have to separate them from our society.

Well, I will go along with the recommendation. You will learn in time or else you will have to pay for the penalty with the law because the law grinds slowly but exceedingly well. If you are going to be a law violator—you have to make up your mind whether you are going to observe the law or not. If you can't observe the law, then, you have to be put away.

{ STATE OF CALIFORNIA
{ COUNTY OF SANTA CLARA   ss.

I, SUSAN K. STRAHM, do hereby certify that the foregoing is a true and correct transcript of the STATEMENTS OF THE COURT had in the within-entitled action taken on the 2nd day of September, 1969; that I reported the same in stenotype, being the qualified and acting Official Court Reporter of the Superior Court of the State of California, in and for the County of Santa Clara, appointed to said Court, and thereafter had the same transcribed into typewriting as herein appears.

Dated: This 8th day of September, 1969.

SUSAN K. STRAHM, C.S.R.

THE CHICANO MIGRANTS

Anne Brunton

Each year about 1 million people in the United States leave their homes to perform agricultural tasks in other areas. These migratory workers did 9 per cent of the nation's agricultural seasonal work in 1968, working in 900 counties of forty-six states (Committee on Labor and Public Welfare 1969:1). They travel to agricultural areas where the local labor force, though sufficient for most of the season, is too small to carry on the total harvest of fresh fruits and vegetables. These migrants also do some pre-harvest work, such as thinning and weeding. Thus, they move during peak seasonal demands to areas with relatively sparse agricultural populations.

There are three major routes of migration and three cultural groups migrating yearly (Fig. 1). The first is along the Atlantic coast. This East Coast stream is made up primarily of Florida Negroes who work their way into New York and the New England states, with some migrating as far as the Great Lakes states. Since 1953 a few Mexican Americans have also entered this migrant stream (Kurth 1960:206).

The second and largest migrant stream stems from south Texas. These migrants are predominantly Mexican Americans traveling in family groupings, nuclear and extended. Some migrate only within Texas, but the majority travel north for the summer to work in the Mountain, Great Plains, and Great Lakes states. In the winter they return south to work in the Texas Valley (vegetables), in the Panhandle (cotton), or in Florida (citrus fruits) (Kurth 1960:206). Also in this migratory group are a number of southern Anglos, usually small farm owners or displaced share-croppers. Along the routes, the Anglos are usually employed in tree crops, the Mexican Americans in stoop labor.

Besides the difference in ethnic affiliation of the members of these two major routes, there are other differences in their composition. In 1968, for example, 74 per cent of the second (Texas) stream consisted of family groups, whereas 84 per cent of the Florida stream were crews. Further (Table 1), 18 per cent of 5,000 people were nonworkers in the Florida group as compared with 31 per cent, or 30,000 nonworkers in the Texas stream. In southern Texas the average Mexican American family size was 6.5 members as compared with the average Negro migrant family from Florida with 2.8 persons (Committee on Labor and Public Welfare 1969:11).

Reprinted with permission from doctoral thesis by Anne Brunton (Pullman, Wash.: Washington State University, 1971).

Anne Brunton received her doctorate in anthropology from Washington State University in 1971. This article is from her dissertation on Chicano migrants in Walla Walla, Washington. She now teaches at Moorhead State College in Minnesota.

Table 1.   Number of Nonworkers and Average Family Size of the
Two Major Migrant Streams

MIGRANT STREAMS	NONWORKERS		AVERAGE FAMILY SIZE
	No.	*Per Cent*	
Florida	5,000	18	2.8
Texas	30,000	31	6.5

Source: Cronemeyer 1969A:14.

The third migrant stream originates in California and is composed of
both Mexican Americans and Anglos. Again, in this group one finds whole
families moving: both from county to county within California, and also
north along the Pacific Coast into Oregon and Washington. A few migrate
inland as far as Idaho (Kurth 1960:206).

The total number of domestic migrants remained stable at approximately 400,000 workers from the end of World War II to 1967. At that
time (Kurth 1960:206) the number dropped to 276,000 (Fig. 2). The
Mexican American migrant stands out in this total, both because he is
different culturally and because he is concentrated in specific geographical areas. The 1960 census listed 3.5 million Americans with Spanish
surnames concentrated in five states: Arizona, California, Colorado, New
Mexico, and Texas. Nearly 3 million reside in California and Texas alone.
In this five-state area, known as Aztlán after the Aztec name for their
mythical origins, the Mexican American minority consists of 12 per cent of
the population. It is projected that there will be about 5 million Spanish
surname persons in the nation in the 1970's (Grebler, Moore, and Guzmán
1970:14). [Current figures indicate that there are about 15 million Spanish
surname persons living in the continental United States.—*Eds.*] As can
been seen from Tables 3 and 4, 40 per cent or 103,000 Mexican American
farmworkers engage in migratory labor, accounting for 25 per cent of the
total migrant stream (Committee on Labor and Public Welfare 1969:5).

Migrants travel because they must for economic reasons. Some move
because local work is not available, others because local competition is
too great and wages too low. This latter is particularly true in south
Texas, where Mexican nationals are available as workers for extremely
low wages.

Table 2.   Frequency of Migration of Mexican American Farmworkers

MEXICAN AMERICAN FARMWORKERS	NUMBER	PER CENT
Mexican American nonmigrant farmworkers	158,000	60
Mexican American migrant farmworkers	103,000	40
Total	261,000	100

Source: Committee on Labor and Public Welfare 1969:5.

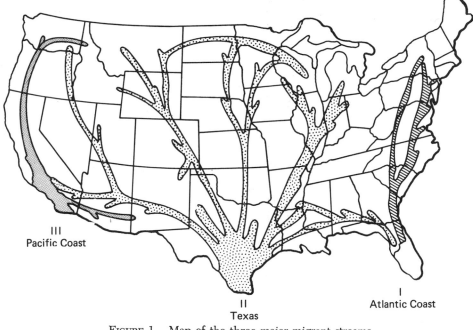

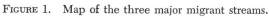

FIGURE 1.   Map of the three major migrant streams.

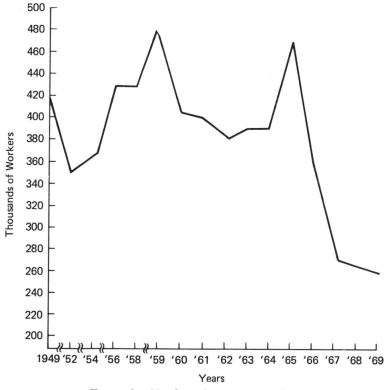

FIGURE 2.   Number of migratory workers.

Table 3.   1960 Distribution of Migrant Workers

ETHNIC GROUPS	MIGRANT WORKERS	
	Number	Per Cent
Mexican American	103,000	25
Other	306,000	75
Total	409,000	100

Source: Committee on Labor and Public Welfare 1969:5.

Table 4.   Man Months of Migratory Labor by State
United States 1968–1969

STATE	THOUSANDS OF MAN-MONTHS OF MIGRATORY WORKER EMPLOYMENT	
	1968	1969
United States	1368.9	1298.7
California	349.4	337.6
Florida	144.7	128.2
Michigan	119.4	112.1
Texas	74.4	72.4
Washington	58.2	60.0
New Jersey	55.7	45.1
New York	50.3	45.8
Ohio	49.9	41.1
Oregon	48.7	48.2
Other States	418.2	407.5

Source: Committee on Labor and Public Welfare 1969:7; Cora Cronemeyer 1970:26.

Although they migrate principally for farmwork, 40 per cent of the migrants in 1968 did other work, too. The particular route taken by individual family groups or crews and the specific areas of employment for each varies. Despite these variations, however, and the fact that almost every state uses some migratory labor, in 1969 more than half of the total men-months of migratory worker employment occurred in five states: California, Florida, Michigan, Texas, and Washington (Table 4).

The yearly activity of migrants begins with early spring employment in southern areas where work in cotton, sugar beets, fruits, and vegetables is available. Overall employment during these early months is very low, numbering about 40,000 workers. Then, as the crops begin to mature in the north, the seasonal workers begin to fan out—up both coasts and the central part of the country. They work their way northward as the crops mature, and then return south for the winter. Peak employment of migrants in 1968 occurred in August, with 235,000 workers employed (Committee on Labor and Public Welfare 1969:8).

The actual number of workers employed, however, has been decreasing since 1967 for two reasons: (1) new regulations on housing requirements for migrants leading to a housing shortage and (2) the increase in mechanized farming. The December, 1969, issue of *Farm Labor Developments* presents the findings of a colloquium on mechanization (Cronemeyer 1969b:1–6). Diverse opinions were expressed on the blessings of this "advancement." At one point it was argued that farmers must accept mechanization because they face a labor shortage at harvest. Others maintained that mechanization had been undertaken for the benefit of the growers (and hardship of the farmworkers). They pointed out that the workers are already subjected to wasted time, vulnerability to exploitation, and inadequate laws and institutions to aid in necessities. Further, Fujimoto (Department of Applied Behavioral Sciences, University of California at Davis) said, "Despite the employer's claims that mechanization is geared to eliminate drudgery, the politics of agriculture show that the large impetus for mechanization comes out of fear of the worker rather than out of concern for him—fears that a malleable labor supply or a comparable foreign labor would diminish, or that the domestic labor force would unionize" (Cronemeyer 1969b:3). The main question discussed from both angles was whether mechanization was a cause or an effect. Does mechanization result from labor shortages, or is the machine a cause of unemployment among farmworkers? Whatever the answer, mechanization is a *de facto* condition. A number of crops have already been mechanized; mechanized handling and harvest are already found for asparagus, cucumbers (pickling), cabbage, peaches, apples, and apricots. Mechanized potato cutting was also reported from Washington.

Projections to 1975 present a very dim future for migrant workers, especially those employed harvesting vegetables. In 1968 about 2 per cent of the fruit and nut crops were harvested mechanically. Projections for 1975 raise this figure to 17 per cent (Davis 1970:11). These figures are, of course, averages for all types of fruit and nuts. For instance, in 1968 one single crop, tart cherries, was 50 per cent mechanized, whereas the mechanization for all others was below 5 per cent. The 1975 projection is based heavily on increased mechanization of wine grapes, cling peaches, and tart and sweet cherries. The total decrease in man-hours required in the production of these crops will be about 8 per cent.

The conditions projected for vegetable workers are less optimistic. By 1968 mechanization had reached 56 per cent in overall vegetable crop production, and the major vegetable crops were almost 100 per cent mechanized. Estimates for 1975 show 75 per cent overall mechanization, which would result in a 27 per cent reduction of man-hour labor requirements. This decrease would affect the unskilled farm laborers, notably the Mexican American migrant in the western stream (Davis 1970:12).

Another change from the traditional picture of the migrant that is becoming more evident is a permanent change of home residence. Though most migrant workers still live in the southern states, there has been some shift to the north. Sixty per cent of the seasonal workers lived in the south in 1960; yet by 1965 only 40 per cent still resided there (Committee on Labor and Public Welfare 1969:7). The remainder was spread in the northern and western regions of the United States. . . .

The income of migrant workers is very low, especially when account is taken of the cost of migration itself. Therefore, when one reads statements such as "there are many low income families in the Nation in the same income bracket as the migrant worker" (Metzler and Sargent 1960:5), it is important to ascertain who these "families" are and what their economic behavior involves before such equations are made. In fact, one could ask if the additional money earned through migration is really sufficient to cover its cost. For instance, looking at the 1956 figures for south Texas migratory workers (Table 8), it can be seen that those households employed only in Texas had an average annual income of $1,496. This is compared to $2,465 earned by south Texans employed only outside of Texas and $2,583 gained by employment both within and outside of Texas. Wages paid in Texas are particularly low, with those paid in the Lower Rio Grande Valley the lowest. This is the area from which most migrants come.

Table 8.   Annual Income of Texas
Migratory Workers (1956)

Area of Employment	Annual Income
Texas only	1,496
Texas and other states	2,465
Outside Texas only	2,583

Source: Metzler and Sargent 1960:6.

The average pay for a migrant within Texas was $5.14 a day, whereas outside the state the average was $6.57 per day. Further, Arizona, California, and Washington were the highest-paying states; Texas and Colorado were the lowest (Table 9).

Table 9.   Average Daily Migrant Pay in 1956 per State

State	Average Daily Earnings	State	Average Daily Earnings
Arizona	$10.72	Ohio	$6.84
California	8.84	Michigan	6.64
Washington	8.39	Idaho	6.20
Illinois	7.84	Colorado	5.35
North Dakota	7.75	Texas	5.14
Minnesota	7.34	Other States	5.76
Wisconsin	7.16		

Source: Metzler and Sargent 1960:13.

Comparisons also should be made between the income of migrants and the average national income. In 1956 a single migrant averaged $781 per year, family income was approximately $2,240 (Metzler and Sargent 1960:1). This latter figure may be compared with the national average household income of $4,785. In 1957 the individual yearly migrant income was $859; family income averaged around $1,900 (Kurth 1960:207). Income levels have changed little over the past decade. Although migrant wages have risen, their relative position remains the same. In the survey conducted by the Economic Research Service of the United States Department of Agriculture (1967:18–23), the average income for a single migrant had reached $1,000 with agriculture alone or $1,700 if both agricultural and nonagricultural jobs were undertaken. Meanwhile, the national average for all workers had risen to $3,700. This income discrepancy between migrant workers and workers in general comes from the very low rate of pay in agriculture: $10 per day as compared with $20 per day in manufacturing. The actual daily migrant wage varies by area, with the lowest in the south and the highest in the west (Table 10).

Table 10.   Average Daily Wage for
Agricultural Employment in 1965

AREA IN UNITED STATES	AVERAGE DAILY WAGE
South	$7.70
North	9.45
West	13.20

Source: Economic Research Service 1967:18.

Such wage increases are in part the effect of the termination of the Bracero program. This loss of foreign labor stimulated payment of higher wages to domestic workers.

In 1966 the Fair Labor Standards Act was amended to include some farmworkers. This act called for a minimum wage of $1 per hour by February 1, 1967; $1.15 per hour by February, 1968; and $1.30 per hour by February, 1969. The extended coverage, however, affected only the largest farms and hence only a small per cent of the total migrant population. Thus, in 1968 wages varied around an average hourly farm wage of $1.32, with Mississippi lowest at $.69 per hour and Connecticut and Washington highest at $1.71 per hour (Babre 1969:5). The lowest overall wage rates were paid in Alabama, Arkansas, Florida, Louisiana, Mississippi, and Texas (Table 11). Conditions in Texas, the homeland of most Mexican-American migrants, warrant a closer look. In 1968 Texas farm wages ranged from $1.25 per hour in the northern Panhandle, to $1 in the Edwards Plateau, and finally to $.80 per hour in the Lower Rio Grande Valley, where most of these migrants reside (Wilson 1969:13).

Besides the low hourly wage, migrants are often unemployed and/or underemployed several months a year. They must plan very carefully in order to arrive in an area as jobs become available. Such jobs, however, are subject to local variations in weather which can speed up or slow down a particular crop by a week or two. Therefore, throughout the work season, migrant families face days or weeks of unemployment while waiting for a crop to mature. Further, the total number of working days per year is very low, ranging from 131 to 150 days. Even this low number was more than they could have worked had they chosen not to migrate.

Table 11.   1968 Average Hourly
Wage for Seasonal Farmworkers

STATE	HOURLY WAGE
Mississippi	$ .69
Alabama	.73
Louisiana	.89
Arkansas	.93
Texas	1.07
Florida	1.18
Oregon	1.42
Ohio	1.50
Connecticut	1.71
Washington	1.71

Source: Wilson 1969:12.

Injuries and occupational diseases are also uncommonly frequent among migratory laborers. A study conducted in California found that agricultural workers "have the third highest rate of disabling work injuries" (Department of Public Health 1965:2). These same workers had the highest rates of both disabling and nondisabling occupational diseases (12.4 per 1,000). Seventy-six per cent of these were skin conditions, 10 per cent were systemic poisoning, 3 per cent were respiratory conditions caused by noxious agents, and 3 per cent were infections and parasitic disease (Table 12).

Table 12.   Disabling and Nondisabling
Occupational Diseases

	PER CENT
Skin conditions	76
Systemic poisoning	10
Respiratory diseases	3
Infectious and Parasitic Diseases	3
Other	8

Source: Kleinman 1965:2.

And finally, "in the nine-year period, 1955–63, there have been 15 deaths attributed to sunstrokes among agricultural workers; 5 due to infectious disease; and 28 due to toxic materials" (Kleinman 1965:2).

Maintenance of health is also a problem faced by migrant families. Since they are not members of a community, such community health services as immunization programs are generally not available to them. Migrants are usually housed in labor camps or barracks provided by their employers and may lack even the benefit of controlled water purity and sewage disposal. Crowded camp conditions without satisfactory sanitation procedures can and do lead to the rapid spread of disease, especially respiratory disease (Kurth 1960:213). Migrants also possess very little education concerning preventive medicine. Thus, parents are often unaware of the benefits of immunization, welfare clinics, and periodical physical examinations. They are also seldom aware of the symptoms of serious health conditions or of the means for help. In many states the migrant is not qualified to receive welfare help with medical problems so that even if the knowledge is there, the money may not be. The Mexican American migrant is further handicapped in this area because of his language. A mother of an obviously ill child may be unable to communicate with the local agencies sufficiently well to obtain assistance.

The children of migrants often incur injuries or conditions resulting from the lack of day-care facilities. For instance, a child may be overcome by heat while sleeping in a car in the fields while the parents work. Another example would be an injury occurring at "camp" while the child was being watched by a young sibling who did not know how to respond to such a situation.

Lastly, many communities have definite discrimination policies toward migrants. It may be almost impossible to find a doctor or clinic which will admit Mexican American people. Or the hours open for these outsiders to come may conflict with the time spent in the fields.

Some of these conditions are changing now. With the advent of day-care centers, most often sponsored by the federal government, children are provided a place to stay while their parents work. Further, these centers usually function to provide both immunizations to children and health information to parents. Thus in many areas health problems of migrants are decreasing in both number and severity.

Because migrants leave their homes seasonally to work elsewhere, they must find housing in the area in which they work. This housing is set up specifically for their use and is used only seasonally. There is an increasing concern about the condition of this housing on both the state and federal levels. At present at least thirty states have regulations or laws to govern the condition of seasonally used housing (U.S. Department of Agriculture 1965:2). In fact, there are now many publications specifically designed to recommend facilities for housing suitable for migrant use while meeting legal standards (cf. U.S. Department of Agriculture 1965 and U.S. Department of Labor 1962).

The earliest form of migrant housing was the rather picturesque bunk-house, consisting of accommodations primarily for single men. The depression of the 1930's caused a large number of people to turn to farm-work for a living. The large number of people entering the agricultural ranks displaced foreign workers and swamped existing housing. "Many lived out of automobiles, tents, crudely constructed huts and whatever else they could improvise" (Economic Research Service 1965:23). Clusters of people were found residing in the shade of trees or along stream or canal banks. In 1935 the federal government sought to alleviate this situation by building housing units. By 1941 the Farm Security Administration operated seventy-four camps serving 13,000 families. World War II caused a labor shortage, with the result that the federal housing was made available to foreign laborers. Following the war these governmental facilities were given to local public or semipublic agencies or nonprofit organizations to be maintained as agricultural housing. When this transfer took place in 1947, the government owned fifty-three perma-nent and 110 temporary camps (Economic Research Service 1965:24). These same camps, now directed by housing authorities and growers associations, constitute a sizable portion of today's migrant housing. Some have been upgraded since 1947, others are unimproved, leaving a wide range of facilities available. Most, however, have at least a few defi-ciencies. A study of 760 camps in 1966 (Table 13) showed 717 with deficiencies, although 432 of these were approved by state authorities. Most of these deficiencies were connected with problems of sanitation, followed in frequency by unrepaired screens and generally unhealthy camp conditions. In only fourteen cases was the water supply found to be below acceptable standards.

Table 13.   Physical Deficiencies in Migrant Housing, 1966

DEFICIENCY	NUMBER
Campsite (general conditions, safety hazards)	79
Building disrepair, lack of sufficient doors or windows	56
Poor mattresses, not enough beds	28
Absence or disrepair of screens	102
Unsanitary privies; privies in disrepair	245
Unsanitary storage and improper disposal of garbage and refuse	146
Water supply: improper well construction	14
Others	47
Total number	717

Source: United States Department of Health, Welfare and Education 1967:11.

Most housing is owned by the growers, either singly or in an associa-tion. To assure these growers of workers, a single camp ordinarily houses both single men and families. If the housing is owned by an individual grower, normally it is rent free. The migrant lives in the housing while working that grower's crops. He may also be allowed to stay there without charge while working neighbors' crops, providing this is done either before or after the owner's needs are satisfied. Association housing, on the other hand, generally requires small weekly rental payments, but allows the migrant independence with respect to employers. When living in such a camp, migratory workers are free to work for any grower in the association. The third most frequent type of housing is that provided by a housing authority, which, in general practice, is similar to association housing. Occasionally commercial housing is available but this is more expensive and is used by workers who are looking for the particular crop or phase of a crop which will pay the most, rather than for steadier employment from a particular grower. This latter kind of housing is unpopular with growers who are concerned with obtaining help for their entire agricultural needs, not just the more "expensive" jobs.

The educational level of migrant workers is very low. According to the United States Office of Education, migrants have the lowest educational level of any single group in the country. This lack of schooling is as much an effect of as a cause of their migratory status. There are many factors which work against school attendance, such as:

1. Migrants often deem school to be useless while they are migrating from one area to another without spending sufficient time in one place for their children to gain an education.
2. Discrimination by both teachers and parents often occurs in schools. Often the migrant child is not welcome and not allowed to associate with the community's children.
3. Despite the fact that migrants contribute to the wealth of the community, this money does not reach the school system in sufficient amounts to cope with the number of migrant children. Thus, local schools often cannot afford the influx of migrant children.
4. Some school boards are either unaware of or unconcerned with migrant needs in education. If the school year is nearly completed, it may be easier to overlook the needs of such children, even if they are realized.
5. Migrant children, because of their frequent moves, are usually behind their age group. It is sometimes very difficult to ascertain just where each student should be placed and exactly what his needs are. This was particularly true in the past when children moved from one school to the next with no records at all. Current procedures are aimed at either providing the children with records or sending the records ahead to the next anticipated school. Both of these techniques are designed to alleviate his fifth difficulty.
6. Migrant parents are not always concerned about the benefits of education. They may regard school as simply an additional expense that they cannot afford. To have children in school requires certain basic equipment in shoes and clothing and eliminates the earning power of an older child. Therefore, unless a school system is particularly de-

signed to teach migrant children skills they can use as measured by their parents, it will probably not be attended with any regularity (Kurth 1960:209–210).

Because of these factors migrant children do not usually attend school any more regularly, nor for many more years, than did their parents.

Many agencies today are trying to increase the migrant educational level. In 1963 the federal government passed three legislative measures designed to provide a means for such an increase. One bill provided assistance to state adult education programs. One placed a limit on child employment in agriculture, whereas the other provided funds for day-care centers. These latter are to serve both as child-care centers for working parents and as educational centers for preschool children. Other agencies aiding migrant education are the Migrant Ministry of the National Council of Churches, various state committees (official and citizen-organized), community action programs, and private groups such as church societies.

Literature Cited

Babre, William E. 1969. Farm wage developments in 1968. Farm Labor Developments, June.

Committee on Labor and Public Welfare. 1969. The migratory farm labor problem in the United States. United States Senate. Washington, D.C.: Government Printing Office.

Cronemeyer, Cora, ed. 1969a. The annual worker plan in 1968. Farm Labor Developments, June.

———. 1969. Manpower implications of fruit and vegetable mechanization: A colloquium. Farm Labor Developments, December.

———. 1970. Farm employment trends. Farm Labor Developments, April–May.

Davis, Velmar W. 1970. The demand for fruit and vegetables in 1975, Farm Labor Developments, April–May.

Ecomonmic Research Service. 1965. Termination of the Bracero program: Some effects on farm labor and migrant housing needs. In Agricultural economic report No. 77, U.S. Department of Agriculture. Washington, D.C.: Government Printing Office.

Grebler, Leo, Joan W. Moore, and Ralph C. Guzmán. 1970. The Mexican-American people: The nation's second largest minority. New York: The Free Press.

Kleinman, Goldy D. 1965. Occupational health of agricultural workers in California, State of California Department of Public Health.

Kurth, Anne, ed. 1960. Children and youth of domestic agricultural migrant families. In Children and youth in the 1960s. U.S. Department of Health, Education and Welfare. Washington, D.C.: Government Printing Office.

Metzler, William H., and Frederic O. Sargent. 1960. Incomes of migratory agricultural workers. Texas Agricultural Experiment Station Bulletin 950.

U.S. Departmnt of Agriculture. 1965. Housing for seasonal farm workers:

Design and design suggestions. Agriculture information bulletin No. 296. Washington, D.C.: Government Printing Office.

Wilson, Mildred G. 1969. Impact of the federal minimum wage on employment and wages of seasonal farmworkers 1967–1968. Farm Labor Developments, June.

MIGRANT WORKERS: WORST-HOUSED GROUP IN THE NATION

Donald Janson

Traverse City, Mich., November 25. The cherries and apples have all been picked, so the people have moved out of the barn and it is time to move the cattle back in.

Oliver M. Tompkins keeps up to 100 head in his century-old red barn during the winter, using the manure they produce there as fertilizer for his orchards. During the picking season, he keeps migrant farm workers in the same red barn.

The big, gray-haired farmer denies state charges that the drafty barn, its dank basement and a shed attached to one side are "unfit for human habitation" after the cattle depart in the spring. "We fix it up as homey as can be," he says. "The Mexicans never complain, just the do-gooders."

Few Mexican-American or other migrants complain about housing conditions anywhere in the country, for fear of losing work. But because of such quarters as the Tompkins barn, the million seasonal farm workers are the worst-housed group in the United States.

Slums in the major cities offer palatial accommodations—at least in terms of space, construction, kitchen equipment, plumbing and furnishings—compared with many of the chicken coops, tarpaper shacks, cage-size quonset huts and filthy barracks that growers provide for migrant workers.

A comprehensive Federal housing code for migrant camps is matched to varying extents by state codes in 32 states. But because of lax enforcement, clusters of rural hovels across the country serve as seasonal homes for American citizens who accept such housing, along with long-distance travel to reach it, because they prefer punishing field labor at meager pay to charity or welfare.

Federal regulations requiring adequate, safe, healthful housing conditions are enforceable by the Department of Labor when it recruits workers for a farmer from another state (the permanent residence for most migrants is Florida, Texas or California) or when hand-harvested crops are sold in interstate commerce. Departments of health are the usual enforcement agencies for state codes.

But few inspectors have been assigned to the task by either the Labor Department or the states. The job is often delegated to local sanitarians. Some of these are reluctant to crack down on growers because of friendship or local political considerations.

Even when a permit for a farm labor camp is denied, operation often continues on an unlicensed basis, with inspectors looking the other way.

The Tompkins camp, worse than some but representative of many farm labor camps around the country, has operated in violation of the code, both with and without a permit.

"Mr. Tompkins always tells us he is going to put up better housing but he never does," said Ricardo Lopez, who began migrating to the Tompkins farm from Texas 11 years ago.

Since then he and his family have lived not only in the barn but in other Tompkins outbuildings, sometimes squeezing with 100 other migrants into space specified for 55.

Overcrowding makes privacy difficult. Inspectors found temporary partitions installed in the barn while the cattle are out were too low to meet standards.

Mr. Lopez's daughter-in-law, Rebecca, said the Tompkins cabin she and her husband lived in last summer had been a chicken coop and "the chickens continued to come into our cabin."

She noted that no bathing facility, not even a communal shower, was available after a day of hard, sweaty work in trees sprayed with pesticide.

"They can go to the bay," Mr. Tompkins said. "We've got lots of water around here." Grand Traverse Bay is half a mile away.

The Lopezes and State Inspector Jack E. Judd reported cattle feces on barn walls used as living units, a family shoehorned into a 10-by-12-foot space on the barn floor with no cooking facilities, overflowing garbage cans that attracted swarms of insects, unscreened windows, ill-fitting doors, broken furniture and unprotected electric wires.

And adding to the misery of occupants was the absence of laundry facilities. The housing had neither hot nor cold running water for any purpose.

The damp, dark barn basement resembles a medieval dungeon except for the wooden feeding troughs that line the walls, but Mr. Tompkins said his employes "love it" compared with the tents he formerly provided.

Mr. Lopez said his family had decided to speak up, even though it would mean they could not return next year, because "many people come all the way from Texas and babies get sick and it's pretty hard for them to live in a barn like that."

Growers often say that if the Government wants more expensive housing for workers who use it only a month or two at a time, the Government should provide it. They argue that no other industry erects rent-free homes for its labor force. Mr. Tompkins said he could not afford to build "luxury motels" for temporary employes. If forced to, he said, he would have to sell the orchards.

But there are growers who disagree, not many but some in every state in which seasonal farm workers are employed. They contend that profit margins are not too thin to permit substantial investment in migrant housing, that good housing in fact is good business.

In New York's apple-growing Wayne County, Lester Bobb, a migrant from Sanford, Fla., pointed to the neat, elongated building where he and 49 fellow Floridians live two or three to a room.

"It's the best camp I've ever seen," he said, "and I've been coming to New York to work since 1941."

It was built by John Pirello, for $55,000 on a bank loan three years ago, for migrants who harvest his 200 acres of celery.

"You get better workers if you offer good housing," said the genial grower. "Also, people are pleased to have a nice place and they take good care of it. We hire a woman just to keep the camp clean."

Mr. Pirello provides amenities unheard of in most migrant housing: indoor plumbing, a modern kitchen, hot water baseboard heat, insulated partitions, fire-resistant walls.

He agrees with Bernard Swindeman, who is praised by United Migrants for Opportunity for the camps he operates at his apple orchards near Deerfield, Mich., that good housing is profitable because the grower who provides it can attract his choice of harvesters and insist upon no bruising of valuable fruit and vegetables.

The most common arguments by growers against new or improved housing, in addition to the immediate financial one, are that migrants come from worse housing at home in the South and therefore should not object, that they would not keep a good place clean anyway, and that it would be unwise to make long-term investments in an out-of-date system when the trend is toward harvesting by machinery rather than hand labor.

Cornell University, when it came under criticism for bad migrant housing, called in the bulldozers this year, obliterated the housing on its 200 acres of orchards at Sodus, N.Y. and shifted to experimental apple-picking machinery.

Mrs. Joseph Hassle of Keeler, Mich., after three Hassle camps were condemned, said the family was cutting back on strawberry production, shifting entirely to machine-harvested vegetables, and selling its migrant housing to others as tool sheds.

But hand labor will be needed for some crops for a long time to come and housing inspectors who hear farmers tell of plans to sell out or shift crops year after year usually see more threat than action or intention in their words.

Rental housing in the barrios of the Rio Grande Valley and the labor camps in rural ghettos of Florida include some of the worst in the country, but some seasonal farmer workers who migrate north to supplement earnings own their home-base homes and take pride in keeping them clean and attractive.

Workers worth rehiring, Mr. Pirello says, will take good care of good migrant housing away from home so they will have a job for future years. Prudent camp supervision by the grower is a further guarantee of good care.

But housing that meets minimal standards remains a rarity. Reeking outhouses, polluted water, unrefrigerated food and vermine-infested mattresses add to the peril to health of making a home for even a few weeks in dilapidated, cardboard-patched buildings that can be sweltering in the daytime and chilling at night.

"Our clinic spends 80 per cent of its time treating illnesses that shouldn't have happened if health and housing laws had been enforced," said Dr. James R. Tobin of Rochester, director of a rural health program in Wayne County.

State Senator Earl Wilson, a farmer who heads a task force on migrants for the Indiana Legislature, said recently that farm workers were probably immune to most diseases associated with camp conditions. As he made the statement, a migrant child lay hospitalized in Anderson, Ind., with pneumonia attributed to lack of heat at the Del Monte camp at nearby Frankfort.

In New Jersey, Jill Brothers, Inc., was fined for maintaining a camp in Salem County with infestations of mice and roaches.

Overcrowding is common throughout the country and not only hinders privacy but adds to discomfort and contagion also.

With four families living in a single trailer in the Windmill camp at Ontario, N.Y., one child had to sleep in a drawer of a chest.

At West Olive, Mich., Billy Joe Kirk and his wife and six daughters, aged 4 to 16, shared a rank, grimy room unscreened against insects. While not picking blueberries in the adjacent fields of Robert L. Brady this summer, they cooked, ate, dressed and slept on mattresses on the floor of their unpartitioned 12-by-18-foot "home."

Fire is a constant hazard. Dangling, exposed wiring is common. Bettie Cadou shivered for five nights at the Del Monte camp during the recent pickle harvest rather than trust a suspect heater, then went to the hospital with bronchial pneumonia.

William Beckett died July 31 when the trailer he occupied burned at night. The spot where it stood on the Bruce Thompson camp for apple pickers in Wayne County is now just a gap between other migrant houses. Henry Matthews of Haines City, Fla., occupant of a nearby cabin, said in an interview he could not quench the blaze with a garden hose that Mr. Thompson, a county supervisor, had provided instead of the required fire extinguisher.

Migrant-aid groups, long hesitant to take drastic action for fear it might cost farm workers their jobs and the only housing available, sued the states of Michigan and New York this year, seeking court orders to force their health departments to perform their assigned function of enforcing state housing and sanitation codes.

In Colorado, the Colorado Migrant Council and Colorado Legal Services sued 65 growers last month, charging gross violations of that state's housing code.

All of these cases are pending. In Michigan, United Migrants for Opportunity contends that failure of the state Health Department to inspect and prosecute has meant some 80,000 migrants in 2,000 camps "must endure conditions . . . unfit for human habitation."

Its allegations include a single sink on one wall of a barn as the water supply for 15 families; one bed for a family of six; a single room with no partition for two families, and the drowning of a nine-year-old girl while she was trying to bathe in a drainage ditch because the shower did not work.

Other "wretched conditions" cited include flimsy construction, leaking roofs and floors, poor or nonexistent drainage, scarce supplies of safe water, badly ventilated and overflowing privies too few in number and too close to living units, exposed wiring, missing fire extinguishers, faulty heaters, lack of storage for food and clothing, missing refrigerators and cooking facilities, unscreened doors and windows, and inadequate lighting.

All of these conditions are prohibited by state law.

The suit against the New York Health Department charges failure to correct such violations in 49 camps throughout Wayne County.

It also charges Health Department officials "maliciously and willfully conspired with growers . . . in a scheme to circumvent" the law by advising growers that if pressed to bring a camp into conformity with the code they could convey ownership of a shack to the occupying migrant for a token sum and have it reconveyed to the owner at the end of the harvest season.

This ruse has been tried in several states. Attorney General Louis J. Lefkowitz in New York, alerted by the Wayne County suit, charged that Vincent E. Poray deeded his camp near Williamson to migrants from Florida for the season in "a sham and an obvious attempt by the defendant to evade the provisions of the public health law and the state sanitary code."

Last month the State Supreme Court found Mr. Poray to be "still the owner" and enjoined him from violating the housing code.

The suit in Michigan charged that it was the State Health Department's "common practice to cooperate with prosecutors who do not wish to prosecute."

John E. Vogt noted in his annual report as Director of the Michigan Health Department's Migrant Health Project that in rural counties where the prosecutor's position is part-time it is difficult to obtain warrants because growers often retain the public prosecutor as their private attorney.

Minimal fines also render prosecutions ineffective. Mr. Vogt cited the example of a grower who was fined $15 for operating a camp without a license. It is cheaper at such rates for farmers to absorb repeated fines than to comply with the law.

Only in occasional cases such as that of Mr. Tompkins are contempt citations sought. The Grand Traverse County farmer annually got provisional license for his migrant housing on the promise to bring it into compliance. When finally denied a license in 1969 he simply operated without one, then ignored a restraining order last year.

He was jailed for contempt for a weekend. After operating without a license again this year he was sued again, but delays made it possible to complete the harvest without a judgment.

Migrant-oriented groups see no widespread housing solution so long as the responsibility for providing it is left to growers and canneries. Few have applied for even the limited funds available in grants and loans from the Farmers Home Administration in the Department of Agriculture.

When they do, says Lee P. Reno of the Rural Housing Alliance, they are inclined to build "company towns" that unduly limit freedoms and bargaining power of occupants by holding over their heads the threat of a sudden loss of home and job if they voice complaints about pay, accommodations or anything else.

The alliance would like to see a multibillion-dollar Government housing program for farm workers in the "migrant stream" states as well as home-base states unless a 1970 liberalization of the Farmers Home Administration funding program, which has just become effective, proves adequate.

But the program has only about $6-million to allocate, barely enough for even the first handful of applicants.

Mr. Reno found that communities view year-round housing for farm workers much as they do housing for other low-income groups, as lowering real estate values, adding to school costs and increasing welfare potential.

"And running throughout these fears," he said, "is the racism which follows most farm workers throughout their lives, since they are, by and large, minority group members."

So housing in the "migrant stream" states has remained largely seasonal, on-farm and ramshackle. State Senator Thomas Teague of Indiana described it last month, following a tour of farm labor camps, as "worse than anything I ever saw while serving in Vietnam."

Suggested Readings

Southwest Cultural Traditions

Benrimo, Dorothy. 1966. *Camposantos.* Fort Worth, Tex.: Amon Carter Museum of Western Art.

A collection of photographic essays on the last cultural expression of the Spanish-American. Benrimo et al. portray the uniqueness of *camposantos*, or holy fields, in northern New Mexico as a cultural trait untainted or influenced by the Anglo. In this form of art is found the expression of honest devotion, love, and passion.

Campa, Arthur L. 1963. *Treasure of the Sangre de Cristos: Tales and Traditions of the Spanish Southwest.* Norman: University of Oklahoma Press.

A collection of stories from the Spanish period to the near present. Campa writes about tales of lost mines stacked with bars of gold, of mule loads of silver cached away in outlaw hoards, of fabulous Jesuit treasures buried when that order was expelled from New Spain, and other nonmaterial wealth stories.

Davila, Mario. 1971. "'Compadrazgo: Fictive Kinship in Latin America," in *Readings in Kinship and Social Structure,* Nelson Graburn, ed. New York: Harper & Row, Publishers.

An attempt to present a possible explanation of the differences in form and function of a fictive kinship relationship, *campadrazgo,* in Latin American "peasant" communities. The ethnographic data is limited to Mexico and Central America. The importance here is that the areas dealt with are centers of contact, conquest, and merging of Spanish culture with the high Indian cultures.

Kiev, Ari. 1968. *Curanderismo: Mexican-American Folk Psychiatry.* New York: The Free Press.

Through psychological and anthropological investigation, Kiev presents information dealing with successful therapy for mental disturbances. Kiev feels that *curanderos* (folk psychiatrists) play an important role because they relate to the patients' institutional environment and belief systems.

Mintz, Sidney W., and Eric R. Wolf. 1950. "An Analysis of Ritual Co-Parenthood (Compadrazgo)," *Southwestern Journal of Anthropology,* Vol. 6, Winter.

An analysis of the complex relationships established by godparent-hood. The writers describe the system in terms of its functions in Mexican society. There is also an excellent discussion of the dynamics of the *compadrazgo* ritual and its historical antecedents.

Paredes, Américo. 1958. *With His Pistol in His Hand: A Border Ballad and Its Hero.* Austin: University of Texas Press.

This is an excellent study of the attitudes and life style of Mexicans living along the Texas–Mexico Rio Grande border. The border hero, Gregorio Cortez, is presented through a historical and folklore analysis. Moreover, Paredes presents the development of the *corrido*, or Mexican folksong. He also offers a comparison between the Cortez ballad and other legends of border heros, e.g., Scottish and English.

Tanner, Clara Lee. 1968. *Southwest Indian Craft Arts.* Tucson: University of Arizona Press.

A superb volume identifying the art of the southwest Indian. It shows the intimacies of design and form which separate the products of various tribes, making each distinctive.

Trent, Elwood Sanford. 1950. *The Architecture of the Southwest.* New York: W. W. Norton & Company, Inc.

Trent describes the southwestern people's adaptation and survival in this harsh land. He offers a state-by-state description of settlement patterns and architecture.

Chicano Problem Areas

Barrio, Raymond. 1969. *The Plum Plum Pickers.* Sunnyvale, Calif.: Ventura Press.

A novel depicting the bleak existence of migrant farmworkers in Santa Clara County, California, and how they fall prey to exploitation.

Ferman, Louis A., et al. (editors). 1969. *Poverty in America: A Book of Readings,* second edition. Ann Arbor: The University of Michigan Press.

The issues raised by this book of readings are the problems of poverty in its larger context and how these problems meet the issue of the Great Society. Individual articles focus on definitions and prevalence of poverty, the structure of poverty, the relationship of poverty to the economy, the values and life styles of poor people, and various programs dealing with problems of social, economic, and cultural deprivation.

Galarza, Ernesto. 1964. *Merchants of Labor: The Mexican Bracero Story.* San Jose, Calif.: The Rosicrucian Press.

The classic study of the bracero in California. The labor movement is traced from 1880 to 1942. Galarza's focus is on the adverse effects of the bracero program on domestic labor. He also discusses the problems encountered in the recent attempts to organize farmworkers.

————. **1970.** *Spiders in the House and Workers in the Field.* Notre Dame, Ind.: University of Notre Dame Press.

A case study of political manipulation aimed at oppressing the poor people of America. This is the case of Di Giorgio Corporation in the San Joaquin Valley and the National Farm Workers' Union. It deals with a series of lawsuits for libel brought by Di Giorgio against the NFWU and the producers of the allegedly libelous motion picture "Poverty in the Valley of Plenty."

Matthiessen, Peter. 1969. *Sal Si Puedes: César Chávez and the New American Revolution.* New York: Delta Publishing Co., Inc.

Sal Si Puedes presents a portrait of César Chávez' crusade, the greatest agricultural labor strike in the history of the United States, and its implications extending beyond the San Joaquin Valley.

Sánchez, George I. 1940. *Forgotten People: A Study of New Mexicans.* Albuquerque: University of New Mexico Press.

This important work calls attention to the plight of the Chicanos of New Mexico by showing how the governing body ignores the Hispano population. Because of the lack of positive response to his work, Sánchez believes, "mine are still the forgotten people. *Paso por aquí.*" As a native of New Mexico, Sánchez writes this historical and sociological account with feeling, insight, compassion and love for his people.

Valentine, Charles A. 1968. *Culture and Poverty: Critique and Counter Proposals.* Chicago: University of Chicago Press.

A challenge to Oscar Lewis' "Culture-of-Poverty" concept. Valentine refutes many theories which blame the poor for being in poverty. Valentine notes that "the cultural values of the poor may be much the same as middle-class values, merely modified in practice because of situational stresses."

PART III
Tomorrow

The articles in this section all represent Chicano efforts to rectify social, economic, and political inequities. The first selection, by Antonio Camejo, relates the events and aftermath of the bloody street riots in East Los Angeles in August, 1969. In those riots Chicanos took to the streets when all other efforts to redress legitimate grievances had failed. Patricia Blawis recounts the development of the Alianza under Reies Tijerina in New Mexico. Having tried unsuccessfully to reclaim Chicano land through the courts, the Alianza has reopened the Mexican-American War. An excerpt from the Plan de Santa Barbara puts forward the basic philosophy for the development of Chicano studies programs on college campuses. César Chávez describes the development of the United Farmworker's Union. Camejo reports on the founding and achievements of the La Baza Unida party in south Texas, and Alfredo Cuéllar surveys the whole range of Chicano political movements, including such lobbying groups as MECHA, MAYO, and so on.

All of these cases represent the philosophy of cultural pluralism and ethnic group self-determination in action. There is nothing really revolutionary about these cases, however. They all have mainstream precedents; they are all in the great American tradition. Local control of education is deeply rooted in the system of parent-controlled school boards. The formation of lobbying groups is an established practice at all levels of American politics. The use of the strike and the right of collective bargaining are commonly understood guarantees established in bloodshed and consolidated by such institutions as the AFL–CIO, UAW, USW, ILGWU, and Teamsters. Community rule by majority vote is a pillar of American national philosophy, and the appeal by political leaders for bloc ethnic voting in order to obtain and maintain power is as American as Carmine de Sapio, Jimmy Walker, Richard Daley, and Bobby Kennedy. The riots *of East Los Angeles and the confrontation politics of the* Alianza *are no less American than the Boston Tea Party. The political guarantee of self-determination—rule of the people, by the people—is the most sacred tenet of the American way of life. The Chicano movement is an attempt to have that guarantee extended to include Americans of Mexican descent.*

Once the basic right of self-determination is acknowledged, many of the current conflicts between Anglos and Chicanos will be automatically resolved. At one time the greatest problem faced by Chicanos was that they were ignored by the system. Discrimination, poverty, hunger, disease, and lack of education were simply not recognized by the society at large as constituting problems. At present, the situation seems to be changing. Chicanos are now apparently recognized as ill fed, ill housed, under-educated, and discriminated against in such areas as employment and health care. Presidential commissions have filed official reports making Chicano poverty a legitimate concern of the system, and blue-ribbon panels of experts have been charged with making recommendations for change. Government and industry are making rather flamboyant gestures to solve these problems now that they have become legitimate. Special education programs for migrant children, retraining centers for farm-workers who have been rendered obsolete by mechanization, surplus commodity programs, and health clinics are examples of such gestures. But few, if any, of these efforts are undertaken in the spirit of self-determination. Anglos define the problem and Anglos figure out their solution.

This relationship between problem definition and problem solution reduces the effectiveness of such programs. The Anglo definition of Chicano poverty, for instance, includes a component which blames the Chicano for this condition. This, in turn, leads to solutions that are oriented toward changing the Chicano rather than the conditions (created by Anglo society) which cause the poverty.

If Spanish is a hindrance to acceptance by white society, the reasoning goes, then eliminate Spanish. If machismo is seen as preventing Chicano men from fulfilling their responsibilities as husbands and fathers, then get rid of it by educating children away from it in Anglo schools. If extended family ties prevent individualism and independence and keep Chicanos from amassing critical amounts of capital, then surely the answer must be to strike at the heart of this cultural complex and undermine it.

The Chicano understanding of the problem is rather different, and so therefore are the solutions.

1. The Spanish language is not a hindrance to economic success; Anglo refusal to accept Spanish as a legitimate tongue is the hindrance. Anglos fail to understand, as Ortego (1970) has shown, that a Spanish accent is no worse than a Boston accent (John F. Kennedy) or a German accent (Werner Von Braun) or a New York accent (John Lindsay) or a Texas accent (Lyndon Johnson). Anglos need to be educated to understand this and Spanish needs to be perpetuated in school rather than discouraged. Chicanos are bilingually advantaged, not disadvantaged. Gingos suffer from a disease known as terminal monolingualism; they will go to their graves knowing only one language and lacking the mind-expanding ability to think in two tongues. Pobrecitos.

2. Machismo is not a peculiarly Chicano or Mexican complex, nor is it destructive of personality and family life, as Anglos would like to believe. Under conditions of abject poverty and despair, where there seems to be no hope of getting out from under the repression of human dignity that such conditions breed, men may be driven to irrational acts of bravado. But to confuse this with the normal cultural complex of machismo is absurd. John Wayne and Audie Murphy have provided a socialization image of machismo for several generations of gringitos. Machismo is a generally Mediterranean trait which encompasses the development and maintenance of a strong masculine image, as well as the knowledge that the image is only safe so long as women allow it to be. Although it is never articulated (some things always remain unsaid in every culture), every Chicano knows that strong machismo depends on strong feminismo—that is, a sense of identity and security of personality on the part of women. If there is any adjustment in the macho–feminino relationship that needs to be made, Chicanos will make it. Meanwhile why not create some programs for the gringos so that they can discover again who they are and stop bickering about male and female roles. Pobrecitos.

3. Extended family obligations are not an obstacle to amassing capital. The wealthiest families in America got that way through family enterprise. The Greeks, Chinese, Jews, and other ethnic groups have used the extended family system as a means of economic mobility for generations. This technique is hardly un-American. And extended kinship obligations do not undermine individuality and independence. If rugged Yankee individualism depends upon cheating between brothers, cutthroat business practices among relatives, abandonment of the aged as an economic drain, and so on, then it is the Anglos who need cultural retraining. Pobrecitos.

The chapters in this section reflect our view of the relationship between problem definition and problem solution. They are examples of Chicanos defining Chicano problems and advocating solutions that fit those definitions.

LESSONS OF THE LOS ANGELES CHICANO PROTEST

Antonio Camejo

The events in East Los Angeles of Aug. 29 through Sept. 16 constituted the most significant upsurge and mobilization of the Chicano people in recent years. The Chicano struggle for self-determination was taken to a higher level, with repercussions not only for La Raza but for the entire Third World struggle in the United States.

The Aug. 29 National Chicano Moratorium against the War in Vietnam, which mobilized some 30,000 Chicanos, was the largest antiwar protest in Los Angeles history and the largest organized, independent mobilization of an oppressed national minority in the present radicalization. Likewise, the Sept. 16 action was a mass response to the police attack of Aug. 29.

All together, within a brief two-and-one-half-week period, the huge East Los Angeles Chicano community was thrown into motion in protest over oppressive conditions, especially the actions of the Los Angeles County sheriffs on Aug. 29. No less than 100,000 people appeared on Sept. 16 to vent their protest in spite of intimidation tactics and an extended occupation of the community by the police.

Originally canceled by its conservative leadership, the usually establishment-oriented Sept. 16 Mexican Independence parade this year was infused with militant protest because of the community outrage which was brought to bear.

This mass upheaval in East Los Angeles is part of and a continuation of the radicalization and independent organization that has occurred throughout Aztlan in the last two years. The Los Angeles events confirmed the validity of the independent, mass-action concepts developed by the Texas Raza Unida Party, the Colorado Raza Unida Party, and the Chicano Moratorium.

The history of Aug. 29 to Sept. 16 can be described as an intense period of debate, education, discussion and struggle for a correct tactical political course of action.

The Aug. 29, 30,000-strong Chicano Moratorium demonstration against the Vietnam war was something new in American political life. Never before had an oppressed nationality in this country so consciously mobi-

Reprinted with permission from *The Militant*, Vol. 34, No. 38 (October 16, 1970).
Antonio Camejo is a Chicano activist and scholar. He is instructor in the department of Latin and Mexican studies at Merritt College in Oakland, California. In 1970 he was the Socialist Worker's party candidate for superintendent of public education in California.

lized in such large numbers to protest a war from which they suffer disproportionally.

The successful action came as a result of a correct political outlook and painstaking organizational efforts by the National Chicano Moratorium Committee (NCMC) leadership. Rosalio Munoz and others in the NCMC built the Aug. 29 action on the basis of involving as large a number as possible around the demand "Bring our *carnales* [brothers] home now." Anyone who supported that demand and action was welcome to help—regardless of their opinions on any other questions. As the date drew nearer, more and more sections of the community became involved in the preparations.

To seasoned observers of the antiwar movement, the Aug. 29 action was something to behold. This was a powerful march—30,000 people marched and loudly chanted slogans which expressed their pride and confidence. Thousands lined the streets to cheer the demonstration, indicating the overwhelming community support for the antiwar action. Clearly this was the beginning of a significant movement in the United States.

For whatever reasons, the Los Angeles County sheriffs attacked and dispersed that demonstration, and apparently planned it that way.

The police did much to provoke that peaceful demonstration, filming events "carefully" to gather "evidence" of "violence" for later use. Over 500 specially trained deputies fully armed with riot gear were on the scene, stationed on every corner.

The police finally used an incident at least a block away from the rally as a pretext for their attack. In the course of the assault, they managed to kill three *carnales*, including Ruben Salazar, who was respected and known by the entire community. The reaction went much deeper than they had anticipated or bargained for. In an explosion of anger, a number of Anglo-owned businesses in the Chicano community went up in flames. The police attack mobilized the entire Chicano community in Los Angeles and drew sharp protest across the country.

The unprovoked police assault brought virtually every segment of the Chicano community (as well as many other people) to their feet in protest. Many not previously involved now sought a militant and effective answer to the police. Newly aroused forces were brought into contact with the Moratorium's outlook.

In the face of this unforeseen development, the ruling class began a concerted effort to block the growing protest. The Democratic Party sent its ward heelers around to cool it. Simultaneously, Los Angeles mayor Yorty, Los Angeles County sheriff Pitchess, and Los Angeles police chief Davis began cries of "outside agitators," attempting to isolate the Moratorium leadership from the community.

The line of argument expressed by Yorty and his friends came down to: "They were seen running around throwing bottles! They were from outside. They weren't from your community! We know you are 'good meskins.' They were from Texas, Denver, Oakland, and not only that, they were communists!" Los Angeles County sheriff Peter J. Pitchess talked about all the "inflammatory literature" they had found at the park. The sheriff pointed out how a pamphlet with Mao's picture on it had been distributed to marchers.

The whole intent of this slander attack was to confuse the community about where the violence came from, telling people that the violence came from those protesting, that is, from the oppressed.

The truth is that the capitalist system commits violence every day in many different forms. When a *chamaquito* [child] walks into school and the teacher can't speak Spanish, that's violence. When such students are held back year after year, or classified as "mentally retarded," and finally drop out of high school at the rate of 70 per cent, as in Los Angeles, that's violence against people. The police brutality against Brown people which goes on every day in the barrio is violence.

Since this is the overriding reality of this capitalist society, the first thing the ruling class attempted after Aug. 29 was to make the victim look like the criminal and the criminal look like the victim.

What was the required response of the Chicano community in this situation? An attempt to intimidate the Chicano community into silence had obviously occurred. What was necessary was a massive and clear response to that attack. It was necessary to go out and mobilize the masses of Chicano and Latino people in a militant protest of the police repression and the war in Vietnam.

To deepen what had been started Aug. 29 and involve new and broader layers of the community was the task at hand. To bring the power of the entire community to bear, it was essential to involve large numbers of people in the formulation, planning, and organization of whatever response was to take place.

On Sept. 1, at the first mass community meeting called to discuss the question, a peaceful and legal mass march and rally to be held on *el 16 de septiembre* was unanimously agreed to. The action was to focus around three things: (1) to protest the police attack and murders of Aug. 29, reaffirming the constitutional rights of free speech and assembly; (2) to complete the antiwar protest which was cut short; and (3) to commemorate the 160th anniversary of Mexican independence. It was assumed that everyone who supported the demands of the action should be mobilized to participate.

The meeting wanted to show the police that they had not succeeded in intimidating anyone and that in fact they had awakened so many people that if they tried it again on the 16th there would be perhaps 1,000,000 people in the streets.

Also needed was a reaffirmation of non-exclusion in the movement and an answer to the red-baiting. It was necessary to clearly state that the police were solely responsible for the violence that had taken place.

How could gringo politicians talk about "outsiders" and about Corky Gonzales "crossing state lines"? No Chicano is an outsider in Aztlan.

But the issue also went much deeper. The ruling class uses the same slander tactics against all movements in order to divide them and obscure the real political issues. A resolute rejection of such tactics, a response by masses of people, was necessary.

The first move after Aug. 29 by the NCMC and the Congress of Mexican-American Unity (CMAU) was to raise bail money to get *everyone* out of jail as soon as possible.

They did not, however, act quickly to answer the red-baiting, the cries of "outside agitator," or the hints of the district attorney that perhaps Corky Gonzales could be indicted for violation of the Civil Rights Act for "crossing state lines to foment a riot."

When the idea of *el 16 de septiembre* was first proposed and unanimously passed by the Sept. 1 community meeting of 600, the NCMC leadership tended to go along with it but then delayed in actually organizing the community for it. You might say that some of the leaders had either lost confidence in their own ability to mobilize people or weren't interested in involving broader layers of the community. This was reflected in their reluctance to call mass community meetings, a reluctance which grew more pronounced as time went on.

The NCMC leadership was confronted with a genuine mass movement and then was hit with intense pressure from conservative groups who feared and opposed the mass mobilization that was occurring. Rather than turning to newly radicalizing layers of the community for support and mobilizing people around the ideas that made the Moratorium successful, the Moratorium leaders began accommodating to the desires of the right, especially the desires of the Comite Civico Patriotico Mexicano, the group of businessmen and "civic leaders" who normally put on the Sept. 16 parade.

The Comite initially called off the parade for "fear of violence" after the first wave of red-baiting by Yorty and others. This met with such outrage from the aroused community that the Comite realized a demonstration would occur anyway. They then reversed themselves and rescheduled the parade—to throttle the militancy they feared by tightly organizing the parade. Many behind-the-scenes meetings then ensued.

It was at this point that the NCMC leadership faltered. Instead of trying to involve the Comite on the basis of a militant protest, they accommodated to the conservative leanings of the Comite. When red-baiting occurred in the movement, they let it pass.

An organization called LUCHA (League of United Citizens to Help Addicts) became involved during this period, attempting to bureaucratically take control of the monitor system for the march and set the tone for what would take place on the 16th.

LUCHA, which has worked closely with the apparatus of the Democratic Party in the past and having at least one of its members on Mayor Yorty's staff, deepened the red-baiting, talking about "getting tough" with "left-wing elements." Their aim was to get the planning for the demonstration out of the hands of the militants and back into the hands of the so-called responsible elements such as the Comite and all the other businessmen, *vendidos* [sellouts] and gringo politicians who traditionally run the Independence Day parade.

The leaders of the NCMC and the Congress of Mexican-American Unity did not answer Moe Aguirre of LUCHA when he got up and said that "we must make sure that outside agitators and left-wing elements do not cause any violence on the 16th." They remained silent. That is a critical mistake when a struggle like this begins to take place. That is always the first step, the opening of the door, to coopting the entire movement and throttling any militant protest by the masses.

Abe Tapia, president of the Mexican American Political Association (MAPA), correctly asked San Francisco MAPA president John A. Ramirez to answer an attack by San Francisco supervisor Bob Gonzalez to the effect that "white long-hair radicals" had caused the "rioting" in Los Angeles. Ramirez stated that "the only group that routinely incites riots in our community is the police department."

But, unfortunately even Tapia didn't think the question out thoroughly. In the mass community meeting, Sept. 1, he got up and said, "Progressive Labor is having a demonstration in Atlantic Square tomorrow, and I want 20 *vatos* [guys] to go down there with me and take care of them."

Progressive Labor Party is rightly despised in the Chicano community because of its anti-nationalist line. But MAPA, the NCMC and CMAU, while disassociating themselves from the action, should have defended PL's right to hold that rally. What was *needed* was a statement that said, "We are not going to play the role of cop in doing to PL what the police did to us the 29th. We are for the right of assembly whether we agree with those who are assembling or not. That's what the right of freedom of speech and assembly is all about." Unfortunately the situation wasn't answered in that manner and so this fed the fire of the red-baiting attack.

We must look carefully at this question because it will occur again and again in future struggles. What is the ideology used by the ruling class to justify the war in Vietnam? Anti-communism. That's what the Democrats and Republicans have used to justify the devastation of Vietnam, the slaughter of the Vietnamese people, and the murder of over 8,000 *carnales* in Vietnam. Aug. 29 began breaking down the anti-communist myth and so the gringo capitalist politicians reintroduced it right into the movement in Los Angeles.

When you don't answer red-baiting correctly you can end up in league with some strange people. For example, the following letter from the Atlantic Square Retail Merchant's Association was addressed to Esteban E. Torres, president of the Congress of Mexican-American Unity, and Rosalio Munoz, Chicano Moratorium Committee:

> Gentlemen: In behalf of all of the Atlantic Square community, I want to express our appreciation for your statement regarding the "proposed Atlantic Square Rally" of September 2. That statement and its wide circulation by your organizations cooled what may have resulted in an explosive situation. This responsible action is deeply appreciated by all Atlantic Square merchants and employees.
>
> Signed Martin Brooks, president.

Even Sheriff Pitchess issued a statement in "appreciation" for stopping the PL rally!

So you see, one must be very careful how these attacks are answered. The way to deal with PL and their incorrect politics is not to go beat them up. That doesn't clarify anything. PL says that nationalism is reactionary. If you go down and break up their demonstration, they can use that to confuse people. The way to answer PL is to expose their politics, that is, to take them on on the basis of their ideas and to educate people as to why they are wrong.

As a result of the accommodation by the NCMC leaders to the conservative orientation of LUCHA and the Comite, a change began to take place in the character of the 16th. The original leaflet put out by the NCMC and CMAU calling for the Sept. 16 action clearly stated:

> Ruben Salazar, Gilberto Diaz, Lynn Ward, We shall not forget you! . . . There will be a peaceful, legal parade and rally to commemorate the 160th anniversary of Mexican Independence and to protest the unprovoked police attack on the Saturday, August 29, rally against the war in Vietnam, reasserting our constitutional right of freedom of speech and assembly.

Suddenly a few days prior to the 16th, the NCMC came out with a new leaflet which read: "16th of September parade and rally. . . . Traditional route . . . everyone is cordially invited to participate. . . ." It listed the assembly point and that's it.

What happened to Ruben Salazar? What happened to the police repression? What happened to the talk of protest? Another little sheet of paper put out by the monitors committee, controlled by LUCHA, stated as point number 11 in a "Code of Conduct," "No inflammatory signs will be carried by marchers."

It was clear that they were on the way to changing the character of the 16th from a protest to a "respectful, responsible show of unity," as Munoz himself favored. Members of the Young Socialist Alliance and Socialist Workers Party, along with other people from the community, passed out a statement to one of the mass community meetings, expressing concern with what was happening and outlining a course of action to correct it. The statement read in part:

> Yorty, Nixon and Pitchess would like to see a 16th confined to a few *vendido* and gringo politicians eating enchiladas. They would like to see us parade in our "colorful, picturesque" clothes and terminate the day with a picnic. They don't want to see our entire community, enraged by the death of three innocent *carnales* (murdered by the police) protest the *chango* [cop] brutality. They want us to forget about the war, to forget about why we marched four miles in the hot sun on Saturday, Aug. 29.

We outlined the need to answer the red-baiting and reaffirm the three-pronged purpose of the 16th: (1) an antiwar protest; (2) a protest against the police repression; and (3) a commemoration of Mexican

Independence. The statement continued, "If we fail to respond in this way, we will be helping to continue and to intensify their victimization of our community and our leaders."

The militancy of that statement reflected the sentiments of many, as was shown on Sept. 16. In spite of the Comite's attempts to throttle the militancy, a minimum of 100,000 people appeared for the action in a mood to protest. The militant contingents in the parade were vigorously cheered. The Chicano Moratorium contingent which led the march grew from around 300 at the start to some 3,000 by the end of the route.

Those who had read the first leaflet issued, or who had made up their minds long before to protest, came prepared for that. There were several militant contingents, including the NCMC contingent, interspersed throughout the march. The Chicano community of Lincoln Heights brought their own protest banners against the war and against the police murders. One of their large signs read: "Stop the War, Stop the Cops." Another contingent carried a huge portrait of Ruben Salazar which was later taken to West Los Angeles Community College and placed above the entrance to the campus. Militant chants of "Chicano Power" and "Raza Si, Guerra No!" could be heard along the march.

Usually march organizers delay the start of a march to maximize participation. The 16th started on time to *minimize* participation. Thousands of people were still pouring into the assembly point by the time the parade was already on its way. They were greeted with a sound truck which told them that the last contingent had left and that everything was over. Some demonstrators asked another sound truck following the last contingent to call on spectators to join the march. The truck began to do this but was immediately stopped by monitors.

Each contingent was surrounded by LUCHA monitors, and the more militant they were the more monitors were around them. Because of the tight monitoring system, only about 10,000 actually marched, contrary to the *People's World* claim that the "demarcation between marchers and spectators was all but erased. . . ."

The fact that the march occurred, that over 100,000 gathered, and that the mass militancy was expressed—these were significant victories. The cops did not dare attack this march. But in light of what could have been done, the march represented a partial, inadequate answer to the police riot of two and one-half weeks earlier.

The Comite's influence on the parade insured that it would have an aspect that can only be described as disgraceful.

The police were there in force on every street corner. All the traditional floats were there in a spirit that made you wonder whether Salazar had died at all or whether it was just a rumor. The Sept. 26th issue of *People's World*, apparently in ecstasy, reported, "Bands, horsemen, and women dressed in brilliant Mexican national costumes, several floats, and cars carrying politicians led off the parade." They don't bother to inform us that two of the floats belonged to the U.S. Navy. A destroyer and a missile launcher! And this was supposed to be a protest against the war!

Some people overheard a conversation among a few Chicanas who were watching the parade go by. "The pigs are laughing at us! They're laughing at us!" they said. In the eyes of the police, these were the "good Mexicans," the "peaceful Mexicanos," the "humble Mexicanos." And those police were just smiling.

When the Lincoln Heights contingent came by, I was standing among the spectators to get a feel for their reaction. In front of me was an older woman who had just watched several floats go by, including the U.S. Navy's, a savings and loan company, and Sloan's cleaners. When she saw that militant contingent approaching she lit up and began yelling to them, "*No se vendan, no se vendan!*" [Don't capitulate. Don't sell out!] And that was the spirit of thousands of people along the parade route.

The "responsible" leaders had their day. Jesse Unruh, the gringo Democrat running for governor of California, who recently stated that "An attack on violent crime ought to be the number one priority in California," had a truck with signs saying "*Arriba con Unruh*" [Up with Unruh] and two additional cars in the parade! And while this gringo politician, who has never done a thing for the Mexicano was shaking hands with some of the spectators, LUCHA monitors were running onto the sidewalks and ripping bundles of *The Militant* out of the hands of YSAers and SWPers.

And all the enchilada-eating politicians were there on a reviewing stand at the conclusion of the parade. Members of the Mexican consulate, including a military officer of the same army that slaughtered hundreds of students in Tlatelolco, also paraded.

On the reviewing stand was some *vendido* who was announcing all the floats as they went by, including identifying the various contingents in a a happy, friendly manner, as if to say, "The community is all out here together, isn't that wonderful?" And down the road came the contingent from Casa de Carnalismo, a barrio youth group with a beautifully painted banner. The announcer began, "Ah, Casa de Carnalismo. . . ." He took one look at the slogan on that banner and almost turned pale. It read "*Tierra y Libertad, Tenemos el Derecho de Armarnos para Defendernos.*" [Land and Liberty, we have the right to armed self-defense.] Needless to say, the announcer didn't read it out loud, and I don't think there were any LUCHA monitors who were about to take the banner away from those youth.

The scheduled rally at the end of the parade was canceled by the NCMC because of the denial of a permit for the East Los Angeles Community College stadium. Instead, a short rally of about 5,000 was held in a college parking lot where Munoz and Torres spoke briefly about having a rally on Oct. 12, to be called, of all things, "*El Dia de La Raza.*" (Oct. 12 traditionally commemorates the arrival of the Spaniards in the new world and is not a holiday popular with those who are proud of their Indian heritage.)

Young Chicanos angered and frustrated with what had occurred in the face of their expectations, vented their anger on the police, resulting in at least one Chicano and a deputy wounded and some 68 arrests, including some damage to Atlantic Square businesses.

How did the various political tendencies claiming to have a program for struggle and change respond to the events of Aug. 29–Sept. 16?

Prior to Aug. 29, the Progressive Labor Party attacked the NCMC as being "divisive of the working class" because it was organizing a nationalist antiwar action under the slogan "Bring the *Carnales* Home." PL, which considers Chicano nationalism to be "reactionary," opposed the slogan because it didn't call for bringing Anglo GIs home as well. They argued that if all the Chicano soldiers were withdrawn from Vietnam the war would continue with those remaining!

It is patently absurd to believe that the Chicano masses could build a movement strong enough to force the government to bring all the *carnales* home, and that the Afro-American and Anglo GIs would simply say, "That's OK. We'll continue fighting." Any movement that was so successful would affect the entire Army, Anglos as well as Blacks.

Nevertheless, PL participated with their own banner (Smash Racism) in what they had characterized as a basically reactionary movement. After the attack of the 29th, PL called their own sectarian action in the Atlantic Square business district of East Los Angeles on the very day of Ruben Salazar's funeral. In terms of a program of action for the masses of the Chicano people in response to the police attack, PL had nothing to say.

The Communist Party did not play a role in its own name in the Chicano Moratorium Committee, nor did it project any concrete response to the repression of Aug. 29. However, the general approach of those sympathetic to the line of the CP was to "let things cool down." They favored a toned-down *16 de septiembre*, after it was proposed, with an emphasis on Mexican Independence rather than on a protest of the war and the police repression.

While Ricardo Romo of the Peace and Freedom Party participated in several press conferences organized by the NCMC just prior to and after Aug. 29, the PFP played no role in the aftermath. Romo himself did not project any course of action for the community. Apparently not grasping the significance of the upsurge in the Chicano community of Los Angeles, Romo left the scene and played no role in organizing for the Sept. 16 action.

The Brown Berets initially played a role in the first two Chicano Moratoriums but did little to build the Aug. 29 action. A few days before the march they published an attack on the Moratorium committee and on Rosalio Munoz personally, accusing him of having "stolen" the NCMC from them. Although the Berets did participate in the Aug. 29 march and rally, they played no role in the aftermath. Individual members of the Brown Berets did participate in the work of building for the 16th, but not the organization nor any of its recognized leaders.

The Los Angeles events involved a social confrontation of great importance. This upheaval mobilized tens of thousands and foreshadowed greater social conflicts to come. One can easily imagine what could have transpired in Los Angeles if a Raza Unida Party with an experienced, independent, authoritative leadership and a correct program had existed. A mammoth protest of the entire Chicano community backed by its supporters could have rocked Los Angeles and been a giant stride toward Chicano control of the Chicano community.

While the Los Angeles events marked a new stage in the Chicano struggle, the Sept. 16 action fell short of its potential. The responsibility for that lies squarely on the shoulders of the Moratorium leadership, who had the credibility and authority to lead an enormous, effective, militant protest.

The debate and struggle that took place within the movement over correct policy has important lessons for future social battles of this nature. The mobilization of an entire community including its most conservative elements will occur many times again, and the debates and underlying issues will be much the same. The experience gained by the militants in the Los Angeles struggle will be important for the future development of the Chicano movement.

TIJERINA AND THE LAND GRANTS

Patricia Bell Blawis

Making of a Leader

Reies Lopez Tijerina was born in Falls City near San Antonio, Texas, on September 21, 1923 in an area torn from Mexico by the United States. Although this conquest took place 80 years before his birth, it fixed his place in society as a member of a Mexican minority. His grandfather was nearly lynched by a ruling majority that spoke English.

At an early age he heard accounts of cruelties carried out by Mexican-hating ranchers and Texas Rangers. These ruthless men were determined to keep Mexicans at work in fields where black slaves had once grown the cotton that made the owners rich.

Reies himself became a worker when he was four years old. His father showed him how to pile into a heap the cotton that fell to the ground. This small pile was added to the family pickings.

Things were tough in Texas. Even whole families couldn't make it on

From *Tijerina and the Land Grants*, by Patricia Bell Blawis. Reprinted by permission of International Publishers Co., Inc., Copyright © 1971.

Patricia Bell Blawis has written many articles and pamphlets regarding the situation of Chicanos in the Southwest. She was Northern New Mexico coordinator of the Poor People's March to Washington and during that campaign acted as Reies Tijerina's press secretary.

25 or 35 cents an hour. They headed north, to the beet fields of Colorado, Wyoming, or even Michigan. Forget about school. There has always been a double standard of school attendance—one for the children of migrants and one for everybody else. Reies Tijerina did not learn English until he was eleven, to read and write until still later.

In the spring, the highways north from San Antonio were filled with truckloads of human beings, packed too tight to breathe, 60,000 of them, grandparents, parents, children and even babies. They made the long and difficult trek to the Michigan beetfields that supply our tables with sugar. In six months they might average $500–$600 total pay and to earn this everyone had to work, including little children. Low as these earnings were, they were more than they would have made by staying in Texas and picking cotton.

Every April, they rode north in trucks and sometimes in cattle cars. The Texas ranchers, enraged when agents for the sugarbeet companies began tapping their great reserves of cheap labor, passed a law to bar out-of-state recruiters (Texas Emigrant Agent Law of 1929). But the law didn't keep the people from leaving and the ranchers were forced to bring in more Mexican workers to pick cotton.

The people of Mexico have always resented the way Mexican labor is treated in Texas, and bitter charges of racial discrimination against those workers appeared in the Mexican press. "We are not the Servants of the Continent," declared an article published in Mexico City during World War II. "The Nazis of Texas are not political partisans of the Fuehrer of Germany nor do they desire his triumph; but indeed they are slaves of the same prejudices and superstitions."

When Tijerina was in his teens, the family spent four years harvesting crops in Michigan, Ohio and Indiana. Neighbors from San Antonio, the Escobars, also made the trip north, and whichever family finished their row first hurried to help the other. Attractive Maria Escobar later was to become Reies' first wife, travel the country with him, and bear his five older children.

During the depression, Reies and his brothers occasionally worked in factories in Pontiac. But there was ugly discrimination in Michigan, as well as Texas. It was a hard life, and young Reies thought about ways of improving it. One day an evangelist came along, and Reies wondered whether the brotherhood of Christ could provide the solutions he had not found in the beetfields. He was 17 when this itinerant preacher offered him a chance to go to a three-year Assembly of God school near El Paso, There he is remembered by those who taught him as a "sincere, reform-conscious student and as a fiery and effective preacher with sometimes unorthodox views."

After graduating from Bible School, Tijerina did international evangelistic work on both sides of the Mexican border. "Entering Mexico as an itinerant religious leader, he left it deeply motivated by the philosophy of the Mexican revolution," wrote Dr. Knowlton.

During this period he wrote a book, *¿Habrá Justicia en La Tierra?*

(Will There Be Justice on Earth?), but did not seek to have it translated into English or published when he returned to the United States because, "At that time, I believed all Anglos to be the enemy."

In 1955, with 19 families, he established a cooperative village in Arizona called Valley of Peace. They built homes, a school and church, raised and marketed their own cotton.

The growers of Arizona's million-dollar crops, however, saw this effort by former migratory workers as a threat, and drove them out in 1957. "The village was all burned down and we had to leave Arizona. We were invited to come to northern New Mexico. There I learned of the land grants. I inquired and investigated and learned the people's dream. So strong, it was strong enough to move me.

"I felt New Mexico was the only spot in the Southwest where there was a spark of hope for Spanish-Americans—where they could make their rights felt in the eyes of the government." [1]

But more information was needed to prove these rights, and for the next three years Tijerina and his whole family picked cotton to raise funds for his research in Mexico. They saved every penny. "We did not even spare the children money for a pair of socks," he said later.

Between seasons, while he pored over the archives in Mexico City, Reies' wife and children waited in the border city of Juarez, assisted financially by his brothers.

This feeling of kinship, binding the most distant relatives to stand by one another in time of need or danger, is a significant factor that the ruling class has failed to take into account in its efforts to destroy Tijerina and the land grant organization he founded, the Alianza. It is apparent in Tijerina's own family, where his brothers Anselmo, Ramón, and Cristobal have all taken part in Alianza struggles. Active supporters are Reies' children: particularly his oldest son Reies Hugh, known in the family as "David," who says of his father, "he is the only real teacher I have ever had."

Alianza members usually join by family groups, and when one of them appears before a court, the face of the defendant seems to be repeated many times among the spectators. As Dr. Margaret Mead has observed, "To be Spanish-American is to belong to a family."

The Tijerina family next moved to Albuquerque, where Reies broke with his church, maintaining that tithes should go to the poor, not to buy the minister a new car. Some have said that the biblical framework of his speech is a gimmick, others that he is a religious fanatic. Neither is true. Like his dark suit, Tijerina's religious terminology stems from the days of his itinerant evangelism. He spices his rhetoric with biblical references, as did the silver-tongued orators of our grandfather's day, and for the same reason.

Although Tijerina is basically a religious man, he does not attend

[1] Tijerina's statements are from testimony at the Bernalillo County Courthouse, December 10, 1968.

church nor urge others to seek salvation in prayer. When Reies describes events in biblical terms, it is because these are the allusions most familiar to his listeners. It is cultural, literary expression rather than a religious one. Most of the Alianza members are at least nominally Catholic. Reies' former Protestant denomination embodies a militant anti-Catholicism. So there is no question of what some have called a "religious rebellion." Tijerina's is a rebellion against impossible conditions of life.

"After considerable research in Washington, after spending a whole year looking into the archives in Mexico City, after visiting Spain, and then examining microfilms of the grants in Albuquerque, I began to learn what had happened to all the documents," explained Tijerina.

"When I had become satisfied of the accuracy of the facts, I began daily radio programs [Station KABQ] in Spanish for two whole years, explaining the historical and legal background, the fraud perpetrated on the grantees, the destruction of records and other crimes against the people.

"The people were totally dependent on this land, physically, morally, spiritually. I saw the land question as the hope of the Southwest."

Throughout one cold winter, Tijerina talked to the people of the northern counties, and the first thing he concluded was that one grant alone could not win. To amass the strength necessary for the battle to regain the land, it was necessary to unite all the heirs of all northern grants. This he did, through meetings, the radio and by means of a widely distributed newspaper column in the Albuquerque *News Chieftan*, starting September 7, 1963.

Listening to the painful narrative of cases that had been thrown out of court by New Mexico judges who often were landowners themselves, he decided that wider public support must be created, both by education and by demonstrative actions. The first of these projects was aimed at obtaining the aid of the Mexican Republic for a petition to the United Nations.

And so 1959 found Tijerina in Mexico with a delegation representing 107 dispossessed families. Mexican writer Mario Gill reported at the time that the loss of their grants in New Mexico, "with the connivance of venal judges and the indifference of Washington authorities," had caused Mexican-Americans to seek help from the government of Mexico.

"From among them there has arisen a leader, a sort of apostle of the cause of Mexican-Americans, the symbolic man in whom the ideals of a people are embodied—the Mexican people oppressed in the US."

"Dedicated to the task of raising a wave of solidarity among his racial brothers," Tijerina and the delegation were in Mexico to turn over to President Lopez Mateos a memorial signed by thousands of Mexican-Americans. It asked that the Mexican government intervene with Washington to demand the fulfillment of the Treaty of Guadalupe Hidalgo, and adherence to the Universal Declaration of Human Rights, "which is today being violated to the injury of the Mexican residents of the Southwestern States of the United States."

The people of Mexico received their brothers warmly, but their government did not challenge U.S. violations of the Treaty. On two subsequent occasions the grantees sought to renew their mission to Mexico, but both attempts failed. In the spring of 1964, the Alianza planned a motorcade from Albuquerque to Mexico City, but Tijerina was arrested when he went to Chihuahua to map the route of the caravan. "The shock and anger which this abrupt and unexplained action aroused throughout Mexico, where festivities for the New Mexico pilgrims were being planned, was reflected in news reports."

Again in 1967 plans to visit Mexico were frustrated when the FBI threatened to arrest a motorcade of delegates if it should attempt to cross the border.

When Reies Tijerina began to unite the heirs to land grants, slander and rumor were widely spread concerning their intentions. Therefore, although the most forceful expression of Tijerina's ideas has always been in speech, he found it necessary to issue a pamphlet summarizing the Alianza position. It was printed in Spanish and English, and distributed throughout the State.

He began by presenting the legal basis for claims to the *pueblos* (villages) that originated in Spanish law, were affirmed by the Treaty of Guadalupe Hidalgo and upheld by the Constitutions of New Mexico and the United States.

From a delineation of these rights, Tijerina drew political, legal and judical conclusions concerning the privileges vested in the heirs to the grants. The booklet described the Alianza's attitude toward the courts, and forecast the tactics that were to determine the Alianza's actions in the three years that followed.

Tijerina opened with a reminder that more than a century had passed since the United States invaded and occupied New Mexico, "yet the question of the land grants, far from being resolved, has sunk into a morass of fraud, forgery and perjury."

After quoting from the Treaty, drawn up to protect property rights in New Mexico, Tijerina cited those sections of the U.S. and State constitutions that forbid depriving any person of property without due process or just compensation.

Next he went to the heart of today's struggle: "None of these grant lands and waters which the United States asserts it acquired from Mexico under the Treaty . . . ever formed any part of the *public domain*. These lands and waters cannot be taken for any purpose."

Then, in a forewarning ignored by the authorities, he declared:

"There are many trespassers on these Land Grants who have through various and devious means seized these lands both contrary to law and the true owner's interest. The true owners of these lands have the legal right to use all the force necessary to oust these trespassers."

In a further chapter, Tijerina explained that the majority of these grants were to *pueblos*, that is, to villages. A *pueblo* had a political jurisdiction, being governed by six or twelve councilmen, according to size. It had a judicial existence, and in addition was allowed to own property.

He quoted an 1859 decree of the first Surveyor General: "the existence of a town when the United States took possession of the country being proven, it is to be taken as evidence of a grant to said town, and when recognized as a town by the Mexican Government, it is believed to be a good and valid grant, *and the land claimed severed from the public domain.*"

"Consequently," wrote Tijerina "the villages have the legal right to use all the force necessary and all the police power necessary to insure their constituents the peaceful enjoyment of their rights."

The pamphlet ends with an appeal to Anglos: "The Indo-Hispano people of New Mexico are no longer a disunited people, but are uniting for the first time to recover and preserve their birthright and cultural heritage . . . each day they are getting stronger and have more confidence in themselves.

"The just cause of the Indo-Hispano people is their struggle to restore authority vested in the community, the natural unit of society, and down with all Anglo anarchists."

Enemy in the Forest

In Febuary of 1963 the Alianza was born. "The object of the Alianza," Tijerina said, "was to give the Indo-Hispanic people of the Southwest pride in their heritage, and force the Anglo to respect him, just like we respect them."

The full name of the new organization was "Alianza Federal de Mercedes"—Federated Alliance of Land Grants—and the first convention, held in September of that year, was attended by more than 800 delegates representing 48 New Mexico land grants.

Of over 50 land grants in the state, the Alianza resolved to concentrate on two, the Tierra Amarilla and the San Joaquín del Río Chama, both in Río Arriba County. Later, activity was also developed around two smaller grants, Piedra Lumbre adjacent to San Joaquín, and the Los Trigos Grant in San Miguel County.

At the convention, the main discussion centered around plans to pool the efforts of the assembled grantees. They would hire attorneys and bring political pressure to bear on Washington. A highlight of the convention was a report on Reies Tijerina's trip to Washington, recently made to enlist the aid of the Attorney General on the land-grant issue. On the same trip, Tijerina had attended the American Emancipation Centennial in Chicago and invited its Negro president, Dr. Alton Davis, to be keynote speaker at the Alianza convention. Mexico's former president, Miguel Alemán, had been a speaker at the centennial and expressed interest in the land-grant struggle.

Alianza membership increased rapidly in the following years, due to an influx of villagers angered by what appeared to them to be harsh, unfair and capricious decisions by the National Forest Service that were forcing many of them to migrate.

The Forest Service determines the number of animals that may be grazed in a specific area.[2] In 1965, in a deliberate effort to oust the small farmers, their grazing permits were reduced by 45 per cent. "Such measures hit the 50,000 northern Spanish-Americans where it hurts, in the stomach as well as the heart," wrote a Santa Fe reporter.

By 1967 more than 20,000 were forced to leave their hamlets for temporary work as migrants—some going as far as Wisconsin to can tomatoes and cucumbers.

While logging firms contracted with the Forest Service for immense areas on their ancestral land, the grantees were forbidden to cut stovewood without a permit. Moreover, the men had lost their jobs at the locally run lumber mill because it was unable to compete with the larger outfits, which hired out-of-county help.

Hatred of the *rinche*, the Forest Ranger, was increasing. Separated by language and social outlook from the local population, the Ranger often assumed the arrogant stance of a member of an army of occupation toward recalcitrant natives.

Of ten million acres of National Forest land in the state, nearly a million were taken from communal grant lands which had already been confirmed by the courts. In the northern counties, the U.S. Forest Service is today the biggest landowner—60 per cent is now in federal hands. "The establishment of the National Forest System in New Mexico alienated millions of acres from the village ejidos without compensation."

The theft continues. Tobias Leyba of Canjilón points in the distance to the former boundaries of the village pasture. "Now, look what they've left us," he says, indicating the Forest Service fence a few feet from his front porch. "This is why I'm with the Alianza." For Mr. Leyba's eleven children, a milk cow is a barrier against hunger.

"A cold war has come into existence between the villagers and the Forest Service," Dr. Knowlton warned. "They believe that they are being deliberately squeezed out of the National Forests to make room for larger Anglo-American cattle and sheep outfits."

It may seem strange that the villager of the north should consider the Forest Ranger to be his ever present enemy, hemming him in and depriving his family of food and fuel. The image of the Forest Service created by a high-powered public relations campaign is that of "A romantic figure of the West . . . a lone rider of the mountains and guardian of the Forests," to quote an example from the stream of self-laudatory publications that pours forth from Washington.

The facts are far from "romantic." The Forest Service is an army of men, 11,000 strong, with 16,000 seasonal employees, whose chief is appointed by the Secretary of Agriculture. It includes a hierarchy of executives

---

[2] For lush grasslands, it might be one cow a month for each 1½ acres. For poor scrub timber land, it might take 20 acres to sustain a cow for one month.

whose function is to administer 186 million acres of land—eight per cent of the area of the entire nation. It commands one-quarter of the total land area of the eleven western states, yielding invaluable forest and mineral products.

In volume of timber sales alone, it is a big business. Over 30,000 individual sales of timber are made each year, with a total value that exceeds 200 million dollars. Proceeds go to the U.S. Treasury. The local Forester has complete authority to negotiate these contracts. "Some are inclined to foster large sales to large companies, whether local or not, to simplify problems of policing the terms of the contracts."

Far exceeding timber sales are mineral prospecting and development on national forest lands. Nationwide, close to 10,000 leases are in force. In the final hours of his administration, former Secretary of the Interior Stewart L. Udall called for a complete overhaul of the nation's antiquated mineral-leasing law as a means of curbing "an outright giveaway of vital natural resources."

In New Mexico, most of these leases are to out-of-state corporations, at a great loss to the local population. The wealth and variety of New Mexico's mineral deposits are enormous, and their value increases daily; in 1968 the state's mineral production approached a billion dollars.

Efforts to force mining companies to pay their share of severance and excise taxes are made each legislative session, but state administrations tied directly to big business won't act. Subsidies and bonuses to new arrivals in the State have been the order of the day.

Kerr McGee, incorporated in Delaware and part of the Morgan group, is one of several giants that have acquired leases on federal lands. It has extended its activities from Nigeria, Angola, Canada and Venezuela to "colonial" New Mexico, where it holds close to 28,000 acres for the extraction of gas, oil and nuclear fuels, and is pursuing an aggressive program for discovery of uranium deposits.

Kennecott, another member of the Morgan group, in 1968 alone sent close to a hundred thousand tons of copper to its Baltimore refinery from New Mexico, adding the precious ore to what it had stolen from the Chilean people. It is also digging in the land grant area along the Río Arriba–Táos County line for rare metals used, among other things, to coat rocket nozzles.

Phelps Dodge not only extracts valuable minerals from Peru, Zambia and Puerto Rico but has developed a $110-million plant in New Mexico to tear out irreplaceable copper, leaving behind nothing but a big hole. In this water scarce section, it has somehow acquired rights to the entire flow of the Gila River.

The Forest Service also provides big business with 55,000 "special use" permits that cover more than three million acres and a wide variety of enterprises. Private concerns are permitted to build and operate hotels, boat docks, and ski lifts in forest preserves, not to mention sawmills, pipelines and roads for the benefit of large corporations.

The Forest Service is evidence of the colonial policy of the Federal government toward the entire West. There are large forests in New York State, for example, but no National Forests. Through this Service, resources of the West are exploited by Washington, D.C. and its friends.

Morris Garnsey, University of Colorado economist, wrote: "the federal government is an absentee landlord in the West. It owns some 275 million acres, nearly 50 per cent of the area of the Mountain States, in national forests, parks and mineral reserves. The fact that the federal government pays no taxes on these lands is a constant source of irritation to state and local governments. Through a policy of getting control of raw materials, the region becomes a colonial dependency of an industrial empire."

To intensify the grievance of the former owners, federal control has not prevented serious damage to the land. Huge tracts of exhausted land testify to the butchery practiced by get-rich-quick newcomers. For settlers in an arid country, such methods would have meant suicide. From the Indians they learned the techniques of irrigation, and the numerous little mountain valleys, with their fields still green and fertile after centuries of use, are eloquent witnesses to the fact that neither the Spaniards, the Mexicans nor the Indians were ever "land butchers"—of necessity, all were eminent conservationists.

The conflict is intensified by the methods of the Forest Service. It operates almost as a law unto itself, unresponsive to the people of the communities it is supposed to serve. In his revealing study of the behavior of the Forest Ranger, Kaufman quotes a letter from the former head of the Bureau of Land Management: "Many Forest Service men will fight for a certain course of action and against others, almost without regard to . . . public criticism and opposition."

In a description that could equally well fit the FBI or the Marines, Kaufman says of the Ranger: "His experiences and his environment gradually infuse into him . . . a militant and corporate spirit, with a fierce pride in the Service."

Throughout the West, the Forest Service is accused of discriminating in favor of large owners. In New Mexico, their "preference for large, corporate leasers as against small stock-raisers has all but shut Hispano stockmen out from their ancestral rangelands."

Justice William O. Douglas has criticised the management of national forests; which he says is left to Federal agencies that promulgate regulations governing the use of these properties, "but seldom allow a public voice to be heard against any plan of the agency."

In New Mexico, the Rangers run true to form. At a border conference held in El Paso in the fall of 1967, Reies Tijerina told Secretary of Agriculture Freeman that the Forest Service discriminated against Spanish-speaking people in their grazing-permit policies. The Secretary promised an investigation. Two months later, no investigation had been ordered, and when reminded, Freeman said he had discussed the charges with the Forest Service chief and been convinced that "their policy is fair enough."

An act of Congress in 1891 gave power to establish forest reserves for the public domain. This power was not used for the stated purpose of preserving natural resources. Instead, Forest Service policies were largely responsible for the hated timber monopoly that ravaged the forests of the West. Big interests such as those of Lumber Baron Frederick Weyerhaeuser and Railroad Magnate J. J. Hill were among the most prominent influences in the program of "conservation."

In this period extensive depredations of the public timber were carried on by the railroads, in some cases relying on the unsurveyed land grants and often with no pretense of legality. Large quantities of timber in New Mexico were cut from the public lands by the Santa Fe railroad, and transported out of the territory, contrary to law.

Recently, Senators Dale McGee of Wyoming and Frank Church of Idaho called hearings, where scores of opponents of Forest Service logging practices descended on the Capitol to protest what they saw as destruction of National Forests simply to benefit the lumber industry. Speaking in defense of the Forest Service, representatives of the Weyerhaeuser Company and the American Plywood Association defended the practice of "clear-cutting," where trees were levelled like the reaping of a wheat field. After the hearings, Senator McGee demanded a two-year moratorium on timber cutting by the Forest Service, which he said had left great forests "depleted to the point that would shame Paul Bunyan."

Hostility to the National Forests began long before New Mexico became a state, and was generated by the Lacey Bill of 1906, which included agricultural lands in the forest reserves. A Colorado congressman attacked the bill because "it left the Secretary of Agriculture with too much discretion in regard to the opening of agricultural lands," and Representative Smith of California secured the exclusion of his state from provisions of the bill, because it was "no part of a proper forest reserve policy" to control range land.

The Forest Service was accused of atrocities—miners had been shot for refusing to vacate ground from which they had been ordered by a Forest Ranger. These, Senator Heyburn of Idaho declared, were "merely illustrations of the manner of administration."

This "manner of administration" again asserted itself at Coyote in August 1969, when James Evans, Forest Service investigator, pointed a gun at Reies Tijerina's head, endangering the lives of his two-year-old daughter and over a hundred Alianzistas.

Even the Service function personified by "Smokey the Bear," protecting forests from fire, is questioned by many. By refusing farmers the right to graze, the Forest Service has increased the fire hazard. Grasses allowed to grow year after year form a mat through which fire, under a wind, runs with great rapidity.

It is in limiting grazing land that the Service most often comes into collision with the Indo-Hispanic farmer. The Rangers make unilateral decisions as to the number of grazing permits they will issue and the fees to be charged.

"The Forest Service has consistently been reducing grazing rights and slowly causing the total economic decline of the communities of Northern New Mexico," said Tomás Atencio of the Migrant Council, "only to open the Forest to private outside investors for recreation purposes." They insult the farmers by declaring that cows overgraze the range, and that horses should be raised instead to provide recreation for the tourists. "But," Mr. Atencio observed, "one horse eats as much as two cows, and a cow they can eat, a horse they cannot."

Land grant heirs must pay fines when their cows wander into the 1.4 million acre Carson National Forest, onto land that was lately theirs. If they cannot pay, the Service sells the cows and keeps the money. "Animals not sold will be destroyed," said a Standard Forest Service Form given to farmers in the San Joaquín land grant.

Tijerina has charged that Forest Service Chief Investigator Evans was brought into the area to drive the people off what land they have left. Since coming to New Mexico, Evans has led in the effort to decapitate the Alianza. Brandishing weapons at every confrontation, then declaring that a "potentially violent situation" exists, he is one of those who have succeeded in converting the Alianza's peaceful struggles into a series of criminal prosecutions of Reies Tijerina.

In the years before the Alianza was founded, resistance to Anglo encroachment was kept up by secret organizations such as the Gorras Blancas (White Caps), east of Santa Fe, and the Mano Negra (Black Hand) in Río Arriba County. They engaged in acts of desperation—fence cutting, burning haystacks and sometimes houses. Tijerina, on the contrary, built the Alianza by education of the public, stressing peaceful mass action. The structure of the organization provided for a ruling "cosmic table" of representatives of the various land grants, that passed on all major decisions. Tijerina, not being an heir, had no vote on this body. His leadership was exercised through membership meetings and conventions, that involved everyone supporting the fight for first-class citizenship.

Attendance at mass meetings sometimes reached a thousand —a significant portion of the state's population which is barely one million. Although most of the 300,000 Spanish-speaking people in New Mexico are land grant heirs, as well as their thousands of relatives in other states, not all belong to the Alianza. The press repeatedly placed the number of actual members at 50,000, the purpose of this overstatement being to accuse Tijerina of amassing a fortune from the one dollar monthly dues, which were actually one dollar a month per *family*.

The organization was maintained by donations from individuals, collections at meetings, and proceeds of meals served at the hall. Tijerina helped serve food to the crowd, working quickly as he hailed friends in the waiting line.

No one drew a regular salary—"Hired leaders are like hired gunslingers," said Tijerina, "they work for the side that pays most." The Alianza provided his living quarters, but expenses for trips were debated and voted on by the elders, and often raised at a rally called for the purpose.

Tijerina's habit was to consult everyone around him, vigorously and enthusiastically discuss a budding idea, consider challenges and arguments against it. Once a course of action was fixed, he threw great quantities of energy into carrying it out—on the phone late at night, starting trips by daybreak, pulling young and old into a swirl of activity: a man used to hard work who had found something worth working for.

Language and Culture

The home of the Alianza in Albuquerque is a two-story, concrete-block building, originally used as a frozen food-packing plant. Its owner had traded the sprawling structure for Tijerina's share of land on the ill-fated Arizona cooperative, plus a monthly sum not always raised.

Reies Tijerina and his second wife, Patsy, lived upstairs with their two little children. Various male members of his family and of the organization slept in the basement. Efforts by Alianzistas to improve the cavernous interior were constantly under way, and later when the building became an object of bombings, the construction extended to blocking in the windows.

English was seldom spoken at the Alianza, and when the building resounded with the music of a dance, the tune was either a New Mexico folk melody or a popular Mexican song, interspersed with rock-and-roll as an occasional concession to the youth.

For the tie that bound all Alianza members together was the fight to preserve their culture. Their right to speak Spanish was fiercely defended in spite of opposition from the dominant class that controls the schools and newspapers and tries to eliminate speaking Spanish on the job.

Since the early days of the State, the Spanish language has been fought for. When the New Mexico Constitution was drawn up in 1910, guarantees of Mexican-American civil and political rights were written into it, because their leaders insisted on them and because Anglo representatives of mining, railroad and commercial interests needed Indo-Hispano support to achieve their own goals.

One half of the 70 Republican delegates to the 100-member convention were Indo-Hispano. "They formed a comparatively solid block welded by a common interest . . . the preservation of their traditional way of life and the language of their forefathers."

Against the Enabling Act of 1910, through which President Taft demanded as a condition for statehood that ability to read and speak English be a qualification for holding office, the New Mexicans counterposed the Treaty of Guadalupe Hidalgo. They wrote two unprecedented clauses into their Constitution, the first providing that: "The right of any citizen of the state to vote, hold office or sit upon juries, shall never be restricted . . . on account of religion, race, language or color, or inability to speak, read or write the English or Spanish languages."

And in order to make it practically impossible to take away this right, the article made a vote of three-fourths of the electors necessary for its amendment, with a further requirement that at least two-thirds of those voting in each county of the State shall vote for such amendment (Article 7, Section 2).

The second article obliged the legislature to provide for the training of teachers "so that they may become proficient in both English and Spanish, to qualify them to teach Spanish-speaking pupils," and followed with the provision that "children of Spanish descent shall never be denied the right and privilege of admission and attendance in the public schools . . . and shall never be classed in separate schools."

The first part of this Article of the Constitution was ignored until Tijerina revived and popularized it. It has yet to be put into force. The second clause, however, prevented a completely segregated school system from arising such as in Texas, where until 1954 three separate schools were the rule in districts with Black, Chicano and white students.

The Alianza's fight against the forced imposition of English won sympathy from the entire Spanish-speaking world and procured for Tijerina considerable publicity when he went to Spain in 1966. In spite of being ruled by a fascist dictatorship, Spain maintains ties with all the countries of Latin America, including socialist Cuba. Sent there by the Alianza in order to pursue the facts about the grants to their source, he was interviewed in ABC (May 7, 1966) by a Seville newspaperman, Antonio Burgos.

Burgos described Reies Tijerina as "a man of 39 years, self-educated, who speaks perfect Castilian . . . a knight crusading for the rights of Hispanos in the Southwest of the United States, much as Rev. Martin Luther King might be of the aspirations of Black North Americans."

Tijerina was in Seville preparing documentation which the Alianza intended to present to the U.S. Supreme Court, Burgos explained. "The lands populated by the Spanish explorers, who left behind, together with their language, the singular legacy of *mestizaje*, became in 1821 a Mexican province. And New Mexico was Mexican until 1846."

"The government of Mexico respected our rights," Tijerina told him, "but the United States dispossessed us. Fifty thousand hectares[3] of pasture were stolen. In addition they kept us in a state of second-class citizenship, without representation or vote, until 1912."

Burgos then asked: "Does Spanish culture still exist in the southern states of North America?"

"Our culture is Spanish. We want to speak Spanish. But the Anglos press for this cultural legacy to be abandoned—lost," Tijerina answered. "Little children who dare to speak Spanish are run out of school. Everything is English. We are not free to express ourselves in our own language." Referring to New Mexico, Reies added, "Outside of the big cities purely Span-

[3] A hectare is approximately 2.5 acres.

ish is spoken. Fifteen per cent of the rural population cannot speak English."

"Suppose the Alianza should win its case from the government at Washington?" asked Burgos.

"Then we would build schools where Spanish may once more be taught, we will once more organize the cultivation of the common lands, some of which are rich in minerals. For example, one single *ejido* that now belongs to an Anglo who lives elsewhere yielded him six million dollars worth of uranium."

When Tijerina returned from Spain he brought with him three large volumes containing the laws decreed by Spanish monarchs in their capacity as rulers of the Indies. This code governed a large part of the Western Hemisphere for well over 300 years—from 1492 to 1821. Tijerina made a detailed study of these tomes. They were prominently displayed in the Alianza office and often quoted. One of these decrees, "the first civil rights law in the Americas," as Tijerina called it, was proclaimed in 1573. It established absolute equality of the offspring of Spaniards and Indians. With this edict, says Reies, a *new race* was founded, the Indo-Hispano, to which most of the people of northern New Mexico belong.

Today, many Alianza members proudly mention that they have an Indian grandma or grandpa. It proves that one "belongs" in the area, is a "true native" of the region. Of himself, Tijerina says, "I come from the Tejas tribe: big nose, tall, red skin."

The Fourth of July Was No Picnic

The Alianza held its first mass action the weekend of July 4, 1966. For Tijerina, years of striving to share the results of his research were bearing fruit. Now, together with several hundred Alianzistas, he was on his way to petition New Mexico's governor, Jack Campbell.

They started out in Albuquerque early Saturday, July 2 and trudged for three days in 100-degree heat to the capital at Santa Fe. Holiday weekend drivers slowed on the steep hills to read signs that demanded not only return of the land, but first-class citizenship too. "US Movie Industry Slanders Spanish and Indian-Americans," read a placard carried the 62 miles by a young woman. The procession was led by bearded José Luis Sanchez of Alburquerque, who rode a burro, waving the flag of the Tierra Amarilla grant.

"For the first time in history, we're doing this in a united way," Tijerina told the press. "Today, politicians won't listen until the people come out with something spectacular."

When they reached Santa Fe, the marchers found the Governor had gone to California, having detailed Frank McGuire, Director of the Office of Economic Opportunity, to face them. But Tijerina told McGuire that they had not come seeking charity but to present the Governor with their demand for land and full civil rights guaranteed in the Treaty with Mexico, and the Alianzistas voted to wait for him.

Camped in a vacant lot on Santa Fe's main artery, they attracted attention. Several carloads drove by to jeer at their banners. Mrs. Gallegos, mother of a large family, was indignant.

"They rode past our camp last night shooting into the air," she said, "and they called out, 'Wet-backs, go home.' But it is we who belong here, and they who should go home if they don't like it, because we were farming this land when they got here from across the sea."

A vigorous middle-aged farmer, reduced to eking out a meager living from less than ten acres, spoke up. "We will occupy the State Capitol buildings if necessary," he declared. "We will not be bought off. If they offer us money it might help us or our children. But we are fighting for our grandchildren and great-grandchildren who have a right to the land granted our families."

They waited all week, and leaning over the backs of pickups or crowded around a borrowed picnic table, talked to visitors and curiosity-seekers. They had time for long discussions, and to the surprise of those who had taken the jingostic "patriotism" of some Mexican-American politicians as typical of the whole people, emerged as the most outspoken anti-war group in the State. Some compared the war in Vietnam to the aggression against Mexico, and argued about what kinds of minerals the United States was after in that distant country. All were agreed in denouncing the disproportionate number of Mexican youth drafted and killed.

As a result of the attention they attracted, facts on the land struggle began to appear in the State's newspapers. One article described the methods by which an avaricious rancher seeking land might gain control of it, "with full right to throw the previous owner off."

"Several famous murders, range wars, and other squabbles (*sic*) erupted from such activities toward the close of the last century in New Mexico. Yesterday's marchers, however, had more on their minds than repossession of Spanish land grants taken away from their grandfathers. A common theme among the marchers was protest against the war in Vietnam. Many held signs and expressed opinions to the effect that minority groups are sent to Vietnam to 'fight the white man's war.'" Paul Vigil, of Bueyeros in Harding County, argued, "I'd rather be on the side of the Viet Cong than with those ranchers in Harding and Union counties." Vigil asserted that a Texas-born rancher told him, "You've had it, because you're not white."

Another reporter commented: "The U.S. Courts have many times ruled against attempts by heirs to old land grants to reassert their claims. Tijerina blames this consistent attitude on racial discrimination. He asserts that Spanish Americans have been discriminated against for more than a century in New Mexico and that they have been consistently squeezed out of the land holdings and livelihood."

Governor Campbell eventually received the marchers on July 11. He promised to investigate this "thorny matter" and personally send the results of his study to President Johnson. Campbell also finally agreed to ask Johnson for an investigation to be conducted at the executive level. When Campbell protested that the executive had no authority to settle such issues, Tijerina countered, "the Constitution requires the executive to see that the laws are enforced."

Furthermore, Tijerina said, New Mexico Senator Joseph Montoya had once offered to introduce a bill in Congress creating a commission to investigate land grant claims, and Representatives Henry Gonzalez of Texas and Edward Roybal of California agreed to support Montoya's proposal, "but they didn't feel the time is right yet."

The President's intervention was necessary, Tijerina told the Governor, because the Claims Court set up by Congress to settle land disputes in 1891 did not adjudicate the cases fairly, as the people had no proper legal representation. "There were no Spanish-American lawyers in the state at that time."

Immediately after the confrontation with the Governor, Tijerina called a meeting of the marchers and a crowd who had joined them. He spoke in Spanish, reviewing the grievances that had brought them from all over New Mexico and from California and Colorado.

Over 60 per cent of our people he said, are chained to the pink card of public welfare and powdered milk, because their land has been taken from them. I suppose we should be grateful that they keep us alive with food handouts while they steal our heritage, but we must remember that they feed us only so that when we are needed to fight their wars they can strike up a military band and say "Come on, Martinez, into the army."

Our children go to school and what do they teach them? That we are born of Spanish and Indian blood? [*Crowd:* "No!"] Our great mountains, rivers and cities carry Spanish names. Do they tell our children why? ["No!"]

They commit their greatest crime when they try to take away the language our fathers left us: "Shut up, don't speak Spanish!" they yell. Real justice has no language. The Treaty of Guadalupe Hidalgo did not say that we must speak English. The Constitution of the United States nowhere says that we must speak English. We will protect our language and our land, not with pistols but with the law.

Reports of this meeting will be heard from Texas to California. The whole world will know that our stepmother [the U.S. government] has us on bread and water. For justice has no frontier. Justice has no language.

When the great day comes, when we have won this fight, we will have a great burning. Of Anglos' homes, as they fear? No. Of pink [welfare] cards. When that great day comes, when the Mexican-American has awakened, we will end poverty and the shameful stain of powdered milk.

THE FORMATION OF CHICANO STUDIES PROGRAMS

Manifesto

For all people, as with individuals, the time comes when they must reckon with their history. For the Chicano the present is a time of renaissance, of renacimiento. Our people and our community, el barrio and la colonia, are expressing a new consciousness and a new resolve. Recognizing the historical tasks confronting our people and fully aware of the cost of human progress, we pledge our will to move. We will move forward toward our destiny as a people. We will move against those forces which have denied us freedom of expression and human dignity. Throughout history the quest for cultural expression and freedom has taken the form of a struggle. Our struggle, tempered by the lessons of the American past, is an historical reality.

For decades Mexican people in the United States struggled to realize the "American Dream." And some—a few—have. But the cost, the ultimate cost of assimilation, required turning away from el barrio and la colonia. In the meantime, due to the racist structure of this society, to our essentially different life style, and to the socio-economic functions assigned to our community by anglo-american society—as suppliers of cheap labor and a dumping ground for the small-time capitalist entrepreneur—the barrio and colonia remained exploited, impoverished, and marginal.

As a result, the self-determination of our community is now the only acceptable mandate for social and political action; it is the essence of Chicano commitment. Culturally, the word Chicano, in the past a pejorative and class-bound adjective, has now become the root idea of a new cultural identity of our people. It also reveals a growing solidarity and the development of a common social praxis. The widespread use of the term Chicano today signals a rebirth of pride and confidence. Chicanismo simply embodies an ancient truth: that man is never closer to his true self as when he is close to his community.

Chicanismo draws its faith and strength from two main sources: from the just struggle of our people and from an objective analysis of our community's strategic needs. We recognize that without a strategic use of education, an education that places value on what we value, we will not realize our destiny. Chicanos recognize the central importance of

From *El Plan de Santa Barbara* 1970. © La Causa Publications, Santa Barbara, California, P.O. Box 4818.

institutions of higher learning to modern progress, in this case, to the development of our community. But we go further: we believe that higher education must contribute to the formation of a complete man who truly values life and freedom.

For these reasons Chicano Studies represent the total conceptualization of the Chicano community's aspirations that involve higher education. To meet these ends, the university and college systems of the State of California must act in the following basic areas:

1. Admission and recruitment of Chicano students, faculty, administrators and staff.
2. A curriculum program and an academic major relevant to the Chicano cultural and historical experience.
3. Support and tutorial programs.
4. Research programs.
5. Publications programs.
6. Community cultural and social action centers.

We insist that Chicano students, faculty, administrators, employees, and the community must be the central and decisive designers and administrators of those programs. We do so because our priorities must determine the nature and development of such programs. Only through this policy can the university and college systems respond efficiently and justly to a critical reality of this society. Through such a policy universities and colleges will truly live up to their credo, to their commitment to diversification, democratization, and enrichment of our cultural heritage and human community.

We assume the sacrifices and responsibilities inherent in our commitment. It was in this spirit that we met in Santa Barbara in mid-April: over one-hundred Chicano students, faculty, administrators, and community delegates representing the northern, central, and southern regions of la Alta California, Aztlan. Away from the sensationalism of the mass media, and from the alarms of self-seeking politicians, we set out to formulate a Chicano plan for higher education.

Workshops on recruitment, support programs, campus organizing and the curricular institutionalizing aspects of Chicano Studies produced analyses and recommendations. We never lost sight of the simple fact that these programs will be effective only to the extent that we can influence decision-making within and without the university and college systems. What follows, El Plan de Santa Bárbara, reflects one critical dimension of the Chicano struggle.

The destiny of our people will be fulfilled. To that end, we pledge our efforts and take as our credo what José Vasconcelos once said at a time of crisis and hope: "At this moment we do not come to work for the university, but to demand that the university work for our people."

Organizing and Instituting Chicano Programs On-Campus

Introduction

Rhetorical liberalism is omnipresent in higher education perhaps more so than in other sectors of society. Unquestionably, the contradiction between rhetoric and reality that is characteristic of 'America' is a feature of the campus also. The existing interests and traditional structures have no intention of sharing power, providing access, extending prestige, and permitting plural participation. Power must be taken, here, as elsewhere.

The institutionalization of Chicano programs is the realization of Chicano power on campus. The key to this power is found in the application of the principles of self-determination and self-liberation. These principles are defined and practiced in the areas of control, autonomy, flexibility, and participation. Often imaginary or symbolic authority is confused with the real. Many times token efforts in program institutionalization are substituted for enduring constructive programming. It is the responsibility of Chicanos on campus to insure dominant influence of these programs. The point is not to have a college with a program, but rather a Chicano program, at that college.

If Chicanos do not exert dominant influence over the program, better no program at all. For without the requisite control, Chicano participation provides an ersatz legitimization for the continuance of the pattern of dominant-subordinate relations that characterizes Chicano colonial status within the larger society. The demand for self-determination in higher education is not a question of puerile power discussions, but, in this area as in others of community life, a matter of survival, progress, and dignity. The practice of self-determination serves best the interest of the Chicano community and the long range interests as a whole.

But old patterns may persist, the anglo may move to deny and limit Chicanos, and there will be "Mexican-Americans" to serve him. Chicano faculty and administrators and even student groups, can function as "tio tacos," the same as politicians, store managers, radio announcers, police officers, ad nauseum. It is all too easy for programs to be co-opted, for them to function as buffers of denial and agencies of control. In that case, better no program at all. Yet the colleges and universities, through Chicano programs, may serve the community.

The premises for Chicano programs are:

- The colleges/universities must be a major instrument in the liberation of the Chicano community.
- Colleges/universities have a three-fold responsibility: education, research, and public service to the Chicano community.
- Only by comprehensive programs instituted and implemented by Chicanos and for Chicanos that focus on the needs and goals of the com-

munity will the larger purposes of the academic institutions and the interests of the Chicano community be served.

These premises are in turn local particularizations of a wider system of values, beliefs, ideas, organizational modes, and commitments to which the Chicano is dedicated. One of these that has a direct bearing on Chicano-university relations is that the concept of "community" is all inclusive. The Chicanos on campus are an organic, integral part of the Chicano community. Among Chicanos on campus there can be no distinctions or separations because of personal occupational differentiations. Moreover, the Chicano community on campus is an extension of the larger community. The base of the Chicanos on campus is the Chicano community. Participation for the Chicano means total access to institutions by the total community.

The primary goals of the various programs must be to serve the interests of the Chicano people through the institutions of higher learning. In education, as in other matters, there is one loyalty—the community, one criterion—service, to La Raza. In higher education, the thrust is directed toward the creation of parallel institutions that are controlled by Chicanos serving the interests of the community. These interests are defined only by Chicanos. Education cannot be isolated from other factors determining the situation of the Chicano in this society.

The base, the strength, of any action on campus depends on the Chicano community at that campus—employees, students, faculty, and administrators. This base must be well organized, and the group must possess general agreement as to its orientation before moving to secure programs. Without a position of strength, it will not be able to exercise control over the programs, and without unity of goals, the programs would be constantly in jeopardy because of internal differences. It is no accident that programs that best fulfill expectations are to be found where the student groups are strong, more sophisticated, and most demanding. Before moving overtly, the Chicano must assess the situation; he must be organized and committed; otherwise, co-optation and tokenism will result. The Chicano cannot depend on the good will and false promises of others. He must recognize that he will secure his rights only to the extent that he is strong.

Initial Steps

Usually there are three preliminary steps toward the institutionalization of programs on campus involving the areas of organization, intelligence and advocation. They are for the most part political; in fact the whole process of institutionalization may be considered a political one:

1. Organize a Junta Directiva composed of Chicano students, employees, administrators, faculty, and other members of the community to initiate, organize, direct, and supervise all aspects of the institution's im-

plementation of its obligation to serve the community. This will be the top policy and decision-making body for the programs.

2. Make a thorough investigation and analysis of the climate within the institution and the surrounding locality. Research the legal/theoretical structure of the institution, and assess its actual functional operations.

3. Secure from the institution the commitment that it will give the highest priority to the needs of the Chicano community, not because of morals or politics, but because it has the obligation as a public institution charged with serving all of society. This is not a novel responsibility, but rather both a past and present one on which the institution has defaulted. The commitment must be clear as to the seriousness of the institution's intent in bringing its facilities, personnel, and resources to bear on the deplorable conditions that exist for the Chicano community, and it must entail more than a strictly educational aspect. If the commitment is first made in the form of a verbal and private understanding between the institution and the Chicano Junta, it should be in this form for only as long as expedient: eventually the relation must be overt and defined.

As pledge of the commitment in higher education, a tangible first step is the designation of these programs as Chicano or La Raza, in their descriptive titles. These are self-denoting, affirmative and positive from the perspective of the Chicano people. These terms, Chicano – La Raza, inherently embody the national and universal philosophical and ideological values and principles which Chicanos affirm as a people and that the programs are charged with fulfilling.

Experience in organizing on and off campus suggests nine principal guidelines to be observed for the creation of satisfactory and viable programs. These fall into the areas of control, autonomy, participation, and responsibility. The guidelines by necessity are expressed in general terms, and it is up to the local groups to apply them to the particular context:

1. *Control:* Chicanos must exercise maximum control over all programs initiated. This will be resisted, but without control the program is worthless. Minimum of control is a simple majority in the governing board, with the Chicano element holding the directorship. Optimum is, of course, total control, vertical and horizontal. This is not unrealizable, for it has been secured in some programs. If non-Chicano participation is necessary, then the Chicano element should have the right of nomination and selection of all participants. Policy and executive responsibility is to be held by the Junta; if there is to be a predominant element within the Junta, it should be the student. This insures a continuous fresh input and avoids the entrenching of personal interests.

2. *Autonomy:* The programs at the different phases must have the maximum autonomy feasible within the context of the institution. This applies to both operating procedures as well as structure, and also to traditional guidelines and conventions of the institution. For the programs to be

effective, independence and wide latitude of operation must be assured from inception. New programs cannot be hampered by old restrictions developed for different interests and needs. Often, as a rationale for denial of legitimate demands, regulatory and legal limitations are invoked. Often the only answer to this is pressure, until it is clear that for the sake of larger interests existing regulations should be changed. In addition to pressure, more politic means for bridging existing prohibitions can be devised. Once the Chicano programs become operational and their viability and attractiveness apparent, it is likely that other sectors of the college or university will endeavor to co-opt and restrict them to protect their own interests and maximize their area of operation. The Chicano programs must be as free and independent of all existing programs as possible.

3. *Structure:* The administrative unit under which the Chicano program operates would be the largest sub-unit within the institution, which facilitates most the desired control and autonomy. The structural label is not important, i.e., college, center, department, etc. What is important is the freedom. Lines of communication must be direct to the highest executive officer or body of the campus, and independent of existing structural hierarchy. In time, a top level general administrative position must be secured. If a designation or structural concept that suits the need doesn't exist, invent one.

4. *Organization:* Internally, the Chicano operation must be designed for efficiency and harmony. The program or programs must be centralized in terms of ultimate policy and executive responsibility to maintain control, insure coordination, and maximize the use of resources. Essential to the success of any program is the reduction and/or elimination of unnecessary friction, duplication, and internecine competition within the program. Coordinating the program effectively means the harmonization of relationships with its sub-components.

5. *Flexibility:* Flexibility must be built into the programs in order to insure sufficient latitude for a constantly increasing effectiveness. As the programs unfold, experience will dictate adaptations, changes, or eliminations; these must be anticipated. Moreover, flexibility must exist within the Chicano operation and in its relationships to the larger institution. Administrative options must be kept open.

6. *Finances:* Chicano programs must have a permanent adequate proportional budgeted allocation of funds from the institution. In addition, the freedom to seek and obtain funds independently must be secured. Not abrogating the strictest accountability, the programs should have the minimum of restrictions in disposing of these funds. The major decisions on expenditures must belong to La Junta.

7. *Participation and Support:* Participation and support at every level and in any position must be open to all Chicanos. It should not be restricted by temporary or artificial status. Participation should include the total Chicano community. Special efforts should be made to include sectors of the community not usually concerned with campus-based activities. In every case the total community must be constantly informed as to

plans and actions on campus, and its active participation and support sought. Emphatically, when the situation arises that there is need for more support than that provided by on-campus Chicano personnel, this support should be obtained from the Chicano community rather than from non-Chicano campus groups. This is not saying, reject all non-Chicano support or participation. Mobilize it, but clearly define the quality and quantity of this support and participation.

8. *Staff:* Staff for the programs must meet four qualifications: knowledge and expertise in the area of concern, experience in the field, sensitivity as a person, and a firm proven commitment to the goals of the programs and the welfare of the community. Delegated, specific, administrative responsibility is best vested in those who have an "overall" conceptual grasp of the programs and its goals. Any effort is dependent on the quality of the individuals involved. Unfortunately, some programs are already being subverted by individuals whose commitment to La Raza is questionable. Keep the "tios" and the reactionaries out.

9. *Responsibility:* Chicano programs demand the highest standards, the strictest sense of responsibility, and the most complete fidelity. This is an integral part of the commitment to the Chicano community.

Integral Components

A complete program that codifies the college or university's obligation in education, research, and public service includes the following minimum components:

1. Department
   a. design and administer degree program
   b. counseling of enrolled students
   c. faculty
2. Recruitment, financial support, and tutorial services for students
   a. identification and recruitment of students for the college/university
   b. maintenance and support
   c. tutorial services
   d. housing
3. Research
   a. design, sponsorship, and administration of research projects that serve actual needs of the Chicano community
   b. graduate fellowship programs
4. Publication
   a. publish materials of research projects
   b. publish materials needed by local community
   c. publish materials by Chicano writers and artists
5. Community Social Action
   a. sponsoring of community services
   b. community organizing, education/cultural programs, information dissemination

6. Policy and Executive Body
   a. nominated by Chicanos representing students, faculty, administrators, employees, and other members of Chicano community
   b. propose policy and specific projects and activities
   c. oversee staff
   d. secure community support

Proposals

Usually, at a certain stage, the specifics of the goals and structure of the Chicano program are spelled out in proposal form. There are two general types of proposals each according to the type of structure desired.

Department proposals outline the framework for the academic unit, detail requirements, curriculum, and the faculty resources, etc. They divide into five parts:

Part I: Introduction. (1) designation of degree, (2) objectives and values of degree, (3) precedents, (4) relationship to existing curriculum and research programs, and (5) timetable for development.
Part II: (1) Admissions criteria, (2) curriculum, definition of proposed degree program, (3) recommended electives, (4) foreign language requirements, (5) criteria for granting degree, (6) relationship to existing masters and doctoral programs.
Part III: Staff resources existing and to be recruited.
Part IV: (1) Course descriptions, existing and to be designed, (2) the instructors and biliography.
Part V: Library resources, actual and anticipated.

Proposals for centers, institutions, schools, colleges, etc., include the following: introduction, statement of justification, precedents, purposes, specific focus, components, administrative design, anticipated effect on current structure of college or university, relationship to existing programs and structures, number and criteria for staff, participating students, necessary research resources, physical plant, timetable for implementation, project budget, and regulatory changes. Proposals for Chicano units should be advanced by the entire Chicano group.

The type of structures possible for the Chicano programs ranges from departments to the ideal, a university. A Chicano Studies department is the best vehicle for the development and implementation of a Chicano curriculum and for securing the necessary staff. A department offers courses, either unilaterally or in association with other departments; it, of course, enjoys the autonomy proper to it. The department may be uni-disciplinary or inter-disciplinary; often the combination of both is the most practical and flexible. Centers, institutes, and schools are organized around a broad multi-faceted program which includes academic and community service activities that cut across various intra-college/university boundaries. The college is perhaps the most suitable structure for a wide set of programs because of its defined autonomy in nearly all areas considered as integral for a viable Chicano program. Of course, a university is the optimum institute for Chicano higher education—and it will be realized, i.e., Universidad de le Raza, Chicano University of the Southwest, Universidad Autónoma de Aztlán.

Problem Areas

There are several external factors that affect Chicano programs which should be considered. Obviously, the general political climate within the state is worsening. Reactionary attitudes held by politicians will affect the context of innovative programs, especially those whose mission is social and educational and whose focus is the disenfranchised ethnic minorities. To compound the problem, the institutions through which the Chicanos are trying to work are, per se, the current political scapegoat. In the area of public attitudes, there are several other factors influencing programs. Though the colleges and universities believe themselves to be progressive, often the opposite is true. They share and harbor the more reprehensible idiosyncracies of the general society. College and university personnel can be racist and reactionary, and so can sectors of the student body. They will refuse to accept the legitimacy of needs and corresponding programs that are not orthodox; further, consciously or unconsciously, they will endeavor to prevent and subvert them. One target where hostility can focus most damagingly is funding. Academic validity is another point of attack; often the question of standards, criteria, etc., merely cloaks racist attitudes and assumptions. Another focus of attack is the socializing aspects of the programs; by exaggerating their political content, critics can undercut their public support.

In some instances, programs are not only beset by difficulties from external sources, but suffer from within. Most of the problems are common to pioneering efforts of any sort. Experience indicates that problems and difficulties in the process of institutionalization are compounded when they are joined to similar efforts carried on by other minority groups. To date, joint efforts have been counter-productive; they should be considered carefully. The Chicano programs develop internal bottlenecks for a number of reasons. One is that the sponsoring individuals are not in full agreement as to the basic propositions of the program, and the implementation phase becomes the battleground for these disagreements. In some cases, difficulties develop from the lack of clear definitions of the roles of staff and students in the program. Of course, all programs are hampered by the lack of proper staff, but many are undermined by staff who do not share movement values and who were hired without thorough evaluation.

Recommendations

Given the current difficulties and the project needs of the future, the following recommendations are made:

1. The establishment of a central information bank on course descriptions, proposals, programs, and personnel.

2. Directory of potential and current students, and faculty, available for distribution.

3. Design and financing of an in-service training and support program for graduate students to enable them simultaneously to obtain higher degrees while filling teaching and staff positions in the programs.

4. Priority in hiring for program positions be given to graduates of Chicano student groups and those Chicanos who have a record of community service.

5. The possible recruitment of Mexican nationals for faculty positions to fill special temporary needs, provided they have the necessary orientation and commitment.

6. Chicano departments, centers, colleges, etc., as they become operational should mutually support each other by the sharing of resources and the development of joint programs.

7. A just number of student slots in "Study Abroad" programs must be secured for Chicano students, and these must be nominated by the student organizations.

8. Chicano student and faculty exchange programs should be implemented.

9. The various students groups, MAYA, MASC, UMAS, etc., should adopt a unified name as symbol and promise, such as CAUSA (Chicano Alliance for United Student Action) or MECHA (Movimiento Estudiantil Chicano de Aztlán).

10. Chicano authored or sponsored publications should be given preference as course materials. Chicanos should publish through Chicano journals. Chicano publishing houses should be established.

11. Chicano students, faculty, staff must organize a united statewide association for the advancement of La Causa in the colleges and universities.

Conclusions

In the last two years, across the state, student organizations on college campuses have addressed themselves to the following objectives: increased admittance of Chicano students, the vindication of their cultural heritage, the utilization of institutional resources for the benefit of the larger community, and the implementation of courses relevant to the Chicano. During this time a coherent set of vital components for a satisfactory program have emerged: admissions and recruitment, curriculum, research, publications, and community action. The process has taught that in any and all programs the guiding determinants must be the principles of self-determination for self-liberation.

A modicum of success has been obtained at a few institutions; but these were not freely given, and they were secured not without cost. The Chicano was here before and has been present these hundred odd years, but it was only in the last two years that the institutions have been moved to satisfy their obligation to our community. This resulted because of the self-sacrifice, militancy, dedication and political maturity of student organizations. There have been a few, isolated conscientious Chicanos who tried to gain the attention of the colleges for the community prior to the last two years. They were ignored, though the need was no less urgent, and the arguments no less valid than today. It is because of the spirit and style of the present generation that progress has been made. Adelante!

THE ORGANIZER'S TALE

César Chávez

It really started for me 16 years ago in San Jose, California, when I was working on an apricot farm. We figured he was just another social worker doing a study of farm conditions, and I kept refusing to meet with him. But he was persistent. Finally, I got together some of the rough element in San Jose. We were going to have a little reception for him to teach the *gringo* a little bit of how we felt. There were about 30 of us in the house, young guys mostly. I was supposed to give them a signal—change my cigarette from my right hand to my left, and then we were going to give him a lot of hell. But he started talking and the more he talked, the more wide-eyed I became and the less inclined I was to give the signal. A couple of guys who were pretty drunk at the time still wanted to give the *gringo* the business, but we got rid of them. This fellow was making a lot of sense, and I wanted to hear what he had to say.

His name was Fred Ross, and he was an organizer for the Community Service Organization (CSO) which was working with Mexican-Americans in the cities. I became immediately really involved. Before long I was heading a voter registration drive. All the time I was observing the things Fred did, secretly, because I wanted to learn how to organize, to see how it was done. I was impressed with his patience and understanding of people. I thought this was a tool, one of the greatest things he had.

It was pretty rough for me at first. I was changing and had to take a lot of ridicule from the kids my age, the rough characters I worked with in the fields. They would say, "Hey, big shot. Now that you're a *politico*, why are you working here for 65 cents an hour?" I might add that our neighborhood had the highest percentage of San Quentin graduates. It was a game among the *pachucos* in the sense that we defended ourselves from outsiders, although inside the neighborhood there was not a lot of fighting.

Reprinted from *Ramparts Magazine*, Vol. 5, No. 2 (July 1966). Copyright 1966. By permission of the author, César Chávez.

César Chávez is head of UFWOC (the United Farmworkers' Organizing Committee) and leader of the struggle against Anglo farmowners who continue to exploit Chicano labor. When he wrote the article we have reprinted here, *La Huelga* (the strike movement) was in its infancy. Today, with the success of the grape boycott and the growing success of a similar boycott against nonunion lettuce, César Chávez and *La Huelga* are nearly synonymous with the Chicano movement.

After six months of working every night in San Jose, Fred assigned me to take over the CSO chapter in Decoto. It was a tough spot to fill. I would suggest something, and people would say, "No, let's wait till Fred gets back," or "Fred wouldn't do it that way." This is pretty much a pattern with people, I discovered, whether I was put in Fred's position, or later, when someone else was put in my position. After the Decoto assignment I was sent to start a new chapter in Oakland. Before I left, Fred came to a place in San Jose called the Hole-in-the-Wall and we talked for half an hour over coffee. He was in a rush to leave, but I wanted to keep him talking; I was that scared of my assignment.

There were hard times in Oakland. First of all, it was a big city and I'd get lost every time I went anywhere. Then I arranged a series of house meetings. I would get to the meeting early and drive back and forth past the house, too nervous to go in and face the people. Finally I would force myself to go inside and sit in a corner. I was quite thin then, and young, and most of the people were middle-aged. Someone would say, "Where's the organizer?" And I would pipe up, "Here I am." Then they would say in Spanish—these were very poor people and we hardly spoke anything but Spanish—"Ha! This *kid*?" Most of them said they were interested, but the hardest part was to get them to start pushing themselves, on their own initiative.

The idea was to set up a meeting and then get each attending person to call his own house meeting, inviting new people—a sort of chain letter effect. After a house meeting I would lie awake going over the whole thing, playing the tape back, trying to see why people laughed at one point, or why they were for one thing and against another. I was also learning to read and write, those late evenings. I had left school in the 7th grade after attending 67 different schools, and my reading wasn't the best.

At our first organizing meeting we had 368 people: I'll never forget it because it was very important to me. You eat your heart out; the meeting is called for 7 o'clock and you start to worry about 4. You wait. Will they show up? Then the first one arrives. By 7 there are only 20 people, you have everything in order, you have to look calm. But little by little they filter in and at a certain point you know it will be a success.

After four months in Oakland, I was transferred. The chapter was beginning to move on its own, so Fred assigned me to organize the San Joaquin Valley. Over the months I developed what I used to call schemes or tricks—now I call them techniques—of making initial contacts. The main thing in convincing someone is to spend time with him. It doesn't matter if he can read, write or even speak well. What is important is that he is a man and second, that he has shown some initial interest. One good way to develop leadership is to take a man with you in your car. And it works a lot better if you're doing the driving; that way you are in charge. You drive, he sits there, and you talk. These little things were very important to me; I was caught in a big game by then, figuring out what makes people work. I found that if you work hard enough you can usually shake people into working too, those who are concerned. You work harder and they work harder still, up to a point and then they pass you. Then, of course, they're on their own.

I also learned to keep away from the established groups and so-called leaders, and to guard against philosophizing. Working with low-income people is very different from working with the professionals, who like to sit around talking about how to play politics. When you're trying to recruit a farmworker, you have to paint a little picture, and then you have to color the picture in. We found out that the harder a guy is to convince, the better leader or member he becomes. When you exert yourself to convince him, you have his confidence and he has good motivation. A lot of people who say OK right away wind up hanging around the office, taking up the workers' time.

During the McCarthy era in one Valley town, I was subjected to a lot of redbaiting. We had been recruiting people for citizenship classes at the high school when we got into a quarrel with the naturalization examiner. He was rejecting people on the grounds that they were just parroting what they learned in citizenship class. One day we had a meeting about it in Fresno, and I took along some of the leaders of our local chapter. Some redbaiting official gave us a hard time, and the people got scared and took his side. They did it because it seemed easy at the moment, even though they knew that sticking with me was the right thing to do. It was disgusting. When we left the building they walked by themselves ahead of me as if I had some kind of communicable disease. I had been working with these people for three months and I was very sad to see that. It taught me a great lesson.

That night I learned that the chapter officers were holding a meeting to review my letters and printed materials to see if I really was a Communist. So I drove out there and walked right in on their meeting. I said, "I hear you've been discussing me, and I thought it would be nice if I was here to defend myself. Not that it matters that much to you or even to me, because as far as I'm concerned you are a bunch of cowards." At that they began to apologize. "Let's forget it," they said. "You're a nice guy." But I didn't want apologies. I wanted a full discussion. I told them I didn't give a damn, but that they had to learn to distinguish fact from what appeared to be a fact because of fear. I kept them there till two in the morning. Some of the women cried. I don't know if they investigated me any further, but I stayed on another few months and things worked out.

This was not an isolated case. Often when we'd leave people to themselves they would get frightened and draw back into their shells where they had been all the years. And I learned quickly that there is no real appreciation. Whatever you do, and no matter what reasons you may give to others, you do it because you want to see it done, or maybe because you want power. And there shouldn't be any appreciation, understandably. I know good organizers who were destroyed, washed out, because they expected people to appreciate what they'd done. Anyone who comes in with the idea that farmworkers are free of sin and that the growers are all bastards, either has never dealt with the situation or is an idealist of the first order. Things don't work that way.

For more than 10 years I worked for the CSO. As the organization grew, we found ourselves meeting in fancier and fancier motels and holding expensive conventions. Doctors, lawyers and politicians began joining. They would get elected to some office in the organization and then, for all practical purposes, leave. Intent on using the CSO for their own prestige purposes, these "leaders," many of them, lacked the urgency we had to have. When I became general director I began to press for a program to organize farmworkers into a union, an idea most of the leadership opposed. So I started a revolt within the CSO. I refused to sit at the head table at meetings, refused to wear a suit and tie, and finally I even refused to shave and cut my hair. It used to embarrass some of the professionals. At every meeting I got up and gave my standard speech: we shouldn't meet in fancy motels, we were getting away from the people, farmworkers had to be organized. But nothing happened. In March of '62 I resigned and came to Delano to begin organizing the Valley on my own.

By hand I drew a map of all the towns between Arvin and Stockton—86 of them, including farming camps—and decided to hit them all to get a small nucleus of people working in each. For six months I traveled around, planting an idea. We had a simple questionnaire, a little card with space for name, address and how much the worker thought he ought to be paid. My wife, Helen, mimeographed them, and we took our kids for two or three day jaunts to these towns, distributing the cards door-to-door and to camps and groceries.

Some 80,000 cards were sent back from eight Valley counties. I got a lot of contacts that way, but I was shocked at the wages the people were asking. The growers were paying $1 and $1.15, and maybe 95 per cent of the people thought they should be getting only $1.25. Sometimes people scribbled messages on the cards: "I hope to God we win" or "Do you think we can win?" or "I'd like to know more." So I separated the cards with the pencilled notes, got in my car and went to those people.

We didn't have any money at all in those days, none for gas and hardly any for food. So I went to people and started asking for food. It turned out to be about the best thing I could have done, although at first it's hard on your pride. Some of our best members came in that way. If people give you their food, they'll give you their hearts. Several months and many meetings later we had a working organization, and this time the leaders were the people.

None of the farmworkers had collective bargaining contracts, and I thought it would take ten years before we got that first contract. I wanted desperately to get some color into the movement, to give people something they could identify with, like a flag. I was reading some books about how various leaders discovered what colors contrasted and stood out the best. The Egyptians had found that a red field with a white circle and a black emblem in the center crashed into your eyes like nothing else. I wanted to use the Aztec eagle in the center, as on the Mexican flag. So I told my cousin Manuel, "Draw an Aztec Eagle." Manuel had a little trouble with it, so we modified the eagle to make it easier for people to draw.

The first big meeting of what we decided to call the National Farm Workers Association was held in September 1962, at Fresno, with 287 people. We had our huge red flag on the wall, with paper tacked over it. When the time came, Manuel pulled a cord ripping the paper off the flag and all of a sudden it hit the people. Some of them wondered if it was a Communist flag, and I said it probably looked more like a neo-Nazi emblem than anything else. But they wanted an explanation. So Manuel got up and said, "When that damn eagle flies—that's when the farmworkers' problems are going to be solved."

One of the first things I decided was that outside money wasn't going to organize people, at least not in the beginning. I even turned down a grant from a private group—$50,000 to go directly to organize farmworkers—for just this reason. Even when there are no strings attached, you are still compromised because you feel you have to produce immediate results. This is bad, because it takes a long time to build a movement, and your organization suffers if you get too far ahead of the people it belongs to. We set the dues at $42 a year per family, really a meaningful dues, but of the 212 we got to pay, only 12 remained by June of '63. We were discouraged at that, but not enough to make us quit.

Money was always a problem. Once we were facing a $180 gas bill on a credit card I'd got a long time ago and was about to lose. And we *had* to keep that credit card. One day my wife and I were picking cotton, pulling bolls, to make a little money to live on. Helen said to me, "Do you put all this in the bag, or just the cotton?" I thought she was kidding and told her to throw the whole boll in so that she had nothing but a sack of bolls at the weighing. The man said, "Whose sack is this?" I said, well, my wife's, and he told us we were fired. "Look at all that crap you brought in," he said. Helen and I started laughing. We were going anyway. We took the $4 we had earned and spent it at a grocery store where they were giving away a $100 prize. Each time you shopped they'd give you one of the letters of M-O-N-E-Y or a flag: you had to have M-O-N-E-Y plus the flag to win. Helen had already collected the letters and just needed the flag. Anyway, they gave her the ticket. She screamed, "A flag? I don't believe it," ran in and got the $100. She said, "Now we're going to eat steak." But I said no, we're going to pay the gas bill. I don't know if she cried, but I think she did.

It was rough in those early years. Helen was having babies and I was not there when she was at the hospital. But if you haven't got your wife behind you, you can't do many things. There's got to be peace at home. So I did, I think, a fairly good job of organizing her. When we were kids, she lived in Delano and I came to town as a migrant. Once on a date we had a bad experience about segregation at a movie theater, and I put up a fight. We were together then, and still are. I think I'm more of a pacifist than she is. Her father, Fabela, was a colonel with Pancho Villa in the Mexican Revolution. Sometimes she gets angry and tells me, "These scabs —you should deal with them sternly," and I kid her, "It must be too much of that Fabela blood in you."

The movement really caught on in '64. By August we had a thousand members. We'd had a beautiful 90-day drive in Corcoran, where they had the Battle of the Corcoran Farm Camp 30 years ago, and by November we had assets of $25,000 in our credit union, which helped to stabilize the membership. I had gone without pay the whole of 1963. The next year the members voted me a $40 a week salary, after Helen had to quit working in the fields to manage the credit union.

Our first strike was in May of '65, a small one but it prepared us for the big one. A farmworker from McFarland named Epifanio Camacho came to see me. He said he was sick and tired of how people working the roses were being treated, and he was willing to "go the limit." I assigned Manuel and Gilbert Padilla to hold meetings at Camacho's house. The people wanted union recognition, but the real issue, as in most cases when you begin, was wages. They were promised $9 a thousand, but they were actually getting $6.50 and $7 for grafting roses. Most of them signed cards giving us the right to bargain for them. We chose the biggest company, with about 85 employees, not counting the irrigators and supervisors, and we held a series of meetings to prepare the strike and call the vote. There would be no picket line; everyone pledged on their honor not to break the strike.

Early on the first morning of the strike, we sent out 10 cars to check the people's homes. We found lights in five or six homes and knocked on the doors. The men were getting up and we'd say, "Where are you going?" They would dodge, "Oh, uh . . . I was just getting up, you know," We'd say, "Well, you're not going to work, are you?" And they'd say no. Dolores Huerta, who was driving the green panel truck, saw a light in one house where four rose-workers lived. They told her they were going to work, even after she reminded them of their pledge. So she moved the truck so it blocked their driveway, turned off the key, put it in her purse and sat there alone.

That morning the company foreman was madder than hell and refused to talk to us. None of the grafters had shown up for work. At 10:30 we started to go to the company office, but it occurred to us that maybe a woman would have a better chance. So Dolores knocked on the office door, saying, "I'm Dolores Huerta from the National Farm Workers Association." "Get out!" the man said, "you Communist. Get out!" I guess they were expecting us, because as Dolores stood arguing with him the cops came and told her to leave. She left.

For two days the fields were idle. On Wednesday they recruited a group of Filipinos from out of town who knew nothing of the strike, maybe 35 of them. They drove through escorted by three sheriff's patrol cars, one in front, one in the middle and one at the rear with a dog. We didn't have a picket line, but we parked across the street and just watched them

go through, not saying a word. All but seven stopped working after half-
an hour, and the rest had quit by mid-afternoon.

The company made an offer the evening of the fourth day, a package
deal that amounted to a 120 per cent wage increase, but no contract. We
wanted to hold out for a contract and more benefits, but a majority of
the rose-workers wanted to accept the offer and go back. We are a democratic union so we had to support what they wanted to do. They had a
meeting and voted to settle. Then we had a problem with a few militants
who wanted to hold out. We had to convince them to go back to work,
as a united front, because otherwise they would be canned. So we worked
—Tony Orendain and I, Dolores and Gilbert, Jim Drake and all the organizers—knocking on doors till two in the morning, telling people, "You
have to go back or you'll lose your job." And they did. They worked.

Our second strike, and our last before the big one at Delano, was in
the grapes at Martin's Ranch last summer. The people were getting a
raw deal there, being pushed around pretty badly. Gilbert went out to the
field, climbed on top of a car and took a strike vote. They voted unanimously to go out. Right away they started bringing in strikebreakers,
so we launched a tough attack on the labor contractors, distributed leaf-
lets portraying them as really low characters. We attacked one—Luis
Campos—so badly that he just gave up the job, and he took 27 of his men
out with him. All he asked was that we distribute another leaflet reinstat-
ing him in the community. And we did. What was unusual was that the
grower would talk to us. The grower kept saying, "I can't pay. I just
haven't got the money." I guess he must have found the money somewhere, because we were asking $1.40 and we got it.

We had just finished the Martin strike when the Agricultural Workers
Organizing Committee (AFL-CIO) started a strike against the grape
growers, DiGiorgio, Schenley liquors and small growers, asking $1.40 an
hour and 25 cents a box. There was a lot of pressure from our members
for us to join the strike, but we had some misgivings. We didn't feel ready
for a big strike like this one, one that was sure to last a long time. Having
no money—just $87 in the strike fund—meant we'd have to depend on
God knows who.

Eight days after the strike started—it takes time to get 1,200 people
together from all over the Valley—we held a meeting in Delano and
voted to go out. I asked the membership to release us from the pledge not
to accept outside money, because we'd need it now, a lot of it. The help
came. It started because of the close, and I would say even beautiful relationship that we've had with the Migrant Ministry for some years. They
were the first to come to our rescue, financially and in every other way,
and they spread the word to other benefactors.

We had planned, before, to start a labor school in November. It never
happened, but we have the best labor school we could ever have, in the
strike. The strike is only a temporary condition, however. We have over
3,000 members spread out over a wide area, and we have to service them
when they have problems. We get letters from New Mexico, Colorado,

Texas, California, from farmworkers saying, "We're getting together and we need an organizer." It kills you when you haven't got the personnel and resources. You feel badly about not sending an organizer because you look back and remember all the difficulty you had in getting two or three people together, and here *they're* together. Of course, we're training organizers, many of them younger than I was when I started in CSO. They can work 20 hours a day, sleep four, and be ready to hit it again; when you get to 39 it's a different story.

The people who took part in the strike and the march have something more than their material interest going for them. If it were only material, they wouldn't have stayed on the strike long enough to win. It is difficult to explain. But it flows out in the ordinary things they say. For instance, some of the younger guys are saying, "Where do you think's going to be the next strike?" I say, "Well, we have to win in Delano." They say, "We'll win, but where do we go next?" I say, "Maybe most of us will be working in the fields." They say, "No, I don't want to go and work in the fields. I want to organize. There are a lot of people that need our help." So I say, "You're going to be pretty poor then, because when you strike you don't have much money." They say they don't care about that.

And others are saying, "I have friends who are working in Texas. If we could only help them." It is bigger, certainly, than just a strike. And if this spirit grows within the farm labor movement, one day we can use the force that we have to help correct a lot of things that are wrong in this society. But that is for the future. Before you can run, you have to learn to walk.

There are vivid memories from my childhood—what we had to go through because of low wages and the conditions, basically because there was no union. I suppose if I wanted to be fair I could say that I'm trying to settle a personal score. I could dramatize it by saying that I want to bring social justice to farmworkers. But the truth is that I went through a lot of hell, and a lot of people did. If we can even the score a little for the workers then we are doing something. Besides, I don't know any other work I like to do better than this. I really don't, you know.

TEXAS CHICANOS FORGE OWN POLITICAL POWER

Antonio Camejo

The formation of La Raza Unida Party, an independent Chicano political party, has raised the Chicano struggle for self-determination to a new level.

On April 4, 1970, the slate of La Raza Unida Party swept the school board elections in Crystal City, Texas, defeating the candidates of the

Reprinted with permission from *The Militant*, Vol. 34, No. 24 (June 19, 1970).

Democratic Party. Although the elections were officially "non-partisan" the party affiliations were known to all.

Jose Angel Gutierrez, 25, founder and former state chairman of the Mexican-American Youth Organization (MAYO), headed a slate of three Chicanos. Elected with Gutierrez were Arturo Gonzales, 21, a gas station attendant, and Miguel Perez, 31, operator of a Chicano dance hall.

Defeated were two Democratic *vendidos* [sellouts], Luz Arcos, 61, a county employee, and Rafael Tovar, 54, a supervisor in the local Delmonte packing plant. Also defeated was rancher E. W. Ritchie, Jr., 46, who in desperation began claiming he was "half Mexican."

On April 7, 1970, La Raza Unida candidates again swept to victory in the city council elections in three cities. In Carrizo Springs, regional headquarters for the Texas Rangers, Rufino Cabello was elected first Chicano mayor in the city's history. In Cotulla, Raza Unida candidate Alfredo Zamora was elected mayor. In both cities, an additional Raza Unida councilman was elected. In Crystal City two Raza Unida councilmen were elected to the five-member city council, which for several years has been all-Chicano.

The racist anglo ruling class in Crystal City (or gringos as they are referred to in Texas) gave up trying to run their own people for the city council there eight years ago. Their tactic has been to run *vendidos*, or coconuts (brown on the outside, white on the inside), Chicanos who think like gringos. That is why the city council is composed of five Mexican-Americans and no gringos.

How did it come about that in these elections young militant Chicanos were able to defeat the gringo and *vendido* candidates of the Democratic Party who were backed up by the ranchers and the other interests?

To understand this we must look at the city of Cristal, as the Chicanos there refer to Crystal City. Cristal is 85 per cent Chicano and 15 per cent gringo, with a small number of anglos friendly to La Raza Unida Party. The people there are primarily migrant laborers who must follow the harvest north into Colorado, North Dakota, Minnesota and Wisconsin each spring, work for miserable wages throughout the summer and return home in the fall.

In many cases, families are forced to put all their possessions into hock to raise enough money for the trip to the beet fields. The small amount of money they bring back barely gives them enough to get out of hock and survive the winter months.

Median family income in Zavala County where Cristal is located, is $1,754 per year. The median educational level is 2.3 grades, which is lower than some impoverished Latin American nations. All the agricultural land is owned by gringos, 95 per cent of the businesses in the city are also owned by gringos.

In 1962 an attempt was made to give the *mexicano* in Cristal some political representation. PASO (Political Association of Spanish-speaking Organizations) got some Mexican-American Democrats together and ran them for office against the gringo incumbents. In the 1963 elections they succeeded in throwing out the gringo mayor of some 38 years in Cristal, as well as creating the all-Chicano city council. They also had successes in other surrounding counties.

PASO, which had not built up any kind of an independent mass movement, became frightened by the unexpected victory. It abandoned the candidates, eventually losing almost all posts within four years. PASO today is the Texas version of the California Mexican-American Political Association (MAPA)—vote getters for the Democratic Party.

But in 1970 something new was added to the picture. La Raza Unida Party came out of a mass movement which developed as a result of the school walkouts in Cristal. Secondly, unlike PASO, La Raza Unida Party does not view itself as simply an electoral coalition to elect candidates, but as a political party in the full sense of the word—participating in strikes, boycotts of gringo-owned businesses, and the fight for community control of the schools.

In the spring of 1969, Cristal students raised a series of demands for improvement of the schools. The school board and the administration, however, succeeded in intimidating the students into capitulation.

The resentments and desire for change were not dissipated, however, and remained under the surface until December when again the Chicano students rallied around demands calling for bilingual education, participation in federal programs, such as a lunch program, better physical plant conditions, Chicano counselors, scholarships, the right to bring whatever literature they wanted into the schools, and an end to racist practices in selection of cheer leaders.

The result was one of the best organized and most successful school walkouts in Texas, and probably in the Southwest. Approximately 1,700 out of 2,300 students in grades one through 12 walked out, virtually closing all the schools in the city.

During the Christmas holidays, teachers came from surrounding areas, Chicano restaurants and beer halls closed and turned over their facilities for classroom space, and workers used their trucks for buses to transport students to a Chicano freedom school.

Many of the students who at first were not very political quickly began seeing things in their true light. The assistant principal of the high school, a Chicano, was mayor of the city. But it wasn't until they saw his reactionary role during the strike that they made the connection that he was also a *vendido* Chicano. Likewise with the two Chicano teachers who also served on the city council. Thus the real basis for the independent campaign of La Raza Unida Party came out of the desire of the parents and students to throw out the existing racist school board and city council.

But the involvement of the Chicano community quickly went beyond the issue of the schools. Students who were fired from their jobs in local stores for participating in mass marches and rallies were quickly backed up by the entire community which proceeded to boycott those stores.

But they didn't stop there. They contacted the parent company and applied for their own franchises to compete with the gringo stores. This resulted in the opening up of community-controlled Chicano businesses. Much of the financing for La Raza Unida Party and other community projects has come out of these small businesses.

Furthermore, to show their attitude toward Chicano *vendidos*, they boycotted the cleaners owned by the *vendido* Chicano school board member.

For about a week, the community went to the gringo cleaners in town to drive home the point that they would not tolerate one Chicano exploiting another. They then proceeded to set up a community cleaners. As result of these actions no more students were fired from their jobs.

Students put a coat of brown paint on a statue of Popeye, symbol of the spinach industry, that stands in front of City Hall. After two and a half months (17 actual school days) the school board capitulated.

This would have been a resounding victory in itself. But the Chicano community was not about to let up on its initiative. The high school students, together with the adults, mounted a voter registration campaign which put La Raza Party on the ballot in three cities and netted an almost 100 per cent registration among *mexicanos*.

This was a first in the history of Texas and without a doubt in all of Aztlan. Maximum voter registration had varied from 15 to 30 per cent, as is the case throughout Texas. The power of this burgeoning movement rightly frightened the local ruling class (100 per cent gringo) who desperately tried to hinder the party legally.

Pablo Puente, Raza Unida candidate for city council, was ruled off the ballot in Cristal on the basis of a municipal law requiring candidates to own property. But they succeeded in having the law ruled unconstitutional in the federal courts. Puente was placed on the ballot and subsequently won the election along with Ventura Gonzales, Jr.

La Raza Unida Party also succeeded in forcing the Civil Rights Commission to come to Cristal to observe the elections so that ranchers and agri-businessmen could not blatantly intimidate people with threats of violence, loss of job for voting, or tamper with the ballots.

The real significance of the electoral victory for the Chicano community in Cristal was apparent at a board of education meeting I attended May 11. The meeting was held in the high school cafeteria, which was packed to overflowing with at least 250 people, predominantly Chicano.

While the board had previously consisted of six gringos and one *vendido* Chicano, it now consisted of three Raza Unida members, three gringos, and the *vendido* who decided to move to the left, giving La Raza Unida Party a majority.

Jose Angel Gutierrez, new president of the board by a 4-3 vote, called the meeting to order.

Among the points discussed were the following: The school district would build houses for school employees, but rent would be based on a percentage of the individual's salary. From now on the school buses had to patronize all gas stations equally, including the Chicano gas stations, such as the one where board member Arturo Gonzales works (previously all business had gone to anglo-owned service stations). Employment of personnel for school maintenance must reflect the composition of the community which is 85 per cent Chicano.

On all controversial points such as the denial of contracts for the fall to two racist teachers, the vote was four Chicanos, *si*, three *no*.

The most controversial point, however, was reflected in the minutes of a special meeting of the school board held on April 27. At this meeting Gutierrez suggested that Cristal accept transfers from the Uvalde School District. The motion itself was routine and harmless enough—on the surface. It touched off a heated fight and a lawsuit.

Uvalde is a town similar to Cristal about 40 miles to the north. It had been the scene of a militant strike by Chicano students around 14 demands such as: the right of teachers to be politically active without intimidation (Josue Garcia, candidate of La Raza Unida Party for county judge, was fired from his teaching job); bilingual education; Chicano studies; more Chicano teachers; the right to bring any literature into the schools; revision of racist text books; and amnesty for striking students upon returning to school.

As in Cristal last December, the Uvalde school board refused to accept the demands of the students and used every means of intimidation, such as arrests, and denial of graduation to seniors, in an attempt to break the walkout.

The students in Uvalde, many of them MAYO activists, turned to Cristal for aid. Attorney Jesus Gamez, now the official attorney of both the Cristal school board and the city council, represented the students before the Uvalde board.

But aid was even more direct. Gutierrez held that if Uvalde wouldn't graduate the striking seniors, then Cristal High School would. The vote: four Chicanos, si, three gringos, no.

The defeated minority on the board then took the board of education to court. Jesus Gamez as the attorney for the board successfully won the case in court, and at the May 11 meeting, Gutierrez matter-of-factly presented the superintendent, a gringo at least twice his age, with a bill for $2,500 for services rendered by Attorney Gamez and told him, "See that it's taken care of."

The comeuppance of the gringo board members evoked a very apparent manifestation of pride and elation in the Chicano audience.

Toward the end of the board meeting, Armando Trevino, brother of walkout leader Mario Trevino, pointed out to the board that in a school that was 85 per cent Chicano, 20 out of the 25 chosen for the National Honor Society were anglos. (The five Mexican-Americans were considered vendidos by the Chicano students.)

One anglo teacher denied that there had been any discrimination, that it was only because more Chicanos "weren't qualified." Armando Trevino replied, "This happened when I was in school, and it is still happening that qualified students are not elected by teachers . . . I would like the school board to look into it."

One of the gringo board members, typically, objected to discussing this point because it wasn't on the agenda. But this was a new school board now, a Chicano school board. Gutierrez quickly responded: "If there is any problem that any one student or parent has we will always incorporate it into the agenda."

He then added, "This board is not going to stand for any kind of discrimination. And any time an allegation of this nature is made we are going to look into it." A committee headed up by Gutierrez was formed on the spot to investigate the charge.

One could not help but be overcome by what was occurring in that room in South Texas. For the first time, the majority of the people, the Chicano people, were running the schools and beginning to mete out justice to racist teachers and administrators. The Chicano community was being heard before its own school board, rather than being insulted by a gringo board representing a tiny minority.

This reality has already resulted in important gains for the entire Chicano community. By a simple motion of the Chicano Board, for example, free breakfast is now provided for every child in every school.

Gutierrez aims to improve the schools and make the education there relevant to Chicanos and thus cut down the 71 per cent dropout rate.

The Chicano community has been faced with difficult problems from the beginning of this endeavor. Over 16 anglo teachers resigned from the schools because of the victory of La Raza Unida Party. The community needs and wants Chicano teachers, administrators and educators who could help turn the schools of Cristal into real learning centers for the children there. For the first time in its history Cristal has the possibility of providing real education for Chicano youth and adults alike.

The city council is also looking into possible courses of action to improve the living conditions of the population, which every day faces greater unemployment due to the rapid mechanization of agriculture.

It has been revealed, for instance, that the oil companies in Texas have been cheating on taxes by digging wells and then capping them. As long as they are capped, they don't pay taxes. But they have received lucrative loans from banks on the basis of the value of the wells.

If La Raza Unida Party is victorious in the county elections in November, a lawsuit may well follow which could bring in tax revenues to the predominantly Chicano counties. It is easy to understand why the ruling powers in Texas are worried about the turn of events.

At almost every meeting of the school board since the elections, anglo lawyers, from as far away as Dallas and Houston, have been present in the hope of catching La Raza Unida board members on something. But the Chicano community is standing firm. An oppressed people have gotten a little taste of freedom and they are not about to let that go without a fight.

Rather than being intimidated, the new Chicano party is projecting an ambitious organizing drive which could see the party on the ballot in 26 South Texas counties by 1972.

As the result of an open nominating convention of La Raza Unida Party

May 2, the gringo power structure (i.e., the Democratic Party) will face some 40 Chicano candidates in the Nov. 3 elections. La Raza Unida is running a full slate of candidates in the counties of Zavala, La Salle, Dimmit and Hidalgo for all county offices.

The giant step that has been taken in South Texas is an example of what can be done throughout Aztlan. There are scores of cities in Aztlan where the Chicano is a majority. But even in cities where the Chicano makes up only 10 or 20 per cent of the population, significant gains can be made by breaking politically from the two capitalist parties. The fight for community control can be a dynamic force if properly led by an independent Chicano political party.

What is needed, however, is to *mobilize* people into action around such demands as community control of the schools in the Chicano community.

What is needed are Raza Unida parties everywhere throughout Aztlan. Such a party will have to continually struggle against those who want to channel every movement for social change into support of the gringo ruling class through the Democratic Party, on the one hand, and those ultra-leftists who consider electoral activity "meaningless" and therefore give a free hand to capitalist politicians in keeping the Chicano and Latino communities under illusions and "under control."

The success of La Raza Unida Party in South Texas should be an inspiration to create two, three, many Cristals. As Gutierrez pointed out on May 4, 1970: "Aztlan has begun, in the southwest part of Texas."

PERSPECTIVES ON POLITICS

Alfredo Cuéllar

The political development of Mexican Americans can be traced through roughly four periods of political activity that begin with the American conquest of the Southwest.

Such a survey must begin with conflict. Though the first three generations of American rule (from the late 1840s until about 1920, the first phase of political development for Mexican Americans) can be termed "apolitical," it is a period that covers widely disparate activities. Through the first generation (until perhaps the mid-1870s) there was widespread violence and disorder accompanying the consolidation of the conquest. In the following 50 years throughout most of the Southwest Mexican Americans were politically submerged. Neither the violence of the first genera-

Alfredo Cuéllar, "Perspectives on Politics," in Joan W. Moore with Alfredo Cuéllar, *Mexican Americans*, © 1970. Reprinted by permission of Prentice-Hall, Inc., Englewood Cliffs, New Jersey.
Alfredo Cuéllar is a candidate for a doctorate in political science at the University of California at Berkeley.

tion nor the quiesence of the second and third can be considered "normal" American political participation. Force and its aftermath of suppression were the rule.

There were two exceptions to the dominant apolitical pattern. Organized political activity was very much present in New Mexico. Here the political system, even during the long period of territorial government, reflected the demographic and social weight of a large Spanish-speaking population. In southern California, moreover, a wealthy land-owning group of Mexicans retained substantial, although declining, political power until the late 1880s and the coming of the railroads.

In the second period, what may be considered conventional political activity began, born in a context of violence and suppresion. This period (beginning roughly in the 1920s) was a time of adaptation and accommodation, reflecting the changing position of Mexican Americans in the social structure of communities in the Southwest. A small Mexican American middle class began to gain some strength and tried to come to terms politically with a still hostile and still threatening social environment.

This period of accommodation was typified by the efforts of the new Mexican American groups to prepare and to "guide" the lower-class and newly arrived immigrant Mexican Americans to "become Americans." Notably, they did *not* press for full political participation. As we shall see, it was also during this period that at least some of the negative ideological assumptions about Mexicans held by the majority were reflected in their political activity.

The third period, beginning in the 1940s, saw increased political activity. Although the results fell far short of full participation in American political life, this period was characterized by a more aggressive style and more organization. During this time, so to speak, the Mexican Americans began to "play the game" according to Anglo political rules. The new idea of progress became associated with exercising the franchise and attempting to gain both elective and appointive office. The political achievements of Mexican Americans in New Mexico exemplified political progress. There, they had kept a political voice through the change from Mexican to U.S. rule: there were Mexicans in the state legislature and in Congress. Most areas, however, fell short of the accomplishment in New Mexico, especially south Texas, where political exclusion and manipulation were the heritage of violence and suppression. This exclusion and manipulation continued in many communities to be enforced by the local Anglo power structure.

The new aggressiveness that appeared after World War II was largely a phenomenon of urban life and reflected again the changing situation of Mexican Americans. They were becoming more urbanized, and more were middle class; they were increasingly American-born. World War II itself was one of the most important forces for change: hundreds of thousands of Mexican Americans served in the armed forces and gained radically new experiences, being sent outside their five-state "*barrio*" and given opportunities to develop a drastically changed view of American society.

In recent years a fourth type of political activity is becoming important. For convenience, it may be called the radicalization of Mexican American political activity. This new style is exemplified in the growth of the *Chicano* movement. Although this movement assumes different forms in various parts of the Southwest and although its acceptance is far from uniform, it is a very different concept of political activity. It questions and challenges not only the assumptions of other generations of Mexican American political leaders but some of the most basic assumptions of American politics as well.

These four phases are roughly sequential, as noted in this outline, but they also overlap a good deal. Violence continues to suppress Mexican American political activity in many communities and to foster an apolitical attitude. In other areas there is a tentative and fearful kind of accommodation politics. Conventional political activity is slowly bringing a quite new political visibility to the Mexican Americans, which is particularly evident in Washington with the recent creation of the Inter-agency Committee on Mexican American affairs. Radical politics is also becoming institutionalized in some parts of the Southwest. Despite this confusing and complex overlapping and coexistence, we will discuss each type of political activity separately.

Conflict and Apolitics

Conflict between Mexicans and Anglo Americans characterized the American Southwest for the better part of the nineteenth century.[1] Let us recall some of the history of the region with specific reference to its political consequences. . . . The first sizeable number of Anglos who entered this region settled in Texas in 1821 under the leadership of Stephen Austin. Alarmed by their rapid increase in numbers and their failure to accept Mexican law and custom, the Mexican government shut off further Anglo immigration in 1830. The end result was the Texas Revolution of 1835–1836, just 15 years after the first legal immigration began. In spite of the Texas declaration of independence from Mexico, there were then 10 years of sporadic warfare, culminating in open warfare between the United States and Mexico in 1846 after the annexation of Texas by the United States.

The Treaty of Guadalupe Hidalgo ended the declared war, but it did not end the fighting between Mexicans and Anglos. Even in New Mexico, acquired "bloodlessly," an abortive rebellion followed the American occupation. In Texas, the next generation lived through an almost endless

---

[1] The historical material in this chapter is drawn heavily from the historical source materials cited in Chapters Two and Three, and also on Walter Prescott Webb, *The Texas Rangers: A Century of Frontier Defense* (Boston: Houghton Mifflin Co., 1935), and on Ralph Guzmán, "The Political Socialization of the Mexican American People" (unpublished manuscript, 1967). Cuéllar is referring to Chapters Two and Three of *Mexican Americans* by Joan Moore, from which Cuéllar's article is taken.

series of clashes, which reached the status of international warfare again in the late 1850s. Mexico's defeat and the humiliating invasion she suffered cost her nearly a third of her territory. For years afterward elements in Mexico dreamed of reconquest. On the American side the new territories were vast and remote from the central forces of government. The feeble hold that the United States had on the Southwest, the recurrent fears of Indian rebellion, and the divisive forces unleashed by the Civil War were all reflected in American fears of reconquest. Today, with the United States stretching from sea to sea, we rarely question the inevitability of this pattern. But a hundred-odd years ago, this "Manifest Destiny" had something of the character of a crusade, a national mission to be accomplished despite the acknowledged existence of great obstacles. In this climate of opinion, defeating Mexico was a very special victory, and holding these territories a special cause.

Anglos used force to gain control, and Mexicans retaliated with force. Texas, the scene of virtually all of this activity and the home of most Mexicans resident in the United States, saw hostilities between substantial armies and a nearly constant state of guerilla warfare. Many Mexicans, perhaps the most dissident, chose to return to Mexico. From the Texas point of view, many of those who remained were ready as always to join any successful marauder from across the border.

Of these, the most successful was Juan Cortina, who first invaded Texas in 1859 in a series of skirmishes known now as the Cortina Wars. These long "wars" illustrate many of the important themes in Texas-Mexican-American history, showing the comparative lack of distinction between "Mexican" and "Mexican American." They illustrate the racial nature of the conflicts, and they also show that these early decades of conflict were inextricably linked with some larger American problems, most notably the Civil War.

The changes in the Texas economy during this period were detailed (in Chapter Two). It should be reiterated that the shift in land use entailed a shift in ownership. Often, political promises were made and broken; legal contracts were made and broken; legal protection for Mexicans—landowners and others—was promised and withheld. As Webb concludes in his history of the Texas Rangers, "The humble Mexicans doubted a government that would not protect their person and the higher classes distrusted one that would not safeguard their property. Here, indeed, was the rich soil in which to plant the seed of revolution and race war." [2]

Juan Cortina's expeditions began as a personal vendetta in Brownsville, Texas against an Anglo sheriff who used unnecessary force in arresting one of Cortina's former ranchhands. Cortina soon extended his campaign to a call for the general emancipation of Mexicans from American rule. He exhorted Mexicans to rise against their oppressors, to claim their lands and to drive out the *gringos*. Mexicans on both sides of the Rio Grande flocked to his camp. His army engaged troops in Texas in numerous

[2] Webb, *Texas Rangers*, p. 176.

battles, although eventually he and his army were forced to retreat into Mexico.

A few years later, after the Civil War, Cortina "helped" U.S. federal troops in the skirmishes and military occupation that preceded Reconstruction, an act that confirmed his unpopularity among Texas Anglos. Cortina went on to become brigadier general in the Mexican army and later, governor of the border state of Tamaulipas in northern Mexico. But as late as the middle of the 1870s he was still leading raids into Texas.

Hundreds of other leaders led groups ranging from the pseudomilitary to the simple bandit (though Mexicans often viewed such bandits as *guerrilleros* fighting for their people). In California, "outlaws" such as Tiburcio Vásquez and Joaquín Murieta (the latter so romanticized that it is difficult to separate fact from fantasy) and in Texas, Juan Flores Salinas, were variously remembered by Anglos anxious for law and order and by Mexicans unwilling to recognize the legitimacy of the American regime. A monument to Salinas was erected in 1875 and carries the inscription: *que combatiendo murió por su patria* ("who died fighting for his country").

The end of the Civil War, however, released troops for the "pacification" of the southwestern Indians, and the railroads could bring in hordes of Easterners looking for land and a new frontier. The era of overt violence between Anglo and Mexican American came to an end and was followed by a long period of quiet. With the beginning of revolution in Mexico in 1910 came the beginning of large-scale immigration. This process rekindled the historical distrust of Mexican Americans, especially now that their numbers were being rapidly increased by refugees from Mexico. It was therefore not surprising that this process would have a depressive effect on political participation among Mexican Americans at this time.

There seemed always to be incidents to keep the Americans fearful. In 1915, for example, a Mexican agent was arrested in a Texas border city with a detailed "Plan de San Diego, Texas," for an insurrection in the Southwest in which "all Anglos over the age of 16 would be put to death." Bandit activities in Texas were being carried out to finance the revolutionary plans of the Flores Magon brothers, who were then operating out of Los Angeles in an effort to begin yet another revolution in Mexico. I.W.W. and anarchist activities among the Mexicans added to the anxiety. Then, in 1916 General Pancho Villa climaxed a number of border raids with an attack on Columbus, New Mexico. The United States retaliated with the Punitive Expedition of General John Pershing into northern Mexico. This comic-opera rerun of the tragic war with Mexico 70 years earlier increased distrust and resentment toward the Mexican American population. Then come the famous Zimmerman Note of 1917, which appeared to confirm all suspicions: the Germans offered to unite Mexico and Japan with Germany for a war against the United States to restore the Southwest to Mexico and give the Far West to Japan. Mexico showed no interest in the scheme, but it touched a sensitive nerve in the United States. As usual, the Mexican Americans in the Southwest were caught in the middle.

Given the background of distrust and violent suppression it is not surprising that the style of the first important Mexican American political groups should have been very circumspect. They could not have been anything but accommodationist.

The Politics of Adaptation

The politics of accommodation can be traced from the 1920s with the appearance of several new political organizations. A good example was the *Orden Hijos de America* (Order of the Sons of America), founded in San Antonio in 1921.[3] The founding members came almost entirely from the newly emerging middle class. Apparently, though, a few refugees from the Mexican Revolution were also involved. More important, both the social and the economic position of these founding members were precarious, and one can note in their announced objectives important concessions to the Anglo definition of the proper role for Mexicans in politics. For example, the goals of the OSA did *not* include demands for equality, either between Mexican Americans themselves or in terms of the dominant majority. Thus, only "citizens of the U.S. of Mexican or Spanish extraction, either native or naturalized" were eligible to join.[4] This exclusion by citizenship was meant—and acted—as an exclusionary mechanism. The implication was that Mexican Americans were more trustworthy to Anglos than Mexican nationals, and also more deserving of the benefits of American life.

This can be understood partly as a reaction to the Anglo conception of Mexicans as an undifferentiated group of low status, regardless of social achievement or citizenship. Hence, all were equally to be distrusted. As an organization of upwardly mobile individuals (albeit of modest achievements) OSA was concerned to show the dominant Anglo majority that they were different from other, "trouble-making" Mexicans. Of course citizenship would have been functionally useful if the *Orden* had been a truly political group, but the symbolic meaning of the requirement is indicated by another regulation. The organization declared itself "to assume no partisan stand, but rather to confine itself to training members for citizenship."

Obviously, "training members for citizenship" is not a strong political position, although presumably this included some activities aimed at increasing political participation, such as by voting. In general, though, this

---

[3] This section draws heavily on Guzmán, "Political Socialization." See also Miguel D. Tirado, "Mexican American Community Political Organization" (unpublished manuscript in files of Ralph Guzmán, University of California Santa Cruz, 1969), and Robert A. Cuéllar, "A Social and Political History of the Mexican-American Population of Texas, 1929–1963" (unpublished Master's thesis, North Texas State University, Denton, Texas, 1969).

[4] Article III, constitution of OSA, cited by O. Douglas Weeks, "The League of United Latin-American Citizens," *The Southwestern Political and Social Science Quarterly*, X (December 1929), p. 260, cited in Tirado, "Mexican American Political Organization," p. 5.

adaptive position could be interpreted as a reflection of the great social and economic vulnerability of Mexican Americans during the 1920s. Validation and recognition meant being as noncontroversial as possible—and preferably with declarations of loyalty to the United States of America.

OSA functioned for nearly ten years. By that time some splintering had begun to occur in the group and its chapters, and on February 17, 1929, several Mexican American groups, among them the OSA itself, the Order of Knights of America, and the League of Latin American Citizens, met in Corpus Christi, Texas. Out of this meeting a new organization emerged to meet the need for harmony and to present a unified front to the Anglo American community. The theme of unity was embodied in the name of the new organization: the League of United Latin-American Citizens, or LULAC. Once again, membership was restricted to citizens of Mexican or Spanish extraction, one of the group's aims being "to develop within the members of our race the best, purest and most perfect type of a true and loyal citizen of the United States of America." [5]

This obvious sensitivity to Anglo opinion was intensified by the debate in Congress and in the press at the time concerning the rising tide of Mexican immigration. This affirmation of loyalty and citizenship may therefore be interpreted as one further example of a protective device used by middle-class Mexican Americans vis-à-vis the Anglo society.

Thus in 1929, to protect themselves from social and economic sanctions, the willingness of Mexican Americans to assert minimum political demands was tempered at all times and in all expressions by a desire to reaffirm citizenship and loyalty to the United States. It is not surprising that there was at this time no pressure for Mexican civil rights, particularly if it might have involved any kind of open demonstrations. (As a matter of fact, Article 1 of the LULAC's by-laws contains one item that states, "We shall oppose any radical and violent demonstration which may tend to create conflicts and disturb the peace and tranquility of our country.") Once again, a statement designed to appease, to reassure those Anglos who feared the worst. And it also served as a warning to Mexicans who might conceivably entertain such radical notions.

Notable by its omission among 25 articles is any demand for any form of cultural pluralism, despite the willingness of some members to preserve a semblance of their ethnic identity.

Throughout, the aims and purposes of the new organization reflected its middle-class orientation, a conformity to the standards of Texas Anglo society, and above all, an emphasis on adapting to American society, instead of emphasis on aggressive political participation, and much less on any kind of political participation based on a separate ethnic identity.

Such circumspection must, as we have noted earlier, be judged in the context of the political milieu of Texas in the 1920s. Both Mexicans and Negroes "knew their place." Although Mexicans did vote in Texas, in some

---

[5] Weeks, "League," p. 260, cited in Guzmán, "Political Socialization," p. 355.

counties the votes were under the control of an Anglo political boss.[6] In other counties Mexicans seldom voted because of the poll tax and other such limitations. The influence of the Anglo *patrón* may be seen in the following letter written by one such boss, who felt it necessary to scold his "Mexican-Texas friends" for forming such a group as LULAC:

> I have been and still consider myself as your Leader or Superior Chief . . . I have always sheltered in my soul the most pure tenderness for the Mexican-Texas race and have watched over your interests to the best of my ability and knowledge. . . . Therefore I disapprove the political activity of groups which have no other object than to organize Mexican-Texas voters into political groups for guidance by other leaders. . . . I have been able to maintain the Democratic Party in power with the aid of my Mexican-Texas friends, and in all the time that has passed we have had no need for clubs or political organizations.[7]

Between hostility and economic vulnerability Mexican Americans were making the best of a difficult situation, which was very slow to change. LULAC gained power among the middle class and ultimately became a spokesman for those Mexican Americans who had achieved a measure of economic and social advancement. In Texas it is still an important political group. Other organizations (as well as branch chapters of LULAC) appeared throughout the Southwest, and many were modeled after LULAC. All of them skirted the question of aggressive political action with considerable skill. Accommodation was the style in the 1920s and 1930s; it may very well have been the only possible style. Since World War II LULAC has taken a much more aggressive stance, a change preceded by a number of changes in the structure of the Mexican American population.

The Politicization of Mexican Americans

The politicization of Mexican American communities in the Southwest dates only from the years following World War II. For the most part politicization was prefaced by deep social changes among the Mexican American population, discussed elsewhere in this book. In sum, they brought Mexicans into new and partly unforeseen contact with American society, particularly in urban areas. The word "urbanization" hardly conveys their impact. A demand for labor brought hundreds of thousands of Mexicans

---

[6] Mexican American voting was "managed," in V. O. Key's term. For a specific discussion of Texas Mexican American politics see his *Southern Politics* (New York: Vintage edition, Alfred A. Knopf, Inc., 1949), pp. 271–76. Key also puts the Texas pattern into the general Southern political context.

[7] Letter published in the *Hidalgo County Independent*, Edinburgh, Texas, March 8, 1929, cited in Weeks, "League," pp. 275–76, cited in Guzmán, "Political Socialization," p. 160.

into cities from rural areas, and at the same time many hundreds of thousands of young Mexican American men found themselves in uniform—and racially invisible to Anglos from other areas of the United States and to other peoples in foreign lands. At the same time, however, their families began to find that the urban areas of the Southwest, like rural ones, were highly discriminatory (this was the time of the "zoot suit riots" in Los Angeles and San Diego, California[8]). (In the rural areas, however, the social fabric that supported and justified discrimination was hardly changed.)

In the cities the urban migrants could find only poor housing, the lowest unskilled employment, and restricted access to schools and other public facilities. As before, few Mexican Americans took part in political activity, although the tradition of political accommodation now seemed outmoded. So did the political organizations built to formalize this relationship to the larger community. A middle class had begun to increase rather rapidly as a result of wartime prosperity, and it was increasingly dissatisfied. Against this background a group of articulate former servicemen (helped substantially by the educational and training benefits of the G.I. Bill of Rights) began to press for changes in the community. In Los Angeles a more open environment facilitated a new alliance with labor elements, Anglo civil leaders, and religious leaders.

One outcome of this alliance was the California-based Community Service Organization (CSO). In Los Angeles the CSO tried to develop indigenous leaders to organize community activity around local issues, using the techniques of larger-scale grassroots community organization. In this manner the Community Service Organization mobilized large segments of the Mexican American community into activities directed against restricted housing, police brutality, segregated schools, inequitable justice, and discriminatory employment, all problems endemic in the Mexican American areas of southern California as much as in other parts of the Southwest. In this process CSO became an important and meaningful post-World War II political phenomenon in the Mexican American community.

In general CSO pressed for full and equal rights for Mexican Americans. The new emphasis was the extra appeal for active and increased participation by as many elements of the community as possible. Therefore, in contrast to previous organizations, CSO tended to be more egalitarian. Under the influence of an outside catalyst (Saul Alinsky's Industrial Areas Foundation) it became a group that no longer served as

---

[8] The zoot suit riots were a series of racial incidents in Los Angeles during the summer of 1943—later called "race riots"—between U.S. servicemen and Mexican American youth (also called "pachuco riots"). These battles, the humiliation of Mexican Americans, ensuing mass arrests of Mexicans (not of the servicemen who were later shown to have provoked them) had a deep impact on the Mexican American community. It resulted immediately in a sharp increase in Anglo discrimination of all kinds against Mexicans and laid the ground for a deep anger and bitterness among the Mexican American community which had been largely impotent to deal with the situation. McWilliams gives an account of the riots in *North from Mexico*.

the vehicle of a relatively few and successful Mexican Americans. Although the leadership tended to be new middle class, on the whole it made an effort to recruit members of the working class and other lower-class elements, including new arrivals from Mexico. CSO also had some non-Mexican members, although they were comparatively few.

This idea of an alliance of equals from various strata of Mexican American society became important. In contrast to the paternalism of previous organizations such as LULAC, there was little concern with the assimilation of lower-class elements into the mainstream of American life. Nor, for that matter, did CSO show any interest in "Mexican culture." The guiding idea of CSO was to cope with concrete and immediate social, economic, and political problems.

The founders of CSO assumed that American institutions were basically responsive to the needs and demands of the Mexican American population. There were no questions about the legitimacy of these institutions; it was always assumed that proper community organization and action would force Anglo institutions to respond to the needs of Mexican Americans. Accordingly, getting Mexicans to exercise the right to vote became a prime CSO objective. Members organized large-scale nonpartisan community drives to register voters. In Los Angeles these registration drives rather significantly increased the number of Spanish-surname voters. The immediate results were electoral victories by Mexican American candidates, there and in nearby communities. Furthermore, CSO pressure on public housing authorities, on the Fair Employment Practices Commission (FEPC), and against police brutality also yielded results. Housing authorities eased discriminatory practices, Mexican American representation was included in the FEPC, and the police department agreed "to go easy on Mexicans" on the Los Angeles East Side.

At the time members considered CSO tactics radical and militant, and throughout the 1950s the CSO remained a politically powerful organization that emphasized direct, grassroots community action. Numerous CSO chapters were organized throughout the state of California, each duplicating the Alinsky approach to community organization.

In recent years CSO has declined as a potent community organization, in part because of the withdrawal of financial support from the Industrial Areas Foundation, and in part because it lost some of its most energetic members. For example, the single most well-known former member of CSO, César Chávez, split with the urban-centered CSO to organize a union of farm workers. Also contributing to the decline of CSO was the rise of competing organizations of Mexican Americans.

Other organizations in the Southwest reflect the aggressive political style growing after World War II. In Texas, there is the important American G.I. Forum. The G.I. Forum was founded by a south Texas physician, Dr. Hector Garcia; the immediate cause of its formation was the refusal of a funeral home in Three Rivers, Texas, to bury a Mexican American war veteran in 1948. The incident attracted national attention, and the idea of the G.I. Forum spread rapidly not only in Texas but also throughout the Southwest, to several midwestern states, and to Washington, D.C. Although the Forum is concerned with nonpartisan civic action, it has moved increasingly toward more direct and aggressive political activities. In Texas, where its main strength lies, the G.I. Forum launched intensive "Get out the vote" and "Pay your poll tax" drives in the 1950s. Subsequently, it has continued voter registration drives since the repeal of the Texas poll tax. On a number of other issues, the Forum continues to act as a spokesman against the problem that beset the Mexican American community in Texas.

If the CSO and the American G.I. Forum reflect the goals of the immediate postwar years, two political groups founded in the late 1950s show a shift in both the political goals and the resources available in the community. In California the Mexican American Political Association (MAPA), founded in 1958, and in Texas the Political Association of Spanish-speaking Organizations (PASSO) were organized essentially as groups pressuring the political system at the party level. These were not primarily attempts to organize the Mexican American poor to register and vote; they were efforts to use growing middle-class strength to win concessions for Mexican Americans from the Anglo-dominated political parties. Essentially the goal of both associations was simply to get Mexican Americans into political office, either as nominees for elective office in the regular parties or as appointees of elected Anglo officials. Thus the best-publicized effort of either group was the successful deposition of the Anglo political structure in Crystal City, Texas, in the early 1960s. In this venture, PASSO joined with some non-Mexican groups, notably the Teamsters and the Catholic Bishops' Committee for the Spanish Speaking. (Although the victory in Crystal City was short-lived, it was as significant to Texas Mexicans as the more recent victory of a Negro mayor in Mississippi was to the black community.)

Both MAPA and PASSO gain strength by virtue of their statewide connections, which are particularly important in the outlying rural areas where repression has been a norm. Statewide ties give courage and support to local efforts. (At this writing one of the strongest MAPA chapters in California is the chapter in the Coachella valley, a citrus- and date-growing area not far from Palm Springs. The local chairman, a vociferous spokesman for Mexican American laborers, is constantly subject to harassment. He is also constantly in demand outside the immediate area. The intervention of outside elements in a local and rather repressive situation has reduced isolation and repression. As in Crystal City, one of MAPA's victories has been the election of Mexican American officials in the grower-dominated town of Coachella.)

Although both MAPA and PASSO are still largely confined to California and Texas, respectively, there are branches and organizational efforts in other states. The two associations once considered amalgamation into a regional group; but, incredibly, the effort failed because the two groups could not agree on a common name. Texas Mexicans could not afford the then too overt ethnic pride suggested by "Mexican American," and the

California group would not accept the euphemism "Spanish-speaking." At these discussions, one disgusted delegate finally proposed "CACA" (a Spanish equivalent of the English "doo-doo") to represent the "Confederated Alliance of *Chicano* Associations." Interestingly, only in such an intensely in-group situation could the name *Chicano* be suggested. At the time this word could not be used for a serious political discussion.

The Chicano Movement

Throughout this chapter we have suggested that Mexican American political activity has often been related to social structural factors. Because much of this political activity was possible only after certain structural changes in Mexican American life, there were seldom any real alternatives beyond simple reaction to Anglo pressure. The importance of the *Chicano* movement as an alternative to pressures from the majority society can hardly be overemphasized. It is a distinctively novel development in the Mexican American community. The *Chicano* movement developed in southern California no earlier than 1968, and it is already a sharp new force in the political expression of Mexican Americans throughout the southwest.

The *Chicano* ideology includes a broad definition of political activity. Ironically, such thinking was possible only for a new generation of urbanized and "Anglicized" (that is, assimilated) young Mexican Americans, who were much less burdened by social and class restrictions than their elders were and whose education had exposed them to new ideas.

The exact beginnings of the movement are obscure. There is some evidence that the *Chicano* movement grew out of a group of conferences held at Loyola University in Los Angeles in the summer of 1966. As originally conceived by its Catholic sponsors, the conferences were to create a fairly innocuous youth organization for the middle-class Mexican students attending various colleges throughout California. Very quickly the movement grew beyond the intent or control of its sponsors (Loyola has never been very noted for its interest in Mexican American education) and it drew in yet others, not students and not middle class, who were attracted by the ideology of *chicanismo*. Thus it cannot be understood as a movement limited to the young, to students, or even to urban areas. It must be understood as including the followers of Reies Tijerina in northern New Mexico and César Chávez' embattled union of striking farm workers in central California. In 1969 Rodolfo (Corky) González was the principal leader and inspiration of the *Chicano* movement in Denver although his interests were mainly in urban civic action. Moreover, "Corky" has organized regional youth conferences and his influence spreads far beyond the local area. No one leader has yet emerged in southern California or in Texas.

As this wide range of activity shows, the *Chicano* movement is extremely heterogeneous, and its elements have different aims and purposes.

In this way the movement cuts across social class, regional, and generational lines. Its aims range from traditional forms of social protest to increasingly more radical goals that appear as a sign of an emerging nationalism. It is a social movement, in that it can be described as "pluralistic behavior functioning as an organized mass effort directed toward a change of established folkways or institutions." [9] The dynamic force of the movement is its ideology—*chicanismo*.

The new ideology is advanced as a challenge to the dominant Anglo beliefs concerning Mexicans as well as to the beliefs of Mexican Americans themselves. Although we have emphasized that students are by no means the only element of the *Chicano* movement, we will reconstruct *chicanismo* primarily as it has been developed among students. Actually, this is only one of several ideological strands but it is the most consistently developed, thus the best illustration of the change from protest to nationalism and a synthesis of the ideology of *chicanismo*.

The first student form of the *Chicano* movement coincided with the development of new student organizations in California universities and colleges in 1966 and 1967. Some of these groups were the United Mexican American Students (UMAS), the Mexican American Student Association (MASA), Mexican American Student Confederation (MASC), and Movimiento Estudiantil Chicano de Aztlán (MECHA). More recently the Mexican American Youth Organization (MAYO) has appeared, with particular strength in Texas. (MAYO is also the name adopted by the new organizations of *Chicanos* in California prisons.) These student groups were at first concerned with a rather narrow range of problems in the field of education, particularly those concerned with increasing the number of Mexican American students in college. To the extent that these student groups were active in the Mexican American community, they were involved with various forms of protest against specific and longstanding grievances, such as police brutality and inferior educational facilities, although other forms of community activity also involved political campaigns.

Chicano student groups thus have never repudiated ordinary forms of political activity, although for them such forms as voting constitute only one political alternative. Actually, given the wide range of problems facing the Mexican American community, *Chicanos* view conventional forms of political activity as perhaps the least effective. Instead, they favor forms of confrontation as the most effective means to gain access for the traditionally excluded *Chicano*, even though it has, on occasion, led to violence. In general, this conception of politics contrasts sharply with the ideas of more conservative Mexican American leaders, most of whom adhere to very limited and "safe" politics with an emphasis on voting and "working within the system" to gain political leverage. This is not to say that *Chicanos* reject working for social change within the system; as a

---

[9] As defined by Abel, in *Why Hitler Came to Power*, as cited in Martin Oppenheimer, *The Urban Guerilla* (Chicago: Quadrangle Books, 1969), p. 19.

matter of fact, much recent activity has focussed on bringing about change in the universities and colleges as well as in the public school systems. Nevertheless, whereas the moderates seek to bring major change in American society through nonviolent means, the more militant speak of the need for "revolutionary activity," though they often leave the details and direction of this revolution unspecified. While they admire the life style and aspirations of revolutionary leaders like Ché Guevara, they have thus far made no systematic theoretical connection between the *Chicano* movement and the general literature on revolution. The theoretical underpinnings of the *Chicano* movement thus often lack a strong direction.

And yet, the advent of the *Chicano* movement does represent a revolutionary phenomenon among Mexican Americans. As we shall see, most of the change from traditional forms lies in (or is reflected in) the ideology of *chicanismo*. Basically eclectic, *chicanismo* draws inspiration from outside the United States and outside the Mexican American experience. The Cuban Revolution, for example, exerts some influence, as do the career and ideals of Ché Guevara. For instance, the Brown Berets (a *Chicano* youth group) affect the life style of this revolutionary. Black Power also offers something of a model. Most recently, *Chicanos* have resurrected the Mexican revolutionary tradition.

Basically, however, *chicanismo* focuses on the life experience of the Mexican in the United States. It challenges the belief system of the majority society at the same time that it attempts to reconstruct a new image for Mexican Americans themselves. *Chicanos* assume that along with American Indians and black Americans, Mexicans live in the United States as a conquered people. This idea allows *chicanismo* to explain the evolution of the *Chicano* as essentially conflictful. In each conflictual relationship with Anglos, the Mexicans lost out and were thus forced to live in the poverty and degradation attendant upon those with the status of a conquered people. This is no better illustrated than by the Mexicans' loss of communal and private property. As a result, they had no choice but to work the land for a *patrón* (usually an Anglo, but sometimes a Mexican, who exploited his own people). When the Mexican was thrown off the land, he was forced to become an unattached wage-earner, often a migrant farm worker; or he might migrate to a city, where the exploitation continued. In any event, *chicanismo* emphasizes that the Mexican was transformed into a rootless economic commodity, forced either to depend on migrant farm work or to sell his labor in the urban centers, where his fate depended upon the vicissitudes of the economy. Ironically, indispensable as Mexican labor was for the economic development of the Southwest, the Mexican got little recognition for his contribution and even less benefit from it.

Chicanos therefore see the economic expansion of the Southwest as essentially a dehumanizing process. They also point out that during periods of economic depression in the United States, when the Mexican became "superfluous" and "expensive," Anglo society had no qualms about attempting to eliminate Mexicans from the United States, as in the repatriations of the 1930s (see Chapter Three).[10] The repatriations are viewed as a conscious attempt to eliminate the *Chicano* from American society.

The thrust of *chicanismo* is not only economic, but also cultural. In many ways, the exploitation and suppression of his culture is what most angers the *Chicano*, who views the attempt to deracinate Mexican culture in the Southwest as the reason why Mexican Americans are disoriented about their culture and often attempt to deny it. The *Chicano* points out that the Anglo himself often views Mexicans with a great degree of ambivalence. Anglos oftentimes take over aspects of "Spanish" (which is really Mexican) culture and at the same time deny it to the Mexican himself. In this fashion Mexicans were denied the development of a more autonomous cultural life, especially as it touches upon Spanish language use, the arts, and so on. (This was done in spite of the agreements made in the signing of the Treaty of Guadalupe Hidalgo. Early drafts of the treaty contained Mexican government efforts to make formal recognition of language rights for Mexicans who chose to remain in the United States after the Mexican War. These provisions were not approved by the U.S. Senate.)

Worse yet, the ideology goes on, the cultural suppression continues to the present day, reinforced by Anglo institutions, particularly the schools. The extreme position (although by no means infrequent) is represented by the fact that Mexican American students in the public schools are corporally punished for using Spanish, their native language. Under these circumstances, it is understandable that the Mexican American student remains ignorant and often ashamed of his past. When the Mexican is mentioned in textbooks, it is in a romanticized and stereotypically Anglicized version of "Spanish culture" that may be congenial to Anglos but is remote and irrelevant to the Mexican American. The *Chicano* considers this type of whitewashed "Spanish" culture particularly galling because he feels that while Anglos may selectively choose certain motifs from Mexican culture, the person behind the culture, the Mexican himself, is given neither recognition nor respect.

Chicanismo also focuses on race, and in some ways this emphasis constitutes one of the most controversial aspects of *chicanismo*. It is argued that Anglo racism denies the Mexican his ethnicity by making him ashamed of his "Mexican-ness." Mexican ancestry, instead of being a source of pride, becomes a symbol of shame and inferiority. As a consequence, Mexicans spend their lives apologizing or denying their ancestry, to the point that many dislike and resent being called "Mexican," preferring "Spanish American," "Latin," "Latin American," and similar euphemisms. For these reasons, the term *"Chicano"* is now insisted upon by activists, as a symbol of the new assertiveness.

Advocates of *chicanismo* therefore hope to reconstruct the Mexican Americans' concept of themselves by appeals to pride of a common his-

[10] Not printed here.—*Eds.*

tory, culture and "race." *Chicanismo* attempts to redefine the Mexicans' identity on the basis not of class, generation, or area of residence but on a unique and shared experience in the United States. This means that appeals for political action, economic progress, and reorientation of cultural identity are cast in terms of the common history, culture, and ethnic background of *la raza*.

Chicano ideologues insist that social advance based on material achievement is, in the final analysis, less important than social advance based on *la raza*; they reject what they call the myth of American individualism. The *Chicano* movement feels that it cannot afford the luxury of individualism; if Mexicans are to confront the problems of their group realistically they must begin to act along collective lines. Hence, the stirrings of a new spirit of what *chicanismo* terms "cultural nationalism" among the Mexican Americans of the Southwest.

Chicanismo has led not only to increased participation in community activities, but also to a heightened and often intense interest in cultural life. *Chicano* poets, playwrights, journalists, and writers of all varieties have suddenly appeared. There are *Chicano* theater groups in several large cities (often known as the *teatro urbano*) and one nationally known and well-travelled group from Delano, California (*El teatro campesino*), which tells the story not only of the striking California farmworkers but of *Chicanos* in general. Newspapers and magazines also reflect this desire to disseminate the idea of *chicanismo*. Throughout the Southwest numerous *Chicano* "underground" newspapers and magazines publishing literary materials have emerged. There is even a *Chicano* Press Association, a regional association representing *Chicano* publications from Texas to California. Furthermore, because of the strong base in colleges and universities, a serious and generally successful drive to develop "ethnic studies" programs has appeared, especially in California. As part of the drive to spread the idea of *chicanismo* in education, *Chicanos* place an emphasis on Mexican contributions to American society, thus giving *Chicano* college students a new conception of their past and present.

Chicano student groups share an orientation similar to that of black students, and on occasion they cooperate and support each other on similar demands. (There is more mutual support between black and brown students than between their counterparts at the community level.) The alliance between black and brown students, however, has not been close, harmonious, or continuous. *Chicano* student organizations have not yet been significantly involved with Anglo radical student groups, although these groups sometimes claim their support or claim that they are working for the benefit of *Chicanos*.

The Echo of Chicanismo

How much has this student manifestation of the *Chicano* movement affected the larger Mexican community? At this writing the ideological reverberations have been considerable, particularly among the young people of college age and including also those in the secondary schools. We must not forget that the Mexican American population is very young. Some counterparts of *Chicano* college militancy have appeared throughout the Southwest in high schools as, for example, among students in Denver, Los Angeles, San Francisco, and many smaller cities.

The demands have often been modest, in most instances no more than for increased counselling services for Mexican American students and other changes in the methods and content of instruction. In some Texas cities and in Denver, Colorado, the student militants further demanded the end of punishment for using Spanish on the school grounds. In most cases the school boards have acceded to this particular demand. But the reaction of the Anglo community has often been fierce. In Los Angeles a school "walk-out" by Mexican American students in 1968 resulted in the arrest of 13 alleged leaders for criminal conspiracy. In Denver a sharp reaction by the police resulted in the injury of 17 persons and the arrest of 40. In other areas in the Southwest there have been similar, if less publicized, responses to *Chicano* militancy.

Neither the Anglo reaction nor the rapid spread of *chicanismo* should be taken to mean that a full-blown social movement is in progress among Mexican Americans. In many areas, on the contrary, established Mexican American leaders have dissociated themselves from the *Chicanos*. For instance, a school walkout by Mexican students in Kingsville, Texas brought an angry denunciation from a Mexican American Congressman from Texas and other community leaders. At the same time, the *Chicano* movement poses a very difficult dilemma for most older Mexican Americans. They sympathize with the goals of *chicanismo*, yet they fear the radical means used to pursue these ends will undermine their own hard-earned social and economic gains. The Anglo community expects a denunciation of what it considers to be irresponsible acts of these young people. But for the older leaders to oppose the *Chicano* protest might be a slow form of personal political suicide as well as acting to exacerbate divisiveness in the Mexican American community.

In California, *Chicano* student groups have grown rapidly; they have acquired the power to pass on Mexican American faculty appointments in many high schools and colleges. Typically such faculty members are avidly sought to assist with the new ethnic studies programs and centers. Ultimately, though, *Chicano* students are faced by responsibility to the community. These students are aware that the popularity of *chicanismo* among Mexican American students means a major opportunity for the development of an entire new generation of young professionals to carry these ideas back to the Mexican American community.

Beyond the universities there have been other sources of support, some of them quite substantial. Grants and direct organizing assistance have come from American Protestant denominations, notably the National Council of Churches. In 1968 a substantial ($630,000) grant from the Ford Foundation to the Southwest Council of La Raza (headquarters in

Phoenix) helped the organization of a number of militant *Chicano* groups. The Southwest Council of La Raza considers itself permanent and accepts money for "*barrio* development" from not only the Ford Foundation but churches, labor groups, and other interested organizations. Both the announced ideals of the council and its membership assure commitment to the ideals of *chicanismo*.

The *Chicano* movement began as a protest. Only later did its dynamics carry it toward an increasing cultural nationalism. The first steps toward social change did not go beyond demands for equality of opportunity for Mexican Americans, which are still being made (by the less militant in the movement). Until recently no Mexican American had tried to define the problems of the community in any terms except those of assimilation. It is precisely these ideas of assimilation and social "adjustment" that the *Chicano* militant rejects. As a new alternative, *chicanismo* represents a conception of an autonomous and self-determining social life for Mexican Americans.

It is interesting that it was not until the 1960s that the *Chicano* leaders emerged to question some of the oldest and most fundamental assumptions of Mexicans in American society. This protest probably would not have been possible in a period of general social calm and stability. That the *Chicano* protest emerged when it did is perhaps due in large part to the emergence of other social groups that also began to question basic notions about American society. But if these other groups feel a sense of alienation in American society, the *Chicano's* alienation is doubly acute. It is not only from American society that he feels alienated; he also feels left out of the mainstream of Mexican history and, simultaneously, he feels a sense of guilt for having "deserted" the homeland. It is this sense of being in two cultures yet belonging to neither (*ni acquí ni allá*) that is the source of his most profound alienation and now, anger. It is against this background that the *Chicano* is attempting with a deep sense of urgency to reconstruct his history, his culture, his sense of identity.

In practical terms the result is increasing radicalization, with which comes a new set of problems. Cultural nationalism has emerged, bringing with it questions that must be answered if the *Chicano* movement is to become a potent force for all Mexican Americans in their diverse circumstances throughout the Southwest and other parts of the United States.

Suggested Readings

Abelardo. 1971. *Chicano: 25 Pieces of a Chicano Mind*, second printing, Santa Barbara, Calif.: La Causa Publications.

This is a collection of poems by one of the most noteworthy Chicano poets, Abelardo, of El Paso, Texas. The poet reveals the soul of a Chicano in this inspiring collection of writings in Pocho, Spanish, and English.

Alisky, Marvin. 1967. "The Mexican-Americans Make Themselves Heard," *The Reporter*, 36 (February 9, 1967), pp. 45–62.

In this article, the author discusses the growing political involvement of Chicanos. Although many events have occurred since this publication, the document presents evidence that the Chicano community is striving for self-determination by attempting to break away from insensitive Democratic politicians who use the ghetto and barrio poor for their own political gain.

Altman, Robert A., and Patricia O. Snuder, ed. 1971. *The Minority Student on the Campus: Expectations and Possibilities*. Boulder, Colo.: WICHE.

This is an anthology of papers presented at the 12th Annual College and University Self-study Institute. Young and articulate social activists in the field of higher education express their views as representatives of the spectrum of American minority communities.

Carranza, Eliu. 1969. *Pensamientos on los Chicanos: A Cultural Revolution*. Berkeley, Calif.: California Book Co., Ltd.

Carranza prefaced his "Pensamientos" by stating that it was a project for thought, that it was "a piece of abrasive rhetoric intended not for the settlement of problems, but for the arousal of feeling and the pricking of thought," Carranza sees the Chicano movement as a "cultural revolution."

Gardner, Richard. 1970. *Grito! Reies Tijerina and the New Mexico Land Grant War of 1967*. Indianapolis: The Bobbs-Merrill Co., Inc.

An objective account of the events that transpired in June, 1967, when a group of Chicanos in northern New Mexico engaged in an armed conflict that resulted from a culmination of disputes over Anglo-American usurpation of Spanish land grants.

Gonzales, Rudolfo "Corky." 1967. "I Am Joaquin" Denver, Colo.: Crusade for Justice.

A movement in itself. "I Am Joaquin" is a pride-instilling poem which portrays the proud heritage and historical events that led to the evolution of the Chicano. It is a poem that gives the Chicano positive reinforcement and a reason to be proud of his past.

Romano-V, Octavio I., ed. 1969. *El Espejo—The Mirror: Selected Mexican American Literature.* Berkeley, Calif.: Quinto Sol Publications.

El Espejo is an outstanding literary source containing short stories, essays, and poetry by Chicanos.

Steiner, Stan. 1969. *La Raza: The Mexican Americans.* New York: Harper & Row, Publishers.

Steiner presents a national panorama of the Chicano movement, covering four major areas: the New Mexico land movement; the California youth movement; La Huelga, or farm labor movement; and the Crusade for Justice.

Magazines and Newspapers

Bronze. 1560 34th Street; Oakland, Calif. 94601
Con Safos. P.O. Box 31322; Los Angeles, Calif. 90031
El Gallo. 1265 Cherokee Street; Denver, Colo. 80204
El Grito. Quinto Sol Publications, Inc.; P.O. Box 9275; Berkeley, Calif. 94719
El Grito del Norte. Rt. 2, Box 5; Espanola; N.M. 87532
El Malcriado. P.O. Box 1060; Delano, Calif. 93215
El Paisano. United Farm Workers Organizing Committee of Arizona. Box 155; Toffeson, Ariz.
El Papel. P.O. Box 7167; Albuquerque, N.M. 87104.
International Socialist Review. 14 Charles Lane; New York, N.Y. 10014
La Causa. 4715 East Olympic Boulevard; Los Angeles, Calif.
La Raza. 2808 Altura; Los Angeles, Calif. 90031. 2445 Gates Street; Los Angeles, Calif. 90031
The Militant. 14 Charles Lane; New York, N.Y. 10014
Times of the Americas. P.O. Box 1173; Coral Gables, Fl. 33134

Annotated Bibliographies

The best general source is *The Mexican-American, A Selected and Annotated Bibliography*. Stanford University, 1969; the interested student is encouraged to consult it. Others include:

Heathman, James E., and Cecilia J. Martinez. *Mexican American Education —A Selected Bibliography*. Las Cruces, New Mexico, Educational Resources Information Center, Clearinghouse on Rural Education and Small Schools, New Mexico State University, 1969.

Inter-Agency Committee on Mexican American Affairs. *The Mexican American, A New Focus on Opportunity: A Guide to Materials Relating to Persons of Mexican Heritage in the United States*. (Washington, D.C.) March, 1969.

Mexican-American Study Project Revised Bibliography. With a Bibliographical Essay by Ralph Guzmán. Advance Report 3. Los Angeles: Division of Research, Graduate School of Business, University of California, 1967.

Riemer, Ruth. *An Annotated Bibliography of Material on Ethnic Problems in Southern California* (preliminary draft). Los Angeles, the Haynes Foundation and the Department of Anthropology-Sociology, University of California (1947).

Sánchez, George I., and Howard Putnam. *Materials Relating to the Education of Spanish-Speaking People in the United States: An Annotated Bibliography*. Austin, University of Texas, Institute of Latin American Studies, 1959.

Glossary

Entries in this glossary are only those words and phrases not adequately defined in the text.

alcalde   mayor; justice of the peace. (Not to be confused with *alcaide,* "warden.")

alquacil   constable; peace officer.

Ahuitzotl   Aztec king of Tenochtitlan, ruled 1486–1502.

arcabuceros   men who used an early type of portable gun, fired by a matchlock and trigger and supported on a hooked staff or forked rest during firing. (From *harquebus.*)

batea   wooden tray or trough; washing trough; the pan used by early gold prospectors in California.

bracero   a farm worker imported temporarily from Mexico. (From *brazo,* "arm." The governments of the United States and Mexico implemented a program for the importation and employment of temporary farm labor. The first program was initiated in 1942; in July 1951, under Public Law 78, the bracero contracting system became a major element in the agricultural business. It was terminated in 1964.)

caballero   literally, a horseman; gentleman. (In Medieval feudal Europe the peasants and serfs were forbidden to ride horses. They were permitted only mules and oxen for transport. Thus, people who were *caballeros* were considered gentlemen or part of the nobility. Today the word *caballero* is used as a form of respect in addressing adult males.)

cacique   originally, a native chief; later a person employed by the Spaniards to collect tribute and maintain order within their village or locality. (Today the word is commonly employed to denote a political boss.)

calpulli   see *pilli.*

campesino   rural person; countryman, countrywoman.

Carranza, Venustiano   provisional president in 1916 throughout most of Mexico. (Presided over the most corrupt administration in the history of Mexico.)

Castillo, Bernal Diaz del   one of Cortés' men who wrote the only extant history of the conquest as seen by a conquistador.

Classic period   the archeological period in New World prehistory from about the time of Christ to about 700 A.D. (During this time the greatest development took place in the Valley of Mexico and in Yucatan.)

cofradia   brotherhood; association of persons with a common purpose; slang, gathering of thieves.

congregación   *during colonial times*, the bringing together of Indians to live in what the Spanish felt were "proper communities." (This practice was instituted in order to control Indian labor better and to promote Christianization. In many areas of Mexico today the government is still trying, with more or less success, to convince Indians to live in centralized pueblos rather than in dispersed settlements.)

creole   see *criollo*.

criollo   a person of direct Spanish descent born in Latin America.

Cuauhtemoc   the last Aztec king during the Conquest of Mexico by Hernán Cortés. Cuauhtemoc is one of Mexico's national heroes and his statue dominates the central crossroad of Mexico City.)

Cuzco   the second largest city in Peru and ancient capital of the Inca Empire.

charro   originally, a peasant from Salamanca, Spain; a cowboy type. (The attire of the *charro* resembles that of the traditional *mariachi*.)

chinampas   the floating gardens built by the Aztecs in the lake which surrounded their capital. (These gardens grew in huge baskets of earth anchored to the bottom. They were built to feed the growing population of Tenochtitlan, much as Holland is now filling in its inland sea to feed its population.)

cholo (chola)   half-breed, mestizo; civilized Indian. (In California the term was used to refer to a male or female member of a pachuco gang.)

gauchupín   see *criollo*. (*Gauchupín* is specifically Mexican and is very derogatory. It was used by the mestizos during the Mexican Revolution of 1810 to refer to the hated Spanish ruling class.)

hacienda   a large agricultural estate. (The dominant land–man relationship system during most of the past 500 years of Latin American history.)

hidalgo   lesser noble; *adj.*, illustrious. (From *hijo de algo*. A title that could be acquired or purchased by Spaniards during the Reconquest Period of Spain and during the conquest of Latin America.)

Hidalgo y Costilla, Miguel   the parish priest who raised the first banner of Mexico's War of Independence from Spain on September 15, 1810. (On the same day he rang the bell and so began the *Grito de Dolores*.)

Huitzilopochtli   War God. (Principal deity of the Aztecs.)

Juárez, Benito   constitutional president of Mexico during the Reform Period in the mid-1800's.

la chingada   generally a woman who has been conquered by being vanquished sexually, and has been totally exploited even to the depths of her soul. (This term refers specifically to *La Malinche*. La Malinche, of course, was the Indian woman who symbolically represents the giving over of the native culture to the conquering Spaniards by the very act of becoming Cortés' mistress.)

La Malintzín a Nahuatl rendering of *La Malinche.*

lambiscon bootlicker; apple-polisher; one who flatters powerful people in order to obtain a favor.

Las Casas, Fray Bartolome the colonial priest who denounced the practice of the Spaniards toward the Indians. (His written indictment of policy and practices became the basis for the Black Legend.)

léperos a sly, scheming person; a thief; *adj.*, wretched.

macana the Aztec war club.

macehual see *pilli.*

machismo literally, the quality of being masculine. (This is a cultural trait inherited from Mediterranean peoples. There are many interpretations as well as misinterpretations of this concept. See Paz' and Ramos' articles in this volume.)

maestro teacher. (In Chicano as well as in Mexican Spanish, *maestro* is used as a term of respect when addressing mechanics, musicians, and other skilled craftsmen.)

Maximilian Archduke of Austria and brother of Emperor Francis Joseph. (Maximilian landed in Veracruz in 1864, the instrument of Napoleon III, who wished to establish his influence in the New World. His regime was maintained by the French troops in Mexico. When they were withdrawn, he was captured and executed.)

mestizage see *mestizaje.*

mestizaje literally, miscegenation. Also refers to cultural mixing, especially the process by which Indians become Mestizo-ized and thus part of the Mexican national culture.

mayeques see *pilli.*

mestizo a person of European and Indian ancestry; *particularly in Mexico,* a person of Indian and Spanish ancestry.

Mexica the "Aztec" people occupying the Valley of Mexico and builders of Tenochtitlan.

Mexicano *in Chicano Spanish,* a native of Mexico; a person of Mexican descent born in the U.S. but who identifies with Mexico; *in Mexican Spanish,* a modern speaker of Nahuatl.

mita the pre-Spanish system whereby Inca men were obliged to give a certain amount of their labor to the state as a form of taxation. (This form of extracting labor became instituted during the silver and mercury mining period in El Cerro de Potosi, Peru.)

Moctezuma two Aztec-Tenochtitlán kings: the first, Moctezuma I, ruled 1440–1469; the second, Moctezuma Xocoyotzin II, ruled 1502–1520.

Monte Alban Zapotec site in the Valley of Oaxaca in southern Mexico during middle and late formative times. (Monte Alban lies in the heart of the region still occupied by the Zapotec people. Most of the constructions at Monte Alban are of the Classic period.)

mordida a bribe; literally, a bite. (The verb *to bribe* is appropriately translatable as "to put the bite on someone.")

Motocuhzoma   see *Moctezuma.*

Nahuatl   language of the Aztecs; a member of the Yuto-Aztecan family.

Obregon, Alvaro   President of Mexico in 1920. Elected in 1920; re-elected in 1924; assassinated in 1928.

Onate, Juan de   Spanish conquistador who led a small group into northern New Mexico and established settlements in 1598.

padre   the father of a family. (Also used to address the grandfather or great-grandfather. Commonly used to refer to a priest.)

patria potestas   *Latin:* power of a father.

pelado   literally, plucked; bare; penniless; also a down-trodden, put-upon person. (The *pelado* encompasses a category of negative attributes. He is a sort of social parasite.)

peón   hired hand; employee. (Used as derogatory term to denote low-class status.)

pilli   the noble class of the Aztecs. (Most of the population were commoners, called *macehuales*. They were organized into clans called *calpulli*. At the bottom of the social order were the *mayeques*, or serfs, who worked for the *pilli*. The *tamines* were also a kind of serf, but worked for merchant-noblemen rather than for agriculturalists. Warriors constituted a separate class, as did the long-distance traders, known as the *pochteca*.)

pochteca   see *pilli.*

primus inter pares   *Latin* first among equals. This was the title given to the Roman Emperor who was theoretically the equal and not the superior of any citizen of Rome.

pueblo   community; village; *cap.*, the tribe of Indians whose ancestors invented the magnificent adobe-brick, apartment-houselike architecture of the Southwest.

pulque   the fermented juice extracted from the agave plant. (An alcoholic beverage used since pre-conquest times.)

puros   liberal intellectuals of nineteenth-century Mexico.

Quetzalcoatl   the feathered Serpent. (One of the oldest of Mexican deities, he is one of the national symbols of Mexico. *The Eagle, the Jaguar, and the Serpent* by Miguel Covarrubias is an excellent source for understanding these major themes in Mexican art and culture.)

Quevedo y Villegas, Francisco de   poet of the early sixteenth century. (Wrote defiantly during the mid-1500's at which time the silver mining business had corrupted society and the public service.)

real   a Spanish silver coin; *adj.*, royal, genuine, kinglike. (Commonly used today in Chicano Spanish in such expressions as *dos reales*, or "quarter of a dollar," "two bits.")

tamine   see *pilli.*

Tenochtitlán   the capital of Aztec power, built on a lake connected to the mainland by causeways. (That lake is filled in today, and Mexico City, the second largest urban center in the western hemisphere, stands on it. The town of Xochimilco is still surrounded by the remnants of the lake and the *chinampas*, or floating gardens of the Aztecs, may still be seen there.)

Teotihuacán the major site of urban civilization during the Classic period; it is situated in the Valley of Teotihuacán, 26 miles from Mexico City.

Tezcatlipoca Smoking Mirror, or the "Eagle God" representing the sun; *in the Aztec period*, the deity who carried a mirror through which he observed deeds of men on earth and punished them accordingly. (He demanded human sacrifices in his honor. There were four Tezcatlipocas, indicating the four cardinal directions.)

Tlacaelel an economic and military advisor to several Aztec kings between 1427 and 1480. A remarkable planner, he formulated a doctrine of manifest destiny very much like that of the North Americans 400 years later. Immediately after he died his dream of a powerful confederacy, dominated by Aztecs, was brought to reality by Ahuitzotl.)

Tlaloc the Rain God of ancient Mexico.

Toltec the civilization which dominated the Valley of Mexico prior to Aztec times. (Their capital was Tula, from which they dominated northern and central Mexico.)

Tonalpohualli the name of the 260-day Aztec ritual calendar.

Villa, Francisco (Pancho) revolutionary general of the Army of the North, which later became Army of Convention. (Assassinated in the summer of 1923 by members of the federalist government.)

Virgin of Guadalupe one of the most important national symbols of Mexican culture; the patron saint of Mexico. (See Wolf's article, this volume.)

Xipe God of Spring, "Our Lord the flayed one." (His priests dressed in the skin of the sacrificed victim.)

Zapata, Emiliano revolutionary leader in the Mexican Revolution of 1910. (An excellent biography, *Zapata*, has been written by Womack, 1969.)

Zapotec the language spoken by Indians in the state of Oaxaca today. (Zapotec civilization was one of the Classic cultures of Middle America. See *Monte Alban*.)